SUMMONED TO GLORY

The Audacious Life of Abraham Lincoln

Richard Striner

ROWMAN & LITTLEFIELD
Lanham • Boulder • New York • London

Rowman & Littlefield
An imprint of The Rowman & Littlefield Publishing Group, Inc.
4501 Forbes Blvd., Ste. 200
Lanham, MD 20706
www.rowman.com

Distributed by NATIONAL BOOK NETWORK

British Library Cataloguing in Publication Information available

Library of Congress Cataloging-in-Publication Data available

ISBN 978-1-5381-3716-1 (cloth : alk. paper)
ISBN 978-1-5381-3717-8 (electronic)

♾️™ The paper used in this publication meets the minimum requirements
of American National Standard for Information Sciences—Permanence of
Paper for Printed Library Materials, ANSI/NISO Z39.48-1992

CONTENTS

Preface vii

Part One: Preparations

Chapter One: Rough Beginnings 3
Chapter Two: Initiations 15
Chapter Three: Rites of Passage 26

Part Two: Crisis of Ambition

Chapter Four: Improvising 55
Chapter Five: Into the Maelstrom 79
Chapter Six: Quest for Purpose 95

Part Three: Rise to Destiny

Chapter Seven: Containing Slavery 111
Chapter Eight: Thwarting Douglas 140
Chapter Nine: Disunion 164

Part Four: At the Helm

Chapter Ten: Crisis 189
Chapter Eleven: Chain of Steel 229
Chapter Twelve: Transformation 272
Chapter Thirteen: Race against Time 326

Part Five: Triumph

Chapter Fourteen: Death Struggle 383
Chapter Fifteen: Stolen Future 428

Epilogue 463
Notes 469
Index 515

PREFACE

L incoln.

The very name conveys powerful associations, especially for those who admire him. And those who admire him see in him a figure with so many different aspects, a funny, humane, and enjoyable man who at one and the same time possessed such austere reserve, a man with the far-seeing vision to behold the course of events and see—in a flash—how to change them.

Of course many great people in history have possessed these qualities. So what was it about Abraham Lincoln that made him unique? What sets him apart in certain ways from the other great American presidents, even Washington and the Roosevelts?

Beyond the man's overwhelming decency, it was surely his power to take strong stands and carry the day in a crisis whose severity and magnitude surpassed any other in American history that made Lincoln pre-eminent among our great presidents. Surely that is why so many people think of him *immediately* when they look to our heritage of presidential leadership for inspiration. That is why so many citizens ponder his life as they ask themselves how such qualities in leaders can be recognized.

This study of his life will emphasize the one single thing that must be grasped to understand him well: the workings of his mind. The mental power he commanded was immense. But the qualities that single him out among so many intelligent leaders whose deeds may be studied with profit may be laid out as follows: his ability to orchestrate power, his adroitness in using that power strategically, his commitment to use the power that he wielded in order to protect, and—a critical point that is often under-appreciated by students of Lincoln—his audacity.

He was a man who used power with *audacity* in order to *protect*—and that made him great.

At least that is what this book will argue.

Lincoln was a pivotal figure in American and world history not only for what he achieved but for what he *prevented*. Admirers of Lincoln are right when they say that he both saved the Union and unleashed the events that would banish the evil of slavery. But those achievements emerged from an underlying mission that he chose.

His contribution to history began with his decision to challenge a process that was ruining the American idea. He saw a monstrous change spreading over his country—a change that could lead over time to *the establishment of slavery in every single state*—and he sounded the alarm with great success. We will never know the full extent of the horror that Lincoln prevented.

Because he never allowed it to happen.

Lincoln of course was merely one among thousands, even millions, of people who fought against slavery. Indeed, there were thousands of determined people who fought against the *expansion* of slavery before Lincoln chose to join them. But once he rose to the decisive position of leadership, history was changed.

His leadership of the "Free Soil" movement led to his nomination for the presidency by the Republican Party. His election triggered the secession movement in the South. His fight against secession gave him leverage to move beyond slavery containment and strike at the evil directly.

So he did.

But in doing so, he took tremendous risks that put everything he treasured on the line. The case can be made that without the strategic brilliance of Lincoln, the anti-slavery movement might have failed. It took a certain kind of leadership to do what he did.

These are the conclusions that pervade this new biography of Lincoln—this latest among a great many books that have told his life story and have tried to make sense of the forces that shaped him. Building on decades' worth of scholarship, this account is for general readers. It will show how this man who was born to poverty cultivated his gifts, but it will also show how the full potential of his brilliance was catalyzed only by historical crisis—a crisis that unleashed so much anger in Lincoln that his destiny at last became apparent to him and his powers exploded into action. It was only a convergence of inner capability and outward challenge that summoned forth the full magnificence of Lincoln's leadership.

Several historians have illuminated the emotional development that was integral to Lincoln's mental power. Specifically, Michael Burlingame, Douglas L. Wilson, and Joshua Wolf Shenk have provided special insights into Lincoln's "inner world," as Burlingame called it.[1] But the fundamental impetus for this new one-volume Lincoln biography is my own work in Lincoln studies. In 2006, I argued in *Father Abraham: Lincoln's Relentless Struggle to End Slavery* that Lincoln was an extraordinary moral strategist and that his achievements displayed intellectual power of the highest order.

Paradoxical as it might seem, a key element in Lincoln's mastery was his power to deceive—or to deal in half-truths—*for ethical reasons.* This book will show the many admirers of Lincoln that the reputation of "honest Abe" must make allowance for his power to pursue an honesty of purpose through strategic methods as crafty as the circumstances demanded.

A corollary to the honest Abe image is the commonplace portrait of Lincoln as a moderate who fought to prevent disunion through endurance unsullied by guile. Any elements of truth in this stereotype must be qualified by a recognition of Lincoln's fiery will, his capacity for manipulation, his power to command while projecting sweet innocence.

A few statesmen in recent centuries have approached this degree of virtuosity: Winston Churchill is one of the most obvious examples of a leader who combined moral values with cunning. But Lincoln's achievement in the mastery of this art was simply superb.

It is time for a Lincoln biography to present its subject in a manner that emphasizes such things. Lincoln was one of the most brilliant orchestrators of power to achieve noble ends that America has ever produced and perhaps is ever destined to produce.

But it was only profound emotional struggle, not least of all his struggle with depression, that enabled Lincoln to summon his powers, then shape them in a fashion that would save his country from a great deal more than the disaster of mere disunion. Any life that resulted in achieve-ments such as these must be understood for what it was: a life of genius.

There are some points to bear in mind about my method. In the first place, I make no attempt to examine every single detail of Lincoln's life or to pile up a bulky and redundant mass of data. A wealth of documentation on Lincoln already exists and any effort to present it all would lead only to a long series of books. My book serves a different purpose, and I cover the facts I deem important. Anyone seeking a Lincoln biography containing an encyclopedic amount of detail should consult Michael Burlingame's excellent two-volume work, *Abraham Lincoln: A Life* (2008).[2]

In the second place, I have striven to make this book vivid while stick-ing to the facts. In their enthusiasm—in their search for details that will liven up their books—some Lincoln biographers have gone too far: they have written out colorful passages to describe events as they imagine them to have happened "in real life." That's fine if the documentary record sup-ports such "true to life" accounts. But when the evidence is lacking—as it frequently is in such cases—there's a problem.

Consequently, this book is grounded in the best documentation avail-able. In the case of reminiscences by others that paraphrase what Lincoln purportedly said on various occasions, I have limited myself to the best and most authoritative compilations. Such compilations have been edited by Lincoln scholars who are in the surest position to render judgments as to the probable accuracy of such material. But we need to be mindful of the fact that reminiscences are imperfect.

Naturally, the best of all documentation is the record that Lincoln produced in his own writings, so my use of quotations will be generous. It is very important for readers who are after the truth to be able to review Lincoln's statements in detail, since his meanings could at times be very subtle. Among its other points, this book will demonstrate the necessity of asking good questions as we read Lincoln's statements in relation to the context in which he was making them.

Within the past few decades, much groundbreaking work has been done by Lincoln scholars. Commonplace notions—within the world of scholarship—have been turned upside-down. This book will present these revaluations of Lincoln for general readers but it will go further by chal-lenging one of the most wrong-headed stereotypes of all: the stereotype of Lincoln as—how to put it exactly?—a slow-moving moderate who somehow achieved true greatness.

Here are some examples of this influential and persistent idea. In 1952, one Lincoln biographer offered the following portrait: "Physically he was always a powerful man whose body, like his mind, moved slowly, as is likely to be the way with country people."[3] In 1995, another Lincoln biography served up a similar notion; according to this biographer, Lincoln's personality bred an "essential passivity," a "reluctance to take the initiative and make bold plans." Moreover, this "basic trait of character" was supposedly "evident throughout Lincoln's life."[4]

Nonsense. Of course Lincoln could *at times* "move slowly," but he did so for different reasons. Sometimes he suffered from depression. Sometimes he took his time in light of hazards. Sometimes his careful sense of timing and pace led to different decisions as to tempo.

But he was brilliant, and his mind at its best could move with dazzling and lightning-like speed.

The work of biography is grounded in character analysis and writers who take up the challenge must arrive at conclusions. There is much to be learned from the lives of great people and the various things they accomplished. But certain people within the historical profession think it wrong to write books that sing the praises of historical figures. They worry that books of this type can succumb to uncritical hero-worship and they call such books "hagiography."

I admit that this danger applies to the study of Lincoln, but the danger can surely be averted. The way to do it is through critical analysis, through scrutiny as thorough and demanding as the minds of conscientious people can make it. Have I met this rigorous standard? I hope so. But the effort has been made, so the conclusions that I reach must be judged accordingly and fairly.

Like many Lincoln scholars in recent years, I have not made any attempt to correct misspellings in the nineteenth-century texts that I quote and I have not seen fit to clutter things up with bracketed notations—notations to acknowledge the obvious fact that the original writing was eccentric. In my opinion, such notation is unnecessary since the nature of the original writing speaks for itself. And there are even advantages in retaining old misspellings; at times they convey some pleasant hints of pronunciations that are now long-vanished, and they savor of dialects and usages that can still be detected now and then in different parts of America. Why let pedantic custom spoil the tang of these lovely written clues?

I

PREPARATIONS

ROUGH BEGINNINGS

The parents of Abraham Lincoln got married in their twenties after meeting in the back country of Kentucky. They were a common social type in early nineteenth-century America: drifters who wished to settle down. There were thousands of others who had grown up living in the country and were looking for a homestead. Thomas Lincoln and his young wife Nancy were familiar with the ways of the Kentucky frontier, so they decided to stay there. They lived in a town right after their wedding, but they moved within a year to a location a few miles away.

Nancy gave birth to the couple's second child in a one-room cabin south of Hodgenville, Kentucky, and they called him Abraham. He was named in honor of his paternal grandfather, who was murdered by an Indian decades earlier.

February 12, 1809, was the day when he came into the world at a place called the Sinking Spring Farm, so-named for its fresh-water spring. The farm was near the south fork of Nolin Creek a few miles below Hodgenville. This region was known as "the Barrens," and the farmland was not very good (or so it was said) for a number of reasons.

His father worked on and off as a carpenter, but he was mostly a subsistence farmer who sometimes sold provisions. Problems with the title to the land at the homestead where Lincoln was born forced the family to move in 1811.

Abraham looked back upon his youth with the feeling of having been impoverished and it made him feel ashamed. Others were just as badly off, but the thought gave him little consolation at the time and in his memories later. When he reflected on his youth in middle age, he used a phrase that he remembered from Thomas Gray's *Elegy*, "the short and simple annals of the poor."[1]

The homesteads selected by his father had problems, and one was too close to a stream known as Knob Creek that flooded. Lincoln remembered all the times "when there came a big rain in the hills [and] the water would come down through the gorges and spread all over the farm."[2] He remembered one occasion when the pumpkin seeds that he had helped to plant were all washed away.

It was the eyes of a prodigy that saw these disasters, and the little boy came to conclusions. He could see all around him what life would be like if he could not find a way to transcend the limitations of ignorance and poverty.

Life was raw, full of hardship, and throughout it was the ever-present threat of dying young. Lincoln encountered early on the desolation that came with the loss of loved ones who were cut down in their prime—robbed of the chance to be all that they could be—and the theme of mortality would haunt him.

Even so, he was a mischievous boy. He liked to play with a friend named Austin Gollaher, whom he remembered years later with affection. He wore linsey-woolsey clothing and straw hats woven by his mother. The cabins in which he lived had dirt floors and crude furniture, and the schools he attended were primitive. "No qualification was ever required of a teacher," he recalled later on, "beyond 'readin, writin, and cipherin,' to the rule of three."[3]

But the crudeness of his situation and the limitations imposed by his frontier environment did not hold him back in his quest to develop his mind. He seemed to believe from a very early age that he was capable of doing great things.

Though he took an interest in his father's side of the family—he eventually traced his paternal lineage all the way back to one Samuel Lincoln, who arrived in Massachusetts in 1638—he was deeply ashamed of his father's illiteracy and his lack of intellectuality. But his mother was different.

She was born Nancy Hanks in Virginia and she married Lincoln's father in 1806. According to Lincoln's future law partner William Herndon, Lincoln called her a "woman of genius," adding that he "got his mind from her."[4] There were rumors, which Lincoln believed, that his mother was born out of wedlock to a poor girl named Lucy Hanks. And Lincoln was convinced that the man who got Lucy pregnant was the source of both his mother's brilliance and his own.

He speculated, according to Herndon, that this grandfather—whom Lincoln believed to be a wealthy Virginia planter—had passed along an intellectuality that would prove to be the source of Lincoln's "power of analysis, his logic, his mental activity, his ambition, and all the qualities that distinguished him from the other members and descendants of the Hanks family."[5]

Lincoln had an older sister named Sarah. A brother named Thomas died in infancy.

Enmity between Lincoln and his father started early. Thomas seemed to feel as if Abraham's quest to develop his potential might put his own weakness in a very bad light, and Lincoln did regard his father as an ignoramus. He wrote years later that Thomas Lincoln "never did more in the way of writing than to bunglingly sign his own name."[6]

So Thomas tried to thwart Lincoln's rise and to punish his precocious ways. A cousin named Dennis Hanks remembered that "when strangers would ride along and up to his father's fence, Abe always, through pride and to tease his father, would be sure to ask the stranger the first question, for which his father would sometimes knock him a rod." Thomas "would pick up a big clod and knock little Abe off the fence, crying: 'Let older people have the first say, will you boy?'"[7]

The situation worsened when Thomas decided to relocate the family to Indiana. In 1816, he set out by himself on a journey by flatboat from the Rolling Fork of the Salt River in Kentucky to the Ohio River, which he crossed at Thompson's Ferry.

Hacking his way through dense underbrush, he staked a claim at Little Pigeon Creek. In early winter, he brought his family to a three-sided shelter he had built of poles and animal hides. Abraham Lincoln was seven years old at the time.

The new farm site that Thomas selected was far from water, and one of the chores that Abraham would face in this new location was the task of trudging a mile and back to fetch water for a family that would soon be growing. Thomas built a cabin and Abraham, who was growing into a muscular boy, helped to clear the land, chop firewood, and plant crops.

Within a year after the move to Indiana, the composition of the Lincoln family changed. From Kentucky came Thomas and Betsy Sparrow, an aunt and uncle of Nancy Hanks Lincoln, and they brought along Lincoln's cousin Dennis Hanks. But an outbreak of a malady that Hoosiers called the "milk sickness" soon killed not only the Sparrows but Lincoln's mother as well.

"Milk sickness," for which there was no treatment at the time, was induced by a toxin that cattle ingested from weeds and then passed along to humans in their milk. On October 5, 1818, Lincoln's mother passed away within a week after coming down with the disease.

Lincoln helped to build a coffin for his mother and he dragged it on a sled to the hill where the Sparrows were buried. Lincoln's twelve-year-old sister Sarah, by most accounts a pretty if heavyset girl—and apparently possessed of an intelligence comparable to Abraham's—assumed the duties of housework.

Her duties increased when Thomas Lincoln went back to Kentucky for the purpose of courting a widow with whom he had been smitten years earlier: Sarah Bush Johnston. "Sally," as Lincoln's stepmother was known, brought her children John, Elizabeth, and Matilda to the Lincoln cabin, which was soon (literally) crowded to the rafters, since Abraham, Dennis Hanks, and Lincoln's new stepbrother John Johnston all slept in a small attic loft.

In most respects, the arrival of Sarah Bush Lincoln was providential. An intelligent, tidy, and kind-hearted woman, she spruced up the cabin and brought good furniture as well as clothing. The families blended, and Sally soon loved Abraham as if he were her own son.

Indeed, two years after Lincoln's death she stated that "Abe was the best boy I Ever Saw or Ever Expect to See."[8] And she knew right away that he possessed rare gifts. He was "a Boy of uncommon natural Talents," she was quoted as saying.[9] She saw that while "he didn't like physical labor," he was "diligent for knowledge," he "wished to know," and "if pains & Labor would get it he was sure to get it."[10]

For that reason, she interceded with his ornery father on behalf of Lincoln's studious ambitions. "I induced my husband," she recalled, "to permit Abe to read and study at home as well as at school. At first he was not easily reconciled to it, but finally he too seemed willing to encourage him to a certain extent."[11]

Lincoln adored his stepmother, saying (on the eve of his presidency) that she had been "his best Friend in this world & that no Son could love a Mother more than he loved her."[12]

Sarah Bush Lincoln was deeply impressed by the manner in which young Abraham's curiosity and penchant for analysis made him pay close attention to adult conversation. "Abe," she recalled, "when old folks were at our house, was a silent & attentive observer—never speaking or asking questions till they were gone and then he must understand Every thing— even to the smallest thing—Minutely & Exactly."[13] Lincoln himself confirmed his stepmother's recollection in the following reminiscence:

> I remember how, when a mere child, I used to get irritated when anybody talked to me in a way I could not understand. . . . I can remember going to my little bedroom, after hearing the neighbors talk of an evening with my father, and spending no small part of the night walking up and down, and trying to make out what was the exact meaning of some of their, to me, dark sayings. I could not sleep, though I often tried to, when I got on such a hunt after an idea, until I had caught it; and when I thought I had got it, I was not satisfied until I had repeated it over and over, until I had put it in language plain enough, as I thought, for any boy I knew to comprehend.[14]

With his stepmother's encouragement, young Lincoln read every book he could get. He re-wrote the lines that he found most interesting; his stepmother observed that "when he came across a passage that Struck him he would write it down on boards if he had no paper & keep it there till he did get paper—then he would re-write it—look at it repeat it."[15] If he lacked proper writing instruments, he would write with a carving knife in wood or use a piece of charcoal for scrawling.

Among his other interests, Lincoln showed a keen aptitude for mathematics, and several examples of his boyhood computations in workbooks have survived.[16]

This was nothing less than self-liberation—self-empowerment—as far as Abraham Lincoln was concerned. Later on he observed that "the great mass of men, at that time, were utterly unconscious, that their *conditions*, or their *minds* were capable of improvement. They not only looked upon the educated few as superior beings; but they supposed themselves to be naturally incapable of rising to equality." And in that regard, he wrote, one of the greatest benefits that the printing press had brought to mankind was that it helped to "immancipate the mind from this false under estimate of itself."[17]

Thus Lincoln associated his self-education with *emancipation*, a principle that he applied as much to the advancement of others as he did to the cultivation of his own intellectual gifts.

And Lincoln's concern for the well-being of others ran deep. Among the first things he wrote at the school that he attended near Little Pigeon Creek was an essay denouncing cruelty to animals. Years later, when some roughnecks ridiculed him for stopping in the midst of a journey to rescue some birds that had fallen from their nest, he replied, "Gentlemen, you may laugh, but I could not have slept well to-night, if I had not saved those birds. Their cries would have rung in my ears."[18]

This sensitive streak in Lincoln became more pronounced, in the view of some neighbors, after the death of his mother. Perhaps the empathy of Lincoln for those who were in pain was accentuated by the "melancholy" feelings in general that would cause a great emotional crisis for him in early adulthood. Regardless, Lincoln's personality was already a many-sided thing. The sensitive bookworm could also be a raucous young fellow, and the earthy sense of humor that emerged in these years would grow apace.

Lincoln's teenage years were taken up with immense physical labor, which he took to be drudgery. He wielded axes, dug ditches, built fences, planted crops, husked corn, and butchered hogs. Almost six feet tall by the time that he turned fifteen, he was strong but awkward-looking, and careless about his attire—which according to one of his schoolmasters included buckskin clothing and coon-skin hats. According to many, his awkward appearance made it hard to succeed with girls. But he was an outstanding athlete and he excelled at the various games and competitions that were contests in strength and agility.

His life took a turn for the worse when his father removed him from school and hired him out to work for neighbors in 1825. Worse still, he had to turn over his earnings to his father until he was twenty-one years old. "I used to be a slave," he remarked significantly in the 1850s.[19]

Some of his labors, however, brought compensations of other kinds. In addition to farm work, his chores included service as a store clerk for a merchant named William Jones. This job gave Lincoln access to newspapers, which kindled his interest in politics.

Lincoln used his status as a rented laborer to move beyond the paternal orbit. In 1827, he and his stepbrother went to Louisville, Kentucky, to work on the Louisville and Portland Canal. Then he worked as a ferryman, and his work brought an offer from a merchant named James Gentry, who proposed to hire him to carry a cargo of goods on a flatboat to Louisiana. With Gentry's son Allen, Lincoln built the flatboat, loaded it, and guided it down the Ohio River to the Mississippi. They peddled the cargo at plantations along the river bank.

Once their boat was attacked by seven slaves, who attempted to rob it, and both young men were injured. But of great importance, these early dealings with plantation owners—together with the hostile encounter with slaves—did nothing to endear the world-view of southern slave owners to Lincoln.

Quite the contrary: when arriving in New Orleans, Lincoln and his friend beheld the spectacle of a slave market, and Lincoln is supposed to have turned to Gentry and said, "Allen, that's a disgrace."[20] He knew too well what it felt like to be the equivalent of a slave himself.

Lincoln's rough-and-tumble experiences during these years helped cultivate a life-long penchant for ribald humor, along with a powerful streak of irreverence that served to spice up his intellectuality. According to Dennis Hanks, he made up "little smutty songs" and told off-color jokes.[21]

Though Lincoln's readings included an immersion in the Bible, he satirized the antics of backwoods preachers and the goings-on at camp meetings. Among his other comic gifts, he was by many accounts a talented mimic. However important religion would become to him later in life, he took it lightly in his teenage years. "Abe read the bible some," his stepmother recalled, "but not as much as [is] said: he sought more congenial books—suitable for his age."[22]

Still, though Lincoln was irreverent, he was drawn to a kind of spirituality if only through the superstitions he imbibed from the Indiana locale. Henry C. Whitney, a lawyer who befriended Lincoln in the 1850s, claimed that Lincoln confided his belief in the supernatural through the following reminiscence. As a boy, he said,

> I used to wander out in the woods all by myself. It had a fascination for me which had an element of fear in it—superstitious fear. I knew that I was not alone just as well as I know that you are here now. Still I could see nothing and no one, but I heard voices. Once I heard a voice

right at my elbow—heard it distinctly and plainly. I turned around, expecting to see some one, of course. No one was there, but the voice was there.[23]

A tragic event led to consequences that neatly illustrate the way in which sorrow, mirth, and profanity could play out in those days for Lincoln. In 1826, his sister Sarah married a neighbor named Aaron Grigsby. Lincoln loathed his sister's husband and believed he mistreated her. Then suddenly his sister died in childbirth. Abraham was devastated by the news.

A dark feud between Lincoln and the Grigsby family gradually developed. When the members of the Lincoln family were pointedly excluded from the double wedding of Reuben and Charles Grigsby to Elizabeth Ray and Matilda Hawkins, Lincoln pounced upon the opportunity for vengeance by writing a bawdy satire, "The Chronicles of Reuben," that spun a yarn about confusion on the wedding night, confusion that resulted in the grooms inadvertently sleeping with the wrong spouses.[24]

By 1829, this restless young man was intent on striking out for himself and rebelling against constraints. "I don't always intend to delve, grub, shuck corn, split rails, and the like," he is supposed to have remarked to a neighbor, Elizabeth Crawford.[25] After he and Allen Gentry had returned from New Orleans, he asked another neighbor, William Wood, to help him run away so he could get a job of his own, a job on the river. Wood urged him to bide his time and then make his move when he turned twenty-one.

Lincoln took the advice.

In 1830, Thomas Lincoln decided to relocate his family again, this time to Illinois. John Hanks, another cousin of Abraham's who had lived near the Lincoln family in Indiana, had moved to a place near Decatur, Illinois, and he sent back letters describing the advantages of his new location. Thomas decided that was good enough for him, so he and his son built some wooden wagons and the trek westward began.

The hardships of the move from Kentucky to Indiana were greatly surpassed by the travails of this latest move. The spring thaw started, and the Lincolns confronted muddy roads and the floodwaters of the Kaskaskia River. Even after they had reached the destination that Hanks picked out for them on the Sangamon River, miseries abounded. Summer brought mosquitoes and malaria. And the succeeding winter brought below-zero temperatures along with mountains of snow.

Disenchanted, Thomas Lincoln made a series of relocations back in the direction of Indiana, until Sarah Bush Lincoln at last put her foot down and refused to move again, so the couple settled down in Coles County, Illinois.

Even though Abraham had reached the age of twenty-one, he helped the family relocate. Then he struck out on his own, and he would seldom see his father again for the rest of his life.

In the summer of 1830, Lincoln and John Hanks sought work together as laborers. This, above all, was one of those times in Lincoln's life when he earned the reputation as a "rail-splitter." It was also during this period that Lincoln began to emerge as a serious public figure.

When Peter Cartwright, a Methodist circuit-riding preacher, toured the area, Lincoln challenged him for being "too dogmatic."[26] And in a public debate between two candidates for the state legislature, Lincoln made a speech that drew praise from both candidates.[27]

In March 1831, a businessman named Denton Offutt approached John Hanks with the proposition of running a flatboat of goods to New Orleans. Hanks brought Lincoln and his stepbrother John Johnston into the deal. The three men travelled by canoe from Decatur to Springfield, where they met Offutt in the Buckhorn Tavern. Then they built the flatboat at Sangamotown, Illinois, and piloted it along the Sangamon River with Offutt. Their plan was to follow the Sangamon northwest from Springfield, then float along the Illinois River to the Mississippi.

But the boat got stuck on a milldam at New Salem and its stern began to fill with water. Lincoln figured out a clever way to drain the water, free the boat, and proceed on their journey: he levelled out the boat by moving cargo to the front, bored a hole in the bow—which was protruding across the dam—to drain the water, then patched up the hole and eased the boat across. They reached New Orleans in May.

Offutt was so pleased with Lincoln's work that he offered him a job running a new store that the businessman was planning to open in New Salem. Lincoln readily accepted the offer.

New Salem was a small and primitive settlement overlooking the Sangamon River. It was a village set up to serve the needs of farmers. It had stores, a blacksmith shop, an inn, a post office, a ferry, and the previously mentioned mill. New Salem was also a place to let off steam in the local saloon. Law enforcement was almost non-existent, so the town could be extremely dangerous.

Drunkenness abounded and a local gang of bullies who were known as the Clary's Grove Boys caused trouble. They engaged in sadistic games such as gander pulling: a goose would be tied by the feet to the limb of a tree and then contestants on horseback would ride by trying to yank its head off.

But New Salem had a higher class of residents, exemplified by people such as Mentor Graham, Dr. John Allen, James Rutledge, and Bowling Green. Graham was a teacher, Allen a physician, and Rutledge, a decent well-educated man, was the owner of the local tavern. He had a pretty young daughter named Ann. Green was a justice of the peace and a man of local influence. There was also a character named Jack Kelso, a drifter with remarkable literary knowledge.

Lincoln rapidly won the admiration of almost everyone in town. And the fact that he could pull this off was a demonstration not only of his well-rounded personality but also of his great potential as a leader.

It was, moreover, the achievement of a man whose emotions were in fine equilibrium. Compared to the emotional crises that were over his horizon, these early days in New Salem show Lincoln in a confident, exuberant condition.

He was in superb form that summer. In Sangamotown, as he and his friends built the flatboat, he became a local celebrity because of his off-color wit and high spirits. A resident named Clark E. Carr recalled that he had never "seen another who provoked such mirth, and who entered into rollicking fun with such glee."[28] And these very same qualities commended themselves to the rougher crowd in New Salem.

Many anecdotes concerning the Lincoln humor during this period were piled up later by aspiring biographers. Here is an example of an early Lincoln joke that William Herndon was able to extract later on from a New Salem storekeeper named Abner Y. Ellis. The gist of it was the proposition that Ethan Allen went to England after the Revolution and was taunted by Britons who resented the United States. When he was told that a portrait of George Washington had been hung in a privy, he jauntily replied that he found it especially appropriate that this particular thing had been done by *Englishmen*.

When his listeners took the bait and asked him why that was so, he replied as follows: because there was "nothing that will make an Englishman Shit So quick as the Sight of Genl Washington."[29]

One can easily imagine the effect of such a joke if Lincoln told it to the New Salem rowdies.

The clinching event in Lincoln's initiation into the world of the New Salem roughnecks was a wrestling match with the champion of the Clary's Grove Boys, Jack Armstrong. Offutt had wagered that no one in New Salem would be able to throw Abe Lincoln. Armstrong took the bet, and, though Lincoln was reportedly irked by the fact that Offutt had acted without his consent, he agreed to wrestle Armstrong. Varying accounts of this match were recorded, but one common element in all of the stories was the upshot: Lincoln performed so well that he made Jack Armstrong an ardent admirer and friend.[30]

Lincoln projected a very different image when he took up his duties as storekeeper. Lincoln became extremely popular with customers for several reasons, but mostly because he was impeccably polite and he treated the ladies with decorum. Hannah Armstrong, who was married to Jack, said she liked Lincoln "first rate" because he was "so pleasant and kind."[31]

His service in Offutt's store began to cement his reputation as "Honest Abe," the fair-dealer who would never—ever—overcharge a customer, and who, if he found that he had made a mistake, would promptly bring the refund right to the customer's door.

This was, of course, one of many different sides to Lincoln's protean personality. To be sure, there was always an overall honesty of purpose that would guide him throughout his life. But his capacities for mischief, satire, and cunning were also at the ready, though he kept these talents suppressed when the demands of his situation dictated simple and straightforward action.

Finally, Lincoln endeared himself to the intellectual elite of New Salem. As he took up his duties in Offutt's store, he asked Mentor Graham, the local teacher, to supply him with an English grammar textbook.

His speech would always continue to bear the twang of his border state origins but his sedulous quest for the mastery of high English usage started to make his statements distinguished. And his eloquence increased as his literary interests turned him toward the poetry of Pope, Byron, Edgar Allen Poe, and the Scottish bard Robert Burns. No doubt he liked the fact that Burns was a religious skeptic with a bawdy sense of humor, like himself. So he turned his talent for mimicry to mastering the Scottish accent in order that his recitations of Burns would come off properly.

Most of all, he turned to Shakespeare, and according to some accounts he and Jack Kelso regaled one another with the beauties of the various plays. For years after living in New Salem, he would carry along with him copies of the plays as he travelled, and later he told an actor that he re-read the most political plays, such as *Julius Caesar*, *Hamlet*, and *Macbeth*, "per-haps as frequently as any unprofessional reader."[32]

In the winter of 1831, he was initiated into a Literary and Debating Society that genteel residents of New Salem had founded to improve the tone of civic life. James Rutledge, the tavern keeper, was in charge. After Lincoln's first address to the group, Rutledge told his wife that "there was more in Abe's head than wit and fun, that he was already a fine speaker; that all he lacked was culture to enable him to reach the high destiny that he Knew was in store for him."[33]

In all, the ascent of Abraham Lincoln from the tedium of manual labor had been swift, confident, and joyous. To achieve his full potential, he was moving just as quickly as his mind performed. The "high destiny" before him was mysterious and cloudy, but he reached out toward it just the same.

INITIATIONS

aving established himself as a man to be reckoned with, Lincoln assessed his situation when the store in which he worked appeared to be entering a decline. In 1832, he reached a decision that was striking for a young man of only twenty-three: he decided to get into politics by running for the Illinois state legislature.

All through the winter he had honed his literary skills. One of his mentors, Dr. Jason Duncan, stated that in the course of this winter (1831–1832) "he seemed to master the construction of the English language and apply the rules . . . in a most astonishing manner."[1] In addition, the time he spent perusing newspapers and chatting with people paid off in well-considered positions on the major controversies of the day.

The year 1832 was the mid-way point in the presidential career of Andrew Jackson, who was running for a second term. Jackson regarded himself as the common man's friend, thus establishing himself in political terms as something of a liberal. But early liberals were government-bashers. They believed that government tends to be controlled by the rich and the privileged, so the slogan adopted by the party that Jackson and his friends were creating—the Democratic Party—was the famous dictum that "the government that governs best, governs least."

Lincoln disagreed. He believed that government could be used in ways that helped everybody, so he rallied behind the presidential aspirations of Jackson's most powerful rival, Henry Clay, who was an advocate of "internal improvements"—the sorts of projects that later generations would call "public works." Clay proposed that the federal government should augment the power of the nation by giving Americans up-to-date transportation systems, especially roads and canals. He and his followers were building their own political party. Known as "National Republicans" in 1832, they would call themselves "Whigs" by the middle of the decade.

Lincoln wrote his first political platform in March 1832. It appeared in the *Sangamo Journal,* which was published in Springfield. In addition to supporting the proposition of education for all, Lincoln applied Clay's principles to the situation of New Salem; he called for improvements to the Sangamon River that would make it a more efficient channel for inland navigation.

But Lincoln had to postpone his campaign for the legislature when an Indian war broke out in Illinois.

The war involved the Sac and Fox (or Meskwaki) peoples, Native Americans whose settlements had once stretched all the way from Canada to the American plains. Under the 1804 Treaty of St. Louis, representatives of the tribes gave up their lands in Illinois, as well as territory in Missouri and Wisconsin.

A number of Sac and Fox leaders regarded the 1804 treaty as fraudulent. They charged that the signatories did not represent their peoples and did not understand what they were signing. One of these chieftains, a leader named Black Hawk, led a band of his followers back into Illinois in 1832.

In April, Governor John Reynolds issued a militia call-up, and Lincoln and others in New Salem responded. Militiamen in Illinois had the right to elect their officers, and Lincoln, to his surprise and gratification, was elected captain of his unit.

He proved an effective officer in most respects. His command was challenging since some of Clary's Grove boys were members of his outfit—the Fourth Illinois Regiment of Mounted Volunteers—and while his followers admired Lincoln, they did not submit readily to orders.

His resourcefulness was demonstrated in the way that he improvised commands when he was unsure of military terminology. Once, when he wanted his men to pass through a gate, he could not remember the proper command for that maneuver. So he made the matter simple by saying, "This company is dismissed for two minutes, when it will fall in again on the other side of the gate."[2]

The "Black Hawk War" in Illinois would rage until August, when the state militia, assisted by Army regulars, drove Black Hawk and his followers into Wisconsin, where they were defeated.

Lincoln and his troops did not see combat. But they had some harrowing experiences in their thirty-day enlistment. They were ordered to march north to Rock Island, where they were mustered into federal service under the command of Col. Zachary Taylor. Along the way, they saw corpses of whites who had been slain in the battle of Stillman's Run; the corpses were mutilated, some scalped and others beheaded. Later in May, they found the corpses of women and children who were scalped and hung upside down.

On a memorable occasion, Lincoln interceded on behalf of a peaceful Indian whose life was in danger. When an old Indian entered their camp with an introductory note from Lewis Cass, the secretary of war, attesting to his good character, some of Lincoln's men threatened to kill him. According to one account, Lincoln bristled with indignation. "Men this must not be done," he said. One of Lincoln's men defied him and accused him of cowardice. "If any man thinks I am a coward let him test it," Lincoln retorted. When the challenger complained that Lincoln's height and strength were an overmatch in physical combat, Lincoln said, "this you can guard against—Choose your weapons."[3]

The old Indian's life was spared.

After the thirty-day enlistment ended, most of the volunteers from New Salem went home. But Lincoln re-enlisted, first in late May and then again in June.

Before this service was over, Lincoln had time to enjoy himself, not only in the kinds of athletic games in which he excelled, but in other ways as well.[4] He and some fellow militiamen wandered into the town of Galena seeking diversion. One of his colleagues, John Todd Stuart—who would soon become one of his most important associates—recalled that they "went to the hoar houses. . . . All went purely for fun—devilment—nothing else."[5]

In mid-July, Lincoln's third enlistment ended when the troops reached Wisconsin, and he walked back most of the way to New Salem—except for a brief excursion by canoe—since his horse had been stolen.

For the most part, Lincoln chose to make light of his military service. In 1848, when Democrats were touting the military background of their presidential nominee, Lewis Cass (who had served in the War of 1812),

Lincoln used self-mockery to ridicule the Democrats' pretensions. "By the way, Mr. Speaker," he quipped on the floor of the U.S. House of Representatives, "did you know I am a military hero? Yes sir; in the days of the Black Hawk War, I fought, bled, and came away.... It is certain I did not break my sword, for I had none to break; but I bent a musket pretty badly on one occasion. If Gen. Cass went in advance of me in picking huckleberries, I guess I surpassed him in charges upon the wild onions. If he saw any live, fighting Indians, it was more than I did; but I had a good many bloody struggles with the musquetoes; and, although I never fainted from loss of blood, I can truly say I was often very hungry."[6]

When Lincoln returned from his service, he had precious little time for campaigning, since the election for the Illinois legislature would be held on August 6. And while he was very well known and well liked in New Salem, the far-flung residents of the surrounding Sangamon County would have to be courted in a whirlwind series of speeches.

One observer, Stephen T. Logan, who listened to a speech that Lincoln was giving in Springfield, was impressed. Even though Lincoln was "tall and gawky and rough looking," Logan remembered, "after he began speaking I became very much interested in him. He made a very sensible speech." Logan, who went on to become both a friend and a law partner of Lincoln's, reminisced that throughout his campaigning in 1832 "he had the same individuality that he kept up through all his life."[7]

Though Lincoln was not elected to the legislature in 1832, he won 277 of the 300 votes cast in New Salem, and political observers took note.

Until the next election, Lincoln had to support himself, and so he turned to the best alternative to manual labor he had found thus far: running a store. But this time he set his sights higher and aspired to be an owner rather than a clerk.

He soon had a chance to buy a half-interest in a general merchandise store in New Salem owned by J. Rowan Herndon and William F. Berry. Herndon was ready to sell. Lincoln and Berry got a license permitting them to sell liquor by the glass. The fact that the store dispensed liquor was part of its undoing, for Berry would dip into the stock.

For a number of reasons, Lincoln and Berry were unsuccessful merchants. Lincoln, for one, found it hard to keep his mind on the work. In his own account of the failure of his store, Lincoln stated that he and his partner sank "deeper and deeper in debt" and that eventually the store "winked out."[8]

Berry died in 1835, which left Lincoln holding the bag for $1,100 in debt, which was a monumental sum in those days. "That debt was the greatest obstacle I have ever met in life," he reportedly told a friend. He assured his creditors that if only they "would leave me alone, I would give them all I could earn, over my living, as fast as I could earn it."[9] It took him years to pay off the debt.

Lincoln scraped up enough money to pay for room and board at different New Salem addresses: in the Lincoln-Berry store after it "winked out," at a series of private residences, with the Rutledge family, and with Mentor Graham. In the spring of 1833, good fortune arrived: he was nominated and appointed as the New Salem postmaster.

Lincoln held this job for three years until the New Salem post office closed in 1836. He found another source of income in 1833 that was more consequential: he became a surveyor. John Calhoun, the official surveyor of Sangamon County, hired Lincoln as an assistant because the demands upon the office were growing. Calhoun, who knew Lincoln from the Blackhawk War, was a Democrat, so Lincoln put to him a very sharp question: "Do I have to give up any of my principles for this job," he reportedly asked. If so, he continued, he would not "touch it with a ten foot pole."[10]

Calhoun assured Lincoln that his Whiggish principles could be maintained without jeopardizing his position. So Lincoln procured the necessary tools, along with textbooks. He had long had a penchant for mathematics, and he mastered the art of surveying by himself. His first recorded work as a surveyor dates to January 1834.

These facts suggest a line of inquiry into the workings of Lincoln's mind that may be worth pursuing. The interest in geometry kindled by his initiation into the art of surveying led him to study Euclid in the 1850s. In 1860 he declared that he had "studied and nearly mastered the Six-books of Euclid."[11]

This interest in geometry, whereby the precepts of mathematics are applied to spatial propositions, suggests the possibility that Lincoln was developing a power that would manifest itself later in what might be called an architectonic sense of strategy. Consider the following message from Lincoln to General George B. McClellan in 1862: "You are now nearer to Richmond than the enemy is. . . . Why can you not reach there before him[?] His route is the arc of a circle, while yours is the chord."[12]

It is not far-fetched to wonder if Lincoln could *visualize* the ebb and flow of power, both political and military, by the time he reached the height of his abilities. One of the keys to his intellectual mastery was his power to see the big picture in a flash and then relate the subsidiary parts of a problem to the whole.

As 1834 was an election year, Lincoln had every intention of trying again for the legislature. This time, his network of friendships led him to a much closer collaboration with John Todd Stuart, who, like him, was a Whig and a follower of Henry Clay. Stuart—already a member of the legislature—was the son of a professor of classical languages, and he was a practicing attorney with an office in Springfield. It was Stuart who suggested to Lincoln that he take up the study of law.

Lincoln had already considered this idea; in his Indiana days he had sometimes dropped into courthouses and listened to trials. In New Salem he had served on juries and he even argued a few cases for friends before Bowling Green, the justice of the peace. He had borrowed some law books from Green, who was gradually becoming a paternal figure in his life. Until 1834, however, he had felt that his lack of a college education was a fatal impediment to the prospect of becoming an attorney.

Stuart convinced him otherwise, and so did Green.

He borrowed more law books from Stuart. He read Blackstone's *Commentaries*. Whenever he had a spare moment, he would find a secluded place and read law. When a neighbor named Russell Godbey saw Lincoln reading one day, he asked him what kind of a book it might be. "Studying law," was the laconic reply. "Great God Almighty," Godbey said.[13]

Stuart and Green were becoming extremely consequential figures for Lincoln. Abner Y. Ellis alleged later on that Lincoln actually "loved Mr. Green" as "his almost Second Father."[14] If there was truth in this statement, its importance is surely self-evident.

And if there was also truth in a statement made later on by Edward D. Baker—another important future associate of Lincoln's—Bowling Green could display an audacity that perhaps encouraged the very same quality in Lincoln. Baker recalled that he had once asked Green whether justices of the peace could hear slander suits, contending that only a court of general jurisdiction could hear such cases. "Well, think again," Green replied, "you have not read law very well, or very long; try it again; now, have I jurisdiction; can I not do it?" No, said Baker, you cannot. Green replied, "I know I can; for, by Heaven, I have done it."[15]

In the election of 1834, Lincoln had bipartisan support because of his popularity in Sangamon County. When the election was held on August

4, he came in second in a field of thirteen, and so—at the age of twenty-five—he would be one of the four legislators to represent the county in Vandalia, which was then the state capital of Illinois. He borrowed some money to pay his more urgent financial obligations and bought himself his first tailor-made suit.

At this point John Todd Stuart became even more consequential as a figure in Lincoln's career. A well-educated and (by the standards of the time) handsome young man, he became a political as well as a legal mentor, for he was nothing less than the Whig floor leader in the Illinois House of Representatives—and Lincoln roomed with him in the same Vandalia tavern where other Whig members of the legislature were staying.

The legislature was in session from December 1834 until April 1835. Lincoln was generally quiet as he learned the legislative routine.

One of the measures that Lincoln supported was a bill to construct a canal between Chicago and La Salle on the Illinois River and to pay for it with $500,000 worth of state bonds. This canal, completed in 1848, would be known as the Illinois and Michigan Canal and it helped to make Chicago a bustling city. Another important bill that Lincoln supported was a bill to establish a state-chartered bank.

This was a very important measure because of a pre-eminent issue in national politics that was being fought out in Washington: the so-called "Bank War" of President Andrew Jackson, who aimed to destroy the federally chartered Second Bank of the United States.

Created by Congress in 1816, this bank was given a twenty-year charter that would have to be renewed in 1836. During the presidential election of 1832, Henry Clay, the most prominent congressional supporter of the bank, pushed through a recharter bill four years before it was needed.

This was a high-risk maneuver, since Jackson hated banks in general and the enemies of the Bank of the United States were calling it a "monster" bank. Clay was forcing the issue as he ran for president, forcing the hand of his opponent. Sure enough, after Congress passed the recharter bill, Jackson promptly vetoed it.

After Jackson was re-elected, he proceeded to destroy the bank. He did this by withdrawing federal deposits, which were then redeposited in commercial banks around the country. It remained for Jackson's successor, Martin Van Buren, to establish a complete divorce between the federal government and banks by pushing through a measure in 1840 that established a system of "sub-treasuries," depositories around the country where federal funds would sit idle until they were needed.

The Whigs, on the other hand, believed that government-chartered banks served important functions. And the destruction of the Second Bank of the United States was tantamount to what would have happened if Parliament had destroyed the Bank of England. So the action of Lincoln and the Illinois Whigs in creating a state-chartered bank in Illinois was important; indeed, the issue would become extraordinarily important after the Panic of 1837 ushered in an economic depression.

Jackson's "Bank War" was supported by a tough, if diminutive, Democrat, Stephen A. Douglass (who later dropped the second "s" from his last name). A transplanted Vermonter, Douglas taught school and then entered the legal profession. As Lincoln began his legislative career, Douglas was campaigning for the position of state's attorney for Morgan County, Illinois.

Lincoln learned a great deal in this initiation into legislative politics. When the session adjourned, he returned to New Salem, where he resumed his duties as postmaster and surveyor. And of course he returned to his study of the law.

On August 25, 1835, a lovely young woman named Ann Rutledge, the daughter of Lincoln's friend and admirer, the tavern keeper James Rutledge, died in New Salem. Ever since Lincoln's own death, his biographers have disagreed as to whether the death of Ann Rutledge did or did not constitute a turning point in Lincoln's life.

In 1866, William Herndon in a public lecture claimed not only that Abraham Lincoln was deeply in love with Ann Rutledge but that her death, which nearly drove him insane, made him utterly incapable of loving any other woman for the rest of his life.

The seeming extravagance of that claim plunged the whole affair into the mists of legend—disreputable legend—and that is where the matter remained until the end of the twentieth century. One Lincoln biographer in 1952 wrote that the supposed love affair with Ann Rutledge was "a legend for which no shred of contemporary evidence has been found."[16] Another Lincoln biographer stated in 1977 that "there is no evidence that Ann and Lincoln ever had anything more than a platonic relationship."[17]

But in 1993, a full-scale study of the subject by John E. Walsh would reverse this climate of opinion.[18] Indeed, Douglas L. Wilson, on his way to becoming one of the foremost scholars of Lincoln's early life, declared five years after Walsh's study that the Lincoln-Rutledge affair was without a doubt quite real.

Even though "the principal thing that most present-day Lincoln students have been taught about Lincoln's love affair with Ann Rutledge is that it is largely a myth," Wilson wrote, "the character and weight of the evidence ultimately show that this view is very much mistaken."[19]

Lincoln possibly encountered Ann Rutledge as early as 1831, at which time she was engaged to be married to a man named John McNamar. But McNamar left New Salem and his long absence and silence led Ann to conclude that their engagement was broken. Then a courtship with Lincoln began, and though few details have survived, the overall evidence is impressive.

Ann's sister Nancy stated years later that Lincoln "declared his love and was accepted for she loved him with a more mature and enduring affection than she had ever felt for McNamar. No one could have seen them together and not be convinced that they loved each other truly."[20] It appears that the two of them were secretly engaged in the early months of 1835.

But then she died.

Hannah Armstrong, the wife of the Clary's Grove champion, reportedly told her daughter that she watched Lincoln "weep like a baby over the death of Ann Rutledge."[21] Elizabeth Abell, a neighbor, wrote that "he was staying with us at the time of her death" and that "I never seen a man mourn for a companion more than he did for her."[22]

This emotional thunderbolt hurled Lincoln into clinical depression; of this there can be no doubt. William Greene told Herndon that "after this sudden death of one whom his soul & heart dearly loved," Lincoln's many friends felt compelled to "keep watch and ward over Mr. Lincoln" who was "temporarily deranged. We watched during storms—fogs—damp gloomy weather Mr. Lincoln for fear of an accident. He said 'I can never be reconciled to have the snow—rains & storms to beat on her grave.'"[23]

Bowling Green's wife reported to the father-in-law of William Herndon that her husband, the justice of the peace, "went to Salem after Lincoln [and] brought him to his house and kept him a week or two" because Lincoln took the death of Ann "verry hard so much so that some thought his mind would become impaired."[24] John Hill, whose father was a merchant in New Salem, claimed that his family "had to lock him [Lincoln] up and keep guard over him for some two weeks . . . for fear he might

Commit Suicide. The whole village engaged in trying to quiet him and reconcile him to the loss."[25]

Henry McHenry recalled that "after the Event he seemed quite changed"; he "had little to say, but would take his gun and wander off in the woods by himself." And "his depression seemed to deepen for some time, so as to give anxiety to his friends in regard to his Mind."[26]

As Wilson has affirmed, this evidence of Lincoln's emotional breakdown "is massive and relatively unmixed.... While some of the testimony is admittedly hearsay, much of it is too specific or too particular or comes from too knowledgeable a source to be discounted or explained away."[27]

An old friend and legal protégé of Lincoln's named Isaac Cogdal reported on a visit with Lincoln in the White House. He found that the president wished to reminisce about New Salem days. According to Cogdal, Lincoln said that "when we lived in Salem there were the Greens, Potters Armstrongs—& Rutledges. These folks have got scattered all over the world—some are dead." Cogdal then asked Lincoln frankly whether he had ever feared for his own sanity after the death of Ann Rutledge.

And Lincoln reportedly replied, "I did really—I run off the track; it was my first. I loved the woman dearly & sacredly; she was a handsome girl—would have made a good loving wife—was natural & quite intellectual, though not highly Educated—I did honestly—& truly love the girl & think often—often of her now."[28]

When Lincoln said that the episode was "my first," he implied that this crisis was his first encounter with the kind of depression that would haunt him for the rest of his life. In the opinion of Joshua Wolf Shenk, who has done the most extensive research on Lincoln's emotional development, there can be no doubt that this episode was indeed Lincoln's first major brush with the tendency toward "melancholy" that would remain a persistent part of his character from that time forward.[29]

It is a psychological commonplace that innate tendencies toward depression, which can be inherited, may remain nothing more than mere potentialities until such time as a crisis draws them to the surface. Shenk has observed that while his struggle to stave off recurrences of what he would later call "the hypos" would constitute a vulnerability for Lincoln, there was a mental flip-side to this proposition: the "hypos" (at least over time) would generate a countervailing mental strength in the form of the coping devices that Lincoln would learn how to use to pull himself back from the depths.

Even so, this double-edged new development was without a doubt a major complication for Lincoln in every respect. Insofar as emotional and intellectual processes interpenetrate each other, it does not seem unwarranted to say that Lincoln's intellectual growth would be hindered in one sense and helped in another by onset of clinical depression.

The grief that he suffered with the loss of his sweetheart was not a completely new feeling for him since the deaths of his mother and sister years before had prefigured it. But in its magnitude, duration, and terrible intensity, this crisis was a turning point indeed.

RITES OF PASSAGE

L incoln recovered from the crisis that followed the death of Ann Rutledge, but his life had been profoundly changed. Before the crisis, his rise had been meteoric. After 1835, the picture became a good deal more complex. Uncertainties about his love life and his political future drove him deep into reflection. Yet his status as a public man whose career combined politics and law was established.

Questions about the nature of Lincoln's love life are difficult to answer since the evidence we possess is contradictory. Some of the anecdotes about Lincoln's early sexual relationships, for instance, portray him in opposite ways. A few of the raconteurs whom William Herndon and others interviewed after Lincoln's death implied he had been indifferent to women. Others portrayed him as hungry for heterosexual excitement. To add to the difficulties, some writers have theorized that Lincoln might have been either homosexual or bisexual.

Lincoln's stepmother recalled that he was "not very fond of girls."[1] Herndon, on the other hand, insisted that Lincoln had "terribly strong passions for women, could scarcely keep his hands off them . . . and yet he had honor and a strong will, and these enabled him to put out the fires of his terrible passion."[2]

What are we to make of such evidence? Abner Y. Ellis acknowledged that while "Lincoln was in those days a Verry shy Man of Ladies," he ascribed this situation to Lincoln's embarrassment about "his awkward appearance and his wareing apparel."[3] There is much to commend this view, since the evidence suggests that young women gave Lincoln precisely this impression, at least during his adolescence. One later recalled that "the young girls my age made fun of Abe," that they would "laugh at him right in his face." She added emphatically that Lincoln "tried to go with them, but no sir-ee, they'd give him the mitten every time, just because he was . . . so tall and gawky."[4]

It appears that Ann Rutledge was one in a series of women who showed Lincoln a charmingly different response as he came of age in his twenties, perhaps because—according to their own taste in masculine attributes—his appearance suggested to them an attractive sense of manly ruggedness.

What of the recent speculations that Lincoln might have had sexual relationships with men?[5] Much has been made of the fact that he bedded down with men in the course of his lodgings. But Lincoln scholar Charles B. Strozier insists that such arrangements were normal in frontier conditions, asserting that "on the frontier as Lincoln experienced it there was never any measure of private space. As a young boy, he slept on a cot in the same room with his parents and one older sister in a tight log cabin" where "everyone dressed—and undressed—in the common space." Moreover, shortages of housing forced men to bunk down with each other all the time as a matter of course.[6]

Regardless, those who believe that Lincoln was gay—or bisexual—will probably cling to this belief since the circumstantial evidence is ambiguous.

So is the evidence regarding the issue of whether he ever had sex with prostitutes. As previously noted, John Todd Stuart told Herndon about a visit to "hoar houses" in the Black Hawk War, and the anecdote seems to imply that Lincoln was a member of the group who went along. But in the view of some, the disjointed form in which Herndon set down the statement leaves the matter in doubt. Herndon recorded the words of Stuart in phrases that are broken up between dashes: "Lincoln & myself were in Iles—Spy Battalion" [i.e., in the spy battalion commanded by Captain Elijah Iles]—Got to Galena—went to the hoar houses—Gen Henry went—his magnetism drew all the women to himself—All went purely for fun—devilment—nothing Else." So did Lincoln go along with Stuart? When Stuart said that "all went," what did he mean? Did he mean that Lincoln was one of the men who "went," or did it simply mean that all those who *did* go—whoever they were—"went purely for fun"?[7]

There is other anecdotal evidence that Lincoln patronized prostitutes, especially an allegation that he visited a prostitute in Beardstown, Illinois, and then began to fear that he had contracted syphilis. Lincoln scholars disagree as to whether this tale—which was set forth by Herndon—should be believed.[8]

One of the problems with such material is that the bawdy humor that was so pervasive in New Salem makes it possible that some or all of these anecdotes were nothing more than jokes. Sometimes statements that begin as jokes are taken seriously after a while and there is no way for anyone to ascertain the truth years later. Others retain their identity as jokes and there is never any misunderstanding.

To provide an example, Jack Armstrong was so addicted to racy humor that he bantered with a perfectly cheerful demeanor that Lincoln had fathered an illegitimate son with his own wife, Hannah. But a neighbor, James Taylor, told Herndon that this tale was crude blarney: "Jack Armstrong used to plague Abe a great deal about his—Abe's son, which he had by Mrs. Armstrong; it was a joke—plagued Abe terribly."[9]

Mrs. Armstrong, with whom Lincoln did have a long but apparently platonic relationship, agreed that it was a joke; she wrote that when she visited Lincoln years later in Springfield (in the months between his election to the presidency and his departure for Washington, D.C.), "the boys got up a story on me that I went to get to sleep with Abe &c—. I replied to the Joke that it was not every woman who had the good fortune & high honor of sleeping with a President. This stopt the sport."[10]

James Short told Herndon that Lincoln would sometimes relate the following racy story:

> Once, when Mr L was surveying, he was put to bed in the same room with two girls, the head of his bed being next to the foot of the girls' bed. In the night he commenced tickling the feet of one of the girls with his fingers. As she seemed to enjoy it as much as he did he tickled a little higher up; and as he would tickle higher the girl would shove down lower and the higher he tickled the lower she moved. Mr L would tell the story with evident enjoyment. He never told how the thing ended.[11]

Douglas L. Wilson has concluded that the story's "authenticity as a Lincoln yarn" seems probable.[12]

But what kind of a yarn was it? Even if this was a tale that Lincoln actually told to others, was it true? Or was it just another exercise in bawdy humor from a man who for years had told off-color stories—most of them nothing more than obvious examples of good-natured nonsense—for their amusement value?

Among all the doubts that surround the details of Lincoln's love life prior to his courtship of Mary Todd, there is one episode about which there can be no doubt at all: his very odd courtship of a woman named Mary Owens.

Mary was the sister of Elizabeth Abell, a friend of Lincoln's who got to know him when he boarded with her family. Elizabeth and her husband Bennett were from Kentucky, but—unlike Lincoln—they were fairly well-to-do. Elizabeth was favorably impressed by Lincoln, who was clearly on his best behavior when he lodged with the Abells in 1833.

Lincoln got to know Mary Owens when she visited the Abells in 1833 and they found each other congenial. After a month, Miss Owens returned to Kentucky.

Then, about a year after the death of Ann Rutledge, Elizabeth suggested to Lincoln that he marry her sister. She offered to bring Mary Owens from Kentucky if Lincoln would be interested in such a match.

It is perhaps a commentary on Lincoln's shaky state of mind as he recovered from depression that he pounced upon the suggestion so fast as to suggest extremely rash action. But it does make emotional sense for a person on the rebound from suicidal grief to be more than normally receptive to life-affirming possibilities, especially if they seem to hold out the prospect of bringing back some measure—*any* measure—of what had been lost.

Lincoln's own account of the episode, which he described a few years later to another married female friend, Eliza Browning, tells the tale in a peculiar manner. Perhaps since the letter to Eliza was written on April Fool's Day (April 1, 1838) Lincoln chose to write in a humorous tone of self-mockery. Just the same, the letter is as notable as much for what it leaves out as for what it says. Here is an excerpt:

> It was, then, in the autumn of 1836, that a married lady of my acquaintance, and who was a great friend of mine, being about to pay a visit to her father and other relatives residing in Kentucky, proposed to me, that on her return she would bring a sister of hers with her, upon the

condition that I would engage to become her brother-in-law with all convenient dispatch. I, of course, accepted the proposal; for you know I could not have done otherwise, had I really been averse to it; but privately between you and me, I was most confoundedly well pleased with the project.[13]

We can only guess what Lincoln had in mind when he wrote that he could "not have done otherwise" even if he had "been averse" to the idea. This sentence suggests something very sad: he seemed to think that he might as well settle for a so-so marriage since the chance of ever finding a woman who could make him completely happy after the loss of Ann was next to nil.

After stating that he had "seen the said sister some three years before," and that he "thought her intelligent and agreeable," he concluded that he "saw no good objection to plodding life through hand in hand with her."[14]

He "saw no good objection" to "plodding" through life with Mary Owens. Hardly an auspicious beginning for a romance.

Sure enough, when Mary arrived, she was a disappointment. It seems that she had put on weight since Lincoln last saw her. He wrote that he knew she "was over-size," but now she was "a fair match for Falstaff." "Nothing," he wrote, "could have commenced at the size of infancy, and reached her present bulk in less than thirtyfive or forty years; and, in short, I was not all pleased with her. But what could I do? I had told her sister that I would take her for better or for worse; and I made a point of honor and conscience in all things, to stick to my word."[15]

Not surprisingly, the courtship of Lincoln and Mary Owens was awkward and strained, full of tension. Lincoln said that he was "continually repenting the rashness" that led him to make the promise to marry Elizabeth Abell's sister. "Through my life," he wrote, "I have been in no bondage, either real or immaginery from the thraldom of which I so much desired to be free."[16]

Lincoln's torment lasted for the better part of a year, and his final letter to Mary, dated August 16, 1837, makes painful reading. As exit strategies go, this missive from a guilt-stricken and obviously miserable young man is transparent:

I want in all cases to do right, and most particularly so, in all cases with women. I want, at this particular time, more than any thing else, to do right with you, and if I knew it would be doing right, as I rather suspect it would, to let you alone, I would do it. And for the purpose of making the matter as plain as possible, I now say, that you can now drop the subject, dismiss your thoughts (if you ever had any) from me forever, and leave this letter unanswered, without calling forth one accusing murmur from me. And I will even go further, and say, that if it will add any thing to your comfort, or peace of mind, to do so, it is my sincere wish that you should. Do not understand by this, that I wish to cut your acquaintance. I mean no such thing. What I do wish is, that our further acquaintance shall depend upon yourself. If such further acquaintance would contribute nothing to your happiness, I am sure it would not to mine. If you feel yourself in any degree bound to me, I am now willing to release you, provided you wish it; while, on the other hand, I am willing, and even anxious to bind you faster, if I can be convinced that it will in any considerable degree, add to your happiness. [17]

In Lincoln's account of the matter to Eliza Browning, he said that after he "delayed the matter as long as I thought I could in honor do," he concluded he "might as well bring it to a consumation without further delay," and so he "made the proposal [i.e., the proposal of marriage] to her direct; but, shocking to relate, she answered, No."

He told Eliza that he found himself "mortified," believing he had "made a fool of myself." But he might as well "let it go," he wrote; he had come to the conclusion "never again to think of marrying; and for this reason; I can never be satisfied with any one who would be block-head enough to have me."[18]

As Lincoln struggled through the Mary Owens episode, his career grew apace. His legal studies had been crowned with success when he was granted a law license on September 9, 1836, and his new law career abetted his law-*making* career, which in turn was integral to his rise as a politician. But the election of 1836 was a strange affair, and the devious tactics of the Whigs brought a new complexity to Lincoln's political situation.

In the previous election, the Whigs ran their very best candidate, Henry Clay, a smart, charismatic, popular, and forthright politician whose program was grounded in public works. But Clay was defeated by Andrew Jackson. Many Whigs came to a glum conclusion: if a man like Clay could be beaten by a demagogue like Jackson—for that was the way that a great many Whigs viewed Jackson—it was a sad commentary on the democratic process. And this led to another sad conclusion: if intelligent and forthright proposals could not succeed, other ways would have to be found to give America the programs that were needed.

And so the Whigs turned to devious tactics. The very name they had chosen for their party—Whig—was something of a trick. Jackson was a government-basher, while the Whigs favored "big government." But since Jackson had succeeded by posing as the people's champion, the Whigs decided to turn the tables on their foe.

For a long time, "Whiggery" denoted resistance to arbitrary power. So the enemies of Jackson in the 1830s tried to twist the term in convenient ways to their uses. Jackson, they said, was a wolf in sheep's clothing who posed as a defender of liberty. But he was really "King Andrew the First," a stubborn despot who thwarted the wishes of the people by using his veto to overturn the wise legislation that the people's own elected representatives in Congress had passed. Consequently, a new form of "Whiggism" was needed to resist the tyranny of Jackson and give the people what they wanted.

But by adopting a name that denoted the protection of liberty by *limiting* governmental power, the Whigs were disguising the important fact that they *favored* bold federal action. They were trying, in an odd and misleading sort of way, to out-Jackson Jackson.

The Whig strategy in the 1836 election was also devious: instead of running one candidate against Martin Van Buren, who was Jackson's anointed successor, the Whigs ran *four* different candidates in different parts of the country: William Henry Harrison, Daniel Webster, Hugh Lawson White, and Willie Person Mangum. Their goal was to prevent *any* candidate from gaining enough votes in the Electoral College. If they succeeded, the election would be thrown into the House of Representatives, where political deals could be made to put a Whig in the White House. But the Whigs' tricky strategy failed and so Van Buren, the successor of Jackson, became the next president.

Meanwhile, Lincoln campaigned for another term in the Illinois legislature. In a letter that was published in the *Sangamo Journal* on June 13, he seized upon the following opportunity: "In your paper of last Saturday," he wrote, "I see a communication over the signature of 'Many Voters,' in which the candidates who are announced in the Journal, are called upon to 'show their hands.' Agreed. Here's mine!"

He went on to announce he would support the enlargement of the electorate by broadening the qualifications for voting. He even supported giving women the vote. In something of an anticlimax, he proclaimed that "if alive on the first Monday of November, I shall vote for Hugh L. White for President."[19]

The campaigning was robust, and Lincoln participated in election-year tactics that went beyond partisanship and at times became bitterly personal. The victim of anonymous handbills, he struck back, calling one particular writer a "liar and a scoundrel" and promising to "give his proboscis a good wringing."[20]

Many anecdotes from Lincoln's associates attest to his gifts in these years as a writer of anonymous satires.[21] Such productions typify not only the scurrility of American politics during the Jacksonian period but also the side of Lincoln's high spirits that could generate humor of the sort that any roughneck would enjoy.

Quite troubling, however—especially in regard to the issue of whether Lincoln ever succumbed to any notions of white supremacy—is the fact that some polemical productions attributed to him employed the tactics of race-baiting against an array of Democratic opponents who were also using those tactics.[22] If Lincoln was indeed the writer of the pieces in question, his authorship raises the issue—to be considered at length in subsequent chapters—of whether this was a sign of an inner conviction in Lincoln or a demonstration of no-holds-barred opportunism that members of both parties, the Whigs and the Democrats, displayed.

The Whig ticket swept Sangamon County, and Lincoln was returned to his seat in the legislature, along with a group of Whig colleagues who were known as the "Long Nine" since their average height was roughly six feet.

The session began in a melancholy fashion for Lincoln. Not only was he in the early stages of the Mary Owens affair, he was seriously ill when he arrived in Vandalia. Regardless, big proposals were churning in the legislative mill, not the least of which was the relocation of the state capital from Vandalia to Springfield. New patterns of settlement in the state were reducing Vandalia to a backwater. Indeed, New Salem would soon become a ghost town because of these rapid demographic changes.

Lincoln made some important new connections with prominent Whigs in the course of this session. He met Orville Browning, the husband of the lady to whom he would later confess those details of the Mary

Owens affair, along with Ninian W. Edwards, a wealthy politician who was also the son of a former Illinois governor. Lincoln's influence was rising.

And so was his reputation for legislative accomplishment. In fact, he was quickly becoming the floor leader of the Whigs, thus following in the footsteps of his friend John Todd Stuart.

One colleague mused that Lincoln "had a quaint and peculiar way, all of his own, of treating a subject, and he frequently startled us by his modes—but he was always right." The Whigs "followed his lead, but he followed nobody's lead; he hewed the way for us to follow, and we gladly did so."[23]

Lincoln played an important role in the movement to relocate the capital. On February 28, 1837, the measure passed and the relocation of the capital to Springfield was scheduled to take effect in 1839.

In the same session, Whigs and Democrats agreed on a $10 million program of internal improvements such as roads, canals, even railroads. The popularity of these measures was such that many Democrats on this one occasion put aside their government-bashing and went on record in support.

On the other hand, many Democrats vilified the state-chartered bank that was the Illinois counterpart to the controversial Second Bank of the United States. One of them was Stephen A. Douglas, who was serving with Lincoln in the Illinois legislature. Lincoln took to the floor to defend the state bank and he assailed his Democratic foes in the following terms:

> Mr. Chairman, this movement is exclusively the work of politicians; a set of men who have interests aside from the interests of the people, and who, to say the most of them, are, taken as a mass, at least one long step removed from honest men. I say this with the greater freedom because, being a politician myself, none can regard it as personal.[24]

This joke typified the way Lincoln used self-deprecation to protect his flanks while employing the most adroit techniques of sarcasm against his foes. Small wonder that he rose so quickly to become the new Whig floor leader. Another illustration of his oratorical techniques is the way he used populistic ridicule to dispose of controversies regarding the disbursement of the state bank's stock and to deflect a Democratic motion to conduct a formal inquiry into the matter:

It is clear that no question can arise on this portion of the resolution, except a question between capitalists in regard to the ownership of stock. Some gentlemen have the stock in their hands, while others, who have more money than they know what to do with, want it; and this, and this alone, is the question, to settle which we are called on to squander thousands of the people's money. What interest, let me ask, have the people in the settlement of this question? . . . These capitalists generally act harmoniously, and in concert, to fleece the people, and now, that they have got into a quarrel among themselves, we are called upon to appropriate the people's money to settle the quarrel.[25]

The most significant action that Lincoln took in this session was his vote on an issue that would gradually define the very meaning of his life: the issue of slavery. The issue was becoming more heatedly disputed in the 1830s, and positions on both sides of the argument were becoming more radical.

For example, defenders of slavery were creating new laws in southern states to crack down on abolitionist activity. These were actually laws that criminalized anti-slavery speech.

This suppression of free speech was held to be constitutional, inasmuch as the First Amendment of the Federal Constitution begins with the word "Congress." "*Congress* shall make no law . . . abridging free speech" is the operative clause. State governments in fact suppressed free speech all the time and this state of affairs would remain the case until 1925 when the Supreme Court applied the First Amendment to the states.

Illinois was a hotbed of white supremacist doctrine in the nineteenth century. In 1848, for instance, Illinois voters adopted a new state constitution that was harshly negro-phobic; its most draconian provisions prohibited free blacks from even entering the state. Indeed, *pro-slavery* sentiment in Illinois (at least in the southern portions of the state) was so strong that an abolitionist named Elijah Lovejoy would be murdered in 1837, murdered by a pro-slavery mob on November 7 in the town of Alton.

It was in this context that the Illinois legislature passed some anti-abolitionist resolutions in January 1837, resolutions passed in the House by the lopsided margin of seventy-seven to six. Lincoln was a member of the tiny minority who opposed the resolutions.

Then he and a fellow legislator named Dan Stone (a member of the Long Nine) co-authored an anti-slavery protest stating in part that "the undersigned ... believe that the institution of slavery is founded on both injustice and bad policy," though Lincoln and Stone went on to declare that "the promulgation of abolition doctrines tends rather to increase than to abate its evils."[26]

Like his mentor Henry Clay—indeed, like many of the Founding Fathers—Lincoln hoped that a gradual phase-out of slavery could be instituted in America.

Lincoln's innermost feelings on race at this point must remain conjectural, in spite of the pervasiveness of racism in his region. Lincoln scholar Don E. Fehrenbacher once argued that Lincoln "had little contact with Negroes while growing up in backwoods Indiana or as a young man in New Salem, Illinois." That may be true, though his early encounters with slaves on his trips to New Orleans were surely significant.

In any case, Fehrenbacher was correct when he observed that "there is scarcely any record of his thoughts on race until he was past forty years of age." Most importantly, "the assumption that his racial attitudes were shaped more or less permanently by his early social environment does not take account of the fact that youth may rebel against established opinion." And Lincoln was already rebelling when he voted against the resolutions that were passed by the Illinois legislature in January 1837.[27]

In March, as the legislature prepared to adjourn, Lincoln got a welcome offer: he was invited to join John Todd Stuart's law firm in Springfield. He accepted this offer, and thereupon decided—especially in light of the fact that the growing city of Springfield would soon become the new state capital—that it was time to bring his days in New Salem to an end. So in April he took his belongings and headed off toward the place that he would soon call home.

Springfield was changing in 1837, and according to many accounts, it was changing for the better. In some respects it was still a frontier settlement, but in other ways it was shaping up into a dignified and commodious location for the new state capital.

With a population of around two thousand, the city had private schools, a Young Men's Lyceum, and a lecture circuit that sometimes brought famous people to town. A local aristocracy flourished and some fancy residences were already local ornaments. The most prosperous neighborhood in Springfield was "Quality Hill" in the southwest quadrant of the city.

Even though he was exhilarated by the promise of the new law partnership, Lincoln was dejected and listless as the time approached to leave New

Salem. After the legislative session, he was traveling with a friend, William Butler, who reminisced later about Lincoln's low spirits at the time.

According to Butler, Lincoln said that "all the rest of you have something to look forward to, and all are glad to get home, and will have something to do when you get there. But it isn't so with me. I am going home, Butler, without a thing in the world. I have drawn all my pay I got at Vandalia, and have spent it all." Lincoln then explained how deeply indebted he was.[28]

Butler accompanied Lincoln on a preliminary trip to Springfield and paid off some of his debts. He even offered to let Lincoln board at his Springfield home free of charge. Lincoln considered this offer when he traveled back to New Salem to tie up some loose ends in early April. He stayed until April 15.

When he arrived back in Springfield, however, he decided to sleep in an office adjacent to Stuart's when he set up shop at the law firm. Acting upon this plan, he walked to a store that sold dry goods, groceries, hardware, books, and sundries at the corner of Fifth and Washington streets. This store was run by a friendly young man named Joshua F. Speed, who, like Lincoln, hailed from Kentucky.

Years later, Speed set forth a reminiscence of this first meeting. Lincoln threw his saddlebags onto the counter and told Speed he wanted to buy materials to construct a bed. After Speed had calculated the cost, Lincoln said, "it is probably cheap enough, but I want to say that cheap as it is I have not the money to pay. But if you will credit me until Christmas, and my experiment here as a lawyer is a success, I will pay you then. If I fail in that I will probably never be able to pay you at all."

Hearing this, Speed took pity on Lincoln and said that he had "a very large room" upstairs in the store with "a very large double bed in it; which you are perfectly welcome to share with me if you choose."

When Lincoln walked into the store he was downcast—Speed said that he "never saw so gloomy, and melancholy a face"—but after Lincoln inspected the room and accepted Speed's offer, he was "beaming with pleasure and smiles."[29] Lincoln had just met the man who for several years would be his best friend in the world.

Speed later reflected on the fact that such emotional shifts were not unusual for Lincoln. The "mobility of his nature" made his moods change quickly. When sadness yielded to high spirits, "his face was radiant and glowing, and almost gave expression to his thoughts before his tongue could utter them."[30]

The episode when Lincoln met Speed was in many ways a commentary on his development. The contrast between the brilliant and successful Whig floor-leader and the penniless and forlorn supplicant who shambled into Speed's store was—and remains—rather striking.

These changes of mood would continue as he settled into life in Springfield. On May 7, when he wrote to Mary Owens, he had slipped back into dejection. He told her that "this thing of living in Springfield is rather a dull business." He was "quite as lonesome here as ever was anywhere in my life."[31] Even so, his career as an attorney was beginning in earnest.

The *Sangamo Journal* ran an announcement to the effect that "J.T. Stuart and A. Lincoln, Attorneys and Counsellors at Law, will practice conjointly, in the courts of this Judicial Circuit." The second-story office of their firm was located in the same building where the circuit court held its sessions.

Stuart and Lincoln would work together for the next four years and Lincoln at last began to prosper. Stuart's practice was the largest in the city.

At the same time, Lincoln and Speed were becoming close friends, not only as roommates but also as members of a male social circle whose members got together after work in Speed's store to share jokes and to regale each other with their triumphs and tribulations as bachelors. No doubt this male camaraderie, which put Lincoln back in his element as a humorist *par excellence*, helped him greatly through the final phases of the Mary Owens ordeal. The men also belonged to a "Poetical Society" that conversed about a great many subjects, some of them racy and some of them serious.

Many of the friends Lincoln made—people such as James C. Conkling, a rising Whig attorney—would remain consequential figures in his life down the years.

Speed reminisced years later about the mental power that Lincoln displayed at such times—as well as in the moments when Speed had the opportunity to watch him at work. He had a mind that could break off any train of thought, digress upon a completely different subject, then resume his earlier discourse as if nothing had happened.

"He might be writing an important document," Speed remembered, or "be interrupted in the midst of a sentence, turn his attention to matters entirely foreign to the subject on which he was engaged, and take up his pen and begin where he had left off without reading the previous part of the sentence. He could grasp, exhaust, and quit any subject with more facility than any man I have ever seen or heard of."[32] In all, "his analytical powers were marvelous."[33]

In the first week of May, a financial panic shook the nation and it ushered in the worst economic depression that Americans had ever experienced. The Panic of 1837, as it was called, was international. And yet mistakes by Andrew Jackson during his "war" with the Second Bank of the United States created preconditions for the panic to spread in America.

Thousands of people were thrown out of work across the country. Others lost their homes or their farms through bank foreclosures, and many banks failed and went out of business. Tax receipts plummeted and so did the receipts from governmental land sales. Nine states defaulted on their bonds, and the Illinois state bank, which Lincoln had supported so vigorously since the Whigs created it in 1835, was in danger.

The depression that resulted from the Panic of 1837 would last for almost six years. It spelled doom for the presidency of Martin Van Buren, who was prevented by his party's ideology—"the government that governs best, governs least"—from taking much action to stimulate the economy.

But Whigs such as Henry Clay and his young acolyte Lincoln insisted that governmental public works (or "internal improvements" as they were called at the time), especially projects that expanded the nation's transportation infrastructure, should be pushed, not least of all to usher in economic recovery.

The Whigs' governor, Joseph Duncan, called the legislature into special session. He was frightened as he confronted the effects of this depression, and he urged his fellow Whigs to back away from the expensive program of state internal improvements that Lincoln and others had voted for a few months earlier. But Lincoln and his like-minded Whig legislators refused to do so.

Meanwhile, another crisis was brewing in 1837, a crisis in regard to the controversy over slavery. For defenders of slavery, not only in the slave states, but also in many of the free states, were becoming more aggressive.

Partially due to the fear of slave rebellions (such as the 1831 Nat Turner revolt in Virginia), they had been suppressing free speech within the slave states, as previously noted. Even federal post-masters in these states were forced to intercept the mail in order to find and destroy anti-slavery tracts. Moreover, the United States House of Representatives

had been forced in 1836 to adopt a "gag rule," whereby anti-slavery petitions would have to be tabled and could never be debated or put to a vote.

By 1837, pro-slavery southerners were starting to demand that even
free states should be forced to take similar action and suppress the free
speech of abolitionists. That was how the resolutions on slavery that Lincoln and Dan Stone had opposed back in January had come before the
Illinois legislature in the first place.

On February 6, 1837, Senator John C. Calhoun of South Carolina
made a speech in the Senate on slavery, a speech that showed how radical
the pro-slavery position had become. Many white southerners, Calhoun
proclaimed, defended the existence of slavery as a "necessary evil," but
slavery, he thundered, was not an evil at all: *it was a "positive good."*

All great civilizations, Calhoun asserted, shoved the inferior folk down
below. And that was how these civilizations achieved their greatness: they
created a degraded class of drudges who would do the hard physical labor
so that the minds of superior people would be free to create greater things.

Southern slave owners had nothing to apologize for, Calhoun asserted.
It was the abolitionists, the attackers of slavery, who should be forced to
apologize.

And so it was that pro-slavery southerners began to threaten even the
physical safety of northern abolitionists. The state legislature of Georgia
offered a bounty of five thousand dollars to anyone who would capture the
abolitionist William Lloyd Garrison and bring him to Georgia for trial.
People in other slave states offered rewards of up to fifty thousand dollars
for the capture and delivery—dead or alive—of New York abolitionist
Arthur Tappan.

It was against this background that anti-abolitionist riots started
breaking out in the North. And it was in this context that the Illinois
abolitionist Elijah Lovejoy was murdered in November 1837. After killing him, the mob threw his printing press into the Mississippi River.

Lincoln was aware of these events and he brooded upon them. Indeed,
he was meditating on some larger themes that would lead to the first great
speech of his life, a speech that stands as a historical and biographical
milestone in his rise to national statesmanship. He would deliver this
speech on January 27, 1838.

When Lincoln addressed the Young Men's Lyceum of Springfield on
that January day in 1838, his topic was nothing less than the American

experiment in self-government—past, present, and future. He spoke in words that foreshadowed the leadership challenge he would face at the height of his greatness in the decades to come. And some of the things that he said on this occasion were expressed in words that were not only memorable but electrifying.

He said that America's Founding Fathers had embarked upon an extraordinary experiment: to determine whether a free society, a society ruled from within by its own people instead of by a despot, could survive in the modern world. And given the realities of human nature, he said, there were all too many ways for this experiment to go wrong. He believed that this was happening already.

Things could degenerate into chaos or mob rule, he warned. He was alluding to the murder of Lovejoy a few months earlier when he said that democratic institutions were eroding whenever "the vicious portion of the population shall be permitted to gather in bands of hundreds and thousands, and burn churches, . . . throw printing presses into rivers, shoot editors, and hang and burn obnoxious persons at pleasure, and with impunity." When such things happened, Lincoln said, "depend upon it, this Government cannot last."

Most interestingly, he said that the emergence of such disorders might lead to the rise of a Napoleonic or Caesar-like figure, a "genius" who would straighten things out, but at the cost of abolishing democratic institutions.

A man who "thirsts and burns for distinction, and, if possible . . . will have it, whether at the expense of emancipating slaves, or enslaving free- men" will emerge at some time, Lincoln said. And whenever that happens, he continued, Americans should be on their guard against him. Was it not to be expected "that some man possessed of the loftiest genius, coupled with ambition sufficient to push it to its utmost stretch, will at some time, spring up among us? And when it does, it will require the people to be united with each other, attached to the government and laws . . . to suc- cessfully frustrate his designs."

More than half a century ago, the critic Edmund Wilson was trans- fixed by that passage, and he wondered about its hidden meanings. Specif- ically, he wondered whether Lincoln might have been conjuring—perhaps in unconscious ways—with the destiny awaiting him, with the possibility that he himself might become that "genius," that he himself might be able to wield such enormous power that he would find himself eventually able to emancipate slaves . . . or enslave free men.[34]

Was Lincoln afraid that the temptation of *abusing* such power would be too much for any man to handle? Was he somehow afraid of rising to his full potential, afraid that the powers he possessed, the powers that awaited self-discovery, might lead him into ways of arrogance?

Perhaps the most memorable passage of his Lyceum address was this one:

> At what point shall we expect the approach of danger? By what means shall we fortify against it? Shall we expect some transatlantic military giant, to step the Ocean, and crush us at a blow? Never! All the armies of Europe, Asia, and Africa combined, and with all the treasure of the earth (our own excepted) in their military chest; with a Buonaparte for a commander, could not by force, take a drink from the Ohio, or make a track on the Blue Ridge, in a trial of a thousand years. . . . If destruction be our lot, we must ourselves be its author and finisher. As a nation of freemen, we must live through all time, or die by suicide.[35]

Re-elected to the legislature in 1838, Lincoln participated in battles that prefigured the upcoming presidential election of 1840. Incumbent Martin Van Buren would be seeking re-election in the midst of hard times. Everyone could see that the circumstances would give the Whigs a precious opportunity if they knew how to use it.

During the congressional elections of 1838, Lincoln's law partner, Stuart, ran for Congress. His opponent was Stephen A. Douglas, whose ascent within the statewide Democratic Party had been almost as spectacular as Lincoln's rise among the Whigs.

Diminutive but extremely aggressive, Douglas was nearly always on the attack. He and Stuart loathed each other, and they actually engaged in a street brawl during the campaign. When Stuart was sidelined briefly due to illness, Lincoln took his place and debated with Douglas. And then, when Stuart won election to Congress, Lincoln was put in charge of their law firm.

By 1839, he was a member of the Whig "Junto," a group of Springfield lawyers who coordinated the selection of Whig candidates throughout the state. Other members of the Junto were Stuart, Stephen T. Logan, and the British-born Edward Baker. By October Lincoln was serving on the five-man state central committee of the Whig Party.

As the relocation of the state capital to Springfield drew nearer, the city's social whirl centered increasingly on the rivalries between the self-styled "Young Democrats," led by Douglas, and their Whig counterparts. Local dramas involving the these groups became bitter, and their mutual denunciations were often channeled through newspapers, with the *Sangamo Journal* serving as the Whigs' house organ and the *Illinois Republican*, soon to be renamed the *Illinois State Register*, as the Democratic mouthpiece.

When the legislature convened in Springfield for the 1839–1840 session, debates about economic policy resumed. Once again, Lincoln defended the state's program of internal improvements and resisted all efforts to cut it back. And he continued to defend the controversial state bank of Illinois.

The economic issues in contention would continue to resonate. The essential controversy continues in America right down to the present. Clay and other Whigs—including Lincoln—argued that government needed to work in creative synergy with business. When economic contractions occurred, a strong stimulus was needed to propel economic expansion, and spending by government could provide exactly that stimulus. John Maynard Keynes would come to the same conclusion a century later.

But this stimulus would have to make use of a special financial mechanism, since tax receipts would shrink in economic contractions. As Keynes would do later, the Whigs turned to bond sales (i.e., deficit spending), to supply the funds that would propel the spending that was needed to give the economy a jolt.

It bears noting that Lincoln came up with an innovative plan to help Illinois achieve economic recovery. He wanted to increase state taxes on the wealthy and then use this revenue to buy up federal lands within the state and re-sell them at a profit. This scheme would have generated funds to be used for internal improvements. The legislature did raise taxes on the wealthy. But Lincoln's suggestion regarding the purchase and resale of federal public lands within the state was not adopted.

Instead, the Whigs found themselves on the defensive in regard to the state's ever-growing debt-load. They were also facing a renewed assault upon the charter of the Illinois state bank.

Democrats were generally primitive in those days when it came to money and banking. America's money supply was based upon precious-metal coinage. Coins were created at the mint whenever people who owned gold or silver chose to have their treasure melted and stamped into coins. That was how money entered circulation in the first place in those days. But the supply of gold and silver was limited.

So a larger "circulating medium" would have to be created if the money supply of the United States were to meet the demands of the economy. By the 1830s, this expansion of the money supply was accomplished through the issuance of "bank notes." These notes started out as printed paper receipts for cash that was deposited in banks. But banks were gradually allowed—under law—to print up bank notes vastly in excess of cash deposits and make their loans in the form of these notes instead of in cash.

People were not required under law to accept such notes in market transactions. But when the banks that printed up the notes were deemed sufficiently trustworthy—if they kept enough cash "on reserve" to pay it out on demand when their notes were presented for redemption—these notes would often circulate and then re-circulate, expanding the nation's supply of purchasing power beyond what a system that was based upon coinage alone could provide.

The Democrats' position on these issues was simplistic. The most extreme "hard money men" within the party (the Whigs often called them "locofocos") wanted to abolish all forms of paper money and to limit the nation's money supply to hard cash. How a growing economy could function on cash alone was a question that they left unanswered.

Andrew Jackson had worked very hard to destroy the Second Bank of the United States. He hated banks in general, and his attack upon the banking system started at the top. His successor, Martin Van Buren, went further and created a system of government finance that would not make any use of banks: federal funds would sit idle in government vaults ("subtreasuries") around the country until they were needed. On the day after Christmas in 1839, Lincoln made a speech attacking this Democratic subtreasury plan.

Before the Second Bank of the United States had been destroyed, Lincoln said, it had been "the depository of the public revenues" for the federal government. And since the bank was permitted to take these government deposits and lend them out, "the large amount of money annually collected for revenue purposes . . . was kept almost constantly in circulation" instead of being "locked up in idleness."

But the Democrats' plan "would rob the people of the use" of public money "while the government does not itself need it, and while the money is performing no nobler office than rusting in iron boxes."The results would be predictable, Lincoln warned: the sub-treasury plan would "reduce the quantity of money in circulation," thus worsening the depression.

Further, Lincoln charged, the Democrats' inclination to accept only cash for the payment of taxes or for purchases of public lands would reduce the operational money supply of the United States even more. Every time a citizen bought government land, he observed, cash would have to be withdrawn from the money supply and then put aside in a vault, doing nobody good and doing the economy very great harm.

Only the supplementation of cash by paper extensions of the money supply could meet America's needs, Lincoln said. And the Democrats' plan would "injuriously affect the community by its operation on the circulating medium."[36]

The Whigs made a very big mistake when they decided not to run Henry Clay against Van Buren in 1840. Their inclination was to keep on using political tricks, whether simple or fancy, in their effort to "out-Jackson" the Democrats.

They nominated William Henry Harrison, a military hero like Jackson. He had become a hero back in 1811 in the battle of Tippecanoe, where, as Indiana's territorial governor, he defeated a Native American uprising. Jackson's nick-name had been "Old Hickory," so the Whigs dubbed Harrison "Old Tippecanoe" and they made it known that he was just as tough as Jackson had been. As Harrison's running mate, they turned to a candidate who was not even a Whig: John Tyler of Virginia, in most respects a Jacksonian Democrat except for the fact that he hated Jackson personally—and he also hated the followers of Jackson (like Van Buren). The Whigs tapped Tyler as a way to twist the knife against Van Buren and divide the Democratic Party.

The campaign of 1840 was a low-brow affair in which the Whigs sang the following lyrics to their campaign song: "Tippecanoe and Tyler too, Tippecanoe and Tyler too, and with them we'll beat little Van, Van, Van, Van, oh he's a used-up man. And with them we'll beat little Van." They beat little Van, but then Harrison died about a month after his inauguration, so the Whigs would be stuck with John Tyler until 1844.

Lincoln was re-elected to the legislature in 1840, but his margin of victory was smaller than it was in the previous elections. Moreover, Van Buren carried the state. Worst of all, the Democrats gained control of the legislature, promising to resolve the state's "debt crisis." And when a special session of the legislature was convened in November, the Democrats continued their attacks against the state-chartered bank.

Lincoln was pushed to devise clever tactics to defend the bank and find revenue sources that would service the state's bonded debt. He was also increasingly busy with his law firm's case-load. In truth, he was close to another emotional breakdown, especially due to another crisis in his love life, one that would drive him into his next episode of clinical depression.

One of the many advantages of Joshua Speed's friendship was the status of Speed's family connections, which could open up a great many doors to high society. One of Speed's relations was a cousin named Elizabeth Edwards, the wife of Ninian Edwards, who was the son of a former Illinois governor.

The Edwardses lived in a mansion that was one of the toniest destinations for social gatherings in Springfield. It was also a place that drew eligible bachelors and women who were ready for suitors. And so it was that in December 1839, at a cotillion party at the mansion, Lincoln met Mary Ann Todd, who was Elizabeth's younger sister.

She was pretty, petite, vivacious, high-strung, and a kindred spirit politically, for like Lincoln she was a Whig and she had even met Henry Clay, who knew her father. They seem to have attracted each other and a "friendship" began—much to the consternation of Elizabeth Edwards who regarded Lincoln as far too inferior in social standing to converse with her sister. But Joshua Speed interceded on Lincoln's behalf, so the doors of the Edwards mansion were open, at least for a time.

Like Lincoln, Mary hailed from Kentucky; her father, Robert Smith Todd, was a wealthy banker in Lexington. She had attended fine private schools and she moved in refined social circles. Her background was totally different from Lincoln's primitive backwoods origin.

For years, controversies have raged in regard to the relationship between Abraham and Mary Lincoln. Their relationship was certainly tempestuous and there were people at the time—and ever since—who have argued that Lincoln never loved her, that she had been the one to initiate and sustain the romantic pursuit, and that the opposite tendencies in their personalities would make for a disastrous marriage.

For what it is worth, it seems obvious enough that Lincoln and Mary Todd were initially attracted to one another. Beyond that, the story gets tangled—and painful.

Off and on through the summer of 1840 they apparently flirted and eventually, toward the end of the year, they made preliminary plans to be married. But then Lincoln started to fall in love with another woman: Matilda Edwards, a beautiful eighteen-year-old cousin of Ninian Edwards. Various residents of Springfield made the allegation that Lincoln was deeply under her spell. Orville Browning, to cite a representative and prominent example, asserted that Lincoln fell ardently in love with her.[37]

Sometime in January 1841 he asked Mary to release him from the engagement, which she did. And then, after Speed announced that he was selling his store and moving back to Kentucky, Lincoln's mental condition plummeted. Everything that he had built seemed worthless to him and the bottom fell out of his world.

Many people talked with alarm about Lincoln's condition at the time and this bout with depression loomed large in the reminiscences of friends and acquaintants. Ninian Edwards said later that Lincoln "in his Conflicts of duty—honor & his love went Crazy as a Loon."[38] A Springfield acquaintance named Martin McKee wrote at the time that "we have been very much distressed, on Mr. Lincoln's account; hearing that he had two Cat fits and a Duck fit."[39]

Jane D. Bell wrote that Lincoln "is in rather a bad way. . . . The doctors say that he came within an inch of being a perfect lunatic for life. . . . They say he don't look like the same person. It seems he had addressed Mary Todd and she accepted him and they had been engaged some time when a Miss Edwards of Alton came here, and he fell desperately in love with her and found he was not so much attached to Mary as he thought."[40]

Lincoln did see a doctor: Dr. Anson Henry, whom he visited from January 13 through January 18. He confirmed his condition in a letter to Stuart, writing that "I have, within the past few days, been making a most discreditable exhibition of myself in the way of hypochondriaism, and thereby got the impression that Dr. Henry is necessary to my existence."[41]

Several days later he wrote that "I am now the most miserable man living. . . . Whether I shall ever be better I can not tell; I awfully forebode I shall not. To remain as I am is impossible; I must die or be better, it appears to me."[42]

In Browning's opinion, the depression was obviously triggered by anxiety mixed with guilt; this "aberration of mind resulted entirely from the situation he . . . got himself into—he was engaged to Miss Todd, and in love with Miss Edwards, and his conscience troubled him dreadfully."[43]

Lincoln was recuperating at the home of the Butlers, and—much as it was back in 1835—friends worried about the possibility of suicide. According to Speed, the Butlers "had to remove razors from his room—take away all Knives and other such dangerous things."[44]

There were other situations that contributed to Lincoln's new depression. The Democrats were running the show in Illinois and they acted with speed and ruthlessness to wipe away everything that Lincoln had supported. They passed a bill to pack the Illinois Supreme Court; they added five new justices, one of them Stephen A. Douglas. They killed off the Illinois state bank, and they also killed the program of internal improvements.

Lincoln's days in the Illinois legislature were over; he no longer commanded sufficient support among the Whigs of Sangamon County. Furthermore, his partnership with Stuart began to dissolve as this sequence of events played out. At least Lincoln managed to salvage his career as a lawyer by forming a new law partnership with Stephen T. Logan.

Toward the end of this crisis, Lincoln made another interesting and revealing public address—a speech about the virtue of temperance. He supported prohibiting the use of alcoholic beverages, and his reason was *mental health*. By banning intoxicants like liquor, he said, Americans could rejoice in the triumph of mental self-control and the conquest of irrationality.

He put it this way: "Happy day, when, all appetites controlled, all passions subdued, *mind*, all conquering *mind*, shall live and move the monarch of the world. Glorious consummation! Hail fall of Fury! Reign of Reason, hail!"[45] The relationship between these words and Lincoln's emotional crisis should be clear enough.

In the summer of 1841, he took a vacation. He spent six relaxing weeks with Joshua Speed at his parents' plantation—"Farmington"—near Louisville, Kentucky. He was a welcome guest at Farmington and he got along nicely with the Speed family. He particularly enjoyed the time he spent with Speed's brother, James, and his half-sister, Mary.

Speed accompanied Lincoln when he returned to Springfield. As the men traveled aboard an Ohio River steamer, Lincoln had an experience that proved consequential for a number of reasons. He encountered a group of slaves, and his existing revulsion against slavery was rekindled. But he also took time to observe how these African Americans coped with their plight by attempting to keep one another cheerful.

Lincoln wrote about this in a letter that he sent to Mary Speed in September. He told her that he observed twelve slaves on board the steamer chained together "precisely like so many fish upon a trot line." They were being "separated forever from the scenes of their childhood, their friends, their fathers and mothers, and brothers and sisters, and many of them, from their wives and children."

Worse, they were being sent to the deep South "where the lash of the master is proverbially more ruthless and unrelenting than any other where," and yet somehow they kept themselves sane. "One, whose offense for which he had been sold was an over-fondness for his wife, played the fiddle almost continually" and the others "danced, sung, cracked jokes," and played card games. Lincoln philosophized: God "renders the worst of conditions tolerable, while He permits the best, to be nothing better than tolerable."[46]

After their return to Springfield, Lincoln continued to recuperate, and his correspondence with Speed played a role in his recovery. It seemed that his torment had a very close counterpart in Speed's romantic situation.

Speed was in love with a woman named Fanny Henning, but he couldn't decide whether to marry her because of deep worries—some of them neurotic and others quite normal. He worried in particular whether he loved her enough. And he wondered whether he could take the emotional blow if she should die. This of course touched Lincoln in ways that were painfully acute.

After Speed headed back to Kentucky, the men continued to support one another via letters—letters providing great insights into Lincoln's condition. In February 1842, Lincoln wrote that "I do not feel my own sorrows much more keenly than I do yours, when I know of them." He continued: "I hope and believe that your present anxiety and distress about *her* health and *her* life, must and will forever banish those horrid doubts, which I know you sometimes felt, as to the truth of your affection for her."

Here were themes that were germane to Lincoln's own situation as well as to the memories of his first bout with depression. The letters that he sent to Speed were *therapeutic* and they deepened the bond between the men as they helped one another get stronger and face the risks of life. Lincoln closed his February letter with the observation that "I have been quite clear of hypo since you left—even better than I was along in the fall."[47]

Speed decided to marry Fanny Henning, and when Lincoln congratulated him he observed that while "your nerves will fail you occasionally for a while," it should be always be remembered that "once you get them fairly graded now, that trouble is over forever."[48]

He kept thinking about Mary Todd as he gave this advice to his friend. In March, he told Speed how happy it made him to hear that after marrying Fanny he was *"far happier than you ever expected to be."* That news gave Lincoln "more pleasure than the total sum of all I have enjoyed since that fatal first of Jany. '41." Since then, he continued, "I should have been entirely happy, but for the never-absent idea, that there is *one* still unhappy whom I have contributed to make so. That still kills my soul."[49]

In other words, he still felt guilty about the way he had treated Mary Todd. For whatever it might be worth, that sentiment reprised the kind of guilt that he had felt in the Mary Owens affair. Was this new romantic situation fundamentally different?

In any case, by the summer of 1842, he had made the decision to try again with Mary Todd. He told Speed that he wanted to "regain my confidence in my own ability to keep my resolves when they are made. In that ability . . . I once prided myself as the only, or at least the chief, gem of my character; that gem I lost—how, and when, you know too well." But he hoped that Speed's experience would inspire him with the confidence to try again.[50]

In the meantime, he got embroiled in an episode that brought him to the brink of a duel. He went back to writing pseudonymous satires directed at Democrats. This time he singled out state auditor James Shields. In a series that appeared in the *Sangamo Journal*—letters that were signed by a fictitious woman named "Rebecca"—Lincoln poked fun at Shields in a manner that enraged him beyond endurance.

A short extract from one of these "Rebecca" letters—one that has been authenticated as a Lincoln composition—illustrates his style of polemical humor.

"Aunt Becca" and a neighbor named "Jeff" are complaining that the notes of the Illinois state bank are no longer accepted in payment of state taxes. This was the result of the Democrats' "hard money" policy. "Jeff" complains that "I've been tugging ever since harvest getting out wheat and hauling it to the river, to raise State Bank paper enough to pay my tax this year . . . when, lo and behold, I find a set of fellows calling themselves *Officers of the State*, have forbidden the tax collectors and school commissioners to receive State paper at all; and so here it is, dead on my hands."

Jeff blames this policy on Shields. So he blasts the state auditor as "a fool as well as a liar" and he says that both Shields and his minions should be jailed.[51]

Shields demanded to know who had written these letters and Lincoln took the blame (or credit) for writing some of them. Shields challenged Lincoln to a duel, and the men agreed to fight across the border in Missouri, where dueling was legal.

The matter was resolved through humor and diplomacy; Lincoln had the right to name the weapons, so he stipulated terms as preposterous as he could make them in the hope that the episode would dissipate. He proposed that he and Shields should fight one another with cavalry broadswords at a distance of ten feet.[52]

Lincoln also said that the "Rebecca" letters had been prompted by political animus, that he had never intended any *personal* damage to Shields. Intermediaries persuaded Shields to call the matter off, so the duel never had to be fought.

But Lincoln had learned a lesson he would never forget and from that point on he was cured of the habit of firing off *sub rosa* compositions of ridicule and abuse.

He met Mary Todd again at a wedding on September 27, and one thing led to another. They rapidly began another courtship, one that played out in the form of conversations at the home of Simeon Francis, who edited the *Sangamo Journal*. When Lincoln made bold to ask for Mary's hand again, she accepted.

Kept in the dark until the very last moment, Elizabeth and Ninian Edwards—indignant and flustered—decided that if Mary were fool enough to disregard their advice, the marriage should at least take place in respectable surroundings.

And so it was that the Lincolns were married in the parlor of the Edwards mansion on the evening of November 4, 1842.

II

CRISIS OF
AMBITION

IMPROVISING

The suddenness of the Lincolns' wedding raised eyebrows, and those who wonder about the nature of the bond between Abraham and Mary Lincoln also wonder why the couple tied the knot abruptly. There was very little time for preparation.

Lincoln might have had last-minute misgivings, if a number of reminiscences by others are to be believed. In light of all the turmoil that led to the on-again/off-again courtship, such doubts would not have been surprising. But historians who view the Lincoln marriage as disastrous have deeper suspicions.

One of Lincoln's groomsmen, James Matheny, alleged in an interview with Herndon that Lincoln looked "as if he was going to the Slaughter" on the day of his wedding and that Lincoln supposedly confessed that "he was driven into the marriage."[1]

One historian, Wayne C. Temple, has gone so far as to hypothesize that Mary, sensing Lincoln's residual ambivalence, seduced him on the night before the marriage in order to force the issue and bind him, for the sake of her honor, to go ahead and have the ceremony quickly.[2]

The Lincolns were married by an Episcopal clergyman, Dr. Charles Dresser. Then they rented a room at the Globe Tavern, an unimpressive establishment that had nonetheless been good enough for some of their relatives, friends, and acquaintances—including John Todd Stuart and his wife—to call home right after their weddings.

Their marriage was rocky in a great many ways. Mary Lincoln reflected more than once upon their "opposite natures."[3] William Herndon was one of the sharpest critics of the Lincoln marriage. Indeed, he and Mary came to loathe one another. His statement that Lincoln and his wife were "the exact reverse . . . in everything" squares with a great deal of testimony from others.[4]

There is no denying that Mary Lincoln could at times be a terrible scold. Herndon said that while Mary had been "affable and even charming" during their courtship, she changed once they took the vows. "After she got married," he wrote, "she became . . . a she-wolf."[5]

The issue of Mary Lincoln's personality is controversial, and the sharp disagreements continue. Among Lincoln scholars, Michael Burlingame has taken the strongest position on the negative side; he argues that Mary was a shrew and an abusive spouse who made Lincoln's life miserable. He cites many incidents when Mary displayed uncontrollable rage that bordered on hysteria. But others regard her as a victim of anxiety, a fragile and struggling soul. Those who sympathize with Mary tend to doubt the worst of the horror stories about her behavior.

The nature of the Lincoln marriage is extremely important. Herndon (naturally) argued that Lincoln fled his home as often as possible and sought satisfaction as a public figure. If there was truth in that view, and perhaps there was some, we can wonder whether Lincoln's rise to greatness would have happened if Ann Rutledge had lived. Regardless, it was Mary whom he married.

Did they love each other? It is tempting to conclude that they did not. Lincoln's attitude toward love had been peculiar for a number of years. In his courtship of Mary Owens, for instance, he had gone through the motions of romance in an oddly fatalistic fashion. Perhaps, after suffering the heartbreaking loss of Ann Rutledge, he convinced himself that it was hopeless to try to find another love as beautiful as that one.

Maybe this conviction arose in his mind to protect him from another such loss in the future—a loss so crushing that it might have wiped out his sanity. Did the loss of Ann ruin his chances of finding real love for the rest of his life? Herndon believed that it did. It is reasonable to wonder whether Lincoln was *afraid* to fall deeply in love again.

In the course of the Lincoln-Speed correspondence in regard to the emotional challenges of love, Lincoln wrote some guardedly pessimistic lines. He warned not "to dream dreams of Elysium far exceeding all that any earthly thing can realize." He then invoked a most surprising authority: "My old Father," he continued, "used to have a saying that 'If you make a bad bargain, *hug* it the tighter."[6]

Strange for Lincoln to claim to find wisdom in a saying of the father he despised. Or perhaps the psychology was not so strange, for by invoking *in this particular case* the saying of a man who (in Lincoln's view) amounted to nothing, perhaps he was unconsciously saying to himself that his own hopes for ardent love would amount to nothing, so he might as well resign himself to the situation and make the best of it.

Did he and Mary love one another by the standards that were (and are) conventional? In light of the misery that she was to cause him, we can wonder. But there are different kinds of love—different in their quality, different in the types of emotional needs that they address, and different in the hard-to-articulate dynamics of the human mind in action.

By many accounts, Lincoln brought a fatherly tone to his behavior as a husband, a quality that calmed his wife down and healed her stricken spirit for a while. Perhaps Lincoln, who for years had felt the absence of paternal love, found a deep if unconscious satisfaction in acting like a soothing father, at the cost of other kinds of marital fulfillment. Having suffered from the lack of a decent father, he could *be one* for many other people, including his wife.

Still, Mary's tantrums were sometimes horrendous. At her worst she lashed out at Lincoln and scolded him in front of others. But Lincoln took it.

Sometimes martyrs experience a beauty that no one else would ever ask for, or even understand. Who can say what Lincoln's innermost feelings might have been on these occasions? At times he used humor to soften Mary up when she was riled.

He deferred to her in most respects at home. According to one reminiscence, Lincoln said that "in little things I have got along through life by letting my wife run her end of the machine pretty much in her own way."[7]

This was easier to do during Lincoln's long absences from home, riding circuit in the course of his law practice with Stephen T. Logan. There can be little doubt that he needed these opportunities to get away. One fellow attorney reminisced about Lincoln's "strange disinclination to go home."[8] To Herndon there was nothing strange about it: "his home was Hell," Herndon proclaimed, and his "absence from home was heaven."[9]

Lincoln forged some enduring friendships out on the circuit. One of the most consequential of these was his friendship with Judge David Davis, who was destined to play a consequential role in Lincoln's future political career.

One of his circuit-riding trips took him to Coles County, Illinois, where his father and step-mother lived. He informed them of his marriage, though he never invited them to visit him in Springfield. It is easy to explain his aversion to inviting his father, but he did continue to love his stepmother, Sarah.

According to Herndon, it was Mary's behavior that kept her in-laws away; he claimed that "Mrs. Lincoln held the Hanks tribe in contempt and the Lincoln family generally—the old folks—Thomas Lincoln & his good old wife. Mrs. Lincoln was terribly aristocratic and as haughty & as imperious as she was autocratic."[10]

And she seemed perpetually dissatisfied. Though Lincoln was prospering in his partnership, it seemed like he could never earn enough, or earn it fast enough, to grant Mary's wish for more luxurious surroundings.

In one respect, at least, Abraham and Mary Lincoln were well suited to each other, since she shared his ambition and encouraged him to pursue it.

Slightly less than nine months after their marriage, Mary bore them a son whom they named Robert Todd, after Mary's father. The boy's nickname was Robby or Bobby. Two years later came a second son, whom they gave the name Edward in honor of Lincoln's friend Edward Baker. Lincoln delighted in playing with Robby and Eddy—delighted in the pleasures of parenthood.

All through the first year of their marriage they lived at the Globe Tavern as they waited for Lincoln to earn enough money to buy a home. He was earning a good income in 1843 through his partnership with Logan, and in May of the following year they bought a house from Rev. Charles Dresser, the clergyman who married them.

It was a modest one-and-a-half story wood frame house at the corner of Eighth and Jackson streets. In 1850, they would add another story above the front rooms and then in 1856 Mary had this story expanded to the rear.

Lincoln's partnership with Logan was successful. Logan was thriving as a litigator, and his junior partner's skills in the courtroom increased as he worked with a man who was widely regarded as the best lawyer in Springfield.

Logan was a strange character in several respects. Though wealthy, he was slovenly. Though he eagerly sought greater wealth in his profession, he disdained the outward signs of status. By most accounts, though, he had a brilliant legal mind—at least when it came to strategy.

The two partners got along well, and they were very close friends before long. They worked on over eight hundred cases together.

By the time of his marriage, Lincoln expanded his ambitions by running for Congress. His district, the seventh, was heavily Whiggish. But to win the congressional seat he would have to defeat two competitors. One was John J. Hardin, an attorney, the son of a U.S. senator, and a cousin of Mary Todd Lincoln.

The other Whig who sought the nomination was such a close friend that Lincoln and Mary would name their second son after him: Edward D. Baker. English-born, Baker practiced law with Lincoln on a few occasions—during Lincoln's partnership with Stuart—and, like Hardin, he served with Lincoln in the legislature. Though he and Lincoln didn't always agree, there was a powerful bond between them.

This election would be for an unusually short term in Congress. In 1839, the legislature postponed the next congressional election from 1840 to 1841—due to the 1840 census.[11] Stuart, re-elected in 1841, chose not to run again in 1843. So the congressional seat was up for grabs, but it would soon be up for grabs again since the normal election cycle would resume in 1844.

Lincoln plunged into the race for the congressional seat with zeal. On March 1, 1843, he met with Whigs who had come from all over the state to set policy. Of great importance, they endorsed the use of nominating conventions to avoid intra-party divisions.

Illinois Democrats led by Stephen Douglas had already developed such a system. The Whigs' resolutions called for a nominating convention in each congressional district on or before May first. The delegates would be elected county by county through "primary meetings."[12]

The Whigs in Sangamon County were divided in their loyalties between Lincoln and Baker. To Lincoln's chagrin, Baker won when the "primary meeting" of Sangamon Whigs was convened. After losing the Sangamon delegates to Baker, Lincoln ruminated about the reasons for his defeat.

One of the reasons, he wrote to an ally in nearby Menard County, was ludicrous: due to Mary Todd Lincoln's aristocratic background, some

Baker supporters called Lincoln the candidate of the high and mighty. Lincoln wrote that the people of Menard, who knew him much better—New Salem being located in that county—could remember him as a "friendless, uneducated, penniless boy, working on a flat boat."[13]

A more telling reason for his loss was religious fervor. "It was everywhere contended," he explained, "that no Christian ought to go for me, because I belonged to no church, was suspected of being a deist, and had talked about fighting a duel."[14]

Moreover, some members of the temperance movement viewed him with distrust. In his temperance address of the previous year, he urged compassion for alcoholics in the name of Christian charity. Staunch members of the movement felt that Lincoln was challenging the depth of their Christian convictions. It bears noting that Lincoln would later invoke the same principle of compassion and forgiveness for those who were involved in the sin of owning slaves.

Lincoln harbored no resentment toward Baker after losing the Sangamon vote. In any case, it was Hardin who eventually prevailed at the nominating convention that was held on May 1 in Pekin, Illinois. Therefore Hardin would be the new congressman for the seventh district. His victory was a foregone conclusion since the district was dominated by the Whigs.

Lincoln accepted this outcome with grace. One of the reasons for his composure was the fact that he had introduced a successful resolution that would pre-commit the Whigs to nominate Baker the next time around, unless the next convention should rule otherwise. This was part of a strategy that Lincoln would use to gain the nomination himself—after Baker.

The strategy behind this "Pekin agreement" was simple: rotation in office. After Hardin had served a single term in Congress it would then be Baker's turn. Then, after Baker, the congressional seat would go to Lincoln—or so Lincoln hoped.

In any case, the 1844 election held momentous implications for America. For Lincoln, this was a long-awaited chance to support the presidential aspirations of his first great political hero, Henry Clay. After playing tricks in the previous two presidential elections, the Whigs decided to play it straight again in the election of 1844. They ran their best candidate, Clay.

It is one of the tragedies of American history that Henry Clay never won the presidential office, though he did come close—maddeningly close—in this final attempt in 1844.

Lincoln made enthusiastic speeches for Clay, both in Illinois and out of state. In October, his campaigning took him back to Indiana, where he had a chance to see his boyhood locale. This visit made a profound impression on him—so profound that it prompted Lincoln to express his feelings in poetry.

He visited some neighbors, the Gentrys, and discovered that one of them—a lad named Matthew who had lost his mind at the age of nineteen—was in worse condition than ever. Lincoln was struck not only with an overwhelming sadness as he gazed upon Matthew but also with the cold pangs of dread, which he later expressed in a poem.

His own second emotional breakdown had occurred just three years earlier. And back home he was setting up housekeeping with a woman whose stability was open to question. He had come very far since those long-ago days in Indiana. Yet the miseries and the fears of his past were still vivid.

By 1844, the issue in American politics that would catapult Lincoln to his destiny was surging to the forefront of election-year controversies. By 1850 it would dominate American politics and threaten the Union's existence. The issue: opposition to the westward spread of slavery. The origins of the movement to restrict the spread of slavery went all the way back to the days of the Founding Fathers.

As soon as the Revolutionary War was over, key American leaders began a campaign to contain the evil of slavery—and then get rid of it. In 1783, Thomas Jefferson drafted a new constitution for the state of Virginia that would, if adopted, have forbidden the importation of any more slaves after 1800. But this new state constitution was not adopted.

In 1784, Jefferson introduced legislation in the Confederation Congress—the United States was still operating under its first constitution, the Articles of Confederation and Perpetual Union—that would have prohibited the spread of slavery into any western territory beyond the Appalachians. But this legislation was defeated by the margin of one vote.

In 1787, however, the Confederation Congress passed the Northwest Ordinance, which did ban the spread of slavery into western territories *above the Ohio River*. No territory from that region could petition for admission to the Union as a slave state. This precedent would be essential to the "Free Soil" movement as it developed in Lincoln's time.

Another political action in 1787 could be viewed as something of a blow against slavery. The new federal Constitution that was being drafted in Philadelphia gave the federal Congress clear power to stop any further importation of slaves after twenty years. Even so, the delay of twenty years permitted the continued importation of vast numbers of additional enslaved people, thus making the problem of eradicating slavery all the more difficult.

Indeed, pro-slavery leaders among the Founding Fathers struck back against these measures. At the Constitutional Convention, for instance, Charles Cotesworth Pinckney of South Carolina strove incessantly to safeguard the interests of slave-holders. And when the federal Congress passed a Southwest Ordinance in 1790, there was no restriction on the spread of slavery below the Ohio River. Accordingly, two brand-new slave states—Kentucky and Tennessee—were admitted in the 1790s.

As the northern states began the process of gradually eradicating slavery, the institution spread in the South. Accordingly, the United States could be said to have been dividing into two very different ways of life by 1800: a slave-holding society south of the Ohio River and south of the Mason-Dixon Line, and a vastly different society above those lines.

Within these two ways of life—within the states that were phasing out slavery and the states that continued to permit it—there were also divisions. For instance, white supremacy sentiment was common in both of the regions, but there were also whites in both regions who opposed slavery due to a commitment to racial equality. Moreover, just as there were definitely anti-slavery whites in the South, there were also *pro*-slavery whites in the North.

We will never know how much anti-slavery sentiment existed among southern whites. As previously noted, slave-holders began a successful campaign to clamp down on free speech in the slave states by the 1830s. Until then, it had been possible to debate the morality of slavery in most of the slave states.

Pro-slavery thought was generally grounded in two basic forces: economic interest and white supremacist doctrine. However, a third force became important in the 1790s: a fear of violence—even race war—if slavery were challenged. There had been a few attempts at slave insurrections before the American Revolution, but a slave rebellion that broke out in the island of Hispaniola (comprising the present-day Dominican Republic and Haiti) in 1794 led to fear in almost all of the slave states, especially the coastal states, that the same thing could happen in America. Right up to the Civil War, white southerners were terrified of black retribution if the shackles of slavery were broken.

Until the 1830s, most opponents of slavery embraced the strategy of gradualism, since the power of the slave-holders was formidable and their opposition would be hard to overcome. For many people, gradualism seemed to be the only sensible method for eradicating slavery.

And that was the way it seemed to Abraham Lincoln.

Containment seemed to be the obvious pre-condition for a slavery phase-out. If slavery spread, it would be hard for Americans later on to roll it back. Phase two of the gradualist vision—the actual phase-out—was envisioned as a peaceful and voluntary process based upon the proposition of paying the slave-holders to unshackle their slaves and set them free.

In 1790, Elbridge Gerry proposed that the revenues from the sale of public lands be used for this purpose. In 1819, former President James Madison developed a secret proposal exploring the idea. In a letter to a friend, Madison calculated that $600 million from the sale of public lands would be necessary to get rid of slavery.[15]

Linked to the idea of a compensated phase-out was the concept of "colonization" (i.e., the emigration of emancipated slaves). It stood to reason that Lincoln would embrace this idea since his hero, Henry Clay, was one of its champions. Clay, who struggled for years to eradicate slavery in his home state of Kentucky—even though he owned slaves himself—served as president of the American Colonization Society, which was founded in 1816.

The colonization idea was controversial on both sides of the anti-slavery dispute. Some slave-holders supported it, while others believed it was dangerous. Some African Americans found it extremely insulting, while others embraced it as a means of escaping from a land of oppression. But a common theme in the writings of anti-slavery gradualists was the conviction that race prejudice among whites was ineradicable, so the races would have to be separated to avoid racial violence. It was above all this pessimistic outlook that prompted such people to proclaim that the two races should eventually go their separate ways in peace.

By the end of the 1810s, there were an equal number of free and slave states in America: eleven of each. But in 1819, a sudden crisis erupted over the fate of slavery. Missouri, within the Louisiana Purchase, petitioned for admission as a slave state and a political firestorm resulted. Slavery already existed in Missouri; the French had permitted it before the vast region of Louisiana was sold to the United States.

Led by a New York congressman named James Tallmadge Jr., opponents of Missouri statehood insisted that Missouri should be required to eliminate slavery as a requirement for admission. But many slave state leaders were enraged by this demand. They threatened to break up the Union if Missouri were denied admission as a full-fledged slave state.

The crisis was resolved through the soon-to-be-famous Missouri Compromise of 1820. Henry Clay brokered a deal through which Missouri's admission as a slave state would be counter-balanced by the creation of a new free state—Maine—so that the number of the free states and slave states would be kept equal. But there was more to the compromise, for Congress also adopted the proposal of Senator Jesse Thomas of Illinois to draw a dividing line across the rest of the Louisiana Purchase, a line to separate the lands that would be open to slavery from the lands in which slavery would be banned.

The most important fact about the new dividing line was that the lion's share of the territory in the Louisiana Purchase would be *off-limits to slavery*. This meant that the number of free states in America would gradually exceed the number of slave states. When that happened, pro-slavery southerners would no longer have enough votes in Congress to stop anti-slavery legislation. Even if they claimed that such legislation was in violation of the Constitution, the Constitution, as everybody knew, could be amended. All it would take would be a three-quarters super-majority of free states to kill off slavery—kill it off by ratifying an anti-slavery amendment to the Constitution.

The most militant pro-slavery leaders like John C. Calhoun foresaw the danger. To forestall it, Calhoun started building up the doctrine of state sovereignty. That doctrine, if pushed to the limit, might eventually provide a springboard for slave state secession, which of course would put the seceded states beyond the power of the federal Constitution.

But there was another way for the advocates of slavery to head off an anti-slavery amendment. If additional western lands—beyond the Louisiana Purchase—could be annexed to the Union for the purpose of creating new slave states, a free-state super-majority might very well be prevented.

And a handy opportunity to build such a strategy developed when the Mexican province of Texas proclaimed independence. Texas broke away from Mexico in 1836, and the Texans were led by some wealthy white slave-owners from the United States. A steady stream of American expatriates had drifted into Texas. And when Mexico prohibited slavery in 1829, the white Texans refused to comply. Instead, they rebelled.

Accordingly, the constitution of the Texas republic protected slavery. And if Texas could be added to the United States, the result would be a huge augmentation of political power for the slave-holding South.

President John Tyler was ardently in favor of Texas annexation. He made Calhoun his secretary of state, and Calhoun went to work on an annexation treaty.

These were the reasons why the issue of Texas annexation loomed large in the election of 1844. And behind the controversies surrounding Texas annexation, an interesting change was brewing in the anti-slavery movement: opposition to slavery was becoming more prevalent *among white supremacists*. It is hard to overstate the importance of this development for without it there might have been no Civil War—and no Lincoln presidency.

As long as the opposition to slavery flowed predominantly from believers in racial equality, it was impossible for the anti-slavery movement to gain enough support to become a majority. But as soon as more whites began to turn against slavery because *they viewed it as a threat to themselves*, a sea change in public opinion became possible.

And that is precisely what was happening in the 1840s. By the time of the 1844 election, the bipartisan "Free Soil Movement"—a powerful movement to stop the further spread of slavery—had attracted enough support among white supremacists to establish itself as a force to be reckoned with in American politics.

Why would white supremacists oppose the spread of slavery? One answer to this question was simple enough: if slavery spread into western territories, *blacks* would be moving into those western territories, and people who believed that the West should be reserved for whites only did not savor the idea that African Americans would live in the vicinity of whites. But there were other significant reasons why northern white supremacists came to view the spread of slavery as a threat—a threat to themselves, to their children, and to the way of life that they supported.

John Tyler—the accidental president who had succeeded to the presidency upon the death of William Henry Harrison—had been expelled from the Whig party in 1841. Regardless, he nursed the hope that by playing off different factions he might somehow find a way to run for re-election in 1844. But that was not to be.

The Whigs ran their best and most popular candidate again in 1844: Henry Clay. The Democratic nomination was contested and former president Martin Van Buren had hopes of capturing the nomination and regaining the presidency. But the Democrats nominated a "dark horse" candidate instead: James K. Polk of Tennessee.

The election was a close one, and to the shock of Lincoln and many other Whigs, Polk eked out a narrow victory. The most important factor in the 1844 election was probably the slavery issue, especially as manifested in the issue of Texas annexation. Clay opposed annexation and Polk enthusiastically supported it.

To be sure, Polk's support was framed within a broader vision. He attempted to incorporate Texas annexation in a program of national expansion that included a pledge to settle the long-standing boundary dispute with Great Britain concerning the size of the Oregon territory, which America had claimed.

A number of Whigs including Lincoln blamed Clay's defeat upon the third party candidacy of James G. Birney, who had founded an anti-slavery party called the Liberty Party in 1840. Lincoln was convinced that Birney drew anti-slavery votes away from Clay by arguing that Clay was unworthy of support since he owned slaves himself.

In an interesting letter, he admonished a Birney supporter as follows: "If the whig abolitionists of New York had voted with us last fall, Mr. Clay would now be president, whig principles in the ascendant, and Texas not annexed; whereas by the division, all that either had at stake in the contest, was lost."

Lincoln went on to hammer home a lesson in moral strategy—a lesson that places his subsequent actions on the slavery issue in perspective. In effect, he called Birney supporters who refused to support Henry Clay self-indulgent perfectionists. And he took a dim view of perfectionism when it came to achieving moral ends. "As I always understood, the Liberty-men deprecated the annexation of Texas extremely," Lincoln began. And yet, he continued, they threw away a realistic chance to prevent it by insisting that their candidate must be immaculate.

"Their process of reasoning," Lincoln explained, "I can only judge from what a single one of them told me. It was this: 'We are not to do *evil* that *good* may come.'" While Lincoln acknowledged that "this general proposition is doubtless correct," he went on to criticize the position of the Birney people as follows:

If by your votes you could have prevented the *extension*, &c. of slavery, would it not have been *good* and not *evil* so to have used your votes, even though it involved the casting of them for a slaveholder? By the *fruit* the tree is to be known. An *evil* tree can not bring forth *good* fruit. If the fruit of electing Mr. Clay would have been to prevent the extension of slavery, could the act of electing him have been *evil?*[16]

The direction in which Lincoln's mental development was moving is clear—a direction that would lead him over time to excel in power orchestration. He was thinking *strategically*, and thus relating the parts of any problem, including moral problems, to the whole.

Even so, it is important to note that he showed little of the fervor that would fire him up as a Free Soiler a decade later. The transformation that would blaze his path to the White House had not yet occurred when he set down the following reflections on Texas annexation in 1844:

> Individually I was never much interested in the Texas question. I never could see much good to come of annexation [and] I never could very clearly see how the annexation would augment the evil of slavery. It always seemed to me that slaves would be taken there in about equal numbers, with or without annexation. . . . It is possibly true, to some extent, that with annexation, some slaves might be sent to Texas and continued in slavery, that otherwise might have been liberated. To whatever extent this may be true, I think annexation an evil.

Then he added the following reflections on the overall issue of slavery:

> I hold it to be the paramount duty of us in the free states, due to the Union of the states, and perhaps to liberty itself (paradox though it may seem) to let the slavery of the other states alone; while, on the other hand, I hold it to be equally clear, that we should never knowingly lend ourselves directly or indirectly, to prevent slavery from dying a natural death. . . . Of course I am not now considering what would be our duty, in cases of insurrection among the slaves.[17]

In the final months of his presidency, John Tyler claimed that the electoral victory of Polk was a mandate for Texas annexation. So Texas was annexed by Congress on March 1, 1845, and then admitted to full-fledged statehood within the year.

The state constitution of Texas made provision for dividing the state into five smaller states. If that had happened, it would have added greater clout than ever to the power in Congress of the slave-holding South. But Texas would never be divided into five smaller states, and the balance of the free states and slave states would continue to remain in a tense equilibrium—at least for a while.

In December 1844 Lincoln's law partnership with Stephen Logan was dissolved. There had been no estrangement between the partners, so the break-up was perfectly friendly. Logan had simply developed other plans and Lincoln was eager to become the senior partner in a brand new law firm. And that provided the occasion for the storied partnership of Abraham Lincoln and William Herndon.

Herndon became a major figure in Lincoln's life. After Lincoln's death, Herndon's interviews with people who knew the young Lincoln bequeathed an abundance of biographical information to scholars. "Billy" Herndon came to idolize Lincoln, whom he always called "Mister Lincoln."

Herndon had studied law under the supervision of Lincoln and Logan. When Lincoln approached him with the idea of entering into a new partnership, he was flabbergasted. He believed himself unworthy. Later he wrote that in 1844 he was just "a young, undisciplined, uneducated, wild man."[18] He told Lincoln he did not deserve the honor—but then he quickly accepted Lincoln's offer.

A colorful figure, Herndon was intelligent, but his mental energies were more diffuse than Lincoln's. Gabby and opinionated, he aspired to intellectuality and he delved into the philosophic classics. Like Lincoln, he was deeply estranged from his father, in his case because his own anti-slavery convictions conflicted with his father's views.

Like Lincoln, Herndon was an ardent Whig, and like Lincoln he struggled to better himself. His personal life was a mess when Lincoln took him on. He had fallen into drunkenness and Lincoln helped him get a grip on his behavior. It is not at all far-fetched to see in Lincoln's attitude toward Herndon yet another demonstration of paternal behavior toward others.

Herndon and Lincoln set up their firm in a second-floor office across the street from the public square. The messiness of their office became almost legendary. These congenial eccentrics got along—though Lincoln's habit of reading aloud from the newspapers as he sprawled across a sofa in the office sometimes drove Billy Herndon to distraction.

As previously noted, Herndon and Mary Lincoln came to loathe one another. Lincoln's wife regarded Herndon as a tavern-haunter, a reprobate, a man who was too uncouth for words—a man who threatened the Lincolns' social standing. Herndon regarded Mary Lincoln as a shrew.

In the course of their partnership, which lasted right down to Lincoln's election to the presidency, the two men would handle over three thousand cases, roughly half of which were concerned with the collection of debts. Most of Lincoln's work throughout the course of his career as a lawyer covered civil cases, including divorce cases, slander cases, and other such disputes. Once in a while he got involved in criminal proceedings, including some cases of murder or assault.

Lincoln's law practice drew heavily upon his gifts as a strategist, an orator, and a humorist. "The strongest jury lawyer we ever had in Illinois," was the way that one professional colleague remembered him. He could "compel a witness to tell the truth when he meant to lie. He could make a jury laugh, and, generally, weep at his pleasure."[19]

Life as a trial lawyer demanded such theatricality, especially out on the circuit, in the rural hinterland. Herndon recalled that in the country towns "the courthouse was the center of interest for the mass of people who were generally uncultured and ignorant. When court commenced people flocked to the county seat to see and hear and to learn."[20] Accordingly, newspapers often commented on the legal skills of Lincoln.

One common theme of these accounts was the strategic sense that lay behind the various devices that Lincoln employed. In 1850, one account emphasized the "intellect" at work when Lincoln performed in the courtroom: "seizing upon the minutest points, he weaves them into his argument with an ingenuity really astonishing."[21] Several years later, an editor observed that keen strategy and shrewd judgment governed Lincoln's choice of tactics: "He never makes a big fight over a small or immaterial point, but frankly admits much, though never enough to damage his case. In this he differs from little lawyers, who adhere with unyielding pertinacity to trifles."[22]

Lincoln frequently chose to handle his case in a friendly manner. But this manner was grounded in strategy. A fellow attorney observed that Lincoln

had the manner of treating his antagonist with such perfect fairness, as to make the jury and bystanders think that he could not be induced to take advantage of him—a manner which was the hell-firedest lie that was ever acted, because the very fairness he assumed was an ambuscade to cover up a battery, with which to destroy the opposing counsel, and so skillfully laid, too, that after it had done its work, only occasionally would the defeated party, and almost never would the uninitiated, discover the deception.[23]

Attorney Leonard Swett remembered that Lincoln "had few equals and no superiors" in the courtroom. "He was as hard a man to beat in a closely contested case as I have ever met. . . . He was wise as a serpent in the trial of a case, but I tell you I have got too many scars from his blows to certify that he was harmless as a dove."[24]

Swett recounted how Lincoln would lull his opponents with amiable behavior to draw them into a trap:

> As he entered trial, where most lawyers object, he would say he "reckoned" it would be fair to let this in, or that; and sometimes when his adversary could not quite prove what Lincoln knew to be the truth, he would say he "reckoned" it would be fair to admit the truth to be so and so. When he did object to the court, after he heard his objections answered, he would often say: "Well, I reckon I must be wrong." [But] by giving away six points and carrying the seventh, he carried his case, and the whole case hanging on the seventh, he traded away everything which would give him the least aid in carrying that. Any one who took Lincoln for a simple-minded man would very soon wake up on his back, in a ditch.[25]

When Lincoln chose to be gentle, his humor was sometimes so indirect that its magic was almost impossible to pin down. Judge John M. Scott recalled a case in which Lincoln was defending a client whose hog had crossed the fence into a neighbor's land and damaged crops. Lincoln simply

> told a little story about a *fence* that was so *crooked* that when a hog went through an opening in it, invariably it came out on the same side from whence it started. His description of the confused look of the hog after several times going through the fence and still finding itself on the side from whence it started was a humorous specimen of

the best story telling. The effect was to make the plaintiff's case appear ridiculous and while Mr. Lincoln did not attempt to apply the story to the case, the jury seemed to think it had some kind of application to the fence in controversy—otherwise he would not have told it and shortly returned a verdict for the defendant.[26]

When Lincoln chose to put on displays of anger, he could rise to indignation. In an 1843 libel action in which Lincoln defended the reputation of a school teacher from slurs upon her chastity, one observer recalled that Lincoln's abuse of the defendant was "as bitter a Philippic as was ever uttered."[27]

At times Lincoln tried to use sarcasm to undermine the credibility of a witness—and to do it through sheer insinuation. On one occasion, he needled a witness who identified himself as J. Parker Green in the following manner:

Why J. Parker Green? . . . What did the J. stand for? . . . John? . . . Well, why didn't the witness call himself John P. Green? . . . That was his name, wasn't it? . . . Well, what was the reason he did not wish to be known by his right name? . . . Did J. Parker Green have anything to conceal?[28]

One of Lincoln's most famous trials took place in 1858: a murder trial in which he won an acquittal for a young man named William "Duff" Armstrong, the son of his old friends Jack and Hannah Armstrong. Young Armstrong was accused of killing James Preston Metzker in a fight that broke out at a camp meeting on a moonlit night. The trial would be known forever after as the "Almanac Trial."

Interrogating the prosecution's star witness, Charles Allen, Lincoln took pains to go over the events of the evening with meticulous care. Lincoln's slow and patient questioning elicited the following account from Charles Allen: he saw Armstrong do the deed, saw him plainly by the light of the moon, around 11 o'clock at night, at which time the moonlight was clear, since the moon was riding high in the sky, shining almost as clear as daylight. Then Lincoln sprang the trap, producing an almanac showing that the moon, on the night in question, was low in the sky and almost settling behind the horizon at the time in question.

Armstrong was acquitted.

One case of Lincoln's bore a strange and ironic relationship to the destiny awaiting him. In 1847, he took on the case of a Kentucky slave-holder named Robert Matson who was trying to recover possession of some slaves whom he had brought to Illinois and kept there for several years.

Illinois law permitted the temporary residence of slaves as seasonal workers but forbade their presence in the state on a permanent basis. Two abolitionists took legal action to prevent Matson from recovering the slaves. Matson retained Lincoln's services in his efforts to get the slaves back.

Accounts of the trial are in some ways inconsistent. In any case, Lincoln lost.[29] And he limited his arguments to technicalities.

There can be little doubt that Lincoln was not at all happy to be in this position. Why did he take the case at all? Perhaps he believed that he had to do it to uphold professional standards. Many at the time subscribed to the doctrine of David Dudley Field, who held that "a lawyer is not at liberty to refuse anyone his services."[30]

Edward Baker was elected to Congress in 1844. As the next election approached, Lincoln made his preparations to run, per the terms of the 1843 "Pekin agreement" for rotation in office. John Hardin had run for the seat back in 1843 and then it was Baker's turn. In 1846, it would be Lincoln's turn.

But then Hardin denied he had ever agreed to the principle of rotation in office. He tried to reclaim the congressional seat he had won in 1843. Lincoln was very angry. But he refrained from any personal attacks upon Hardin. Instead, in the autumn of 1845 and in the early months of 1846, he made the rounds in the seventh congressional district, lining up one Whig leader after another with a catchy slogan: "Turn about is fair play."

By 1846, recollections of the Pekin agreement were inconsistent or hazy. Still, Whig leaders found it telling that Hardin stepped aside in the 1844 election. That seemed to imply that the Pekin agreement had been more or less what Lincoln always claimed. After attempting a number of ploys, including attempts to sow division between Lincoln and Baker, Hardin withdrew from the race in early February. Lincoln won the Whigs' nomination at the May 1 convention, which was held in Petersburg, Illinois.

That was less than two weeks before Congress declared war on Mexico. The war was in many ways a power grab to push the goal of American expansion at Mexico's expense. The pretext for war was a boundary dispute between Mexico and Texas.

The Mexicans disputed the border claims of the Texans, who asserted that their lands extended all the way to the Rio Grande. The Mexicans insisted that Texas proper extended no farther than the Nueces River. At stake were vast amounts of territory that both sides claimed as their own.

James K. Polk sent American troops to Texas in July 1845, and he declared that the proper border of Texas was the Rio Grande, as the Texans were claiming. But beyond acquiring the territories between the Nueces River and the Rio Grande, Polk wanted much more: he wanted nothing less than *all* the lands stretching westward from Texas to the Pacific Ocean.

In November 1845, he sent an emissary to Mexico City with a secret offer. He offered $25 million to pay not only for a Texas boundary settlement but also for the Mexican provinces of Alta California and Santa Fe de Nuevo México (i.e., the territories of California and New Mexico).

The Mexicans refused.

Polk ordered American troops to cross the Nueces and proceed to the Rio Grande. Mexican forces attacked them and the president of Mexico proclaimed that his country would fight a "defensive war" against American encroachment. Polk brazened it out, contending that American troops were attacked upon American soil. Since the fighting had already begun, Congress declared war on May 13, 1846.

Though many Whigs were opposed to the war, some rallied to the patriotic standard. But Lincoln avoided taking any position on the war in its first year.

Looking back upon the situation two years later, he claimed that when the war began "it was my opinion that all those who, because of knowing *too little*, or because of knowing *too much*, could not conscientiously approve of the conduct of the President . . . should, nevertheless, as good citizens and patriots, remain silent on that point, at least till the war should be ended."[31] Before long, however, Lincoln's stance toward the war became harsh.

In Polk's own party, the war provoked a controversy in regard to a much larger issue: the spread of slavery.

On August 8, 1846, Polk sent to Congress a war appropriations bill. Immediately, Congressman David Wilmot of Pennsylvania, a Free Soil Democrat, proposed the following rider: "Provided, That, as an express and fundamental condition to the acquisition of any territory from the Republic of Mexico by the United States, by virtue of any treaty which may be negotiated between them, and to the use by the Executive of the moneys herein appropriated, neither slavery nor involuntary servitude shall ever exist in any part of said territory, except for crime, whereof the party shall first be duly convicted."

This was the famous "Wilmot Proviso." Though it passed the House easily, it was quickly defeated in the Senate. Nonetheless, it was a gauntlet hurled: a gesture of defiance to the slave-holding South that would make Polk's victory in the course of the Mexican War an empty triumph for the Democratic Party. And it would lead the United States straight to the brink of disunion by 1850.

Importantly, Wilmot was a white supremacist: he said so himself. "I plead the cause of white freemen," he wrote. "I would preserve to free white labor a fair country, a rich inheritance, where the sons of toil, of my own race and own color, can live without the disgrace which association with negro slavery brings upon free labor."[32]

These events had little effect upon Lincoln's congressional campaign when the war broke out in 1846. Instead, his opponent made religion the election's central issue. The Democrats nominated Peter Cartwright, the circuit-riding Methodist preacher whom Lincoln had criticized back in the 1830s for being "too dogmatic." Now Cartwright went on the attack with a whispering campaign accusing Lincoln of being an infidel, a scoffer, a pagan, an enemy of orthodox Christianity.

And Cartwright's accusations were in most respects true. For years, Lincoln had gained the reputation for being a scoffer. He had, in point of fact, been a skeptic in the tradition of the eighteenth-century secular Enlightenment. John Todd Stuart called him "an avowed and open Infidel" who "went further against Christian beliefs—& doctrines & principles than any man I ever heard." More particularly, he "always denied that Jesus was . . . the son of God."[33] According to Herndon, Lincoln told him "a thousand times that he did not believe that the Bible, etc., were revelations of God, as the Christian world contends."[34]

In the course of his congressional campaign, Lincoln handled these issues in an interesting way. On July 31 he issued a handbill that was highly deceptive. "That I am not a member of any Christian church," he wrote, "is true; but I have never spoken with intentional disrespect of religion in general, or of any denomination of Christians in particular."

This was pettifoggery. Though Lincoln had never spoken with disrespect about *"religion in general,"* that was beside the point since the issue at hand was the *Christian* religion, toward which he had indeed expressed scorn. And the fact that he had never spoken with disrespect about "any denomination of Christians" was again irrelevant—beside the point—because his scorn was for *Christianity in general.* And so the differences between Christian denominations never entered into the question. Lincoln's handbill, so seemingly forthright, was in fact quite evasive, if not misleading.

This was yet another demonstration of the formidable powers that Lincoln would use later on as a political strategist.

Lincoln did include in this handbill a venture into metaphysical speculation that was probably sincere—and also quite significant. He wrote that "in early life I was inclined to believe in what I understand is called the 'Doctrine of Necessity'—that is, that the human mind is impelled to action, or held in rest by some power, over which the mind itself has no control." In both psychological and philosophic terms, that was an interesting statement to make.

Even so, Lincoln soon retreated to his thicket of clever disclaimers. He claimed that this "habit of arguing" for the so-called "doctrine of necessity" was a thing of the past. "I have entirely left off" propounding this argument, he claimed, "for more than five years."

In any case, Lincoln concluded this document by saying he did "not think any man has the right . . . to insult the feelings, and injure the morals, of the community in which he may live."[35]

Cartwright's campaign against Lincoln developed little momentum. According to one reminiscence, a Democrat reportedly told Lincoln in confidence that "such is my utter aversion to the meddling of preachers in politics, that I will vote for you even at the risk of losing cast with my party."[36]

Lincoln at last won his seat in Congress—though because of the congressional schedule, he would not take it until December 1847. He would then be thrown into the maelstrom of controversy regarding the Mexican War and free soil. He would at last take his place as a figure in national politics.

Sometime around 1846, Abraham and Mary Lincoln had themselves photographed. This earliest photograph of Lincoln shows him as a well-groomed and serious-looking young man. Clean-shaven and sporting side-burns, he wears a handsome black vested suit.

He would always have the tendency to look awkward because of his angular and long-proportioned frame. And some described his movements as clumsy, especially when he was emphasizing a point in the course of a speech. Gustave Koerner, a German immigrant who was elected to the Illinois legislature and who got to know Lincoln well in the 1840s, recalled that his "appearance was not very prepossessing" because his "exceedingly tall and very angular form made his movements rather awkward." Moreover, "his complexion had no roseate hue of health, but was then rather bilious."[37]

The carefully groomed appearance he arranged for his earliest photograph was, according to many, at odds with the unkempt look that had long since become habitual for him—perhaps because his mind was so busy that grooming and poise were details he regarded as trivial. His thoughts were elsewhere.

The Mexican War continued, and Lincoln kept practicing law as he waited to begin his term in Congress. Yet well before his race for Congress, he took some time to look back and reflect upon the distance he had traveled in his life. He did it in the form of poetry.

For years Lincoln's interest in poetry seems to have prompted him to turn his hand to composition; Lincoln scholars have unearthed some very interesting verse exercises—published anonymously in newspapers—that appear to have been Lincoln's work. But in 1846, Lincoln chose to leave a record with regard to his authorship.

He sent a letter with some verse to a friendly attorney named Andrew Johnston. The theme of the poetry was drawn from his 1844 campaign swing through Indiana. He visited people he had not seen for years and saw places where he played long ago. He also visited the place "where my mother and only sister are buried."

As he walked the old grounds, he found himself once again in the throes of melancholy. But the sadness was mixed with some pleasant reflections and the interplay of these emotions was developed in the poem as follows:

My childhood's home I see again,
And sadden with the view;
And still, as memory crowds my brain,
There's pleasure in it too.

It seems that these memories were idealized in certain respects, and the experience of comparing them with the actual state of the people and landscapes that he encountered gives the poem much of its poignancy.

> O Memory! Thou midway world
> 'Twixt earth and paradise,
> Where things decayed and loved ones lost
> In dreamy shadows rise,
>
> And, freed from all that's earthly vile,
> Seem hallowed, pure, and bright,
> Like scenes in some enchanted isle
> All bathed in liquid light.

But when the memories were compared to the decay of people and surroundings, the effect was depressing, a reminder of the fleeting and evanescent nature of life itself:

> Near twenty years have passed away
> Since here I bid farewell
> To woods and fields, and scenes of play,
> And playmates loved so well . . . .
>
> The friends I left that parting day,
> How changed, how time has sped!
> Young childhood grown, strong manhood gray,
> And half of all are dead.[38]

Lincoln sent this poem to Johnston in an exchange of letters on the subject of poetry. A few months later, he sent another poem about the condition of Matthew Gentry, who was locked in incurable madness. Lincoln explained that Matthew had once been "a bright lad," but at age nineteen he went "furiously mad, from which condition he gradually settled down into harmless insanity." He was still in that "wretched condition" when Lincoln saw him twenty years later:

But here's an object more of dread
Than ought the grave contains—
A human form with reason fled,
While wretched life remains.

Poor Matthew! Once of genius bright,
A fortune-favored child—
Now locked for aye, in mental night,
A haggard mad-man wild. . . .

O death! Thou awe-inspiring prince,
That keepst the world in fear;
Why dost thou tear more blest ones hence,
And leave him ling'ring here?

Early in 1847, Lincoln gave Johnston permission to have his poems published, while keeping his authorship a secret. "I am not at all displeased by your proposal to publish the poetry, or doggerel, or whatever else it may be called, which I sent you," Lincoln wrote. "But let names be suppressed by all means. I have not sufficient hope of the verses attracting any favorable notice to tempt me to risk being ridiculed for having written them."[39]

INTO THE
MAELSTROM

As Lincoln prepared himself for his service in Congress, the migration to Washington became a vacation of sorts for the Lincolns. They rented their house in October 1847. After traveling to St. Louis, they proceeded by train on a rambling inter-state journey.

In Kentucky they paused for a leisurely visit with the Todds. Lincoln and Mary's father had grown to like one another and the latter had provided the family with financial assistance. In the course of this visit Lincoln heard a speech by Henry Clay, who condemned the Mexican War as an act of aggression.

On December 2, 1847, the Lincolns arrived in the nation's capital, a city whose bad sanitation, summertime humidity, and plagues of insects were notorious. They stayed at the Indian Queen Hotel and then moved to a rooming house near the Capitol. Run by a landlady named Ann Spriggs, the place was known in some quarters as "Abolition house" because one of the most outspoken foes of slavery in the House of Representatives, Rep. Joshua Giddings of Ohio, resided there.

Though a freshman in Congress who needed to "learn the ropes," Lincoln was immediately popular. One observer reported that whenever he "addressed the House, he commanded the individual attention of all present."[1] This was a notable achievement since the floor of the U.S.

House of Representatives was boisterous. One journalist called him the "universal favorite here."[2]

His gregariousness was in fine form as he made his way among political insiders, his high spirits projected—at least in male company— through the usual off-color jokes. A colleague from Tennessee recalled that whenever he noticed "a knot of Congressmen together laughing, I knew that they were surrounding Lincoln and listening to his filthy stories."[3] In a way, he was re-enacting his youthful achievement when he took New Salem by storm with his ribald sense of humor.

Lincoln was unusual in bringing his family along with him, for most of the congressmen at that time chose to leave their wives and children at home. But Mary was lonely in Washington and before very long she was miserable. In April she departed with the children and returned to her father's home in Kentucky, leaving Lincoln by himself.

For all the gratification that his instant popularity brought him, Lincoln found the life of a freshman congressman depressing. Much of the work was routine: answering correspondence, seeking special favors for constituents, attending dull committee hearings.

A few weeks after Mary's departure, Lincoln wrote to her as follows: "When you were here, I thought you hindered me some in attending to business; but now, having nothing but business—no variety—it has grown exceedingly tasteless to me. I hate to sit down and direct documents, and I hate to stay in this old room by myself."[4]

Lincoln's letters to Mary in 1848 provide interesting documentation regarding their family life. In the letter just cited, he included an inquiry regarding her health: "And you are entirely free from head-ache? That is good—good—considering it is the first spring you have been free from it since we were acquainted. I am afraid you will get so well, and fat, and young, as to be wanting to marry again."[5]

The homely details of these letters were rich in paternal solicitude. He inquired about their boys as follows: "What did [Bobby] and Eddy think of the little letters father sent them? Don't let the blessed fellows forget father." He went shopping for them, taking care to find precisely what Mary said they needed: "I went yesterday to hunt the little plaid stockings, as you wished; but found that McKnight has quit business, and Allen had not a single pair of the description you give, and only one plaid pair of any sort that I thought would fit 'Eddy's dear little feet.' I have a notion to make another trial to-morrow morning."[6]

He also bought a few things for himself, including—an unusual event—a little something to spruce up his appearance: "Very soon after you went away, I got what I think a very pretty set of shirt-bosom studs— modest little ones, jet, set in gold, only costing 50 cents a piece, or 1.50 for the whole."[7]

A month after Mary's departure, she wrote to Lincoln in terms that were at odds with her intermittent abuse. "Dear boy," she wrote, "I must tell you a little story." She told how Bobby and Eddy found a kitten that they wanted to adopt. "I feel very sad away from you," she wrote, adding that she was writing on a Saturday night when "our *babies* are asleep."[8] When she expressed an interest in returning to Washington for a visit, Lincoln sent her this reply: "Will you be a *good girl* in all things, if I consent? Then come along, and that as *soon* as possible. . . . I want to see you and our dear—*dear* boys very much."[9]

As soon as he took his seat in Congress, Lincoln began a campaign to discredit James K. Polk, whom he accused of sordid aggression in fomenting war. Like a great many Whigs, Lincoln hated Polk and blamed him for putting the United States in the wrong.

But while many Whigs at the national level shared the views of Clay, some Illinois Whigs were in favor of the war, and so Lincoln took a significant risk in his attacks on Polk.

On December 22, 1847 he introduced a series of resolutions that were known as his "spot" resolutions since they directed Polk to respond to some legal interrogatories as to whether the spot where the war had begun was indeed American soil or merely land that the nations disputed. Polk had claimed that the Mexicans started the war by spilling American blood "on our own soil," a proposition that in Lincoln's opinion was so patently weak as to constitute treachery.[10] On January 3, he voted for a Whig resolution contending that the war had been "unnecessarily and unconstitutionally begun by the president."

On January 12, he followed up with a speech attacking Polk directly. When Congress agreed to Texas annexation, he observed, Congress did so "leaving all questions of boundary to future adjustment." But the legalities had never been settled, notwithstanding Polk's claims, which were so specious and flimsy that they could never survive cross-examination in a court of law.

No, Polk was a guilt-ridden man, Lincoln claimed—and probably conscience-ridden, too, since he knew that "the blood of this war, like the blood of Abel, is crying to Heaven against him." He had "some strong motive . . . to involve the two countries in a war," Lincoln said. And so, "by fixing the public gaze upon the exceeding brightness of military glory—that attractive rainbow, that rises in showers of blood—that serpent's eye, that charms to destroy—he plunged into it, and has swept, *on* and *on*, till, disappointed in his calculation of the ease with which Mexico might be subdued, he now finds himself, he knows not where."[11]

But since the Mexican War would be settled on terms that were favorable to the United States, Lincoln's stance became unpopular among his constituents, not only among the Democrats but even among some Whiggish friends, including—most awkwardly—his partner Billy Herndon.

Lincoln would not be moved by their arguments. He defended his vote to condemn Polk's behavior as *refusal* to condone a shameful act. He was proud of the fact that when a fellow congressman from Illinois proposed a resolution supporting the president, he voted "no." He put Herndon on the spot as follows: "Would you have voted what you felt you knew to be a lie?"[12]

Lincoln's indignation was sincere. That being the case, we must consider his attacks upon Polk in a sophisticated context. Lincoln himself was no saint, and he used the methods of deception many times, when he believed they were necessary. So perhaps we are justified in asking ourselves this question: beyond the obvious influence of Clay, whence came the moral outrage that Lincoln was displaying in his vilification of Polk?

It appears that his contempt for Polk's actions came down to his belief that the president acted like a bully. And there was nothing quite as ugly in Lincoln's estimation as abuse of power by the strong.

Since Polk had been a "dark horse" candidate in 1844, he declined to run again in 1848. That was probably wise, since the war had caused a crisis for his party, and indeed for the nation as a whole. Polk's success wrought disaster for the Democrats in 1848 and it destabilized the Whigs. By 1850 it would lead the United States of America to the brink of disunion.

Polk never lived to see much of this, for he died three months after he left the White House in 1849.

The Mexican War created two new military heroes: Generals Zachary Taylor and Winfield Scott. Both appeared to be presidential prospects by 1847. Taylor was of interest across party lines since his views on most public issues were unknown and perhaps would prove to be malleable. But he was a southern slave-holder from Louisiana, which made him objectionable to anti-slavery leaders in both parties.

Nonetheless, a Taylor boom was under way among Whigs by the summer of 1847. The party turned back to the strategy that worked for them in 1840 when they beat Van Buren with the opportunistic candidacy of William Henry Harrison—another war hero.

And even though Clay entertained some lingering hopes for another presidential bid, a great many of his previous supporters—including Lincoln—started switching to Taylor. In August 1847 some Illinois Whigs including Lincoln had a meeting to discuss the merits of a Taylor candidacy. Democratic strength in the state had been surging and the Whigs were receptive to propositions that were based upon imperatives of strategy.

As soon as Lincoln got to Congress he consulted with Taylor supporters, including southern Whigs such as Alexander Stephens of Georgia. Lincoln was the only Illinois Whig to be serving in the House of Representatives, so his voice carried weight.

He argued the merits of a Taylor candidacy on pragmatic grounds. "I am in favor of Gen. Taylor as the whig candidate," he wrote to one correspondent, "because I am satisfied we can elect him . . . and that we cannot elect any other whig."[13] On another occasion he wrote that "our only chance is with Taylor. I go for him, not because I think he would make a better president than Clay, but because I think he would make a better one than Polk, or Cass, or Buchanan, or any such creatures, one of whom is sure to be elected, if he is not."[14]

Lincoln even drafted some text that he hoped might be used by Taylor if he gained the nomination. The text included a promise not to veto legislation except in rare instances—thus smoothing the way for the Whig public works agenda—and to take as little territory from Mexico as possible.

"In a final treaty of peace," Lincoln wrote in his scripted lines for Taylor, "we shall probably be under a sort of necessity of taking some territory; but it is my desire that we shall not acquire any extending so far to the South, as to enlarge and agrivate the distracting question of slavery."[15]

But the "distracting" issue of slavery could not be avoided, for the Free Soil implications of the Treaty of Guadalupe-Hidalgo—preliminarily signed on February 2 and ratified (with modifications) by the Senate on

March 10—were vast since the amount of territory gained by the United States was also vast.

The Democrats nominated Congressman Lewis Cass of Michigan at their Baltimore convention in May. A few weeks later the Whigs nominated Taylor, who agreed to support the Whigs' agenda. Just the same, the Whigs decided to adopt no platform. Lincoln traveled to Philadelphia to attend the Whig convention.

He was exultant—full of expectations for the Whigs to win a big victory. He wrote to Herndon on June 12, predicting that "we shall have a most overwhelming, glorious, triumph." The Whigs' decision to run a war hero, he said, "takes the locos on the blind side. It turns the war thunder against them. The war is now to them, the gallows of Haman, which they built for us, and on which they are doomed to be hanged themselves."[16]

A few weeks later he encouraged Herndon to establish a "Rough and Ready Club" in Springfield—"Old Rough and Ready" being one of Taylor's nicknames. "Gather up all the shrewd wild boys about town," Lincoln wrote, and "let everyone play the part he can play best—some speak, some sing, and all hollow [i.e., holler]."[17]

After the Whig convention, Lincoln spoke twice on the floor of the House of Representatives. One of these speeches defended the Whigs' public works agenda, and the other was an election-year commentary poking fun at the Democrats. These speeches provide some interesting glimpses of Lincoln in action as a congressman.

The speech on public works showed Lincoln's serious and analytical side. Polk had vetoed a Whig measure for river and harbor improvements and Cass had announced he would adhere to his party's opposition to "internal improvements." Lincoln decided it was time for someone to make the case for bold federal action so persuasively that even Democrats might pause for a moment and *think*.

This speech places Lincoln in a long tradition stretching all the way back to Alexander Hamilton, who interpreted the Constitution broadly and who wished to use the powers of the federal government to maximum advantage. Lincoln felt the same way. "No one who is satisfied with the expediency of making improvements," he said, "needs be much uneasy in his conscience about its constitutionality."

Lincoln addressed what seemed to him a tiresome view among opponents of internal improvements: the notion that the taxes to be levied to support public works "would be *general*, while their benefits would [be] *local* and *partial*, involving an obnoxious inequality." It was time, Lincoln said, to acknowledge that "there are few things *wholly* evil, or *wholly* good," that common goals should be advanced through the use of common sense, and that churlish haggling served the interests of no one.

Lincoln offered precedents for bold federal action—and federal expense—along with comparisons to show how the goals of some projects commanding universal support were no different from the goals of controversial projects. "The Navy, as I understand it," he reasoned,

> was established, and is maintained at a great annual expense, partly to be ready for war when war shall come, but partly also, and perhaps chiefly, for the protection of our commerce on the high seas. This latter object is, for all I can see, in principle, the same as internal improvements. The driving of a pirate from the track of commerce on the broad ocean, and removing a snag from its more narrow path in the Mississippi river, cannot, I think, be distinguished in principle.

Then he gave a more pointed example for his audience to ponder:

> This capitol is built at the public expense, for the public benefit; but does anyone doubt that it is of some peculiar local advantage to the property holders, and business people of Washington? Shall we remove it for this reason? And if so, where shall we set it down and be free from the difficulty?

Endless objections could be raised against public works, he argued, and he gave more examples:

> One man is offended because a road passes over his land, and another is offended because it does *not* pass over his. One is dissatisfied because the bridge, for which he is taxed, crosses the river on a different road from that which leads from his house to town; another cannot bear that the county should be got in debt for these same roads and bridges; while not a few struggle hard to have roads located over their lands, and then stoutly refuse to let them be opened until they are first paid the damages.

The way to minimize such wrangling, he said, was to base the planning of internal improvements on "facts"—"statistics," for instance, regarding "hindrances, delays, and losses of life and property during transportation"—as opposed to mere "whim, caprice, or local interest." "Determine that the thing can and shall be done," Lincoln said, "and then we shall find the way."[18]

This exercise in pragmatism was followed up a week later by a venture in partisan humor—a discourse on the "presidential question" of 1848. Lincoln strove in this speech to defend the candidacy of Taylor while poking fun at Lewis Cass. The jokes that he employed were so effective that even Democrats laughed.

Lincoln reveled in the Democrats' charges that the candidacy of Taylor was opportunistic. According to eyewitness accounts of this speech, Lincoln strode back and forth, trading barbs with opponents, spinning out rhetorical questions and following up with funny answers.

So the Whigs' nomination of a military hero was an act of desperation? So the Whigs were hanging onto the "coat-tails" of Taylor as they put Henry Clay out to pasture like an old horse? Who were Democrats to say such things when for years they had shamelessly depended on the image and reputation of their own pet hero, Andrew Jackson? Lincoln needled his opponents with gusto:

> Your campaign papers have constantly been "Old Hickories" with rude likenesses of the old general upon them; hickory poles, and hickory brooms, your never-ending emblems: Mr. Polk himself was "Young Hickory" or something so; and even now, your campaign paper here is proclaiming that Cass and Butler are of the true "Hickory stripe." No sir, you dare not give it up.

He was having the time of his life as he brought the old skills that served him so well in the Illinois legislature to the floor of the House of Representatives:

> If you have any more old horses, trot them out; any more tails, just cock them, and come at us. . . . I wish gentlemen on the other side to understand, that the use of degrading figures is a game at which they may not find themselves able to take all the winnings. (We give it up). Aye, you give it up, and well you may. . . . The point—the power to hurt—of all figures, consists in the *truthfulness* of their application; and understanding this, you may well give it up. They are weapons which hit you, but miss us.

This banter was a warm-up for the roasting Lincoln gave to Lewis Cass. The Democrats were trying to present Cass as a hero because of his service in the War of 1812. Here was an occasion for Lincoln to mock his own service in the Black Hawk War: if Cass were a hero, Lincoln gibed, then surely he was such a hero himself for his charges against patches of huckleberries and battles with mosquitoes.

Then Lincoln had more fun by implying that Cass, while traveling— during his tenure as governor of Michigan Territory and as a commissioner who helped to implement Jackson's policy of "Indian removal"—had looted the public by helping himself to double or triple stipends for meals and by tallying expenses for duties he performed simultaneously in different places:

> I have introduced Gen: Cass's accounts here chiefly to show the wonderful physical capacities of the man. They show that he not only did the labor of several men at the same *time*; but that he often did it at several *places*, many hundreds of miles apart, at the same time. And, at eating too, his capacities are shown to be quite as wonderful. From October 1821 to May 1822, he ate ten rations a day in Michigan, ten rations a day here in Washington, and near five dollars worth a day on the road between the two places! .... Mr. Speaker, we have all heard of the animal standing in doubt between two stacks of hay, and starving to death. The like of that would never happen to Gen: Cass; place the stacks a thousand miles apart, he would stand stock still midway between them, and eat them both at once; and the green grass along the line would be apt to suffer some too at the same time.

There was more of such humor in the speech, but there was also serious content. Most importantly, Lincoln declared his support for the Wilmot Proviso. "I am a Northern man," he said, "or rather, a Western free state man, with a constituency I believe to be, and with personal feelings I know to be, against the extension of slavery."[19]

On the slavery issue, Cass proposed that white settlers in western territories should decide the question for themselves—a policy that would be known before long as the doctrine of "popular sovereignty." Lincoln ridiculed the record of Cass on this issue as shifty and opportunistic.

The Free Soil issue was whipping people into a frenzy by the summer of 1848. The balance of power between the free states and the slave states depended on how the vast amount of territory seized from Mexico in the treaty of Guadalupe-Hidalgo would be handled in regard to slavery. Would these lands be open to the spread of slavery or not?

President Polk had a simple solution: extend the Missouri Compromise line due west to the Pacific Ocean. Cass proposed a different solution: let the whites in these territories work out the matter for themselves. But neither of these ideas was acceptable to the Free Soil militants.

The two parties were internally divided on the issue of slavery: "Conscience Whigs" and "Cotton Whigs" debated whether Zachary Taylor was a fit nominee for the presidency in light of the fact that he owned slaves. And the Democrats were so divided that in August a faction of New York Democrats known as "Barn-Burners" joined with Conscience Whigs to form a new party: the Free Soil Party, which was created in improvised conventions. Their presidential candidate was none other than former president Martin Van Buren.

More and more, Free Soilers viewed slavery as an urgent threat to themselves. In 1847, white workers at the Tredegar Iron Works in Richmond, Virginia, went on strike for better hours and wages. The owner of the factory, after firing them all, used a gang of slaves to run the factory. And he didn't even *own* the slaves in question: he *rented* them. Here was a strong demonstration of the threat that slave labor could pose for working-class whites: slaves could be used as rented strike-breakers.

By 1848, Free Soilers referred to the southern plantation aristocracy as a "Slave Power" that threatened the common man everywhere. They were tyrants who suppressed white freedom of speech in the slave states and even tried to silence free whites in the sacred halls of Congress through the "Gag Rule" that tabled all petitions on slavery. Former President John Quincy Adams—the only president to serve in Congress after serving in the White House—defied the Gag Rule ever since it was enacted and fought to have it repealed. He finally succeeded in 1844.

With the launching of the Free Soil Party, the prospects of both Taylor and Cass were imperiled. Lincoln decided that he had to protect his party from a third-party movement that could tip the election to the Democrats, just as the Liberty Party had blighted the chances of Clay in the previous election.

Lincoln was recruited to give pro-Taylor speeches in Massachusetts, where the situation was doubtful. He toured the state giving speeches, beginning on September 13 with an address to the Whig state convention in Worcester.

According to the Boston *Daily Advertiser*, Lincoln presented "a very tall and thin figure, with an intellectual face, showing a searching mind, and a cool judgment." He began his hour-and-a-half speech "by expressing a real feeling of modesty in addressing an audience 'on this side of the mountains,' a part of the country where, in the opinion of the people of his section, everybody was supposed to be instructed and wise."

After this crowd-pleasing gesture, he laid out the issues in a manner that the *Advertiser* deemed "masterly and convincing."[20]

Two days later, he gave a speech in Boston that was equally well received. According to the Boston *Atlas*, it was a speech that "for sound reasoning, cogent argument, and keen satire, we have seldom heard equaled." Lincoln "pointed out the absurdity of men who professed Whig principles supporting Van Buren, with all his Locofocoism, while the Whigs were as much opposed to the extension of slavery as the Van Buren party."[21]

In Lowell, Lincoln's speech was according to the local *Daily Journal* "replete with good sense . . . and spoken with that perfect command of manner and matter which so eminently distinguishes the Western orators."[22] Even a Democratic paper reported that the speech Lincoln gave in Taunton was "such as to give unlimited satisfaction to the disheartened Taylorites," adding that "such a treat it is indeed seldom their good luck to get, and they were in ecstacies."[23]

In most of these accounts, Lincoln seemed to be stiff as he began the speeches, but he limbered up and gave vent to the exuberant side of his nature. One Lowell citizen remembered that after Lincoln made jokes he often "joined in a comical way in the laugh they occasioned, shaking his sides, which peculiar manner seemed to add to the good humor of the audience. He had a voice of more than average compass, clear and penetrating, pronouncing many of his words in a manner not usual in New England."[24]

In Boston, Lincoln spoke right after a speech by former Governor William H. Seward of New York. Seward declared that the Whigs should go further than opposing the extension of slavery; they should seek to abolish it wherever federal power made it possible to do so, especially in Washington, D.C., the nation's capital.

The next day Lincoln reportedly told Seward he had "been thinking about what you said in your speech. I reckon you are right."[25]

Lincoln returned to Illinois in late September via the Great Lakes: he sailed from Buffalo to Chicago from September 23 to October 5, having visited Niagara Falls on the way. Niagara Falls put him in a meditative mood, and he set down the following observations:

Contemporary with the whole race of man, and older than the first man, Niagara is strong, and fresh to-day as ten thousand years ago. The Mammoth and the Mastadon—now so long dead, that fragments of their monstrous bones, alone testify, that they ever lived, have gazed on Niagara. In that long—long time, never still for a single moment. Never dried, never froze, never slept, never rested.[26]

In the course of this trip, Lincoln saw a lake steamer that had run aground near Detroit. So he designed a boat with extensions that could free other boats from such obstacles. Lincoln actually went on to obtain a patent for this invention. Here was another demonstration of the ingenuity by which he had freed the flatboat that got stuck on the milldam at New Salem so many years before.

Taylor won the election of 1848. The Free Soil candidacy of Van Buren turned out to be more damaging to the Democrats than the Whigs.

In any case, Lincoln's term in Congress was expiring. Per the terms of the Pekin agreement, he did not run for re-election.

In the lame duck session of the Thirtieth Congress, Lincoln sized up his prospects for advancement. Perhaps his support for Taylor might lead to some new opportunities. In any case, he decided to take Seward's advice in regard to the slavery issue: he would start to address it more directly.

The fight about slavery emerged with great force after the Treaty of Guadalupe-Hidalgo was ratified. It caused rifts in both parties and it threatened to cause a huge breach between the North and South.

A few months after the ratification, one congressman reported that "we are just now in an awful state of excitement. A dissolution of the Union is threatened on every side."[27]

The proposal to extend the Missouri Compromise line to the Pacific was rejected by the House. Oregon was secured as a free soil territory with little controversy but the vast Mexican Cession remained unorganized and potentially up for grabs.

Moreover, the anti-slavery bloc in Congress became more ambitious, beginning with attempts to abolish slavery in the nation's capital, where Congress had the power to do so.

The most odious signs of enslavement could be seen from the Capitol itself. Lincoln remembered a few years later that "in view of the windows of the capitol, a sort of negro-livery stable, where droves of negroes were collected, temporarily kept, and finally taken to Southern markets, precisely like droves of horses, had been openly maintained for fifty years."[28] This was the "Georgia Pen," which opponents of slavery regarded as an international disgrace.

When Lincoln returned to Washington after the election, the final session of the Thirtieth Congress was dominated by the slavery fight. Disputes regarding California and New Mexico became so fierce that fistfights erupted in the House and Senate.

This was merely a prelude to the confrontation that would bring the nation to the point of disunion in 1850.

The central figure in the drama was Senator John C. Calhoun of South Carolina, who had served as one of the foremost architects of pro-slavery strategy since the 1820s. In the midst of the crisis regarding the Mexican Cession he wrote a pro-slavery manifesto entitled "Address of Southern Delegates in Congress to their Constituents."

Released on January 22, 1849 and signed by forty-eight congressmen, it stated that the slavery controversy was an all-or-nothing struggle in which the white South should unite to frustrate every move by opponents of slavery.

Calhoun got to the point when he warned that an amendment to the Constitution ratified by three quarters of the states could eliminate slavery, and that the struggle to protect the institution must focus on preventing the establishment of a three-quarters super-majority of free states.

The South had "no cause to complain prior to the year 1819," he wrote, when the Missouri crisis erupted. But that crisis prefigured the subsequent attempts to prevent the spread of slavery and thus isolate the existing bloc of slave states. The obvious "determination avowed by the North to monopolize all the territories," he wrote, would "add to the North a sufficient number of States to give her three fourths of the whole; when, under the color of an amendment to the Constitution, she would emancipate our slaves."[29]

Only one course of action could avert the catastrophe, Calhoun insisted: militant and united resistance by the slave-holding South.

For years Calhoun had been concocting strategies designed to thwart the anti-slavery movement. After the Missouri Compromise—which gave the free-state system most of the territory in the Louisiana Purchase—he championed the doctrine of state sovereignty as a means of "nullifying" federal action. His logic was simple: if the free states outnumbered the slave states, the latter would be powerless to stop anti-slavery measures in

Congress, so the best way to deal with that threat was to limit the power of Congress through the doctrine of states' rights.

Though many students of history believe that his intent in the 1828–1832 "Nullification Crisis" was to oppose a federal tariff (import tax), he admitted in private that the tariff was nothing but a pretext, an excuse for establishing a precedent supporting state sovereignty. "I consider the Tariff," he confided, "but as the occasion, rather than the real cause of the present unhappy state of things," which resulted from the fact that the "domestic institutions of the Southern States [have] placed them in . . . opposite relation to the majority of the Union."[30]

He also tinkered with constitutional doctrines that could be used to declare anti-slavery legislation unconstitutional. On February 19, 1847, he introduced a series of resolutions stating that Congress had no power to bar slavery from federal territories—or anyplace else. He grounded this doctrine in the Fifth Amendment, which states, among other things, that "no person shall be . . . deprived of life, liberty, or property, without due process of law."

Since slaves were property, Calhoun reasoned, any ban on slavery would "deprive" slave-holders of the use of their property "without due process of law."

Ironically, this reading of the Fifth Amendment—a reading that would shape Lincoln's destiny profoundly a decade later when the U.S. Supreme Court embraced it—was countered by a reading that gave to the very same text an *anti*-slavery meaning. Salmon P. Chase, an Ohio Free Soil Democrat, argued that the presence of slavery in federal territories deprived the slaves of their *liberty* "without due process of law," since slavery was merely a *state*-sanctioned institution.

The very same words in the Constitution could be construed in opposite ways.

By 1849 Calhoun was determined to whip up southern resistance to the Wilmot Proviso, which never passed the Senate, though the House had passed it repeatedly. After the adjournment of the Thirtieth Congress, Calhoun called for a convention to unify southern resistance. Two conventions ensued: the first met in Jackson, Mississippi, on October 1, 1849. The next would meet in Nashville during the Crisis of 1850.

It was against this background that Lincoln, in his last few months in Congress, wrote a bill that would have abolished slavery in the nation's capital.

Even though Lincoln's bill was ambitious, it was grounded in the gradualist school of thought. The bill provided that children born to slave mothers in Washington after 1850 would be gradually emancipated and compensation would be given to the owners of adult slaves who agreed to emancipate them. To soften opposition, Lincoln provided that the law would only go into effect if a majority of District of Columbia voters approved, and that residents of Washington would have to return any fugitive slaves who entered the city.

The bill never had a chance. Though Lincoln had visited Washington's mayor and other local leaders to organize support, pro-slavery leaders struck back. Lincoln later recounted what happened:

> I visited Mayor [William S.] Seaton, and others whom I thought best acquainted with the sentiments of the people, to ascertain if a bill such as I proposed would be endorsed by them.... Being informed that it would meet with their hearty approbation I gave notice in congress that I should introduce a Bill. Subsequently I learned that many leading southern members of Congress, had been to see the Mayor, and the others who favored my Bill and had drawn them over to their way of thinking. Finding that I was abandoned by my former backers and having little personal influence, I *dropped* the matter knowing it was useless to prosecute the business at that time.[31]

After Taylor's inauguration Lincoln found himself besieged by a horde of office-seekers who wanted his assistance. Before long, these requests embroiled him in tawdry complications, not least of all because Lincoln himself was considering the next steps in his career.

One of the most important of the jobs to be filled by Taylor was the lucrative position of commissioner of the General Land Office in the brand-new Department of the Interior. Several prominent Illinois Whigs were contenders, and when Lincoln backed one of them, he ran afoul of his old friend Edward Baker, who was backing a different candidate.

Meanwhile, Lincoln was troubled by the fear that his law practice was dwindling due to his absence. Even so, he had finally begun to enjoy the social life of the nation's capital with its opportunities to hob-nob with luminaries like Daniel Webster, who had taken a liking to Lincoln. In April he returned to Springfield in a wistful state of mind.

As he did so, Illinois Whigs began to worry that both of the state's candidates for the commissionership of the Land Office might fail to get the job: the position might go to someone else. So Anson Henry and other Whig leaders told Lincoln that he ought to seek the job himself, lest it go to a politician from another state.

He came back to Washington and battled it out with the other candidates. A number of political friends supported him, and Lincoln even made a direct application to President Taylor. But the president chose someone else.

After denying Lincoln the commissionership of the Land Office, the administration tried to make it up to him by offering him two different jobs in the Pacific Northwest—first the secretaryship of the Oregon Territory and then the territorial governorship of Oregon. According to John Todd Stuart, Lincoln was interested in this position; it was lucrative and it might have led to greater things over time, perhaps even a seat in the U.S. Senate after Oregon became a state.

But Mary Lincoln had no desire to relocate to the other side of the Rocky Mountains, so Lincoln turned down the offer. He went back to his old routine in Springfield.

He tried to be philosophical in the aftermath of these disappointments, but the truth was obvious: he was out of office, at loose ends, and faced with the possibility that his days as a public figure were over: he was just another lawyer in Springfield. And then another blow in the procession of tragedies that seemed to dog him struck on February 1, 1850: his little boy Eddy passed away just a few months before his fourth birthday.

QUEST FOR PURPOSE

ddy's death was a terrible blow to the Lincolns, and Mary sought comfort through religion. A Presbyterian minister, Rev. James Smith, conducted Eddy's funeral, and he gave the Lincolns a book he had written, *The Christian's Defense*. Mary later claimed that Lincoln's heart was "directed towards religion" by the death of their son, and Lincoln rented a pew for the couple at Smith's First Presbyterian Church.[1]

Mary soon became pregnant again, and another son, William Wallace Lincoln ("Willie"), was born on December 21, 1850.

The next year Lincoln's father died, and—not surprisingly—Lincoln took little time to grieve. Though his father wished to see him, Lincoln remained so estranged that he declined. He told his step-brother, John Johnston, that if he visited his father "it is doubtful whether it would not be more painful than pleasant." But he asked John to speak some words of comfort, and suggested that he tell Thomas Lincoln to "call upon, and confide in, our great, and good, and merciful Maker; who will not turn away from him in any extremity. He notes the fall of a sparrow, and numbers the hairs on our heads; and he will not forget the dying man, who puts his trust in Him."[2]

Perhaps Mary was telling the truth when she wrote that Lincoln became more receptive to religion after Eddy's death.

Lincoln's beloved step-mother, Sarah, survived, and Lincoln was determined to make her financial situation secure. When Johnston proposed to sell part of the farm where Sarah lived, Lincoln—who had come to regard his step-brother as a wastrel—shot down the proposal in words that make for darkly funny reading.

Johnston was thinking of moving to Missouri, but Lincoln was unsympathetic. "You have idled away all your time," Lincoln wrote, and then he warned his step-brother against selling any farm land to finance his own relocation:

> I learned that you are anxious to sell the land where you live, and move to Missouri. I . . . can not but think such a notion is utterly foolish. What can you do in Missouri, better than here? Is the land any richer? . . . Will any body there, any more than here, do your work for you? If you intend to go to work, there is no better place than right where you are; if you do not intend to go to work, you can not get along any where. Squirming & crawling about from place to place can do no good. You have raised no crop this year, and what you really want is to sell the land, get the money and spend it. . . . Now I feel it is my duty to have no hand in such a piece of foolery. I feel that it is so even on your own account; and particularly on *Mother's* account. The Eastern forty acres I intend to keep for Mother while she lives—if you *will not cultivate it*; it will rent for enough to support her—at least it will rent for something.

Lincoln closed with a rhetorical kick in the posterior, telling Johnston that "your thousand pretenses for not getting along better, are all non-sense—they deceive no body but yourself. *Go to work* is the only cure for your case."[3]

Lincoln took his own advice as he buried himself in his legal practice. "I was losing interest in politics," he later wrote, and "practiced law more assiduously than ever before."[4] He maintained Whig connections, and he gave a few speeches in the 1852 presidential election—speeches ridiculing the Democrats' nominee, Franklin Pierce. But it was a half-hearted effort.

His law practice was becoming more lucrative, and Lincoln began to earn a lively income by representing railroads. One of his earliest cases in 1851 was *Barrett v. Alton and Sangamon Railroad*. Lincoln won the case, and went on to earn handsome fees in this new legal specialization.

All the while, however, he was brooding, reflecting on the question of whether the most exciting years of his career were already behind him.

Mary gave birth to another son on April 4, 1853. He was christened Thomas, but the Lincolns called him Tad. According to many recollections, Lincoln doted on his sons, but his relationship with his eldest son Robert was distant. Herndon (typically) ascribed the situation to the baleful personality of Mary, proclaiming that Robert Lincoln "is a Todd and not a Lincoln . . . his mother's baby all through."[5]

The sectional confrontation over California and New Mexico escalated to the point where a crisis of the Union seemed possible. The California gold rush had flooded the West Coast with settlers whose views about slavery rang alarm bells throughout the South.

A California constitutional convention was called in June 1849, and it voted in October to seek admission to the Union as a free state. Pro-slavery leaders perceived that they and their social system were about to be deprived of the power base that the Pacific West Coast represented.

In addition to California, lingering issues regarding the borders of Texas had implications for slavery in New Mexico.

Though President Taylor was a slave-holder, he proclaimed he was ready to support the admission of California and New Mexico as free states if their settlers wished to have it so.

He called for the admission of both in his annual message to Congress in December 1849, and he urged Congress to "abstain from the introduction of . . . exciting topics of a sectional character" when debating the issues. Furthermore, he stated that since "this Union has stood unshaken," he would "maintain it in its integrity to the full extent of the obligations imposed and the powers conferred upon me by the Constitution."[6]

Under the leadership of Calhoun, pro-slavery resistance had stiffened. The Alabama and Georgia legislatures approved measures that were known as the "Alabama Platform," since Congressman William Lowndes Yancey of Alabama drafted them. They opposed any restrictions on slavery in federal territories and they also opposed "popular sovereignty."

Henry Clay was working with Lincoln's old enemy Stephen Douglas to resolve the crisis. Both men were serving in the Senate. This was to be Clay's last performance as America's "Great Pacificator"—the peacemaker who had played the central role in the Missouri Compromise in 1820. Clay was motivated by considerations that were very different from those that animated Douglas.

Douglas was enjoying a meteoric rise that began in 1847 when the Illinois Democrats had placed him in the U.S. Senate, whose members were still chosen by the state legislatures. By 1850, he chaired the powerful Committee on Territories. As Clay sought to build bipartisan support for a sectional compromise, he reached out to Douglas as a matter of course.

But Calhoun would have none of it, and he wrote out a fiery speech to encourage pro-slavery resistance. Too ill to deliver this speech, he had it read on his behalf by Senator James Murray Mason of Virginia on March 4, 1850. "I have, Senators, believed from the first," Calhoun's speech began, "that the agitation of the subject of slavery would, if not prevented by some timely and effective measure, end in disunion."

He accused northerners of seeking to destroy slavery. If the Wilmot Proviso should ever be passed, he predicted, "the North" (i.e., the free-state bloc) would control three-fourths of the nation's territory. And then, such a super-majority of states would ratify an anti-slavery amendment to the Constitution. Only a pre-emptive pro-slavery amendment could forestall that possibility, he said. In the meantime, the moment for a show-down had arrived. "It is time, Senators," the speech concluded,

> that there should be an open and manly avowal on all sides as to what is intended to be done. . . . If you, who represent the stronger portion, cannot agree to settle [the issues] on the broad principles of justice and duty, say so; and let the States we both represent agree to separate and part in peace. If you are unwilling we should part in peace, tell us so; and we shall know what to do. . . . If you remain silent, you will compel us to infer by your acts what you intend. In that case California will become the test question. If you admit her under all the difficulties that oppose her admission, you compel us to infer that you intend to exclude us from the whole of the acquired territories, with the intention of destroying irretrievably the equilibrium between the two sections.[7]

Within weeks after Mason had delivered this speech on his behalf, Calhoun died.

President Taylor was prepared to face the southern threats. After three southern Whigs arrived to discuss the territorial situation, Taylor reportedly said to them that "he would take command of the army himself" in the case of any threats to the Union. As for any secessionists who might be "taken in rebellion against the Union, he would hang them with less reluctance than he had hung deserters and spies in Mexico."⁸ But then Taylor himself died—from an intestinal illness that he contracted on the Fourth of July.

After Calhoun's death, talk of southern secession abated. The convention in Nashville that Calhoun and others had summoned met in June, but, instead of supporting secession, the delegates proposed reviving the compromise that Polk and others had suggested: extending the Missouri Compromise line to the Pacific, thus dividing California in two.

But it was not to be.

Clay and Douglas made deals in Congress and they pushed through a messy compromise package of their own. Five separate bills encompassed this "Compromise of 1850." All were passed by September and signed into law by Zachary Taylor's successor, Millard Fillmore.

The compromise was ragged and its provisions boded ill for the future. California was admitted as a free state. But the rest of the Mexican Cession would be open to slavery on the principle of popular sovereignty. The Texas land claims in New Mexico were over-ruled. The slave *trade* in Washington, D.C.—but not the institution itself—was abolished, but a harsh new Fugitive Slave Law was passed to appease southern militants.

Lincoln, in a state of political drift, did little to support these measures. But he did pay tribute to Clay when the Great Pacificator passed away in 1852.

In a eulogy delivered in Springfield, Lincoln emphasized Clay's opposition to slavery while lauding him for saving the Union during sectional crises. Clay resisted both extremes in the slavery dispute, Lincoln said: he resisted both the abolitionists "who would shiver into fragments the Union of these states . . . rather than slavery should continue a single hour" as well as the pro-slavery militants who, "for the sake of perpetuating slavery, are beginning to assail and to ridicule the white-man's charter of freedom—the declaration that 'all men are created free and equal.'"

Lincoln was still a supporter of gradualism when it came to the slavery issue. He believed it would be best to pay compensation to the owners of the slaves and then encourage the emancipated slaves to live elsewhere. In eulogizing Clay, Lincoln heralded the vision of colonization and he did so in biblical terms—as the exodus of a latter-day African Israel.

This notion was current at the time among the African Americans who found colonization attractive rather than insulting. Lincoln made the biblical analogy to their situation explicit:

Pharaoh's country was cursed with plagues, and his hosts were drowned in the Red Sea for striving to retain a captive people who had already served them more than four hundred years. May like disasters never befall us! If as the friends of colonization hope, the present and coming generations of our countrymen shall . . . succeed in freeing our land from the dangerous presence of slavery; and, at the same time, in restoring a captive people to their long-lost father-land, with bright prospects for the future; and this too, so gradually, that neither races nor individuals shall have suffered for the change, it will indeed be a glorious consummation.[9]

When Lincoln delivered this speech, he believed that the threat of secession had vanished. "In our last internal discord," he said, "when this Union trembled to its center," Clay "gave the death blow to fraternal strife."[10]

But two years later, Lincoln found himself radicalized—along with thousands of other Free Soilers—by the prospect that slavery was spreading so far and so fast that it would ruin the United States forever.

The Compromise of 1850 postponed the sectional showdown—but not for long. Opponents of slavery loathed the new Fugitive Slave Law and they sought to impede its operations. Conscience Whigs vilified Fillmore and denied him the party's 1852 nomination to punish him for signing the 1850 Compromise. Instead, the Whigs nominated General Winfield Scott, who went on to get beaten by the Democrats' "dark horse" nominee, former Senator Franklin Pierce of New Hampshire.

Supporters of slavery were also disgusted by the Compromise of 1850. The loss of California enraged them. The pro-slavery journal *De Bow's Review* called California "the new El Dorado" and complained that if slavery had only been given a chance on the West Coast, it would have been perfect for California mining operations.[11]

Before long, the urge to seize more territory for slavery became over-powering. As early as 1850, Governor John A. Quitman of Mississippi called for detaching Cuba from the Spanish empire and bringing it into the Union as a slave state. In 1853, a Tennessean named William Walker led a band of marauders into Mexico. They hoped to foment another Mexican war that would lead to the seizure of Baja California. Mexico expelled these American terrorists but a few years later they were back at work. In 1855 they invaded Nicaragua, and instituted slavery there.

A pro-slavery Virginian named George Bickley created a secret society called the "Knights of the Golden Circle." The "circle" in question was the Caribbean rim, and Bickley envisioned the creation of a huge tropical empire for slavery.

These pro-slavery imperialists were known as "filibusterers," a term derived from the Spanish word "filibustero," meaning pirate. One of them, Mississippi Senator Albert Gallatin Brown, proclaimed that he wanted "Cuba . . . and one or two other Mexican States; and I want them all for the same reason—for the planting or spreading of slavery."[12]

There was another reason behind this wave of pro-slavery expansionism: the belief that slave rebellions were likely unless the "excess" black population could be siphoned away by means of new territorial conquests.

North Carolina Congressmen Thomas L. Clingman declared that both masters and slaves should not "be pent up within a territory or a state which after a time will be insufficient for their subsistence, and where they must perish from want, or from collision that would occur between the races."[13]

The new Democratic president, Franklin Pierce, was receptive to these ideas. He was a "dough-face," in the parlance of the times—a "northern man of southern principles" whose foremost goal in political life was placation of the slave-holding South.

In 1854, Pierce dispatched three diplomats—Pierre Soulé, John Y. Mason, and James Buchanan—to Europe in the hope of laying the groundwork for the annexation of Cuba. They drafted a document that would soon become known as the "Ostend Manifesto," a declaration setting forth the benefits of purchasing Cuba and justifying its seizure by the United States if the Spanish refused to sell. After it was leaked and published, this manifesto triggered an international furor.

But it was a more shocking act of pro-slavery aggression in 1854 that rekindled the sectional crisis. This development shattered the existing two-party system and incited such wrath in Abraham Lincoln that his life took on a new meaning.

All of a sudden, the Missouri Compromise of 1820 was repealed. This meant that slavery could spread into any part of the Louisiana Purchase that had not yet been admitted to statehood.

The reaction in the Free Soil movement was disbelief, and then rage. Almost everyone had expected the next major sectional collision to occur in New Mexico. Few had imagined that federal lands that were already off-limits to slavery would again be put at risk. Now nothing was safe any longer.

Stephen Douglas, smitten with presidential ambitions and eager to aggrandize the power of his state, was promoting the construction of a trans-continental railroad that would reach the new state of California. He wanted it constructed on a line that would stretch from Chicago to St. Louis, and then proceed west. He introduced legislation that would organize the land directly to the west and northwest of Missouri into a territory known as Nebraska. The idea was to hasten the settlement of that area to make it more attractive as a route for the railroad.

But the lands to the west of Missouri were forbidden to slavery. So opposition from the slave states erupted. Senator David Atchison of Missouri proclaimed that he would rather see Nebraska "sink in hell" than consent to the creation of any more free states.

And then, pro-slavery leaders decided to turn this situation to their own advantage by holding the Nebraska bill hostage in the hope that they could force the repeal of the entire Missouri Compromise. This would open the floodgates for slavery expansion in a part of the country that for years they had regarded as lost.

And it worked.

On January 4, 1854, Douglas introduced a revised Nebraska bill that would institute popular sovereignty in the open territories that were left in the Louisiana Purchase.

But pro-slavery leaders in the Senate demanded even more: Senator Archibald Dixon of Kentucky introduced an amendment *explicitly* repealing the dividing line that kept slavery out of the northern part of the Louisiana Purchase. And Douglas consented. The new bill divided the territory of Nebraska in two smaller segments so that the lower portion—directly to the west of Missouri—could be groomed for quick admission as a slave state. This new subdivided portion of Nebraska would bear the name of Kansas.

The Kansas-Nebraska bill was passed by Congress and signed into law by President Pierce on May 30, 1854. All the old restrictions on the spread of slavery within the Louisiana Purchase were suddenly gone.

Anti-slavery Americans were livid, not least of all because this burst of pro-slavery aggression was so unexpected. It was a surprise attack upon the Free Soil movement and a harbinger of much worse to come. The anti-slavery movement was convulsed and Free Soilers across party lines began talking of a "fusion" movement that would help them join forces more effectively.

This was the process that shattered the existing two-party system and created the brand-new Republican Party—a party that would make the cause of Free Soil its top priority.

Free-Soil Democrats and Conscience Whigs began organizing, and within two years—by the election of 1856—the Whig Party was gone. The Democratic Party survived, but it was greatly transformed. Most of the Free Soil Democrats left and became Republicans. That left the hard-core supporters of slavery in firm control of the Democratic Party.

All through the summer of 1854, the outrage of Free Soilers increased, and then another provocation was added: a pro-slavery Virginian named George Fitzhugh published a radical and inflammatory book, *Sociology for the South*. This book supported slavery in such extravagant terms as to constitute a frontal assault on the ideals expressed by Thomas Jefferson in the Declaration of Independence.

In a famous letter written just before he died, Jefferson proclaimed that "the mass of mankind has not been born with saddles on their backs."[14] Quite wrong, said Fitzhugh, for precisely the reverse was true; "it would be nearer the truth to say," he wrote, "that some were born with saddles on their backs, and others booted and spurred to ride them; and the riding does them good."

He went further, proclaiming that enslavement was such a wonderful system that it ought to extend across the race line. "Slavery," he wrote, "is the natural and normal condition of the working man, whether white or black."[15]

There it was: exactly what the Free Soil activists had been predicting, the growth of American slavery into a force that was truly un-American. It was a threat to American whites as well as to blacks, a force that would pull the United States downward and backward into medieval regression, with lords of the manor in command and their wretched vassals down below.

This was the sequence of events that led Lincoln to transform his life and his career. What he saw going on was obscene—so obscene that he would make it his business to punish Stephen Douglas, the man who disgraced Illinois and set in motion these horrible events.

To the accomplishment of that objective he consecrated himself.

Douglas was in trouble. In September he came back to Illinois to mend fences. As he traveled through the state he could see his own effigy burning in one town after another.

So he went to work, giving speeches that he hoped would defend what he had done. And his rationale was seductive by the standards of Illinois white supremacists.

He said that popular sovereignty was nothing less than a demonstration of American democracy at work. It was time to let whites, he contended, decide for themselves if they wished to own Negroes or not. What difference should it make to any whites who took time to think the matter through? Nothing that happened to blacks, declared Douglas, was important, so if some whites decided to own them, fine, and if other whites decided not to own them, that was also fine with Stephen Douglas. White Americans should live and let live when it came to the ownership of blacks.

Congress had already turned to this new and intelligent policy, he argued, when the Compromise of 1850 applied it to New Mexico. So popular sovereignty was already to some extent the law of the land. All that he had done in the Kansas-Nebraska Act was to extend this wise policy to the Louisiana Purchase.

Besides, Douglas said, it was unlikely that slavery would really move west in any case. Slavery, he reasoned, was a product of the South's unique climate. So if Free Soil whites would just relax and stay calm, they would probably get their own way. The most important thing, he said, was to calm down the owners of slaves so they did not try to break up the Union.

It all sounded very convincing to some—until Abraham Lincoln struck back.

Day by day, Lincoln followed Douglas and attacked him. Lincoln hounded Douglas, giving speeches that demolished his arguments.

In Springfield, on October 3, as Douglas spun out his web of slick justifications, Lincoln paced back and forth in the hall. Then he told the crowd that he would answer Douglas point for point the very next day. No record of Lincoln's remarks has survived, but a few weeks later, in Peoria, Douglas agreed to something close to a debate with Lincoln—a series of sequential speeches with Douglas speaking first and last.

It was Lincoln's speech—his "Peoria Speech" of October 16, 1854— that would be remembered. As Lincoln scholar Lewis Lehrman has observed, this single speech was "the foundation of his politics and principles, in the 1850s and in his presidency."[16]

In this speech Lincoln started calling his opponent "Judge Douglas" as an act of ridicule. Perhaps he intended to remind his listeners that Douglas and his friends were full of tricks—like the time that they packed the Illinois Supreme Court, making Douglas a judge.

Allowing Douglas to have the last word on this occasion was crafty strategy, and Lincoln used the ploy for all it was worth. He even confessed what he was doing and he turned it into something of a joke—a good-natured joke that would amuse both his friends and his foes. Here is his confession:

> I do not arise to speak now, if I can stipulate with the audience to meet me here at half past 6 or at 7 o'clock. It is now several minutes past five, and Judge Douglas has spoken over three hours. . . . Now every one of you who can remain that long, can just as well get his supper, meet me at seven, and remain one hour or two later. The Judge has already informed you that he is to have an hour to reply to me. I doubt not but you have been a little surprised to learn that I have consented to give one of his high reputation and known ability, this advantage of me. Indeed, my consenting to it, though reluctant, was not wholly unselfish; for I suspected if it were understood, that the Judge was entirely done, you democrats would leave, and not hear me; but by my giving him the close, I felt confident that you would stay for the fun of hearing him skin me.[17]

When the audience convened after dinner, Lincoln's tone became serious. With precision, he went after every specious argument that Douglas had concocted.

Was it true that the institution of slavery was nothing but a product of the South, an institution that would never spread anywhere else? Nonsense, said Lincoln: slavery could root itself anywhere and it might spread all over America. For proof, Lincoln said, take a look right across the Mississippi River—take a look at Missouri, standing side-by-side with Illinois. Slavery had spread itself throughout the state of Missouri, and from there it could spread into Kansas. Missouri was not the deep South and neither was Kansas.

Indeed, Lincoln asked, what had stopped the institution of slavery from coming right into Illinois—from Kentucky, just across the Ohio River? One thing alone, Lincoln said, had kept slavery out of Illinois: the prior prohibition put in place by the Founding Fathers in the Northwest

Ordinance of 1787. And that was the precedent for everything that Free Soilers were trying to achieve.

But the heart of Lincoln's Peoria speech was his direct attack upon the racism of Douglas—an attack that was risky business in the bigoted state of Illinois, a state that had banned racial intermarriage and had banned free blacks from even entering the state. It would have been easy—very easy—for Lincoln to attack Stephen Douglas by harping on the threat of slavery to whites.

But he chose not to do that. He chose to work upon the conscience of his hearers by declaring that blacks were human beings and that the act of enslaving them was monstrous.

It is important to note that pseudo-science at the very same time was making use of genetic discoveries to argue that blacks were not really human beings at all. "Scientific racists" were calling blacks *subhuman*, a species that was totally distinct from the full-fledged *homo sapiens*. An internationally renowned scientist, Louis Agassiz, was spreading this creed of "polygenism," as people were calling it.

No one can say whether Lincoln had heard about this pseudo-scientific movement. But notions such as these were "in the air" at the time and it was notable that Lincoln took some time to address and emphasize the issue of blacks' full humanity.

"Nearly eighty years ago," he said, "we began by declaring that all men are created equal; but now . . . we have run down to the other declaration that for SOME men to enslave OTHERS is a 'sacred right of self-government' [original emphasis]." How on earth had such a transformation happened? Most of the Founders, Lincoln said, had known perfectly well that slavery was wrong and they said so. And that was probably the reason why they shunned the very word when they wrote the Constitution. "At the framing and adoption of the Constitution," Lincoln argued, the Founders

forbore to so much as mention the word "slave" or "slavery" in the whole instrument. In the provision for the recovery of fugitives, the slave is spoken of as a "PERSON HELD TO SERVICE OR LABOR" . . . Thus, the thing is hid away, in the constitution, just as an afflicted man hides away a wen or a cancer, which he dares not cut to the bone at once, lest he bleed to death; with the promise, nevertheless, that the cutting may begin at the end of a given time.[18]

Even white southerners, Lincoln argued, acknowledged that blacks were human beings when they chose to free some slaves in their wills. Why do such a thing, Lincoln wondered, if blacks were less than real people? "There are in the United States and territories 433,643 free blacks," he pointed out. "How comes this vast amount of property to be running around without owners? We do not see free horses or free cattle running at large. How is this?"

There was only one answer: "All these free blacks are the descendants of slaves, or have been slaves themselves, and they would be slaves now, but for SOMETHING which has operated on their white owners, inducing them, at vast pecuniary sacrifices, to liberate them."

He went on: "What is that SOMETHING? Is there any mistaking it? In all these cases it is your sense of justice, and human sympathy, continually telling you, that the poor negro has some natural right to himself—that those who deny it, and make mere merchandise of him, deserve kickings, contempt, and death. . . . If the negro is a *man*, why then my ancient faith teaches me that 'all men are created equal.'"[19]

Slavery, he argued, "is founded in the selfishness of man's nature—opposition to it is his love of justice. These principles are an eternal antagonism. . . . Repeal the Missouri Compromise—repeal all compromises—repeal the declaration of independence—repeal all past history, you still cannot repeal human nature. It still will be the abundance of man's heart, that slavery extension is wrong; and out of the abundance of his heart, his mouth will continue to speak."[20]

Douglas and the leaders of the slave states should take this speech as a warning, Lincoln said. The Louisiana Purchase had been opened up to slavery by Douglas because he "took us by surprise—astounded us—with this measure. We were thunderstruck and stunned; and we reeled and fell in utter confusion. But we rose each fighting, grasping whatever he could first reach—a scythe—a pitchfork—a chopping axe, or a butcher's cleaver. We struck in the direction of the sound, and we are rapidly closing in upon him."[21]

The life of Abraham Lincoln was changed beyond question by the Kansas-Nebraska crisis. No longer would he advocate the Union-saving methods of his first great hero Henry Clay. He would fight to make certain that the evil of slavery would spread no further in America.

No further: the issue simply had to be forced, and the days for compromise were over.

In the years that followed, an aura developed in Lincoln's demeanor, a radiance that scores of people felt. An ally observed that when Lincoln spoke out, a "magnetic influence . . . brought him and the masses into a mysterious correspondence with each other."[22] An Illinois congressman wrote of "the invisible chords of his marvelous power" and the "spell" of his "voice and presence."[23] Yet another observer wrote that Lincoln's voice had developed "some quality which I can't describe, but which seemed to thrill every fiber of one's body."[24]

Yes, something had changed in Abraham Lincoln, and the people all around him could feel it.

He had found his life's work—and he would carry on and never turn back.

Earliest known photograph of Abraham Lincoln, taken in 1846 or 1847 by photographer Nicholas H. Shepherd. (Credit: Illinois History and Lincoln Collections, University of Illinois at Urbana–Champaign)

Earliest known photograph of Mary Lincoln, taken in 1846 or 1847 by photographer Nicholas H. Shepherd. (Credit: Library of Congress)

A photograph of
Lincoln taken in 1857 by
photographer Samuel
Alschuler. (Credit: Library of
Congress)

Stephen Douglas in the
1850s (Credit: Library of
Congress)

The Lincoln home in 1860. Photograph by John Adams Whipple. (Credit: Library of Congress)

A photograph of Lincoln taken on June 3, 1860 by Alexander Hesler. (Credit: Library of Congress)

Lincoln in 1860. (Credit: Library of Congress)

Lincoln and political supporters in front of his home in 1860. Lincoln, who towers over everyone else, was wearing his white suit on this occasion. (Credit: Illinois History and Lincoln Collections, University of Illinois at Urbana–Champaign)

William H. Seward. (Credit:
Library of Congress)

Mary Todd Lincoln. (Credit:
Lincoln Financial Foundation
Collection)

Lincoln photographed at Mathew Brady's studio on May 18, 1861. (Credit: Library of Congress)

Lincoln with General George McClellan and other officers at the Antietam battlefield, October 3, 1862, photographed by Alexander Gardner. (Credit: Illinois History and Lincoln Collections, University of Illinois at Urbana–Champaign)

Lincoln photographed on August 9, 1863 by Alexander Gardner. (Credit: Library of Congress)

Lincoln with John Nicolay (left) and John Hay (right) on November 8, 1863. Photograph by Alexander Gardner. (Credit: Library of Congress)

Lincoln as photographed by Mathew Brady on January 8, 1864. (Credit: Library of Congress)

Lincoln reading to his son Tad, as photographed on February 9, 1864 at Mathew Brady's gallery by Anthony Berger. (Credit: Illinois History and Lincoln Collections, University of Illinois at Urbana–Champaign)

The famous Lincoln profile as photographed on February 9, 1864 by Anthony Berger. (Credit: Library of Congress)

Lincoln photographed in his White House office on April 26, 1864 by Anthony Berger. The limited light in the office made the imagery appear faded. (Credit: Lincoln Financial Foundation Collection)

Ulysses S. Grant at Cold Harbor. (Credit: Library of Congress)

William Tecumseh Sherman. (Credit: Library of Congress)

Lincoln and his son Tad on February 5, 1865, as photographed by Alexander Gardner. (Credit: Illinois History and Lincoln Collections, University of Illinois at Urbana–Champaign)

Lincoln photographed at Alexander Gardner's studio on February 5, 1865. (Credit: Library of Congress)

Spectators on the U.S. Capitol grounds on the morning of Lincoln's Second Inauguration. The crowd has turned away from the building to watch a military procession. (Credit: Library of Congress)

To the left of the white lectern, Hannibal Hamlin, Andrew Johnson, and Lincoln are seated from left to right on the ceremonial platform at Lincoln's Second Inauguration. (Credit: Illinois History and Lincoln Collections, University of Illinois at Urbana–Champaign)

III

RISE TO DESTINY

CONTAINING
SLAVERY

I n 1853, Stephen Douglas was re-elected to his seat in the U.S. Senate. That was before the furor over his Kansas-Nebraska Act cut into his support.

The other U.S. senator from Illinois, James Shields, had to seek re-election in 1855. With the encouragement of his wife, Lincoln made up his mind to campaign for this position and thereby re-enter the world of national politics.

In the autumn months of 1854 he worked hard to line up support among the Illinois Whigs. His situation was complicated by the fact that some Whigs had placed him without his approval on the ballot for the Illinois legislature. When he found himself elected, he resigned in order to stay eligible for consideration as a candidate for the U.S. Senate.

He also declined to participate in efforts to advance the new Republican Party—the "fusion" party that was being set up to put the Free Soil issue front and center in American politics. It was too early for him to believe that the old Whig Party was dead.

The same sort of belief prevailed among a number of Free Soil Democrats, who declined to abandon their party. Such men were often called "Anti-Nebraska Democrats." In February, 1855, the Illinois legislature voted in joint session, and Lincoln fell just five votes short of what he needed to become a U.S. senator. The few votes he needed were withheld by some Free Soil Democrats who refused to vote for a Whig. As the balloting continued, Lincoln's base of support began to melt, and at last the Senate seat went to a Free Soil Democrat named Lyman Trumbull.

Within the next few years, more and more Free Soilers deserted their parties and became Republicans. By 1856, the old Whig Party was for all intents and purposes dead. The Democratic Party survived—but after the Free Soil shake-out, its identity was changed. Those who remained within the party were supporters of slavery or temporizers who were trying to avoid the issue.

Lincoln's depression in the aftermath of this disappointment—though mild in comparison with his earlier crises—merged with feelings of overall bitterness as he beheld what was happening in Kansas. He predicted that the situation out there would turn violent, and events were proving him right.

In his Peoria speech, he observed that the Kansas-Nebraska Act said nothing in regard to the procedures for instituting "popular sovereignty" in Kansas or Nebraska. The people in those territories—the white people, at least—would decide the question of slavery, but as to "WHEN they are to decide, or HOW they are to decide . . . the law does not say. Is it to be decided by the first dozen settlers who arrive there? Or is it to await the arrival of a hundred? Is it to be decided by a vote of the people? Or a vote of the legislature? Or, indeed, by a vote of any sort?"

This vagueness in the law would lead to conflict before very long, he predicted. "Some Yankees are sending emigrants to Nebraska," he observed, "to exclude slavery from it. . . . But the Missourians are awake too. They are within a stone's throw of the contested ground. . . . They resolve . . . that abolitionists shall be hung, or driven away. Through all this, bowie-knives and six-shooters are seen plainly enough."[1]

Late in 1854, the "New England Emigrant Aid Society" sent a large expedition of Free Soil settlers to Kansas. But pro-slavery "border ruffians" from Missouri crossed over into Kansas and they voted in a special election for a non-voting delegate to Congress. They prevailed.

Over and over, pro-slavery Missourians would cast illegal votes in Kansas. And the administration of Franklin Pierce always ruled in their favor.

The situation worsened in 1855. In March, elections for a territorial legislature were held under the supervision of the appointed territorial governor. Border ruffians thronged to the polls and a pro-slavery legislature was elected. The fraud was so massive and so obvious that even the governor that Pierce had selected—a Democrat from Pennsylvania named Andrew Reeder—invalidated some of the results and he called for new special elections. But in July, the new legislature seated all of the fraudulent delegates.

Then the legislature requested Pierce to remove Andrew Reeder and appoint someone else as territorial governor. Pierce happily complied. Reeder eventually fled when a pro-slavery grand jury in Kansas indicted him for treason.

But Free Soilers were pouring into Kansas, determined to strike back hard. The abolitionist Henry Ward Beecher had given them Sharps rifles, which were soon to be known as "Beecher's Bibles." In August, they elected a rival legislature and they drafted a free state constitution. President Pierce declared that they were nothing but outlaws.

Reacting, Lincoln poured out his thoughts in a letter to his old friend Joshua Speed. He was furious—and deeply pessimistic. "Kansas," he wrote, "will form a Slave constitution, and, with it, will ask to be admitted to the Union."

He was sick at heart as he thought about the evil of slavery and the millions of lives that it was ruining. Pro-slavery southerners, he wrote, could not imagine how people like himself were forced to "crucify their feelings" for the sake of maintaining the Union. He reminded his friend of the trip that they had taken together on a steam boat in 1841. "There were," he reminded him, "ten or a dozen slaves" aboard the ship, and they were "shackled together with irons. That sight was a continual torment to me; and I see something like it every time I touch the Ohio or any other slave-border." The very concept of slavery, he wrote, has "the power of making me miserable."

As a follower of Clay, he had supported the Compromise of 1850, even with its Fugitive Slave Law. Now he started to wonder if he had made the right decision. "I hate to see the poor creatures hunted down, and caught," he wrote, "but I bite my lip, and keep quiet."

Even so, the day was arriving *when the Union might not be worth defending.* "Our progress in degeneracy," he told Speed, was "pretty rapid." He continued as follows: "As a nation, we began by declaring that '*all men are created equal.*' We now practically read it, 'all men are created equal, *except negroes*'" and soon it might read that "'all men are created equal, except negroes, *and foreigners and Catholics.*'"

When it came to that, he declared, "I should prefer emigrating to some country where they make no pretense of loving liberty—to Russia, for instance, where despotism can be taken pure, and without the base alloy of hypocrasy."

The Union would have to be rescued from this degradation and rededicated to its founding proposition that all men are created equal. And "if for this you and I must differ," Lincoln informed his old friend, then "differ we must."[2]

To another correspondent he shared the same thoughts, and in terms that were equally bitter. His hopes for the phase-out of slavery were dashed—at least for the moment. "There is no peaceful extinction of slavery in prospect for us," he wrote.

Indeed "the Autocrat of all the Russias will resign his crown, and proclaim his subjects free republicans sooner than will our American masters voluntarily give up their slaves." Again he expressed deep despair about America's condition:

> When we were the political slaves of King George, and wanted to be free, we called the maxim that "all men are created equal" a self evident truth; but now when we have grown fat, and have lost all dread of being slaves ourselves, we have become so greedy to be *masters* that we call the same maxim a "self evident lie." The fourth of July has not quite dwindled away; it is still a great day—*for burning fire crackers*!!![3]

America was at odds with itself because its creed—"all men are created equal"—required an allegiance to the golden rule that was beyond the power of people whose consciences were no longer active. They were so intoxicated by the thrill of domination that they did to others precisely what they never wanted done to themselves. Conscience-bearers like Lincoln were struggling to stop the *expansion* of slavery but their prospects appeared to be dim.

The question was whether a republic that was so deeply divided could—or really should—be allowed to survive. "Our political problem now," he concluded, "is 'Can we, as a nation, continue together *permanently—forever*—half slave, and half free?' The problem is too mighty for me. May God, in his mercy, superintend the solution."[4]

In the final months of 1855, the open violence in Kansas that Lincoln foretold blazed forth in a showdown called the "Wakarusa War." Blood was being shed on the prairies.

All the while, his work as an attorney proceeded. In 1855, a patent-infringement case took Lincoln to Cincinnati. The McCormick Reaper Company had sued the John H. Manny Company of Rockford, Illinois, and the latter corporation put Lincoln on its high-powered legal team. But when Lincoln arrived in Cincinnati, he found himself shoved to the sidelines.

The lead attorney, George Harding of Philadelphia, chose Edwin Stanton of Pittsburgh as his principal associate. Lincoln, though paid a retainer, was virtually ignored. Even worse, he was reportedly snubbed by the egotistical Stanton, who regarded him as an awkward country bumpkin. At least that was what Harding would claim years later.

Harding wrote that "he had never seen one man insult another more grossly . . . than Stanton insulted Lincoln on that occasion."[5] Stanton supposedly called Lincoln a "giraffe" and a "long-armed baboon."[6]

The presidential election of 1856 drew Lincoln at last into the ranks of the new Republican Party. More and more Free Soilers from both of the old parties were concluding that a "fusion" party to resist the expansion of slavery was urgently needed. The short-lived Free Soil Party of 1848 had come and gone, but this newer party would last.

But one of the problems confronting the Republican Party was the fact that significant numbers of Whigs were moving in a different direction: they were becoming members of an emerging "American Party" whose stock-in-trade was prejudice against white ethnic minorities. Often called "Know Nothings"—supposedly because some of them refused to divulge details about the party's organization—they had been eliciting Lincoln's contempt.

In his letter to Speed about the fate of the American republic, Lincoln made it clear that he found the Know Nothings repulsive. "I am not a Know Nothing," he wrote; "that is certain. How could I be? How can any one who abhors the oppression of negroes, be in favor of degrading classes of white people?"[7]

The American Party convention was held in February 1856, and the party's nominee for the presidency was former president Millard Fillmore. At the very same time, a group of newspaper editors were meeting in Decatur, Illinois, to launch the Republican Party in Lincoln's home state. Lincoln attended this meeting and his hopes for the party took fire.

His fervor was quickened by his growing indignation on the slavery issue. Nonetheless, his shrewdness as a strategist balanced his anti-slavery fervor and channeled it in practical directions. As the work of building the Illinois party began, he helped unify disparate political forces so the party would be built upon the strongest possible foundation.

Some of the editors at this meeting spoke of running Lincoln for governor, but he demurred. Nonetheless, he played an active role in drafting a preliminary platform, and his partner Billy Herndon was placed on the party's central committee.

Those in attendance at the Decatur meeting called for a statewide Republican nominating convention to be held in Bloomington on May 29. This convention would be very successful and its unforgettable highlight would be a speech by Lincoln that is legendary for two reasons, one of them tragic: it was apparently one of the greatest orations that he ever gave and no record of it was ever made.

He was in brilliant form at the Bloomington convention, as many would recall years later. John Locke Scripps reminisced that "no other man exerted so wide and salutary an influence in harmonizing differences."[8] Henry C. Whitney "never saw him more busily engaged," noting that he "kept his mental balance" so well that he never "swerved a hair's breadth from perfect equipoise in speech or action."[9]

Whitney observed the full range of Lincoln's work since the two men were rooming together at the home of a mutual friend, Judge David Davis.

But the "perfect equipoise" of Lincoln would be whipped into outraged fervor as the news that was arriving from Kansas stoked the fires of Republican anger.

In the week before this convention had gathered, the violence in Kansas turned savage and it led to an outrageous act in the U.S. Capitol building in Washington, D.C. On May 21, pro-slavery thugs invaded the Free Soil settlement at Lawrence, Kansas. They destroyed a hotel and newspaper offices and wrecked some settlers' homes. Three days later, the abolitionist John Brown struck back. With help from his sons and some other followers, he kidnapped five pro-slavery men at Pottawatomie Creek and ordered his followers to hack them to death with broadswords.

Andrew Reeder, the territorial governor who had fled from Kansas, arrived at the Bloomington convention to share all the news about what was going on.

Meanwhile, Senator Charles Sumner of Massachusetts gave a long oration in the Senate on May 19 and 20. "The Crime against Kansas" was the title that he chose for his speech. Sumner made his hatred of the authors of the Kansas-Nebraska Act—Stephen Douglas and Senator Andrew Butler of South Carolina, who co-authored the bill—quite apparent.

On May 22, Representative Preston Brooks of South Carolina, a relative of Butler, confronted Sumner in the Senate. Brooks began beating Charles Sumner with a cane—he hit him over and over. The senator, blinded with his own blood and groping desperately to defend himself, sank down to the floor and got trapped below his desk. Brooks kept right on beating him. Even when his cane snapped in two, he kept it up. He beat Sumner senseless.

Amid this news, Lincoln gave the keynote address at the Bloomington convention on May 29.

The "Lost Speech," as it has been known, was impromptu. There were no prepared notes, and Lincoln's performance was so highly charismatic that reporters got carried away in the excitement of the moment. They just put down their pencils and listened.

Many reminiscences exist among those who heard the speech and they are impressive. Delegate Thomas J. Henderson recalled that as Lincoln gave the oration he was standing "as if on tip-toe, his tall form erect, his long arms extended, his face fairly radiant."[10] Judge John M. Scott called it "the speech of his life in the estimation of many who heard it," adding that the tone of the speech was one of "impressive grandeur."[11]

In his coverage of the convention, John Locke Scripps described the scene. "For an hour and a half," Scripps wrote, Lincoln "held the assemblage spell bound."[12]

He brought the members of the crowd to their feet at least once in the course of the oration. Henderson remembered that at one point "everybody present rose as one man ... and there was a universal burst of applause ... such as I have never seen on any other occasion."[13] John Scott agreed; "Every man," he wrote, "stood upon his feet. In a brief moment every one in that ... assembly came to feel as one man, to think as one man and to purpose and resolve as one man."[14]

Both the Democratic and Republican party conventions of 1856 were held in June. The Democrats declined to re-nominate Pierce. And they spurned the controversial Douglas. Instead, they settled on James Buchanan of Pennsylvania—a former congressman, senator, secretary of state, and diplomat. Buchanan was out of the country when the Kansas-Nebraska Act was passed. He was therefore free from any connection with "Bleeding Kansas," a term that was coming into use among writers for the *New York Tribune*.

But Buchanan's politics were similar to those of Pierce; both of them were "northern men of southern principles"—"doughfaces"—pro-slavery Democrats who sought to placate the slave-holding South.

The Republicans, whose convention met at Philadelphia, nominated John C. Frémont, a soldier, explorer, and politician who was famed in connection with the new state of California. He served there during the Mexican War and he was one of the first two senators elected after California joined the Union as a free state in 1850.

Meanwhile, the fighting in Kansas continued. Pierce sent troops to disperse the Free Soil legislature. In August, John Brown and his men fought with hundreds of pro-slavery settlers in the "battle of Osawatomie." The new territorial governor, John W. Geary, tried to work out an armistice.

There was talk of disunion in 1856. Southern "fire-eating" nationalists were threatening secession if Frémont won the election. Conversely, the abolitionist William Lloyd Garrison called for the North to secede from the South. "No Union with Slaveholders" was his battle cry. The new Republican Party was often attacked in the 1856 campaign as a threat to the Union since its Free Soil platform might push the leaders of the slave states over the brink.

In the course of campaigning for Frémont, Lincoln talked about the secession threat, not only to defend his party but also to reply to the southern "Fire Eaters." In a speech at Galena, Illinois, Lincoln ridiculed the very idea of disunion on July 23. He said that attempts at secession would be stamped out quickly and effectively. He said the Union

> won't be dissolved. We don't want to dissolve it, and if you attempt it, *we won't let you.* With the purse and the sword, the army and navy and treasury in our hands and at our command, *you couldn't do it.* This Government would be very weak, indeed, if a majority, with a disciplined army and navy, and a well-filled treasury, could not preserve itself, when attacked by an unarmed, undisciplined, unorganized minority. All this talk about the dissolution of the Union is humbug—nothing but folly. *We* WON'T dissolve the Union, and *you* SHAN'T.[15]

Lincoln regarded the talk of secession as "humbug"—as blackmail and bluff. Southern tricks should be resisted, he thought, for it was largely through manipulation of northern public opinion that defenders of slavery succeeded. In notes for a campaign speech, he reflected sarcastically on the way that pro-slavery leaders had been propping up northern Democrats for reasons of their own:

> If a Southerner aspires to be president, they choke him down instantly, in order that the glittering prize of the presidency, may be held up, on Southern terms, to the greedy eyes of Northern ambition. . . . The Democratic Party, in 1844, elected a Southern president. Since then, they have neither had a Southern candidate for *election*, or *nomination*. Their Conventions of 1848, 1852, and 1856, have been struggles exclusively among *Northern* men, each vying to out-bid the other for the Southern vote—the South standing calmly by to finally cry going, going, gone to the highest bidder.[16]

Buchanan was merely the latest in this series of northern pro-slavery puppets.

And Buchanan was the winner of the 1856 election. Still, the Republicans had good reason to be hopeful as they analyzed the patterns of the voting. For in their very first national election—an election complicated by the presence of a new third party—they had won so many of the northern states for Frémont that they almost captured the White House. If they could figure out a way to win the lower-northern swing states, they could easily win the presidential election of 1860 without winning any of the slave states.

The leaders of the slave states were noticing the very same thing. And it made them all the more desperate—all the more ruthless.

The leaders of the slave-holding South were determined to defy the Free Soil movement. And the leaders of the Free Soil movement were determined to block the spread of slavery. Lincoln was right: America was at odds with itself. The situation was becoming too excruciating to continue. It would have to be resolved one way or the other.

And the time for compromising was over. Neither side would allow the other to place it in a "one-down" power position. The result, in the last four years before war, was an all-out struggle for control of the federal government. Pro-slavery southerners only turned to secession when their bid to control the federal government—and to construe the highest law of the land, the federal Constitution, in ways that would protect their social system—had failed.

It all came down to a fight about the federal Constitution, as Calhoun predicted. The Free Soil movement, if successful, would usher in a super-majority of free states. Those states would be able in time to approve an anti-slavery amendment to the Constitution—unless the South could find a way to head them off with a pre-emptive constitutional amendment, an unamendable amendment, to make slavery permanent.

In the meantime, defenders of slavery would twist the Constitution their way. And Calhoun had come up with ingenious new doctrines that would help them to accomplish that purpose. In 1857 the U.S. Supreme Court applied those doctrines in a manner that constituted another surprise attack—another stab in the back that was aimed at the Free Soil movement. The *Dred Scott* decision was nothing less than a declaration that the Free Soil movement itself was unconstitutional.

Dred Scott was a Missouri slave who had been trying to gain his freedom—along with the freedom of his wife and daughter—in court for over a decade. His legal expenses were covered by donations from abolitionists. The case turned upon the question of whether a slave who had been taken into a free state or a free territory and kept there should be declared free.

Scott's master had taken him out of Missouri and brought him to several places where slavery was against the law—the free state of Illinois, for example, and Wisconsin Territory, where slavery was banned per the terms of the Missouri Compromise. Scott contended that his presence for extended periods on free soil should have made him free.

Case law varied in regard to the status of slave "sojourners" (i.e., slaves who were taken out of slave states and brought to free soil). In some free states—like Illinois—the courts had recognized the right of slave-holders to send their slaves to the state but only for limited periods. That had been the nub of the *Matson* case that Lincoln had argued in 1847.

Conversely, the courts in some of the slave states—including Dred Scott's home state of Missouri—held that if residents took their slaves into free states or territories and kept them there for extended periods, they forfeited their ownership (i.e., the slaves would become free).

That was the conclusion of a court in Missouri where Dred Scott was suing for his freedom: in 1850, it decided that Scott (along with his wife and his daughter) should be free. But Scott's owner appealed to the state

Supreme Court, which in an ominous ruling handed down in 1852 over-turned many years of Missouri case law and ruled that the Scotts should be kept enslaved.

Then, Scott's owner moved away to New York and left Scott behind in Missouri. His services were leased out to others. Scott found a way to take his case to federal court, since the dispute could be held to extend across state lines.

In 1854, a federal jury deferred to the Missouri Supreme Court and refused to free Scott. So he appealed to the Supreme Court, which heard preliminary arguments in February 1856. The court was ready to hand down its ruling in the weeks before the inauguration of James Buchanan. And there were rumors—later confirmed—that Buchanan improperly conferred with some of the justices in order to sway the court's decision.

Pretending to be impartial, Buchanan vowed in his Inaugural Address to abide by the court's decision and he urged all Americans to do the same.

The *Dred Scott* decision was handed down on March 6, 1857. It hit the Republican Party like a thunderbolt. A seven-to-two majority ruled that the Free Soil platform of the party was unconstitutional, that neither Congress nor a territorial legislature had the power to keep slavery out of a federal territory. But that was just the beginning. The majority opinion, written by Chief Justice Roger Taney, declared that blacks possessed no rights at all.

According to Taney, the case should never have come to court since blacks were not citizens of the United States or of any state. Taney's opinion was both bigoted and ignorant—bigoted, since its reasoning was grounded in raw white supremacy emotions, and ignorant, since he believed in an oversimplification of history. Despite the anti-slavery sentiment among the Founding Fathers, Taney asserted that blacks were universally regarded as inferior beings when the nation was founded.

He claimed that for "more than a century" before the founding, blacks had "been regarded as beings of an inferior order, . . . altogether unfit to associate with the white race either in social or political relations, and so far inferior that they had no rights which the white man was bound to respect." And "this opinion," Taney continued, "was at that time fixed and universal in the civilized portion of the white race," an opinion that "no one thought of disputing."[17]

Consequently, he reasoned, the proclamation in the Declaration of Independence that all men are created equal could not apply to blacks, since the Founders "universally" regarded them as inferior. After all, Taney wrote, if they did believe that blacks were the equals of whites, they would surely have freed their own slaves—but they declined to do so.

Why?

Because the notion of racial equality never entered their minds, in Taney's opinion. Blacks had been brought to the English colonies as "articles of merchandise," said Taney, nothing more.

Even though Taney contended that the case should not have come to court, he could not resist the opportunity to enshrine the doctrines of Calhoun in case law.

The court ruled that Congress *never* had the power to prevent slave owners from taking their slaves into territories purchased by the United States after independence—territories such as the Louisiana Purchase, where the Missouri Compromise applied.

The Missouri Compromise, according to the court, was unconstitutional from the moment Congress created it.

In the first place, Taney declared, the provision in Article Four of the Constitution granting Congress the power to make "all needful Rules and Regulations respecting the Territory or other Property belonging to the United States" was limited to territory that was in the possession of the United States *when the Constitution was ratified.* Things were different, Taney asserted, with respect to the newer territories that America gained later on.

More fundamentally, Taney invoked the Bill of Rights—and here was where the doctrines of Calhoun were employed—in a way that prohibited Congress from excluding slavery from territories acquired after the ratification of the Bill of Rights. The Fifth Amendment, wrote Taney, "which provides that no person shall be deprived of life, liberty and property, without due process of law" made Congress powerless to stop the territorial expansion of slavery, for "an act of Congress," he continued,

> which deprives a citizen of the United States of his liberty or property merely because he came himself or brought his property into a particular Territory of the United States, and who had committed no offence against the laws, could hardly be dignified with the name of due process of law.[18]

Congress, wrote Taney, cannot "assume discretionary or despotic powers which the Constitution has denied to it." And such was the action of Congress when it passed the Missouri Compromise, he said. Moreover, he concluded, "if Congress cannot do this—if it is beyond the powers conferred on the Federal Government—it will be admitted, we presume, that it could not authorize a Territorial Government to exercise them."[19]

As to the question of whether Dred Scott's stay in Illinois should make him free, that was up to the authorities of Scott's home state to determine.

Two justices—John McLean and Benjamin Curtis—dissented from the court's decision. And the dissent of Curtis influenced a great many people who protested and sought to resist the *Dred Scott* decision, including Lincoln.

As to Taney's allegation that blacks were "universally" held to be inferior at the time of the founding, Curtis showed that when the Articles of Confederation (the constitutional predecessor to the federal Constitution) were ratified, five states had given the status of citizenship to free blacks, and their citizenship held good when the Constitution was ratified.

Curtis dismissed as ridiculous Taney's claim that only lands in the possession of the United States in 1787 were covered by the Constitution's grant to Congress of the power to make regulations for federal territories. Since the Constitution grants Congress the power to make war and to negotiate treaties, Curtis wrote, it stood to reason that its power over territories would have to extend to any lands that the nation might acquire as a consequence of war or pursuant to a treaty.

As to Taney's assertion that the Fifth Amendment barred Congress from excluding slavery from territories—such action, Taney claimed, would amount to a deprivation of property "without due process of law"— Curtis reasoned as follows. The possession and use of slave "property" was never an *absolute* right, for the use of such property was governed by different state laws, and the states that permitted the use of slave property differed in their rules and regulations for controlling it.

And so Congress could exercise the very same prerogatives in regard to the *use* of slave property—including a prohibition on its *presence*—in the federal territories. A prohibition against bringing human property to federal lands did not "deprive" the owners of the property. After all, the slaves would *remain* their property as long as they were used in places that permitted it.

Curtis's dissent from the *Dred Scott* decision was disseminated far and wide among Americans who were enraged by the action of Taney's court. For the message of the *Dred Scott* decision to Lincoln and his fellow Republicans was clear: they would have to give up their attempt to contain the evil of slavery because their intention was unconstitutional and dead on arrival in Washington.

They refused to do any such thing. Taney and Buchanan apparently believed that the court's pronouncement would end the controversy over slavery expansion and defeat the Free Soil movement. But that belief was sadly mistaken. Republican defiance was kindled all over the free states in 1857.

Stephen Douglas was placed in a quandary by the *Dred Scott* decision. His doctrine of popular sovereignty rested on the view that white settlers in federal territories should determine whether slavery ought to be permitted. But the *Dred Scott* decision barred the territorial legislatures (as well as Congress) from prohibiting slavery, and that appeared to make Douglas's policy unconstitutional. After all, how could settlers ban slavery if their own representatives in the territorial legislature lacked the power to do so? Douglas would have to find an answer to that question.

On the other hand, Douglas endorsed the white supremacy content of Taney's opinion, and echoed Taney's view of the Declaration of Independence: its statement that "all men are created equal," Douglas affirmed, applied to whites, and the equality clause was nothing but a flourish to justify the action of some white men, English colonists, in breaking away from the control of other white men, the British.

On June 7, 1857, Douglas made a speech in Springfield setting forth his new position. He endorsed the *Dred Scott* decision, defended its white supremacy provisions, and taunted the "Black Republicans" by accusing them of altering race relations in a manner that would lead to "amalgamation" (i.e., to racial intermarriage), which of course would feature inter-racial sex.

As to the Supreme Court's declaration that no territorial legislature had the power to ban slavery, Douglas argued that whites in any territory could do so whenever they wished. They could do it in a very simple way: by telling the members of their legislature *to do nothing*. Everyone knew, Douglas said, that the institution of slavery required police protections to prevent slave rebellions and to aid in the capture of runaways. The owners of slaves would never risk their human property in places where such protections were lacking. So, Douglas reasoned, if settlers wished to ban slavery, they could simply tell the members of their legislature to sit on their hands—decline to pass the sorts of laws that the owners of slaves would demand.

On June 26, 1857, Lincoln made an important speech in Springfield refuting Douglas. The doctrines that Lincoln set forth in this speech must be examined with patience and care. First, however, another issue has to be considered: Lincoln's feelings on the subject of race. For despite the fact that he opposed the evil of slavery on moral grounds (the golden rule) and for reasons of humanitarian empathy, Lincoln said some things in the course of this speech (and in other speeches) that have led some observers to conclude that he was something of a racist.

If answers are sought to this extremely vexed question, other questions must first be explored.

What were Lincoln's innermost feelings on the subject of race? Did he harbor racial aversions? We will never really know—but we can make some educated guesses.[20]

There is a basic problem with the evidence: it is hard to be sure that we can trust it. Lincoln said what he said, there is no denying that, but we know very well that his statements were sometimes misleading. We know this from his work as a lawyer. He could use tricky language on occasion, so we need to confront the unpleasant (or pleasant) possibility that Lincoln might not have been completely truthful when he made certain troublesome statements.

Illinois was one of the most virulently racist of the free states before the Civil War. Here is evidence to illustrate the moods with which Lincoln had to deal.

In 1847, when a state constitutional convention approved a ban on black immigration to the state, a supporter expressed direct doubt as to whether Africans "were altogether human beings." If anyone suspected that they were, he continued, "let him go and examine their nose; (roars of laughter) then look at their lips. Why, their skulls were three inches thicker than white people's." The *Chicago Times* proclaimed that there "is in the great masses of the people a natural and proper loathing of the negro, which forbids contact with him as with a leper."[21]

Examples of this racist abuse could be piled up endlessly. The *Chicago Herald* referred to blacks as members of an "imbecile race." The *Herald* dared abolitionists to peer down into the hold of a slave ship and take a good look at "a couple of thousand of those naked, musky, greasy cannibals."[22]

Douglas and the Illinois Democrats regaled the voters with such rhetoric. They stoked the fires of racial hatred, portraying the Republicans as "negro-lovers" whose opinions on slavery were nothing but excuses for their real and secret agenda: to initiate by stealthy degrees the "amalgamation" of the races to the point where intermarriage would pollute the racial purity of Illinois.

When Lincoln gave his speech refuting Douglas on June 26, 1857, he strove to neutralize this charge. The prurient fixation on inter-racial sex was quite pervasive at the time, and his attack upon Douglas and the *Dred Scott* decision was grounded in this realization.

So he proclaimed that he understood the "disgust in the minds of nearly all white people, to the idea of an indiscriminate amalgamation of the races." He said that Douglas was "evidently . . . basing his hope, upon the chances of being able to appropriate the benefits of this disgust." But Douglas would fail, Lincoln said, because his reasoning was totally illogical:

> If he can, by much drumming and repeating, fasten the odium of that idea upon his adversaries, he thinks he can struggle through the storm. He therefore clings to this hope, as a drowning man to the last plank. . . . He finds the Republicans insisting that the Declaration of Independence includes ALL men, black as well as white; and forthwith he boldly denies that it includes negroes at all, and proceeds to argue gravely that all who contend it does, do so because they want to vote, and eat, and sleep, and marry with negroes! . . . Now I protest against this counterfeit logic which concludes that, because I do not want a black woman for a *slave* I must necessarily want her for a *wife*. I need not have her for either. I can just leave her alone.[23]

So far, this statement provides little basis for concluding that Lincoln was a racist himself. But he continued to talk about the hypothetical black woman in a manner that commands our attention: "In some respects she certainly is not my equal; but in her natural right to eat the bread she earns with her own hands, without asking leave of anyone else, she is my equal and the equal of all others."[24]

This was one of the statements by Lincoln that have prompted some people to conclude that, for all of his decency, he shared a few of the bigoted notions that were common at the time in Illinois.

He made another statement on racial intermarriage that provides yet another reason for concluding that he had racial bias. "Judge Douglas," he said, "is especially horrified at the thought of the mixing of the white and black races: agreed for once—a thousand times agreed."[25]

That would seem to be absolute proof that Lincoln harbored racial prejudice, for he admitted it himself—did he not?

But the problem is not quite so simple. For Lincoln said some other things about racial intermarriage on this and on other occasions that sound very different. In the same 1857 speech—the speech in which he claimed that, like Douglas, he was "horrified" by the thought of racial intermarriage—he made light of the subject with a joke that made the issue sound trifling—not "horrifying," but a subject for light entertainment. He said there were "fortunately white men enough to marry all the white women, and black men enough to marry all the black women, so let them be married. . . . On this point we fully agree with the Judge."[26]

He made similar jokes on other occasions, if the reminiscences of others can be trusted. Two years later, in the aftermath of a speech in Ohio, someone turned to Lincoln and asked him how he felt about the Illinois law that forbade racial intermarriage. Lincoln reportedly answered this way: "The law means nothing. I shall never marry a negress, but I have no objection to anyone else doing so. If a white man wants to marry a negro woman, let him do it—*if the negro woman can stand it* [original emphasis]."[27]

In the same year (1859) he gave a passionate speech in Columbus, Ohio, attacking white supremacist doctrine.

And there was also a personal fact about Lincoln that needs to be considered: he was on cordial terms with a Haitian-born African American barber in Springfield, a man for whom he did some legal work and with whom he exchanged favors. This barber's name was William Fleurville and they exchanged friendly letters in the course of Lincoln's presidency. There were free blacks living in the Lincolns' own neighborhood, blacks who had come to the state before the racist crack-down on black immigration.

So the question simply has to be asked: when Lincoln said some things in his political speeches that appear to be racist, was he telling the truth, or was he . . . faking it?

The question is serious, for Lincoln was willing on occasion to concoct slick deceptions for the purposes of strategy. His presidential behavior in the Civil War years will establish this fact beyond a doubt. He was sometimes a master of deception. His private memoranda demand to be consulted if we wish to put his public statements in perspective. When his public statements are compared to his private reflections, the complicated truth may emerge.

Circa 1854, he jotted down an interesting reflection on race. His statement was grounded in the fact that variations in color could be found within each of the so-called races. Lincoln framed this reflection as an exercise in logic that was centered on the issue of enslavement:

> If A. can prove, however conclusively, that he may, of right, enslave B., why may not B. snatch the same argument, and prove equally, that he may enslave A.?—You say A. is white, and B. is black. It is *color*, then; the lighter, having the right to enslave the darker? Take care. By this rule, you are to be the slave of the first man you meet, with a fairer skin than your own.

Even mental qualities were subject to the same sort of logic, and he laid out the issues like this:

> You do not mean *color* exactly—You mean that whites are *intellectually* the superior of blacks, and, therefore, have the right to enslave them? Take care again. By this rule, you are to be slave to the first man you meet, with an intellect superior to your own.[28]

Individual traits in his opinion—the traits of the "first man you meet" who may possess a fairer skin and a bolder mind—were more important than the physical appearance of people when taken in the aggregate. After all, his own physical appearance had been ridiculed by others since his teens.

In the same year (1854) he made a statement on race in the course of his Peoria speech that was revealing. He said a number of things to protect himself against the "negro-loving" charge while at the same time testing how far he might go—how much he could safely get away with—in challenging the prejudice of the day. At one point he asked what should happen to American slaves if the time should ever come when they were free. Here is the gist of his statement:

What next? Free them, and make them politically and socially, our equals? My own feelings will not admit of this; and if mine would, we well know that those of the great mass of white people will not. Whether this feeling accords with justice and sound judgment, is not the sole question, if indeed it is any part of it. A universal feeling, whether well or ill-founded, can not be safely disregarded.[29]

He said he could not support the idea of making former slaves the equals of whites because his "feelings" would "not admit of it." Yet an instant later he confessed that those feelings might change. Then he raised the issue of whether the "universal feeling" on race that was common in the state of Illinois could be consistent with the principles of "justice and sound judgment." What was Lincoln trying to accomplish in this roundabout and highly ambivalent passage?

He was probably trying to unsettle the members of his audience—to make them question the nature of their feelings.

In his 1857 Springfield speech was a statement on the meaning of the Declaration of Independence for people of all races—a statement that should not be omitted from a reckoning with Lincoln's racial views. He was taking on the assertion of Taney and Douglas that the declaration's equality clause was intended to apply to whites only. He was also contesting their assertion that if Jefferson and others had believed in race equality, they would have shown it more clearly in their deeds.

No, said Lincoln, the truth was a great deal more complex, but it was easy enough to comprehend. "Chief Justice Taney," Lincoln said,

> admits that the language of the Declaration is broad enough to include the whole human family, but he and Judge Douglas argue that the authors of that instrument did not intend to include negroes, by the fact that they did not, at once, actually place them on an equality with the whites. Now this grave argument comes to just nothing at all, by the other fact, that they did not at once, *or ever afterwards*, actually place all white people on an equality with one another.

The signers of the Declaration "did not intend to declare all men equal *in all respects*," Lincoln reasoned. "They did not mean to say that all were equal in color, size, intellect, moral developments, or social capacity." What they did mean to say was that everyone was equal "in certain inalienable rights, among which are life, liberty, and the pursuit of happiness."

They never intended to assert the "untruth, that all men were then actually enjoying that equality," nor yet "that they were about to confer it immediately upon them. In fact they had no power to confer such a boon."

But what they did mean to do, Lincoln said, was to

> declare the *right*, so that the *enforcement* of it might follow as fast as circumstances should permit. They meant to set up a standard maxim for free society, which should be familiar to all, and revered by all; constantly looked to, constantly labored for, and even though never perfectly attained, constantly approximated, and thereby constantly spreading and deepening its influence, and augmenting the happiness and value of life to all people of all colors everywhere.[30]

But history was moving in the *opposite direction*, Lincoln said, and the rights that the Founders had declared were being thwarted and reserved for whites only in a drive to make American slavery permanent. The American slave was being pushed into an endless confinement from which there would never be a hope of escape:

> They have him in their prison house; they have searched his person, and left no prying instrument with him. One after another they have closed the heavy iron doors upon him, and now they have him, as it were, bolted in with a lock of a hundred keys, which can never be unlocked without the concurrence of every key; the keys are in the hands of a hundred different men, and they [have] scattered in a hundred different and distant places; and they stand musing as to what invention, in all the dominions of mind and matter, can be produced to make the impossibility of his escape more complete than it is.[31]

Lincoln the humanitarian—he who had told his best friend that the thought of enslavement had the power of making him miserable—was urging racists to renounce the ways of cruelty and embrace the ways of compassion.

Many knew that this speech, which Lincoln gave in the Illinois state Capitol building, was an opening shot in his campaign to throw Stephen

Douglas out of the U.S. Senate in 1858 and take his place. But the time that he could spare for the practice of politics in 1857 was limited. He had to spend more time as an attorney, earning a living. A great deal of his time had gone into politics in 1856.

Nonetheless, he had won a major courtroom victory in 1856 in which huge amounts of money were at stake.

Back in 1851, when the Illinois legislature chartered the Illinois Central Railroad, the state had exempted that corporation from taxes in return for a fixed percentage of the railroad's earnings. Some county officials then complained that this action was an unconstitutional abridgment of their own taxation authority. So McLean County started taxing the railroad, and the corporation filed suit.

Lincoln was a member of the corporate legal team that prevailed on behalf of the railroad in the Illinois state Supreme Court in 1856. The case was recorded as *Illinois Central Railroad v. McLean County, Illinois and Parke.*

But when Lincoln tried to collect his $2,000 fee from the railroad, its officials complained that his fee was excessive. He consulted with some other attorneys who told him that he actually ought to be charging the railroad $5,000, in light of all the work that he had done.

So Lincoln sued the corporation for $5,000 in the summer of 1857—and he won.

In July, he and Mary took a trip to New York, coming back by way of Niagara Falls. In a letter to her sister, Mary wrote that "this summer has strangely & rapidly passed away—some portion of it, was spent most pleasantly in travelling east, we visited Niagara, Canada, New York & other points of interest. . . . When I saw the large steamers at the New York landing, ready for their European voyage, I felt in my heart, inclined to sigh, that poverty was my portion, how I long to go to Europe. I often laugh & tell Mr. L—that I am determined my next Husband *shall be rich.*"[32]

In September, Lincoln won another legal victory that some regard as one of his greatest. The case of *Hurd v. The Rock Island Bridge Company* was tried in the U.S. Circuit Court of Chicago with Supreme Court Justice John McLean presiding.

The plaintiff, Jacob S. Hurd, owned a river boat, the *Effie Afton*, that crashed into the Rock Island railroad bridge, which spanned the Mississippi River from Rock Island, Illinois, to Davenport, Iowa. Both the river boat and the bridge had caught fire. Hurd alleged in his suit that the bridge

was a menace to navigation. The company hired Lincoln, upon the recommendation of Norman B. Judd, who was both a railroad attorney and
a political ally of Lincoln.

Lincoln won the case, and many people who heard his summation
to the jury regarded it as a masterpiece—a masterpiece of logic. Lincoln
had to study a great many technicalities of engineering and navigation in
the course of this trial and then explain these complicated matters to an
audience of laymen. An observer reminisced about the trial as follows:

> Lincoln's examination of witnesses was very full and no point escaped
> his notice. I thought he carried it almost to prolixity, but when he
> came to his argument I changed my opinion. He went over all the
> details with great minuteness, until court, jury, and spectators were
> wrought up in the crucial points. Then drawing himself up to his full
> height, he delivered a peroration that thrilled the court-room and, to
> the minds of most persons, settled the case.[33]

Throughout these courtroom battles of Lincoln, his mind never
strayed from the moral and political issue of slavery. In his Springfield
office he made a practice of reading the many southern newspapers to
which Billy Herndon subscribed: the *Charleston Mercury*, for instance, and
the *Richmond Enquirer*, both of which editorialized fiercely on behalf of
slavery. Ever the strategist, Lincoln paid careful attention to the thoughts
and the deeds of his enemies.

Out in Kansas, the supporters of slavery were on the attack, and their ally
President Buchanan was working as ruthlessly as Pierce had done to back
them up.

After Pierce's actions against the insurgent Free Soil legislature, the
pro-slavery legislature summoned a convention to draft a state constitution for Kansas. In September 1857, this constitution was drafted in
Lecompton. Buchanan would use all of his presidential authority to push
this Lecompton constitution in Congress. Like Pierce, he was committed
to forcing Kansas into the Union as a slave state.

But Buchanan made a serious mistake. In choosing a new territorial
governor, he tapped a Mississippian named Robert Walker, presuming
no doubt that he would rig the system for the pro-slavery Kansans. But
Walker turned out to be honest. A new Kansas legislature was due to be
elected in October, and Walker guaranteed a fair election.

This put the Free Soilers in control of the new and officially sanctioned Kansas legislature.

Walker also insisted that the pro-slavery Lecompton constitution would have to be submitted to the voters in a referendum. This referendum was scheduled for December 1857.

The constitutional convention struck back in a way that destroyed the integrity of the referendum. They submitted two different constitutions to the voters: the pro-slavery constitution and a different constitution set up to give the voters a choice. But the choice was a trick, since the alternative constitution also permitted the institution of slavery. The only difference was the fact that the alternative constitution forbade the importation of *more* slaves into Kansas. But the slaves who were already in Kansas would remain and their status as slave property would be upheld.

Either way, Kansas would enter the Union as a slave state.

The Free Soilers boycotted this fraudulent election, so the pro-slavery Lecompton constitution stood approved.

But the Free Soil legislature called for a second and honest referendum in which the voters would be given a chance to reject the Lecompton constitution completely. And they rejected it in January 1858.

Buchanan declared that the *first* referendum was valid and he sent the Lecompton constitution to Congress with a recommendation that Kansas be admitted as a slave state.

Then . . . something spectacular happened. Douglas broke with his own party's presidential leader. The Lecompton fraud was so blatant and obvious that he had no choice but to resist. He could not allow his doctrine of popular sovereignty to get a reputation for being a fraud. If the settlers in Kansas did not want slavery, they should not be forced to have it.

Republicans were both surprised and delighted in the spring of 1858 by this spectacle of their rival party torn asunder in an all-out fight between supporters of the administration and supporters of Douglas, who called the followers of Buchanan "Buchaneers."

Indeed, the spectacle was so satisfying that some national Republican leaders began to urge their Illinois counterparts to throw their support behind Douglas in his 1858 campaign for re-election to the Senate. And that was bad news for Abraham Lincoln, not only in light of his own senatorial ambitions but also in light of his belief that Douglas was a threat to the Free Soil movement. His white supremacist demagoguery could undermine the moral commitment that Lincoln was trying to instill among whites in Illinois—and elsewhere.

At the very same time he was thinking some more about the *Dred Scott* decision. Then it hit him: there was something in that decision that could spread the institution of slavery into every single one of the free states. There was no doubt about it, so he had to speak out about the threat in a way that would be heard far and wide.

He would have to sound the alarm.

The *Dred Scott* decision was a frontal attack upon the Free Soil movement. Taney had declared that both Congress and the territorial legislatures lacked the constitutional power to keep slavery out of federal lands. A life-and-death struggle was playing out in Kansas, a federal territory. Naturally, Republicans were preoccupied with the *territorial* issue.

But Dred Scott had also been taken by his master to *the free state* of Illinois and then kept there from 1833 until 1836. Slavery was prohibited in Illinois. True, slave "sojourners" were permitted to remain in the state temporarily. And yet Scott had been kept there for *three long years*, and when he later claimed that his stay in Illinois should have freed him, the Supreme Court turned him down.

His residence for three long years in a free state did nothing to free him. The laws of his home state, Missouri, would govern his fate, said Taney, and the federal Constitution itself would also govern his fate. For Taney's reading of the Fifth Amendment made Dred Scott nothing but property, an article of merchandise, nothing more.

He remained a slave and he would always be nothing but a slave—no matter where he might travel in America.

A number of people had been musing about that situation. If the Constitution protected slave property in federal lands, perhaps it was only a matter of time before defenders of slavery would start claiming that even *states* lacked the power to ban the institution. And then, sure enough, on November 17, 1857, the *Washington Union*, a pro-slavery newspaper, claimed that every state law restricting the institution of slavery was unconstitutional.

In the springtime of 1858, Lincoln pondered that claim and he foresaw the rise of slavery to national dimensions.

As soon as that happened, the United States of America would be ruined—*permanently* ruined.

Lincoln wrote down his thoughts in a private memorandum in May. The fact that "the bringing of Dred Scott into Illinois by his master, and holding him there for a long time as a slave, did not operate his emancipation" was of great importance. Taney and his friends could perceive that fact, and yet they chose not to emphasize it greatly. Why not? Because they were probably getting things ready for another surprise attack against the anti-slavery movement. The point was

> not to be pressed immediately; but if acquiesced in for a while, then to sustain the logical conclusion that what Dred Scott's master might lawfully do with Dred in the free State of Illinois, every other master may lawfully do with any other one or one hundred slaves in Illinois, or in any free State.[34]

And then—the United States of America, founded on Jefferson's equality creed, would become not only hypocritical but monstrous, a nation positioned to lead the new "master race" movement that was gathering strength on both sides of the Atlantic.

Perhaps it was not accidental that this transformation was in play. Ever since 1850, one surprise attack after another had been launched against the Free Soil movement. Consider: Free Soilers expected the next confrontation over slavery extension to come in New Mexico territory. Then, surprise: the Louisiana Purchase was opened up to the spread of slavery. It was done very suddenly. The great Kansas struggle began, and as the Free Soil settlers shed their blood on the prairies, surprise: they were informed that the Free Soil movement itself was unconstitutional.

Perhaps more of these surprises were in store. And perhaps this sequence of events had been orchestrated—planned in a movement that could never be *proven* but could surely be *inferred* by observers who had their wits about them. Calhoun had laid the groundwork for the scheme in the years before his death. Who could say what manner of secret consultations had occurred in the dark recesses of Washington after his death?

Lincoln worked in the early months of 1858 to line up Illinois Republicans behind his Senate candidacy. He was assisted by his friend Norman Judd, who chaired the Republican State Central Committee, as well as by his partner Billy Herndon, who told Republicans that the eastern Free Soilers who were flirting with Douglas—people like the Republican editor Horace Greeley—were nothing but fools.

The idea that Stephen Douglas might seduce the Republicans of Illinois might seem to be grotesque—but it was plausible. Lincoln brooded in a private memorandum that if Illinois Republicans should "drop their own organization" and "fall into rank" behind Douglas, they would soon be "haltered and harnessed," betrayed. They would "stand ready" to be

> handed over by him to the regular Democracy [i.e., Democratic Party], to filibuster indefinitely for additional slave territory,—to carry slavery into all the States, as well as Territories, under the Dred Scott decision, construed and enlarged from time to time according to the demands of the regular slave Democracy,—and to assist in reviving the African slave-trade in order that all may buy negroes where they can be bought the cheapest.[35]

Lincoln was certain that Douglas would love to see slavery nationalized and extended throughout the western hemisphere and beyond. He had to be stopped. In fact, the whole pro-slavery conspiracy had to be stopped.

The Republicans scheduled a nominating convention to be held on June 16 in Springfield. To hold a convention to recommend a candidate for the United States Senate was a daring move. The constitutional prerogative of state legislatures to choose U.S.Senators was closely guarded. But now, for the first time, the issue would be fought in the open, in a general election campaign among the voters, with candidates for the legislature pledged to vote for either Douglas or Lincoln when the legislature convened.

As the June 16 convention approached, there was no doubt at all as to who the Republican opponent of Douglas would be. Lincoln's efforts to line up unanimous Republican support in Illinois had been crowned with success.

On the evening of June 16, 1858, Illinois Republicans thronged to the House of Representatives chamber in the Illinois state Capitol building to hear Lincoln. That was the very same place in which he had addressed them the year before—in his attack upon the *Dred Scott* decision. And since that time he had become the undisputed champion of Illinois Republicans. He had no rivals.

He began this speech—sermon-like—with a familiar and biblical quotation:

> A house divided against itself cannot stand.
>   I believe this government cannot endure, permanently half *slave* and half *free*.

I do not expect the Union to be *dissolved*—I do not expect the house to *fall*—but I do expect it will cease to be divided. It will become *all* one thing, or *all* the other. Either the *opponents* of slavery, will arrest the further spread of it, and place it where the public mind shall rest in the belief that it is in course of ultimate extinction, or its *advocates* will push it forward, till it shall become alike lawful in *all* the States, *old* as well as *new*—*North* as well as *South*.

Have we no *tendency* to the latter condition?[36]

Lincoln showed how things had been *trending* since the *Dred Scott* decision, and he showed how the trend would push the institution of slavery—unless stopped—to national dimensions.

Taney alone could not have caused this dreadful transformation. He had help: help from the likes of Stephen Douglas, Franklin Pierce, James Buchanan, and who could say how many other pro-slavery schemers who had labored long and hard to transform the American Republic into the biggest prison in the world.

They had been laboring to hammer into place a new legal edifice of tyranny, the provisions of which (to date) were as follows:

First, that no negro slave, imported as such from Africa, and no descendant of such slave can ever be a *citizen* of any State. . . .

Secondly, that "subject to the Constitution of the United States," neither *Congress* nor a *Territorial Legislature* can exclude slavery from any United States Territory. . . .

Thirdly, that whether the holding [of] a negro in actual slavery in a free State, makes him free, as against the holder, the United States courts will not decide, but will leave to be decided by the courts of any slave State the negro may be forced into by the master.

This point is made, not to be pressed *immediately*; but, if acquiesced in for a while, and apparently *indorsed* by the people at an election, *then* to sustain the logical conclusion that what Dred Scott's master might lawfully do with Dred Scott, in the free State of Illinois, every other master may lawfully do with any other *one*, or *one thousand* slaves, in Illinois, or in any free State.[37]

Free Soilers had to stay vigilant. Otherwise, Lincoln warned, "we shall *lie down* pleasantly dreaming that the people of *Mississippi* are on the verge of making their State *free*," but "*awake* to the *reality*, instead, that the Supreme Court has made *Illinois a slave State*."[38]

And it could happen with terrifying speed.

Coming back to his theme of the "house divided," Lincoln spoke about the *unified* house—the *prison house* of *enslavement*—that would *stand complete* if the schemers and conspirators were allowed to finish their work.

In oratory as polished as anything that he would ever compose, Lincoln spelled it all out in a statement that reads, as it gathers momentum, like a rolling incantation—especially so when he chants out the names of "Stephen and Franklin and Roger and James" in a rhythm of defiance. One can easily imagine him wagging an extended finger as he did so, for the pace of the statement (at the end of the paragraph in question) would be perfect for a gesture like that:

> We cannot absolutely *know* that all these exact adaptations are the result of preconcert. But when we see a lot of framed timbers, different portions of which we know have been gotten out at different times and places by different workmen—Stephen, Franklin, Roger, and James, for instance—and when we see these timbers joined together, and see they exactly make the frame of a house or mill, all the tenons and mortices exactly fitting, and all the lengths and proportions of the different pieces exactly adapted to their respective places, and not a piece too many or too few—not omitting even scaffolding—or, if a single piece be lacking, we can see the place in the frame exactly fitted and prepared to yet bring such piece in—in *such* a case, we find it impossible not to *believe* that Stephen and Franklin and Roger and James all understood one another from the beginning, and all worked upon a common plan or draft drawn up before the first lick was struck.[39]

But there was time for the nation's Republicans to tear down the edifice. There was still enough time to stop the pro-slavery conspirators. "Two years ago," Lincoln observed, "the Republicans of the nation mustered over thirteen hundred thousand strong" in the 1856 election. They did so under the single impulse of resistance to a common danger. . . . Of *strange, discordant,* and even, *hostile* elements, we gathered from the four winds, and *formed* and fought the battle through, under the hot fire of a disciplined, proud, and pampered enemy. Did we brave all *then,* to falter now?—*now*—when that same enemy is wavering, disserved and belligerent?[40]

No, he proclaimed, the Republicans in Illinois and elsewhere would not fail. They would halt the conspiracy, tear down the house of enslavement, brush aside all distractions—and stop them.

They would stop the supporters of slavery from ruining America.

THWARTING DOUGLAS

On the evening of July 10, 1858, Lincoln stood upon a balcony of Chicago's Tremont House hotel and gave a charismatic speech. He was speaking extemporaneously to a crowd composed of thousands of people. Torches blazed.

He did not speak from notes. But journalists recorded his fiery oration in shorthand.

Stephen Douglas spoke from the very same balcony the day before. His speech was preceded by fireworks and a parade; it was the kick-off event in his campaign for re-election to the Senate. Lincoln was there, and he listened very carefully to what Douglas said.

Along with his usual racist abuse, Douglas bragged that the events in Kansas (and in Washington, D.C.) proved that popular sovereignty worked. He claimed most of the credit for resisting the Lecompton fraud. And he said that Lincoln was fomenting war between the sections in his "House Divided" speech.

The very next day Lincoln answered him point for point.

But what gave Lincoln's speech its great power was a discourse on the meaning of the Declaration of Independence in light of all the furor over race. In order to appreciate the dynamism of the way Lincoln worked this crowd—to get a feel for the "electricity" in the air that evening—it is useful to read some generous extracts from his remarks, paying heed to the reactions of the crowd, which the journalists recorded.

Lincoln spoke without notes, and yet his speech possessed strong oratorical qualities—qualities distinctive to speeches that are given off the cuff.

Though we can only guess about how quickly or slowly this speech was delivered, Lincoln probably delivered it fast. If one reads aloud the extracts below in a slow and deliberative manner, the result may be a tangle of words. But if read at a good fast clip, it just snaps into place and releases an on-rushing flow of great force.

He used a clever tactic when he spoke about the meaning of the Declaration of Independence. He spoke of white ethnicity, undermining notions of white solidarity and forcing certain members of the audience to think about the way they had been mistreated by the Know Nothings:

> Now, sirs, for the purpose of squaring things with this idea of "don't care if slavery is voted up or down," for maintaining the Dred Scott decision [A voice—"Hit him again"], for holding that the Declaration of Independence did not mean anything at all, we have Judge Douglas giving his exposition of what the Declaration of Independence means, and we have him saying that the people of America are equal to the people of England. According to his construction, you Germans are not connected with it.[1]

That surely got the attention of a good many people that evening, and Lincoln moved along quickly to establish the global context of America's struggle.

Douglas was blind to the real implications of America's founding document, Lincoln said. The language of the declaration was more than just an exercise to justify colonial separation from Britain. It was a manifesto of world significance. Douglas (like Taney) was draining the declaration of its power by insisting that certain groups are *better* than others, that the "better" people have the right to rob others of their freedom:

> Now I ask in all soberness, if all these things, if indulged in, if ratified, if confirmed and endorsed, if taught to our children, and repeated to them, do not tend to rub out the sentiment of liberty in this country, and to transform this Government into a government of some other

form. Those arguments that are made, that the inferior race are to be treated with as much allowance as they are capable of enjoying; that as much is to be done for them as their condition will allow. What are these arguments? They are the arguments that kings have made for enslaving the people in all ages of the world. You will find that all the arguments in favor of king-craft were of this class; they always bestrode the necks of the people, not that they wanted to do it, but because the people were better off for being ridden. That is their argument, and this argument of the Judge is the same old serpent that says you work and I eat, you toil and I will enjoy the fruits of it.[2]

America was a republic. But how long could this republic protect its institutions when subversives were using white supremacy to eat away the foundations of the system that protected the rights of everyone? Reduce other people to bondage, Lincoln said, and you are setting the stage for some future lord and master to trample down your very own freedom:

Turn in whatever way you will—whether it come from the mouth of a King, an excuse for enslaving the people of his country, or from the mouth of men of one race as a reason for enslaving the men of another race, it is all the same old serpent, and I hold if that course of argumentation that is made for the purpose of convincing the public mind that we should not care about this, should be granted, it does not stop with the negro.[3]

No, it did not stop with the Negro, and that was exactly why the Free Soil movement had begun. Would you like to be slaves yourselves, Lincoln asked: if so, just keep on diminishing the truths of the Declaration of Independence and see where it gets you. Already in the South was the notion that "inferior" *whites* should be enslaved. Perhaps the time was approaching when people would repudiate the Declaration of Independence altogether:

I should like to know if taking this old Declaration of Independence, which declares that all men are equal upon principle and making exceptions to it where will it stop. If one man says it does not mean a negro, why not another say it does not mean some other man? If that declaration is not the truth, let us get the Statute book, in which we find it and tear it out! Who is so bold as to do it! [Voices—"me" "no one," &c.] If it is not true let us tear it out! [cries of "no, no,"].[4]

It was time, Lincoln said, to "discard all this quibbling about this man and the other man—this race and that race and the other race being inferior.... Let us discard all these things, and unite as one people."[5]

But Douglas had no intention of desisting from his race-baiting tactics. The Lincoln-Douglas battle of 1858 would be driven by the politics of race.

Lincoln was uncertain about the prospects for toppling Douglas. The Democrats controlled the Illinois legislature and many Democratic legislators did not have to stand for re-election in 1858 due to staggered terms. Lincoln predicted that "we shall have a very hard run to carry the Legislature."[6]

And he knew that Stephen Douglas, a bombastic but powerful orator, would fight ferociously to hold his seat in the Senate. In sizing up the enemy's strength, Lincoln acknowledged that Douglas was "a very strong logician," and that, while he had "very little humor or imagination," he was "an exceedingly good judge of human nature." He "knew the people of the state thoroughly and just how to appeal to [their] prejudices." In all, he was a "very powerful opponent."[7]

Lincoln might have been comforted if he had known that Douglas reciprocated such feelings. Douglas privately confessed to a friend that "I shall have my hands full. He is the strong man of his party—full of wit, facts, dates, and the best stump speaker, with his droll ways and dry jokes, in the West."[8]

Win or lose, Lincoln believed that his challenge to Douglas would resonate down the years and contribute, if only in a very small way, to the cause of eradicating slavery. He thought about the long anti-slavery struggle in Britain—a struggle that finally succeeded. He consoled himself, in a private reflection, that abolitionism in Britain had its "open fire-eating opponents; its stealthy 'don't care' opponents; its dollar and cent opponents; its negro equality opponents; and its religion and good order opponents." But, he continued,

> I have also remembered that though they blazed, like tallow candles for a century, at last they flickered in the socket, died out, stank in the dark for a brief season, and were remembered no more, even by the

smell.... Remembering these things I can not but regard it as possible
that the higher object of this contest may not be completely attained
within the term of my natural life. But I can not doubt either that it
will come in due time.[9]

In July, the rival senatorial candidates made speeches in different
localities, and Douglas lashed out at Lincoln again and again with the
charge that he meant to let African Americans have full-fledged equality
with Illinois whites.

In Springfield on July 17, Douglas prophesied that blacks would
overrun the state if Lincoln's brand of politics prevailed. "When he lets
down the bars," Douglas railed, then the "floods shall have turned in upon
us and covered our prairies thick with them till they shall be as dark and
black as night in mid-day.... We must preserve the purity of the race not
only in our politics but in our domestic relations."[10]

Surely everyone knew what Douglas meant by "domestic relations."

Lincoln's reply, which he gave in a speech that he delivered the very
same day, was defensive. He knew how effective the racist appeal of Stephen Douglas was, and this is obvious enough from the way that he framed
the issues. Douglas "tormented himself with horrors," Lincoln said,

> about my disposition to make negroes perfectly equal with white men
> in political and social relations. He did not stop to show that I have
> said any such thing, or that it legitimately follows from anything I
> have said, but he rushes in with his assertions. I adhere to the Declara-
> tion of Independence. If Judge Douglas and his friends are not willing
> to stand by it, let them come up and amend it. Let them make it read
> that all men are created equal except negroes.

But Lincoln could sense that this invocation of the Declaration of Independence would not be enough to deflect the charge that he was a . . .
"negro lover." So he followed up with a carefully composed disclaimer that
again raises questions about what he secretly felt regarding race.

"Certainly the negro is not our equal in color," he said, and "perhaps
not in other respects," but "in the right to put into his mouth the bread
that his own hands have earned, he is the equal of every other man, white
or black.... All I ask for the negro is that if you do not like him, let him
alone."[11]

If the tricky-language theory on Lincoln's racial statements is correct, this statement shows him struggling to *sound* the way that racists demanded but to do it in the least offensive manner. His language was mild—indeed, it was *weak* by the standards of racists—when compared to the virulence of Douglas.

The only thing that was "certain," he said—he used the word "certainly"—was that "the negro is not our equal in color." Beyond the fact that the colors of the races were *different* (not "equal"), there was no way to know whether other forms of "inequality" existed, according to Lincoln. He used the double-sided word "perhaps"—so his statement had an obvious escape clause. Racists might have taken him to mean that perhaps inequalities *did* exist, but others might have understood him to mean that perhaps inequalities between the races did *not* exist . . . beyond color.

Regardless, he insisted, the races were equal when it came to the right to be free.

All through July the candidates traversed Illinois. Douglas continued his race-baiting, while denying he had ever conspired with Pierce, Taney, and Buchanan, as Lincoln had suggested in his House Divided speech. Lincoln kept fending off the "negro-loving" charge, while trying to revive the inspirational power of the Declaration of Independence.

Douglas traveled the state in style. George B. McClellan, an executive of the Illinois Central Railroad, offered him the use of a private railroad car. McClellan, a West Point graduate who had served in the Mexican War, was a white supremacist Democrat. Douglas luxuriated in these accommodations and indulged between speeches in the heavy smoking and drinking that were steadily taking a toll on his health. His tall and beautiful wife accompanied him throughout the state.

Lincoln traveled in second-class accommodations. Mary stayed mostly at home. But he often looked stylish in a new white suit—one that was strikingly at odds with the black that he usually wore when he had his picture taken. He reportedly wore the white suit back in May when he defended young Duff Armstrong—the son of his longtime friend Hannah Armstrong—in the "Almanac" murder trial.

The power he commanded as a public speaker was vividly displayed on that occasion. His co-counsel reminisced about his presentation to the jury: "Such [was] the power, & earnestness with which he Spoke, that jury & all, Sat as if Entranced, & when he was through found relief in a gush of tears. I have never Seen such mastery Exhibited over the feelings and Emotions of men."[12] No doubt Lincoln used all of that skill in the course of his run for the Senate.

At Lewistown on August 17 he delivered a speech very similar to his off-the-cuff oration in Chicago. But this time he wrote it all out in some meticulously crafted lines. The Founding Fathers, he said, had a reverence for the dignity of the human spirit that they meant to pass on to their descendants. They believed that nothing "stamped with the divine image and likeness" was meant to be "trodden on, and degraded, and imbruted by its fellows." So they

> erected a beacon to guide their children, and their children's children.
> ... Wise statesmen as they were, they knew the tendency of prosperity to breed tyrants, and so they established these great self-evident truths, that when in the distant future some man, some faction, some interest, should set up the doctrine that none but rich men, or none but white men, or none but Anglo-Saxon white men, were entitled to life, liberty, and pursuit of happiness, their posterity might look up again to the Declaration of Independence and take courage to renew the battle which their fathers began—so that truth, and justice, and mercy, and all the human and Christian virtues might not be extinguished from the land.[13]

That was the message that Lincoln kept sending in 1858. He meant to hold aloft the principles that guided America. He might be awkward in physical terms, but his speeches had a radiant intensity. In contrast, his opponent Stephen Douglas came off like a boorish sot.

Many expressed their belief that Douglas was drunk when he delivered at least some of his speeches in 1858. One observer reported that Douglas "was very bitter; he shook his shaggy locks, rolled his eyes, stamped his feet, flourished his arms, pointed his fingers and gnashed his teeth." Another expressed the opinion that "a sober man would hardly talk and act as he did," adding that many "thought that Douglas was under the influence of liquor."[14]

For whatever reasons, Douglas drew bigger crowds than Lincoln in July. So some of Lincoln's supporters suggested that he ought to challenge Douglas to a series of debates—encounters where the rivals would face one another directly. On July 24, Lincoln asked Norman Judd what he thought of the idea. Judd replied that Lincoln ought to do it. So Lincoln wrote a letter to Douglas and requested Judd to hand-deliver it.

When Judd tracked Douglas down and delivered this challenge, Douglas was at first resentful. He was reluctant to face his competitor in open debates. He confessed his misgivings to a confidante:

> I do not feel, between you and me, that I want to go into this debate. The whole country knows me and has me measured. Lincoln, as regards myself, is comparatively unknown, and if he gets the best of this debate, and I want to say he is the ablest man the Republicans have got, I shall lose everything and Lincoln will gain everything. Should I win, I shall gain but little.[15]

But Judd and others put pressure on Douglas by warning him that he would look like a coward if he turned Lincoln down. The *Chicago Press and Tribune* charged that Douglas "is afraid of 'Long Abe' on the stump," and "would rather go about the country like a strolling mountebank, with his cannon, and toadies and puffers, to shoot, cheer, and blow for him than to stand up to the work with a full grown man to confront him."[16]

So Douglas agreed, but he insisted he would only face Lincoln in seven debates, to be held in each of the state's congressional districts, except for the districts in which he and Lincoln had already exchanged attacks—namely in the districts containing the cities of Springfield and Chicago.

On July 29, Lincoln accepted Douglas's terms for the seven debates.

By the time the first Lincoln-Douglas debate occurred on August 21 in Ottawa, the county seat of LaSalle County in northern Illinois, the campaign was being covered by out-of-state reporters. Over ten thousand people watched the rivals attack one another on a platform in the public square. Many had come from great distances, by train or by boat (along the Illinois and Michigan Canal) to witness the event. The hotels were jammed and an Ottawa resident recalled that the "campfires that spread up and down the valley for a mile made it look as if an army was gathered."[17]

Douglas arrived with all the usual fanfare—in a horse-drawn carriage, accompanied by band music and flag-waving followers. Lincoln arrived by train from Chicago and he spent the night at the home of Ottawa's mayor.

For three hours the candidates debated on the unshaded platform. Ottawa was a Republican city, but supporters of Douglas had turned out in force. Audience reactions were recorded as the journalists took their notes in shorthand.

Douglas was on the attack, and he employed the oratorical devices that admirers regarded as formidable and detractors dismissed as disgusting: he stamped his feet, made fists, flailed the air, and vented outrage at the "Black Republicans."

Defending his doctrine of popular sovereignty, he claimed that the Founding Fathers had supported it. The Union they created contained both free states and slave states, depending on the choices of the whites who lived there. Accusing Lincoln of threatening the Union with his "House Divided" doctrine, Douglas said that America's divided house could last forever in a state of division if whites would only practice a live-and-let-live policy in regard to the ownership of blacks.

As to blacks, Douglas roared out his principles by asking the voters of Ottawa to say how they felt about the following propositions:

> I ask you, are you in favor of conferring upon the negro the rights and privileges of citizenship? ("No, no.") Do you desire to strike out of our State Constitution that clause which keeps slaves and free negroes out of the State, and allow the free negroes to flow in, ("never") and cover your prairies with black settlements? . . . If you desire negro citizenship . . . then support Mr. Lincoln and the Black Republican party. . . . For one, I am opposed to negro citizenship in any and every form. (Cheers.) . . . I do not question Mr. Lincoln's belief that the negro was made his equal, and hence is his brother (laughter) but for my own part, I do not regard him as my equal, and positively deny that he is my brother or any kin to me whatever ("Never," "Hit him again," and cheers).[18]

Douglas posed "interrogatories" for Lincoln, questions designed to put him on the spot. Did Lincoln "stand pledged" to prevent the admission of any more slave states "even if the people want them"? Did he stand pledged to prevent the acquisition of more territory if slavery were permitted there?

"I ask Abraham Lincoln to answer these questions," he said, "in order that when I trot him down to lower Egypt"—"Egypt" was the southern-most part of Illinois where white supremacy sentiments were strongest—"I may put the same questions to him. (Enthusiastic applause.) My principles are the same everywhere. (Cheers, and 'hark.')"[19]

Douglas foresaw that Lincoln's tone on the subject of race would start changing as the bigotry of his audiences changed for the worse. Even in Ottawa, the race-baiting tactics of Douglas had elicited cheers.

Lincoln was on the defensive. He made no reply to the "interrogatories" but recited a carefully composed disclaimer on the subject of race, a disclaimer that he obviously hoped would pass muster later on with the voters in Egypt when Douglas raised the same issues.

"I have no purpose to introduce political and social equality between the white and black races," Lincoln said. "There is a physical difference between the two, which in my judgment will probably forever forbid their living together upon the footing of perfect equality, and inasmuch as it becomes a necessity that there must be a difference, I, as well as Judge Douglas, am in favor of the race to which I belong, having the superior position."[20]

Of all the statements by Lincoln that appear to be racist, this one looks obviously bad. But again, the language was slippery. His statement as to whites maintaining their "superior position" was framed in the language of *contingency*: he used the phrase "inasmuch as" (equivalent to "if") regarding the proposition that there *had* to be a difference in the social status of the races. The flip-side of the proposition was the chance that such a difference might no longer be necessary if *attitudes* regarding the "physical difference" between the two races should change for the better.

And his declaration that he "had no purpose" to introduce a program of civil rights reform is rather curious if we compare it to the things *that he actually did* years later when his presidential power made it possible. By 1864, he began suggesting in secret that some blacks should be allowed to vote. He *did* "have the purpose" to introduce a measure of "political and social equality" between the two races at the time, as his actions would prove.

Yet in 1858 he had told the Illinois racists he had no such "purpose."

Had his feelings on the issue really changed? Or had he felt the same way all along? Was he secretly thinking to himself "no purpose *at the moment*" when he issued his disclaimer about civil rights in Ottawa? One thing is certain: if he *had* embraced civil rights in his confrontation with Douglas, he might very well have been jeered off the stage—even in Ottawa.

Lincoln did his best in this first debate with Douglas to regain the initiative. He renewed his attack upon Douglas for working with Pierce, Buchanan, and Taney to pave the way for the nationalization of slavery.

But Douglas brushed aside what he called "that nonsense about Stephen, and Franklin, and Roger, and Bob, and James." He even made fun of the literary craftsmanship that Lincoln had employed in the composition of that sentence:

> He studied that out, prepared that one sentence with the greatest care, committed it to memory . . . and now he carries that speech around and reads that sentence to show how pretty it is. (Laughter.) His vanity is wounded because I will not go into that beautiful figure of his about the building of a house. (Renewed laughter.) All I have to say is, that I am not green enough to let him make a charge which he acknowledges he does not know to be true, and then take up my time in answering it, when I know it to be false and nobody else knows it to be true. . . . Let him prove it if he can.[21]

It was obvious that Lincoln would have to become more aggressive in the second debate. So he consulted with advisers such as Joseph Medill of the *Chicago Tribune*, Norman Judd, and other members of the Republican State Central Committee.

The second debate was held on August 27 in Freeport, the county seat of Stephenson County at the very top of Illinois. This town was a Republican bastion.

Lincoln arrived by train and found himself deluged with supporters. He was carried in a Conestoga wagon to the speakers' platform that stood in an open-air grove.

He began by taking up the matter of the "interrogatories" posed by Douglas. He took the offensive by agreeing to answer them "upon the condition that he will answer questions from me not exceeding the same number. I give him an opportunity to respond." Douglas seemed to be caught off-guard, and so Lincoln seized the welcome opportunity: "The Judge remains silent. I now say to you that I will answer his interrogatories, whether he answers mine or not; [applause] and that after I have done so, I will propound mine to him."[22]

Lincoln took advantage of the way that Douglas posed the questions; he had asked whether Lincoln "stood pledged" to certain propositions. Lincoln made it clear that his answers were sly when he showed his hand with perfect candor:

Now my friends, it will be perceived upon an examination of these questions and answers, that so far I have only answered that I was not *pledged* to this, that or the other. The Judge has not framed his interrogatories to ask me anything more than this, and I have answered in strict accordance with the interrogatories.... But I am not disposed to hang upon the exact form of the interrogatory. I am rather disposed to take up at least some of these questions, and state what I really think upon them.[23]

In this priceless declaration, Lincoln made it clear—to his listeners and also to posterity—that public statements may be clever evasions. One cannot just *presume* that public statements by prominent figures are the whole truth and nothing but the truth. Secret thoughts will remain secret thoughts until such time (if ever) that the speaker sees fit to reveal them. Such a time had arrived in this case, and so Lincoln agreed to reveal "what I really think" about *some* of the matters in question.

He declared that he was absolutely "pledged to a belief in the *right* and *duty* of Congress to prohibit slavery in all the United States Territories. (Great applause.)"[24]

Then he hurled his own questions at Douglas. First, "can the people of a United States Territory, in any lawful way, against the wishes of any citizen of the United States, exclude slavery from its limits prior to the formation of a State Constitution?" And second, "if the Supreme Court of the United States shall decide that States cannot exclude slavery from their limits, are you in favor of acquiescing in, adopting and following such decision as a rule of political action?"[25]

Douglas answered the first question easily, since he had already answered it the year before. Slavery, he affirmed, "cannot exist a day or an hour anywhere, unless it is supported by local police regulations."[26]

But his answer to the second question—about a Supreme Court decision that would strike down the constitutions of the free states and thus nationalize slavery—was revealing. Working himself into a state of indignation, he said he was "amazed that Lincoln should ask such a question.... He casts an imputation upon the Supreme Court of the United States by supposing that they would violate the Constitution of the United States. I tell him such a thing is not possible. (Cheers.)"[27]

Then Douglas went on the attack with his standard white supremacy routine. But this time his insinuations about the possibilities for inter-racial sex were more salacious. Though some of the people in the crowd were resistant, Douglas used this particular pitch for all that it was worth. He talked about an incident from 1854, when he had been making speeches all over the state to defend his authorship of the Kansas-Nebraska Act:

> The last time I came here to make a speech, while talking from the stand to you, people of Freeport, as I am doing to-day, I saw a carriage and a magnificent one it was, drive up and take a position outside the crowd; a beautiful young lady was sitting on the box seat, whilst Fred. Douglass [i.e., the black abolitionist Frederick Douglass] and her mother reclined inside, and the owner of the carriage acted as the driver. (Laughter, cheers, cries of right, what have you to say against it, &c.) I saw this in your own town. ("What of it.") All I have to say of it is this, that if you, Black Republicans, think that the negro ought to be on a social equality with your wives and daughters, and ride in a carriage with your wife, whilst you drive the team, you have a perfect right to do so.[28]

It is tempting to wonder whether Douglas had been reading the new novel by Gustave Flaubert—*Madame Bovary*—that was published just the year before. In this sensational tale of adulterous sex, the title character gets ravished in a coach by one of her innumerable young paramours.

In September the debates moved to "Egypt," the southern-most portion of Illinois. On September 15 the candidates debated in Jonesboro, the county seat of Union County. In contrast to the crowds that turned out to hear the two previous debates, the turn-out in Jonesboro was meager.

Douglas used the same anecdote about the carriage that had drawn such a mixed response in Freeport. But in Jonesboro the response was what Douglas intended and it led to some banter with the crowd that was tinged with the imagery of violence.

"In the extreme northern counties," he began, "they brought out men to canvass the State whose complexion suited their political creed, and hence Fred Douglass, the negro, was to be found there." He went on:

> Why, they brought Fred Douglass to Freeport when I was addressing a meeting there in a carriage driven by the white owner, the negro sitting inside with the white lady and her daughter. (Shame.) When I got

through canvassing the northern counties that year and progressed as far south as Springfield, I was met and opposed in discussion by Lincoln, Lovejoy, Trumble, and Sidney Breese. . . . Father Giddings, the high priest of abolitionism, had just been there and Chase came about the time I left. ("Why didn't you shoot him?") I did take a running shot at them, but as I was single-handed against the white, black and mixed drove, I had to use a short gun and fire into the crowd instead of taking them off singly with a rifle. (Great laughter and cheers.)[29]

In this ugly atmosphere, Lincoln was obliged to change his tactics, so he plied these people with some carefully contrived tomfoolery. Douglas, he told them, had predicted that "I would not come to Egypt unless he forced me—that I could not be got down here, unless he, giant-like, had hauled me down here (Laughter)." Well,

Judge Douglas, when he made that statement must have been crazy, and wholly out of his sober senses, or else he would have known that when he got me down here—that promise—that windy promise—of his powers to annihilate me, wouldn't amount to anything. Now, how little do I look like being carried away trembling? . . . Did the Judge talk of trotting me down to Egypt to scare me to death? Why, I know this people better than he does. I was raised just a little east of here. I am a part of this people. But the Judge was raised further north, and perhaps he has some horrid idea of what this people might be induced to do. (Roars of laughter and cheers.)[30]

Notwithstanding the low-brow tone that Lincoln knew was required, he made some interesting points in this debate. He argued, for instance, that the proposition that "slavery cannot enter a new country without police regulations is historically false." It had to be false, he reasoned, since the slave Dred Scott had been brought into the free state of Illinois and then kept there for three years.

In Charleston, the county seat of Coles County, in the central part of Illinois, where the next debate occurred on September 18, Douglas kept up the race demagoguery. This time the level of attendance was close to the first two debates.

Douglas charged that the Republicans were shifty when it came to the politics of race: "Their principles in the North are jet black, (laughter), in the centre they are in color a decent mulatto, (renewed laughter), and in lower Egypt they are almost white. (Shouts of laughter)." Indeed, said Douglas, the party presented "the extraordinary spectacle of a house divided against itself."[31]

Lincoln, after reciting his standard disclaimers on the subject of race, thrust back at Douglas with some sharply honed humor of his own. Douglas was "in constant horror," Lincoln said, with regard to the prospect of equal rights for blacks. He went on to assert that there was no way at all to bring about "an alteration of the social and political relations of the negro and the white man . . . except in the State Legislature." That being the case, he concluded, it would probably be best for everyone if Douglas could "be kept at home and placed in the State Legislature to fight the measure. (Uproarious laughter and applause.) I do not propose dwelling any longer on the subject."[32]

In October the Lincoln-Douglas debates became more focused. The men exchanged sharp accusations in regard to the larger issues of the Union and slavery extension.

On October 6 the scene moved to Galesburg, the county seat of Knox County in northern Illinois. The turn-out for this debate was huge and the debate took place on the campus of Knox College.

Douglas took aim at Lincoln's House Divided speech, claiming that the Union could continue forever in a state of division. Whites should do whatever they pleased in regard to the ownership of blacks, he insisted, and the legacy of the Founding Fathers supported him. Suppose, he reasoned, that the House Divided doctrine had been raised in the days of the Founding Fathers: would the Union itself have been created?

Lincoln responded with a forthright denunciation of Douglas's moral nonchalance, which amounted to amorality. Douglas seemed to be incapable of feeling any moral sense at all when it came to slavery: "Everything that emanates from him or his coadjutors in their course of policy, carefully excludes the thought that there is anything wrong with Slavery," he said.[33] And this was monstrous in light of the fact that the Founding Fathers had wanted to initiate a long-term elimination of the evil.

Furthermore, the callousness of Douglas was preparing the way for the nationalization of slavery. He told people not to care about the issue. So with Douglas lulling public opinion, Lincoln said, it was easy for Taney and his ilk to insert their pernicious new doctrines into constitutional law. Lincoln went on to set forth the full danger of what was going on:

The essence of the Dred Scott case is compressed into the sentence which I will now read . . . "The right of property in a slave is distinctly and expressly affirmed in the Constitution!" What is it to be "affirmed" in the Constitution? Made firm in the Constitution— so made that it cannot be separated from the Constitution without breaking the Constitution—durable as the Constitution, and part of the Constitution. Now, remembering the provision of the Constitution which I have read, affirming that the instrument is the supreme law of the land, that the Judges of every State shall be bound by it, any law or Constitution of any State to the contrary notwithstanding; that the right of property in a slave is affirmed in that Constitution, is made, formed into and cannot be separated from it without breaking it; durable as the instrument; part of the instrument;—what follows?[34]

What followed was the overturning of the northern free state constitutions.

Douglas was complicit in the effort to nationalize slavery, Lincoln charged—complicit by telling his fellow whites not to care. Perhaps Douglas never *meant* to pave the way for the nationalization of slavery, Lincoln said, but his actions were leading in that direction just the same:

I call upon your minds to inquire, if you were going to get the best instrument you could, and then set it to work in the most ingenious way, to prepare the public mind for this movement, operating in the free States, where there is now an abhorrence of the institution of Slavery, could you find an instrument so capable of doing it as Judge Douglas? Or one employed in so apt a way to do it? (Great cheering. Cries of "Hit him again," "That's the doctrine.")[35]

On October 13 the men faced off in Quincy, the county seat of Adams County in the central part of Illinois. Douglas continued attacking the House Divided speech; since Lincoln said that he hoped to see slavery extinguished, Douglas asked, how exactly did he anticipate the process unfolding in the South? "How can he extinguish it in Kentucky, in Virginia, in all the slave states by his policy if he will not pursue a policy which will interfere with it in the States where it exists," Douglas asked.[36] The answer was simple: Republican policies would *have* to interfere with the institution in all of the slave states at some point in time. And this would cause a rupture of the Union.

"Let each State mind its own business and let its neighbors alone," Douglas said. That was the only realistic way to preserve the Union—to preserve it *in peace.*[37]

Douglas also demanded to know how Lincoln intended to overturn the *Dred Scott* decision. "Will he appeal to a mob," Douglas asked. "Does he intend to appeal to violence, to Lynch law? Will he stir up strife and rebellion in the land and overthrow the Court by violence?"[38]

The audience found Lincoln's answer to this question absolutely hilarious. He made it clear that he would overturn the decision by packing the Supreme Court with Republicans:

> He is desirous of knowing how we are going to reverse the Dred Scott decision. Judge Douglas ought to know how. . . . Didn't Judge Douglas find a way to reverse the decision of our [state] Supreme Court, when it decided that Carlin's old father—old Governor Carlin—had not the constitutional power to remove a Secretary of State? (Great cheering and laughter.) Did he not appeal to the "MOBS" as he calls them? Did he not make speeches in the lobby to show how villainous that decision was, and how it ought to be overthrown? Did he not succeed too in getting an act passed by the Legislature to have it over-thrown? And didn't he himself sit down on the bench as one of the five added judges, who were to overslaugh the four old ones—getting his name of "Judge" in that way and no other? (Thunderous cheers and laughter.)[39]

In the final debate held in Alton, the county seat of Madison County in southern Illinois, Lincoln decried the Democrats' tendency to "dehumanize the negro—to take away from him the right of ever striving to be a man. I combat it as being one of the thousand things constantly done in these days to prepare the public mind to make property, and nothing but property of the *negro in all the States of this Union.*"[40] Lincoln's wife was in attendance at this final debate.

As Election Day neared, Lincoln sized up his chances. He theorized about the possibility of election fraud, and on October 20 he wrote a letter to Norman Judd about the difficulty of proving it:

On alighting from the cars and walking three squares at Naples on Monday, I met about fifteen Celtic gentlemen, with black carpet-sacks in their hands. I learned they had crossed over from the Rail-road in Brown county, but where they were going no one could tell. They dropped in about the doggeries, and were still hanging about when I left. At Brown County yesterday I was told that about four hundred of the same sort were brought into Schuyler, before the election, to work on some new Railroad; but on reaching here I find Bagby thinks that is not so. What I most dread is that they will introduce into the doubtful districts numbers of men who are legal voters in all respects except *residence* and who will swear to residence and thus put it beyond our power to exclude them. They can & I fear will swear falsely on that point, because they know it is next to impossible to convict them of Perjury upon it. Now the greater remaining part of the campaign, is finding a way to head this thing off. Can it be done at all?[41]

Notwithstanding Lincoln's fears, the candidates pledged to support his senatorial quest got more votes than the candidates pledged to Douglas in 1858. But it was not enough, since the Democrats retained their control of the legislature, thanks to the staggering of terms and the malapportionment of Illinois electoral districts. The Democratic legislature would send Stephen Douglas right back to the U.S. Senate.

Lincoln of course was crestfallen for a while in the aftermath of the election. He told supporters on a wistful note that "though I now sink out of view, and shall be forgotten, I believe that I have made some marks which will tell for the cause of liberty long after I am gone."[42] But he had altered the political balance of power decisively, and so his spirits revived as he realized more and more what he had actually achieved. To one supporter he wrote: "I believe you are 'feeling like h—ll yet.' Quit that. You will soon feel better. Another 'blow up' is coming, and we shall have fun again."[43]

To another supporter he was much more specific: "I hope and believe the seed has been sown that will yet produce fruit.... Douglas managed to be supported both as the best means to *break down* and to *uphold* the slave power. No ingenuity can long keep those opposing elements in harmony. Another explosion will come before a great while."[44]

By 1859, Lincoln started to learn how great his achievement in running for a seat in the U.S. Senate really was. He had out-polled the Democratic presidential contender Stephen A. Douglas—the much-renowned "Little Giant"—in his own home state, and Illinois was one of the critical lower-northern swing states that the Republicans would have to be targeting in the presidential election of 1860. If the Republicans could manage to capture Illinois and the rest of the lower-northern swing states, their capture of the White House was certain.

These facts would make Lincoln a presidential contender if he could manage to set his sights a good deal higher than a mere legislative career.

And that was exactly what began to happen in 1859. Lincoln's rise to destiny resulted from his realization that he had the power to change the course of history if he could find a way to summon his gifts and then use them to the fullest extent. The great process of mental self-discovery for Lincoln had begun in his youth but its crucial transformative surges occurred in two years: in 1854 and 1859.

The political situation changed rapidly. The attempt to bring Kansas into the Union as a slave state failed; Free Soilers controlled the ground out in Kansas and a free state constitution would be drafted there in 1859.

To compensate the South for this loss, Buchanan renewed the attempt of Franklin Pierce to seize Cuba and groom it as a slave state. There were even proposals to re-open the African slave trade. Pro-slavery leaders were increasingly militant in 1859, and their anger was a threat to the presidential candidacy of Douglas. They began to demand the creation by *Congress* of a territorial slave code that the federal government would enforce.

Douglas could not support such a measure—he had too much capital invested in his doctrine of popular sovereignty—so he faced the challenge in 1859 of shoring up his southern support base within the Democratic Party.

Meanwhile, Republican presidential contenders were emerging: Senator William H. Seward of New York and Governor Salmon P. Chase of Ohio—an erstwhile Free Soil Democrat. Chase gained national fame as a legal theorist who challenged the constitutional doctrines of Calhoun. He had also been a prominent leader in the founding of the Republican Party. Seward gained national attention for a speech he delivered on October 25, 1858. This oration was in many ways similar to Lincoln's House Divided speech. Seward proclaimed there was an "irrepressible conflict" between the principles of slavery and freedom. He was widely regarded as the clear front runner for the Republican nomination in 1860.

Lincoln's interest in the presidential possibility grew steadily. He feigned modesty—or else pessimism in regard to his chances—but when

Jesse W. Fell, a Bloomington businessman who had become a close friend, suggested that he seek the Republican presidential nomination, Lincoln reportedly replied that he would certainly "like to be president."[45]

So he tried to take advantage of the heightened visibility his race against Douglas had given him. He positioned himself as a strategist who could guide his fellow Republicans with trenchant observations. In that way he would continue to draw attention to himself.

In December 1858, he wrote to Senator Lyman Trumbull about the predicament that Douglas faced in a divided Democratic Party. Douglas, Lincoln wrote, had "gone South, making characteristic speeches, and seeking to re-instate himself in that section." His Democratic enemies "mean to kill him; but I doubt whether they will adopt the aptest way to do it."

The best way for them to block Douglas, he explained, would be to "present him with no new test," let him do his best at the Democratic national convention that was set to be held in Charleston, South Carolina, then "outvote him, and nominate another. In that case, he will have no pretext for bolting the nomination, and will be as powerless as they can wish." But "on the other hand," Lincoln wrote,

> if they push a Slave Code upon him, as a test, he will bolt at once, turn upon us, as in the case of Lecompton, and claim that all Northern men shall make common cause in electing him President as the best means of breaking down the Slave power. In that case, the democratic party go into a minority inevitably; and the struggle in the whole North will be, as it was in Illinois last summer and fall, whether the Republican party can maintain its identity, or be broken up to form the tail of Douglas's new kite.[46]

He told a Republican rally in Chicago on March 1, 1859, that "if we, the Republicans of this State, had made Judge Douglas our candidate for the Senate of the United States last year and had elected him, there would to-day be no Republican Party in this Union."[47]

Months later, he called Douglas "the most dangerous enemy of liberty, because the most insidious." He argued that Douglas "would have little support in the North, and by consequence, no capital to trade on in the South, if it were not for our friends thus magnifying him and his humbug." Popular sovereignty, Lincoln continued, was a poisonous doctrine that "nationalizes slavery, and revives the African Trade inevitably." Look at it this way, he reasoned:

> Taking slaves into new territories, and buying slaves in Africa, are identical things—identical *rights* or identical *wrongs*—and the argument which establishes one will establish the other. Try a thousand years for a sound reason why Congress shall not hinder the people of Kansas from having slaves, and when you have found it, it will be an equally good one why Congress should not hinder the people of Georgia from importing slaves from Africa.[48]

More and more, Lincoln tore into Douglas as the bearer of subversive evil, subversive to the moral, philosophic, and political foundations of America. The amorality of popular sovereignty was symptomatic of a moral declension that dehumanized millions of blacks in the minds of susceptible whites. In April, Lincoln wrote to the organizers of a Jefferson's birthday celebration in Boston as follows:

> It is now no child's play to save the principles of Jefferson from total overthrow in this nation. They are denied, and evaded, with no small show of success. One dashingly calls them "glittering generalities"; another bluntly calls them "self-evident lies"; and still others insidiously argue that they apply only to "superior races." . . . Those who deny freedom to others, deserve it not for themselves; and, under a just God, can not long retain it. All honor to Jefferson—to the man who . . . had the coolness, forecast, and capacity to introduce into a merely revolutionary document, an abstract truth, and so to embalm it there, that to-day, and in all coming days, it shall be a rebuke and a stumbling block to the very harbingers of re-appearing tyranny and oppression.[49]

In notes he prepared for himself, he vowed that the Republicans "must, by a national policy, prevent the spread of slavery into new territories, or free states, because the constitution does not forbid us, and the general welfare does demand such prevention. We must prevent the revival of the African slave trade, because the constitution does not forbid us, and the general welfare does require the prevention. We must prevent these things from being done either by *congresses* or *courts*. The people—the people—are the rightful masters of both congresses and courts—not to overthrow the constitution, but to overthrow the *men* who pervert it."[50]

In August, Lincoln accepted invitations to speak in Ohio and elsewhere on behalf of Republican candidates. This would also provide him with an opportunity to demonstrate his appeal beyond the state of Illinois. He bore down harder than ever on Douglas-style racism. White supremacy, he argued, was the foremost threat to the American idea.

In some notes that he jotted down in mid-September, he focused on a statement that Douglas had made the year before. "At Memphis," Lincoln wrote, "Douglas told his audience he was for the negro against the crocodile, but for the white man against the negro. This was not a sudden thought spontaneously thrown off at Memphis. He said the same thing many times in Illinois last summer and autumn, though I am not sure it was reported then." The remarks in question were delivered by Douglas on November 30, 1858:

> If old Joshua Giddings should raise a colony in Ohio, and settle down in Louisiana, he would be the strongest advocate of slavery in the whole South; he would find when he got there his opinion would be very much modified; he would find on those sugar plantations it was not a question between the white man and the negro but between the negro and the crocodile. He would say that between the negro and the crocodile, he took the side of the negro. But between the negro and the white man, he would go for the white man.[51]

Lincoln extracted from this statement the essence of Douglas's racist brutality. The statement was "a carefully framed illustration of the estimate he places on the negro and the manner in which he would have him dealt with. It is a sort of proposition in proportion. 'As the negro is to the crocodile, so the white man is to the negro.' *As* the negro ought to treat the crocodile as a beast, *so* the white man ought to treat the negro as a beast."[52] In phonetic imitation of his rival's bombastic oratorical manner, Lincoln wrote that this dehumanization of blacks was the gist of that "gur-reat pur-rinciple" that Douglas called popular sovereignty.[53]

On September 16, in Columbus, Ohio, Lincoln gave a major speech—a speech that sheds a great deal of light on the subject of his racial views.

Douglas, said Lincoln, was pandering to the bigotry of whites when he told them not to trouble their minds about the fact that many blacks were enslaved. That was none of our business, said Stephen Douglas—and whites should unite around the principle that nothing that was done to black people was very important. Lincoln warned that

> if this principle is established, that there is no wrong in slavery, and whoever wants it has the right to have it, is a matter of dollars and cents, a sort of question as to how they shall deal with brutes, that between us and the negro here there is no sort of question, but that at the South the question is between the negro and the crocodile ... where this doctrine prevails, the miners and the sappers will have formed public opinion for the slave trade. They will be ready for Jeff. Davis and Stephens and other leaders of that company, to sound the bugle for the revival of the slave trade, for the second Dred Scott decision, for the flood of slavery to be poured over the free States, while we shall be here tied down and helpless and run over like sheep.[54]

Pro-slavery Americans, said Lincoln, had been weakening the Declaration of Independence, draining its maxims of substance to the point where the principles of Jefferson would soon be little more than the vestiges of a lost or repudiated age:

> Did you ever five years ago, hear of anybody in the world saying that the negro had no share in the Declaration of National Independence; that it did not mean negroes at all; and when "all men" were spoken of negroes were not included? ... I have been unable at any time to find a man in an audience who would declare that he had ever known any body saying so five years ago. But last year there was not a Douglas popular sovereign in Illinois who did not say it.[55]

As for you in Ohio, Lincoln asked, do you currently subscribe to the notion that people of African descent were excluded from the Declaration of Independence? "If you think that now," Lincoln said, "and did not think it then, the next thing that strikes me is to remark that there has been a *change* wrought in you (laughter and applause), and a very significant change it was, being no less than changing the negro, in your estimation, from the rank of a man to that of a brute." He continued, his outrage against white supremacy leading to a powerful chanted indictment:

They are taking him down, and placing him, when spoken of, among reptiles and crocodiles, as Judge Douglas himself expresses it. . . . I ask you to note that fact, and the like of which is to follow, to be plastered on, layer after layer, until very soon you are prepared to deal with the negro everywhere as with the brute. If public sentiment has not been debauched already to this point, a new turn of the screw in that direction is all that is wanting; and this is constantly being done by the teachers of this insidious popular sovereignty.[56]

Lincoln's fight to stop Douglas came down, in the end, to his revulsion toward his white supremacist doctrines.

Lincoln was fifty years old at the time and his rise to destiny was accelerating in 1859. The circumstances of his private and family life remained largely the same, and he appeared to be in very good health.

Tall, clean-shaven, his thick black hair sweeping up and around his broad forehead, his face made a strong impression on people. His prominent nose, square jaw, high cheekbones, and sallow complexion were striking and he towered above most companions. His likeness was captured in a multitude of photographs that were taken in the years when he challenged Stephen Douglas.

He still practiced law with Billy Herndon. His pleasure in his children led to playful indulgences that Herndon had reason to resent. When Lincoln brought Willie and Tad to the office, Herndon wrote, they would "take down the books—empty ash buckets—coal ashes—inkstands—papers—gold pens—letters, etc., etc., in a pile and then dance on the pile."[57] Mary wrote that her husband would declare his satisfaction with the fact that "my children are free—happy & unrestrained by parental tyranny. Love is the chain whereby to Lock a child to its parents."[58]

He had to enjoy these children as much as he could, because his life was moving toward a crisis—the crisis of war. On October 16, John Brown raided Harper's Ferry, Virginia, with the aim of fomenting a slave insurrection.

He was stopped by force, but in the months that followed white southerners were saying more and more that a Republican victory in 1860 must lead to secession.

Lincoln continued to believe that this talk was largely bluff, and yet his pledge to block the spread of slavery was leading to a challenge that was vastly more daunting. And there were many signs in 1859 that he knew it.

DISUNION

L incoln's thoughts began to shift from the threat of Douglas to the threat of disunion before the Harper's Ferry raid. He jabbed at secessionists during his speaking tour in Ohio, but his remarks had a humorous tone that disappeared after John Brown's attack.

In Cincinnati on September 17, 1859, he called Douglas a proxy for the South. And he said that the defenders of slavery—Douglas included—would lose as the Free Soil movement gathered strength.

At one point, he aimed some remarks at the slave-holders themselves. "I should not wonder," he joked, "that there are some Kentuckians about this audience; we are close to Kentucky; and . . . we are on elevated ground, and by speaking distinctly, I should not wonder if some of the Kentuckians would hear me on the other side of the river. (Laughter)."[1]

He told them that Douglas was their very best candidate—whether they knew it or not. Though he said he didn't care about slavery, Douglas *normalized* it, thus protecting it, and southerners ought to realize the value of that. Still, said Lincoln, "we, the Republicans and others forming the Opposition of this country, intend to 'stand by our guns,' to be patient and firm, and in the long run to beat you whether you take him or not. (Applause.)"[2]

Then he spelled out the Republicans' intentions regarding the slave-holding South. "When we do as we say, beat you," he told the

Kentuckians, "you perhaps want to know what we will do with you. (Laughter)." As to that,

> we mean to treat you as near as we possibly can, like Washington, Jefferson and Madison treated you. (Cheers) We mean to leave you alone, and in no way to interfere with your institution; to abide by all and every compromise of the constitution. . . . We mean to recognize and bear in mind that you have as good hearts in your bosoms as other people.[3]

Secession would backfire if southerners attempted it, he said, for it would not protect the institution of slavery. Look at it this way, he reasoned:

> Are you going to split the Ohio down through, and push your half off a piece? Or are you going to keep it right alongside of us outrageous fellows? Or are you going to build a wall some way between your country and ours, by which that movable property of yours can't come over here any more, to the danger of your losing it?[4]

After all, he continued, if America divided, the Fugitive Slave Law would no longer operate. And if northerners "cease to be under obligations to do anything for you, how much better off do you think you will be?" If slaves crossed the Ohio in massive numbers, what recourse would slave owners have? Then he asked them a startling question: "Will you make war upon us and kill us all? Why, gentlemen, I think you are as gallant and as brave men as live . . . but, man for man, you are not better than we are, and there are not so many of you as there are of us. (Loud cheering.)"[5]

Lincoln's joking on the subject of secession subsided after John Brown's raid. Then his statements turned blunt. In December he travelled to Kansas to praise the Free Soilers, who were getting ready for the next territorial election. Fierce winter winds on the plains made him wrap himself up in a buffalo robe as he made his way from one settlement to another.

In a speech that he delivered on December 3 at Leavenworth, he warned that attempts at secession would be stopped. He compared the situation of pro-slavery southerners as they faced the election of 1860 with the plight of Free Soilers who struggled for years against the policies of pro-slavery presidents. "While you elect [the] President," he warned secessionist southerners,

> we submit, neither breaking nor attempting to break up the Union. If we shall constitutionally elect a President, it will be our duty to see that you submit. Old John Brown has just been executed for treason against a state. We cannot object, even though he agreed with us in thinking slavery wrong. That cannot excuse violence, bloodshed, and treason. It could avail him nothing that he might think himself right. So, if constitutionally we elect a President, and therefore you undertake to destroy the Union, it will be our duty to deal with you as old John Brown has been dealt with.[6]

Shortly after he issued that warning, his ally Norman Judd struck a blow for his presidential chances. On December 21, Judd persuaded the members of the Republican National Committee to hold the party's nominating convention in Chicago instead of New York (the obvious choice of Seward and his supporters) or Cleveland (favored for similar reasons by Ohio's favorite son, Salmon Chase). Since Illinois had no presidential candidate (at the moment), Judd argued, Chicago would constitute a "neutral" location for the party's convention in 1860. The ploy worked.

Lincoln's name had been bandied about for months as a presidential contender. Seward was perceived as the clear front runner, with Chase as a competitive rival. But Seward was subjected to vilification after Harper's Ferry for the tone of his "Irrepressible Conflict" speech, which some were calling an incitement to sectional warfare. Moreover, Seward's flaunting ambition was playing into the hands of detractors. Senator William Pitt Fessenden of Maine, for instance, complained that Seward had "forgotten everything else" in his quest for the presidency. He had even forgotten "that he is a Senator, & has duties as such." Fessenden wrote that he was "getting disgusted" with Seward.[7]

As Seward's chances began to appear more questionable, other candidates entered the field, especially men who could boast of "conservative" credentials that might make them more electable than Seward. One of them was Edward Bates of Missouri, who had gained the support of

Horace Greeley. Another was Simon Cameron, an ambitious politician from Pennsylvania, which would be a key swing state.

Illinois Republicans were divided as to which candidate they should support. The year presented the party with a chance to capture the White House, and so Republicans wanted to be certain that they made no mistakes. Some were musing that it might be best if Lincoln sought the second-place slot on the ticket as the vice-presidential nominee.

Lincoln's reaction to the situation was understandable. Uncertain about his chances, he hedged his bets. In November, he told a Cameron supporter that he had "enlisted for the permanent success of the Republican cause; and, for this object, I shall labor faithfully in the ranks, unless, as I think not probable, the judgment of the party shall assign me a different position."[8] But in December, when his friend and supporter Jesse Fell suggested he compose a brief autobiography for the use of journalists, he decided to take the advice.

The supporters of Lincoln's presidential bid—Fell, Norman Judd, David Davis, and Leonard Swett—were uncertain as to how to proceed. Some of them believed it might be best to angle for the vice-presidential slot in the beginning. Judd disagreed, saying that "the proper and only thing to do was to claim the Presidency for him."[9] Judd believed it might be wise to hold back for a while and let the rival candidacies of Seward, Chase, Bates, and Cameron wear each other down. Swett favored plunging right ahead.

At an Illinois Republican caucus in January 1860, Lincoln maintained his pose of modest doubtfulness. Swett—a particularly ardent supporter—lost his temper, saying, "see here, Lincoln, this is outrageous. We are trying to get you nominated for the presidency, and you are working right against us. Now you must stop it."[10] Lincoln laughed and said he would not interfere with such efforts.

All the while, he predicted with canny accuracy that the Democrats would split in 1860 due to southern opposition to Douglas. Herndon recalled him saying that Douglas would "split the Convention wide open and give it to the devil; & right here is our future success."[11]

In October 1859, Lincoln received an exciting and welcome invitation to speak at the Plymouth Church in Brooklyn, New York, where the Reverend Henry Ward Beecher was minister. Beecher was a very famous man. Indeed, the whole Beecher family was celebrated for its intellectuality and literary flair; one of Beecher's sisters was Harriet Beecher Stowe, the author of *Uncle Tom's Cabin*.

This invitation had been engineered by a Chase supporter named James A. Briggs. The idea was to undermine the presidential prospects of Seward by upstaging him in his home state of New York.

Here was a chance for Lincoln to outshine the Republican front-runner and prove to the eastern literati that he was a man of distinction. Seward himself had been dismissing Lincoln as a "country lawyer," and it was time to lay that stereotype to rest.

First, however, Lincoln had to rid himself of the notion. He worried that he lacked sufficient poise to address such an audience. But an Illinois newspaper editor named William H. Bailhache received an encouraging letter from the organizer of the Plymouth Church lecture series, a letter praising Lincoln's Cincinnati speech. So Bailhache told Lincoln to put aside his misgivings and accept the invitation. Billy Herndon said the very same thing.

Lincoln took their advice, but he flirted for a while with the idea of giving a lecture on a topic more elevated than politics. By the time he dismissed the idea, there were no longer any speaking dates left in the Plymouth Church lecture series. But the friendly Chase supporter who had engineered the invitation—James Briggs—turned the matter over to the Young Men's Republican Union of New York, a group that was dominated by enemies of Seward. Lincoln was booked to give his speech in New York City in late February.

The speech that he composed was a command performance that would elevate him to the top of the Free Soil movement. Indeed, as Lincoln scholar Harold Holzer has argued, it was in many ways "the speech that made Abraham Lincoln president."[12]

Much of the speech would be targeted on the *Dred Scott* decision. After reviewing the dissent of Justice Curtis, Lincoln did some research of his own. He immersed himself in records of congressional proceedings that he found in the Illinois State Library in Springfield.

In time, Lincoln learned that he would be speaking at the Cooper Union (or "Cooper Institute"), a school founded two years earlier by the New York philanthropist Peter Cooper. Upon arriving in Manhattan, he checked into the Astor House Hotel. Even though he had visited New York City before, he felt keenly aware of his provincial origins. He was embarrassed by the fact that he could not read the menu in the restaurant because it was written in French.[13] When members of the Young Men's Republican Union paid a call upon him, they found him in a self-effacing mood.

But they took him up Broadway and showed him the sights. Then he stopped at the studio of Mathew Brady to have his photograph taken. At the studio he met the well-known historian George Bancroft. He told Bancroft that after his New York visit he would go on up to New England to visit his eldest son Robert, who had been enrolled at the Phillips Exeter Academy the year before. Robert "already knows much more than his father," Lincoln said.[14]

And so it was that on February 27, 1860—when he would give one of the most brilliant speeches of his life—Lincoln worried a lot about his hard-scrabble origins and lack of a college education. As he groped with these feelings, he summoned the confidence to compose an extraordinary speech that would sweep this cosmopolitan audience off its feet.

Fifteen hundred people were there. The poet William Cullen Bryant introduced Lincoln this way: "I have only to pronounce his name to secure your profound attention." Lincoln remained ill at ease for a moment or two and his gestures were awkward.

Within moments, however, his charisma took over and his manner was completely transformed. An observer reminisced about it later in an interview with the writer Noah Brooks:

> When Lincoln rose to speak, I was greatly disappointed. He was tall, tall—oh, how tall! And so angular and awkward that I had, for an instant, a feeling of pity for so ungainly a man. His clothes were black and ill-fitting, badly wrinkled. . . . He began in a low tone of voice. . . . He said "Mr. Cheerman," instead of "Mr. Chairman." . . . I said to myself: "Old fellow, you won't do; it's all very well for the wild West, but this will never go down in New York." But pretty soon he began to get into his subject; he straightened up, made regular and graceful gestures, his face lighted as with an inward fire; the whole man was transfigured. I forgot his clothes, his personal appearance, and his individual peculiarities. Presently, forgetting myself, I was on my feet with the rest, yelling like a wild Indian, cheering this wonderful man. . . . When he reached a climax, the thunders of applause were terrific. It was a great speech. When I came out of the hall, my face glowing with excitement and my frame all a-quiver, a friend,

with his eyes aglow, asked me what I thought of Abe Lincoln, the rail-splitter. I said: "He's the greatest man since St. Paul."[15]

It is easy to imagine the effect of this speech as one reads it, for the observations of Lincoln were trenchant and his language was superb. In this and in subsequent speeches from the spring of 1860 we hear for the very last time the fiery tone that Lincoln had been using in his speeches on slavery since 1854. In his presidential years, he would have to adopt a very different oratorical style.

He opened his attack upon the *Dred Scott* decision by proving that the claims of Roger Taney were absurd. He reviewed the historical facts about the Northwest Ordinance of 1787, which contained the evil of slavery above the Ohio River. His point was that the Founding Fathers had done exactly what Taney claimed was unconstitutional.

It was true that this law had been passed by the old Confederation Congress, before the federal Constitution was ratified. But once the new Constitution went into effect, a bill was introduced in the first federal Congress affirming that the Northwest Ordinance remained the law of the land. This bill, Lincoln showed, was introduced by one of the men who had signed the Constitution, and both houses of Congress went on to pass it unanimously. Moreover, in this Congress were sixteen of the men who had signed the Constitution at the federal convention in Philadelphia.

And this bill was promptly signed into law by none other than President George Washington, who had presided at the Constitutional Convention.

Taney argued that the Fifth Amendment made Congress incapable of preventing the spread of slavery into federal lands. Well it just so happened, said Lincoln, that the Fifth Amendment was debated and passed by the very same Congress that was going out of its way to confirm that the Northwest Ordinance remained a valid law And the Fifth Amendment and the act re-affirming the Northwest Ordinance were passed by the very same Congress *at the same time.*

So how could the Fifth Amendment be in any way inconsistent with the principles of Free Soil? Who was Taney to declare that he understood the Fifth Amendment better than the men who created it? There was no doubt at all that the U.S. Congress had the constitutional power to do exactly what the Republicans demanded: contain the evil of slavery.

Then, Lincoln turned to the leaders of the South and he refuted their assertion that Republicans were to blame for Harper's Ferry. He spoke to them *in absentia*: "You charge that we stir up insurrections among your slaves," he began; "we deny it; and what is your proof? Harper's Ferry! John Brown! John Brown was no Republican, and you have failed to implicate a single Republican in his Harper's Ferry enterprise. If any member of our party is guilty in that matter, you know it or you do not know it. If you do know it, you are inexcusable for not designating the man and proving the fact. If you do not know it, you are inexcusable for asserting it."[16]

Lincoln accused the pro-slavery Southerners of encouraging treason with their threats of secession: "You will not abide the election of a Republican President! In that supposed event, you say, you will destroy the Union; and then, you say, the great crime of having destroyed it will be upon us! That is cool. A highwayman holds a pistol to my ear, and mutters through his teeth, 'Stand and deliver, or I shall kill you, and then you will be a murderer!'"[17]

Slave-owners, said Lincoln, were tyrants who had to be resisted. They thought they had the right to control what everybody else in the United States should be allowed to think. Nothing less than surrender would appease them. They demanded in effect that Republicans must

> cease to call slavery wrong, and join them in calling it right. . . .
> Silence will not be tolerated—we must place ourselves avowedly
> with them. . . . We must arrest and return their fugitive slaves with
> greedy pleasure. We must pull down our Free State constitutions.
> The whole atmosphere must be disinfected from all taint of opposi-
> tion to slavery, before they will cease to believe that all their troubles
> proceed from us.[18]

All this, Lincoln said, "we could readily grant" if we believed that slavery was right. But "thinking it wrong, as we do, can we yield to them?" No—Republicans should "stand by our duty" and resist all demands to back down:

> Let us be diverted by none of those sophistical contrivances where-
> with we are so industriously plied and belabored—contrivances such
> as groping for some middle ground between the right and the wrong,
> vain as the search for a man who should be neither a living man nor a
> dead man—such as a policy of "don't care" on a question about which

all true men do care—such as Union appeals beseeching true Union men to yield to Disunionists, reversing the divine rule, and calling, not the sinners, but the righteous to repentance—such as invocations to Washington, imploring men to unsay what Washington said, and undo what Washington did. Neither let us be slandered from our duty by false accusations against us, nor frightened from it by menaces of destruction to the Government nor of dungeons to ourselves. LET US HAVE THE FAITH THAT RIGHT MAKES MIGHT, AND IN THAT FAITH, LET US, TO THE END, DARE TO DO OUR DUTY AS WE UNDERSTAND IT.[19]

The roar of approval was deafening as Lincoln concluded. People threw their hats in the air and went wild. William Cullen Bryant called it "the best political speech he ever heard in his life."[20] Horace Greeley called it "the very best political address to which I ever listened."[21]

The Cooper Union speech was a *tour de force*, and by sweeping these sophisticates into delirium, Lincoln made an unforgettable impression on some of the people who would help to determine the presidential choice of the Republican Party in 1860.

The speech was reprinted in pamphlet form and thousands of copies were distributed. Speaking invitations poured in, and so the trip to visit Robert in New England turned into a multi-state speaking tour. By the time it was over, Lincoln had given rapid-fire speeches in New Hampshire, Rhode Island, and Connecticut. The tour did more than just increase his popularity. It gave him an opportunity to weld the different factions of the Republican Party together.

In the previous year he had warned against factionalism, especially when it came to the party's anti-slavery program. In a letter to Schuyler Colfax, he argued that "the point of danger is the temptation in different localities to 'platform' there for something which will be popular just there, but which, nevertheless, will be a firebrand elsewhere, and especially in a national convention."[22] The danger in New England, he sensed, was the temptation on the part of abolitionists to push a more advanced anti-slavery agenda that might jeopardize the party's chances in the critical lower-northern swing states.

So he seized the opportunity in March to convince New Englanders to limit their anti-slavery advocacy (for the time being) to containment of the evil. In New Haven on March 6, he made this case by means of a vivid and entertaining metaphor:

> If I saw a venomous snake crawling in the road, any man might say I might seize the nearest stick and kill it; but if I found that snake in bed with my children, that would be another question. (Laughter.) I might hurt the children more than the snake, and it might bite them. (Applause.) Much more, if I found it in bed with my neighbor's children, and I had bound myself by a solemn compact not to meddle with his children under any circumstances, it would become me to let that particular mode of getting rid of the gentleman alone. (Great laughter.) But if there was a bed newly made up, to which the children were to be taken, and it was proposed to take a batch of young snakes and put them there with them, I take it no man in the world would say there was any question how I ought to decide! (Prolonged applause and cheers.) That is just the case! The new Territories are the newly made bed to which our children are to go, and it lies with the nation to say whether they shall have snakes mixed up with them or not.[23]

In another speech, his defense of free labor—as opposed to involuntary servitude—included an endorsement of the right to go on strike: "I am glad to know that there is a system of labor where the laborer can strike if he wants to! I would to God that such a system prevailed all over the world."[24]

As he prepared to return to Illinois, a New Hampshire editor named George G. Fogg wrote that the "blessings and hopes of many thousands who have seen and heard him for the first time, will go with him."[25] Fogg was a member of the Republican National Committee.

A growing number of people had the feeling that Lincoln might turn out to be one of history's great men. On March 31, on his way back to Springfield, he was invited to the Chicago studio of the sculptor Leonard Volk, who proceeded to create a plaster-cast "life mask" to be used as the basis for a sculpted portrait.

The Republican national convention in Chicago would begin on May 16, and in March and April the supporters of Lincoln were busy. At one and the same time they had to solidify support within the Illinois delegation and position Lincoln to attract support elsewhere. They had to avoid making needless enemies. Seward, the front-runner, and Chase, his most significant rival, had been making a great many enemies. Both had allowed their strong egos to get out of control; they behaved in imperious ways that offended people. Lincoln's obvious move was to turn their character flaws to his advantage.

On March 24, he set down his thoughts in a letter to Samuel Galloway, a supporter. "My name is new in the field," he acknowledged, "and I suppose I am not the *first* choice of a great many. Our policy, then, is to give no offense to others—leave them in a mood to come to us, if they shall be compelled to give up their first love."[26] A month later he began to admit that "the taste *is* in my mouth a little."[27]

As he wrote those words, the disaster for the Democratic Party was unfolding. The Democrats' convention had opened in Charleston, South Carolina, on April 23. When they voted to adjourn on May 3, they did not have a candidate. Douglas failed to win the nomination. But he and his supporters voted down the proposed federal slave code that southern militants demanded. When that happened, William Lowndes Yancey of Alabama led a walk-out of slave-state delegates.

Democratic leaders called another convention that would meet a month later in Baltimore. Meanwhile, southern Unionists created a new party—the Constitutional Union Party—and nominated John Bell of Tennessee for the presidency.

On May 9 and 10, Republicans from all over Illinois got together in Decatur to choose a gubernatorial candidate and write a platform. Lincoln arrived the night before and checked into a hotel.

Over three thousand people assembled in a convention hall that accommodated only nine hundred. Lincoln was sitting in the back. All of a sudden a Lincoln supporter named Richard J. Oglesby made an announcement: "I am informed that a distinguished citizen of Illinois, and one whom Illinois ever delights to honor, is present, and I wish to move that this body invite him to take a seat on the stand." After Oglesby shouted out "Abraham Lincoln," a roar of approval arose and supporters lifted Lincoln high over the heads of the delegates and passed him along until he took his place of honor at the front.

A short while later, Oglesby interrupted the proceedings again to announce that "an old Democrat of Macon County . . . desires to make a contribution to the Convention." Lincoln's cousin John Hanks and a friend burst into the hall. They carried with them two fence rails along with a sign that bore the following text: "Abraham Lincoln, The Rail

Candidate for President in 1860. Two rails from a lot of 3,000 made in 1830 by Thos. Hanks and Abe Lincoln—whose father was the first pioneer of Macon County." More delighted commotion erupted.[28]

The next day, delegate John M. Palmer introduced a resolution "that Abraham Lincoln is the first choice of Illinois for the Presidency, and that our delegates be instructed to use all honorable means for his nomination by the Chicago convention, and to cast their votes as a unit for him." The resolution passed overwhelmingly.

The Republican convention would meet in a huge and newly constructed two-story assembly hall that was built (in less than a month) for the Republican convention. Called the "Wigwam," it could accommodate twelve thousand people.

The supporters of the front-runner, Seward, arrived full of confidence. They had raised vast sums for their candidate, and they bragged that this war chest would make their man unbeatable in the general election.

But many Republicans recoiled from what seemed to them an ugly emphasis on money. They worried that a Seward administration might prove to be corrupt and they feared the influence of Seward's chief political backer, Thurlow Weed. Weed was a publisher and a man of great political influence in New York. He engineered deals in the state legislature that some regarded as sleazy, and his Albany "machine" made significant numbers of Republicans (including some New Yorkers like Horace Greeley) resistant to the candidacy of Seward. Another presidential candidate, Simon Cameron, was also dogged by an evil reputation for corruption, but Seward, the front-runner, was the man to beat.

Seward also continued to suffer from the widespread perception that his "radical" image would ruin the Republicans' chances of carrying the lower-northern swing states. More and more, the candidacy of Chase was raising similar fears.

So Lincoln's managers knew what they needed to do. They had to prevent Seward from gathering enough support to win the nomination on the first ballot. They had to send the message that Lincoln was supremely electable, the most electable of all the candidates, a strong contender in the swing states, and a candidate whose record was unsullied with corruption. The reputation of "Honest Abe"—the reputation that would blind so many to the depth of his shrewdness and cunning—was emphasized in 1860 for a reason that was perfectly germane: he was averse to financial impropriety.

Lincoln's managers had to work steadily, persuading the delegates who supported other candidates to view Lincoln as a smart "second choice" if they were forced to give up their first choice. And they had to work quietly enough to avoid the emergence of a "stop-Lincoln" campaign among the other candidates.

Lincoln's team of supporters checked into the Tremont House Hotel. Lincoln himself stayed behind—waiting in Springfield.

The self-appointed leader of the Lincoln-for-president team was his old friend Judge David Davis. Leonard Swett described Davis as "the most thorough manager of men I ever knew," and his pre-eminence among the other Lincoln supporters appeared to be so natural at the time that no one resisted.[29] Davis urged the other members of the Lincoln team to "put yourself at my disposal day and night."[30]

About twenty-five men were serving as Lincoln's agents, and among them were long-time supporters such as Swett, Norman Judd, and Jesse Fell. Lincoln's old law partner Stephen T. Logan was there, and so was Orville Browning. Others of note included Ward Hill Lamon, a lawyer who had known Lincoln since 1852. Lamon was becoming such an ardent admirer of Lincoln that he would soon appoint himself his unofficial bodyguard.

Davis divided these men into teams of two and three. Their assignment was to greet arriving delegates and win them over through friendliness. One of Lincoln's agents, Nathan M. Knapp, cabled Lincoln before the convention and reported as follows. "Keep a good nerve," he told the candidate, and "be not surprised at any result." Knapp and the other Lincoln agents were "dealing tenderly with delegates, taking them in detail, and making no fuss. Be not too expectant," he cautioned, "but rely upon our discretion. Again I say brace your nerves for any result."[31]

When the convention opened, Lincoln's operatives sensed that the most serious competitor was Edward Bates. Seward's shortcomings would in all likelihood prevent him from receiving a majority on the first ballot. Both Chase and Cameron were widely deemed unelectable. But Bates had gotten support with the same sort of pitch that Lincoln's agents were using: he was thought to be a good, safe choice for carrying the swing states. And since Bates had made inroads with the Indiana and Pennsylvania delegations, Lincoln's people saw where they needed to prioritize their efforts.

Their work paid off with the Indiana delegates. Lincoln's agents used various tactics to win them over. Former Illinois lieutenant governor

Gustave Koerner said that Bates's support for Know Nothings made his candidacy unacceptable for German-Americans. Browning gave an impassioned impromptu speech and he argued that Lincoln was the only man who had a realistic chance of stopping Seward. That convinced Henry Lane, the Republicans' candidate for the governorship of Indiana. Lane hated Seward so much that he threatened to withdraw as a gubernatorial candidate if Seward won the nomination. Meanwhile, a leading Bates supporter in Indiana, Caleb B. Smith, was (according to some) promised a cabinet position in the Lincoln administration.

Lincoln sent a message to his agents instructing them to "make no contracts that will bind me."[32] When the message was read at a Lincoln caucus by Edward Baker, laughter erupted. Davis supposedly chuckled that "Lincoln ain't here, and don't know what we have to meet, so we will go ahead, as if we hadn't heard from him."[33]

Far into the night on May 17, Davis and the others bargained in a caucus of delegates from swing states, including Pennsylvania. According to several sources, a cabinet position was offered to Cameron in return for Pennsylvania's votes—on the second ballot. It was widely understood that Pennsylvania delegates would have to vote for Cameron the first time around. But his supporters would be up for grabs on the second ballot and that was what Davis was counting on.

There can be no doubt that some binding deals were made for Lincoln—and without his knowledge. Swett later told him that the way his supporters had gotten "the Cameron leaders to throw the bulk of their support to you" was the lure of patronage.[34]

On Friday, May 18, the scene at the Wigwam was never to be forgotten by those who were there. One observer recalled that the hall itself was "decorated so completely with flags, banners, bunting, etc.," that it was like "a gorgeous pavilion aflame with color."[35] Both the Seward forces and the Lincoln forces recruited vast throngs who were prepared to shout themselves hoarse.

Seward's supporters brought the house down when his name was placed in nomination. "Looking from the stage over the vast amphitheater," one journalist wrote, "nothing was to be seen below but thousands of hats—a black swarm of hats—flying with the velocity of hornets over a mass of human heads."[36] But according to the very same reporter, when Lincoln was nominated, "the uproar that followed was beyond description."[37]

The result of the first ballot was shocking to Seward's supporters: he needed 233 votes to win but he only got 173. Lincoln was stronger than many had imagined. He got 102 votes on the first ballot and then he picked up more on the second. None of the other challengers to Seward was anywhere close to this level of support. On the third ballot, an avalanche of vote-switching started and a landslide for Lincoln gave him far more votes than he needed to clinch the nomination.

John A. Andrew of Massachusetts recalled the scene when the final tally was announced. There arose from the crowd a great "peal of human voices, a grand chorus of exultation, the like of which has not been heard on earth since the morning stars first sang together, and sons of God shouted for joy."[38]

An artillery salute was fired from the roof of the Tremont House Hotel. The same thing happened back in Springfield. Church bells tolled and the streets of the city filled with people. After speeches at the statehouse, a crowd of well-wishers thronged the Lincoln home, and Lincoln quickly invited them in. "We'll give you a larger house on the fourth of next March," said one of his admirers.[39]

Over the summer of 1860, the prospect of an enormous Republican triumph began to shape up. Lincoln's strategy of good will toward his rivals paid off, and though some of the followers of Seward were bitter, they slowly began to come around. But Seward continued to be bitter.

Lincoln's managers held out the olive branch by offering Seward and his people a say in the choice of Lincoln's running mate. Though neither Seward nor his backers had any interest in the post for themselves, one of them, Senator Preston King, suggested Senator Hannibal Hamlin of Maine. Though Hamlin had no genuine interest in being vice president, he agreed to help out the party.

The Republican platform condemned both popular sovereignty and secession threats. It advocated internal improvements—including support for a transcontinental railroad—of the very sort that Henry Clay had once espoused. It called for homestead legislation and adopted a generous position on immigration, a victory for men like Lincoln.

The Republican National Committee sent a delegation to Springfield to inform Lincoln of his nomination, a standard procedure in the days before nominees gave acceptance speeches.

He did no active campaigning, which was also normal for presidential candidates—though he did write another autobiographical essay for the use of journalists. But Republicans mounted a jubilant campaign on the scale of the Whigs' old "Tippecanoe" campaign of 1840. They made abundant use of the "railsplitter" image and they called their candidate "Honest Old Abe." As to that, even Joshua Giddings, Lincoln's anti-slavery mentor from his days in Congress, told him that the paramount issue for many in election year 1860 was the fact that "you are an *honest* man" and "not in the hands of corrupt or dishonest men."[40]

His demeanor during the 1860 campaign was one of humble dignity. He seemed to be genuinely awed by his new situation. He was aware of the danger that success might go to his head and he even joked about it. Orville Browning observed that he bore "his honors meekly" in 1860.[41]

He seemed averse to all the hoopla, an attitude that certainly contrasts with his feelings back in 1848 when he told Billy Herndon to gather all the "shrewd wild boys" about town to whoop and holler for "Old Rough and Ready." But in 1860 he had a much greater sense of mission and transcendent purpose. He was also self-conscious and he knew he came off as a provincial. So now, as he contemplated the prospect of becoming the nation's highest magistrate, he became introspective.

If he did suffer pangs of residual insecurity, there was a basis for it in the signals he was picking up from others. He was indeed being scrutinized by snobbish easterners.

Thurlow Weed came west to see Lincoln, but he took his time about making the appointment. He did some sightseeing, looking over the Illinois landscape where "candidates for president grew, expanded and developed without the polishing aid of eastern refinement, and the aid of the educating influence of her colleges."[42] But when Weed had his meeting with Lincoln, he came away satisfied.

Lincoln's humble origins turned out to be a considerable asset during the 1860 campaign. Thousands of people found the story of his life inspiring. John A. Kasson, an Iowa politician, wrote that "I never talk to an audience of farmers without noticing the intense interest as they listen to the story of his life & trials in making himself what he is,—the ablest & most eminent man in the West."[43] A farmer in Ohio said he liked the fact that Lincoln was "a self-made man, who came up a-foot. We like his tact—we like his argumentative powers—we like his logic, and we like the whole man."[44]

All summer people came to visit him, consult with him, and take his measure. Artists came to paint his portrait. He was given the use of the governor's office in the Illinois statehouse after his presidential nomination.

Lincoln's office was flooded with massive correspondence, and he soon required a secretary to help him keep up with it. He chose a young man named John G. Nicolay, a German-born writer who had clerked for the Illinois secretary of state. Before long he needed even more secretarial help, so he hired John Hay, a graduate of Brown University and the nephew of an old friend.

Sometime in the spring of 1860, a spontaneous movement arose among young Republicans. Some said the movement began in Connecticut, but no one knew for sure. It was a movement to create new marching clubs with a message—a solemn message. By summer, all over the North and even in the far West, these marching clubs were active. They were called "Wide Awakes," and they usually marched at night. They marched in silence except for the beating of a drum. The members wore oilskin capes and military-style caps. They carried whale-oil lanterns on poles and their insignia was an all-seeing eye.

They were "wide-awake" to the danger of the southern "Slave Power." As if in response to Lincoln's House Divided speech, these clubs sent a stern new message to the South: the attempt to nationalize slavery would fail since the machinations of the plotters were being observed.

The paramilitary air of the Wide Awake clubs could also be seen in the fad for creating new "Zouave" militias. Inspired by the exploits of some elite French colonial troops from Algeria who fought in the Crimean War—soldiers whose uniform was based upon the garb of North African tribesmen—young men in the North began to form such units in 1858. Their outfit consisted of a fez, baggy trousers, and an open-fronted jacket. Their drill routine was extraordinarily athletic and it incorporated elements of gymnastics.

A young clerk named Elmer Ephraim Ellsworth helped found a Zouave militia in Chicago and before long he was a national celebrity. He led his cadets in what was called a "national" tour in 1860—a tour that pointedly excluded the South—and on their way back to Illinois these cadets performed in Springfield. Lincoln joined the crowd of rapt onlookers, and after the performance he struck up a conversation with Ellsworth. The men liked each other and Ellsworth was hired as a law clerk in the firm of Lincoln and Herndon. He befriended Lincoln's sons Willie and Tad.

As attitudes on the slavery question hardened in the North, the same thing happened in the South. In fact, a growing sense of dread gripped the minds of white southerners in the summer of 1860.

A series of fires in Texas were ascribed to abolitionist sabotage. Vigilantes unleashed a reign of terror and scores of people, both black and white, were killed by rampaging lynch mobs. Southern newspapers juxtaposed the imagery of the fires in Texas with the flames in the lanterns of the northern Wide Awakes. Northern "fanatics," it was said, were preparing to spill the blood of white southerners.

Southern editors warned that the election of Lincoln would usher in the kind of apocalypse that John C. Calhoun had foretold. In October 1860, the *Charleston Mercury* described what would happen if Republicans took over the executive branch. With the Republican Party "enthroned at Washington," the newspaper warned, "the *under*-ground railroad will become an over-ground railroad" since the Fugitive Slave Law would not be reliably enforced. And "with the tenure of slave property . . . felt to be weakened, the Frontier States" (i.e., the border slave states that were closest to the North) would "*enter on the policy of making themselves Free States*" and the slaves in those states would "be sent to the Cotton States for sale."

"With the control of the Government of the United States, and an organized and triumphant North to sustain them," the editorial continued, "the Abolitionists will renew their operations upon the South with increased courage." Once Republicans began to appoint southern post-masters, there would be no more censorship of the mail to destroy abolitionist literature. So abolitionism would begin to influence the thoughts and the ethical reflections of more and more southern whites.

Sooner or later, "they will have an Abolition Party in the South, of Southern men," the editorial predicted. "The contest for slavery will no longer be one between the North and the South. It will be in the South, between the people of the South."

In other words, Republican policies would overpower the police state that the southern master class had created.

"If in our present position of power and unitedness, we have the raid of John Brown," the editorial concluded, "what will be the measures of insurrection and incendiarism, which must follow our notorious and abject prostration to Abolition rule at Washington?"[45]

It is likely—indeed probable—that Lincoln read this editorial, since Herndon subscribed to the *Charleston Mercury* and Lincoln made a point of reading it.

But he refused to give credence to the threats of secession. He wrote in August that "the people of the South have too much of good sense, and good temper, to attempt the ruin of the government, rather than see it administered as it was administered by the men who made it. At least, so I hope and believe."[46]

But when a Tennessean urged him to make some new statements to reassure the South, he demurred. "In my judgment," he wrote, "it would do no good. I have already done this many . . . times; and it is in print, and open to all who will read, or heed."[47]

Pro-slavery threats continued and began to escalate. A Georgia newspaper declared that "the south will never permit Abraham Lincoln to be President of the United States. . . . Whether the Potomac is crimsoned in human gore, and Pennsylvania avenue is paved ten fathoms in depth with mangled bodies. . . . The south, the loyal south, the constitutional south, will never submit to such humiliation and degradation as the inauguration of Abraham Lincoln."[48] The voices of southern nationalists—the so-called "Fire-Eaters" such as Edmund Ruffin, Robert Barnwell Rhett, Louis Wigfall, and William Lowndes Yancey—were heeded increasingly. And northern Democrats abetted such feelings with their ugly and maniacal bigotry.

Anti-slavery leaders, who differed among themselves in a great many ways, differed too in their reactions to Lincoln. Some of them were impatient with political temporizing and they had no respect for "the art of the possible." Indeed, a prominent New England abolitionist named Wendell Phillips held Lincoln in contempt. He called him "the slave hound of Illinois" because he would not advocate the repeal of the Fugitive Slave Law.

But other abolitionists were far more reasonable in the way they viewed Lincoln. Lydia Maria Child shared the following observations with Charles Sumner:

> I don't place much reliance on any political party; but I am inclined to think this Mr. Lincoln . . . is an honest, independent man, and sincerely a friend to freedom. *One* thing makes me strongly inclined to like him and trust him. At a public meeting in Illinois, two years ago, in discussion with Stephen A. Douglas, he said "A negro is my equal;

as good as I am." Considering that Lincoln came from Kentucky, and that his adopted state, Illinois, is very pro-slavery, I think he was a brave man to entertain such a sentiment and announce it.[49]

Gerrit Smith, an abolitionist whom the Liberty Party nominated for the presidency in 1860, was also impressed. In a letter to Joshua Giddings, Smith said that Lincoln "is in his heart an abolitionist" and that his victory in November should be regarded quite rightly as "an Abolition victory."[50]

Frederick Douglass, the pre-eminent black abolitionist, was prepared to work in partnership with politicians. He credited Lincoln with "a cool well-balanced head" and with "firmness of will."[51] While Douglass supported Gerrit Smith, he proclaimed that "the Republican party carries with it the anti-slavery sentiment of the North, and . . . a victory gained by it in the present canvass will be a victory gained by that sentiment over the wickedly aggressive pro-slavery sentiment."[52]

The smash-up of the Democratic Party continued when its next convention met in Baltimore. Some of the militants who bolted from the Charleston convention declined to go to Baltimore at all. They met in Richmond by themselves. The rest went to Baltimore but walked out again when Douglas won the nomination. They held their own convention and nominated John C. Breckinridge of Kentucky, who had served as vice president under Buchanan.

The candidacy of Douglas was foredoomed in 1860 since most southern Democrats rallied either to Bell or Breckinridge.

Northern Democrats used the racial issue for all it was worth and they used it with shrill desperation. In Lincoln's home state, for instance, the *Chicago Herald* cited his speech of July 10, 1858, and ridiculed it by calling blacks "naked, greasy, bandy-shanked, blubber-lipped, monkey-headed, muskrat scented cannibals from Congo and Guinea."[53] The *Illinois State Register* condemned Lincoln's "detestable doctrines" that would "mingle the African with the blood of the whites, by intermarriage with your sisters and daughters."[54]

So pervasive was the doctrine of white supremacy that Republicans sometimes declined to challenge it. They used the old logic of the Free Soil movement: they argued that the platform adopted by Lincoln and his party was designed to keep blacks *away* from federal territories. The

Indianapolis Daily Journal declared it was nonsensical to use the cry "'nigger equality' against a party, the first cardinal principle of whose creed is, exclusion of Niggers from the Territories."[55]

But however pervasive race bigotry was, the Republicans were in a very strong position. They benefitted from the Democrats' divisions, and their Whig-derived principles of active government were supported by a great many groups who stood to benefit. The Free Soil movement had been gathering strength for years and white racists had been active from the start.

Perhaps most telling was northern resentment of the southern threats to secede. William Cullen Bryant compared the South to "a spoiled child." Everything the South demanded, he wrote, "has been eagerly given it; more eagerly still if it threatens to cut off its nurse's ears. The more we give it the louder it cries and the more furious its threats; and now we have Northern men writing long letters to persuade their readers that it will actually cut off its nurse's ears if we . . . elect a President of our own choice."[56]

We will never know how pervasive such feelings might have been in 1860, but Republicans swept the free states in congressional and gubernatorial elections in September and October. On November 6, Lincoln sat in the Illinois governor's office, then went out to vote in mid-afternoon. Cheering crowds followed him all the way down to the courthouse and back. By evening, the statehouse crowd was immense, so Lincoln and some friends walked over to the telegraph office to review the returns as they came in.

Despite a few tense moments, the news was very good and it kept getting better. They took a break around midnight to enjoy some refreshments, then returned. In the early hours of the morning, there was no doubt about it: Lincoln had won a massive triumph.

He got 39.9 percent of the popular vote—far more than any of his rivals. More importantly, he won the electoral vote in every one of the free states except New Jersey. As for the slave states—the Republicans had not even bothered to push his candidacy.

On November 9, only three days after the election, the South Carolina General Assembly passed a "Resolution to Call the Election of Abraham Lincoln as United States President a Hostile Act." The next day the assembly called for a "Convention of the People of South Carolina" to consider secession.

Elections for the delegates took place on December 6 and they voted unanimously for secession on December 17. The secession ordinance was issued on December 20, and the convention issued a proclamation explaining its decision.

The proclamation stated that the "ends for which this Government [i.e., the federal government] was instituted have been defeated, and the Government itself has been made destructive of them by the action of the non-slaveholding states." Specifically,

> those States have assumed the right of deciding upon the propriety of our domestic institutions; and have denied the rights of property established in fifteen of the States and recognized by the Constitution; they have denounced as sinful the institution of slavery; they have permitted open establishment among them of societies, whose avowed object is to disturb the peace and to eloign the property of the citizens of other States. They have encouraged and assisted thousands of our slaves to leave their homes; and those who remain, have been incited by emissaries, books and pictures to servile insurrection.

And now, the proclamation continued, "a sectional party" had elected a president "hostile to slavery. He is to be entrusted with the administration of the common Government, because he has declared that 'Government cannot endure permanently half slave, half free,' and that the public mind must rest in the belief that slavery is in the course of ultimate extinction." Moreover,

> on the 4th day of March next, this party will take possession of the Government. It has announced that the South shall be excluded from the common territory, that the judicial tribunals shall be made sectional, and that a war must be waged against slavery until it shall cease throughout the United States. The guaranties of the Constitution will then no longer exist; the equal rights of the States will be lost. The slaveholding States will no longer have the power of self-government, or self-protection, and the Federal Government will have become their enemy.

Republicans would force a reconsideration of the *Dred Scott* decision by a packed Supreme Court. The existing slave states would be powerless to stop an anti-slavery amendment to the Constitution when a supermajority of free states voted to ratify one.

The game was over.

It was time to put slavery beyond the reach of the federal Constitution, beyond the reach of the people in the free states, beyond the reach of the Republican Party, beyond the reach of anyone. There was only one way to do it:

> We, therefore, the People of South Carolina, by our delegates in Convention assembled, appealing to the Supreme Judge of the world for the rectitude of our intentions, have solemnly declared that the Union heretofore existing between this State and the other States of North America, is dissolved, and that the State of South Carolina has resumed her position among the nations of the world, as a separate and independent State; with full power to levy war, conclude peace, contract alliances, establish commerce, and to do all other acts and things which independent States may of right do.[57]

The election of Abraham Lincoln had broken the Union—perhaps forever.

IV

AT THE HELM

10

CRISIS

The election unleashed a reaction so explosive that Lincoln faced the strong probability of war. He would have to measure up to a challenge of vast dimensions.

From November through January he received a flood of visitors and he met with them daily. He continued to use the governor's office in the statehouse until the end of the year. Visitors of all kinds flocked to see him. They offered advice, begged favors, and sought jobs. Some merely wanted to look at the man who would soon get a chance to shape history on the grand scale.

Lincoln was inundated with correspondence, and his secretaries worked hard to keep up with it. He tried to read most of the letters, especially the short ones. Some (not surprisingly) were written by cranks, but others—especially the letters pouring in from the South—were genuinely ominous. Some were laced with obscenities and some of them threatened his life.

It would "do no good to put him out of the way," Lincoln said, since the vice president-elect had "plenty of *Pluck*."[1] But his superstitious streak came to life and it led to a morbid occurrence. According to writer Noah Brooks, Lincoln told him the following story in 1864:

It was just after my election in 1860. . . . I was well tired out, and went home to rest, throwing myself down on a lounge in my chamber.

189

Opposite where I lay was a bureau, with a swinging-glass upon it . . . and, looking into the glass, I saw myself reflected, nearly at full length; but my face, I noticed, had two separate and distinct images. . . . I was a little bothered, perhaps startled, and got up and looked in the glass, but the illusion vanished. On lying down again I saw it a second time—plainer, if possible, than before; and then I noticed that one of the faces was a little paler, say five shades, than the other. I got up and the thing melted away, and I went off and, in the excitement of the hour, forgot all about it nearly, but not quite, for the thing would once in a while come up, and give me a little pang.

A few days later, he "tried the experiment again, when (with a laugh), sure enough, the thing came again; but I never succeeded in bringing the ghost back after that, though I once tried very industriously to show it to my wife." Mrs. Lincoln believed it was "a 'sign' that I was to be elected to a second term of office, and that the paleness of one of the faces was an omen that I should not see life through the last term."[2] Lincoln told the story in substantially the same form to Ward Hill Lamon.[3]

As soon as the election was over, Lincoln turned to the selection of a cabinet. He decided to bring most of his competitors into the cabinet in order to draw upon their individual and collective strengths. He would need as many power sources as possible in the dark days ahead.

He also considered the merits of bringing some Democrats, southerners, and border-state men to his team. But he pondered the problems such people could cause: they might foment dissension that would make the task of governing more difficult.

He did not want a bevy of sycophants. He wanted men of substance, advisors who could see different angles of complicated problems, men of resourcefulness who could be political assets. They would need to be managed, since people like that can sometimes have egos that are out of proportion to their gifts. Lincoln was not afraid to tackle this problem. When someone advised him against giving a post to Salmon Chase because he thought himself "a great deal bigger" than Lincoln, the president-elect asked the following question: "Do you know of any other men who think they are bigger than I am? I want to put them all in my cabinet."[4]

He would always be able to trust his own instincts and rely on his own intuition. So there was little to be risked and a lot to be gained by surrounding himself with men of power. After Thurlow Weed got to know him better (they conferred about cabinet appointments on December 20), he observed that Lincoln "sees all" who approach him, "hears all they have to say, talks freely with everybody, reads whatever is written to him, but thinks and acts by himself."[5]

The first order of business was getting Seward into the cabinet. Touchy, arrogant, charming, gregarious, and prone to delusions of grandeur (depending on his moods), he was a challenge. His strengths would have to be harnessed and his weaknesses kept under firm control.

Lincoln used his vice president-elect as an emissary. In late November Hannibal Hamlin came to Chicago. On December 8, Lincoln gave him two letters to be hand-delivered to Seward, one of them a formal offer to appoint him secretary of state and the other one a personal appeal that was carefully composed. Seward took his time about considering the offer, but he finally accepted it on December 28.

Lincoln and others had been skeptical about the secession threat at first. Indeed, Lincoln regarded the threat as a bluff—"humbug" he called it—as early as 1856. And there was reason to believe that South Carolina could be isolated, for John Bell, the Constitutional Union candidate, and Stephen Douglas (a militant Unionist) won most of the upper South in the election of 1860.

Time would show that the Unionist sentiment in those states was largely concentrated in mountainous areas where the plantation system was weak—in western Virginia, for example, and east Tennessee. Both of those regions would become strategic objectives for Lincoln in the course of the Civil War.

Another reason to be hopeful was the fact that Alexander Stephens took a Unionist position in Georgia. Lincoln remembered him well from their days in the House of Representatives. He wrote to him in December, assuring him that he would make no moves to destabilize the social or political situation in the South. But he could not resist adding this direct observation: "You think slavery is *right* and ought to be extended; while we think it is *wrong* and ought to be restricted. That I suppose is the rub. It certainly is the only substantial difference between us."[6]

It was, and the difference would prove to be substantial enough to cause a war that would kill over six hundred thousand. And Lincoln knew that a war might be brewing.

There had always been a flip side to his skepticism about the possibility of secession. He had a worst-case position: if secession were attempted, he was fully prepared to go to war. He had warned as early as 1856 that a rebellion would be stopped and that the weight of the North's superior resources would be used to simply stamp it out. His power of holistic thinking, his ability to see the big picture in a flash, led him straight to the strategy that would emerge full-blown in the Civil War years as a doctrine of total war.

His commitment to the Union was also a matter of instinct. Like millions, he believed in the rightness of what the Founding Fathers had done and he believed that the United States of America was imbued with the potential to save the world from tyranny.

After all, he saved himself from tyranny—he gained freedom from paternal domination—and he wished to help others to empower themselves as he had done. Moreover, his empathy for those who were in pain made him hate and abominate slavery. He hated it ever since he first encountered it on his trips down the Mississippi River. He was telling the truth in his House Divided speech when he said that he wanted to put slavery on course for extinction, first in America, then everywhere else. America had to stay intact in order to perform that mission for the world.

The mission would never be performed if the South were allowed to create a new empire devoted to slavery.

So he had no intention of allowing any states to secede. And he had no intention of retracting his pledge to keep slavery contained. He made his intentions very clear in some remarks that were attributed to him in the *New York Herald* on January 28, 1861: "I will suffer death before I will consent or will advise my friends to consent to any concession or compromise which looks like buying the privilege of taking possession of this government to which we have a constitutional right."[7]

Reactions in the North to the South Carolina secession claim ran the gamut from sympathy to a willingness to let the slave states go (and good riddance) to calls for immediate war to proposals for new concessions to the South.

The lame duck president, Buchanan, proclaimed in his annual message to Congress that secession was unconstitutional. But he also alleged that the federal government possessed no legal power to stop it. He allowed the secessionists in South Carolina—and elsewhere as secessionism spread—to seize federal property including post offices, court houses, and military installations.

Lincoln was livid; a visitor reported in late December that the president-elect "has not yet had time to examine the list of vessels in our navy suitable for the purpose, but he intends to use them *all* if necessary, for blockading the ports in every seceding State, & the Army to garrison every fort on the coast, from Savannah to New Orleans."[8]

Republicans were generally divided between appeasers—"conservatives," so-called—and militants known as "Radical Republicans." Lincoln for the most part agreed with the Radicals, but Seward—the supposedly fearsome firebrand, the oracle who had spoken of an "irrepressible conflict" regarding slavery—was an appeaser and so was his supporter Thurlow Weed.

On December 18, Sen. John J. Crittenden of Kentucky offered a "compromise" package of six constitutional amendments along with some supplementary resolutions. They were all designed to contain the secession movement and isolate South Carolina. One of the proposed constitutional amendments was in direct violation of the 1860 Republican platform.

It would have revived the old Missouri Compromise line and extended it due West—as Polk had proposed back in 1848. This would have allowed the institution of slavery to spread not only in existing territories below the line but also in territories that might be acquired at some point in the future. Moreover, that amendment would be *unamendable*—as would all of the others, including the following: an amendment to force the federal government to compensate owners of runaway slaves; an amendment to prohibit Congress from abolishing slavery in places within its jurisdiction; and a coup-de-grace amendment to prohibit Congress from emancipating slaves or abolishing slavery in any state.

Seward supported this "compromise" in private, assuring himself that he was acting as a statesman who would save the Union. Lincoln, on the other hand, resisted the compromise in private while emphasizing Unionism in a manner that would *sound* conciliatory while yielding nothing substantial.

He was determined to stand his ground and confront both secessionists and appeasers. He would not back down from his commitments to the Union or to Free Soil. Whatever it took to maintain these positions would be backed up by maximum force. As to the Crittenden Compromise, he intended to kill it.

He dashed off a series of letters marked "Private & confidential" to congressional Republicans. To Illinois Congressman William Kellogg (an appeaser) he wrote the following on December 11: "Entertain no proposition for a compromise in regard to the *extension* of slavery. The instant you do, they have us under again; all our labor is lost, and sooner or later must be done over. . . . Have none of it. The tug has to come & better now than later."[9]

On December 13 he told Elihu Washburne that if Republicans agreed to a deal with the congressional appeasers, "immediately filibustering and extending slavery recommences. On that point hold firm, as with a chain of steel."[10] To Lyman Trumbull he wrote this message on December 17: "If any of our friends prove false, and fix up a compromise on the territorial question, I am for fighting again—that is all."[11]

To John A. Gilmer of North Carolina Lincoln sent this message: "Is it desired that I shall shift the ground upon which I have been elected? I can not do it. . . . It would make me appear as if I repented for the crime of being elected, and was anxious to apologize and beg forgiveness."[12]

He was preparing for war. He told Washburne to contact General Winfield Scott—the Army's general in chief—and have him make preparations to counteract Buchanan's dereliction of duty and reassert the federal authority: "Tell him, confidentially, I shall be obliged to him to be as well prepared as he can to either *hold*, or *retake*" any federal forts that secessionists might have attacked and be ready for action right after the Inauguration.[13]

Though Lincoln's attacks upon the Crittenden Compromise were marked "confidential," the news of his actions spread and his reputation as a man of strong will grew apace. Seward, on the other hand, was showing himself to be a feckless and flighty opportunist.

Lincoln did make a few symbolic gestures to put himself on record as a man of peace. In response to an entreaty from a Unionist Democrat named Duff Green who requested a conciliatory statement, Lincoln said that he did "not desire any amendment of the Constitution," but acknowledged that such questions "rightfully belong to the American people." Moreover, he condemned "the lawless invasion, by armed force, of any State or Territory, no matter under what pretext"—whatever that meant. But he also said he would not release this document unless half of the senators from states that had summoned secession conventions would sign a declaration calling for a halt to secessionism until "some act, deemed to be violative of our rights, shall be done by the incoming administration."[14]

Largely because of Lincoln's opposition, the Crittenden Compromise died. The Senate rejected it on January 16, 1861.

In the meantime, secessionism spread with extraordinary speed. Six states joined South Carolina in repudiating the federal Constitution in the early weeks of 1861: Mississippi on January 9, Florida on January 10, Alabama on January 11, Georgia on January 19, Louisiana on January 26, and Texas on February 1.

On February 4, commissioners from all of these states came together in Montgomery, Alabama, to draft a constitution for a nation to be called the Confederate States of America. A provisional president and vice president were selected, respectively Jefferson Davis of Mississippi and Alexander Stephens of Georgia.

The leaders who founded the Confederacy were acting to protect the institution of slavery and they said so. And the Confederate cause was grounded firmly in racism.

Stephens made this clear in a speech that he delivered in Savannah, Georgia, on March 21, 1861. He proclaimed that the Confederacy's "foundations are laid, its cornerstone rests, upon the great truth that the negro is not equal to the white man; that slavery, subordination to the superior race, is his natural and moral condition. This, our new Government, is the first, in the history of the world, based upon this great physical, philosophical, and moral truth."[15]

The Confederacy was indeed the first nation in the world to be based upon the doctrine of race. And this doctrine would lead in the future to other movements for race-based nationhood—in Germany and elsewhere.

The slow process of assembling a cabinet consumed a great deal of Lincoln's time in December and January. As he worked to get Seward, he reached out to another Republican competitor, Bates, who came to Springfield on December 15. After Lincoln offered him the attorney-generalship and Bates accepted, Lincoln tasked him with the challenge of examining the constitutional issues pertaining to secession. He also asked him to look into the legality of the mail censorship that was performed routinely by southern postmasters who destroyed anti-slavery literature that was sent through the U.S. mail.

Bates responded with a very tough line on both questions. He said he was "inflexibly opposed to secession, and strongly in favor of maintaining the government by force if necessary." As to mail censorship, he condemned the custom that "permitted petty postmasters to examine and burn everything they pleased."[16]

Through December and January, Lincoln struggled to choose the other members of his cabinet. He had a tough time deciding what to do about two politicians who had played key roles in securing him the Republican nomination: Simon Cameron of Pennsylvania and Caleb B. Smith of Indiana. Lincoln tried to find other men from Indiana and Pennsylvania whose appointments would satisfy the Republican leaders of those states, because he didn't like Cameron or Smith.

He knew that both of them were spoilsmen, and he was disinclined to offer them cabinet positions for fear they were corrupt.

He was under great pressure to establish a Republican cabinet with balance between former Democrats and former Whigs. He also wanted geographical balance if he could get it. Eventually he tapped Smith for the interior department.

As for Cameron, Lincoln was inundated with letters of support—some of them elicited by Davis in an effort to carry out the bargain he had made. Cameron was finishing a term in the U.S. Senate and he made it clear that he would like to be treasury secretary.

On December 31 Lincoln told him that he would receive that position or else be considered for appointment as secretary of war. Lincoln had grave doubts about the wisdom of sending Cameron to the treasury. So he introduced the idea of a different departmental position when he made his promise to Cameron—a promise in writing.

But a storm of protest erupted from Cameron's foes, a storm so intense that Lincoln fired off a cable to Cameron informing him that the offer of a cabinet position would have to be retracted. "Since seeing you," Lincoln wrote, "things have developed which make it impossible for me to take you into the cabinet." He told Cameron he was "not at liberty to specify" the trouble.[17] Cameron, angry and insulted, did nothing, and within a few weeks Lincoln had second thoughts. No proof of Cameron's crookedness had yet been delivered, so Lincoln played for time by sending off a mollifying letter that left the matter open.

The problem with Cameron affected Lincoln's offer of a cabinet position to a much more important politician: Salmon Chase. On December 31, Lincoln contacted Chase and requested a meeting as soon as possible. "In these troublous times," Lincoln wrote, "I would much like a conference with you. Please visit me here at once."[18]

Chase, who was both the incumbent governor and a senator-elect from Ohio, came to Springfield on January 4. Lincoln had a genuine respect for

Chase in light of his illustrious record of Free Soil leadership. But he confessed that for political reasons he would have to make him an offer that was far less definite than he wished. "I have done with you," Lincoln admitted, "what I would not perhaps have ventured to do with any other man in the country—sent for you to ask whether you will accept the appointment of Secretary of the Treasury, without, however, being exactly prepared to offer it to you." The problem, Lincoln confided, was "mainly the uncertainty whether the appointment would be satisfactory to Pennsylvania."[19]

Lincoln slowly decided to send Cameron to the war department, a less risky position than treasury in light of his bad reputation when it came to matters of money.

But he told a delegation from Pennsylvania on January 24 that since Cameron's opponents "charge him with corruption in obtaining contracts" the allegations would be scrutinized. And even if he chose to give Cameron a job, he would keep him under close observation. Moreover, Lincoln declared, if "I should be deceived by subsequent transactions of a disreputable character, *the responsibility will rest upon you gentlemen of Pennsylvania who have so strongly presented his claims to my consideration.*"[20]

Meanwhile, Lincoln sought to find a cabinet member from New England and another from a border-state, preferably Maryland. He asked Hamlin to advise him in regard to the New England appointment and Hamlin suggested either Gideon Welles of Connecticut or Nathaniel Banks of Massachusetts. Welles, whom Lincoln had met in his tour of New England in 1860, was an editor and politician.

The front runners for the Maryland position were Congressman Henry Winter Davis, a cousin of David Davis, and Montgomery Blair, who was the eldest son of the old Democratic Unionist Francis Preston Blair Sr., an adviser to Andrew Jackson.

Lincoln put off making any more decisions about cabinet appointments until he reached Washington. But at last he sent Welles to the navy department and appointed Blair postmaster-general. The Blairs had political influence in another one of the important border slave states, Missouri. Montgomery's younger brother Frank (Francis Preston Blair, Junior), was a congressman from Missouri, where a fierce battle against secession would rage throughout 1861.

The question of whether the United States of America constituted a permanent Union—though it might have appeared to be a very simple question—was in fact a conundrum. For the United States had functioned under *two* successive constitutions, and even though the first one, the "Articles of Confederation and Perpetual Union," proclaimed the Union perpetual, the second one—the Federal Constitution of 1787—said nothing whatsoever on the subject.

Those who believed that the permanence proclaimed by the Articles carried over to the new Constitution of 1787—and people such as Daniel Webster had been making that claim for many years—were on shaky ground. For secessionists could claim that the adoption of the Federal Constitution *destroyed* the Union that the Articles created and replaced it with a different sort of Union that was not perpetual at all.

It happened this way. The Constitution provided that as soon as any nine of the thirteen states had ratified it, it would take effect in those states. Any other state that declined to ratify the new Constitution would be on its own—provided that nine other states had adopted it. James Madison made it clear in *The Federalist* # 43 that there could be no constitutional connection between the states that had ratified the Constitution and states that declined to do so. The latter would be on their own in every single respect . . . left out.

And so it was that in the presidential election of 1788, the so-called "wayward sisters," North Carolina and Rhode Island, did not (and could not) participate. Since they had not yet ratified the federal Constitution, they could not choose electors for the Electoral College or send representatives to the new federal Congress.

North Carolina ratified the Constitution in 1789 and Rhode Island ratified it a year later. So they were "back" in the Union, but the question could be asked down the years: were they back within the very same "perpetual" Union or had their temporary absence from the overall polity created a new and very different kind of Union?

It could certainly be argued that the Union had been broken for a very brief time and then put back together in a different way. How could the Union have remained unchanged and "perpetual" if four of the thirteen states had been given a chance to opt out? What would have happened to North Carolina and Rhode Island—and what would have happened to the supposedly "perpetual" Union—if those states had never ratified the Constitution?

Though the constitutional metaphysics might have seemed clear enough in 1861 to opponents of secession, those issues would swirl within

Republican politics throughout the Civil War and then loom with great significance for post-war America when the guns fell silent.

Seward's resentment over losing the Republican nomination—and the presidency—made him restless. In the early months of 1861, he sought to pre-empt Lincoln while convincing himself that he was saving the country as he did so.

In January, as the lower southern states were joining the secession movement, Seward was in Washington. And since Lincoln would not be leaving for Washington until February 11, the secretary of state–designate decided it was up to him to take some action that would keep the so-called "Cotton States" from spreading their contagion. So he pushed for new compromise measures in the hope that he could keep the upper southern states from embracing secession.

Virginia had called for a "Peace Conference" that would meet in Washington beginning on February 4. Every state was invited to send delegates in the hope that they could find a solution to America's crisis. Republicans floundered. Scores of them flirted with the notion of abandoning or watering down their Free Soil principles for the sake of preserving the Union.

Among the symbolic gestures that Lincoln had made in December to show that he was a man of peace, he sent Seward some innocuous resolutions to be introduced in the Senate—resolutions affirming the Union's perpetuality and also affirming the validity (as statute law) of the Fugitive Slave Act. But these were not the resolutions that Seward introduced. Instead, he proposed some resolutions of his own that included an offer to guarantee the continuation of slavery where it already existed.

This was one of the origins of the notorious pro-slavery constitutional amendment—the so-called Corwin Amendment—that was working its way through Congress well before Lincoln took the presidential oath. Lincoln had nothing to do with introducing this "bad thirteenth amendment."

On January 12, Seward gave a major speech in the Senate without consulting Lincoln. He called for dividing the western territories into two enormous new states, with one of them to be designated a slave state and other one a free state. He called for a constitutional amendment to protect slavery where it existed. And he called for a new constitutional convention that would put an end to America's sectional division.

These proposals are extremely suggestive of what a Seward presidency would have been like, and they are also suggestive of what David Davis,

Leonard Swett, and the others accomplished when they stopped Seward's nomination. Seward's proposals might very well have made it impossible for Lincoln or anyone else to eradicate slavery in the United States.

But then—fearful that he might have gone too far—Seward wrote to Lincoln to inform him about what he did. We can only guess about Lincoln's thoughts and feelings when he heard about Seward's speech, but he sent off a tepid and noncommittal message to Seward—a superficially cheery reply that the speech was "doing good all over the country."[21] But there can be little doubt that he realized how treacherous William Seward could be. It would take Lincoln time to decide how to handle him. He could easily have cast him adrift, but he chose not to do that.

Perhaps it struck him that Seward would be far more dangerous outside of the administration than within it.

Apostasy was rife in Republican circles. A measure to admit New Mexico to statehood was gathering support, though New Mexico had already adopted a territorial slave code. In early February the Senate passed a bill organizing Colorado with no exclusion of slavery. Lincoln was privately disgusted: he reportedly told an acquaintance that "Douglas got the best of it in the election last fall. I am left to face . . . a great rebellion, while my own party endorses his popular sovereignty idea and applies it in legislation."[22]

On February 1, he sent a stern letter to Seward informing him that "on the territorial question—that is, the question of extending slavery under national auspices—I am inflexible." He continued:

I am for no compromise which *assists* or *permits* the extension of the institution on soil owned by the nation. And any trick by which the nation is to acquire territory, and then allow some local authority to spread slavery over it, is as obnoxious as any other. I take it that to effect some such result as this, and to put us again on the high-road to a slave-empire is the object of all these proposed compromises. I am against it.

But then he made a few concessions: "As to fugitive slaves, District of Columbia, slave trade among the slave states, and whatever springs of necessity from the fact that the institution is amongst us, I care but little, so that what is done be comely, and not altogether outrageous. Nor do I care much about New-Mexico, if further extension were hedged against."[23]

That concession was important, and it showed that even Lincoln would "give" just a little in this time of unprecedented crisis. But he was not really giving very much, for even if New Mexico became a slave state, the majority status of the free state bloc would remain intact—provided that no other slave states were admitted. The free state majority would continue to grow to the dimensions of a super-majority.

The time was approaching for Lincoln to begin his long journey to Washington—a trip that would be made even longer by the fact that he had accepted invitations to deliver some speeches along the way. People in the North were truly anxious to hear what the president-elect had to say to them.

In the final days of January Lincoln hid himself away so he could write his Inaugural Address. He began composing it in a little back room above a store on Springfield's public square. As to the inauguration ceremony, there were rumors that pro-slavery thugs might try to disrupt it—or disrupt the counting of electoral votes by Congress, or even try to assassinate Lincoln on his way to Washington or at the inauguration—anything to prevent him from taking office as president.

So Lincoln sought to make certain of the loyalty of General Winfield Scott since the general in chief was a Virginian. He sent Thomas S. Mather, the adjutant general of Illinois, to confer with the general, and Scott sent Lincoln a message that was reassuring. He told Mather to inform the president-elect that he should "come on to Washington as soon as he is ready. Say to him also that, when once here, I shall consider myself responsible for his safety. If necessary, I shall plant cannon at both ends of Pennsylvania Avenue, and if any Maryland or Virginia gentlemen who have become so threatening and troublesome of late show their heads or even venture to raise a finger, I shall blow them to hell!"[24]

Slowly Lincoln put his affairs in order and prepared himself and his family for the journey. Mary and Robert had been visiting New York on a shopping trip, and they returned to Springfield on January 25. Lincoln rented out the family's home, visited his elderly step-mother Sarah—she was living near Charleston, Illinois—threw a farewell party, and offered his books to Billy Herndon, who reminisced about their parting years later.

Lincoln observed that they had "never had a cross word" during all the sixteen years that they had practiced law together. He told his partner and friend that the signboard that bore the firm's name should "hang . . .

undisturbed" outside the office. "Give our clients to understand," he continued, "that the election of a President makes no change in the firm of Lincoln and Herndon. If I live I'm coming back some time, and then we'll go right on practicing law as if nothing had ever happened."[25]

He delivered a farewell address to his friends and neighbors at the train depot on the morning of February 11. He and John Nicolay wrote down the words that he had spoken as they sat together on the train. Nicolay, John Hay, and Robert Lincoln would be Lincoln's companions on the first leg of the long and arduous trip. Then Mary and the younger boys would follow and the whole group would proceed together from Indianapolis. Mary and the boys brought along with them Elmer Ephraim Ellsworth, the young "Zouave" militia colonel who had joined Lincoln's firm.

As he faced the crowd of well-wishers, Lincoln looked different from the man they had known. He was growing a beard at the suggestion of an eleven-year-old girl named Grace Bedell who had written to him from her home in Westfield, New York, on October 15, 1860.

He looked different in another way, too, for a friend remembered that Lincoln looked "care worn & more haggard & stooped than ever I saw him."[26] Here is what Lincoln had to say as he gazed out over the crowd on February 11:

> My friends—No one, not in my situation, can appreciate my feeling of sadness in this parting. To this place, and the kindness of these people, I owe every thing. Here I have lived a quarter of a century, and have passed from a young to an old man. Here my children have been born, and one is buried. I now leave, not knowing when, or whether ever, I may return, with a task before me greater than that which rested upon Washington. Without the assistance of that Divine Being, who ever attended him, I cannot succeed. With that assistance I cannot fail. Trusting in Him, who can go with me, and remain with you and be every where for good, let us confidently hope that all will yet be well. To His care commending you, as I hope in your prayers you will commend me, I bid you an affectionate farewell.[27]

So he said goodbye to the house at Eighth and Jackson streets in which he and his wife and his children had lived—the house with its little white picket fence in the front and the vivid wallpaper within. He said goodbye to the yellow dog Fido whom the Lincolns had decided to leave since they worried he might find his new surroundings in the executive mansion disorienting. It was goodbye to everything familiar and comforting as the Lincolns set out on this journey.

But Lincoln was heading toward a city he remembered very well from his days as a congressman, a city in which he would soon have tremendous power to determine the future of his country.

Lincoln's journey from Springfield to Washington took a "winding way," as he put it, because of all the speaking invitations. While they varied in quality, some of the speeches that he made on this trip were extremely important. Most of them explored the looming issues of secession, the meaning of the American Union, and the prospect of war.

He visited eleven cities in a sequence that took him back and forth across state lines. Beginning in Indianapolis, he gave speeches of varying length in Cincinnati, Columbus, Pittsburgh, Cleveland, Buffalo, Albany, New York, Trenton, Philadelphia, and Harrisburg. He also made remarks when the train stopped in villages and towns.

He was protected on the trip by a crew of bodyguards: army officers, the Illinois adjutant general, Ward Hill Lamon (Lincoln's close friend and admirer, who, among his other qualities, had a powerful physique), and Elmer Ephraim Ellsworth.

In Indianapolis he spoke to an audience of thousands from a balcony of the Bates House hotel. He talked about the concept of states' rights in a tone that was superficially jocular. Yet the speech was an interesting exercise in legal analysis.

He examined the easily overlooked but important practice of thinking about states not only as jurisdictions but as *entities with volition*, as when people carelessly talk about states "doing" things or "wanting" things. The statement that "South Carolina seceded" is different in a fundamental way from the statement that *a majority of people with voting rights in South Carolina* had voted to declare that their state was seceding. "By what principle of original right," Lincoln asked, can

> one-fiftieth or one-ninetieth of a great nation, by calling themselves a State, have the right to break up and ruin that nation as a matter of original principle? Now, I ask that question—I am not deciding anything (laughter)— . . . where is the mysterious, original right, from principle, for a certain district of the country with inhabitants,

by merely being called a State, to play tyrant over all its own citizens, and deny the authority of everything greater than itself? (Laughter).[28]

In some of these speeches Lincoln used a conciliatory tone. In Cincinnati on February 12, he talked about the speech that he had given there in 1859—the one in which he said that the Republicans would treat the slave-holding South the way "Washington, Jefferson, and Madison treated you." That statement, Lincoln said, was sincere.[29]

In Pittsburgh on February 15 he addressed a crowd of five thousand people who had turned out in a heavy storm to hear him. He urged calm, proclaiming "there is really no crisis except an artificial one!" He continued: "What is there now to warrant the condition of affairs presented by our friends 'over the river?' Take even their own view of the questions involved, and there is nothing to justify the course which they are pursuing. . . . If the great American people will only keep their temper, on both sides of the line, the troubles will come to an end."[30]

But Lincoln knew that a war might be coming and the pressure of that knowledge was constant. And the work of giving speeches one after another was beginning to wear him down.

His nerves snapped at times, as they did when the carpetbag with copies of his Inaugural Address was misplaced by Robert, who absent-mindedly left it behind a hotel counter. According to Nicolay, a "look of stupefaction" came over Lincoln's face when his son shrugged away his query as to where the bag was with an air of "bored and injured virtue."

Lincoln thereupon "forced his way through the crowded corridor" to the hotel office, and, "with a single stride of his long legs, he swung himself across the clerk's counter, behind which a small mountain of carpetbags" were piled.[31] He worked his way through the pile until he found his own bag, and Lamon mused that he had "never seen Mr. Lincoln . . . so angry."[32]

The stress increased on a number of occasions when the throng of people who came to see him became so huge that things got out of control. In the Ohio state capitol building in Columbus, he was almost crushed by the weight of the crowd and in Buffalo, New York, a crowd of seventy-five thousand surged up to see him as he rode in a carriage.

But the trip had its moments of fun, like the one at Westfield, New York, where the train stopped briefly on its way to Buffalo. Lincoln asked if a little girl named Grace Bedell might be present—the one who had written to him in October suggesting that he grow a beard. "There she is, Mr. Lincum," shouted a boy, and Grace was led by her father to the train where Lincoln kissed her and said, "You see, I let these whiskers grow for you, Grace."[33]

In New York City, it took no less than a thousand police officers to handle the crowds that jammed the streets to see Lincoln on his way to Astor House hotel. He was drawn into a whirl of activity, much of it pleasant but some of it exhausting. He tried oysters on the half shell for the first time and he also went to see a Verdi opera.

Democratic newspapers portrayed him as an awkward and embarrassing hayseed, but even some Democrats in New York were impressed by Lincoln's demeanor on this latest visit to the city. One said that "he was a much better looking & finer man than he expected to see; and that he kept aloof from old politicians here & seemed to have a mind of his own." Another reported that Lincoln "has an eye that shows power of mind & will & he thinks he will carry us safely."[34]

On February 20, Lincoln attended a welcome ceremony that was held at City Hall, and the mayor, Fernando Wood, who was a southern-sympathizing Democrat, called upon him to conciliate the South. Lincoln's reply was affable; he endorsed the proposition of sectional reconciliation. But then he talked about the meaning of the Union in terms that cry out to be understood today by all the people who continue to view him as a "Unionist first" and as an anti-slavery leader "second." He talked about whether the American Union *ought* to be saved. In this speech, which was improvised, he came up with an ingenious nautical metaphor, apt in the great port city through which he was passing:

> There is nothing that can ever bring me willingly to consent to the destruction of this Union . . . unless it were to be that thing for which the Union itself was made. I understand a ship to be made for the carrying and preservation of the cargo, and so long as the ship can be saved, with the cargo, it should never be abandoned. This Union should likewise never be abandoned unless it fails and the probability of its preservation shall cease to exist without throwing the passengers and the cargo overboard.[35]

These remarks provide a powerful link between the House Divided Speech and the Gettysburg Address, for in it Lincoln set forth a fundamental proposition—set it forth to Fernando Wood and to every-body else—that the Union would never *deserve* to be saved if it should cease to embody its founding ideal: universal freedom. The Civil War, he would tell posterity later, was a test to determine whether *any nation that was so conceived and so dedicated* could long endure.

So he would not back down from the Free Soil platform in order to save the Union—and he would face the prospect of war without flinching.

At Trenton, New Jersey, he talked of the heroes of the American Revolution and he prepared the members of the New Jersey legislature for the proposition that such heroism might be needed again:

> I shall do all that may be in my power to promote a peaceful settlement of all our difficulties. The man does not live who is more devoted to peace than I am. (Cheers.) None who would do more to preserve it. But it may be necessary to put the foot down firmly. (Here the audience broke out into cheers so loud and long that for some moments it was impossible to hear Mr. L's voice.) And if I do my duty, and do it right, you will sustain me, will you not? (Loud cheers, and cries of "Yes," "Yes," "We will.")[36]

Then he went to Philadelphia, where he gave two speeches, one of them at Independence Hall, where he had the great pleasure of invoking again the nation's founding manifesto, but this time at the very place where the Founders had approved it.

"I have never had a feeling," he told the mayor and citizens of Philadelphia, "that does not breathe from those walls. All my political warfare has been in favor of the teachings coming forth from that sacred hall. May my right hand forget its cunning and my tongue cleave to the roof of my mouth, if ever I prove false to those teachings."[37]

On the morning of February 22 (Washington's birthday), he rode to Independence Hall, where thirty thousand people were waiting. He was scheduled to raise a huge flag above the building—a flag containing thirty-four stars in recognition of the fact that a brand-new free state, Kansas, had just joined the Union. Before he raised this flag, Lincoln praised the work of the Founders, exclaiming that he had "never had a feeling politically that did not spring from the sentiments embodied in that Declaration of Independence," a document that was not, as Stephen Douglas and others had claimed, "the mere matter of separation of the colonies from the mother land." No, there was "something in that Declaration giving liberty, not alone to the people of this country, but, I hope, to the world for all future time."

And then he started his listeners as follows: "If this country cannot be saved without giving up that principle, I would rather be assassinated on this spot than to surrender it."[38]

The man who had seen the double-vision in the mirror just a few months earlier was making this vow for good reason. There was actually a plan in the works to assassinate him, and he had been warned about it. At this point Lincoln was ready and inclined to take action—to do something—instead of just shrugging the matter away as he would do later on in the days leading up to Ford's Theatre.

News of the assassination plot was brought to him soon after his arrival in Philadelphia. Norman Judd called upon him at his suite in the Continental Hotel and he brought along the detective Allan Pinkerton, whose firm was on retainer for the railroad that Lincoln would be using for the trip from Philadelphia to Baltimore. Pinkerton told the president-elect that secessionists in Baltimore intended to kill him.

He would have to change trains for the final trip to Washington and the murderers in Baltimore intended to attack him on his way to the station where the second train was waiting. Pinkerton and Judd suggested that he break off the tour and leave for Washington at once, but he refused. He had no intention of cancelling his speech at Independence Hall or his visit to Harrisburg.

But shortly after this meeting, a letter was hand-delivered to Lincoln by Seward's son Frederick. This letter, signed by Seward and General Scott, confirmed that the murder plot was real and that something would have to be done.

So on the trip to Harrisburg, Lincoln and Judd decided he would travel back to Philadelphia, and then, in disguise, board a secret coach on a train that was traveling to Washington. That train would pass through Baltimore at night—and arrangements would also be made for it to travel far ahead of schedule. After Lincoln was safely in Washington, the regular presidential train (with his family aboard) would proceed through Baltimore.

Lincoln agreed. He recalled later on that he "thought it wise to run no risk, where no risk was necessary"—and he instructed Pinkerton to make all the necessary arrangements.[39]

At 7:00 on the evening of February 22, Lincoln, with his friend and bodyguard Ward Hill Lamon, returned to Philadelphia. As soon as the train had departed from Harrisburg, the telegraph lines leading in and out of the city were cut. When the train arrived at Philadelphia, Lincoln and Lamon were greeted by Pinkerton and railroad officials.

Lincoln donned his disguise—which consisted of a soft felt hat and an overcoat—and then with Lamon and Pinkerton he sneaked aboard the sleeping car of the train that would take him to Baltimore. He climbed into a berth and drew the curtains. Lamon, armed with four guns, brass knuckles, and knives, stood look-out as Lincoln tried to sleep.

At 3:30 a.m., when the train reached Baltimore, the sleeping car was detached and then a team of horses pulled it from the first railroad station to the second. Lincoln and his companions reached the nation's capital at 6:00 a.m. Congressman Elihu Washburne met them at the station and conveyed them to the Willard Hotel, where the Lincolns would live until Inauguration Day.

When the regular presidential train with Lincoln's family aboard reached Baltimore, a screaming mob created an extremely frightening scene.

The Willard Hotel (which was subsequently rebuilt on a far grander scale) stood five stories high in those days at the corner of Pennsylvania Avenue and 14th Street, N.W. The accommodations were reasonably elegant. But the city was a very rude affair by the standards of the time. A pestilential drainage canal ran right along the Mall, and there were sewage-filled marshes not far from the White House. The climate made things even worse—especially in the summertime, when stifling humidity and torrents of mosquitoes made the city very close to unbearable.

The Lincolns would live in Suite 6 of the Willard Hotel until Inauguration Day. Lincoln was pestered in this suite by a horde of office-seekers. On the morning of his arrival, he ate breakfast with Seward and then visited the White House to meet Buchanan. Seward made no secret of the fact that he was continuing to lobby for sectional conciliation.

Seward had a vision of the best-case future for his country in the winter of 1860–1861. He thought that if the upper southern states could be kept from seceding, the states within the Confederacy would languish. Pro-Union politicians would begin to assert themselves and then the impetus toward reunion would become inevitable. After one or two years, a constitutional convention would settle the sectional difficulties of America.

Or so he thought. He was giving short shrift to the alternative worst-case scenario, which might have gone like this: the energy of nation-building would make the Confederacy robust, and its allure would exert an irresistible pull upon the slave states that continued to dangle just below the northern remnant of the Union. It would only be a matter of time before those states would fall away—one by one.

Seward was too sure of himself to consider that possibility. So he worked away in February with members of the Peace Conference that was summoned by Virginia. That convention was meeting in a dance hall adjacent to the Willard Hotel. Seward also plucked a constitutional amendment from the package that Crittenden had proposed in December and he pushed it hard. This would be an unamendable amendment to prohibit Congress from ever interfering with slavery in states that permitted it.

He was joined in this effort by several like-minded Republicans, most notably Charles Francis Adams, son of John Quincy Adams, and Thomas Corwin of Ohio. Both were serving in the House of Representatives. Before long, the pro-slavery amendment would be known as the "Corwin Amendment."

Lincoln had only a week and a half before taking the helm to come to terms with this atmosphere in Washington. He was exhausted by the arduous trip, and the relentless siege of the office-seekers gave him little time for reflection. Meanwhile, the Democratic press had a field day making fun of the way that he had sneaked into Washington. The papers lampooned him as a coward. And the disguise that he wore was incorrectly described as being a Scottish outfit. Cartoonists depicted him as an awkward and emaciated scarecrow wearing a tam o' shanter and kilt.

It was under these unfortunate circumstances that he waded into the political scene in the capital city of a nation that was breaking apart.

He gave himself some maneuvering room by adopting a charming tone in his dealings with the Peace Conference. He kept his eyes and ears open and the things he saw and heard made him lean toward conciliatory gestures in the short run.

There can be no doubt that his underlying attitude was firm and would remain that way. But he was uncertain about the short-term contingencies, so he decided to give himself as much flexibility as possible as he sought to gain more information.

One of the most alarming things that he heard was the rumor that secession in the upper South and border states would result if the Peace

Conference failed. The governor of Maryland was supposed to have said "that if the conference adjourned without doing anything . . . he should immediately call the Legislature of his state together & the state would at once secede."[40] Stephen Douglas paid a call upon Lincoln to advise him that the threat of secession in Maryland was genuine.

Lincoln knew that the nation's capital city was bordered on three sides by the slave state of Maryland. And the slave state of Virginia was just across the Potomac River. If he handled things wrong, he might find himself in a city surrounded and under assault by the very sorts of people who had threatened to kill him in Baltimore. General Scott stood ready to defend the city, but Lincoln had no time for discussions in regard to its defense.

Perhaps it was due to this single contingency that he decided to play for more time and even back-peddle in his dealings with the Peace Conference.

So when Virginia delegates urged him to evacuate Fort Sumter in the middle of Charleston harbor, he replied that if Virginia would consider adjourning its secession convention he might very well do as they suggested. "Go to Richmond," he told the delegates, and "pass a resolution that Virginia will not in any event secede, and I may then agree with you in the fact a State any day is worth more than a fort."[41] But nothing came of this gesture.

More importantly, when the Peace Conference recommended a watered-down version of the Crittenden Compromise, he decided that he might have to stand aside at that point and let events run their course. This decision could not have been a pleasant one for Lincoln in light of his record when it came to the extension of slavery.

To the contrary, it must have been galling—especially after the stern position he had taken on the issue of slavery extension in his letter to Seward. But the entire lower South had been breaking away, and if Virginia and Maryland left, then the game might be very nearly over.

It is hard to believe—no, it is completely impossible to believe—that his feelings had changed when it came to Free Soil or his long-term vision for America. So it seems that he was saying some things that he did not necessarily believe as he stalled and struggled to maneuver. If events went well, he would be watching for chances to straighten things out later on.

It appears that he was being deceptive—putting on an act—as he dabbled in some of these gestures of conciliation. "May my right hand forget its cunning," he had sworn in Philadelphia, if he ever proved false to his ideals. And he would not prove false to his ideals. But he would use all the cunning he possessed as the time for his swearing-in approached. The emergency was worse than he had thought when he had killed off the Crittenden Compromise back in December, so he played along with Seward for a while in February.

The version of the Crittenden scheme that the Peace Conference sent to Congress would have barred the acquisition of territory unless a majority of the free states as well as slave states approved. That made it only slightly less obnoxious than the original Crittenden plan, since the old Missouri Compromise line would still be revived and the territories to the south of it would be opened to slavery. But happily for Lincoln, this compromise proposal died in Congress.

That was not to be the case with the Corwin Amendment, which squeaked through Congress on the very eve of Lincoln's Inauguration. Henry Adams (son of Charles Francis Adams) claimed later on that Lincoln had engaged in some behind-the-scenes efforts on behalf of the amendment. On the face of it, that proposition sounds dubious. We will never know whether Lincoln did anything at all to intervene in the matter.

The one public statement that he made in regard to the Corwin Amendment, a statement he included in his first Inaugural Address, became all but irrelevant within a few weeks as the swirl of events changed the terms of the political debate.

More on that later.

Though Seward and some of his allies pushed conciliation out of genuine conviction (leavened, perhaps, with a dose of opportunism), Lincoln took their occasional advice without adopting their view of events. He knew that a war would be coming and he knew what he was going to do when the war broke out, at least in the essentials. When others gave him advice that was different from Seward's—advice to be foxy—he paid close attention, though he left no written responses for obvious reasons.

No one gave him better advice of this sort than Orville Browning. In the days before the inauguration, Lincoln passed around copies of his draft Inaugural Address, inviting Browning and others to share suggestions. Browning told him that he ought to tone down a certain pledge that he made in the speech—a pledge to occupy federal forts and installations and reclaim the ones that the secessionists had already seized. The principle was right, Browning said, and yet the threatening language would inflame the situation in the border states, and so the language would need to be softened. Lincoln would have to make this pledge sound almost innocuous. "It is very important," said Browning,

> that the traitors shall be the aggressors and that they be kept constantly and palpably in the wrong. The first attempt that is made to furnish supplies or reinforcements to Sumter will induce aggression by South Carolina, and then the government will stand justified, before the entire country, in repelling that aggression, and retaking the forts. And so it will be everywhere, and all the places now occupied by traitors can be recaptured without affording them additional material with which to inflame the public mind by representing your inaugural as containing an irritating threat.[42]

Lincoln took this advice, and the strategy that he would use in the Fort Sumter crisis would succeed just as Browning had foretold.

It was shrewd of Lincoln to leave his options open in the days before he took the oath of office. Many times in the past he had lulled his opponents as he planned the trap that he would spring, and he would spring a fine trap in the weeks leading up to the war.

Meanwhile, he made his final cabinet selections and he dealt with all the other office-seekers as best he could. Squabbling about the final cabinet appointments was so intense that Lincoln spoke sharply to some Republicans. To those who questioned his decision to make Montgomery Blair his postmaster-general, he had this to say: "I have weighed the matter—I have been pulled this way and that way—I have poised the scales, and it is my province to determine, and I am now going to be master."[43]

Seward, true to form, became more petulant as Inauguration Day approached. He was so convinced that he and Salmon Chase could never work together that he threatened to resign from the cabinet. After asking him to reconsider, Lincoln let it be known that he had a replacement for Seward in the wings if this foolishness did not abate.

The matter was still pending on the morning of March 4, Inauguration Day.

Inauguration Day dawned cloudy over Washington and Lincoln rose early. He looked over the Inaugural Address and asked Robert to read it aloud. He met with Seward, Bates, Welles, Cameron, and various advisers.

Some significant last-minute changes were made to his speech in the wee hours of March 4.

Outside, the streets began filling up with people who came to see the procession that would head down Pennsylvania Avenue to the Capitol. General Scott made elaborate preparations to protect the new president: two thousand troops were on hand along with armed detectives who would circulate among the crowds. Sharpshooters crouched atop the roofs of buildings.

At noon, Lincoln was ready; dressed for once in a well-pressed suit and shined shoes, he wore a stovepipe hat and he walked with a gold-headed cane in his hand. He climbed aboard the carriage that would carry him and Buchanan over cobble-stoned streets as a dense crowd of forty thousand people cheered. The weather began to clear up, and a bright winter's day was at hand.

The carriage was driven to the base of Capitol Hill and then up to the building's East Front. The men entered the building and proceeded to the President's Room. The ceremony's first event would be the swearing-in of vice president Hannibal Hamlin in the Senate chamber.

Buchanan, initially quiet and forlorn, became chatty. According to John Hay (who eavesdropped), Buchanan shared details about life in the White House, telling Lincoln that "I think you will find the water of the right-hand well at the White House better than that at the left."[44]

Then they walked to the Senate chamber, filled with dignitaries: members of Congress, governors, justices of the Supreme Court—the Supreme Court, whose power Lincoln intended to challenge in his Inaugural Address.

Hamlin was sworn in, and the ceremonies moved outdoors, to the Capitol's East Front, where a large wooden platform had been set up. Thousands of people watched as Lincoln and the other officials took their places.

As people gazed at the Capitol building, they could see the big crane that was used to build the great new cast-iron dome that was slowly taking shape. That dome was part of an expansion plan that commenced years earlier under the supervision of Secretary of War Jefferson Davis.

As he rose to give his speech, Lincoln looked for a place to put his hat. Stephen Douglas, who was seated nearby, reached out and offered to hold it. Then Lincoln's old friend Edward Baker, now serving as a senator from Oregon, introduced the president-elect.

Lincoln's speech was a long and spliced-together affair. It had been shaped by suggestions from friends and advisers and polished in the time that was available. Early in the speech he affirmed that he would stand by the Republican platform, but he did so in a mild and circumspect way. Then he confronted the crisis of the day and he addressed it as follows:

> Apprehension seems to exist among the people of the Southern States, that by the accession of a Republican administration, their property, and their peace, and their personal security, are to be endangered. There has never been any reasonable cause for such apprehension. Indeed, the most ample evidence to the contrary has all the while existed, and been open to their inspection. It is found in nearly all the published speeches of him who now addresses you. I do but quote from one of those speeches when I declare that "I have no purpose, directly or indirectly, to interfere with the institution of slavery in the states where it exists."[45]

He talked about the nature of the Union and insisted it could not be broken by secession. In addition to the long-familiar argument that the "Perpetual Union" established by the Articles of Confederation must have carried over into the Federal Constitution, Lincoln offered some arguments of his own—arguments grounded in political theory and common-sense logic.

"It is safe to assert," he began, "that no government proper, ever had a provision in its organic law for its own termination." And for those who would argue that the United States was "not a government proper, but an association of states in the nature of a contract merely, can it, as a contract, be peaceably unmade, by less than all the parties who made it?"[46]

Then he laid out his carefully composed and much revised statement of intent with regard to policy:

> I therefore consider that ... the Union is unbroken; and, to the extent of my ability, I shall take care, as the Constitution itself expressly enjoins upon me, that the laws of the Union be faithfully executed in all the States. Doing this I deem to be only a simple duty on my part; and I shall perform it, so far as practicable, unless my rightful masters, the American people, shall withhold the requisite means, or, in some authoritative manner, direct the contrary. I trust this will not be

regarded as a menace, but only as the declared purpose of the Union that it *will* constitutionally defend, and maintain itself. In doing this there needs to be no bloodshed or violence; and there shall be none, unless forced against the national authority.[47]

So he would "hold, occupy and possess the property, and places belonging to the government," and he would collect the duties on imports. But "beyond what may be necessary for these objects, there will be no invasion—no using of force against, or among the people anywhere."[48]

He acknowledged that violations of minority rights by majorities may sometimes justify revolution—which is what the Confederates claimed was taking place by means of secession. But he argued that no such clear violations could be claimed by the self-styled southern revolutionists. That being the case, he continued, secession was a threat to the integrity of the governing process itself.

When the population of any society divided into majority and minority groups, one of them—the minority—would have to yield (at least to some extent) until the controversies were resolved through the democratic process:

> Plainly, the central idea of secession is the essence of anarchy. A majority, held in restraint by constitutional checks, and limitations, and always changing easily, with deliberate changes of popular opinions and sentiments, is the only true sovereign of a free people. Whoever rejects it, does, of necessity, fly to anarchy or to despotism. Unanimity is impossible; the rule of a minority, as a permanent arrangement, is wholly inadmissible; so that, rejecting the majority principle, anarchy, or despotism in some form, is all that is left.[49]

Minorities needed to hold their position yet submit to the democratic process until such time as they could turn themselves into majorities. This was more than just the only fair and reasonable way to proceed, Lincoln said, it was the only *sane* way to proceed.

Secessionists would quickly discover that their principles could backfire, he warned, "for a minority of their own will secede from them whenever a majority refuses to be controlled by such minority."[50]

Lincoln then applied the principle of majority rule in a very different manner: to challenge the Supreme Court's power of judicial review. There was nothing in the federal Constitution that gave the court the right to act as arbiter in disputes about constitutionality. The court had given that power to itself in the case of *Marbury v. Madison*. Lincoln now became the latest in a series of presidents to question that power of the court.

The Republican challenge to the *Dred Scott* decision was latent in everything he said, and one can only imagine what Roger Taney was thinking as he listened to the following statement. "I do not forget the position assumed by some," Lincoln said, "that constitutional questions are to be decided by the Supreme Court; nor do I deny that such decisions must be binding in any case, upon the parties to a suit, as to the object of that suit." But, he continued,

> at the same time the candid citizen must confess that if the policy of the government, upon vital questions, affecting the whole people, is to be irrevocably fixed by decisions of the Supreme Court, the instant they are made . . . the people will have ceased, to be their own rulers, having, to that extent, practically resigned their government into the hands of that eminent tribunal.[51]

The upshot was clear: when the time seemed right, the Republicans in Congress would do exactly what Roger Taney had told them was beyond their power. They would cheerfully ignore the *Dred Scott* decision as they set their own territorial policy.

In the soon-to-be famous conclusion of this first Inaugural Address, Lincoln emphasized his peaceful intentions—while at the same time throwing down the gauntlet. "In *your* hands, my dissatisfied fellow countrymen," he declared, "and not in *mine*, is the momentous issue of civil war. The government will not assail *you*. You can have no conflict, without being yourselves the aggressors. *You* have no oath registered in Heaven to destroy the government, while *I* shall have the most solemn one to 'preserve, protect, and defend' it."[52]

Seward had convinced him to insert a final gesture of good will. Lincoln took the advice, and he produced a poetic composition—one of his best:

> I am loth to close. We are not enemies, but friends. We must not be enemies. Though passion may have strained, it must not break our bonds of affection. The mystic chords of memory, stretching from

every battle-field, and patriot grave, to every living heart and hearth-stone, all over this broad land, will yet swell the chorus of the Union, when again touched, as surely they will be, by the better angels of our nature.[53]

There was one more passage that Lincoln inserted, and admirers of the sixteenth president have often regretted that he did. At 4:00 a.m.—an hour before Lincoln awoke on the morning of Inauguration Day—the Senate passed, by a razor-thin majority, the Corwin pro-slavery amendment that Seward had championed and the House of Representatives had passed on February 27. This amendment would be sent to the states for their ratification.

Someone (probably Seward) urged Lincoln to insert a brief statement to affirm that the ratification process would proceed as the Constitution provided and that nothing would stand in the way of it. So he did—in the early hours of the morning on Inauguration Day—and the preliminary part of this insertion in his first Inaugural Address was unexceptionable:

I can not be ignorant of the fact that many worthy, and patriotic citizens are desirous of having the national constitution amended. While I make no recommendation of amendments, I fully recognize the rightful authority of the people over the whole subject . . . and I should, under existing circumstances, favor, rather than oppose, a fair opertunity being afforded the people to act upon it.

But then he added the following passage, perhaps under pressure from Seward, who had still not rescinded his threat to resign as secretary of state:

I understand a proposed amendment to the Constitution—which amendment, however, I have not seen, has passed Congress to the effect that the federal government, shall never interfere with the domestic institutions of the States, including that of persons held to service. To avoid misconstruction of what I have said, I depart from my purpose not to speak of particular amendments, so far as to say that, holding such a provision to now be implied constitutional law, I have no objection to its being made express and irrevocable.[54]

Lincoln, who abominated slavery and wanted to place it "on course for ultimate extinction," had endorsed an amendment to the Constitution that would have taken away from Congress the power of doing such a thing. What are we to make of this?

Did this passage reveal that the convictions he espoused from the days of his Peoria speech had been a sham? Did it reveal that when the chips were down he could be just as feckless and spineless as Seward on the slavery issue?

No.

He had always hoped that the containment of slavery would lead to its eventual phase-out. His statements that he "had no purpose" to interfere with slavery were highly misleading. He hoped to set the stage for a gradual process that would kill it off over time.

But when he made his impassioned statement in the House Divided speech that he wished to put slavery "on course for ultimate extinction," he tipped his hand. The South Carolina secession convention had pounced upon that statement as proof that the Republican program would be instituted in stages. Though *Lincoln* might protest that his purposes were harmless, his victory in quarantining slavery would lay the strategic groundwork *for actions by others in the future*. And the South Carolina secessionists were absolutely right to perceive this reality.

Lincoln strove to reiterate his pledge to leave slavery alone in his first Inaugural Address because he had to. He had to do everything he could to keep Maryland, Virginia, and the whole northern tier of the slave states from bolting at once.

But the Corwin Amendment called his bluff and he was forced to respond to what Congress had done. If he refused to endorse the amendment, secessionists would say that his promise of noninterference with slavery was empty. After all, when he had been given a chance to *guarantee* that his promise *would apply to his successors*, he refused to endorse an amendment that would give the South permanent security. And so his pledge was nothing but a trick.

He knew perfectly well that the Corwin Amendment was disgusting. But some consolations might have entered his mind as he made the decision under pressure to insert those painful lines into his first Inaugural Address.

In the first place, the Corwin Amendment would require the ratification of three-quarters of the states. And there was very good reason for presuming that no such thing would ever happen. The rapidly unfolding events that were leading to a war would change everything. The Corwin amendment would be shoved aside and then lost in the shuffle in the weeks when the Civil War began.

But there was another and still more interesting form of consolation for Lincoln. Like everyone else, he understood the kind of fear that was gripping the white southern mind. He knew that if secession were stopped and the containment of slavery achieved, the defenders of slavery would start to feel unbearable pressure as their fears of a slave insurrection grew steadily worse.

As the *Charleston Mercury* warned, Republicans would break down protections that the slave-holding class had put in place. Sooner or later, the Republican post-masters would halt the southern censorship of the United States mail—the censorship that was keeping abolitionist tracts from flooding the region. Lincoln had asked Edward Bates to look into the possibility of doing that.

For years white southerners had feared that their day of reckoning would come if the black population kept growing. And with the Free Soil movement triumphant, they would no longer have any way to keep the situation under their control—there would be no way for them to keep the pot from boiling over—by shipping their "surplus" slaves to the West. The South's "safety valve" would be closed, and then a race war could start at any time.

Meanwhile, the operations of the Underground Railroad would increase at the very same time that the clamp-down on anti-slavery opinion was weakening. Yes, "Republican rule" would start to eradicate the power of the slave-owning master class. The "southern way of life" would unravel as the slave-holding aristocracy lost its power to dominate others.

When that happened, the owners of slaves in the states that were closest to the North would start to ship their slaves to the "Cotton States" or "Gulf States" for sale. The slave population would be shifted from the border states to the states of the very deep South, and then millions and millions of slaves would begin to accumulate there. Their market value would be dropping since the market would be glutted and the danger of a bloody slave rebellion would be getting worse every day.

As slaves became cheaper to buy, less valuable to hold, and more dangerous to keep, the white South might decide to get rid of the "peculiar institution" altogether—to cash in and let somebody else take the problem off their hands. At that point, an offer by a group like the American Colonization Society to buy the slaves, give them freedom, and ship them away to foreign lands would look increasingly attractive. The legislatures of the slave states would also have authority to institute and pay for a buy-out, perhaps through bond sales.

No action by Congress would be necessary. There was nothing that the Corwin Amendment could do to preclude such a sequence of events.

Perhaps thoughts of this kind were occurring to Lincoln as he jotted down the hurried insertion in the early hours of March 4, 1861. We will never know. In any case, he began to disavow the insertion and repudiate what he had done. According to Congressman John A. Bingham, when the matter arose in conversation Lincoln said it was "extraordinary that I should have made such statements in my Inaugural." He went on to say that "he felt that the proposed Amendment had not been correctly reported to him, and that some one had blundered." But "he reproached no one, nor did he intimate how or by whose agency this passage came to be in the Inaugural Address."[55]

Lincoln's speech was enormously successful; even guests on the platform like Douglas joined the crowds on the Capitol grounds in expressing their approval with exclamations and cheers.

When Lincoln finished, he placed his hand upon the Bible, took the oath of office from Roger Taney, kissed the Bible, and shook hands with the people around him. After the ceremony, he and Buchanan rode back to the White House, where a great reception was held—a reception that was followed later on by the inaugural ball in a pavilion adjacent to the White House.

The Executive Mansion was in rather dilapidated shape after more than a half century of use since the days of John Adams. Van Buren had done some refurbishing, and successive presidents installed the rudiments of plumbing. But the place was in need of repairs. On the main floor were state reception rooms, including the East Room and other rooms that were designated by colors: the oval Blue Room with its view of the Potomac, the Red Room, and the Green Room. There were also two dining rooms, a large one for state dinners and a smaller one for the family.

Upstairs were offices and presidential living quarters, with the bedrooms in the mansion's west wing. Willie and Tad would room together. On the other side of the building was the president's office, a modest-sized room with a good view across the river. Lincoln's upright desk stood around the corner from the window. In the middle of the room was a table used for cabinet meetings. Nearby were the offices of the secretaries, Nicolay and Hay, who would soon be joined by a writer named William O. Stoddard. These secretaries had small bedrooms near their offices.

The mansion had its pleasant side, and Mary enjoyed the conservatory that extended from the west wing, where she grew flowers. But the basement was infested with rats and the stench that they created was repulsive. A bronze statue of Jefferson on the lawn in front of the mansion was covered in mold. The summer brought a pestilence of insects. That, and the stifling humidity, would cause the Lincolns to flee the White House on a regular basis in the summertime.

On his first day as president, Lincoln got bad news that demanded his attention. General Scott informed him that Fort Sumter in Charleston harbor was running out of supplies and it could only hold out for six weeks. That was the opinion of Major Robert Anderson, who was in command at the fort.

In light of the fact that Buchanan had allowed the South Carolinians to occupy artillery positions on the shore that could be used to bombard Fort Sumter, it would be best to evacuate it, Scott argued. Another coastal defense installation, Fort Pickens in Pensacola, Florida, was also at risk but the Sumter situation would soon be desperate.

The next day Lincoln met with Scott, Seward, Welles, and others to review the situation. Welles recommended a reinforcement expedition, whereas Seward (not surprisingly) was pessimistic. Lincoln called a cabinet meeting on March 9, and the issue was discussed. Scott said that he would need to have a formidable fleet, twenty-five thousand troops, and several months to defend the fort properly. But the food and supplies in the fort would have run out long before that.

Furthermore, when Buchanan sent an unarmed ship, the *Star of the West*, to resupply Sumter in January, the secessionists had opened fire and the ship was forced to turn back.

Seward, true to form, recommended abandoning Sumter, and as the word about his recommendation spread—there were rumors that Seward himself was the source of unauthorized leaks—a storm of protest erupted, not only from Republicans but also from some Unionist Democrats. On March 13, a caucus of Republicans considered a measure to demand the reinforcement of Sumter. Montgomery Blair was so indignant at the prospect of surrendering the fort that he considered resigning from the cabinet.

But instead of resigning, he introduced his brother-in-law Gustavus Vasa Fox—a retired naval officer—to Lincoln and he told the president that Fox had devised a good plan to resupply Sumter by means of a small flotilla under cover of darkness. Lincoln was impressed by the plan as well as by the man who had devised it. He would later appoint Fox assistant secretary of the navy.

On March 15 Lincoln outlined the plan to his cabinet, but only Blair was willing to support it. Seward warned that a defense of Fort Sumter would antagonize the South and thus ruin his own hopes for a gradual reconciliation. Cameron advised deferring to Scott's opinions. Welles worried that the plan might make the North seem aggressive. Bates complained that he could not see why the fort was so important, and Smith declared he was against the plan unless overwhelming force could be used. Chase reflected that perhaps it might be best to just let the South go—and good riddance.

Lincoln was disinclined to abandon Sumter. And in spite of the division in his cabinet, he took action on his own. He sent Fox to Charleston harbor with instructions to confer with Anderson. And he sent a special agent into Charleston, an Illinois friend named Stephen Hurlbut who was born in South Carolina.

Hurlbut's mission was to gauge the state of public opinion in South Carolina and predict the reactions that Lincoln would elicit if he chose to do . . . certain things. Lincoln also sent Ward Hill Lamon, who had just been appointed U.S. Marshall for the District of Columbia, to accompany Hurlbut.

As usual, Lincoln was averse to snap decisions. He wanted to get as much information as he could. His instincts guided him. But like every good strategist, he tried to explore the different contingencies if he had the luxury of time.

But those not privy to his actions made the understandable mistake of concluding he was weak. Edwin Stanton, the attorney who had formed such a low opinion of Lincoln during the McCormick Reaper case—and who had served as attorney-general under Buchanan—complained that "the administration not only have, as yet, no line of policy but also believe that it *never can* have any—but will drift along, from day to day, without a compass."[56] Like many northerners, he was indignant in the face of secession and he wanted to see southern rebels confronted by a strong show of force.

A like-minded Illinois Unionist complained in a letter to Lyman Trumbull that "we have *compromised* and *truckled* long enough. War is bad. Civil war is worse, but if liberty and the right of the people to govern themselves was worth fighting for in the days of the Revolution, it is worth fighting for now."[57]

Others hoped for reconciliation. Lincoln, they said, should avoid "coercion" at all costs. He should do it for the sake of the country, for the sake of averting bloody carnage, to prevent a catastrophe. They were correct about the cost of the war that was coming, but nobody knew how very bloody or protracted such a civil war might turn out to be. Some thought it would be over in a hurry. And it might have been over very quickly if a number of things had shaken out differently.

Lincoln was paying close attention to all of these opinions while thinking for himself as he measured the situation and developed his own strategic plan.

As he did so, he was under constant and brutal pressure from the throng of office-seekers. Over a thousand had flocked to the White House on the second day after the inauguration, and before very long they were preventing Lincoln from giving enough time to more important matters. He told Henry J. Raymond, the editor of the *New York Times*, that "he wished he could get time to attend to the Southern question . . . but the office-seekers demanded all his time. 'I am,' said he, 'like a man so busy letting rooms in one end of his house, that he can't stop to put out a fire that is burning the other.'"[58]

Senator William Pitt Fessenden wrote that the "poor President is having a hard time of it. He came here tall strong & vigorous, but has worked himself almost to death."[59] To journalist Henry Villard, Lincoln confided that "I hardly have a chance to eat or sleep. I am fair game for everybody of that hungry lot."[60]

Lincoln used his secretaries Nicolay and Hay to help him manage the huge horde of supplicants. Nicolay projected an intense demeanor in an effort to dampen their ardor, whereas Hay deflected the worst of them with light banter. Some yarns about the wit of John Hay began to circulate in Washington. Here is one of them. A visitor declared that he had to see the president immediately. "The President is engaged now," Hay replied, and when the caller asked him, "Do you know who I am?" and when Hay replied that he did not, the man said, "I am the son of God." Very well, replied Hay, "the President will be delighted to see you when you come again . . . and perhaps you will bring along a letter of introduction from your father."[61]

Humor could seldom assuage the hurt feelings of those who made unsuccessful overtures to Lincoln in the confidence that he would give them what they wanted. One of them was James C. Conkling, a man who had befriended Lincoln since the 1830s. "I almost adored him," Conkling wrote a year later, "and spent my time and money freely with him, and did not know but that my feelings toward him were reciprocated." But it seemed evident in light of his failure as a favor-seeker and an office-seeker "that I was viewed by him with contempt."[62]

Under this pressure, Lincoln tried to maintain his friendly poise but he began to be methodically businesslike. When two rival groups of New Yorkers were plying him with their requests and demands, he told them that "one side shall not gobble up everything. Make out a list of the places and men you want, and I will endeavor to apply the rule of give and take."[63]

In the moments of peace that he managed to carve out for himself, he reflected on the past. He thought of his days in New Salem since friends from that time like Hannah Armstrong had visited him before he left for Washington. Perhaps he thought about the years he had allowed to slip away before he paid a belated visit to his step-mother Sarah. One thing we know, if we can trust the reminiscences of a New Salem acquaintance named Isaac Cogdal, who visited Lincoln at the White House.

He was thinking about Ann Rutledge.

William H. Seward, indulged for a while by Lincoln for compelling political reasons—most of all to keep the Republican Party united—was about to engage in some behavior that would force the president to put him in his place.

According to Charles Francis Adams Jr., Seward "thought Lincoln a clown, a clod, and planned to steer him by . . . indirection, subtle maneuvering, astute wriggling and plotting crooked paths. He would be Prime Minister [and] he would seize the reins from a nerveless President."[64] Lincoln would "reign," like a figurehead monarch, while Seward called the shots.

He had come to the conclusion that peace was more important than anything else, and that it had to be achieved at any price. "War must be averted," he was quoted as saying, "the negro question dropped; the 'irrepressible conflict' ignored; & a Union party, to embrace the border States inaugurated."[65]

To achieve these goals, he sent unauthorized messages to Virginia Unionists and also to Confederate emissaries. He was eager to meet with the Confederate agents who had come to Washington demanding the recognition of the Confederacy. Naturally these emissaries presented their "diplomatic" credentials to Lincoln's secretary of state.

Lincoln prohibited Seward from receiving them, but Seward went ahead and communicated with them through intermediaries, thus violating Lincoln's directive. Before long, Seward sent messages through them to Jefferson Davis, assuring him that Fort Sumter would be evacuated.

Gustavus Vasa Fox reached Charleston on March 21. He conferred with Anderson, to whom he explained his plan to re-provision the fort. Anderson was skeptical, but Fox was convinced that his plan could succeed and he reported as much upon his return to Washington.

When Hurlbut returned and reported, his assessment was clear and very grim. He told Lincoln that the victory of secessionism in South Carolina was complete. The Confederates would accept nothing less than the possession or destruction of Fort Sumter. They were determined to fight to achieve their goals if that proved to be necessary.

"A ship known to contain only provisions for Sumpter [sic] would be stopped & refused admittance," he said. The seizure or destruction of the fort would be "followed by a demand for Pickens and the Keys of the Gulf." Moreover, *any* "attempt to fulfill the duties of the Executive Office in enforcing the laws & authority of the U.S. . . . will be war."[66]

Abandoning Sumter had become an untenable option for Lincoln in light of the furor that raged among Unionists. And even if Lincoln had decided to abandon the fort, the result would be nothing like what Seward imagined. The surrender would embolden rather than pacify the secessionists. Hurlbut had described their next moves very clearly.

So there was no way out of a war—or so it would seem—and Lincoln's darkest suspicions were confirmed. That being the case, this was probably the moment when he turned to Orville Browning's advice: his advice to put the rebels in the wrong by maneuvering them into firing the first shot.

The situation came to a head when Scott advised the president on March 28 to surrender both Fort Sumter and Fort Pickens. At the end of his first state dinner, Lincoln summoned the members of his cabinet to the Red Room and quietly told them about Scott's recommendation. Almost everyone was outraged—everyone but Seward and Caleb B. Smith.

Members of the cabinet began to change their minds; Chase, for example, who a few weeks earlier was glad to be rid of the slave-holding South, now recommended the reinforcement of both Fort Sumter and Fort Pickens.

At a cabinet meeting the next afternoon Lincoln called for a discussion. The trap that he was going to spring was already worked out in his mind. He would send an expedition to Sumter and *inform the rebels* well in advance. He would *tell* them that the re-supply mission was on its way and that its purpose was entirely *peaceful*.

That is how the message would sound to northern Unionists: like a mission to feed some hungry men. But Lincoln knew from what Hurlbut had told him that the mission would be regarded in South Carolina as an act of defiance, and it would trigger counter-defiance.

The South Carolinians demanded the surrender of the fort. Lincoln defied them—by sending in supplies. And so what would the Confederates do? Hurlbut told him what they would do: "a ship known to contain only provisions for Sumter [sic] would be stopped & refused admittance." Stopped how? In a hail of gunfire. And that was what Lincoln intended; he would trick them into firing the first shot, so the guilt of the war would be theirs alone.

As historian James M. McPherson has observed, "Lincoln's new conception of the resupply undertaking was a stroke of genius. In effect he was telling Jefferson Davis, 'Heads I win, Tails you lose.'"[67]

At the cabinet meeting on March 29 Lincoln offered some alternative courses of action. He first reviewed Scott's proposal to abandon both of the forts. Then he presented his counter-proposal: to "send an armed force" to Charleston harbor to relieve Fort Sumter, but declare "the intentions of the government to provision the fort, peaceably if unmolested."

Blair, Chase, Cameron, and Welles all supported Lincoln's idea whereas Bates and Smith were noncommittal. Only one member of the cabinet flatly opposed it.

William H. Seward.

Lincoln had Seward just where he wanted him: alone and in complete isolation. It would soon be clear to the rebels that Seward had been speaking for himself alone. He would then be exposed for what he was and he would lose his credibility and influence—unless he turned to some desperate counter-measures.

On April 1 he sent a memorandum to Lincoln suggesting that the best way out of the crisis was to pick a quarrel with a carefully selected foreign nation in the hope of reviving the old patriotic feelings in the North and South. And he offered to take charge of this entire operation personally—take charge of it so that Lincoln would be saved all the trouble.

Lincoln decided it was time to put his secretary of state where he belonged. He ignored the suggestion of a needless foreign war, but he demolished the procedural suggestions that Seward had made as he quoted them one by one. "Upon your closing propositions," Lincoln told Seward, specifically

"Whatever policy we adopt, there must be an energetic prosecution of it"

"For this purpose it must be somebody's business to pursue and direct it incessantly"

"Either the President must do it himself, and be all the while active in it, or"

"Devolve it on some member of his cabinet"

I remark that if this must be done, *I* must do it.[68]

That should have been enough, but Seward's recklessness and insubordination died hard. He attempted to restore his credibility with southerners by finding some way to get Sumter abandoned. On the very same day, April 1, he revived the idea of swapping a state for a fort (i.e., Virginia in exchange for Fort Sumter) by writing to George W. Summers, a Richmond Unionist. This correspondence led to a meeting on April 4 between Lincoln and John B. Baldwin, whom the Richmond Unionists chose as their designated spokesman.

But the talks went nowhere, since the Unionists in Richmond lacked the power to force the state's secession convention to adjourn.

Then Seward tried to interfere with the expedition to Fort Sumter by getting part of it rerouted to Fort Pickens. And on April 6, when Lincoln sent his letter to the governor of South Carolina—the letter informing him of the expedition to Sumter—Seward leaked the information to a journalist named James E. Harvey, who sent a telegram to South Carolina to tip off the rebels.

But that only furthered Lincoln's objectives.

Lincoln did some leaking himself, since he wanted to make sure that northern public opinion would be formed as he wished it to be formed. When his letter reached South Carolina, General P.G.T. Beauregard—in command at Charleston harbor—conveyed the information to Jefferson Davis in Montgomery, Alabama. Davis ordered Beauregard to fire upon the fort without waiting for the arrival of Lincoln's relief expedition.

And so it was that on April 12, 1861, the Civil War began in Charleston harbor, with the rebels firing first, which was just what Lincoln wanted. He would now begin to fight the kind of war that he had always envisioned if the threat of secession proved real.

He could only hope that the generals possessing the audacity to do such a thing would stay loyal.

CHAIN OF STEEL

As Lincoln prepared to spring the Fort Sumter trap, he was mindful of the danger to Washington, D.C. No doubt he was reviewing the steps that he would take if the Confederates did what he hoped they would do—fire first.

He knew that the attack could lead to follow-up assaults that would aim at overwhelming results. He knew that his city was a target since secessionists were swarming all around it—and within it.

He dashed off a message to Governor Andrew G. Curtin of Pennsylvania advising him to summon troops, and the message was succinct: "I think the necessity of being *ready* increases. Look to it."[1]

Confederates were ready to unleash all sorts of attacks in the aftermath of Fort Sumter. Southern plans for aggression were grandiose enough to include the creation of the "golden circle"—the tropical empire for slavery encompassing the entire Caribbean rim—so Confederate troops would be sent to New Mexico in July 1861, with plans for possible follow-up invasions of California and Central America.

In April, however, the Confederates intended to move quickly in the East. For if the Fort Sumter fight tipped the balance toward secession in Virginia, they would roll the momentum into Maryland—just as Lincoln feared. Then Washington, D.C., would be surrounded, and the president would face the equivalent of "check-mate."

So he acted quickly after getting the news of the Confederate attack on Sumter. He had a meeting with General Scott and Governor Curtin of Pennsylvania to discuss the plight of Washington. Scott denied that the city could be taken, but his statements did not convince Lincoln. Curtin took the threat seriously and he pledged to send one hundred thousand men to defend the city. But it remained to be seen how quickly he could summon a force of any size.

On April 15 Lincoln issued a proclamation calling for troops from the state militias who would serve for ninety days. He called up seventy-five thousand men to augment the regular army, which consisted of seventeen thousand. In the same proclamation he called the newly elected Congress into a special session that would start on the fourth of July. Four days later he proclaimed a naval blockade of the rebellious states.

The decision regarding the special session of Congress did not come easily. Lincoln and others were concerned that if Congress were summoned, proposals for appeasement would result. There was also a question of whether Congress should be summoned to a city that might soon be overrun. One reason for postponing the session until July was to give the administration enough time to make Washington secure.

The reactions to Lincoln's April 15 proclamation could not have been more different in the North and South. A tremendous surge of approval emanated from Americans all over the North. Unionist Democrats like Stephen Douglas worked hard to encourage it. But in every slave state, Lincoln's proclamation—which stated that militia forces would be used to "repossess the forts, places and property, which have been seized from the Union"—was fervently denounced. Southern Unionists were almost unanimous in condemning this threat to "coerce" southern states.

Lincoln temporized when Maryland Unionists like former Senator Reverdy Johnson complained about the threat to "invade" rebellious states. Lincoln said that Washington was his chief concern and that he had no intention of "invading" any state "as I understand the term *invasion*." But he added some caveats. "Suppose Virginia erects, or permits to be erected, batteries on the opposite shore, to bombard the city, are we to stand still and see it done?" And what about Fortress Monroe, at the tip of the York-James peninsula, downriver from Richmond? That was a federal installation, Lincoln observed, and he had every intention of holding it.[2]

So he worked at the task of preparing for war, and emergency measures would have to be taken before Congress convened. The immediate military challenge was nothing less than severe.

Scott suggested to Lincoln that a younger man should take field command of U.S. forces. He recommended Colonel Robert Lee of the Second U.S. Cavalry, and Lincoln took this advice. He asked the elder Francis Preston Blair to offer Lee the position on his behalf. Lee, like Scott, was a Virginian, and both of them had opposed secession.

But Lincoln's militia call tipped the political balance in Virginia. The secession convention voted to take the state out of the Union on April 17, so when Blair met with Lee on the following day, the colonel said no to Lincoln's offer. Scott lectured Lee on his patriotic duty, to no avail.

If Lee had followed the example of other Unionist Virginians, some of whom would go on to become Union war heroes, the Civil War might have ended much sooner. It might also have been less bloody. Lee possessed the kind of audacity that Lincoln's leadership instincts demanded. And with Robert E. Lee in command of U.S. forces in 1861, it is easy to imagine the difference in battlefield results.

On the same day that Lee made his decision, some Pennsylvania troops reached Washington. But on April 19, a riot broke out in Baltimore when the Sixth Regiment of Massachusetts volunteers marched through. Secessionists mobbed them—four soldiers died and thirty-six were wounded—and railroad bridges were burned at the order of the city's own officials. That would make the reinforcement of Washington more difficult. The roads into Washington were blocked, the telegraph lines to the city were cut, and the delivery of mail was interrupted.

Baltimore secessionists requested arms from Virginia, and the governor of that state promised two thousand muskets and twenty heavy guns.

So the threat that Lincoln had foreseen—the threat of Washington being surrounded—was real. And there were doubts about the loyalty of troops within the city. One Washington resident wrote that the nation's slave-holding capital city was "rife with treason, and the streets are full of traitors."[3] He worried that the military reinforcements would arrive too late.

Lincoln shared this fear. Journalist Henry Villard wrote that the president "groaned at the inexplicable delay in the advent of help from the loyal states."[4] A congressman who visited the White House on April 22 stated that Lincoln was "especially exercised at the critical condition of the federal capital."[5] On April 23 he was heard to exclaim, "Why don't they come?"[6]

Desperate plans were made to resist a Confederate attack. Scott directed that the treasury building would serve as an emergency shelter for Lincoln and his cabinet. Two members of Congress, Cassius

Clay of Kentucky and James Lane of Kansas, organized volunteer units that included congressmen and their clerks. Clay himself showed up at the White house bearing pistols and a bowie knife. Lane's "Frontier Guards"—some fifty men bearing muskets—moved into the White House on April 18, led by Lane, who brandished a sword.

Lincoln asked Attorney General Bates for an opinion regarding the imposition of martial law in Maryland. And he summoned his cabinet to meet in an emergency session on April 21. All agreed that emergency powers should be invoked by the executive branch. So Lincoln authorized the members of his cabinet to take action for the purposes of raising money, requisitioning supplies, and enlisting troops.

The sense of panic was spreading far and wide in Washington. In the week that followed the Baltimore riot, only the Sixth Massachusetts and a few hundred men from Pennsylvania were on hand. Delegations from Baltimore visited Lincoln and told him to avoid bringing any more out-of-state troops through their city. Lincoln agreed to bring men through Annapolis temporarily, but then another delegation from Baltimore demanded that no more loyal troops should enter Maryland at all.

Lincoln exploded. "You would have me break my oath and surrender the Government without a blow," he told them. Continuing the remonstrance, he said that there was "no Washington in that—no Jackson in that—no manhood nor honor in that." He said that if Baltimore's defiance got worse he would make the secessionists regret it. "Go home and tell your people that if they will not attack us, we will not attack them," he promised, while adding this warning: "if they do attack us, we will return it, and that severely."[7] All over the North aroused Unionists were calling for vengeance against Baltimore.

Meanwhile, reinforcements had still not arrived. Part of the problem was the added time that was needed to bring troops by boat instead of sending them directly through Baltimore by train.

On April 24, Lincoln verged upon despair. "I don't believe there is any North," he told some men from the Sixth Massachusetts, adding that "*you* are the only Northern realities."[8] But on the very next day, the Seventh New York, a dashing and aristocratic outfit known as the "silk stocking regiment," arrived, and Lincoln, immensely relieved, went down to greet them, shaking hands with every soldier.

In the next two days even more troops arrived until at last, by April 27, ten thousand soldiers were present. Washington was suddenly a military camp with martial music filling the air. As the flood of militiamen and volunteers continued to pour in, authorities were hard-pressed to find places to put them. Before long, troops were being quartered in the Capitol building.

Yet even as the invasion crisis subsided, Lincoln took more precautions. On April 29, he instructed Navy Secretary Welles to

> have as strong a War Steamer as you can conveniently put on that duty, to cruise upon the Potomac, and to look in upon, and, if practicable, examine the Bluff and vicinity, at what is called the White House, once or twice per day; and, in any case of an attempt to erect a battery there, to drive away the party attempting it.[9]

The strategic situation confronting the Confederates was highly ambiguous. They possessed an advantage from the start: their claim of nationhood would stand unless federal authorities could topple it. It was up to the Unionists to invade the South—an enormous task—and Confederates would be fighting on their own familiar ground.

On the other hand, the South was totally out-classed by the superiority of the North in manufacturing, agriculture—the ability of the South to raise food was severely compromised by the predominance in the plantation system of cash crops like cotton—and manpower. Lincoln had realized early on that his task would be to mobilize the North's resources to the full and employ them with force.

Confederate strategists knew that they would have to supplement their resources with power from elsewhere. One external resource that they could tap would be the northern white supremacist Democrats. Another would be the foreign nations that needed cotton—nations that might be inclined to recognize the Confederacy and intervene in America's civil war in order to get it. So the Confederates sent emissaries to France and Britain. They also instituted a cotton embargo, creating an artificial shortage that they hoped would eventually give them leverage. And they worked vigorously to pull the remaining slave states out of the Union.

Lincoln's challenge in the spring of 1861 was to take effective countermeasures to thwart these Confederate efforts. He had already appointed Charles Francis Adams ambassador to Great Britain and he and Seward worked closely with Adams to avert recognition of the Confederacy. One immediate problem concerned the blockade of the South that Lincoln had proclaimed. Under international law, blockades could only be imposed by sovereign states upon other sovereign states in a time of war. The very last thing that Lincoln intended was to set a diplomatic precedent confirming Confederate nationhood. But a blockade was essential to his war plan.

All through 1861 the Lincoln administration would wrestle with this issue. Meanwhile, the most pressing immediate challenge was containing the secessionist impulse in the upper slave states.

The second wave of secession that began in Virginia swept on through the upper South. Even before the Confederates decided on May 8 to move their capital from Montgomery, Alabama, to Richmond, Virginia, Arkansas voted for secession on May 6. North Carolina did the same on May 20, and Tennessee followed suit on June 8. Virginia and Tennessee submitted the secession ordinances to the voters for ratification.

It was vital for Lincoln to hold onto the remaining four slave states—the slave states of Maryland, Kentucky, Missouri, and Delaware.

Delaware was not much of a threat, for the secession movement was weak and there were not many slaves in the state. But Maryland, Kentucky, and Missouri were profoundly divided and secessionism was strong.

Lincoln's policies would vary as he dealt with the politics in each of these border slave states. He would carefully play all the angles in Kentucky with discretion and restraint. But Maryland was different—the threat to Washington was fundamental—so he was ready to deploy direct force.

The governor of Maryland summoned the state's legislature to meet on April 26. Some were recommending to Lincoln that he should arrest or disperse the members of the legislature. Lincoln rejected that advice. He explained his reasoning to Scott. "We can not know in advance," he observed in a letter that he wrote to Scott on April 25, "that their action will not be lawful, and peaceful." Besides, it would not be possible to prevent them from voting for secession at a later date if they chose to. "If we arrest them," Lincoln wrote, "we can not long hold them as prisoners; and, when liberated, they will immediately re-assemble, and take their action. And, precisely the same if we simply disperse them. They will immediately re-assemble in some other place." So Lincoln instructed Scott as follows:

> I therefore conclude that it is only left to the Commanding General
> [i.e., Scott] to watch, and await their action, which, if it shall be to arm

their people against the United States, he is to adopt the most prompt, and efficient means to counteract, even, if necessary, to the bombardment of their cities—and in the *extremest* necessity, the suspension of the writ of habeas corpus.[10]

The fact that Lincoln deemed the suspension of habeas corpus more extreme than the bombardment of cities suggests that this letter to Scott had been composed in some haste. But his willingness to command the bombardment of cities shows that his total-war doctrine was forming early.

Even though the Maryland legislature did not vote for secession, Lincoln suspended the writ of habeas corpus along military lines between the cities of Washington and Philadelphia on April 27. In May, thousands of Union reinforcements passed through Baltimore, and Benjamin Butler—a Democrat from Massachusetts who had risen to a general's rank in the state militia through political contacts—ordered his men to occupy Federal Hill, a high prominence in the southern part of the city.

When a secessionist named John Merryman was arrested in Maryland for aiding the Confederates, he took his case to court and his suit was heard by none other than Chief Justice Taney, riding circuit. Taney sided with Merryman and claimed that only Congress had the right to suspend habeas corpus. Lincoln ignored this ruling, not least of all because Taney's logic was slovenly. The Constitution says nothing in regard to the question of *who* may suspend the writ. The relevant provision in Article One, Section Nine, Clause Two was composed in the passive voice: "The privilege of the writ of habeas corpus shall not be suspended, unless when in cases of rebellion or invasion the public safety may require it."

Lincoln certainly stretched the Constitution in a number of respects between April and July 1861. He spent millions of dollars that Congress had never appropriated and he ordered the expansion of the army and navy without congressional authorization. He took that particular step on May 3, when he called for an additional forty-two thousand volunteers who would serve for three-year enlistments. But the emergency he faced was unprecedented, and he counted on the likelihood that Congress would ratify his actions in the special session that was coming. After the emergency was over, Congress could legalize his deeds retroactively. And that was precisely what would happen.

A year later, he confessed that he had sometimes acted outside the law, but the choice was to "let the government fall at once into ruin" or else construe "the broader powers conferred by the Constitution in cases of insurrection" in a free and expansive manner. Though some of the measures he had taken were "without any authority of law," he made certain that "the government was saved from overthrow."[11]

Though Lincoln was bold and audacious when the situation demanded it, he could also be cautious. His strategic sense told him that he needed to avoid miscalculations when the situation was delicate, and such was the case with Kentucky.

The stakes in Kentucky were high and the state was profoundly divided between Unionists and secessionists. The governor, Beriah Magoffin, was an obvious secessionist, and he refused to send troops in response to Lincoln's militia call-up. But in order to consolidate his position—in order to play for time—he advocated "neutrality" for Kentucky in the weeks that followed the attack on Fort Sumter, a position that the legislature endorsed.

Lincoln saw that this "neutrality" was a ruse, but he sent no troops to the state. Instead, he worked with Kentucky Unionists, including his old friend Joshua Speed, to strengthen their position as much as possible. He authorized Major Robert Anderson, who had commanded the troops in Fort Sumter, to establish a recruiting camp for loyal Kentuckians just across the Ohio River.

Lincoln's patience in Kentucky paid off, and the Unionists won key congressional elections and took over the Kentucky legislature in the summer.

In Missouri, the situation was different, for civil war had already broken out. Initially Lincoln had planned on handling Missouri the way that he was treating Kentucky, but the secessionist governor, Claiborne Jackson, was preparing to seize the huge federal arsenal at St. Louis and distribute its weapons to pro-secession militiamen who called themselves the Minute Men.

Missouri Congressman Frank Blair vowed to prevent this. He used his influence to get a fiery and impetuous army officer named Nathaniel Lyon promoted to command the St. Louis Arsenal.

Blair had been organizing thousands of German immigrants who lived in St. Louis into a militia that he dubbed the Home Guards. Many of these Germans had fled from despotic rule and they hated slavery. They had formed Wide Awake clubs in the election of 1860. One of their leaders, Franz Sigel, would serve as a Union general.

Since Governor Jackson refused to cooperate with Lincoln's militia call-up, Blair persuaded Lincoln to allow him to muster over four thousand members of his Home Guard into federal service. They set up camp around the St. Louis Arsenal. Meanwhile, Jackson mustered the Minute Men into state service. They set up a bivouac of their own in St. Louis and they called it "Camp Jackson."

When the governor arranged to get some cannon and muskets from the Confederates, Blair and Lyon took action. On May 10, Lyon marched his men to Camp Jackson and surrounded it. All of the secessionists were forced to surrender. Then fighting broke out in the streets of St. Louis when a pro-Confederate mob attacked Lyon's troops. Dozens of people were killed or wounded. All over Missouri that night secessionists went on the attack and Governor Jackson called for fifty thousand troops to support secession.

On May 30, Lincoln promoted Lyon to command of the army's entire Department of the West on a temporary basis. Then Lyon and his troops marched to Jefferson City, the Missouri capital, where Jackson and Confederate General Sterling Price were gathering forces. They withdrew as Lyon approached and so the Unionists in Missouri would have the upper hand, at least for a while.

By summer, a new provisional Missouri government was formed, and the new governor, Hamilton Gamble, proclaimed the state loyal to the Union.

Maryland, Kentucky, and Missouri were not the only slave states that were deeply divided between Unionists and secessionists. Tennessee and Virginia were divided, especially in geographical terms because the mountainous portions of those states where the plantation system was weak—east Tennessee and western Virginia—were Unionist. One of Tennessee's U.S. senators, Andrew Johnson, refused to go along with secession. He proclaimed that the secessionists were traitors and he continued to represent his state in the U.S. Senate.

In western Virginia a full-scale rebellion-within-a-rebellion began within the western counties. On May 1, a committee of Virginia loyalists from Butler County called upon Lincoln and requested assistance. Lincoln authorized War Secretary Cameron to send them arms, and on May 24 he sent troops from Ohio and Indiana into western Virginia. By June the Unionist movement in western Virginia was strong enough to proclaim—in a convention that met at Wheeling—a "Reorganized Government of Virginia."

Led by Francis Pierpont, they proclaimed themselves the legitimate legislature of the state. But their real aim was to secede from Virginia and establish a new state.

These stark divisions within key states of the Confederacy were representative of patterns that were present throughout the slave states. An underground Unionist resistance would continue within the Confederacy throughout the Civil War. By the same token, Confederate sympathy was present in many parts of the North.

Amid these unprecedented events, the Lincolns began to establish their own routines in the White House.

They had servants to help them out and there were guards on duty to protect them, though the president decided right away that the guards were unnecessary. Stewards and cooks and waiters and drivers and messengers bustled about. A few of these servants were black. One of them, an African American valet named William Johnson, had worked for the Lincolns back in Springfield. Mary Lincoln hired a free black seamstress and dress designer named Elizabeth Keckley who became one of her closest confidantes during her years in the White House.

Lincoln usually rose early and got right to work. After reading the newspapers and drafting correspondence, he would eat a light breakfast and then walk over to the war department building next to the White House and look at the incoming telegrams. After that he would sort out the mail and start receiving visitors at 10 a.m. in his office.

Almost every day he was besieged by supplicants and well-meaning pests of every description. He could have spared himself this ordeal, but he chose to endure it. If cabinet meetings were scheduled, he would end these visiting hours at mid-day, but on other weekdays he continued to receive visitors throughout the afternoon. Through it all, he tried to get some work done.

Sometimes he would take a break to eat lunch in the residential quarters, but visitors accosted him in the hallway as he attempted to leave the office. So he frequently ate lunch and even dinner in his office as he kept on working.

This routine was exhausting, and it slowly began to take its toll on Lincoln in some ways that were observed by others. William O. Stoddard wrote that Lincoln became "like a man who carried a load too great for human strength; and, as the years went on and the load grew heavier, it bowed him into a premature old age."[12] At least Lincoln relaxed now and then with a carriage ride in late afternoon. When he did eat dinner with his family, the meal was served at six. Afterward he would sometimes socialize with friends and members of Congress in the Red Room before retiring.

No doubt the enormous fatigue that resulted from this routine accounted for the shakiness that Lincoln sometimes displayed in the course of state receptions and dinners. The British journalist William Howard Russell, who wrote for the *London Times*, reported that Lincoln would enter a room "with a shambling, loose, irregular, almost unsteady gait."[13] Moreover, he had slipped back into to his accustomed carelessness about attire and personal appearance. The landscape architect Frederick Law Olmsted, who visited the White House, wrote that Lincoln "dressed in a cheap & nasty French black cloth suit," so wrinkled that it looked as if it had just come "out of a tight carpet bag."[14]

The first ceremonial event at the White House was a reception held for foreign dignitaries on March 7. The next day the Lincolns held a public reception, which Attorney General Bates described as a "motley crowd and terrible squeeze."[15] At another reception on March 22, the novelist Herman Melville observed that Lincoln "shook hands like a good fellow—working hard at it like a man sawing wood at so much per cord."[16]

His wit could liven up amid this busy routine when a visitor amused him; when someone reported to him on one occasion that "up our way, we believe in God and Abraham Lincoln," he answered, "My friend, you are more than half right."[17]

William Russell wrote a vivid sketch of Lincoln's appearance and general demeanor. He had "pendulous arms," Russell wrote, large hands and feet, a "thatch of wild republican hair," and a "strange quaint face" that commanded one's attention. His nose probed its surroundings "with an inquiring, anxious air, as though it were sniffing for some good thing in the wind." And his eyes—they commanded attention all the time. They projected a feeling "which almost amounts to tenderness."[18]

Reactions to Mary Todd Lincoln in her role as First Lady were divided. Some found her gracious, even elegant. Gustavus Vasa Fox regarded her as "Lady Like," and he wrote with approval that she "converses easily, dresses well and has the Kentucky pronunciation."[19] But others perceived in her the qualities that had made her so unpopular in many quarters back in Springfield. She struck many people as ostentatious and even gauche.

Mary's less-than-winsome qualities were still a tribulation for Lincoln, just as they had been for many years. She fancied herself a kind of power behind the throne and she flaunted her influence in many different ways. She interfered in political appointments, campaigning for unsavory characters and padding the federal payroll. She helped flatterers to gain access to political documents which they leaked, to the president's embarrassment.

She used emotional blackmail to get her way with Lincoln; she would sometimes threaten to throw public tantrums that would mortify them both if he did not give in and do her bidding. Before long she was involved in quite a number of scandals and her behavior was impossible to control.

Right after the Lincolns moved into the White House she had come to the conclusion that the place should be completely refurbished. There was plenty of justification for this decision and she secured a handsome congressional appropriation. The project was carried out between May and October 1861 under her direction.

She went on numerous out-of-town shopping sprees in the course of this project and there were allegations that she went completely wild in the course of her spending. There were even rumors to the effect that she was taking bribes from contractors who failed to provide the promised goods or else over-charged the government.

Scandal-mongers also whispered that she was having an affair with a man named William S. Wood, a New York business associate of Seward's who had planned the Lincolns' trip from Springfield to Washington.

Mary demanded that Lincoln appoint Wood commissioner of public buildings. She locked herself in her room until the president complied. Wood did not last very long in this position. In June Lincoln received an anonymous letter alleging that Mary and Wood were having liaisons during her shopping trips in New York.[20]

Mary's aberrational behavior was a source of great torment to Lincoln, just as it had been during all the years of their marriage. Orville Browning recalled that Lincoln "several times told me . . . that he was constantly under great apprehension lest his wife should do something which would bring him into disgrace."[21]

But if Mary worsened the emotional pressure for Lincoln in the White House, his boys were a source of great solace.

Lincoln's children made a wonderful impression on everyone in 1861, though their pranks could sometimes arouse the consternation of the White

House staff. Robert was away at Harvard, but Willie and Tad made their presence felt constantly. They "kept the house in an uproar," wrote John Hay, and "drove their tutor wild with their good natured disobedience."[22]

Willie, according to Hay, was a gifted child who inherited many of his father's mental qualities. He was "a child of great promise, capable of close application and study. He had a fancy for drawing up railway time tables, and would conduct an imaginary train from Chicago to New York with perfect precision." Tad on the other hand "was a merry, warm-blooded, kindly little boy, perfectly lawless, and full of odd fancies and inventions." For instance,

> he ran continually in and out of his father's cabinet, interrupting his gravest labors and conversations with his bright, rapid and very imperfect speech—for he had an impediment which made his articulation almost unintelligible, until he was nearly grown. He would perch upon his father's knee and sometimes even on his shoulder while the most weighty conversations were going on. Sometimes, escaping from the domestic authorities, he would take refuge in that sanctuary for the whole evening, dropping to sleep at last on the floor, when the President would pick him up and carry him tenderly to bed.[23]

Unlike Willie, Tad did not succeed at his studies. But Lincoln didn't care very much, according to Hay. "'Let him run,' the easy-going President would say; 'he has time enough to learn his letters and get pokey.'"[24]

The boys' pets included ponies, which they rode all over the White House grounds, goats (named Nanny and Nanko), which they hitched to a cart, and some kittens that Seward, who at last began to settle down and behave himself, presented as a gift.

Lincoln enjoyed playing with these kittens, and he played along with the boys and their friends. The children were smitten with the Zouave military fashions that were suddenly the rage. They asked for Zouave uniforms of their own—a photograph was taken of Tad in his child-sized outfit—and they dressed up a doll named Jack in Zouave attire. Once the boys put Jack on trial for dereliction of duty, and when Lincoln found out about the game, he gave the doll a full pardon.

The boys' Zouave fixation was instilled by their friend and hero, Elmer Ephraim Ellsworth, who had gone to New York to form a special Zouave regiment composed of New York City firemen, renowned for their toughness.

When Ellsworth and his "Fire Zouaves" arrived in the nation's capital, they marched up Pennsylvania Avenue past the White House as Lincoln and his family watched. Then on May 8, they were sworn into federal service. Lincoln and Tad looked on as the oath was administered by General Lorenzo Thomas, the adjutant general of the army, and Major Irvin McDowell, who commanded the troops who were guarding the Capitol. McDowell, after being promoted, would soon command all the troops in Washington.

On May 23 the voters of Virginia approved the secession ordinance, so Lincoln decided it was time to send troops across the Potomac River and occupy the portions of Virginia that were close to Washington. The primary objective was Alexandria, a port city down the river. On the night of May 23–24, troops marched quietly across the two bridges—the Long Bridge and the Chain Bridge—that led over the Potomac into Virginia. Ellsworth and his Zouaves were assigned to an amphibious operation that would land directly in Alexandria.

The town capitulated right away. The Confederate garrison withdrew and the Union troops entered. While securing the telegraph office, Ellsworth noticed that a large Confederate flag was flying on one of the buildings. This flag had been waving over the city for weeks, and one could see it quite easily through a spy glass from Washington. Ellsworth decided it was time to remove this flag. It was flying from the roof of Marshall House, a small hotel that was owned and operated by a fervent secessionist named James Jackson. Ellsworth entered, ascended the stairs to the roof, and came back down with the flag.

Then Jackson appeared and shot him dead. The troops who accompanied Ellsworth fired back. Jackson fell—his face blown away. The whole thing occurred within seconds. The news of Ellsworth's death spread rapidly all over the North.

Lincoln and his sons were devastated by the loss of Ellsworth. Hay remembered that "Lincoln loved him like a younger brother."[25] When Lincoln heard the news he burst into tears, telling people around him, "excuse me, but I cannot talk." When he recovered, he said that Ellsworth's gallantry "shows the heroic spirit that animates our soldiers . . . yet who can restrain their grief to see them fall in such a way as this; not by the fortunes of war, but by the hand of an assassin."[26]

In a letter to Ellsworth's parents, Lincoln reflected on this death by what he called assassination. "So much of promised usefulness to one's country," he wrote them, "and of bright hopes for one's self and friends, have rarely been so suddenly dashed, as in his fall." After writing to them about their "early fallen child," Lincoln signed himself "your friend in a common affliction."[27]

This event marked the start of a process that would gradually constitute a turning point in Lincoln's leadership. Ever since he made the slavery issue the new centerpiece of his politics in 1854—and then written his first reflections on the threat of secession in 1856—his mood was determined and bold. That mood would continue to characterize his wartime leadership. And to the boldness and the determination would be added the brilliance with which he had always delighted in out-maneuvering opponents.

But something else would now be added to his mood, or reawakened from his moods of long ago: the sorrow he had known down the years from the experience of losing his loved ones, combined with his sensitivity to the pain of anyone who suffered. The gentle father who loved to indulge his children would have to put himself into a very different frame of mind when he issued his tough-as-nails orders to annihilate armies. Still, the sorrow and gentility would always be there as he did so. And the intensity of the sorrow would grow with the casualty lists.

Another and more ironic death occurred a few weeks later. After several years of declining health, Stephen Douglas passed away in Chicago on June 3.

The Union occupation of northern Virginia proceeded over the course of the next month. Robert E. Lee's mansion that stood across the river from Washington was seized. Union forces commanded by General Robert Patterson—like Winfield Scott, a veteran of the Mexican War—marched to Harper's Ferry in mid-June, and the Confederate forces there, under the command of General Joseph Johnston, withdrew.

And out in western Virginia, Union troops under the command of Generals George B. McClellan and Thomas A. Morris beat Confederates under the command of Col. George Porterfield at Philippi in a skirmish that occurred on June 3. McClellan in particular was given credit for this action in accounts that were published in the northern press. A West Point veteran who retired from the army to serve as a railroad executive—he was the one who had let Stephen Douglas use his private car back in 1858—McClellan returned to active duty after Fort Sumter and was given the command of the Department of the Ohio, headquartered in Cincinnati.

The Union victories in western Virginia continued in July when Confederates under the command of General Robert S. Garnett were beaten in the battles of Rich Mountain and Corrick's Ford. Garnett was killed. Though Robert E. Lee had been promoted to general and put in charge of all Confederate forces in Virginia, he would not lead men into battle until September.

Meanwhile, the steady flow of Union recruits kept pouring into Washington. News of Ellsworth's murder inflamed northern public opinion, and Lincoln's call for forty-two thousand more militia volunteers had elicited a response from more than two hundred thousand. A great Union army was in the early stages of creation. Lincoln borrowed books on military strategy from the Library of Congress and he read them far into the night.

Winfield Scott had been devising an overall strategic plan for the prosecution of the war. He envisioned a slow campaign that would gradually choke the life out of the Confederacy, causing pressure that would prompt an upsurge of Unionism in the slave states while avoiding heavy casualties. His so-called "Anaconda Plan" envisioned an expansion of Lincoln's naval blockade with the addition of a huge thrust down the Mississippi River to split away Texas and Arkansas from the other rebel states.

Lincoln and Republican members of Congress, who had been gradually arriving in Washington, believed that this grand design should be supplemented by some fast and decisive thrusts. At first, Lincoln favored a plan that would build up troops in Fortress Monroe in Virginia while an expeditionary force was sent to attack Charleston, South Carolina.

Lincoln had begun to meet often with Scott and he requested the general to send him daily reports. On June 25, he brought Scott to a council of war whose participants included the members of the cabinet as well as two other military officers: Irvin McDowell, promoted to general and placed in command of fifty thousand Union troops in northern Virginia, and also Montgomery Meigs, the army's southern-born quartermaster-general.

McDowell was a regular army officer who had attended military school in France. He had an impressive amount of experience in military staff work.

Though Scott was opposed to fast action—believing that the Union recruits required more training—he instructed McDowell to plan for a direct strike at Manassas, a strategic rail junction located roughly thirty miles southwest of Washington. The Confederate general P.G.T. Beauregard, who commanded the bombardment of Fort Sumter, had occupied

Manassas with twenty thousand troops. McDowell would command a force of thirty thousand, thus out-numbering the rebels. Other Confederates under the command of Joseph Johnston were stationed in the Shenandoah Valley at Winchester. These troops would have to be held at bay so they could not be moved to Manassas.

A second council of war was held on June 29, and the decision was made to proceed. McDowell—who shared Scott's aversion to a premature attack—would lead his men to attack the rebels at Manassas. Union troops in Harper's Ferry under the command of Robert Patterson would keep the Confederates at Winchester from joining in the fight.

Lincoln wrote a long and carefully composed message to Congress that was ready for the Fourth of July. It reiterated points that he had made in his Inaugural Address, but his tone was defiant this time.

His purpose was to create a bipartisan politics of Unionism while de-emphasizing the issue of slavery. He needed to secure the approval of Congress for all of the emergency measures he had taken. He also needed the kinds of authorizations and appropriations that a total war would require.

The politics were generally good since Republicans were left in control of Congress when the Democratic members from Confederate states went off to Richmond. But Lincoln was taking no chances on divisiveness. If the war went badly, Democrats could always blame the Republicans not only for the military defeats but also for starting the war in the first place by dint of their Free Soil politics—politics that had pushed the slave states over the brink into secession.

Due to all of these imperatives of strategy, Lincoln wanted a unified political front if he could get one. His message to Congress of July 4, 1861, was designed to achieve that goal.

He reiterated his contention that secession was impossible, insisting that no secession had occurred. This was not a war between nations or a war between sovereign states: it was simply a police action to suppress an illegal insurrection.

"The States," he argued, "have their status IN the Union, and they have no other *legal status*. . . . The Union is older than any of the States; and, in fact, it created them as States."[28]

So he would never refer to the "Confederacy" or to "Confederates," for that would serve to legitimize their claim to nationhood. He spoke of "rebels"—or "Confederates so-called"—who were the members of a huge and illegal rebellion. They invoked "state sovereignty" because "they could never raise their treason to any respectable magnitude, by any name which implies a *violation* of law," Lincoln wrote, and so they perpetrated a gross constitutional fiction. He continued:

> With rebellion thus sugar-coated, they have been drugging the public mind in their section for more than thirty years ... until at length, they have brought many good men to a willingness to take up arms against the government the day *after* some assemblage of men have enacted the farcical pretense of taking their state out of the Union.[29]

And the men who enacted the farcical pretense were members of an arrogant, elitist minority. "There is much reason to believe," Lincoln wrote, that "the Union men are in the majority in many ... of the so-called seceded States." Indeed, "it may well be questioned whether there is, to-day, a majority of the legally qualified voters of any State, except South Carolina, in favor of disunion."

Even in Virginia and Tennessee, where the secession ordinances were sent to the voters for ratification, the results were suspicious, Lincoln claimed, for "the result of an election, held in military camps, where the bayonets are all on one side of the question voted upon, can scarcely be considered as demonstrating popular sentiment."[30]

No, the rebel leaders scorned the principles of popular consent or majority rule, Lincoln charged. Instead of "We the People," their would-be Confederate constitution began with the words "We, the deputies of the sovereign and independent States," so Lincoln asked the question why: "Why this deliberate pressing out of view [of] the rights of men, and the authority of the people?" Because the Confederacy was a hierarchy rigged by a selfish master class, and it would have to be opposed by the sorts of Unionists who would consciously fight "a People's contest:"

> On the side of the Union, it is a struggle for maintaining in the world, that form, and substance of government, whose leading object is, to elevate the condition of men—to lift artificial weights from all shoulders—to clear the paths of laudable pursuit for all—to afford all, an unfettered start, and a fair chance, in the race of life.[31]

It was also a struggle to uphold the principle of majority rule that is integral to such a form of government. It was a struggle to

> demonstrate to the world, that those who fairly carry an election, can also suppress a rebellion—that ballots are the rightful, and peaceful, successors to bullets, and that when ballots have fairly, and constitutionally, decided, there can be no successful appeal, except to ballots themselves, at succeeding elections.[32]

Referring to those like Taney who challenged the things that he had done before Congress was in session—things like suspending the writ of habeas corpus—Lincoln presented a brief that was a fine demonstration of the art of considering the parts in relation to the whole.

He acknowledged the fact that he had sworn a presidential oath to make certain that the laws were faithfully enforced. And yet he found himself in an unprecedented situation since "the whole of the laws . . . were being resisted . . . in nearly one-third of the States." So what was he to do? He had used his very best judgment in a flagrant emergency and called the new Congress to meet in special session just as soon as it was safe for the members to convene. And to make things safe, he had suspended the writ of habeas corpus, which he claimed he had the perfect right to do.

People like Taney should see the big picture and spare the world their perversity, myopia, and foolishness, Lincoln said. He put it this way: were "all the laws, *but one*, to go unexecuted, and the government itself fall to pieces, lest that one be violated?" Why be pedantic when the nation's very life was in danger?

In any case, Lincoln refused to concede that he had taken an unconstitutional step since the Constitution "is silent" as to *who* may suspend the writ of habeas corpus while providing that the writ may indeed be suspended in cases of rebellion. The suspension clause was "made for a dangerous emergency," Lincoln observed, and it was therefore impossible to believe "that the framers of the instrument intended, that in every case, the danger should run its course, until Congress could be called together," since the danger might make it impossible for Congress to meet unless emergency measures were taken.[33]

Lincoln ended his message by declaring he had striven to do his duty as he saw it and that Congress would have to do the same. They should all confront this rebellion together with a courage that was worthy of America. Let us go forward, Lincoln wrote, "without fear, and with manly hearts."[34]

Congress gave him almost everything that he asked for. He requested a war appropriation of $400 million, and Congress exceeded that request by giving him $500 million. He was also given the authority to enlist at least four hundred thousand more soldiers. Congress ratified his emergency actions except for the suspension of habeas corpus. Congress finally ratified that action retroactively in 1863.

On July 16, McDowell and his men marched away to attack the Confederates at Manassas. They had not had very much training, and the maps at their disposal were poor. Moreover, the hot summer weather made the going very slow, and it took them four days to arrive where the Confederates were waiting on heights behind a stream that was known as Bull Run.

No attempts had been made to take the rebels by surprise; the army's movement had been publicized in the newspapers, and a flock of politicians and socialites from Washington had tagged along. Winfield Scott, notwithstanding his objection to launching an attack against the rebels so soon, informed Lincoln that McDowell's troops would win easily. And it looked for a while as if they would.

On Sunday morning, July 21, the men got off to a very good start when they forced Beauregard's troops to make a steady series of retreats. But at last the Confederates established a line that held firm, and the credit for this was largely due to the courage of General Thomas J. Jackson, a West Point graduate who commanded troops in the Mexican War and then taught at the Virginia Military Institute. Jackson earned his nickname "Stonewall" on the spot in the battle of Manassas—or Bull Run, as northerners would frequently call this first great battle of the Civil War.

It bears noting that another commander who was destined for greatness took part in this battle at a lower level of command: William Tecumseh Sherman was serving as a colonel under McDowell.

The tide of the battle turned in the Confederates' favor after Jackson put a stop to their retreat. Reinforcements began to arrive from Winchester by train. General Patterson had been ordered to prevent these troops from joining forces with Beauregard's army, but he did not accomplish that objective.

Then the Union troops panicked. They dropped their weapons and knapsacks and ran for their lives back to Washington. The battle of Manassas had turned into a Union rout.

All day long Lincoln visited the war department seeking news of the battle. Scott told him that everything was fine and that a Union victory was certain. In late afternoon Lincoln went for a carriage ride, and then the news of the disaster reached Washington. Indeed, eyewitnesses were pouring into Washington with lurid accounts. Lincoln took the news calmly, but he stayed up most of the night going over the reports.

The battle was the largest in American history up to that point, and the casualties on each side—killed, wounded, and missing—exceeded one thousand.

The next day, when a drenching rain descended over Washington, Lincoln sent for General George B. McClellan, the commander who had been achieving some success out in western Virginia. To McClellan would be given the task of reorganizing the force that fled from Manassas—reorganizing it and building it up until at last it became a mighty force called the Army of the Potomac.

There was much finger-pointing in the aftermath of the Manassas defeat, and northern newspapers excoriated Lincoln as well as his cabinet. Editorial writers assigned them the blame for an attack that was launched prematurely. But much of what they wrote was unfair since McDowell and his men had come very close to winning in the early phase of the battle. And they might have won, too, if the Confederates out in Winchester had been kept from reinforcing Beauregard.

The men's lack of training did, of course, account for the way in which they panicked and fled, and more training of the Washington garrison was clearly in order.

Scott tried to foist the blame onto others, telling everyone that he opposed the attack when others had first suggested it. It was perfectly true that he had opposed the operation in its earliest stages, but once it was launched he uttered bland and confident predictions. His days as general in chief were clearly numbered.

Lincoln took the attacks upon himself philosophically. On July 23 he wrote a private memorandum sketching plans for future operations. In addition to calling for the troops in Washington to be "reorganized as rapidly as possible," he called for a second and larger attack against Manassas to be followed by attacks against Memphis and East Tennessee.

The defeat at Manassas was a shock to northern public opinion. Victory over the rebellion might not come easily. As the point began to sink in—with the drive to stamp out secession expanding into a great and possibly long civil war—the potential for revolutionary change was felt in many different parts of America.

The most vocal advocates of revolutionary change were the African Americans, abolitionists, and Radical Republicans. Patriotic blacks were overwhelmingly eager to serve in the army, but federal policy forbade it. Abolitionists and Radical Republicans chafed at the delicacies of coalition-building with Democratic Unionists and they sought to strike at slavery.

Lincoln agreed with these people in a great many ways, but he had to be mindful of the border state problem and he had to keep the politics of slavery under control if he wished to prevent the overall political situation from spinning out of control. The political leverage of the Republican Party could disintegrate if a white supremacist backlash started in the North.

Lincoln was right to perceive this risk, and it would shape his strategic calculations throughout the war. Stephen Douglas was dead, but his bigoted attitudes were very much alive in the minds of many Unionists and Free Soilers—the people whose support was essential to preventing the triumph of a powerful pro-slavery Confederacy. The Blair brothers, for instance—Montgomery and Frank—were fervent in their hatred of the Confederacy and just as fervent in their hatred of blacks.

In 1861 Lincoln kept his mind open to the possibility of adding antislavery goals to the war incrementally. He found ways to use the force of abolitionist activity as the basis for some secret anti-slavery work of his own. Indeed, by 1862 he would urge some abolitionists (in private) to continue their moral agitation. His purpose was to set up an insideroutsider power orchestration with them.

This story began as early as May 1861 when Virginia slaves began running away from plantations and crossing Union lines at Fortress Monroe near Hampton Roads. General Benjamin Butler, in command at the fortress, was visited by a Confederate officer under a flag of truce. This officer demanded the return of three runaway slaves who belonged to a fellow Confederate. He demanded their return per the terms of the Fugitive Slave law.

Butler had the exquisite pleasure of refusing. He reasoned that the Fugitive Slave law, a federal act, was not binding in the case of rebellious citizens who claimed to have renounced all federal authority.

Interestingly, Lincoln predicted that situations like this one might arise if southern militants attempted secession. Back in 1859, he warned them in his Cincinnati speech that secession could ironically backfire—to the detriment of slave owners. If the people of the North "cease to be under any obligation to do anything for you," he had asked, "how much better off do you think you will be?"[35]

Of course there was an inconsistency in what Butler was doing in light of the Unionist claim that no secession had occurred. And yet Butler had no intention of letting that inconsistency worry him. Instead, he had fun with it as he classified the runaway slaves as "contraband of war." He made this policy official on May 27. He said that since the Virginians *claimed* to be citizens of a foreign country, they could not *consistently* invoke the laws of the federal government that they had renounced.

Butler notified Winfield Scott of his decision, and Secretary of War Cameron ratified it. Lincoln also upheld Butler's order.

The implications were obvious—and immense. By August over nine hundred fugitive slaves had escaped to Fortress Monroe and Butler put them steadily to work in support of the Union war effort.

The anti-slavery potential of these developments was so powerful that congressional Democrats struck back. On July 22 and 25, the House and Senate approved some resolutions introduced by Senators John Crittenden of Kentucky and Andrew Johnson of Tennessee—resolutions affirming that the war was being fought for only one purpose: to "defend and maintain the supremacy of the Constitution and to preserve the Union, with all the dignity, equality, and rights of the several States unimpaired." The war was *not* being waged for the "purpose of overthrowing or interfering with the rights or established institutions of those States."

The politics of Unionist coalition in the summer of 1861 were so fragile that Congress passed these resolutions with Republican support and Lincoln signed them.

But in the aftermath of the Manassas defeat, the politics regarding the slavery issue were changing. Republicans complained that the rebels' position was strengthened by the fact that slave labor was supporting the Confederate armies. The use of slaves as workers in Confederate camps released whites to bear arms and kill patriots.

As early as July 5, the Radical Republican Zachariah Chandler introduced a bill to seize property that was used in support of the rebellion. In the aftermath of Manassas, the backing for such a confiscation law became stronger. At last, by the end of the special congressional session, the support was strong enough to pass the First Confiscation Act, which Lincoln signed into law on August 6. This act permitted Union armies to seize any property that was helping the rebels to perpetrate their war against the Union—including slaves.

The act did *not* give these "contraband" slaves their freedom, but it did authorize their use in the Union war effort as military workers. In effect, it enshrined the action of Benjamin Butler in the annals of federal law.

The efficacy of the Fugitive Slave Law of 1850 had been dealt a strong blow.

No sooner had Congress adjourned than the war in Missouri intensified. Confederate troops under Generals Sterling Price and Benjamin McColloch approached the Union forces of Nathaniel Lyon that were camped near Springfield, Missouri. Lyon was killed in the battle of Wilson's Creek on August 10. The Union troops, exhausted, deprived of their charismatic leader, and running out of ammunition, withdrew. The engagement was a Confederate victory.

Lyon's appointment as commander of the western department had been temporary from the start. His successor had already been appointed by the time he was killed. John C. Frémont, the Republicans' presidential candidate in 1856, volunteered to fight for the Union after Fort Sumter. He possessed some military experience—as a topographical army engineer and explorer who had served in the Mexican War. But he was really a "political general" in 1861, a politician in search of greater prominence and glory as a military commander.

The same thing happened in the Confederacy, where southern politicians won the right to lead armies into battle. Such political generals would play an important role in the Civil War, for better or for worse.

Lincoln appointed Frémont to command the western department on July 1, and he arrived in St. Louis on July 25. He began well enough in some respects; learning that the Confederates were planning an attack against Cairo, Illinois, he reinforced that strategic position. He also sent troops under the command of Ulysses S. Grant to protect the Missouri state capital, Jefferson City, in the aftermath of Wilson's Creek.

Frémont was making big plans for the thrust down the Mississippi River as envisioned in Scott's Anaconda Plan. He intended to launch an attack against Memphis in line with Lincoln's post-Manassas memorandum. And he was one of the very first people to recognize the potential of Grant to play a major role in the western campaign. On August 27 he gave Grant field command.

But only three days later, on August 30, he issued an order declaring that the slaves of all rebels in Missouri would be freed. Not confiscated— *freed.* And he had not consulted with Lincoln before he did it.

The Lincolns thought about using the summer home in Washington where Buchanan often stayed: a house on the grounds of the Retired Soldiers' Home that was several miles northwest of the White House. With its high elevation, it offered a welcome respite from summertime humidity.

But Lincoln had to be available on rather short notice in light of the urgent political and military situation in August 1861, so he made the reluctant decision to stay in the White House all summer. After an August 3 reception for Prince Jérôme Napoléon of France, Mary took a long vacation with Willie and Tad. They traveled through New Jersey and New York and paid a visit to Niagara Falls. Lincoln remained at work on the many different problems he confronted.

While he paid close attention to the rapidly unfolding events in Missouri, he was preoccupied with the eastern theater and he wanted to get the army that retreated from Manassas reorganized quickly enough to strike again. Lincoln had chosen General George B. McClellan for the job.

The selection of McClellan sheds light upon a problem that confronted both Lincoln and Jefferson Davis in the Civil War. Both of them had to select their commanders on the basis of battlefield results. And even though Davis had the distinct advantages of a West Point background and service as secretary of war, he would face the same challenge as Lincoln: the challenge of finding commanders who were capable of carrying out his orders. And like Lincoln, he would often find himself disappointed by the men he selected.

As the war progressed, both Lincoln and Davis had to face this challenge repeatedly. They had to decide who deserved to be trusted with further command assignments—on the basis of their past performances—and who deserved to be relieved of command or reassigned. The problem was figuring out how to judge the results of particular battles, for the outcomes could be misleading. One general's success might be due to sheer luck while the failure of another could be due to the mistakes of subordinates. Every evaluation of a battlefield outcome could lead to erroneous conclusions.

For example: Robert E. Lee had a well-deserved reputation for excellence in command when the war began. Scott recommended him to Lincoln for field command, and after Lee had decided to support the rebellion, Davis gave him command of all Confederate forces in Virginia. But when Lee led troops into battle *in person* he could not accomplish his objectives. Davis sent him to western Virginia in September 1861 to reverse the ongoing series of Confederate defeats. But when Lee was defeated himself in the battle of Cheat Mountain (September 12–15), his reputation plummeted and Davis sent him off to Georgia and South Carolina to organize coastal defenses. And that was where he had to stay for another four months.

McClellan had been victorious in western Virginia, at Philippi on June 3 and again at Rich Mountain on July 11. So it made good sense when Lincoln summoned him to Washington to take command of the troops who had retreated from Manassas.

But McClellan would prove to be incompetent for major field command—unable to command in heavy battles as opposed to light skirmishes—unable to carry out a sustained and serious offensive. His early successes in western Virginia were just as misleading as the failure there of Robert E. Lee. McClellan did possess some talents: a good engineer, he would prove to be a wizard in constructing defenses, and he oversaw the creation of a magnificent ring of earthen-work forts to protect and surround the city of Washington during the autumn of 1861.

He was also effective in the training and equipping of armies. He took the shattered men who fled Manassas and he turned them into an excellent and well-trained fighting force with very high morale. He was charismatic, and before very long he had earned the fervent loyalty of his men, who called him "Little Mac." He had given them back their pride.

But McClellan would prove to be a terrible field commander. He over-estimated the strength and the number of the enemies he faced while ignoring his very own advantages. And he had no stomach for combat. His forte was textbook maneuvers and he dreaded the moment when the guns would really blaze forth. He had no business leading men into battles.

Even worse, he possessed certain character flaws that ran deep. He was conceited—his sense of self-importance could become so inflated that it made him insufferable to those who saw through his pretenses. He was really just a coward at heart, as his battlefield performance would show. His arrogance was nothing but a cover-up for weakness. At his worst, he was a phony—an imposter—a conceited ass. After Lincoln had summoned him to Washington, McClellan wrote to his wife as follows:

I find myself in a new & strange position here—Presdt, Cabinet, Genl Scott & all deferring to me—by some strange operation of magic I seem to have become *the* power of the land. I almost think that were I to win some small success now I could become Dictator or anything else that might please me—but nothing of that kind would please me—*therefore* I *won't* be Dictator. Admirable self-denial![36]

As is often the case with such creatures of conceit, it stood to reason that he blamed other people when he failed. In his own mind his powers were superb and immaculate: he could do no wrong. And the fact that he was a white-supremacist Democrat who despised Lincoln and Republicans in general did not help matters at all.

Back in the spring, when he was appointed to command the Department of the Ohio, McClellan sent Scott a proposal. He proposed to march directly from Ohio to Richmond with eighty thousand men—over mountain ranges and without any railroad connections for purposes of supply. Scott dismissed the scheme at once.

Now that McClellan commanded the Army of the Potomac—the name that he chose for McDowell's defeated force—he proposed an even grander scheme to Lincoln on August 2: to capture the following Confederate cities in quick succession: Richmond, New Orleans, Charleston, Savannah, Montgomery, Pensacola, and Mobile. He would "crush out this rebellion at its very heart."[37] But the immediate task was to resume the offensive in Virginia, beginning with Manassas, which the rebels still held.

All through September and October, the Army of the Potomac grew in size, and McClellan took Lincoln on grand reviews to see the troops in their various camps around the city of Washington and in northern Virginia. The men sometimes rode on horseback together—a mode of travel that was perfectly familiar to Lincoln after all the years he had spent riding circuit in backwoods Illinois. Nicolay observed the president's horsemanship and wrote that Lincoln "rode as erect and firm in his saddle as a practical trooper—he is more graceful in his saddle than anywhere else I have seen him."[38]

As early as October some Democrats were speaking of McClellan as a possible presidential contender in 1864. They liked the confident tone that he exuded and they thought that if he really turned out to be a military hero he might go on to become a much greater man of destiny. People were beginning to call McClellan "Young Napoleon," and this naturally went to his head.

Republicans were more skeptical, especially due to the fact that McClellan's pro-slavery views were well known. By October, the Radical Republicans were impatient and increasingly suspicious about George McClellan. The grand reviews of the well-trained troops were just repeated over and over as the weather that was suitable for an offensive in Virginia—the roads would become deep morasses of mud in the freeze-thaw cycles of the winter—ebbed away.

Three Republican members of Congress—Benjamin Wade of Ohio, Zachariah Chandler of Michigan, and Lyman Trumbull of Illinois—paid a call on McClellan and told him that they were tired of the inaction—tired of the endless parades. They called for an attack in Virginia while the good weather lasted. McClellan claimed he was eager to attack, but the ineffectual General Scott kept holding him back.

Scott, wrote McClellan to his wife, "is a perfect imbecile" who "knows nothing, appreciates nothing & is ever in my way."[39] The fact of the matter was that Scott was quite willing to retire, for his age and his health were undeniable impediments to action. And he had no desire to be constantly quarrelling with an insubordinate prig like George McClellan.

At least some good news arrived for Lincoln at the very end of August—news that provided consolation for all the inaction. A land-sea task force attacked and captured Forts Hatteras and Clark in the outer banks of North Carolina. The troops were commanded by Benjamin Butler and the naval operation had been planned by Gustavus Vasa Fox. When the two men reported to Lincoln, the president, according to Butler, was so happy that he danced around the room with them.[40]

As Lincoln attempted to size up McClellan, he faced a more immediate problem in John C. Frémont's emancipation decree. On August 30, Frémont declared martial law in Missouri and ordered that the property of anyone supporting the rebellion would be confiscated and their slaves would be freed. Anti-slavery leaders all over the North were jubilant.

But Frémont had not consulted with Lincoln, and the president received many messages from people who were less than jubilant. One of them was his old friend Joshua Speed. Within a week Speed warned him that Frémont's emancipation order could jeopardize everything that Unionists were struggling to achieve in Kentucky. "So fixed is public sentiment in this state against freeing Negroes," wrote Speed, "that you had as well attack the freedom of worship in the North or the right of a parent to teach his child to read as to wage war in the state on such principles."[41]

Robert Anderson reported that Frémont's action "is producing the most disastrous results" in Kentucky "and that it is the opinion of many of our wisest and soundest men that if this is not immediately disavowed, Kentucky will be lost to the Union." He warned Lincoln that Kentucky volunteer units were disbanding.[42]

Lincoln sent off a message to Frémont explaining the problem. "I think there is great danger," Lincoln wrote, "that the closing paragraph" of the proclamation "in relation to the confiscation of property, and the liberating of slaves of traitorous owners, will alarm our Southern Union friends, and turn them against us—perhaps ruin our rather fair prospect in Kentucky." He continued:

> Allow me therefore to ask, that you will of your own motion, modify that paragraph so as to conform to the . . . act of Congress, entitled "An Act to confiscate property used for insurrectionary purposes," approved August 6th, 1861, and a copy of which I herewith send you. This letter is written in a spirit of caution and not of censure.[43]

Frémont resisted. He sent his wife Jessie—an influential figure since she happened to be the daughter of the late Thomas Hart Benton, one of the most prominent political leaders of the previous generation—to meet with Lincoln and try to change his mind. She met with him on September 10, and she did not change his mind one bit. She even subjected him to a tongue-lashing.

Frémont told Lincoln he would only retract his emancipation decree when Lincoln ordered him to do so. Lincoln acted at once. On September 11, he wrote that since Frémont had "expressed the preference . . . that I should make an open order for the modification, I very cheerfully do."[44]

Lincoln's action caused tremendous anger that extended from the abolitionists to rank-and-file Republicans; Joseph Medill of the *Chicago Tribune* declared that the revocation of Frémont's emancipation order was a greater calamity than the battlefield loss at Bull Run. The "frightfully retrograde order," he wrote, "comes upon us like a killing frost in June—which destroys the coming harvest." It created "funereal gloom" like a "pestilence that walketh at noon day."[45] Even Orville Browning, who was appointed to complete the unfinished Senate term of Stephen Douglas, took Lincoln to task in a personal letter.

In his answer, Lincoln poured out his thoughts about the situation on September 22. As to the legalities of what Frémont had done, Lincoln wrote that his action was "purely *political*, and not within the range of *military* law, or necessity." If Frémont wished to put the slaves of the rebels to use, "he can seize them, and use them; but when the need is past, it is not for him to fix their permanent future condition." Lincoln hastened to add that if Congress should pass an emancipation law he might very well support it, but neither he nor Frémont possessed the power to set such a policy.

Beyond the legalities—or legalisms, since Lincoln himself would claim the power to liberate slaves in just over a year—Lincoln turned to the political realities. When news of Frémont's action reached Kentucky, he told his friend Browning, "a whole company of our Volunteers threw down their arms and disbanded." In fact, he had good reason to worry that "the very arms we had furnished Kentucky would be used against us."

And to lose Kentucky, Lincoln wrote, "is nearly the same as to lose the whole game. Kentucky gone, we can not hold Missouri, nor, as I think, Maryland. These all against us, and the job on our hands is too large for us. We would as well consent to separation at once."

But if Browning and others would be patient, "give up your restlessness for new positions, and back me manfully on the grounds upon which you and other kind friends gave me the election . . . we shall go through triumphantly."[46]

After Lincoln overturned the emancipation edict, Frémont continued with his military operations. The Confederates made the mistake of allowing one of their political generals, Leonidas Polk, to bring troops to Kentucky on September 3, and this action violated the state's proclaimed (or supposed) "neutrality." The Unionist legislature seized this opportunity to summon help in repelling the Confederate "invasion," so Frémont sent Ulysses S. Grant to capture the city of Paducah, Kentucky, which he took without firing a shot on September 6.

But Frémont was getting into deeper political trouble and his problems continued to multiply. His imperious demeanor offended many people, not least of all the cantankerous Frank Blair, who became an implacable enemy. Blair and many others had complained to Lincoln that Frémont was running up lavish expenses and allowing corrupt associates to practice graft. Lincoln sent Montgomery Blair and General Montgomery Meigs to investigate. Another investigation was made by General Lorenzo Thomas. Still another investigation was made by a congressional subcommittee.

Both Montgomery Blair and Lorenzo Thomas recommended the removal of Frémont, who went on to commit the extraordinary blunder of arresting the brother of Montgomery Blair—Congressman Frank Blair. Frémont accused the congressman of making "insidious & dishonorable efforts to bring my authority into contempt with the Govt & to undermine my influence as an officer."[47] On September 19, Lincoln drafted an order removing Frémont, but he agreed to postpone the action at the request of Seward.

He decided, however, to find a replacement for Frémont and to get that replacement in position to take over command. Scott suggested approaching General David Hunter, who had been wounded at Manassas and who was on his way to Missouri to serve under Frémont. Montgomery Blair and Meigs met with Hunter in Chicago and they handed him a letter from Lincoln. The letter stated in part that "General Frémont needs assistance which it is difficult to give him. He is losing the confidence of men near him. . . . His cardinal mistake is that he isolates himself & allows nobody to see him. . . . He needs to have, by his side, a man of large experience. Will you not, for me, take that place?"[48] This naturally put Hunter in position to take over the western department on very short notice.

Meanwhile, Lincoln ordered the release of Frank Blair, but Frémont promptly arrested him again. The general's sense of his own political invincibility was almost delusional. Winfield Scott countermanded this second arrest of Frank Blair.

It was absolutely clear to Lincoln by October that Frémont had to go—even though the general had succeeded in recapturing Springfield, Missouri, from the Confederates on October 25. The day before that, Lincoln issued the order relieving him of command. Frémont turned over his duties to Hunter on November 2, to the consternation and outrage of his many defenders.

Opponents of slavery all over the North protested this action and even burned Lincoln in effigy. The editor of the *Cincinnati Gazette* declared that "the West is threatened with a revolution" because people believed that "Frémont has been made a martyr."[49]

The autumn of 1861 was in overall terms a rather grim interlude for Lincoln. True, he had succeeded in holding the border states and averting foreign recognition of the Confederacy. But the lack of military progress was galling and his problems with McClellan were just getting started.

Moreover, he was deeply saddened by the fact that someone else who was close to him was killed by Confederate fire. On October 21, Union forces under the command of General Charles Stone crossed the Potomac River far above Washington at a place called Ball's Bluff in order to conduct a reconnaissance. They got caught by surprise in a Confederate attack, and dozens of the Union troops were killed. One of them was Lincoln's old friend and political colleague Edward Baker, for whom Lincoln's first son Eddie had been named.

Baker, who had introduced Lincoln to the crowd at the Capitol on Inauguration Day, was serving as a senator from Oregon until he joined up to fight for the Union. Now he was dead.

On November 1, Lincoln finally granted the wish of both Winfield Scott and George McClellan: he agreed to accept Scott's retirement. Lincoln and members of the cabinet visited Scott, who by then was too feeble and ill to go out. As Scott lay on a couch, Lincoln read him a letter of appreciation that he had composed.

Then Lincoln called upon McClellan to inform him that Scott had recommended him to be the new general in chief. In reality, Scott wanted General Henry Halleck to become the new general in chief, but Halleck was travelling and thus unavailable when Scott decided to step down.

Lincoln told McClellan that this "vast increase in responsibility" would tax anybody, and that McClellan should always feel free to "draw on me for all the sense I have, and all the information. In addition to your present command, the supreme command of the army will entail a vast labor upon you."

McClellan replied, "I can do it all."[50]

A week later McClellan rearranged both the structure and the personnel of the high command. He broke up the huge "Department of the West" and created a new "Department of Missouri," with its headquarters in St. Louis and encompassing Arkansas and western Kentucky in addition to Missouri.

He appointed Halleck to command this department. Halleck was a military theorist who had written some books about military strategy. He was consequently known as "Old Brains." Hunter, who had taken over from Frémont, was assigned by McClellan to command a newly created Department of Kansas. The Department of the Ohio, which McClellan himself had commanded in the spring, would be run by General Don Carlos Buell, a close friend of McClellan. Buell would have responsibility for covering eastern Kentucky.

McClellan would continue to command the Army of the Potomac while serving simultaneously as general in chief.

All through November and December, Lincoln tried to establish rapport with McClellan and persuade him to take the offensive in Virginia. He visited McClellan every day for a while in the hope that these visits would lead to a working relationship. But McClellan grew increasingly arrogant, insolent, disrespectful, and sluggish.

In private, he poured out his scorn for the president. In a letter to his wife on November 17, he had this to say: "I went to the White House shortly after tea, where I found 'the original gorilla,' about as intelligent as ever. What a specimen to be at the head of our affairs now!"[51]

A few days earlier, McClellan delivered an extraordinary snub when the president, Seward, and Hay dropped by to have a chat. McClellan had been out, attending a wedding. When he returned, he was told that the president was waiting to see him. McClellan just walked past the room where Lincoln and the others were waiting, and proceeded upstairs without a word.

In his diary Hay recorded that after waiting an hour and a half, they "sent once more a servant to tell the General they were there, and the answer cooly came that the General had gone to bed." Hay commented later on "this unparalleled insolence of epaulettes," but Lincoln replied that it was "better at this time not to be making points of etiquette & personal dignity."[52]

Republicans in Congress were incensed that McClellan was taking no action to renew the offensive in Virginia. Lyman Trumbull told Lincoln "that if the federal army did not achieve a decided success before winter set in, it would be very difficult not only to raise a fresh loan in the money market, but to get Congress to authorize a new loan."[53] Benjamin Wade told Lincoln that American taxpayers would not "care to pay forty millions a month simply to retain Maryland in the Union, for that seems to be about all the government is doing, or attempting to do."[54]

Things in general were going very wrong for Lincoln by November. He faced a huge crisis at the war department, for Cameron was turning out to be just as crooked as the pessimists had feared. He was also incapable of creating the managerial infrastructure that was needed to conduct a total war.

Lincoln had been reading a steady flood of complaints about Cameron's inefficiency, favoritism, and incompetence. By September Lincoln let it be known that Cameron was "unequal to the duties of the place" and that "his public affiliation with army contractors was a scandal."[55] In December Montgomery Blair told the president that "he ought to get rid of Cameron at once."[56] Lincoln told Cameron that he would soon be replaced and given other duties.

At first Lincoln was inclined to replace him with Joseph Holt, who had served the Buchanan administration as war secretary. But he turned instead to Edwin M. Stanton, who had served as Buchanan's attorney general. Stanton, a firm and even militant Unionist, had come to the war department a few months earlier to serve as a legal adviser. He was also the lawyer who supposedly belittled Lincoln in the course of the McCormick Reaper case. But Lincoln, characteristically, overlooked that slight because of Stanton's obvious strengths.

Lincoln was usually willing to overlook a slight—as he was willing at the time to overlook the rudeness of McClellan—if he thought that the offender might be useful in ways that transcended his bad manners. It was easy for Lincoln to be magnanimous since he had a towering and justified confidence in his own intellectual superiority. However insecure he had been in the past about his lowly origins, provincial background, and lack of a formal education, he knew perfectly well what powers he commanded by 1861. There were very few people in the country who could even come close to his strategic sense, his self-possession, and his mental creativity.

But the vexations just kept piling up in the autumn months of 1861. A diplomatic incident threatened not only to bring the Confederates foreign recognition but involve the United States in a foreign war. The Confederates had been trying to send two emissaries, James M. Mason and John Slidell, to Europe in their quest for alliances. Mason was bound for England and Slidell for France. They escaped from Charleston in a blockade runner and boarded a British mail packet, the RMS *Trent*, in Havana.

The *Trent* was intercepted by a U.S. naval vessel, the *San Jacinto*, and the rebels were seized. As the news got out, there was exultation throughout the North. Navy Secretary Welles congratulated Charles Wilkes, the captain of the *San Jacinto*, for his achievement.

But Lincoln perceived right away that this welcome success spelled international trouble. For the case could be made that Wilkes had violated international law by seizing men from a neutral ship in its travels between neutral ports. At a cabinet meeting Lincoln predicted that the British might react in a belligerent manner and observed that he could not afford to have two wars on his hands at the same time. Only Montgomery Blair agreed with him.[57]

Events proved that Lincoln was right. Lord Palmerston, the British prime minister, was furious. He demanded an apology, the payment of an indemnity, and the release of the two rebel agents. Palmerston threatened to break diplomatic relations and he sent eleven thousand British troops to Canada. The British demands were sent off in a dispatch from Lord Russell, the British foreign minister.

News of this British reaction was delayed and the demands of Palmerston were not presented to Seward until December 19. Right away the demands of the British led to waves of indignation in the North, where people called the behavior of the British a humiliation of America. But Lincoln feared that the British would use their naval strength to break his coastal blockade of the Confederacy.

So he drafted a conciliatory letter for Seward to present to the British ambassador. "This government," Lincoln wrote, "has intended no affront to the British flag, or to the British nation." Moreover, Captain Wilkes had acted "without orders from, or expectation of, the government." However, Lincoln's letter continued, the British must surely be aware that the emissaries were part of a rebellion that the U.S. government held to be treasonable, and "we too, as well as Great Britain, have a people justly jealous of their rights."[58]

Lincoln offered to submit the case to arbitration. And he expressed the willingness to pay a reparation if the British could prove that the United States was in the wrong.

As news of the war possibility spread, people took a different view of the matter. Their mood of resentment gave way to fear—fear that a foreign war might be more than the nation could bear under civil war conditions. A stock market crisis erupted and bank panics started. These developments could very well have jeopardized the Union's war finances—already strained—if the situation with Britain deteriorated further.

Seward drafted his own response to the British. Its tone was moderate and it explored the legal issues in a desultory way that established a basis for a tactical line of retreat—for releasing the rebels on the grounds that the issues were complex. The cabinet discussed Seward's draft on Christmas Day and this time the general consensus went along with Lincoln's views. Bates acknowledged that "to go to war with England now, is to abandon all hope of suppressing the rebellion."[59] Chase declared that the release of Mason and Slidell was "gall and wormwood to me," but "our commerce will suffer serious harm, our action against the rebels must be greatly hindered, and the restoration of our prosperity . . . must be delayed" unless the rebels were released.[60]

Mason and Slidell were released, and then Palmerston waived his demand for an apology and indemnity. The crisis was over. But Lincoln readily acknowledged that the whole affair was a very bitter pill to swallow.

One of many.

Perhaps the crowning indignity in December was the cost of the White House renovation.

Early in Lincoln's presidency his wife had cultivated the acquaintanceship of the White House gardener, a man by the name of John Watt. He soon became one of the shady hangers-on who were used by Mary Lincoln in her schemes.

According to another White House servant, Watt "suggested to Mrs. Lincoln the making of false bills so as to get pay for private expenses out of the public treasury and had aided her in doing so."[61] In August she charged an exorbitant amount of money for the dinner in honor of Prince Napoleon. When she ran into trouble getting payment through the usual channels, Watt charged it to his gardening expenses.

In October the White House gatekeeper, James Upperman, complained to Caleb Smith about the "sundry petit, but flagrant frauds on the public treasury" that were engineered by Watt at the behest of Mary Lincoln. Many of the bills were for goods and services that were never delivered.[62] Smith covered up the scandal for the sake of Mary's reputation.

Upperman took his complaint to Congress, where the matter was also suppressed. But Watt discovered a way to make use of the fine art of blackmail. He threatened Mary that he would release certain documents that proved she was complicit in fraud. He would do it, he said, if she did not obtain a more lucrative government position for him. The lurid story was bandied about throughout Washington and beyond. Early in 1862 David Davis informed his wife that "I got a letter from Washington & the gossip is still about Mrs. Lincoln and the gardener Watt."[63]

According to the new commissioner of public buildings, Benjamin Brown French—who had replaced Mary's pet and collaborator William S. Wood—Mary came to him in mid-December and asked for his help in interceding with her husband. She had overspent her budget for the White House renovation by $25,000. According to French, Mary told him on December 14 that "I have sent for you to get me out of trouble," and that "if you will do it, I will never get into such difficulty again."

She asked French to make the case that it was "common to over-run appropriations—tell him how *much* it costs to refurnish." Lincoln quickly flew into a rage when he was told about the over-run and he declared that he would not request Congress for an appropriation to cover the deficiency. "It can never have my approval," he exclaimed to French; "I'll pay for it out of my own pocket first—it would stink in the nostrils of the American people to have it said that the President of the United States had approved a bill overrunning an appropriation of $20,000 for *flub dubs* for this damned old house, when the poor freezing soldiers cannot have blankets!"[64]

But through all of the frustrations, Lincoln took the first steps in a process that would move him from the leadership of the Free Soil movement to the work that he would claim to be the greatest achievement of his life: the liberation of others. And there is reason to believe that the things he was doing in secret to undermine slavery in the final months of 1861 gave him real consolation for everything else.

He was painfully aware of the disappointment and the anger he caused when he overturned Frémont's emancipation order and ousted the man who had given it. The abolitionist William Lloyd Garrison spoke for many people in the autumn of 1861when he vilified Lincoln. Though Lincoln was famously a very tall man, the abolitionist wrote, "he is only a dwarf in mind."[65]

This dismissive view of Lincoln as an anti-slavery leader has continued to resonate. Lincoln, in the view of certain critics, was a calculating politician who rose to leadership in the Free Soil movement to advance his own career and who dragged his heels on the challenge of emancipation during his presidency until events at last forced his hand. Such critics regard him as a cold manipulator, as a self-confessed racist, a reluctant reformer who does not deserve his reputation as America's "Great Emancipator."

It was true that Lincoln was something of a latecomer to the ranks of the Free Soil movement, though he did go on record in opposition to slavery as early as the 1830s. It is also true that he compromised on slavery in 1861.

But to dismiss him as nothing but a cold politician is a grievous mistake since the evidence of his emotional development proves otherwise.

As early as the 1840s he recorded his outrage and indignation—on humanitarian grounds—when he beheld the enslavement of blacks during visits to the slave states. He made these feelings very clear in his letters to Joshua and Mary Speed. And throughout the 1850s, his Free Soil speeches condemned the dehumanization of blacks in America in terms that carried great risk in Illinois—and elsewhere. His speech in Columbus, Ohio, offers proof of how much he loathed not only the evil of enslavement but the white supremacy attitudes that supported it.

He was a man of powerful emotions that influenced his thinking. Some critics are misled by an observation of Herndon's, who said years later that "Lincoln's common sense came through his brain and not through his soul" and that Lincoln "was not spontaneous in his feelings and was, as some said, rather cold."[66] Herndon of all people should have known better—he who would tell the world what had happened to Lincoln with the loss of Ann Rutledge. To view Lincoln as somehow aloof and remote by his very nature is absurd. He was a man of changing moods. He was capable of powerful grief—grief that could lead to depression. He was capable of anger and abundant mirth. His elfin sense of humor was active right down to the end. His inner world was rich and complex.

He was not at all "cold"—except when he was thinking *strategically.* When he thought about the uses of *power*, he could surely be dispassionate enough to see the truth of things in hard terms. No doubt Herndon experienced this *side* of Lincoln when he analyzed the issues of a legal problem and determined what strategy to use when the case came to trial.

Lincoln differed from the abolitionists in a fundamental manner that relates to this side of his nature. As a politician, he was by nature and by definition a practitioner of power orchestration. Many of the abolitionists, by contrast, were masters of advocacy—of eloquent denunciation—preachers by preference. They were offering a strong and clear view of an important and urgent moral issue. They were oracles who chose to leave the messy business of deal-making and vote-getting to others.

Garrison and Wendell Phillips, for example, saw their challenge as expressing what was morally right—and that was all. They sought to change the course of public opinion, but their efforts to rid the nation of slavery stopped there.

They had little to offer when it came to the issue—the basic strategic issue—of *how* to eradicate slavery. Garrison's solution in the 1850s was to advocate secession by the free states. That would surely have ended the complicity of northerners in the evil of American enslavement.

But how many slaves would it have freed?

The achievement of Lincoln was to work his way up to the summit of American power and *force* events to go his way. He *forced* the United States to turn the great corner on slavery, to put it on course for extinction, as he said in his House Divided speech. The first step was to prevent the evil from spreading. To this task he would have to add the challenge of *destroying a nation* that others were creating—the Confederacy—that would spread the evil of enslavement.

That was Lincoln's objective in his quest to "save the Union." He meant to save the Union *his way*—with slavery contained and on course for extinction. He delivered this message in New York on his way to be inaugurated: he would save the American vessel *with its precious cargo intact*. He would save not only the Union but its great founding principle of freedom for all.

And it was not at all clear whether he or anyone else could accomplish that objective in 1861.

The key was to maximize the chances for success while protecting the anti-slavery movement from its enemies.

In the course of the Frémont affair, Lincoln talked about this challenge in some private conversations. Of special interest is something that he said to one of Frémont's defenders, an abolitionist named Charles Edwards Lester. "I should never have had votes enough to send me here," he observed, "if the people had supposed I should try to use my power to upset Slavery. Why, the first thing you'd see, would be a mutiny in the army. No! We must wait until every other means has been exhausted. *This thunderbolt will keep.*"[67]

The fact that Lincoln acknowledged that he was keeping a "thunderbolt" is important. This statement aligns with many others to suggest what he was contemplating in 1861. To the abolitionist Moncure Daniel Conway, Lincoln complained that "Frémont is in a hurry."[68] "In a hurry"—it was all a matter of timing for Lincoln—timing and power calculation.

Any premature or ill-grounded action could explode into a white supremacist backlash.

Looking back upon the Frémont affair from the vantage point of 1863, Lincoln told some abolitionists that they and their colleagues in the anti-slavery movement played a necessary role in the events leading up to emancipation, but that "the pioneer in any movement is not generally the best man to carry that movement to a successful issue." He gave them a biblical example. Moses "began the emancipation of the Jews, but didn't take Israel to the Promised Land after all. He had to make way for Joshua to complete the work. It looks as if the first reformer of a thing has to meet such a hard opposition . . . that afterwards, when people find they have to accept his reform, they will accept it more easily from another man."[69]

Interesting, in light of the reputation that Lincoln would enjoy for a while as the "Moses" who led the slaves out of bondage. But that was not the way he saw himself: he was Joshua, the one who took over from the great pioneers and completed the work they had been doing.

And so it was that in November 1861 Lincoln launched a great secret experiment: an experiment to see if he could use the emergency of war as an excuse to begin the long phase-out of slavery that he and many others had envisioned down the years in America. James Madison had toyed with the idea back in 1819. And Henry Clay had supported it throughout his life.

In November Lincoln secretly drafted an anti-slavery bill that he hoped to get introduced and passed in the state legislature of Delaware. The resolution would request financial assistance from the federal government to rid the state of slavery. State action would have had a number of political and legal advantages. In the first place, since the legal underpinning of slavery rested chiefly in state law, state action would be harder for the courts to overturn. In the second place, Delaware was the smallest of the slave states. The slave population was small, so the cost involved in buying and freeing the slaves would be comparatively minimal.

By seeking financial assistance from Congress, Lincoln's plan contradicted the Corwin Amendment—the proposed amendment to the Constitution that would have prevented such congressional action. But that amendment was going nowhere. Only three states had ratified it thus far: Kentucky, Ohio, and Rhode Island.

Lincoln drafted two versions of his bill. "Be it enacted by the State of Delaware," the first one proclaimed, "that on condition the United States of America will, at the present session of Congress, engage by law to pay . . . in the six per cent bonds of the said United States, the sum of seven hundred and nineteen thousand and two hundred dollars, in five equal annual installments, there shall be neither slavery nor involuntary servitude, at any time after the first day of January in the year of our Lord one thousand eight hundred and sixty-seven, within the said state of Delaware."[70] The second version of the bill would have extended the phase-out process over thirty years.

Lincoln consulted with Delaware Congressman George P. Fisher as well as with Benjamin Burton, the largest slave owner in the state. He hoped that Delaware would start a process that would quickly catch on in all the border slave states. Lincoln told David Davis he was "hopeful of ultimate success" and that "if Congress will pass a law authorizing the issue of bonds for the payment of the emancipated Negroes in the border states, Delaware, Maryland, Kentucky, and Missouri will all accept the terms."[71]

Four states would thus be subtracted from the slave state bloc. And if the Confederacy could be defeated later, the basis for further congressional anti-slavery action would be nicely established.

On December 3, Lincoln sent his first annual message to Congress, the equivalent in those days of a State of the Union Address, except it was delivered at the end of the year and in writing.

He reiterated his contempt for the leaders of the Confederacy and he contended that the power of the electorate was shrinking in all the rebel states. That was not surprising, he said, when those states had fallen into the grip of a parasitic elite that lorded it over poor whites as they kept their own slaves in endless bondage. And in that regard, Lincoln made an oracular statement that would serve the American labor movement in its long upward struggle; "labor," Lincoln said, "is the superior of capital, and deserves much the higher consideration" in human affairs.[72]

Turning to the military issues, Lincoln mentioned the appointment of McClellan as general in chief, but he did it in a way that implied he had misgivings about the appointment. He was obviously laying the groundwork for ousting McClellan later if he failed to measure up.

After saying that "the nation seemed to give a unanimous concurrence" to McClellan's appointment, Lincoln shared an old saying to the effect that "one bad general is better than two good ones; and the saying is true," he continued, "if taken to mean no more than an army is better directed by a single mind, though inferior, than by two superior ones, at ... cross-purposes with each other."[73]

Turning to the slavery issue, he portrayed himself in terms of sweet innocence—by the standards of the Democrats who were watching and waiting to pounce if he departed by so much as an inch from the Crittenden-Johnson resolutions, which limited the purpose of the war to preserving the Union. "In considering the policy to be adopted for suppressing the insurrection," he wrote,

> I have been anxious and careful that the inevitable conflict for this purpose shall not degenerate into a violent and remorseless revolutionary struggle. I have, therefore, in every case, thought it proper to keep the integrity of the Union prominent as the primary object of the contest on our part, leaving all questions which are not of vital military importance to the more deliberate action of the legislature [i.e., Congress].[74]

But then he made the transition to a statement that appeared to be a come-on to his fellow Republicans. After citing the passage by Congress of the First Confiscation Act, he wrote that "if a new law upon the same subject shall be proposed, its propriety will be duly considered."[75]

That was slick, because it opened the way for a startling suggestion that would lay the groundwork for his own secret Delaware scheme.

The contraband slaves who were seized and put to use according to the terms of the First Confiscation Act were "already dependent on the United States," Lincoln pointed out, "and must be provided for in some way." And it was "not impossible that some of the States will pass similar enactments of their own for their own benefit respectively."

"Not impossible."

Consequently, he said, "I recommend that Congress provide for accepting such persons from such States, according to some kind of valuation, in lieu, *pro tanto*, of direct taxes, or upon some other plan to be agreed on with such States respectively; that such persons, on acceptance by the general government, be at once deemed free."[76]

"Deemed free." So if the states were to pass some confiscation laws of their own, they could seize the slaves of rebels, determine the value of those slaves in market terms, and then send the slaves to the federal government in lieu of taxes. Whereupon they would all be set free.

It was just a suggestion.

He concluded his message by observing that "the struggle of today, is not altogether for today," but "for a vast future also."[77]

Both congressional and administration policies on slavery were shifting. Secretary of War Cameron—whose days in the administration of course were numbered—called in his annual report for arming the slaves who were being put to military use per the terms of the First Confiscation Act. General Henry Halleck, on the other hand—the general who had taken over in St. Louis—gave an order on November 19 that warned commanders not to welcome any fugitive slaves into their camps.

Congress was more inclined to take action on the slavery issue in December. The ranks of the congressional Democrats were depleted by defections of border state congressmen to the Confederacy. Senator John Breckinridge, for instance, deserted the Union and volunteered to serve the rebels in uniform. This former senator from Kentucky became a Confederate general.

On December 4, Congressman William Steele Holman of Indiana (a pro-slavery Democrat) called upon Congress to reaffirm the Crittenden-Johnson resolutions. Congressman Thaddeus Stevens of Pennsylvania, a Radical Republican, got the motion tabled. This meant, in effect, that the House of Representatives was changing its policy on slavery—that when given a chance to reaffirm the Crittenden-Johnson resolutions, the House of Representatives refused.

At the same time Republicans were taking aim at Halleck's order on fugitive slaves. Though Frank Blair defended the order, some Radical Republicans, led by Congressman James Ashley of Ohio, condemned it. Then Lincoln's Illinois ally, Lyman Trumbull, introduced a bill in the Senate that would seize the slaves of all the rebels and *give them their freedom.*

The signs were auspicious for the huge transformation in policy that Lincoln had in mind. In December he met with Charles Sumner, the Radical Republican leader in the Senate. According to Sumner's account of their meeting, Lincoln said that when it came to the issue of slavery the only real difference between the two of them was "a month or six weeks."[78] It was all just a matter of timing.

He had every intention of expanding the aims of the war during 1862, and his plans to do it were in motion.

12

TRANSFORMATION

There was little improvement for Lincoln or those who supported him in the last days of 1861. And the military situation had fallen into a state of paralysis by the time that the holiday season—such as it was—was over.

Lincoln kept working on the military challenge but there seemed to be little he could do to force action. McClellan was out of the picture for a while because he had contracted typhoid in December. And he had made no arrangements for the supervision of military operations while he was bedridden.

Congress created a Joint Committee on the Conduct of the War on December 9. The growing revelations of Cameron's cronyism at the war department had prompted congressional inquiries, and now the battlefield stalemate was becoming intolerable to members of Congress. The committee was chaired by Senator Benjamin Wade.

Before McClellan fell ill, Lincoln sent him a proposal in early December for a second Manassas campaign. McClellan deferred this proposal by stating that he had a plan of his own that would surprise everyone. He was working on a scheme to move around Manassas by water and slip between the rebel army and Richmond, landing his men at Urbana, on the Rappahannock River. But this plan remained under wraps and it stayed there during McClellan's illness.

Don Carlos Buell proposed to make a move in eastern Kentucky and plunge on into Tennessee. But he would only do it if Halleck's forces in the Mississippi Valley joined in to create a pincer movement. Halleck demurred and said that he could not spare enough troops for a thrust up the Tennessee and Cumberland Rivers, as Buell proposed.

On New Year's Eve, Lincoln wrote to both Halleck and Buell to inquire if the plans for their two theaters were being coordinated. Their replies made it clear that there was no coordination at all.

On January 10, Lincoln wrote to Cameron in a state of exasperation, complaining that "nothing can be done."[1] Later that day he walked over to the office of Quartermaster General Montgomery Meigs. According to Meigs' recollection, Lincoln seated himself by the fire and said, "General, what shall I do? The people are impatient; Chase has no money and tells me he can raise no more, the General of the Army has typhoid fever. The bottom is out of the tub."[2]

The financial situation was indeed rather dire, and Lincoln was correct to place it high on his list of worries.

The financing of the war had depended on deficit spending—the sale of war bonds—from the beginning. Government revenue was largely dependent on the proceeds of tariffs (import taxes), but years of Democratic rule, with its doctrines of small government and low taxes, had put the Union in a very weak position. The tariff was lowered in 1857.

Salmon Chase turned to a prominent banker, Jay Cooke of Philadelphia, to help the treasury department sell war bonds. In order to guarantee the purchasers of the bonds that the government would have financial resources, Congress had passed a revolutionary direct tax—an income tax—in August 1861.

But this tax would not be collected until 1862, and the events of the last three months of 1861 had led the confidence of the financial community to plummet. The Ball's Bluff defeat, the lack of action in Virginia, and the *Trent* affair had led to severe bank panics in December. So when Lincoln told Meigs that the bottom was out of the tub and that Chase could not raise money, he was speaking the truth. There might be no money to pay for the war before very long.

Meigs recommended to Lincoln that he consult with other generals at his discretion, so he called a conference at the White House that very day. He invited Meigs, Irvin McDowell, General William B. Franklin,

Seward, Chase, and Assistant Secretary of War T. A. Scott. According to McDowell, Lincoln said that if McClellan did not want to use the Army of the Potomac, he would very much like to borrow it. McDowell, who seemed to bear no grudge about his own demotion after Manassas, recommended a second attempt to attack the Confederates there. That was of course what Lincoln himself preferred.

Lincoln called the group together on the following evening—the 11th—and the consensus was in favor of a second Manassas campaign. The group met again on the 12th. Meanwhile, McClellan found out about these meetings and reacted with predictable indignation to these conferences "behind his back." On January 13, the group met again with McClellan present.

McClellan was sullen, at times saying nothing and at other times projecting resentment. He refused to reveal his plans unless Lincoln ordered him to do so. But he did say that Buell's army would be taking action fairly soon.

As to Buell, Lincoln sent him a letter on the same day—a letter that demonstrates the big-picture terms in which he was thinking. He said his "general idea of this war" was that "we have the *greater* numbers, and the enemy has the *greater* facility of concentrating forces upon points of collision." For that reason, the Union "must fail . . . unless we can find some way of making *our* advantage an over-match for *his*."

The way to do it, Lincoln said, was "by menacing him with superior forces at *different* points, at the *same* time; so that we can safely attack, one, or both, if he makes no change; and if he *weakens* one to *strengthen* the other, forbear to attack the strengthened one, but seize, and hold the weakened one."[3]

Put simply, the idea was to make the enemy stretch his forces too thin. At this point Buell had similar thoughts since he wanted Halleck to menace the Confederates in the west while he struck them in the east.

Lincoln was a natural strategic thinker and this made him an ideal commander in chief. Attorney General Bates wrote that Lincoln "*must* command—especially in such a war as this."[4] But just as it had taken Lincoln time to achieve self-assurance as he mingled with sophisticated and well-educated easterners, it would take him time to overcome the idea that the generals' West Point training made them better qualified than he to formulate battle plans.

As with so much of his intellectual development, this was a process of mental self-discovery.

But before very long he would find enough assurance to dish out commands to his generals and sack them if they failed or malingered. And yet he would always face a question by the time that he achieved such mastery: if he fired a particular general, did he have someone else lined up to take over?

And would the replacement turn out to be an improvement or another disappointment?

In any case, Lincoln ended the tenure of Cameron at the war department. A diplomatic vacancy opened, and Lincoln used the opportunity to ease Cameron out of the cabinet—and out of the country—by nominating him as ambassador to Russia. On January 13, he nominated Edwin Stanton to be the new secretary of war, and Stanton was confirmed by the Senate two days later. A brilliant and irascible workaholic, Stanton had an intense demeanor and a striking appearance with his long flowing beard and gnome-like visage. He would soon become one of the leading men in Lincoln's cabinet.

Stanton was initially one of the people who found themselves impressed by George McClellan, whose achievements in troop preparation were indeed impressive. Soon Stanton would begin the large task of bringing order out of chaos in the war department, so he naturally looked with approval on the feat that McClellan had performed in reorganizing a beaten army. But before very long, as he got to know the real George McClellan, he found the general insufferable.

At last there was some action in Kentucky, as McClellan had predicted. Kentucky had become a full-fledged battleground ever since the Confederates occupied the city of Columbus in September 1861. That movement had triggered the seizure of Paducah, Kentucky, by Grant. With Kentucky's "neutrality" thus dissolved, both the Union and the Confederacy sent in substantial military forces. Robert Anderson was put in command of a new Department of Kentucky. He was shortly replaced by William Tecumseh Sherman, but Sherman suffered a nervous breakdown and went home to recuperate.

Jefferson Davis appointed General Albert Sidney Johnston—not to be confused with Joseph Johnston, who had taken Lee's place as the commander of Confederate forces in Virginia—to coordinate all of the Confederate forces in the West. Johnston occupied Bowling Green, Kentucky, and sent forces to cover the Cumberland Gap. By the time that Buell took over for the Union in this overall theater of action, Union forces in Kentucky were commanded by General George Thomas. Buell ordered Thomas to confront the Confederate troops near Cumberland Gap in preparation for a strike at Tennessee. The result was the battle of Logan's Crossroads or Mill Springs, which took place on January 19, 1862. Thomas achieved a Union victory.

As Lincoln gradually learned to trust his own military instincts, he asserted himself in other ways. He needed more control of his time, and so he started to screen out distractions. He began to have his secretaries Nicolay, Hay, and Stoddard summarize the salient points of incoming mail and memoranda.

He still kept open office hours, but he started to abandon his long-standing habit of perusing newspapers. There was not enough time any longer to continue that habit, but he had another reason for the change. While he still remained interested in considering the views of other people, the scurrility of editorial attacks upon himself was beginning to hurt his morale, so he limited his intake of such polemics. And since these attacks were so enervating, he tried an old psychological trick, with apparent success. He tried to talk himself into a mood of serenity and tell himself he didn't care.

As he later remarked, "if I were to try to read, much less answer, all the attacks made on me, this shop might as well be closed for any other business. I do the very best I know how—the very best I can; and I mean to keep doing so until the end. If the end brings me out all right, what is said against me won't amount to anything. If the end brings me out wrong, ten angels swearing I was right would make no difference."[5]

But he was always ready to consider the opinions of a certain group of critics in 1862: abolitionists. As his Delaware scheme was playing out, he made an effort to cultivate certain abolitionists and establish the basis for a synergistic partnership with them. There were limits to what he could divulge in January 1862, but he did take pleasure in dropping certain hints about his plans to selected people.

On January 20 he was visited by two abolitionist critics, Moncure Daniel Conway and William Henry Channing, the nephew of a famous Unitarian clergyman. Conway recorded his recollections of this meeting in his memoirs.

Channing opened the discussion by contending that "the opportunity of the nation to rid itself of slavery had arrived." He "suggested emancipation with compensation for the slaves" and Lincoln said "he had for years been in favour of that plan." Then Conway asked Lincoln whether "we might not look to him as the coming Deliverer of the Nation from its one great evil." Lincoln answered that "perhaps we may be better able to do something in that direction after a while than we are now."

Then he revealed how he planned to strike at slavery in secret and by gradual degrees to maintain his political cover. He made the point through a metaphorical joke: "Perhaps it may be in the way suggested by a thirsty soul in Maine who found he could only get liquor from a druggist; as his robust appearance forbade the plea of sickness, he called for a soda, and whispered, 'Couldn't you put a drop o' the creeter into it unbeknownst to yourself?'"

As his visitors prepared to depart, he made a most extraordinary remark to them—one that shows how far he was willing to exert his creativity for the anti-slavery movement.

Conway recalled that "we had, I think, risen to leave and had thanked him for his friendly reception when he said, 'We shall need all the anti-slavery feeling in the country, and more; you can go home and try to bring the people to your views; and you may say anything you like about me, if that will help. Don't spare me!' This was said with a laugh. Then he said very gravely, 'When the hour comes for dealing with slavery, I trust I will be willing to do my duty though it cost my life. And, gentlemen, lives will be lost!'"[6]

We are naturally stricken by that very last statement, but the previous statement is of interest as well. For he was telling these critics to increase their denunciation of himself. He was telling Conway and Channing to encourage their followers to go out and call him names if they chose to do so.

He could turn such abuse into leverage and put it to political use in his own attacks against slavery. Do we know of any other president who actually encouraged his allies to trash his own reputation for the sake of noble purposes?

Lincoln spared himself the ordeal of reading attacks upon himself—but when it came to the issue of slavery, he was willing to go out of his way and *incite* such attacks through this sort of behind-the-scenes maneuvering. That was how important the issue of putting an end to American slavery had really become to him by 1862.

A few months later, he was visited by one of his fiercest abolitionist critics, Wendell Phillips. Phillips reported that Lincoln told him the very same joke that he had used with Conway and Channing.[7]

Lincoln took a major step in assuming more control of the military on January 27, when he issued an order designed to force McClellan into action. Entitled "President's General War Order No. 1," it was composed by Lincoln alone. It commanded that "the 22nd day of February 1862 [Washington's birthday], be the day for a general movement of the Land and Naval forces of the United States against the insurgent forces." Then it listed the particular forces, including the Army of the Potomac, that should "be ready for a movement on that day."[8]

Lincoln followed up on January 31 with an additional "Special War Order No. 1" commanding the Army of the Potomac to attack the rebels at Manassas. When the news of this order got out, it was praised by those who were exasperated by the military inaction.

These orders succeeded in forcing McClellan to reveal his own strategic plans to his commander in chief. He asked permission to submit a different plan for the Army of the Potomac and then he sent Stanton a long memorandum explaining his Urbana scheme—his plan to move the Army of the Potomac in a flanking maneuver around Manassas by water.

Lincoln didn't like McClellan's scheme. He found it ponderous and rather implausible. He worried that it might leave the nation's capital defenseless. McClellan, after all, was proposing to take his army from the vicinity of Washington and send it down the Potomac River by boat to the Chesapeake Bay.

What if the Confederates pounced upon the chance to strike at Washington as soon as McClellan stripped the city of its troops? A direct attack against Manassas would be safer since the army could shield the city of Washington at the very same time that it was moving to attack the enemy.

So on February 3, Lincoln sent off a letter to McClellan with a series of questions that were actually objections to his plan. "If you will give me satisfactory answers," he wrote, "I shall gladly yield my plan to yours." The last of Lincoln's questions was a worst-case query; "in case of disaster," Lincoln wrote, "would not a safe retreat be more difficult by your plan than by mine?"[9]

McClellan defended his scheme in a memorandum that he sent to Stanton.[10] So Lincoln faced a big decision: should he replace McClellan with another commander? Many people were clamoring for Lincoln to remove George McClellan and for very good reason. Lincoln himself would have taken great pleasure in ridding himself of McClellan, but who would be the general's replacement?

Perhaps he might have restored Irvin McDowell to command, but there were too many questions about what had happened in the battle of Manassas when McDowell was ignobly defeated. Lincoln was not at all familiar with the other corps commanders who were serving under McClellan. And time was of the essence: a forward movement by the Army of the Potomac was essential.

Benjamin Wade paid a call upon Lincoln and urged him to get rid of McClellan, telling him that *anybody* would be better than "the Young Napoleon." Lincoln answered him thus: "Wade, *'anybody'* will do for you, but not for me. I must have *somebody*."[11] Lincoln was right, as events confirmed. But the process of finding a replacement for McClellan would be difficult. When Lincoln finally did get rid of McClellan, the replacement commander—who at first looked good when compared to McClellan—proved to be worse.

So Lincoln agreed with reluctance to McClellan's proposal in mid-February. But he insisted that McClellan leave sufficient troops in Washington to defend the city.

Meanwhile, dramatic Union victories in other theaters bolstered Lincoln's morale. When Frémont put Grant in charge of operations in the Mississippi valley, preparations were made for some army-navy operations in the inland rivers. A huge shipbuilding program had commenced in the summer of 1861, not only to enforce the oceanic blockade of the Confederacy but to create the sort of gunboat fleet that would operate inland.

Construction of this fleet was begun in Mound City, Illinois, as well as in a suburb of St. Louis. Many of these ships were "ironclads" with metal-sheathed sides—state-of-the-art naval vessels of the sort that the British and the French had been constructing for several years.

Halleck had retained Grant as the field commander of riverine operations, and Grant developed a plan to attack up the Tennessee and Cumberland Rivers. Gustavus Vasa Fox recommended the construction of a fleet of floating mortars to augment this campaign. Lincoln took a keen interest in these weapons and he wanted them to be ready in time for Grant's use. Lincoln told Navy Lieutenant Henry Wise that "I am going to devote a part of every day to these mortars and I won't leave off until it fairly rains Bombs."[12]

Lincoln was beginning to promote the use of new weapons of many varieties. He supported the use of breach-loading rifles and he even field tested some of these guns himself. He promoted the adoption of a new invention that prefigured the modern machine gun.

Perhaps goaded into action by the victory at Logan's Crossroads under the aegis of Buell, Halleck authorized Grant to proceed. The gunboat fleet was commanded by Navy Captain Andrew Hull Foote, and the targets for attack were two forts that Albert Sidney Johnston, the Confederate commander, had built in Tennessee as a fall-back line to support his army in Kentucky. Forts Henry and Donelson were their names. Fort Henry was constructed on the Tennessee River and Fort Donelson was built on the Cumberland. By striking at these two forts, Grant would be thrusting behind the rebels' lines. And that would make the continued presence of Confederate troops in Kentucky untenable.

Grant's attack was a stunning success. He captured Fort Henry on February 6 and Fort Donelson on February 15. The Confederates were forced to pull out of Kentucky and indeed from most of Tennessee; they withdrew to northeastern Mississippi. Buell's forces were able to occupy Nashville, the Tennessee capital, on February 25.

Though Halleck took most of the credit for these military successes, Grant became a rising presence in the Union command and an instant war hero in the North. On his own initiative, Lincoln promoted Grant to major general.

Meanwhile, another Union victory occurred in the East: a land-sea operation captured Roanoke Island in North Carolina on February 8. The naval forces were commanded by Navy Flag Officer Louis M. Goldsborough and the troops were commanded by General Ambrose Burnside.

These victories brought a huge and welcome sense of relief in the White House. The pressure was mounting on George B. McClellan to back up his words with deeds and turn his grandiose plans into action.

But something terrible occurred for the Lincolns in February and it cast a pall over everything else. Their little boy Willie—the lad who possessed such a gifted mind like his father—took sick and died.

The deaths of Ellsworth and Baker had been awful enough, but this was a blow that hit Abraham and Mary Lincoln with horrific force.

Both Willie and Tad had fallen ill with a fever. Invitations had already gone out for a ball, and the redecorated White House looked as elegant as Mary or anyone else could have wished. The ball was held in the East Room, and it was followed by a midnight dinner in the

State Dining Room. The bill of fare consisted of oysters, pâté de fois gras, canvasback duck, and candied quail. The ball was held as scheduled on February 5, but the host and hostess came and went as they attended to their sick children.

Tad slowly began to improve, but Willie did not. Day after day he got weaker as his father and mother sat at his bedside and applied cold compresses to his feverish forehead. After a while he was delirious, and then at last, on February 20, he passed away.

Words could hardly begin to express what Lincoln was feeling. He walked down the hallway in tears and said, "Well, Nicolay, my boy is gone—really gone!"[13] The next day Elihu Washburne wrote that Lincoln was "completely prostrated with grief."[14] Mary was far beyond grief. After Elizabeth Keckley helped her away from Willie's death bed, she locked herself away in her room and would not come out.

Lincoln asked Orville Browning to arrange the funeral, which was held in the White House on February 24. Much of official Washington was there, and even George McClellan found the grace to show up. Lincoln gazed down sobbing as he looked at Willie's coffin. A nurse who had attended the boys said she heard Lincoln say repeatedly, "this is the hardest trial of my life. Why is it? Oh, why is it?"[15] After the service, Lincoln rode in a gale to the neighborhood of Georgetown, where he saw his little boy laid to rest in the Oak Hill Cemetery.

He said it was the hardest trial of his life—harder even than the death of Ann Rutledge, but this time he faced the death of a dear one armed with all of the accumulated strength that a lifetime of self-strengthening had given him.

Slowly and fitfully he worked his way back to a state that bore a semblance of normality. About a month later, Stoddard wrote that Lincoln had "recovered much of his old equanimity and cheerfulness; and certainly no one who saw his constant and eager application to his arduous duties, would imagine for a moment that the man carried so large a load of private grief."[16]

But the thought of Willie preoccupied him, and he asked an army officer later if he ever found himself "talking with the dead." Lincoln continued: "Since Willie's death I find myself every day involuntarily talking with him, as if he were with me."[17]

A year and a half later, he corresponded with his old friend in Springfield, the African American barber William Fleurville, who remembered Willie very well. The boy was "So Considerate, So Manly," the old friend wrote to Lincoln, and he had "Knowledge and Good Sense, far exceeding most boys more advanced in years."[18]

Mary found it more difficult to recover from this horrible blow. She stayed locked in her room, so Lincoln asked her sister Elizabeth Edwards to come to the White House and stay with them in the hope that she would comfort them both. "You have Such a power & control Such an influence over Mary—Come do Stay and Console me," he wrote.[19] Elizabeth complied. But Mary remained locked in depression and grieving. One day Lincoln pointed out the window to an insane asylum that stood within view and said, "Mother, do you see that large white building on the hill yonder? Try and control your grief, or it will drive you mad, and we may have to send you there."[20]

This experience quickened the process that was changing Lincoln over time from a skeptic and a scoffer in religious matters to a man whose emotional and intellectual sensitivities became receptive to the comforts of religion.

More and more in the months that followed, he began to see his role in the war, the war itself, and the meaning of his life in overtly religious terms.

Mary's grief took her in a different but related direction—to the world of the occult. She conferred with spiritualists and held séances at the White House in an effort to commune with Willie on the "other side." Lincoln attended some of these events.

All the while something else had been going very wrong for Lincoln: his plan to start the phase-out of slavery in Delaware came to nothing. Delaware Congressman George Fisher, who had gotten the measure introduced in the Delaware legislature, secured its passage in the state senate, but a straw poll indicated to him that it would fail in the lower house by the margin of one vote. So he withdrew the bill in February, hoping to be able to reintroduce it later.

Much of the opposition in the Delaware legislature was based in virulent racism; liberation of the slaves in the state, critics said, would start a process that would elevate them to the status of whites, and that was something that the white supremacists vowed that they would never allow to happen.

Meanwhile, support for anti-slavery measures in Congress had increased. Senator Henry Wilson of Massachusetts introduced a bill to eliminate slavery in Washington, D.C. And some Radical Republicans were working on a scheme that would impose Reconstruction in some of the occupied slave states. As early as August 1861 Thaddeus Stevens had proclaimed that any occupied rebel states should be treated as "conquered provinces."

Charles Sumner propounded a slightly different variation of the doctrine. In February he introduced some resolutions declaring that states taken over by secessionists had forfeited their statehood and lapsed into the status of territories. As such, they could be governed by new territorial legislatures that would be created by Congress. Before long, this doctrine was known as the theory of "state suicide."

James Ashley of Ohio went further. He chaired the House Committee on Territories, and he and his Senate counterpart, Ben Wade, met privately with Salmon Chase to discuss the idea of forcing emancipation in occupied states along with land redistribution and integrated public schools. Ashley drafted a measure along those lines and he guided it through his committee. But when it reached the House floor, it was tabled. Still, these efforts showed clearly that the Radical Republicans were becoming very bold.

Lincoln pondered these matters with care. At last he came to a momentous decision. Since his secret effort to initiate a phase-out of slavery through state action failed, he would make a proposal to Congress, a proposal that was totally unprecedented. He would propose to Congress that a compensated phase-out program should be *offered* to all of the slave states by the federal government.

For many years, the advocates of gradualism in the anti-slavery movement had cherished this idea. Madison had written about it in private, Clay had advocated it publicly, Lincoln had adopted it early as the best way to rid the nation of slavery. The British had actually instituted such a plan in the West Indies. But no president of the United States had ever proposed such a thing in the form of legislation.

Lincoln did so on March 6, 1862.

While the reputation of Lincoln as an anti-slavery leader will always rest for good reason on the Emancipation Proclamation, his proposal to Congress of March 6, 1862, should be seen for what it was: an epochal event in American history. For Lincoln it was a now-or-never experiment to see if his long-held vision for abolishing slavery on a gradual basis could be realized. It was a high-risk experiment to determine whether such a plan would actually work. There might never be a better opportunity to try to make this old anti-slavery vision come true.

The timing was good, since the measure could be plausibly justified and rationalized as a way to bring the war to an end. But there might have been another reason why Lincoln took action when he did—an emotional reason.

The bill was framed as a joint resolution with the following preamble: "Resolved that the United States ought to co-operate with any state which may adopt gradual abolishment of slavery, giving to such state pecuniary aid, to be used by such state in its discretion."[21]

In the message to Congress that contained this proposal, Lincoln argued it would strike at the cause of the war. It was the controversy over slavery that triggered the war in the first place, so if a plan to make the problem go away could be offered to all of the slave states, why should men continue to be killed?

The place to start was in the loyal slave states and use them as a way to demonstrate the program—to show both its fairness and its efficacy—to the rebel states. It would also show the rebels that the tide of history was turning against them.

"While the offer is equally made to all," Lincoln wrote, "the more northern" of the slave states would, "by such initiation, make it certain to the more southern, that in no event, will the former join the latter, in their proposed Confederacy." As to the cost, he continued, a comparison to the cost of the war would make the logic of the measure self-evident: "In the mere financial or pecuniary view," he wrote, "any member of Congress, with the census-tables and Treasury reports before him, can readily see for himself how very soon the current expenditures of this war would purchase, at fair valuation, all the slaves in any named State."[22]

Lincoln added strong hints that if the federal offer were refused, more radical measures would be coming. If rebel resistance should continue, he warned, "the war must also continue; and it is impossible to foresee all the incidents, which may attend and the ruin which may follow it." Significantly, Lincoln closed his message with an open declaration of religious feeling: he had been led to propose this measure in light of "my great responsibility to God, and to my country."[23]

He worked very hard in the weeks that followed to make a case for his proposal in terms that he hoped any Unionist would find persuasive. In a letter to the editor of the *New York Times*, he wrote that "one half-day's cost of this war would pay for all the slaves in Delaware, at four hundred dollars per head." Indeed, "eighty-seven days cost of this war would pay for all in Delaware, Maryland, District of Columbia, Kentucky, and Missouri at the same price."[24]

Congress passed this joint resolution on April 10, but the votes shook out along party lines, with almost all of the Democrats denouncing the idea of instituting "taxes to buy Negroes."

Many abolitionists who vilified Lincoln since the ouster of Frémont expressed great surprise and happiness with the advent of Lincoln's plan. Wendell Phillips, who usually took pleasure in dismissing Lincoln in terms of cruel derision, admitted that the new plan was "a wedge—a very small wedge, but it is a wedge for all that."[25] Phillips even exclaimed in the presence of Moncure Conway, "Thank God for old Abe! He hasn't got to Canaan yet but he has set his face Zionward."[26]

The *New York Tribune* called Lincoln's March 6 message to Congress "the day-star of a new national dawn," and "the most important document ever issued from the White House."[27] Abolitionist Elihu Burritt wrote to Lincoln that the "whole civilized world is honoring you with its sincere homage, as the first of all the list of American Presidents that ever had the moral courage to propose a plan for the extinction of slavery."[28]

But the famous abolitionist William Lloyd Garrison was not impressed at all.

As to taxes and the cost of the war, the financial crisis that was troubling Lincoln in January was addressed in a bold piece of new legislation, the Legal Tender Act, which was passed by Congress on February 20. The brainchild of a congressman from New York named Elbridge G. Spaulding, the act was essentially a measure whereby Congress could create new money directly and spend it into use. It authorized the issuance by the Treasury of currency bills that would be called United States Notes.

Like the private-sector notes that were issued by commercial banks, these notes were backed by a promise of payment in precious-metal coin. But whereas all of the bank notes bore the statement "Payable to the Bearer on Demand," the United States Notes just proclaimed that "the United States of America will pay" the face value of the bill. The timing for redemption in cold hard cash was left open-ended. But the bills made it clear and in writing—the statement was printed on the back of the bill in green ink, wherefore the notes became known as "Greenbacks"—that the currency was legal tender for most financial transactions. People were compelled under law to accept it.

This new paper money faced predictable resistance and it led to double-digit inflation over the four-year course of the war. People who proposed to buy anything using this government-issued currency instead of gold coin were eventually charged over double the price.

But the Confederates, who also had recourse to paper money, fared worse, to put it mildly. The rate of inflation in the North was roughly 80 percent (over the course of the war), whereas the Confederacy's rate of inflation was over 9,000 percent. Confederate money was worthless, but the Union Greenbacks would prove themselves indispensable in winning the war. By 1865, over $430 million had been added to the money supply of the United States through the use of this method.

Treasury Secretary Chase had his doubts about the constitutionality of the Legal Tender Act. But he made sure that a portrait of himself was given a prominent place on the front of each United States Note.

The fighting continued to play out in March and the result was more Union victories. In the West, Union forces under Halleck's command were slowly driving the Confederates out of Missouri. Several distinct armies were in operation within the western theater: the Army of the Tennessee, commanded by Grant, the Army of Missouri, commanded by General John Pope, and the Army of the Southwest, commanded by General Samuel Curtis.

On March 13, Pope forced the Confederates to withdraw from New Madrid, Missouri, on the banks of the Mississippi. The rebels regrouped on Island Number Ten, so named because it was the tenth island below the junction of the Mississippi and Ohio Rivers. Pope began a campaign to capture Island Number Ten.

General Curtis defeated the Confederate forces commanded by Earl Van Dorn in the two-day battle of Pea Ridge, Arkansas, which occurred on March 7 and 8. As this battle was fought, a showdown took place in the East in the waters of Hampton Roads—the waters separating Fortress Monroe in Virginia from the cities of Norfolk and Portsmouth to the south.

While the Union maintained its possession of Fortress Monroe, the Confederates captured the strategically important Gosport Navy Yard in Portsmouth, Virginia. During 1861, as the great Union ship-building program began, the Confederates tried to keep pace in the construction of warships.

Their resources were limited, so they tried to place orders for ironclad ships to be constructed in the shipyards of Britain. But they did manage to salvage the hull and the engines of the USS *Merrimac* in the Gosport Yard and then using iron produced at the Tredegar Works in Richmond they converted it into an ironclad warship that they christened the CSS *Virginia.*

Most of the ironclad construction for the Union navy was centered in the creation of the inland gunboats. The oceanic blockade was conducted for the most part by old wooden ships of the line. But in October 1861, a new ironclad began to take shape in the Brooklyn Navy Yard, a ship fitted out with the first revolving turret gun in naval history: the USS *Monitor.*

On March 8, the *Virginia* (née *Merrimac*) steamed into Hampton Roads and attacked wooden warships that were being used to blockade the James River. The *Virginia's* attack was successful, and panic briefly gripped Washington, since people feared that this formidable Confederate ship—impervious to cannon fire—might steam up the Potomac and shell the nation's capital.

Lincoln went to see the commander of the Navy Yard, John Dahlgren, who confirmed that the *Virginia* could attack Washington. The ship could also destroy the transports that were being prepared to take McClellan's army down the Potomac. At a cabinet meeting, Stanton wondered whether the *Virginia* might be sent to bombard other northern cities, beginning with New York.

On March 9, however, the *Virginia* was confronted by the *Monitor*, which had been cruising down the Atlantic coast, and in the epochal battle that followed—known far and wide as the battle of the "*Monitor* and *Merrimac*," the first naval encounter in history between enemy ironclads—the ships fought one another to a draw.

As this was happening, two other important events were occurring. On March 8, Lincoln issued an order commanding McClellan to heed the imperative of keeping the nation's capital safe. The order stated that the Army of the Potomac would not depart from the vicinity of Washington "without leaving in, and about Washington, such a force as, in the opinion of the General-in-chief, and the commanders of all the Army corps, shall leave said city entirely secure."[29]

It was significant that Lincoln required the assent of all the corps commanders. Lincoln clearly distrusted McClellan's judgment.

On the very next day, the Confederates evacuated their position in Manassas and withdrew toward the capital of Richmond. This Confederate move made McClellan's Urbana scheme completely pointless.

On March 11, Lincoln took an important step in the process of ridding himself of George McClellan. He demoted McClellan from his position as general in chief since he was manifestly unfit for the task of coordinating military operations in different theaters. McClellan was still in command of the Army of the Potomac for the time being. But on March 15, Lincoln offered command of the army to General Ethan Allen Hitchcock, whom Winfield Scott had recommended. Unfortunately, Hitchcock declined because of his health.

Lincoln decided to take his own time in selecting McClellan's replacement as general in chief. He kept the post vacant. That meant that the president could serve for a while as his own general in chief, and he could issue orders to individual armies without the need for any intermediary.

On March 13, McClellan proposed to resurrect his Urbana scheme with a major modification. He would still send his troops to Virginia by water, but instead of landing them at Urbana on the Rappahannock River, he would take them all the way to Fortress Monroe at the tip of the York-James peninsula. Then he would march straight up the peninsula to Richmond.

Lincoln still preferred the overland approach via Manassas, but he gave this new plan his approval since at least it promised action. On March 17, the first units of the Army of the Potomac began to depart for the "Virginia Peninsula."

Suddenly things went wrong in the West. The armies of Grant and Buell had continued their conquest of Tennessee and most of that state had been put under Union occupation. Besides Memphis, the only major part of Tennessee that remained in the Confederates' grip was the mountainous region of east Tennessee, whose population was heavily Unionist.

The main Confederate forces under the command of Albert Sidney Johnston had retreated into Mississippi. Johnston's second in command was P.G.T. Beauregard, who was transferred to the West after quarreling with Jefferson Davis. Grant's second in command was William Tecumseh Sherman, back in action after his bout with depression. The Grant-Sherman partnership that would become so consequential over time had begun to take shape in Tennessee.

Grant's army was camped at a place known as Shiloh or Pittsburg Landing on the banks of the Tennessee River in southwestern Tennessee. On April 6, from his base in Corinth, Mississippi, Johnston unleashed a ferocious attack that caught Grant and his forces by surprise. The resulting two-day battle of Shiloh was a Union victory—a victory that almost destroyed the reputation of Grant while changing the overall course of the war in fundamental ways.

For the battle of Shiloh was a gruesome slaughter. The fighting was unspeakably savage and one of the thousands of casualties was the Confederate commander Albert Sidney Johnston, who bled to death after being shot. But he had led his troops to the brink of victory and it was all that Grant could do on the first day of this terrifying battle to avert a catastrophic defeat. Overnight, however, reinforcements arrived from Buell's army and the rebel troops, now commanded by Beauregard, withdrew.

The carnage of this battle defied comprehension at the time, for the casualties at Shiloh were greater than all the casualties in all of the previous U.S. wars put together. Union casualties were 13,047 (killed, wounded, and missing) and Confederate casualties were 10, 699.

The political results of this horror were apparent on both sides. The Confederates were prompted to institute a military draft, and the Union followed suit months later. The reputation of Ulysses S. Grant slipped under a cloud, for reporters started claiming he was drunk at the time of the attack and that his troops were unprepared because of his negligence. At the same time that Grant was being discredited, his future nemesis Robert E. Lee was being rehabilitated. As Grant tried to fend off demands for his ouster, Lee was brought back to Richmond to advise Jefferson Davis. But the Confederate field command in Virginia would remain in the hands of Joseph Johnston.

Not the least of the effects of the battle of Shiloh was its obvious effect upon Lincoln. To the burden of grieving that he bore in the aftermath of losing friends like Ellsworth and Baker, followed by the dreadful loss of his son, an additional burden had been added. He now had to contemplate the onset of a general bloodbath—a bloodbath that in some respects his Free Soil policies had triggered. Over time he would feel an increasing responsibility for all the death.

The news of Shiloh undoubtedly affected the attitudes of George B. McClellan. The extent of the slaughter increased his own innate aversion to attack. But something else should be considered in explaining the extraordinary sluggishness that he would show in his Peninsular Campaign.

He consistently over-estimated the strength of the enemy troops that he faced. At times the illusion of being out-numbered was so great that it magnified the forces that he confronted into twice their actual number. Part of the reason for this was the fact that he was using the services of detective Allen Pinkerton as a source of intelligence and Pinkerton himself overstated the strength of Confederate forces.

The problem of getting reliable intelligence regarding the position and strength of the enemy is fundamental to war. Both the Union and Confederacy employed the services of spies, and another source of information derived from the ability of cavalry units to conduct effective scouting operations. Still another source of intelligence in the Peninsular Campaign would be the use of observation balloons.

The reason for Pinkerton's exaggeration of Confederate strength is a mystery in and of itself. Perhaps—whether consciously or unconsciously—he was inclined to err on the side of exaggeration lest he be held accountable, in case of disaster, for having *under*-estimated the risk of going into battle.

Regardless, the convergence of the sensibilities of these two men— McClellan and Pinkerton—led the former into another long spell of delay and procrastination that began just as soon as he arrived on the Virginia peninsula.

A sound understanding of the enemy's strength can be a crucial precondition for battlefield victory. Commanders who send their troops into fights against impossible odds can be justly held responsible for ordering their men into suicide missions. But while the presence of superior enemy strength is an important battlefield issue, it is seldom an *all-important* issue. Depending on the skill of individual commanders, a victory over numerically superior forces is often attainable.

The key is to demonstrate audacity, to be capable of executing lightning-fast maneuvers, to launch surprise attacks and then follow up aggressively. Robert E. Lee and Stonewall Jackson would demonstrate these principles over and over again as they defeated numerically superior forces. They had exactly the kind of prowess that Abraham Lincoln needed.

McClellan did not.

Still another factor entered into this situation. As the Army of the Potomac embarked for the peninsula, there were widespread concerns in the war department that McClellan had failed to leave sufficient troops in Washington. So in the first week of April, Lincoln held back an entire corps that was commanded by Irvin McDowell—some thirty thousand men—for the purpose of ensuring that the nation's capital could be defended.

When McClellan learned of this action, his sense of being outnumbered by the Confederates was greatly worsened. But he would never in the course of the entire Peninsular Campaign be in truth outnumbered by the enemy.

As McClellan began the long march to Richmond, he confronted Confederate troops at Yorktown. These Confederates, commanded by General John B. Magruder, numbered approximately seventeen thousand and they were protected by entrenchments. McClellan's own troop strength was in the 80,000–90,000 range.

But of course he thought he was outnumbered. So he settled in for an unnecessary siege of Yorktown that lasted all month.

Lincoln, of course, wanted action, and he said so, insistently and often. On April 6, he wrote to McClellan as follows: "I think you had better break the enemies' line from York-town to the Warwick River, at once. They will probably use *time*, as advantageously as you can."[30] Three days he later he wrote that this was "the precise time for you to strike a blow. . . . By delay the enemy will relatively gain upon you—that is, he will gain faster, by *fortifications* and *re-inforcements*, than you can be re-inforcements alone." He could not resist adding the observation that "going down the Bay in search of a field, instead of fighting in or near Manassas, was only shifting, and not surmounting, a difficulty. . . . The country will not fail to note—is now noting—that the present hesitation to move forward upon an entrenched enemy, is but the story of Manassas repeated."[31]

Lincoln seemed to have a strong premonition that McClellan's campaign against Richmond would fail. Much of his correspondence with McClellan during this period suggests the desire to create a good "paper trail" that would put his own dissatisfaction with McClellan's performance on record.

As McClellan dithered, Union victories resumed in the West. On April 8, John Pope, with assistance from the gunboat fleet of Andrew Foote, succeeded in capturing the Confederate stronghold on Island Number Ten. This opened the way for the capture of Memphis two months later. Even more important, another land-sea operation from the Gulf of Mexico captured New Orleans along with the Louisiana capital of Baton Rouge. The naval forces were commanded by Captain David

Farragut, a southerner who refused to support secession. The army troops were commanded by Benjamin Butler.

The campaign began on April 18, when Farragut guided his fleet past the guns of two forts below New Orleans. After heavy bombardment, these forts surrendered on April 28 and then Butler's men marched into New Orleans without resistance. The Confederates abandoned Baton Rouge and Union troops entered the city on May 9.

After Congress passed the joint resolution on the slavery phase-out, Lincoln went to work. He began inviting delegations from the border states to the White House. If he could persuade the leaders of just one slave state to begin the process—to apply for federal funding—perhaps the leaders of the other slave states would follow.

So as the anti-slavery movement in Congress continued, Lincoln tried to keep the legislative efforts consistent with his plan. A bill to abolish slavery in the District of Columbia—introduced in the Senate by Henry Wilson—was working its way through both houses. Congressman James Ashley of Ohio was a key player. The original bill called for immediate and unconditional emancipation. Salmon Chase persuaded Ashley to include a provision for the colonization of liberated slaves who agreed to go abroad. But Ashley refused to accede to a request by Lincoln to make the liberation process gradual.

Democratic racists howled with indignation, predicting a nightmare of black retribution on whites—along with their party's standard and demagogic warnings about inter-racial sex. When it was clear that the bill was moving forward, Senator Garrett Davis of Kentucky proposed an amendment that would force the deportation of the freed slaves. It took a tie-breaking vote by Vice President Hannibal Hamlin to kill that idea. While the bill made provision for colonization, it was just a voluntary option. And that had always been Lincoln's position on the controversial idea.

The bill passed the Senate on April 6 and it passed the House on April 11. The debates in both chambers were ugly. This law provided for immediate abolition with compensation. Lincoln signed it—though he would have preferred to have a gradual phase-out consistent with the joint resolution that Congress was approving at the very same time.

Congressman Owen Lovejoy could see that Lincoln's quiet and measured response to this revolutionary bill reflected shrewd strategy. Lincoln, he wrote, was the kind of rail-splitter who "understands his business," knowing that the "thin end of the wedge must first enter the wood" and that "the blows have to be a little easy at first, or the wedge flies out."[32]

Indeed, the behavior of Lincoln as this bill passed Congress was indicative. He played both sides of the issue to stave off a backlash. He framed his remarks for particular constituencies. Critics of Lincoln down the years have called him shifty and devious. But he was something of a tightrope-walker when it came to the politics of slavery in 1862. He had to maintain his position in a state of equilibrium as he tried to move forward by careful degrees.

So when Maryland Congressman John W. Crisfield expressed the concerns of his constituents about the implications of abolishing slavery in Washington, D.C., Lincoln said that "Maryland had nothing to fear, either for her institutions or her interests." When Crisfield asked for permission to make that statement public, Lincoln said no because it "would force me into a quarrel before the proper time."[33]

But to another observer, Lincoln said he looked forward to the effects upon Maryland of emancipation in Washington. He confessed that he would find a grim sort of satisfaction in responding to Marylanders who complained that their slaves would flee to Washington to gain their freedom. He said that he would tell them "I am engaged in putting down a great rebellion, in which I can only succeed by help from the North, which will not tolerate my returning your slaves, and I cannot try experiments. You cannot have them."[34]

So much for his assurances to Crisfield.

About a month later, General David Hunter did what Frémont had done in Missouri: he gave an emancipation order without consulting Lincoln. After Lincoln had removed George McClellan as general in chief, he rearranged the theaters of command. At the behest of Republican friends of Frémont, he created a new "Mountain Department" that would cover the Appalachian region from western Virginia to east Tennessee and he put Frémont in charge of it. Hunter was transferred from Kansas to a new "Department of the South" that would encompass the states of Georgia, South Carolina, and Florida.

Hunter established his headquarters on Hilton Head Island, one of the "sea islands" off the coasts of Georgia and South Carolina. When these barrier islands had been occupied as bases for the Union blockade, planters fled to the mainland, leaving thousands of their slaves. Salmon

Chase had encouraged northern abolitionists and missionaries to go to the islands and educate the slaves. Hunter supported this effort with enthusiasm and he proposed to go further.

On May 9 he issued an order putting Georgia, South Carolina, and Florida under martial law. And he proclaimed that all the slaves in the Department of the South would be forever free. This was a clear repetition of the Frémont affair, and Lincoln chose to respond in the very same way, though with one important difference.

An extremely important difference.

On May 19, when he countermanded Hunter's order, Lincoln observed that the question of "whether it be competent for me, as Commander-in-Chief of the Army and Navy, to declare the Slaves of any state or states, free, and whether at any time, in any case, it shall have become a necessity indispensable to the maintenance of the government, to exercise such supposed power, are questions which . . . I reserve to myself."[35]

This was a bold new departure from the principle that Lincoln had invoked months earlier when he told Orville Browning that the permanent status of contraband slaves was a matter of law that only Congress had the power to address. He was now declaring that *executive* as well as legislative power could address the issue. He was laying the groundwork for issuing an emancipation order himself.

In the same proclamation, he tried once again to elicit support for his gradual phase-out plan. He addressed the people of the slave states directly. "You can not if you would be blind to the signs of the times," he wrote, going on to observe that

> this proposal makes common cause for a common object, casting no reproaches on any. It acts not the pharisee. The change it contemplates would come gently as the dews of heaven, not rending or wrecking anything. Will you not embrace it? . . . May the vast future not have to lament that you neglected it.[36]

There was very little doubt in his mind as to what he would do if the slave-holders did neglect it. In June, when a group of abolitionists visited him and expressed the hope that he "might, under divine guidance, be led to free the slaves," he replied that "he had sometime thought that perhaps he might be an instrument in God's hands" and was "not unwilling to be."[37]

He had come a long way from the days in his youth when he ridiculed the antics of preachers and told his friends in New Salem and Springfield how foolish it was to regard the Bible as the literal word of God. But even in those days, he mastered the Bible as a literary document, committing long passages of it to memory. And even as he parodied preachers, the rhetoric of biblical exhortation was beginning to enter his lexicon.

Well before his move to New Salem, he experienced the vicarious sensation of acting like a preacher. His step-sister Matilda Johnston recalled that "Abe would take down the bible, read a verse—give out a hymn—and we would sing. . . . He would preach & we would do the Crying."[38]

In the spring of 1862 he turned more and more to the Bible. He read it as something of a "seeker." He was seeking consolation as he grieved for little Willie, but he sought something else of broader scope: a reason that would justify the carnage that his policies on slavery had triggered. He was coming to see the Civil War in terms of Old Testament typology: a divine castigation of a new chosen people who had broken their covenant and drifted into declension.

The United States of America had been founded as a new promised land, and it offered the blessing of freedom—freedom to experience the miracle of life to its fullest extent and to savor the sweetness of living. The nation had been built upon what Jefferson called the "Laws of Nature and of Nature's God." Among these laws were the self-evident truths that all men are created equal and "endowed by their Creator with certain unalienable Rights," among which were "Life, Liberty and the Pursuit of Happiness."

It stood to reason that a covenant was implied by these propositions. More than a mere social compact, this was a *sacred* covenant, resting as it did upon the laws of "Nature's God." All men being equal—all men being equally entitled to live, to be free, to seek happiness—they had to treat one another by the standards of the golden rule if they wished to be worthy of their rights. They had to defend and protect the freedom of others if they wished to be treated the same.

"Those who deny freedom to others, deserve it not for themselves," Lincoln wrote back in 1859—"and, under a just God, can not long retain it."

God was just and his laws were universal. But the pride that keeps raging in the hearts of all people had been prompting Americans to stamp out the rights that God commanded—the rights that everyone deserved, without exception. Americans had been called to be the vanguard of a world-redemptive movement that would make the right to freedom universal. But instead of living up to the creed that their Founders professed, Americans maintained a social system of unparalleled cruelty, one that reduced other people to the status of beasts of the field and made them livestock.

God was just. Americans had tolerated sin and hypocrisy ever since the founding of the nation. And now the moment of reckoning had come. God's wrath was on display for all to see. Julia Ward Howe had proclaimed it that way in the new song lyrics that she offered to America in February 1862. God had "sounded forth the trumpet that shall never call retreat," the lyrics said. God was "tramping out the vintage where the grapes of wrath are stored"—He was "sifting out the hearts of men before His Judgment Seat"—and it was time for Americans to suffer in order to atone.

A "terrible swift sword" would make certain that they did.

At last, on May 3, the Confederate forces in Yorktown—which had since been heavily augmented by Johnston—withdrew to Richmond. McClellan, with his vastly superior forces, had sent for some siege guns. But now the guns were unnecessary. McClellan could occupy the rebel entrenchments unopposed and he claimed a great victory. It was nothing of the kind. The month that he had wasted gave Joseph Johnston more time to prepare the defenses of Richmond. Slowly and painfully, McClellan and his huge army crept up the Virginia peninsula toward the Confederate capital.

As the Confederates withdrew, Lincoln, Stanton, Chase, and several others sailed down the Chesapeake Bay to Fortress Monroe. They wanted more information on conditions at the front. In the course of this visit, Lincoln took direct command of some troops and he issued orders for the capture of Norfolk. Neither McClellan nor anyone else had thought of doing such a thing.

Lincoln suggested the idea to General John E. Wool, in command at Fortress Monroe, and he pointed out that the capture of Norfolk could also result in the capture or destruction of the CSS *Virginia*. "Pooh," Wool reportedly said; "you don't understand military necessity."[39]

But Lincoln took action in defiance of Wool. He ordered Navy Flag Officer Louis M. Goldsborough to conduct a reconnaissance of Norfolk. Lincoln came along in person to supervise. From May 8 to May 10, he took command of the operation. Norfolk, largely deserted by the rebels, was captured, and of equal or greater importance, the Confederates destroyed the *Virginia* to prevent it from falling into Union hands.

Lincoln was an excellent commander in the field. When he learned that the troops commanded by Colonel Joseph R. Carr were not participating in the operation, he demanded to know why not. Informed that Wool had given different orders, Lincoln sharply directed Carr to "send me someone who can write."[40] He quickly dictated an order countermanding Wool.[41]

One of the officers serving aboard the *Monitor* wrote that it was "extremely fortunate that the President came down as he did—he seems to have infused new life into everything."[42] When Lincoln arrived back in Washington, Chase wrote the following: "So has ended a brilliant week's campaign of the President; for I think it quite certain that, if he had not come down, Norfolk would still have been in possession of the enemy, and the '*Merrimack*' as grim and defiant and as much a terror as ever."[43]

Lincoln decided to augment McClellan's advance by ordering McDowell and his corps to move south/southwest in the direction of Richmond. This was precisely the movement that Lincoln had been advocating for months, and now he forced it to happen.

It was a very good move under these particular circumstances. McDowell could continue to shield the nation's capital as he advanced into Virginia. And his advance would reinforce McClellan and create a kind of pincer movement on Richmond. Moreover, if McClellan malingered, McDowell could be ordered to attack—and that would force an engagement with the rebels.

But the rebels struck first. They did it in the Shenandoah Valley.

In the autumn of 1861, Stonewall Jackson had been sent to the Shenandoah. The valley was of very great importance to both sides. Interpenetrated by mountain ranges, it offered troops an excellent corridor for maneuvering. And its farmland offered a superb source of food.

As the Confederates prepared for their defense of Richmond, Jackson withdrew "up" the Shenandoah Valley—"up" meaning higher elevation, which meant that he was actually moving to the *south*—at the same time that Joseph Johnston's troops withdrew from Manassas. The idea was to position these armies to work in coordinated fashion in the overall defense of Richmond.

General Nathaniel Banks—a Union political general from Massachusetts who had served as both governor and speaker of the U.S. House of Representatives—was sent with a corps to Harper's Ferry after Jackson withdrew from the town. Banks pursued Jackson's forces, engaging them on March 23 in the battle of Kernstown. This was the first and only time that Stonewall Jackson was defeated in battle.

In May, as McClellan advanced upon Richmond, Jackson struck again in the valley to create a big diversion that would pin down federal troops. His campaign succeeded brilliantly. It was a whirlwind of action and it did much more than just defeat the army of Banks. It disrupted the movement of McDowell's army in its overland march toward Richmond. Indeed, Jackson eventually pinned down *three* separate Union armies for the better part of a month.

He began on May 8 and his campaign would continue until June 9. He moved with speed, darting in and out of mountain passes, striking quickly by surprise and then vanishing. Then he struck at a different location to knock his opponents off balance.

Lincoln was concerned about the safety of Washington as the news of this fighting arrived. It was entirely possible that Jackson would cross the Potomac River and test the defenses of the city.

But Lincoln's response to the valley campaign would reveal something else that was significant about his military instincts. For Lincoln wanted not only to protect his own capital city, he wanted to *trap Jackson's army and destroy it.* He viewed the valley campaign as both a threat and a golden opportunity.

As he engaged his strategic senses with the challenge of war, Lincoln came to a realization that was quite advanced: it embodied the teachings of the German military theorist Carl von Clausewitz before his doctrines had even been translated in English or taught at the American military academies. It was a doctrine of total war and it taught that the armies of the enemy had to be regarded as more than obstacles, which of course they occasionally were. But those armies were *targets* as well.

By May 1862 Lincoln understood that it would not be enough to capture fixed geographical assets such as cities—not enough to just occupy ground. For as long as the armies of the enemy were active, there could be no overall victory. The enemy's armies would have to be neutralized as sources of power. They would have to be defeated and forced to surrender.

Or destroyed.

So in May Lincoln summoned three armies to converge upon Jackson and defeat him. He ordered Banks to continue his attacks; he re-routed McDowell and sent him off to the Shenandoah, and he pulled the army of Frémont from its newly created "Mountain Department" and hurled it at Jackson from the West.

Lincoln was acting in the role of general in chief, and so he gave direct orders to these armies. He wanted action and speed; he sought to be as fast on the draw as Stonewall Jackson. Alas, the forces at his command were no match for the audacity of Jackson. Lincoln's anger at the sluggishness of his armies—compared to the speed with which Jackson could travel—grew sharper as events played out. His orders were impatient and peremptory.

He was especially impatient with Frémont, urging him on May 24 to "put the utmost speed into it. Do not lose a minute."[44] On May 30 he cabled Frémont again as follows: "Where *is* your force? You ought this minute to be near Strasburg. Answer at once."[45] He also goaded McClellan, wiring him that "the time is near when you must either attack Richmond or give up the job and come to the defense of Washington. Let me hear from you instantly."[46]

All in vain. The tactical audacity that Lincoln required in Virginia was not to be found in such commanders. The time was approaching when Lincoln would decide to bring a new commander from the West and put him straight to work in Virginia. Not Grant—his reputation was under a cloud and it would take him the better part of a year to redeem himself. Lincoln had his eye upon a different commander, the one who had captured Island Number Ten: General John Pope.

The summer of 1862 was a rather momentous time for legislative accomplishment by the Civil War Republican Congress. One historic act after another was passed and then signed by Lincoln.

Some of this legislation had nothing to do with the war or with slavery. It was domestic legislation in the big-government tradition of Alexander Hamilton and Henry Clay. The Democrats were powerless to stop it.

On July 1, Congress passed the Pacific Railway Act that established a brand-new company, the Union Pacific Railroad, whose task would be to make the long-dreamed-of overland link to the West Coast of North America a reality. Congress also passed the Morrill Act, which established the land-grant college system. On May 20, Congress had passed another civilian measure of tremendous significance: the Homestead Act, releasing free acreage on the frontier to western settlers.

And as to the territories in the West, Congress finally passed the long-promised Republican Free Soil measure prohibiting slavery in federal lands. This act was passed on June 19 and Lincoln signed it with pleasure. Stephen Douglas never lived to see the passage of this law overturning the *Dred Scott* decision, but Roger Taney lived to see it.

The act stood squarely in defiance of a terrible case law precedent. The Republicans did exactly what Lincoln had promised to do in the 1860 election.

Some Republicans in Congress were ready to take on the court more directly. In December 1861, Republican Senator John P. Hale of New Hampshire introduced legislation to abolish the existing Supreme Court and replace it with a different one. The existing court, Hale contended, "is bankrupt in everything that was intended by the creation of such a tribunal. It has lost public confidence; it does not enjoy public respect; and it ought not."[47]

He argued that the language of Article III, Section 1 of the Constitution—which stipulated that "the judicial power of the United States shall be vested in one Supreme Court and in such inferior courts as the Congress may, from time to time, ordain and establish"—meant that Congress was free, "from time to time," to ordain and establish *any* new courts, and this meant that the existing Supreme Court could be replaced by a *different* one that was newly "ordained and established."

Other Republicans talked about expanding the size of the court to permit the kind of court-packing that Lincoln himself had hinted at with gusto in the course of the Lincoln-Douglas debates. But since vacancies on the court began to open up as early as 1862, Republicans could start to reshape the court to their liking without expanding its size. Lincoln nominated and Congress confirmed two new justices in 1862, and one of them was none other than Lincoln's old friend and campaign manager David Davis.

The Revenue Act of 1862, which was passed by Congress on July 1, expanded the Direct Tax Act of the previous year and it contained one proviso of vast potential significance for the South. It provided that the real estate of tax evaders could be seized and then sold to pay the tax. That meant that property owners in Confederate states could have their lands seized and sold for non-payment of taxes, since Congress had refused to recognize the Confederacy as a nation.

The Militia Act, passed by Congress on July 16, cheered the hearts of abolitionists and advocates of racial equality. It allowed black men to be accepted into military service, not only as laborers but also as soldiers. And it laid the groundwork for a military draft, creating militia quotas for the states. If the states were unable to meet the quotas, the administration could begin to induct men directly.

Most significant of all was the Second Confiscation Act, which took the much-anticipated step of giving freedom to the slaves who escaped from disloyal owners. This law was the direct culmination of legislation introduced the previous December by Lyman Trumbull. As it worked its way through Congress, Lincoln objected to some of its provisions. Those who still subscribe to the Lincoln-the-moderate legend believe that when he did so he was showing an aversion to what Congress was doing.

But that was not the case at all.

He was trying through his lawyer-sense to *strengthen* the bill by foreseeing the ways in which courts could strike down its provisions. His recommendations for the modification of the bill make interesting reading. He was trying to make it lawyer-proof.

All the while, however, he was pondering a step that was far more radical than anything the bill contained. He was coming very close to the Rubicon. He was almost ready to draft and release an emancipation proclamation.

But first he decided to give his compensated phase-out plan a last chance. The issuance of a presidential freedom proclamation might foment a huge white supremacist backlash—a backlash powerful enough to usher in a Democratic Congress if the voters rebelled in the November mid-term elections. And if Republicans lost control of Congress, who could say how far the damage would extend?

Indeed, the goal of tipping the mid-term elections to the Democrats would soon become central to Confederate strategy.

Though many Radical Republicans were eager to exceed Lincoln's tempo of reform, an influential Radical had faith in Lincoln's judgment. On June 5, Senator Charles Sumner wrote to a colleague (whose name was deleted from the published correspondence) and told him that Lincoln agreed with the Radicals on most of the moral fundamentals and would guide their movement to success.

Sumner, who once expressed support for the concept of a compensated phase-out of slavery, wrote that Lincoln's unprecedented action of March 6 "must take its place among the great events of history." "If you knew the President," Sumner lectured his colleague, you would "be grateful that he is so true to all you have at heart." Give him time, Sumner said, "for from the past" one could easily "discern the sure promise of the future."[48]

Lincoln quietly did many things that made it obvious where his sympathies lay on the issues of slavery and race. He signed a law extending diplomatic recognition to the black republics of Haiti and Liberia. When someone expressed the fear that the president of Haiti would send a black diplomat to Washington, Lincoln said that "I shan't tear my shirt if he does send a negro here!"[49]

Little by little, the administration put policies in place that were tending toward racial equality. Later in the year, Attorney General Bates handed down an important ruling—a ruling that free blacks were American citizens as a matter of birthright. This ruling overturned an important part of the *Dred Scott* decision, which Bates dismissed as having "no authority as a judicial decision" beyond its immediate impact on the freedom suit of the plaintiff.[50]

McClellan's vast army had arrived at the outskirts of Richmond. McClellan refused to attack, believing as always that his army was vastly outnumbered. In fact, the Confederates' strength in the Richmond defense perimeter had increased: reinforcements from North Carolina augmented the size of Johnston's army to approximately seventy-five thousand. The Union and Confederate armies were far more evenly matched at this point than had been the case at Yorktown. Regardless, McClellan was not outnumbered.

On May 31, the Confederates' commander took the offensive. Johnston launched an attack against McClellan that resulted in the two-day battle of Fair Oaks or Seven Pines. About forty thousand troops on each side were involved, and this battle, though a tactical stand-off, was bloody, with over five thousand casualties for each army.

The battle did achieve two significant results. The first was a Confederate change of command; Joseph Johnston was wounded in the shoulder and replaced by Robert E. Lee. Lee at last had a chance to redeem himself after all those months in exile. With a flash of bravado, he christened the force he commanded the "Army of *Northern* Virginia."

The other result of the battle was to make McClellan more averse than ever to combat. He was sickened by the slaughter—as anyone with normal sensibilities would be, but field commanders have to summon the stamina to carry on. McClellan was almost ready to give up. He wrote to his wife that "victory has no charms for me when purchased at such cost."[51]

So he complained that his army would be wiped out completely without reinforcements and he said that the responsibility for "saving" his army would rest in Washington.

On June 26, two consequential things happened simultaneously. First, Lincoln issued an order consolidating "all the forces under Major Generals Frémont, Banks, and McDowell" into "one army, to be called the Army of Virginia."[52] He brought in Pope from the West to command it. Lincoln would now have two separate armies in Virginia—something of a Team A and Team B arrangement that would give the new commander a chance to show up McClellan, thus providing the basis for Lincoln to oust him or to ease him out of the picture as soon as possible.

Second, Lee unleashed a tremendous new assault against McClellan on the outskirts of Richmond. The result was a series of engagements to be known as the "Seven Days Battles." It had started with a minor attack by some Union forces on June 25. But when Lee struck back the next day he seized the battlefield initiative and never let it go. Again and again, he hurled his forces at McClellan, who steadily retreated without doing much to fight back.

McClellan's characteristic whining reached the point of hysteria as he sent this message to Stanton: "I have lost this battle because my force was too small. . . . The government must not and cannot hold me responsible for this result. . . . If I save this army now, I tell you plainly that I owe no thanks to you or to any other persons in Washington. You have done your best to sacrifice this army."[53] He claimed that he faced almost two hundred thousand Confederate troops.

That was nonsense.

Lincoln sent off a message designed to calm McClellan down and protect himself from this obvious attempt to shift the blame. "Save your Army at all events," the president wrote, adding that "I feel any misfortune to you and your Army quite as keenly as you feel it yourself." He hastened to remind McClellan of the reason why McDowell's corps had been held back. "If you have had a drawn battle, or a repulse," Lincoln wrote, "it is the price we pay for the enemy not being in Washington. . . . Had we stripped Washington, he would have been upon us before the troops could have got to you."[54]

By the time these bloody battles ended on July 1, both sides suffered grievous losses. Confederate casualties were around twenty thousand and the Union lost approximately sixteen thousand. The overall result was a

Confederate victory: McClellan's great army was driven back from Richmond to a place called Harrison's Landing on the James River.

But the result could have been very different. Lee's attacks might have failed if McClellan struck back, for in the final battle, at Malvern Hill, Lee's orders were botched in a number of respects and his troops were cut to pieces in a hail of artillery fire. McClellan's corps commanders begged him to order a counter-attack against Lee, but he refused.

Of course he refused.

In Washington Lincoln decided it was time to escalate the war. He was ready to consider the possibility that McClellan *had* been outnumbered, at least to some extent. A vast new infusion of troops might have to be inducted. So Lincoln drafted a letter for Seward to carry to a meeting of Union governors on June 28.

He stipulated that the enemy had concentrated "too much force in Richmond for McClellan to successfully attack." Therefore the best thing to do, he reflected, was "to hold what we have in the West, open the Mississippi, and, take Chattanooga and East Tennessee." Then, "let the country give us a hundred thousand new troops in the shortest possible time, which added to McClellan ... will take Richmond, without endangering any other place which we now hold—and will substantially end the war."

Lincoln pledged to "maintain this contest until successful, or till I die, or am conquered, or my term expires, or Congress or the country forsakes me."[55]

On July 1, he called for *three hundred thousand* new troops, and a recruiting poem began to make the rounds: "We are Coming, Father Abraham, Three Hundred Thousand More." This poem—which would later be set to music by eight different American composers, including Stephen Foster—was written by an abolitionist named James S. Gibbons.

In July, Lincoln took the time to visit some wounded soldiers in the military hospitals of Washington. And he persuaded Mary Lincoln to accompany him on some of these visits. Mary visited the hospitals more and more on her own in the months that followed. The emotional release that such acts of compassion could provide helped her greatly in her effort to recover from the loss of her son.

On the Fourth of July, Charles Sumner visited Lincoln and said that it was time for him to escalate his anti-slavery strategy. This was friendly advice, and Lincoln knew it; Sumner was one of the most sympathetic of the Radical Republicans.

"You need more men," the senator declared, "not only at the North, but at the South, in the rear of the Rebels: you need the slaves." Lincoln said that the danger of a white supremacist backlash worried him. "Half the officers would fling down their arms and three more States would rise," Lincoln said.[56] But the moment was approaching when Lincoln would take perhaps the biggest calculated risk of his political career and take the anti-slavery movement to a point of great fulfillment—and great danger.

Meanwhile, McClellan told Lincoln he would need fifty thousand more men to renew the offensive. Lincoln had to figure out what to do about McClellan, since the Army of Virginia under Pope's command was shaping up quickly. He sounded out Ambrose Burnside, who achieved some success at Roanoke Island, to see if he might serve as McClellan's replacement. Burnside's troops had been brought to Virginia to become a new corps of the Army of the Potomac. But Burnside declined Lincoln's offer.

So Lincoln traveled to McClellan's new base on the James River at Harrison's Landing to inspect the army and review the situation on July 7. After touring the base and conferring with McClellan, he was handed a letter by the general, an openly political letter proclaiming that the issue of slavery should be kept out of the war.

Lincoln made no comment. He had already summoned yet another delegation of border state leaders to the White House. He would make a final pitch for his gradual emancipation plan when he met with these leaders on July 12.

On July 11, he filled the vacant position of general in chief with Henry Halleck. Stanton advised this step, and it was consistent with the earlier decision to transfer Pope to Virginia. The greatest military successes for the Union thus far had unfolded in the western theater.

Lincoln made sure to leave a written record of the things that he said to the border state leaders on July 12. Over two dozen of them came to the White House. "Let the states in rebellion see," the president began, "that, in no event, will the states you represent ever join their proposed Confederacy." It was time to make slavery moot, Lincoln said, time to break the lever that Confederates were using to influence the border states' politics. "Break that lever before their faces," the president said, "and they can shake you no more forever."

Besides, if they ignored this chance to receive compensation for their slaves, they might lose the slaves without getting anything. Slavery might be eradicated through "friction and abrasion—by the mere incidents of war." If so, a huge capital investment would be "gone, and you will have nothing valuable in lieu of it."

Then Lincoln used the ploy he had sketched for Conway and Channing in January; he invoked the attacks against himself to gain leverage for this anti-slavery initiative. He said that by rescinding General Hunter's decree, "I gave dissatisfaction, if not offense, to many whose support the country cannot afford to lose. And this is not the end of it. The pressure, in this direction, is still upon me, and is increasing."

Therefore, seize the moment, Lincoln said. "As you would perpetuate popular government for the best people in the world," he implored them, "I beseech you that you do in no wise omit this. To you, more than to any others, the privilege is given."[57]

But most of the border state representatives had no interest whatsoever in his gradual emancipation scheme.

So he came to one of the most important decisions of his life, and he revealed it to Seward and Welles in the course of a carriage ride the next day. He would issue a decree that would strike down slavery in all of the rebellious states.[58] He would take a step so drastic it surpassed the most far-reaching features of the Second Confiscation Act—the act that Congress would pass a few days later.

Did this mean that Lincoln was abandoning his long-cherished vision of a gradual phase-out of slavery? Not exactly. Since the edict he would issue would have to be grounded—for constitutional reasons—in military need, it could only apply in those slave states where a rebellion was actually occurring. It could therefore not apply in loyal slave states. Since Lincoln was determined to eradicate slavery *everywhere*, he kept his offer to the border states open.

But his secret decision was radical indeed and it was based upon his own tough-mindedness and intellectual candor. He had tried an experiment to see if the gradualist anti-slavery vision he inherited from Henry Clay would work if it were put to the test. The experiment had failed. Slave owners were too stubborn, too addicted to the ways of domination. Their sick self-esteem was so grounded in the ownership of other human beings that they had no conscience. They were lost souls.

So much the worse for them. Their folly and their pride and their arrogance would have to be humbled. He had given them chance after chance to be decent, even offering to *pay* them to do the right thing.

It was impossible. They were so far gone in the ways of enslavement that one couldn't even pay them to be decent.

So they would suffer—as they made others suffer.

That was justice.

His plan had been to start with border states in order to show the rebels that emancipation could be easy. He got nowhere, and so he flipped the whole sequence: he would start with the rebels and go after the border states later. But instead of compensation, the rebels would get nothing— nothing at all—when their slaves were set free.

It would serve them right.

The Second Confiscation Act was weak by the standards of the Radicals. True, it promised freedom to slaves who were owned by rebel masters. But the act's procedures were extremely cumbersome. The issue of whether or not a slave deserved freedom came down to the question of whether the master of that slave could be proven to be a rebel. And the Second Confiscation Act left that matter up to the courts, so the emancipation of slaves who escaped to Union lines would have to be settled case by case through thousands and thousands of court proceedings.

Lincoln, like the Radicals, could see how ineffective this procedure would be. And he was troubled by constitutional issues that he feared might undermine the new law if it were challenged in court. The bill provided for the permanent seizure of real estate, and Lincoln feared that this provision amounted to a "bill of attainder"—a forfeiture of real estate beyond the lifetime of the offender—which the Constitution forbids. A lawsuit challenging that provision could lead to lawsuits challenging other provisions, and the law, already weak, would be weakened even further by the courts.

While Radical Republicans were disappointed by the final form of the Confiscation Act, some conservative Republicans were urging Lincoln to veto the legislation because it went too far.

Congress hastened to pass a new joint resolution confirming Lincoln's stand on the attainder issue, so the president signed the confiscation act into law on July 17. But as he did so, he was putting the finishing touches on a new presidential decree that would sidestep court procedures for liberating slaves.

His new proclamation would declare that *every single slave* within certain geographical areas would be free—*automatically* free if the rebellion continued—and that slaves in those areas would be delivered from their bondage by direct military action.

It could not free all the slaves in the nation since its power could not extend into loyal border slave states. But the Emancipation Proclamation as Lincoln conceived it was a revolutionary act.

On July 22 he revealed his intention at a cabinet meeting and he read the first draft of his decree. "I, as Commander-in-Chief of the Army and Navy of the United States," Lincoln wrote, "do order and declare that on the first day of January in the year of Our Lord one thousand, eight hundred, and sixty-three, all persons held as slaves within any state or states, wherein the constitutional authority of the United States shall not then be practically recognized, submitted to, and maintained, shall then, thenceforward, and forever, be free."[59]

This historic cabinet meeting would be memorialized later in an oil painting by the artist Francis Bicknell Carpenter, who would take up residence in the White House during 1864 as he tried to reconstruct the scene on that summer day two years earlier.

The reactions from the members of Lincoln's cabinet were mixed. Blair said that he could not support the measure and warned of the consequences in the mid-term elections that were little more than three months away. Caleb Smith said nothing. Stanton supported the proposal with gusto. Chase was surprisingly ambivalent. Bates said he could support the measure. Seward and Welles had told Lincoln in the course of their carriage-ride that they thought the proclamation was justified. But Seward, in the cabinet meeting, told Lincoln that he ought to delay until a battlefield victory of obvious and overwhelming magnitude could be achieved.

At least that was what Lincoln remembered when he reminisced about this meeting in conversations with the artist Francis Carpenter.[60]

For all of the quirkiness and the perversity that Seward had shown sometimes in the past, this was one of the times when Lincoln believed that his strategic advice was quite sound. So Lincoln put the proclamation away in a desk drawer.

He would wait. But he did announce on July 25 that he would start to implement the Second Confiscation Act in sixty days.

Meanwhile, in spite of their devastating losses in the western theater, the Confederates were moving toward victory. At last their cotton embargo was having its desired effect upon the British. The backlog of cotton in

British warehouses was running low and a "cotton famine" could have a devastating effect on the British economy.

Moreover, the defeat of McClellan's army at the gates of Richmond had been duly noted abroad. When it was clear that the attack upon the Confederate capital had failed, France's Emperor Napoleon III sent a query to Britain regarding the merits of recognizing the Confederacy. Parliament debated the issue on July 18, though without taking action. The British Prime Minister, Lord Palmerston, was not yet convinced that the decisive moment had arrived. But he did have Confederate sympathies and it might not take much longer for him to act upon them.

Counterbalancing Palmerston was the fact that Queen Victoria and Prince Albert abominated slavery, and so did much of the British electorate. Lincoln's proclamation could help to fend off foreign recognition of the Confederacy. And yet the very same proclamation might give white supremacist Democrats control of Congress.

After Lincoln had signed the Second Confiscation Act, racial violence began to break out in the North. Rioters attacked free blacks, and many Democratic newspaper editorials vilified the Republican "Nigger Lovers." Lincoln had his work cut out for him in the summer of 1862: he would have to prepare northern voters for his revolutionary blow against slavery. Perhaps a decisive battlefield victory in Virginia would help to set the stage. It was up to Pope to deliver that victory. As for McClellan, a decision would have to be made about how to use his army.

The pressure on Lincoln was eased just a little by the fact that he was spending his evenings with his family in the pleasant surroundings of the Soldiers' Home, far away from the oppressive heat and humidity that plagued the White House. Beginning in 1862, he made use of the Soldiers' Home from June through November.

The Soldiers' Home was a complex of five buildings, and the Lincolns probably stayed in a Gothic-style house on the grounds that had been built around twenty years earlier by a banker named George W. Riggs. "We are truly delighted, with this retreat," wrote Mary; "the drives & walks around here are truly delightful."[61] Lincoln rode out to this place around 5 p.m.—either on horseback or in a carriage—and returned to the White House around 8 a.m. the next morning.

A year later, Walt Whitman, who was living very close to the White House, wrote that he liked to watch Lincoln all the time in his commutes back and forth to the Soldiers' Home. The poet left a vivid description of what he saw:

He always has a company of twenty-five or thirty cavalry, with sabers drawn and held upright against their shoulders. They say this guard was against his personal wish, but he lets his counselors have their way. . . . Mr. Lincoln on the saddle generally rides a good-sized, easy-going gray horse, is dressed in plain black, somewhat rusty and dusty, wears a black stiff hat, and looks about as ordinary in attire, etc., as the commonest man. . . . I see very plainly Abraham Lincoln's dark face, with the deep-cut lines, always to me with a deep latent sadness in the expression. We have got so that we exchange bows, and very cordial ones. Sometimes the President goes and comes in an open barouche. . . . Often I notice as he goes out evenings—and sometimes in the morning, when he returns early—he turns off and halts at the large and handsome residence of the Secretary of War, on K Street, and holds conference there. If in his barouche, I can see from my window he does not alight, but sits in his vehicle, and Mr. Stanton comes out to attend him. Sometimes one of his sons, a boy of ten or twelve, accompanies him, riding at his right on a pony.[62]

Whitman added that "none of the artists or pictures has caught the deep, though subtle and indirect expression of this man's face. There is something else there. One of the great portrait painters of two or three centuries ago is needed."[63]

After Henry Halleck, the new general in chief, arrived in Washington on July 23, Lincoln sent for him and told him to visit McClellan and present him with a simple proposition: if McClellan would agree to renew the offensive, the president would send him twenty thousand more troops. If not, his army would be withdrawn from the Peninsula and merged into Pope's. Halleck met with McClellan on July 25 and suggested that he put the issue to a vote among his corps commanders. They accepted the offer. But then McClellan sent off a message demanding *forty thousand* more troops.

So on August 4, Lincoln ordered McClellan to withdraw from the Virginia Peninsula—to send his army back the way it came. The troops would be merged into Pope's new army and participate in its overland advance against the army of Robert E. Lee.

McClellan took his time about implementing this presidential order. He could see that he was being eased out of the picture and he knew that there was little he could do about it, so he took his time, brooding and sulking.

Meanwhile, Lincoln was turning his attention to the task of defending the Second Confiscation Act while preparing the public for the much stronger measure that was waiting in his desk drawer. He began by inserting some hints into private correspondence.

On July 28, he told Cuthbert Bullitt, a lawyer in occupied New Orleans, that he had no patience with complaints that "the relation of master and slave is disturbed by the presence of our Army." "What would you do in my position," he inquired: "Would you drop the war where it is? Or, would you prosecute it in future, with elder-stalk squirts, charged with rose water? Would you deal lighter blows rather than heavier ones? Would you give up the contest, leaving any available means unapplied?"[64]

To financier August Belmont, he wrote on July 31 that "broken eggs cannot be mended. . . . This government cannot much longer play a game in which it stakes all, and its enemies stake nothing. Those enemies must understand that they cannot experiment for ten years trying to destroy the government, and if they fail still come back into the Union unhurt."[65]

On August 14, Lincoln had a long and significant meeting with five free blacks from the District of Columbia. It was a meeting to discuss the subject of "colonization," and for years Lincoln critics have denounced this meeting as insulting to blacks and a demonstration of Lincoln's instinctive racism. Such critics often claim that Lincoln acted in a "condescending" manner toward his guests.

It is easy to refute such charges since Lincoln made sure that his remarks were recorded by a journalist. He wanted everything he said to be brought to the public's attention.

To be sure, one has to acknowledge here the obvious fact that the notion of shipping free blacks to another land—those who were willing to go, for Lincoln always insisted that the program would have to be voluntary—could indeed be regarded as insulting if blacks chose to take it that way. And there were certainly African Americans who found it so in 1862, most famously the black abolitionist Frederick Douglass.

But for those who were pessimistic about the prospects for decent race relations in America—in light of the virulence and power of white supremacy attitudes—the idea made a certain kind of sense. It would be better, said the advocates of colonization, for blacks and whites to go their separate ways in peace than to allow racial conflict to ruin the lives of millions.

Henry Clay was the pre-eminent advocate of colonization and Lincoln had imbibed the idea from Clay. But it is hard to know how fervently he *wished* to see a mass emigration. Did Lincoln really *wish* to see people like his old friend the barber William Fleurville leave the country? Did he wish to see Mary's "modiste" and confidante Elizabeth Keckley leave the country?

The colonization idea was for Lincoln a component of the overall program of gradual and compensated emancipation, and its purpose was purely political: it was a device to reduce white resistance to the liberation of blacks.

Republicans broadly acknowledged these facts during 1862. Pennsylvania Congressman George Biddle said on June 2 that the "alarm" about emancipation "would spread to every man of my constituents who loves his country and his race if the public mind was not lulled and put to sleep with the word 'colonization.'"[66]

There were blacks who supported the idea, and for a very simple reason: they saw no reason to linger in a land where they were subject to cruel and vicious persecution. The black leader Henry Highland Garnet had organized an African Civilization Society to encourage emigration, and Congress had received a petition from 242 blacks in California who wanted help so they could move to some foreign country where their color would not be a "badge of degradation."[67]

Lincoln's meeting with the black delegation on August 14 had been organized by James Mitchell, a Methodist minister who had worked with the American Colonization Society. Lincoln confronted the issue of bigotry head-on, and he told his guests that he shared their feelings in regard to the way that they were treated. Those who have the notion that Lincoln was "condescending" in the tone of his remarks should reflect upon the following statement. "Your race," Lincoln said, "are suffering in my judgment, the greatest wrong inflicted on any people. . . . On this broad continent, not a single man of your race is made the equal of a single man of ours," and this, he continued, was "a fact about which we all think and feel alike, I and you." But it was "a fact with which we have to deal . . . [for] I cannot alter it."[68]

He made it clear that he regarded colonization as a way to reduce white resistance to emancipation. If blacks who were interested in moving to a land that was free of racial prejudice could demonstrate the feasibility of emigration, he said, it could "open a wide door for many to be made free." And "if intelligent men, such as are before me, would move in this matter, much might be accomplished."[69]

He suggested a move to Liberia, or else, if the continent of Africa seemed to be too distant and remote, a move to Central America. "To your colored race," he suggested, the inhabitants of Central America "have no objection," and he had been studying the geography to see if a suitable site for a colony could be found. And he believed that he had found such a place.

"The particular place I have in view," he explained, "is to be a great highway between the Atlantic or Caribbean Sea to the Pacific Ocean, and this particular place has all the advantages for a colony." He was speaking of the Chiriqui province of Panama, and he assured his guests that "if I get a sufficient number of you engaged," he would "have provisions made that you shall not be wronged." Indeed, he would insist that his black colonists should be "made equals" to everyone else in Panama, "and have the best assurance that you should be the equals of the best."

He said that he would like to get an enterprise started "so that you can get your daily bread as soon as you reach there," and he explained more specifically that he was having discussions with entrepreneurs who intended to establish a coal-mining operation in Chiriqui. Even a group of colonists as small as "twenty-five able-bodied men, with a mixture of women and children" would "make a successful commencement," he said.

Lincoln tried to be realistic. "I am not sure you will succeed," he admitted, and "the government may lose the money, but we cannot succeed unless we try. . . . The political affairs in Central America are not in quite as satisfactory condition as I wish. There are contending factions in that quarter; but . . . all the factions are agreed alike on the subject of colonization, and want it, and are more generous than we are here." [70]

Edward M. Thomas, the chairman of the black delegation, said that "they would hold a consultation and in a short time give an answer." "Take your full time," the president replied—"no hurry at all." [71]

A few days later Thomas said that Lincoln's speech had converted him from opposition to colonization to support. Though a majority of the five-man delegation voted against the colonization proposal, five hundred free blacks had signed up for Lincoln's experiment by mid-September and four thousand more were on the waiting list.

On August 20, the editor Horace Greeley provided Lincoln with a new opportunity to prepare northern public opinion for the Emancipation Proclamation. Greeley's *New York Tribune* ran an editorial entitled "The Prayer of Twenty Millions." It criticized Lincoln's performance on the slavery issue and urged more vigorous action to strike at the cause of the rebellion.

Here was another chance for Lincoln to do what he hinted at to Conway and Channing, another chance to "spike the soda" with his anti-slavery policy. By using Greeley's attack upon himself as a foil, he could position himself as a leader with one and only one objective on the issue of slavery: saving the Union.

In lines that remain quite famous—and to this day misleading to a great many people—Lincoln answered Greeley in an open letter as follows:

> My paramount object in this struggle *is* to save the Union, and is *not* either to save or to destroy slavery. If I could save the Union without freeing *any* slave I would do it, and if I could save it by freeing *all* the slaves I would do it; and if I could save it by freeing some and leaving others alone, I would also do that. . . . I have here stated my purpose according to my view of my *official* duty; and I intend no modification of my oft-expressed *personal* wish that all men every where could be free.[72]

Countless Americans have read those statements and come to the predictable conclusion that Lincoln was nothing but a moderate Unionist who "got around to" the issue of slavery in order to save the Union.

At least that's the way it seems to Americans who know little or nothing about the way the Civil War started—those who do not understand that Lincoln's policies *triggered* secession, that he meant to save the Union *his way* with the institution of slavery on course for extinction, that his statement in regard to his "paramount object" cannot survive a very simple question: why did he oppose the Crittenden Compromise? After all, if he was willing to adopt *any* policy on slavery that helped save the Union, he should have joined right in with Seward and the others in appeasing the slave-holding South.

But he refused.

His purpose in writing this deceptive letter is obvious: he was trying to soften up public opinion, to get people used to the idea that he might begin freeing some slaves. Rest assured, he was saying, that whatever he did about slavery—and he might start freeing some slaves—he was doing it for patriotic reasons.

Would it work?

Back in March, he revealed that the relationship between his goals of emancipating slaves and preserving the Union was *the opposite* of what he said to Greeley. Frank Blair had told him to wait—to wait for more battlefield successes—before pushing his scheme for the gradual phase-out of slavery with border state leaders. He replied that the emergency of war was a priceless way to get them committed to anti-slavery measures they would otherwise oppose. So he had to go ahead: he had to use the opportunity for all that it was worth to the anti-slavery movement.

"That is just the reason why I do not wish to wait," Lincoln said to Blair. "If we should have successes, they may feel and say, the rebellion is crushed and it matters not whether we do anything about this matter. I want them to consider it and interest themselves in it as an auxiliary means for putting down the rebels. I want to tell them that if they will take hold and do this, the war will cease."[73]

There would always be a very different way to make saving the Union the "paramount object" of the struggle—the Democrats' way. But Lincoln meant to use the war if he possibly could for the purpose of making people free.

The Democrats did not.

True, if he could save the Union without freeing slaves, he would do it: he would have no other choice. But that was not what he preferred or intended. What he wanted was to set people free.

The military situation began to turn dire in late August and a new emergency erupted. Confederates unleashed a great counter-offensive on every single front.

The Union successes that began in the spring had continued for a while. Both Huntsville, Alabama, and Corinth, Mississippi, had been occupied. Farragut had sailed up the Mississippi River to the stronghold of Vicksburg, where he joined his fleet with the northern flotilla, and both of these forces had subjected the city to bombardment.

But the rebel stronghold resisted them, and a new Confederate ironclad, the CSS *Arkansas*, steamed down the Yazoo River and anchored off Vicksburg. Then the level of the river started dropping, so Farragut was forced to take his deep-water craft back down toward the Gulf of Mexico. The northern gunboat fleet withdrew as well. The campaign to take Vicksburg had stalled.

Lincoln ordered Buell to move eastward toward Chattanooga, Tennessee, in order to complete the Union conquest of the state. But a new Confederate commander, Braxton Bragg, developed other plans. Placed in command of the Confederate Army of Tennessee, Bragg led his own troops to Chattanooga, thus pre-empting Buell. Meanwhile, Confederate cavalry raiders under the command of Nathan Bedford Forrest in Tennessee and John Hunt Morgan in Kentucky wrought havoc behind the Union lines.

In July, Bragg planned to strike back and initiate a major Confederate counter-offensive: he would lunge to the north, re-enter Kentucky, then carry the attack as far north as he could possibly take it. As he moved to the north from Chattanooga, a parallel invasion of Kentucky would be led by General Edmund Kirby Smith, whose troops were in Knoxville.

Smith went on the attack on August 14, and then Bragg followed up on August 28. By September 3, they had seized the Kentucky capital of Frankfort, and Buell, breaking off his approach to Chattanooga, tried desperately to catch up.

Meanwhile, Bragg ordered yet another offensive: he had Confederate troops in Mississippi under the command of Generals Earn Van Dorn and Sterling Price march north in the direction of Nashville. Two relatively small Union armies—the Army of the Tennessee, commanded by Grant, and the Army of the Mississippi, commanded by William S. Rosecrans— would have to confront these Confederates. Both of these Union forces were operating in the vicinity of Corinth and Iuka in northern Mississippi.

All of these southern campaigns were part of a larger rebel counter-offensive. The Confederates intended to take the initiative in every theater of the war. Their purpose went beyond the achievement of battlefield victories. They hoped that this counter-offensive would prompt the British and the French to recognize the Confederacy. And they hoped that it would usher in a Democratic victory in the Union's mid-term congressional elections. With foreign recognition and a Democratic Congress, there was simply no telling how great a coup the rebels would be able to achieve.

And these Confederates' hopes were quite plausible. Indeed, the Confederacy was coming close to an overall victory.

So when Robert E. Lee found out that McClellan's men would be withdrawn from the Peninsula, he too went on the offensive. He struck north at Pope's Army of Virginia, seeking to defeat it before it could be merged with the Army of the Potomac. And in launching his attack, he would achieve one of his greatest battlefield triumphs in partnership with Stonewall Jackson.

Lee's campaign was a masterpiece of speed, deception, and audacity. He outwitted his opponents, overcame superior numbers, and launched his own invasion of the North. In early August he sent twenty-four thousand men under Jackson to menace Pope's Army of Virginia. Lincoln had ordered McClellan to evacuate the Peninsula on August 4, but McClellan did not even begin to carry out the order until August 14.

He was stalling deliberately—stalling in the hope that John Pope would be defeated. He told his wife that Pope "will be very badly thrashed," and that Lincoln and the cabinet "will be very glad to turn over the redemption of their affairs to me. I won't undertake it unless I have full & entire control."[74]

By the time that McClellan began to obey Lincoln's order, Lee was headed north with most of his forces. Leaving some twenty-two thousand men to cover Richmond, he joined forces with Jackson and advanced toward Pope's army. Pope withdrew behind the Rappahannock River.

Then Lee executed a maneuver of real virtuosity: he split his army again, sending Jackson behind Pope's lines. Jackson's forces converged upon Manassas Junction, which Pope had been using as a depot. After plundering food and supplies, Jackson's men set fire to what remained and withdrew to the vicinity of the old Bull Run battlefield.

Pope—who was starting to receive the first advance units of McClellan's army—turned north to find Jackson and attack him. But he was headed straight into a trap.

Jackson's whereabouts were ascertained on August 28, and the next day Pope attacked. What he didn't know was that Lee was already there— he had brought up the rest of his army and was waiting to strike by surprise. In the midst of the campaign against Jackson on August 30, Pope's army was blind-sided by one of the most devastating surprise attacks in military history. What would soon be called the battle of Second Manassas was a Union catastrophe.

All of Lincoln's plans in Virginia were ruined, and his command structure was thrown into absolute chaos. Halleck was revealed to be a feckless bureaucrat: he was completely unable to speed up the arrival of McClellan's troops to give Pope the relief that he needed.

But he tried. He issued repeated orders to McClellan to rush his troops to Manassas. McClellan offered nothing but excuses. He had no intention of extending any help to Pope. On August 29, he showed his insolence in a brazen telegram to Lincoln. He said that the best course of action would be to "leave Pope to get out of his scrape & at once use all our means to make the Capital perfectly safe."[75]

The rank-and-file troops of the Army of Virginia blamed Pope for their defeat, and their rout had indeed been total. Their retreat back to Washington was an eerie reprise of what had happened the first time Confederate and Union armies clashed at Manassas. But several of McClellan's corps commanders blamed *him*, for they knew perfectly well that he had stabbed Pope in the back. He had refused to come to Pope's assistance.

These shocking events caused a panic in Washington, and Lincoln faced one of the war's most frightening emergencies. Once more, an invasion scare gripped the nation's capital, and it was more than Lee's army that frightened the citizens of Washington. Pope's troops were in a very ugly mood, for they knew that they had been betrayed. Attorney General Bates reported that Lincoln "was manifestly alarmed for the safety of the City. He had been talking with Gen Halleck . . . & had gotten the idea that Pope's army was utterly demoralized—saying that 'if Pope's army came within the lines *as a mob*, the City would be overrun by the enemy in 48 hours."[76]

Perhaps the defeated troops would start a riot. There was even some talk about a military coup d'état. Journalist Whitelaw Reid reported on widespread gossip in Washington that "we have more than one General who has been trying to shape events so as to make himself dictator."[77]

All over the North, despair and anger were spreading, not only in reaction to Second Manassas but to all the other Union setbacks. New York banker George Templeton Strong spoke for many when he wrote that "the North is rapidly sinking just now, as it has been sinking rapidly for two months and more."[78]

There was no doubt at all within Lincoln's inner circle that McClellan was to blame for Pope's defeat. Stanton wanted to have McClellan court-martialed and Chase believed that he ought to be shot. Four cabinet members signed a memorandum advocating McClellan's immediate dismissal and the matter was debated on September 2 in an angry cabinet meeting.

Lincoln had come to despise George McClellan, and he fully agreed that the general's character was rotten. He told John Hay that it was "envy jealousy and spite" that shaped McClellan's behavior.[79] But Lincoln needed to sort out his feelings. All at once he felt rage toward McClellan, alarm for the safety of the nation's capital, and an intense inclination to have his troops attack Lee's army again.

Hay wrote that Lincoln was in a "singularly defiant tone of mind. He often repeated, 'We must hurt this enemy before it gets away.'" When Hay expressed some feelings of defeatism on September 1, Lincoln shot back, "No, Mr. Hay, we must whip these people now. Pope must fight them." But he added that if necessary Pope could "gradually retire to these fortifications."[80]

The next day, however, at the cabinet meeting, Lincoln's state of mind was very different. Though he still believed in Pope's skill, he had been hearing from authoritative sources that the troops did not share this opinion. To the contrary, Pope's men had come to loathe him. They blamed him alone for their defeat.

As for McClellan, one of Lincoln's most fundamental instincts—his understanding of the need to put first things first—curbed his impulse to fire McClellan at once. He had come to a lamentable but inescapable conclusion: the safety of Washington had to be paramount, so the safest course of action for defending the city was to give the command of its fortifications to the man who had designed them, McClellan.

The members of his cabinet disagreed, and the effect upon Lincoln was predictable. He felt close to despair. He knew that it was miserable—mortifying—to have to retain this wretch McClellan for any length of time. But while McClellan was unable to take the offensive, his defensive abilities were to be sound . . . or so it appeared. And while some of his men could see his weaknesses clearly, many others had come to regard him as their very best friend. They felt that his reluctance to order attacks showed a deep concern about their safety.

Months later, Lincoln told Congressman William D. Kelley that McClellan "had contrived to keep the troops with him . . . by charging each new failure to some alleged dereliction of the Secretary of War and President." He said that his decision to retain McClellan was "the greatest trial and most painful duty of his official life."[81] But he would summon his strength to confront this crisis—and confront it as boldly as he could.

In the short run it had to be done, though it brought down a chorus of denunciation from people all over the North who had come to the correct conclusion that McClellan was an ignominious failure. Lincoln swallowed down the bitter pill. He told Hay that "McClellan has the army with him" and that "we must use the tools we have. . . . There is no man in the Army who can man these fortifications and lick these troops of ours into shape half as well as he. . . . He is too useful just now to sacrifice."[82]

Lincoln met with Pope on September 3, and according to Chase he told the general that "McClellan's command was only temporary, and led him [Pope] to expect that another army of active operations would be organized at once," with Pope in command. But the reports about Pope's reputation among his own troops kept pouring in, and soon a new emergency was shaping up not far from Washington.

A different field commander would have to be found for the eastern theater, and found in a hurry. For on September 4 and 5, Lee's Army of Northern Virginia crossed the Potomac and began an invasion of Maryland. The Confederate counter-offensive was in full swing in every theater.

On September 6, Lincoln sent Pope back to the West. A Sioux uprising was raging far away in Minnesota, and Pope was assigned to put it down.

Relieved that Washington was safe, Lincoln reveled in the chance of being able to destroy Lee's army in the field. He knew that Lee's forces would be easier to trap when they were far from their base and on the march through unfamiliar country. But he had to find someone to do it, for the threat to every one of his goals for the war—and for the nation—was obvious. With a few stunning victories in Maryland, Lee could hand the Confederates a great diplomatic victory in London and Paris. And the Democrats could win control of Congress.

As historian James M. McPherson has observed, this campaign in Maryland would constitute one of the great turning points of the war. It is often observed that the battle of Gettysburg in 1863 was the "high water mark of the Confederacy." There is reason to challenge that belief. The Confederates were closer to overall victory in 1862—the year before Gettysburg.

Or so it could be argued.

In any case, everything was now on the line for Lincoln, so his thoughts about the meaning of the war turned again to religious reflections. Sometime in early September, he wrote down the following passage, and the themes that it contained would guide his views down to the end:

The will of God prevails. In great contests each party claims to act in accordance with the will of God. Both *may* be, and one *must* be wrong.

God can not be *for*, and *against* the same thing at the same time. In the present civil war it is quite possible that God's purpose is different from the purpose of either party—and yet the human instrumentalities, working just as they do, are of the best adaptation to effect His purpose. I am almost ready to say this is probably true—that God wills this contest, and wills that it shall not end yet. By his mere quiet power, on the minds of the now contestants, He could have either *saved* or *destroyed* the Union without a human contest. Yet the contest began. And having begun He could give the final victory to either side any day. Yet the contest proceeds.[83]

From this meditation emerged a decision that Lincoln would reveal to the startled members of his cabinet a few weeks later: he made a promise to God that if Lee's invasion of Maryland were stopped, he would take it as a sign that he should issue the Emancipation Proclamation without any further delay. He would not hold back any longer—not wait to see the results of the November congressional elections. He would take the great risk.

He sensed, somehow, that he needed to relax his own stewardship for once and let the will of God play out in relation to the meaning of the war.

As soon as Lee's invasion began, Lincoln had to make lightning-fast decisions in regard to the chain of command. With Pope on his way back out to the West, and with the city of Washington secure, he had to find a field commander who was capable of taking on Lee. Time was of the essence.

Once again, he offered the field command to Ambrose Burnside, the commander who had captured Roanoke Island in February. Once again, the general declined. So Lincoln sought some opinions from his cabinet members, and Chase suggested two corps commanders from the Army of the Potomac, Joseph Hooker and Edwin V. Sumner.

But neither Chase nor Lincoln nor anyone else knew if either of these two men would succeed, and if either one of them should fail, the results would be too catastrophic to contemplate.

And the troops kept believing in McClellan. It was galling, maddening to know that a fake like McClellan could inspire these battle-hardened men, but the fact was indisputable. When Pope's troops—in the course of their retreat back to Washington—had been told that McClellan would command in the defense of Washington, they filled the air with a cry of joyous deliverance. Journalists witnessed the event and reported it. And no one could deny that in just a few days McClellan succeeded in blending the army of Pope with the Army of the Potomac almost effortlessly.

So the dreadful conclusion was obvious again: yet another opportunity would have to be given to George McClellan. On September 5, Lincoln and Halleck asked McClellan to assume field command and pursue Lee's army. With the stakes so momentous, the magnificent Army of the Potomac would be sent into battle once again commanded by a fool. If ever Lincoln had occasions to pray, this was one of them.

One advantage for Lincoln was the fact that Lee's invasion was opportunistic: everything was improvised. His troops were exhausted when he made the decision to cross the Potomac on September 3. He wrote to Jefferson Davis that the moment seemed ripe for delivering a coup de grâce that would achieve southern independence, so he meant to press on. And without even waiting for Davis's reply, he crossed into Maryland, intending to live off the land and strike at targets of opportunity. If things went well, perhaps the Army of Northern Virginia could menace Harrisburg or even Philadelphia.

Lee's audacity was great, but he was making up the moves as he went. He was hoping this invasion would give the northern voters a chance "to determine at their coming elections whether they will support those who favor a prolongation of the war, or those who wish to bring it to a termination." He wrote this to Davis on September 8.[84] And he was hoping that the people of Maryland would welcome his troops and assist them. On the same day that he sent his letter to Davis, Lee issued a proclamation in Frederick, Maryland, proclaiming that his troops had come to help the citizens of Maryland join their fellow "States of the South" in "throwing off this foreign yoke."[85]

The doubts about secession that Lee had entertained before the war were now completely gone. He was a zealot—a true believer.

And on foreign shores, the Confederate cause appeared brighter than ever before. The French foreign minister told the American ambassador that the South could never be conquered. And in London, William Gladstone informed John Russell that the time had come to recognize the Confederacy.

As Lee and his men marched on through the state of Maryland with confidence, McClellan and his army came slowly and cautiously behind.

As the drama played out in the foothills of Maryland, Lincoln kept trying to prepare the northern voters for emancipation. Any trick that he could use to soften public opinion was of interest to him. He had to keep building the idea that in this great crisis of the Union he might have to adopt much stronger measures, use every single angle that presented itself, to defeat the Confederates. He had to keep sending the message that nothing at all was too extreme for him to consider.

And he had to keep pretending he was still undecided in regard to the subject matter of his secret proclamation.

Both the hints that he dropped and the deceptions that he used were so artfully contrived that one is tempted to laugh out loud sometimes in appreciation of his cleverness—except that the issues at stake were no laughing matter.

On September 13, a delegation of abolitionists from Chicago paid a call on Lincoln and urged him to free the slaves quickly. He decided to play devil's advocate. "What *good* would a proclamation of emancipation from me do," he asked his guests, "especially as we are now situated? . . . Would *my* word free the slaves, when I cannot even enforce the Constitution in the rebel states?" Besides, he said, if he made the slaves free, "how can we feed and care for such a multitude?"

On the other hand, Lincoln continued, he was raising "no objection . . . on legal or constitutional grounds; for, as commander-in-chief of the army and navy, in time of war, I suppose I have a right to take any measure which may best subdue the enemy." In any case, Lincoln concluded, "I have not decided against a proclamation of liberty to the slaves . . . but hold the matter under advisement."[86]

On the very same day, George McClellan was given one of the greatest windfalls in military history. Lee split his forces again, sending some of them to capture Harper's Ferry and some others in the direction of Hagerstown. By accident, a copy of Lee's secret battle orders was dropped and left behind in a field—the papers were wrapped around three cigars—and by amazing coincidence two soldiers from McClellan's army found the documents and sent them right away up the chain of command to George McClellan.

McClellan was given a priceless opportunity to do exactly what Stonewall Jackson would have done in such a situation: strike the separated parts of Lee's army and annihilate them quickly.

And of course he did no such thing.

As Lee began to bring his army back together at the town of Sharpsburg, Maryland, along Antietam Creek, McClellan's army drew closer. But when McClellan arrived in the vicinity of Sharpsburg, Lee's army was still not ready to confront him. A sudden strike at Lee would have caught him at a huge disadvantage, and McClellan's seventy-five thousand–man army outnumbered Lee's army of forty-five thousand by almost two-to-one.

But McClellan of course was convinced that precisely the reverse was true—that he was the one who was outnumbered. So he waited.

The battle of Antietam of September 17 was the bloodiest day of the war. There had been no time for Lee's men to entrench, and so the battle was fought in the open, with only some sunken lanes and cornfields to give his troops cover from the Union fire.

McClellan never brought all of his forces into action at once. And he never coordinated his attacks in a way that could have stretched Lee's forces even thinner. In fact, McClellan used only two-thirds of his available forces. And that gave Lee time to shift his men back and forth down the line. At one point a gap opened up in Lee's center and a forceful attack by McClellan would have broken Lee's forces in two.

But McClellan never gave the order.

The battle was a frightful slaughter, with approximately eleven thousand casualties for the Confederates and over twelve thousand for the Union. Lee's army was stopped, and yet another attack by McClellan might have forced it to surrender. As it was, Lee retreated to Virginia with no further challenge. An opportunity to end the war in a day had been lost by a general who threw away chance after chance that better generals could have turned to brilliant use.

Nonetheless, Lee's army had been stopped. And that was enough for Abraham Lincoln. On September 22 he revealed to his cabinet that he would issue the Emancipation Proclamation immediately. Chase recalled what Lincoln said to his cabinet as follows: "When the rebel army was at Frederick, I determined, as soon as it should be driven out of Maryland, to issue a proclamation of emancipation. . . . I made the promise to myself, and (hesitating a little)—to my Maker."[87]

The announcement was a thunderbolt. To be sure, abolitionists complained about the legalistic language of the document, but that language was essential to establishing the constitutional basis for such an act. Only the extraordinary circumstances of a military and constitutional emergency could justify a presidential decree of such revolutionary power.

Lincoln framed the proclamation as a warning to the rebels: lay down their arms by New Year's Day or his armies would free all the slaves in any state where the rebellion continued. The most stunning language of the proclamation stated that

> on the first day of January in the year of our Lord, one thousand eight hundred and sixty-three, all persons held as slaves within any State, or designated part of a State, the people whereof shall then be in rebellion against the United States shall be then, thenceforward, and forever free; and the executive government of the United States, including the military and naval authority thereof, will recognize and maintain the freedom of such persons, and will do no act or acts to repress such persons, or any of them, in any efforts they may make for their actual freedom.[88]

The proclamation was a turning point for the American anti-slavery movement. The purpose of the war had been changed.

Two days later, abolitionists arrived at the White House to serenade Lincoln. Afterward, administration revelers gathered at the home of Salmon Chase for a joyous celebration. "They all seemed to feel a sort of new and exhilarated life," John Hay remembered, and they all "breathed freer."[89]

13

RACE AGAINST TIME

The Emancipation Proclamation of September 22, 1862, was preliminary. It was framed as a warning: the rebels were given three months to give up their rebellion if they wished to avoid the threat. If they were still seeking nationhood on the first day of January 1863, then another proclamation would be issued—a proclamation declaring that Lincoln's new policy was in effect.

There was very little chance that the rebels would heed Lincoln's warning as the waiting period started. But another waiting period was playing out at the same time: the period leading up to the mid-term elections of 1862. Lincoln put aside caution when he made his promise to God and proceeded with his proclamation in the aftermath of the Antietam victory. As he tried to assess the reaction, he sought to be as careful as possible in order to prevent the Democrats from gaining control of Congress.

To the serenaders who came to cheer him on September 24, he said that "I can only trust to God I have made no mistake."[1]

On the hopeful side, the Democrats had been dividing into factions. "Peace Democrats" were calling for an end to the war, and this meant that they might be willing to grant the Confederates independence if they could not restore the Union on pro-slavery terms. The "War Democrats" disagreed. Perhaps Republicans would be able to exploit this division in the Democratic ranks.

But the Democrats remained as united as ever when it came to white supremacy. They sought to foment a backlash against the Republicans' anti-slavery policies. This, combined with war-weariness and complaints about the administration's competence, might lead to Democratic victories, if not in 1862, then perhaps in 1864.

Reactions to the Preliminary Emancipation Proclamation were vehement on both sides of the controversy and on both sides of the Atlantic.

Predictably, American opponents of slavery were divided between those who were overjoyed at the potential of what Lincoln did and those who reacted with scorn to the document's legalistic text. "GOD BLESS ABRAHAM LINCOLN," proclaimed Horace Greeley's *New York Tribune*. "Let the President know that everywhere throughout all the land he is hailed as Wisest and Best," the paper declared.[2] The abolitionist Theodore Tilton experienced "a bewilderment of joy" and he said he was "half crazy with enthusiasm."[3]

Such reactions were widespread. Charles Sumner wrote that the "skies are brighter and the air is purer."[4] Lincoln, wrote Ralph Waldo Emerson, "has been permitted to do more for America than any other American man."[5] The *New York Times* called the Proclamation "one of the great events of history."[6] The *Pittsburgh Gazette* called it "the most important document in the world's history" and a "new Magna Charta, before the light of which the other must pale."[7]

But abolitionists who already viewed Lincoln as a disappointment sneered at the Proclamation's legalism. Lydia Maria Child, who had revised her views of Lincoln (downward), contended that "it was done reluctantly and stintedly, and that even the degree that *was* accomplished was done selfishly; was merely a war measure, to which we were forced by our own perils and necessities."[8]

Frederick Douglass proclaimed in October that "we shout for joy that we live to record this righteous decree," adding that Lincoln could be trusted to carry out the new policy, for he was "not the man to reconsider, retract and contradict words and purposes solemnly proclaimed over his official signature."[9] Perhaps Douglass was counting on these words to bind Lincoln to his pledge, for the black abolitionist was harboring some profoundly mixed feelings about the president.

A few months later, Douglass complained that the Proclamation's language "touched neither justice nor mercy." If only the document had contained just "one expression of sound moral feeling against Slavery, one word of regret and shame that this accursed system had remained so long a disgrace and scandal of the Republic," Douglass lamented.[10]

Democrats worked themselves into hysteria when they heard about the Proclamation. In addition to their usual obsession regarding interracial sex, they began to warn that Lincoln's Proclamation would trigger a slave insurrection as slaves rose up to kill their masters.

The *Louisville Democrat* called Lincoln "an imbecile" who meant to encourage "insurrection, lust, arson, and murder." The paper went on to declare that Lincoln had "as much right to abolish the institution of marriage . . . as to nullify the right of a State to regulate the relations of the white and black races."[11] Another paper in Louisville, the *Journal*, declared that "Kentucky cannot and will not acquiesce in this measure. Never!"[12]

Midwestern Democrats called for Lincoln's impeachment and some of them expressed the private hope that he would be murdered. Charles Mason, former chief justice of Iowa, wrote in his diary that Lincoln would have to be stopped "by revolution or private assassination."[13]

George McClellan called the Proclamation "infamous" and told his wife that he might not be willing to fight "for such an accursed doctrine as that of a servile insurrection."[14] He drafted a letter to Lincoln declaring that "the Army would never sustain" the Proclamation. But his corps commanders talked him out of doing such a thing, so instead he issued a general order declaring that the "remedy for political errors . . . is to be found only in the action of the people at the polls."[15]

The Confederate reaction to the Proclamation was totally predictable. Jefferson Davis told the Confederate Congress that Lincoln meant to encourage "millions of human beings of an inferior race" to attempt the "assassination of their masters."[16] Members of the Confederate Congress called the Proclamation an affront to the rules of civilized war and demanded retaliatory measures. The *Richmond Inquirer* called Lincoln a "fiend" and demanded that "the civilized world fling its scorpion lash upon him."[17]

Reactions abroad to the Emancipation Proclamation were as mixed as they were in America. Pro-Confederate journalists in London echoed the sentiments of Confederates and Democratic racists in America. The *London Times* predicted that the Proclamation "will appeal to the black blood of the African; he will whisper of the pleasures of spoil and of the gratification of yet fiercer instincts."[18] The British foreign minister, Lord John Russell, said much the same thing in more restrained language. And the French foreign minister called for intervention in the American Civil War to prevent a servile insurrection.

But a groundswell of anti-slavery opinion in Britain supported the Emancipation Proclamation. The *London Morning Star* called the document "a gigantic stride in the paths of Christian and civilized progress."[19] John Stuart Mill reassured an American friend that the "demoniacal cry" against the Proclamation by Confederate sympathizers in Britain should be ignored.[20] And in the months that followed, mass meetings were organized in Britain to demonstrate support for the Proclamation. By January, Henry Adams reported from London that the Proclamation "has done more for us here than all our former victories and all our diplomacy."[21]

Even so, the Confederate sympathizers in Britain kept trying to persuade Parliament and Palmerston to recognize the Confederacy. In October William Gladstone declared that "Jefferson Davis and the other leaders of the South have made an army; they are making, it appears, a navy; and they have made what is more than either—they have made a nation."[22]

But it was too late: Antietam had convinced Lord Palmerston that recognition of the Confederacy would be a mistake—at least for the time being. "The whole matter is full of difficulty," he told John Russell. "We must continue merely to be lookers-on till the war shall have taken a more decided turn."[23]

The battle of Antietam was a turning point in the war. Lee's invasion failed, and so did the other campaigns that were launched in the Confederate counter-offensive of 1862. The campaign in Mississippi was stopped before the troops even crossed the northern border of the state. The armies of Rosecrans and Grant overpowered the Confederates in the battles of Iuka and Corinth, fought respectively on September 19 and on October 3–4.

The invasion of Kentucky was stopped on October 8 at the battle of Perryville. Both of the Confederate armies—the army of Braxton Bragg, together with the parallel Confederate force led by Edmund Kirby Smith—went back to East Tennessee, by way of the Cumberland Gap. Lincoln was keen to have Buell pursue them: to use the situation to renew the campaign for Chattanooga. But Buell just took his army back to Nashville.

Fed up, Lincoln decided on October 23 to replace Buell with William S. Rosecrans.

That should have left Grant in the pre-eminent position of command in the Mississippi Valley. But Grant was still under a cloud, and in the meantime a Democratic political general named John McClernand came to Washington and laid before the president a tempting proposition: he would raise a force of midwestern Democratic Unionists and then use it to attack the rebel stronghold of Vicksburg.

In October Lincoln decided to give this plan a try. He also decided to make the campaign in the Mississippi Valley a pincer movement.

Ever since the capture of New Orleans, the political general Benjamin Butler had been in charge of that occupied city and his force had been called the Army of the Gulf. His rule had been harsh. But he had done almost nothing else of military value, so by the final months of 1862 Lincoln felt the inclination to replace him. The approval of McClernand's proposal marked the end of Butler's rule in New Orleans. Lincoln decided to put a different man in charge of the Army of the Gulf. He would send it north as McClernand's army moved south. McClernand would descend upon Vicksburg as the Army of the Gulf attacked the rebel stronghold of Port Hudson, Louisiana.

In November, Lincoln sent Nathaniel Banks to New Orleans as Butler's replacement. One political general had replaced another political general, and both were from the same state: Massachusetts.

Meanwhile, Ulysses S. Grant decided to project himself into the action. His campaign to stage a come-back was beginning, and it would continue throughout the winter of 1862–1863. If he could somehow manage to get himself in overall command of the Vicksburg campaign, he might be able to overcome the doubts about his leadership that had been festering in Washington since Shiloh.

And then there was the matter of McClellan. He would have to go—but his ouster would have to be carefully managed, since the Democrats were touting him as a hero for stopping Lee's army at Antietam.

Lincoln said privately he would "remove him at once but for the election."[24] Until then, he did not want to "estrange the affections of the Democratic Party" by making McClellan appear to be a martyr.

Even so, the groundwork was laid in October for McClellan's removal when the danger of the November elections had passed. As he had done in the course of the Peninsular Campaign, Lincoln sent off a series of directives to McClellan. They look, when perused one after another, like a paper trail that was created deliberately to prove that McClellan's performance after Antietam had been defective.

Lincoln would claim to many people in the months that followed that he had been curious—genuinely curious—to see whether McClellan would rise to the occasion in the aftermath of Antietam. That may have been the case, but there is very great reason for doubting it. Lincoln probably knew very well what he could expect from George B. McClellan.

In the first week of October, Lincoln traveled to Antietam to visit McClellan and review the Army of the Potomac. He had his picture taken with the general, and among the results are some priceless images—some of the very best photographs of Lincoln in action that we have.

For months he had been visiting the studio of Mathew Brady to sit for formal photographic portraits. Alexander Gardner ran the studio. On the battlefield he was photographed conferring with McClellan in a tent. Another picture shows him standing out in the open with McClellan and his officers, tall and erect with his stovepipe hat as he gazes out with an expression of serenity.

He conferred with McClellan in regard to the pursuit of Lee's army. He asked pointed questions as to why McClellan made certain decisions and how he could justify them. On horseback he inspected the troops. As he passed the Fifth New York Zouaves, he said, "Boys, your thinned ranks and shattered flags tell the story of your bravery. The people thank you, and so do I."[25] Perhaps at least a part of his purpose in visiting Antietam was to make a good impression on the soldiers—to use his own charisma to break the spell of George McClellan and win the loyalty of rank-and-file troops.

And it seemed to work. Soldiers left accounts of how Lincoln's visit cheered them. One said that the president's "kindly smile . . . touched the hearts of the bronzed, rough-looking men more than one can express. It was like an electric shock. It flew from elbow to elbow; and, with one loud cheer which made the air ring, the suppressed feeling gave vent."[26]

Lincoln visited field hospitals and he even decided to visit some wounded Confederate prisoners. He said that "if they had no objection he would take them by the hand," since they were enemies "through uncontrollable circumstances" and "he bore them no malice."[27] One after another, rebel soldiers walked up to shake his hand.

As for McClellan, Lincoln found himself in the same old bind; he would have to wait a little bit longer to gratify his pent-up desire to be rid of him. To fire him at once might backfire with voters who thought he was a hero. But retaining him was also risky. More than one Republican nursed the dark suspicion that McClellan and other Democratic generals were pulling their punches, shirking opportunities for victory to drag the war out and create a mood of war-weariness among the voters. Even Lincoln told Hay in the course of some reminiscences two years later that he was beginning to suspect that McClellan might be "playing false—that he did not want to hurt the enemy."[28]

An anonymous letter to the *Cincinnati Gazette* warned that "Halleck, McClellan and Buell" planned "not to subdue the South, but to wear out the patience of the North."[29] Even darker suspicions were making the rounds. Some worried that treachery among the Army of the Potomac's officer corps might well lead to treason in the aftermath of the Emancipation Proclamation.

The army's adjutant general, Thomas M. Key, believed that "the 'traitor' element near McClellan had constantly grown bolder. . . . They daily talked of overthrowing the Government and making McClellan dictator." After the Emancipation Proclamation

> this element felt that McClellan would not long remain in command; that then was the time to move or never—that an appeal could be made to the army setting forth that this proclamation was a usurpation, the conversion of the war for the Union into a John Brown Abolition raid and thus was a subversion of the Constitution absolving the army from its allegiance.[30]

Lincoln himself would admit that one of his purposes in visiting Antietam was "to satisfy himself personally without the intervention of anybody, of the purposes intentions and fidelity of McClellan, his officers, and the army."[31]

There was certainly some resentment of Lincoln in the officer corps. Colonel Charles S. Wainwright ridiculed Lincoln, "with his long legs doubled up so that his knees almost struck his chin, and grinning out of the windows like a baboon."[32] This cruel observation was based upon the fact that when Lincoln had to ride a horse that was too small for him, his legs would indeed double up. But when he had the chance to ride a steed that was better suited to him, he was perfectly graceful in the saddle.

On October 6, Lincoln ordered McClellan to cross the Potomac and attack Lee's army as soon as possible. McClellan gave the usual excuses for delay. On October 13, Lincoln sent him a letter containing a proposed plan of action. Above all, what he wanted from McClellan was *speed*, and this letter would demonstrate how painfully slow McClellan was. "You remember my speaking to you of your over-cautiousness," Lincoln wrote. "Are you not over-cautious when you assume that you can not do what the enemy is constantly doing?"[33]

Lincoln went on to observe that since Lee was in or near Winchester, Virginia, McClellan was "now nearer to Richmond than the enemy is. . . . Why can you not reach there before him? . . . His route is the arc of a circle, while yours is the chord." So "to beat him to Richmond on the inside track" should be "easy . . . if our troops march as well as the enemy; and it is unmanly to say they can not do it."[34]

Lincoln also observed (in detail) how McClellan's army could be kept supplied no matter what path to Richmond he used. What he needed to do was to draw Lee out in the open before he could ensconce himself in the Richmond fortifications. Lincoln added that "if we can not beat the enemy where he is now, we never can."[35]

McClellan expressed the fear that Lee might try another invasion of the North. Lincoln responded with gusto: if Lee invaded again, "you have nothing to do but follow and ruin him."[36]

By the end of October, McClellan was still giving Lincoln excuses. This time he said that his cavalry forces were exhausted. Lincoln dashed off a reply that would later become quite famous: "I have just read your despatches about sore-tongued and fatigued horses. Will you pardon me for asking what your horses have done since the battle of Antietam that fatigues anything?"[37]

The Sioux rebellion in Minnesota was suppressed by the end of September. The fiercest fighting occurred in August. The Santee Sioux had been pressured for years to make land cessions, and their reservations kept shrinking. At last their frustration erupted into war. Atrocities were committed upon white settlers in Minnesota.

After the rebellion was broken, 303 Sioux were sentenced to death for murder, rape, and other crimes. The trials before military tribunals often lasted just a few minutes.

Lincoln intervened. In the midst of all his other obligations and cares, he reviewed every one of the verdicts in the months that followed. Then he commuted the sentences of 264 prisoners from death to imprisonment. The others were executed. This outcome has been condemned as both the greatest mass execution in American history and the greatest act of executive clemency in American history.

Lincoln had other dealings with Native Americans in the autumn of 1862. Out in the "Indian Territory" (the future state of Oklahoma), the Cherokee tribe had been swept into Civil War politics. The same hope for westward expansion (and conquest) that prompted the Confederates to invade New Mexico had led them to eye the Indian Territory. After their victory in the battle of Wilson's Creek in August 1861, their power was great enough to prompt some Cherokee leaders to become Confederate allies.

One of them, a chieftain named Stand Watie, became a Confederate general. Another chieftain, John Ross, at first urged neutrality but then came around to support a Confederate alliance.

After the Union victory at Pea Ridge, Arkansas, in March 1862, Lincoln began to challenge the Confederate presence in the Indian Territory. Aware that the tide of war had turned decisively, many Cherokee fled to Kansas. Ross came to Washington to meet with Lincoln and make the case that he and other Cherokee leaders had been coerced by the rebels.

Ross met with Lincoln on September 12, and the president, in the midst of Lee's invasion of Maryland, took time to consider Ross's claims. On September 25, he wrote a letter promising to be fair. "In the multitude of cares claiming my attention," he wrote,

> I have been unable to examine and determine the exact treaty relations between the United States and the Cherokee Nation. Neither have I been able to investigate and determine the exact state of facts claimed by you as constituting a failure of treaty obligations on our part, excusing the Cherokee Nation for making a treaty with a portion of the people of the United States in open rebellion against the government thereof. This letter therefore, must not be understood to decide anything upon these questions. I shall, however, cause a careful investigation of them to be made. Meanwhile the Cherokee people remaining practically loyal to the federal Union will receive all the protection which can be given them consistently with the duty of the government to the whole country. I sincerely hope the Cherokee country may not again be over-run by the enemy, and I shall do all I consistently can to prevent it.[38]

In the autumn of 1862 Lincoln pressed forward with his colonization experiment. He deemed the effort important to containing the white supremacist backlash against emancipation. At the same time, he considered different ways to assist former slaves who decided to remain in America. It is vital to understand the duality of these actions, since they shed significant light on the issue of whether or not Lincoln's colonization plan was "racist."

The new tax act that Congress had passed in 1862 permitted the seizure of real estate for tax evasion. This would open up the possibility of redistributing some land to the freedmen in a manner that could not run afoul of the charge that it constituted "attainder." Since tax evasion—and not treason—would be the issue, there would be no problem with the seizure and sale of rebel lands where this procedure was used.

In October 1862, tax commissioners arrived in the Sea Islands off the coast of South Carolina. Within a year, Lincoln would take direct action to make certain that some of the confiscated land in these islands would be set aside for former slaves.

As to colonization, he changed his plans in October. He had told the black delegation in August that the Chiriqui province in Panama seemed well suited to the project. A land speculator, Ambrose Thompson, had been trying to sell a tract of land in this province to the federal government. Thompson claimed that the land was rich in coal. Lincoln followed up with inquiries into the validity of the land title as well as the value of the coal that the land supposedly contained. In October, he came to the conclusion that the whole thing was a swindle. So he changed his plans accordingly.

In December he signed a contract with a New York businessman named Bernard Kock to resettle up to five thousand free black emigrants on an island off the coast of Haiti: Île-à-Vache.

The results of the November congressional elections could certainly have been much worse, but they could have been better. The Republicans kept control of Congress. But their majority in the House declined, since the Democrats gained thirty-two seats. The Democrats also captured the governorships of New Jersey and New York and took over the legislatures of those states. And in Illinois, the Democrats took over both the congressional delegation and the state legislature.

Lincoln took this as very bad news. "We have lost the elections," he wrote, and "the ill-success of the war had much to do with it."[39] He also believed that his Emancipation Proclamation had caused the kind of white supremacist backlash that he had been fearing. He reportedly said to Wendell Phillips that "he had put himself into a minority with the people, and he well knew that it was impossible for him to carry on a great war against the feelings of the majority of the people."[40]

He began to feel the stress of a person who knows that he is struggling on borrowed time. He was almost half-way through his presidential term and no president had ever been re-elected since the days of Andrew Jackson. He would have to face the voters in 1864. But Jefferson Davis had a six-year term, and this put the Confederates into a position of great comparative advantage.

Lincoln had unleashed a social revolution, but no one could tell if this revolution would succeed. If he were replaced by a white supremacist Democrat in 1864, the slaves he had managed to free might be sent right back into bondage. Already, the Democrats were claiming that his Emancipation Proclamation was unconstitutional.

But he had no intention of backing down. He told a delegation of "unconditional Union Kentuckians" in late November that "he would rather die than take back one word of the Proclamation of Freedom."[41]

Right after the election, Lincoln had the great pleasure of removing George McClellan on November 5. Stanton sent a staff officer to deliver this order to McClellan and to offer the command of the army to General Burnside. Burnside (as usual) declined, but the officer informed him that if he refused again to take command of the Army of the Potomac, the position would be offered to a fellow corps commander, Joseph Hooker. Burnside thought this over and decided to accept.

Burnside seemed to have a fairly good record as a fighting general. He was eager to please, but he doubted whether he had enough strategic sense to command a large army.

He was willing to implement the scheme that the president suggested to McClellan in the letter of October 13. He would move the army south toward Richmond. He proposed to go to Fredericksburg, Virginia, on the Rappahannock River, cross over, and then draw Lee into battle.

Halleck conferred with Burnside regarding this particular plan, and it was duly conveyed to Lincoln. The president preferred to engage Lee's army closer to its existing location near the Shenandoah. But he assented to Burnside's proposal to move via Fredericksburg, farther away, with the proviso that the movement should be rapid enough to take Lee by surprise.

Unfortunately, Burnside's movement was slow. Where he arrived at Falmouth, across the river from Fredericksburg, he could have made the crossing right away, but he preferred to wait for the arrival of some pontoon bridges he had ordered. Yet the bridges were delayed, and by the time that the bridges had arrived, Lee's army had arrived as well.

Lincoln did not like the situation one bit. On November 25, he traveled by boat to Aquia Creek to confer with Burnside. In his record of the meeting, Lincoln wrote that Burnside "thinks he can cross the river in the face of the enemy and drive him away, but that, to use his own expression, it is somewhat risky."[42] Lincoln therefore suggested the idea of sending a force to cross the river in a different location to draw Lee's army away while the rest of the army moved into Fredericksburg.

But both Burnside and Halleck dismissed Lincoln's plan as unrealistic.

Lincoln sent his second annual message to Congress on December 1. There is much to be learned from this document—a great state paper for the light that it sheds upon his long-term vision for America. And it reveals how keenly he sensed the growing pressure of time. There was no turning back from his emancipation program, but he had to protect it from the white supremacist backlash.

Looking over the horizon, he saw the great dangers of a Democratic victory in 1864. He sought to do things that would make the liberation of blacks a *fait accompli* that no Democratic racist could undo.

Consequently, he proposed a package of constitutional amendments that would add his anti-slavery program to the nation's supreme law. That would make the issue of whether or not the Emancipation Proclamation was constitutional completely moot. The language of these amendments was designed to mollify opponents and induce them to cooperate.

He proposed the following amendments: (1) "Every state, wherein slavery now exists, which shall abolish the same therein, at any time, or times, before the first day of January, in the year of our Lord one thousand and nine hundred, shall receive compensation from the United States." (2) "All slaves who shall have enjoyed actual freedom by the chances of war, at any time before the end of the rebellion, shall be forever free; but all owners of such, who shall not have been disloyal, shall be compensated for them." (3) "Congress may appropriate money, and otherwise provide, for colonizing free colored persons, with their own consent, at any place or places without the United States."[43]

If the lame-duck Congress moved quickly, the Republicans could write some new constitutional law that would make their anti-slavery program permanent and beyond political challenge.

But there was something else in this message that deserves to be much better known in relation to the charge that Lincoln's colonization program was racist. As previously noted, the program was set up to be *voluntary*. There would be no forced deportation: any blacks who chose to remain in the United States would be free to stay.

So Lincoln tried to reduce white resistance to the presence of African Americans who *chose* to stay in America (as millions of them obviously would). For that reason, he started arguing with racists in the course of this message to Congress.

He wrote about the dread on the part of great numbers of whites "that the freed people will swarm forth, and cover the whole land." But there was nothing to be feared, he explained, for if the entire population of American blacks were "distributed among the whites of the whole country . . . there would be but one colored to seven whites." Then he made a more daring observation: "There are many communities now, having more than one free colored person, to seven whites; and this, without any apparent consciousness of evil from it."[44]

Americans, he said, should revive the nation's original ideals and reassert the great truths that were declared long ago by the Founders. They had to ask themselves a very simple question: "Can we all do better?"

"The dogmas of the quiet past," he observed, "are inadequate to the stormy present. The occasion is piled high with difficulty, and we must rise to the occasion. As our case is new, so we must think anew, and act anew. We must disenthrall ourselves, and then we shall save our country."

"Fellow citizens," he concluded, "*we* cannot escape history. . . . The fiery trial through which we pass, will light us down, in honor or dishonor to the latest generation. . . . In *giving* freedom to the *slave*, we *assure* freedom to the *free*." One way or another, he wrote, "we shall nobly save, or meanly lose, the last best hope of earth."[45]

On December 13, General Burnside ordered the Army of the Potomac to cross the Rappahannock and unleash an assault against Lee's Army of Northern Virginia—without the peripheral maneuver that Lincoln recommended. The Confederate army was entrenched on impregnable heights behind the town.

This was truly an attack against impossible odds, and the Union troops were cut down and slaughtered. Burnside kept ordering wave after wave of these misguided attacks, and the outcome was always just the same.

Burnside wished to demonstrate the fighting spirit that was missing from McClellan's performance. But this was not the way to do it, and Burnside—so dull, so good-natured and straightforward—proved worse by far than the vain and treacherous McClellan.

The result was 12,600 Union casualties that day, compared to less than 5,000 for the rebels. Lincoln was distraught. "If there is a worse place than hell," he said, "I am in it."[46] Pennsylvania Governor Andrew Curtin observed that when Lincoln heard about the massacre, he "walked the floor, wringing his hands and . . . repeatedly asking: 'What has God put me in this place for?'"[47]

The news of this terrible defeat brought another political crisis to Washington, one that almost tore the Republican Party asunder.

Strains within the party had been building for months and discontent with Lincoln was growing. The extended presence of McClellan in command had exasperated many Republicans. And despite the fact that Lincoln had kept McClellan in command for some compelling political reasons—to avoid making the "hero" of Antietam seem like a martyr—some believed that the continued indulgence of pro-slavery Democrats like McClellan gave the opposition party more strength than it would otherwise have.

After Second Manassas, Senator Henry Wilson expressed the opinion that Lincoln "couldn't get one vote in twenty in New England."[48] After Lincoln had restored McClellan to field command, Zachariah Chandler wrote that the president was "as unstable as water" and called him "a weak man, too weak for the occasion."[49]

As the news from the elections rolled in, the disillusionment with Lincoln grew worse. Indiana Governor Oliver P. Morton warned that unless the Mississippi were re-opened to navigation, his state and other Midwestern states might begin to gravitate into an alliance with the Confederacy. The "fate of the North-West is trembling in the balance," Morton wrote as some early election returns were tallied. "The result of the late elections admonishes all who understand its import that not an hour is to be lost."[50]

The political general Carl Schurz wrote Lincoln a very angry letter on November 8. The "defeat of the Administration is the Administration's own fault," he contended. He blamed electoral reverses on military setbacks, and he blamed the latter on Democratic generals. Lincoln had made the mistake, he asserted, of placing "the Army . . . into the hands of its enemies." "Let us be commanded by Generals whose heart is in the war, and only by such," he said.[51]

Lincoln replied that it was essential for obvious political reasons to create a bipartisan power coalition. Since he had carried the 1860 election with less than a majority of the popular vote, it was inconceivable for the administration to fight a major war "without assistance outside of its party . . . mere nonsense to suppose a minority could put down a majority in rebellion." Besides, he observed, "very few of our friends [i.e., Republicans] had a military education." So he had appointed some Democrats to positions of military command, but all had bipartisan backing. "So it was with McClellan," he wrote; "he was first brought forward by the Republican Governor of Ohio."[52]

But Schurz would not let up. A few weeks later, he reiterated his indictment of Lincoln in terms that the president found intolerably sententious. Schurz scolded Lincoln as follows:

> Let us indulge in no delusions as to the true causes of our defeat in the elections. The people, so enthusiastic at the beginning of the war, had made enormous sacrifices. Hundreds of millions were spent, thousands of lives were lost for nothing. . . . I command a few thousands of brave and good fellows, entitled to life and happiness just as well as the rest of us; and when I see their familiar faces around the campfires and think of it, that to-morrow they may be called upon to die,—and to die for a cause which for this or that reason is perhaps doomed to fail, and thus to die in vain—and when I hear the wailings of so many widows and orphans . . . then, I must confess, my heart begins sometimes to sink within me. . . . I do not know, whether you have ever seen a battlefield. I assure you, Mr. President, it is a terrible sight.[53]

This was more than Lincoln could bear, and so he fired off a scathing reply that shows the toll that the pressure of events had been taking on his nerves. The "purport" of Schurz's letters, Lincoln said,

> is that we lost the late elections, and the administration is failing, because the war is unsuccessful; and that I must not flatter myself that I am not justly to blame for it. I certainly know that if the war fails, the administration fails, and that I *will* be blamed for it, whether I deserve it or not. And I ought to be blamed, if I could do better. You think I

could do better; therefore you blame me already. I think I could not do better; therefore I blame you for blaming me.

He said that he was doing his best to find generals worthy of the nation. He readily acknowledged he had also been "dissatisfied with the slowness of Buell and McClellan; but before I relieved them I had great fears I should not find successors to them, who would do better; and I am sorry to add, that I have seen little since to relieve those fears."[54]

This exchange of correspondence occurred in late November. By December, in the aftermath of the Fredericksburg disaster, the rage among Republicans had become overwhelming. Zachariah Chandler wrote that "the country is gone unless something is done at once. Folly, folly, folly reigns supreme."[55]

Rather than attack Lincoln directly (though some were talking about asking him to resign), disillusioned Republicans pressed for a cabinet shake-up and Seward became their chief scapegoat. The Radicals remembered his support for the Crittenden Compromise and the Corwin Amendment. They believed that he was largely to blame for the appointment of so many weak Democratic generals.

Chandler called Seward "the evil genius of this Nation" and "the bane of Mr. Lincoln's administration."[56] Joseph Medill wrote that Seward "kept a sponge saturated with chloroform to Uncle Abe's nose."[57] And Mary Lincoln, now sufficiently recovered from her grieving to engage in more devious machinations, reached out to the enemies of Seward. She had come to detest Lincoln's secretary of state. Indeed, she distrusted most of his cabinet.

Chase was also involved in the campaign against Seward. The men had never liked one another, and Chase was close to the Radical Republicans. And he was beginning to flirt with the possibility of trying for the Republican presidential nomination in 1864. He regarded Seward as a rival.

On December 16 and 17, thirty-two Republican senators met in a caucus and decided "to ascertain whether any steps could be taken to quiet the public mind." According to some accounts, they believed that Seward was behind "the disasters which had come upon our arms alleging that he was opposed to a vigorous prosecution of the war." Twenty-eight of these senators voted to support a resolution that "the public confidence in the present administration would be increased by a change in and partial

reconstruction of the Cabinet." They decided to send a nine-man delegation to call upon Lincoln.[58]

Seward was aware of this campaign, and he knew that he was the
target. "They may do as they please about me," he wrote, "but they shall
not put the President in a false position on my account."[59] So he sent off
a letter of resignation.

Lincoln was profoundly displeased, and according to Orville Browning, "he had no doubt Chase was at the bottom of all the mischief, and
was setting the radicals on to assail Seward."[60] He had come to value
Seward's judgment—notwithstanding his early acts of treachery in 1861.
Since then, Seward found the grace to calm down. Moreover, he became a
rather pleasant companion for Lincoln, whereas Chase remained on more
formal terms with the president.

Lincoln kept his cool and used strategy. He met with the Republican
delegation on the evening of December 18, and he refused to shake up the
cabinet. "What the country wanted," he said, "was military success. Without that nothing could go right:—with that nothing could go wrong."
And "he did not yet see how the measure proposed . . . would furnish the
remedy required."[61] But he thanked the delegation for expressing their
concerns and asked them to return on the following evening.

The next morning he asked all of his cabinet members—except for
Seward—to attend a meeting. He said that he needed them all, but that
a group of influential senators wanted Seward removed. He asked them
to tell him sincerely whether any of them was unhappy with the way in
which the cabinet functioned. And he asked whether any of them believed
that Seward's dedication to the war effort should be questioned. No one
had a serious complaint. So he asked the cabinet to return that evening to
meet with the senatorial delegation.

When the senators returned to the White House, they had no idea
that the entire cabinet—except for Seward—would be present. It was part
of Lincoln's strategy to create a surprise and put everyone on the spot.

In the four-hour meeting that followed, Lincoln said that key decisions on administration policy were always discussed at cabinet meetings,
and that notwithstanding the inevitable differences that arose from time
to time in those discussions, the members of the cabinet were generally
united when the time had come to reach a consensus. He also said that
"Mr. Seward had been earnest in the prosecution of the war," and then he
asked whether any member of the cabinet thought there had been a real
"want of unity, or of sufficient consultation."[62]

He knew from the previous meeting exactly what would happen in response to his question: nothing at all.

The eyes of the all senators turned toward Chase, who was completely outmaneuvered—and he knew it. He had led his senatorial friends to believe that the cabinet was in a state of near-chaos and that Seward was despised by everyone. But now, if he dared to disagree with Lincoln's characterization of the cabinet's unity, he ran the risk that not a single member of the cabinet would back him up.

He grew indignant and declared that "he should not have come here had he known that he was to be arraigned before a committee of the Senate." But he reluctantly acknowledged there had been "no want of unity in the Cabinet."[63]

In light of Chase's statement, the members of the senatorial delegation began to back down from their previous position.

The next day Chase returned to the White House and said that "he had been painfully affected by the meeting of the last evening, which was a total surprise to him." He then told Lincoln he had written out a letter of resignation. "Let me have it," said Lincoln.

After Chase had departed, Lincoln said, "This cuts the Gordian knot. I can dispose of this subject now without difficulty. I see my way clear."[64] Since Seward and Chase had *both* offered letters of resignation, he could refuse to accept either one. "Now I can ride," he said; "I have a pumpkin in each end of my bag."[65]

Weeks later, he was heard to observe that he could not have let Seward resign "without dismissing Chase also, because, whether rightfully or wrongly, the people regarded them as representatives of the two wings of the party, the Radicals and the Conservatives." And "we can't afford to ignore either wing, for that would sort the party down to altogether too small a heap."[66]

On December 20, he wrote to both Seward and Chase requesting them to withdraw their resignations. Seward agreed right away, but Chase decided to take his time. Nonetheless, on December 22, he agreed to stay in the cabinet.

One cabinet change did occur in December: Interior Secretary Caleb Smith resigned for reasons of health. Lincoln would replace him later on with the assistant secretary, John Palmer Usher.

In December, a tricky problem in constitutional metaphysics played out in the case of West Virginia. The Wheeling Unionists had voted to break away from secessionist Virginia and form a new state of their own. The

Unionist convention in Wheeling had proclaimed itself the legitimate legislature for *all* of Virginia and Lincoln had recognized it as the state's true government. But everyone knew that it represented nothing more than a break-away portion of the state.

Republicans wanted to support the West Virginians, but there was a problem since Article IV of the federal Constitution specifies that new states can only be carved out of old ones "with the consent of the Legislatures of the States concerned, as well as of the Congress." Obviously the secessionist legislature in Richmond would never consent to let the West Virginians break away.

Regardless, on December 10, Congress voted to admit West Virginia and the statehood bill was sent to Lincoln. What followed was a lengthy exercise in political and constitutional casuistry. Lincoln admitted there was a constitutional problem and he asked the members of his cabinet for their opinions. No one knew what the outcome of these deliberations would be and the matter was still left pending on New Year's Eve.

But Lincoln signed the statehood bill and his written opinion on the matter, which he drafted on December 31, provides a tantalizing clue as to the way Reconstruction might have unfolded if he had lived.

Lincoln developed a neat and clever solution to the constitutional problem. He said it was a universal practice in elections to take no cognizance of the voters who declined to vote. Therefore, he argued, "it is not the qualified voters, but the qualified voters, *who choose to vote*, that constitute the political power of the state."[67] In this regard, he concluded, the voters in secessionist Virginia—that is, the rebels in Virginia—had essentially abdicated their voting rights and had chosen *not to vote* when they sided with rebellion.

Lincoln put it this way: "Can this government stand, if it indulges constitutional constructions by which men in open rebellion against it, are to be accounted, man for man, the equals of those who maintain their loyalty to it?"[68] No, he concluded: the rebels had absented themselves from the legitimate governance process by rebelling. For that reason, "we can not deny that the body which consents to the admission of West Virginia [i.e., the Wheeling government] is the Legislature of Virginia."[69]

Lincoln acknowledged the fact that there were loyal men within secessionist Virginia, men "whose voices were smothered by the more numerous secessionists." But he argued that "we know too little of their number to assign them any appreciable value."[70] In any case, "we can scarcely dispense with the aid of West-Virginia in this struggle," and so he could not "break faith" with the loyal West Virginians.[71]

When a supporter of West Virginia statehood called upon Lincoln on New Year's Day, he held aloft the statehood bill with his signature on it and he smiled with a look of sweet innocence.

This action was potent with significance for the post-war future of America. Lincoln's willingness to go along with the breaking up and reconfiguring of a slave state was germane to the theories of Thaddeus Stevens, Charles Sumner, and James Ashley—the theories of "state suicide" giving Congress the power to slice, dice, reform, reconstruct, and reconfigure any state or fragment of a state whose residents, through treason, had caused their states to lose their statehood and lapse into mere territories.

The West Virginia statehood bill required the elimination of all vestiges of slavery. For all practical purposes, a new free state had been added to the Union. Lincoln celebrated this fact by declaring that "the admission of the new state, turns that much slave soil to free."[72]

The time was approaching for Lincoln to carry out the intention that he had announced on September 22. He promised to issue the definitive and final Emancipation Proclamation on New Year's Day. As he readied the document, he considered the advice of many people. Orville Browning, now increasingly cautious and conservative, tried to talk him out of issuing the Proclamation, but Lincoln would not back down.

Montgomery Blair suggested adding some language to dampen the fears of a slave insurrection, and Lincoln took this advice by adding the following sentence: "I hereby enjoin upon the people so declared to be free to abstain from all violence, unless in necessary self-defense, and I recommend to them that, in all cases when allowed, they labor faithfully for reasonable wages."[73]

He also declared in the Proclamation that blacks would be accepted for military service. Congress had provided for this policy already in the Militia Act, but Lincoln had refused to take action to date for fear of worsening the white supremacist backlash. Now, with the mid-term elections behind him, it was time to go forward. Racists would howl, but he would not turn back from the social revolution that he and his fellow Republicans were unleashing.

So instead of resisting black military service any longer, Lincoln *emphasized* it. If blacks could contribute to military victory, they could be hailed as heroes of the Union. And this might propel the social revolution.

So Lincoln added this text to his Proclamation regarding the slaves whom his armies would liberate: "And I do further declare and make known, that such persons of suitable condition, will be received into the armed service of the United States to garrison forts, positions, stations, and other places, and to man vessels of all sorts in said service."[74]

As he readied the document, Lincoln felt the overwhelming righteousness of what he was doing, but he reflected again on some ambiguous religious themes. This tremendous step forward for America was only made possible by thousands of deaths. Lincoln wondered why those who were doing the work of the Lord were made to suffer just as much as the people who were stubbornly resisting.

"If you and I had our way," he observed to a clergyman who called upon him, "we would settle this war without bloodshed, but Providence permits blood to be shed. It's hard to tell what Providence wants of us. Sometimes we, ourselves, are more humane than the Divine mercy seems to be."[75] To a group of abolitionists on New Year's Eve, he confessed that he was "not so certain that God's views and feelings" in respect to slavery "are the same as mine. If his feelings were like mine, how could he have permitted it to remain so long? I am obliged to believe that God may not, after all, look upon it in the same light as I do."[76]

At 11 a.m. on the first of January, Lincoln and the first lady came down to the Blue Room for a reception. Mary left before the reception was over, and Lincoln, his mind on other things, stayed on, shaking hand after hand. In the afternoon he went upstairs to his office to sign the Proclamation. Seward and several other public officials were in attendance.

As he prepared to sign the Proclamation, his hand began to tremble a bit—from all the hand-pumping earlier—so he paused and put down the pen. "If my name ever goes into history," he said, "it will be for this act," and he did not want the Proclamation to bear a shaky signature.[77]

But then he signed the document with confidence. He told Seward and his son Frederick that "I never, in my life, felt more certain that I was doing right, than I do in signing this paper."[78] He then gave the pen that he used to sign the Proclamation to Charles Sumner.

The significance of Lincoln's action was acknowledged far and wide. Jefferson Davis called the Proclamation "the most execrable measure recorded in the history of guilty man."[79] Abolitionists—even those who deplored the legalistic text of the document—rejoiced.

Frederick Douglass was among the abolitionists who complained about the Proclamation's language. Years later, however, he admitted that he felt jubilation on the day it was released. He was in Boston on New

Year's Day. He and others were waiting in a crowd for the expected news from Washington. He recalled the details with great vividness: "Eight, nine, ten o'clock came and went, and still no word. . . . At last, when patience was well-nigh exhausted . . . a man (I think it was Judge Russell) with hasty step advanced through the crowd, and with a face fairly illuminated with the news he bore, he exclaimed in tones that thrilled all hearts, 'It is coming! It is on the wires!'"

Douglass continued: "My old friend Rue, a colored preacher, a man of wonderful vocal power . . . led all voices in the anthem, 'Sound the loud timbrel o'er Egypt's dark sea, Jehovah hath triumphed, his people are free.'" As he read the Proclamation, Douglass "saw in its spirit, a life and power far beyond its letter. Its meaning to me was the entire abolition of slavery, wherever the evil could be reached by the Federal arm, and I saw that its moral power would extend much further."[80]

As Lincoln signed the Proclamation, a battle raged in Tennessee. After his retreat from Kentucky, Bragg attempted to regain the initiative for the Confederates. He took his army from Chattanooga toward Nashville, and Rosecrans, who was now in command of the Union's army—which was now called the Army of the Cumberland—engaged him at the town of Murfreesboro. The battle began on December 31 and it lasted through January 2. Though a tactical standoff, this battle became a Confederate defeat, because Bragg withdrew his force and took it back toward Chattanooga.

Murfreesboro (or Stone's River) was a very costly battle. There were over twelve thousand casualties for the Union and over eleven thousand for the Confederates. Rosecrans appeared to be making a good beginning in his new command, with the help of some excellent subordinates, especially George Thomas and Philip Sheridan. Lincoln needed no encouragement to take the results of this battle as a victory. "God bless you and all with you," he telegraphed Rosecrans.[81]

Meanwhile, Grant had succeeded in getting control of the campaign against Vicksburg. Having found out about McClernand's proposal—as well as Lincoln's approval of it—he went up the chain of command in December and sent Halleck a proposal for a Vicksburg campaign of his own.

He would strike southward into Mississippi following the Mississippi Central Railroad while Sherman marched down to the Yazoo River and approached Vicksburg from the northeast. Halleck was inclined to let Grant have his way in this matter. So he and Stanton arranged with Lincoln that McClernand's expedition would operate in coordination with Grant, who was now officially in charge of this military department.

Grant's initial maneuvers, in the final week of December, were unsuccessful. Sherman ran into impregnable Confederate defenses northeast of Vicksburg while Grant's supply lines and communications were disrupted by Confederate raiders led by Earl Van Dorn and Nathan Bedford Forrest. Nonetheless, Grant resolved to keep trying.

Back East, the defeated Ambrose Burnside—who was willing to assume all the blame for the Fredericksburg defeat—tried to salvage his honor by crossing the Rappahannock River again. But several of his corps commanders, who had lost every bit of their previous confidence in him, wrote to Lincoln and urged him to cancel the maneuver.

Burnside was willing to let go. On New Year's Day he told Lincoln he was ready to resign. For good measure, he urged the president not only to accept his own resignation but to fire both Halleck and Stanton.

Lincoln demurred, but he did order Halleck to confer with Burnside and determine which places, if any, offered suitable conditions for another attack across the Rappahannock. Halleck tried to shirk the duty. He said only the army's field commander could make such determinations. Then he too asked to be relieved of command.

Lincoln might very well have been inclined to accept both Burnside's and Halleck's resignations, but the same old problem confronted him: there were not as yet any obvious candidates to take their places.

Burnside was determined to restore his honor, so he tried to lead his men upstream on January 20, with the intention of building five bridges across the Rappahannock. But torrential rains started, and the condition of the roads became impossible. Burnside called off the maneuver that would soon become known as the "mud march." He returned his men to winter quarters.

On January 26, Lincoln decided to replace Ambrose Burnside with Joseph Hooker, a corps commander who had earned himself the nickname "Fighting Joe." He had also earned a reputation for being somewhat treacherous.

Lincoln's letter to Hooker on January 26 was at the same time direct and sardonic in laying down the terms of this appointment. He wanted boldness, but he also wanted a commander who would carry out presidential orders. So he told Hooker very candidly that in some respects "I am not quite satisfied with you." He continued:

I believe you to be a brave and skillful soldier, which, of course, I like. . . . You are ambitious, which, within reasonable bounds, does good rather than harm. But I think that during General Burnside's command of the Army, you have taken counsel of your ambition, and thwarted him as much as you could, in which you did a great wrong to the country. . . . I have heard, in such way as to believe it, of your recently saying that both the Army and the Government needed a Dictator. Of course it was not *for* this, but in spite of it, that I have given you the command. Only those generals who gain successes, can set up dictatorships. What I now ask of you is military success, and I will risk the dictatorship.

He wanted the resourcefulness that had been missing in McClellan, but without the recklessness of Burnside. Only time would tell if Joseph Hooker would at last provide the long-suffering Army of the Potomac with the kind of leadership that it had always needed and deserved.

In January Grant ascertained that Vicksburg was better approached from the south. So he decided on a roundabout plan: he would cross the Mississippi into Arkansas and then march his men southward—below the city—on the opposite shore. The problem was ferrying them back across the river, since the guns of Vicksburg were formidable and it would be very difficult to send his ships past them in order to rendezvous with the troops when they got below the city.

So from January through March, Grant experimented with plans to dig inland canals in the bayous of Arkansas. The work was difficult, but Grant pushed ahead. Lincoln was reasonably pleased when he learned about this effort, since at least Grant was showing creativity.

Elsewhere, however, things were quiet. In Virginia, Hooker waited for the weather to improve so he could launch a spring offensive. And in Tennessee, Rosecrans was slipping into the same old pattern of procrastination that had characterized the behavior of his predecessor, Buell. Lincoln wanted a campaign into East Tennessee but he would have to wait a long time before he got it.

So the mood in the nation's capital became dismal again in the early months of 1863. Republicans were bitter and divided. There was much concern among conservative Republicans that Lincoln had miscalculated when he issued his Emancipation Proclamation. Browning wrote that the party was "upon the brink of ruin . . . unless the President would change his policy, and withdraw or greatly modify his proclamation."[82]

Democrats were in full cry against the Republican "nigger lovers." The Peace Democrats—whom Republicans were now beginning to call "Copperheads"—talked darkly of a new Midwestern confederacy that could operate in alliance with the southern slave states. Confederate sympathizers were active and pro-Confederate secret societies were beginning to emerge in different parts of the North. Lincoln was all too well aware of these sinister trends.

But some other things lifted his spirits. Mary was sufficiently recovered from depression to host a honeymoon reception in the Blue Room on February 13 for the celebrated midget "General Tom Thumb" (Charles S. Stratton) and his bride Lavinia Warren, who had just been married. The contrast between Lincoln's towering height and the diminutive figures of his guests amused everyone.

And Lincoln went to see some Shakespeare plays in local Washington theaters. On March 13, he attended a performance of *Henry IV, Part One*, with the actor James H. Hackett playing Falstaff. On March 25 he went to see *Hamlet*, with the actor E. L. Davenport in the title role.

Of particular interest—in the aftermath of the bloody Sioux rebellion—was a visit to the White House on March 27 by some Native American chieftains who had come from the far West. They represented the following tribes: Cheyenne, Kiowa, Arapaho, Comanche, Apache, and Caddo.

The *Washington Daily Morning Chronicle* reported that the meeting took place in the East Room. Seward, Chase, Welles, and many other distinguished guests including Joseph Henry of the Smithsonian Institution were present. According to the reporter, the chieftains were seated on the floor and "around them the spectators formed a ring" so dense that people in the crowd were jostling one another to get a look.

"These Indians are fine-looking men," the *Chronicle* reported, and "they listened to everything with great interest. At half-past eleven the President entered the circle, and each of the chiefs came forward and shook him by the hand." Lincoln directed the interpreter to "tell them I am very glad to see them, and if they have anything to say, it will afford me great pleasure to hear them."[83]

After speeches by Lean Bear of the Cheyenne and Spotted Wolf of the Arapaho, Lincoln responded with a kindly presentation. "You have all spoken of the strange sights you see here," he began: "the very great numbers of people that you see; the big wigwams; the difference between our people and your own." He presented a science and geography lesson, while taking care to present the contents as nothing more than "notions" and "beliefs" of the whites.

"We pale-faced people think that this world is a great, round ball," Lincoln said, "and we have people here . . . who have come almost from the other side of it to represent their nations here. One of our learned men will now explain to you our notions about this great ball, and show you where we live." He then invited Joseph Henry of the Smithsonian to give a presentation. Afterward Lincoln spoke to the chieftains about the cultural differences between their own peoples and the whites:

> There is a great difference between this pale-faced people and their red brethren, both as to numbers and the way in which we live. We know not whether your own situation is best for your race, but this is what has made the difference in our way of living. The pale-faced people are numerous and prosperous because they cultivate the earth, produce bread, and depend upon the products of the earth rather than wild game for subsistence.

Then he said a few things that are very significant in light of the troubled relations between whites and Native Americans. "You have asked for my advice," he began. "I really am not capable of advising you whether, in the providence of the Great Spirit, who is the great father of us all, it is best for you to maintain the habits and customs of your race, or adopt a new mode of life." But he said that he would try to mitigate the problems that arose between Native Americans and whites:

> It is the object of this Government to be on terms of peace with you, and with all our red brethren. . . . We make treaties with you, and will try to observe them; and if our children should sometimes behave badly, and violate these treaties, it is against our wish. You know it is not always possible for any father to have his children do precisely as he wishes them to do.[84]

At last there was a break in the military deadlock when Grant achieved preliminary victory. Running his transports below the guns of Vicksburg, he ferried his men across the river to the destination he had chosen for his attacks. On the night of April 16, Admiral David Porter oversaw the high-risk maneuver. Grant brought his men across the Mississippi on April 29 and 30.

What followed was a daring and remarkable campaign—exactly the sort of performance that Lincoln had been seeking from his other generals. Before assaulting Vicksburg, Grant disposed of an inland threat: an army gathered in the state capital of Jackson, Mississippi, and commanded by Joseph Johnston, who had finally recovered from his wounds of the previous year. Grant severed his own supply lines and communications for maximum speed, in the confidence that his men could live off the land.

By May 18, he had won five battles, captured the capital of Jackson, and laid siege to Vicksburg. Lincoln was delighted at this sudden demonstration of audacity, and he wrote on May 26 that "whether Gen. Grant shall or shall not consummate the capture of Vicksburg, his campaign . . . is one of the most brilliant in the world."[85]

But a different campaign had led nowhere. Six months earlier, Gustavus Fox had suggested an attack on Charleston, South Carolina. Lincoln received this proposal with great enthusiasm. On April 7, however, the ironclad fleet of Admiral Samuel F. Du Pont was unable to overcome the Confederate shore batteries defending Charleston Harbor. So the fleet withdrew after only a half hour of fighting.

Lincoln had wanted a lightning-fast strike against Charleston. When the idea of a joint army-navy siege of the city was proposed, Lincoln told an aide of Du Pont that "I fear neither you nor your officers appreciate the supreme importance to us of *Time*."[86]

Lincoln felt the constraints of time more and more as the days and months of 1863 played out.

Early in April, Lincoln traveled to Falmouth, Virginia, across the Rappahannock from Fredericksburg. He wanted to confer with the new commander, Joseph Hooker, in regard to his plans for a spring campaign and he wanted to review the troops. He was accompanied by his wife and by the journalist Noah Brooks, who had become a valued friend.

Soldiers recorded their impressions of him, and they often wrote that he looked extremely fatigued. He confessed to Brooks that "nothing could touch the tired spot within," going on to say that this tired spot was "all tired."[87]

He visited wounded soldiers in the field hospitals, and Brooks recorded how he "moved softly from between the beds, his face shining with sympathy and his voice often low with emotion." The soldiers were often quite moved, and Brooks was struck by the "thundering cheer" that "burst forth from the long lines of men" as Lincoln rode back to the field headquarters.[88]

Mary participated in these hospital visits, which augmented her new reputation for performing mercy missions. But her temper flared up when she heard that some wives of the corps commanders had kissed Lincoln at a reception. She scolded him about it for a quarter of an hour.

Lincoln's conferences with Hooker were significant and he differed with his new commander right away. Hooker was proposing to by-pass Lee and move swiftly to attack the city of Richmond. Lincoln had learned from the Burnside debacle to interpose his own views quickly when he doubted his commanders' judgment. So he said that "just now, with the enemy directly ahead of us, there is no eligible route for us into Richmond." For that reason, he said, "our prime object is the enemies' army in front of us," and he instructed Hooker to draw Lee out into the open.

"I do not think we should take the disadvantage of attacking him in his entrenchments," Lincoln said. Instead, the optimal approach was to "continually harass and menace him, so that he shall have no leisure, no safety in sending away detachments. If he weakens himself, then pitch into him."[89] Lincoln and Hooker agreed that the first step should be a cavalry raid that would cut Lee's supply lines.

By the end of the month, Hooker worked out a plan that was similar to what Lincoln had suggested to Burnside. He decided to conduct a deceptive strike against Fredericksburg while at the same time bringing most of his troops upriver to launch a surprise attack that would hit Lee from the rear.

All through the spring of 1863, the white supremacist backlash against emancipation raged, and it merged with protests against the administration's strong policy against disloyalty behind the lines. Two days after he had issued the preliminary Emancipation Proclamation, Lincoln declared martial law against "all Rebels and Insurgents, their aiders and abettors within the United States, and all persons discouraging volunteer enlistments, resisting militia drafts, or guilty of any disloyal practice."[90] The writ of habeas corpus was suspended for people who were subject to arrest for such activities.

And on March 3, 1863, Congress passed the Enrollment Act, which created a military draft.

Democrats accused Lincoln of assuming dictatorial powers—of stamping out the freedom of whites in his mania to elevate blacks. By the early months of 1863, one of the most vocal leaders of the Peace Democrats or Copperheads was Clement L. Vallandigham of Ohio, a congressman who had just been defeated for re-election. Unfazed, he began to campaign for the Democratic gubernatorial nomination in Ohio in the off-year elections of 1863.

Before he left Congress, Vallandigham accused Lincoln of launching "universal political and social revolution, anarchy and bloodshed." He proclaimed that "the South could never be conquered," and he charged that "the secret but real purpose of the war was to abolish slavery in the States" and to "turn our present democratical form of government into an imperial despotism."[91]

After replacing Burnside with Hooker in Virginia, Lincoln gave Burnside a very different mission that would hopefully fit his capabilities. Lincoln sent him out to Ohio to form an army that could operate in pincer fashion with Rosecrans in East Tennessee. When Burnside arrived in Ohio, he issued an order declaring that disloyalty in his department would not be tolerated and that anyone expressing sympathy for the rebellion would be arrested and tried before a military court.

On May 5, Burnside's troops arrested Vallandigham for a speech in which he denounced the "wicked abolition war."[92] A tribunal found Vallandigham guilty of violating Burnside's order and the Peace Democrat was sentenced to confinement until the war was over.

Copperheads vilified Lincoln throughout the North for condoning this arrest. Governor Horatio Seymour of New York declared that the legal precedent of Burnside's action was "full of danger to ourselves and to our homes."[93] Meanwhile, Vallandigham issued a circular declaring that he had been confined to "a military bastille for no other offense than my political opinions."[94] He went on to win the Democratic gubernatorial nomination.

Lincoln decided to commute Vallandigham's sentence and to banish him to the Confederacy. But he defended his crackdown on war resisters in a letter that he sent to some organizers of a protest meeting in Albany, New York. "Must I shoot a simple-minded soldier boy who deserts," Lincoln asked them, "while I must not touch a hair of a wily agitator who induces him to desert?"

The Constitution, he said, permitted the suspension of habeas corpus in cases of rebellion and insurrection. And he was using this constitutional authority for very good reason. Without such draconian measures, he argued, the enemy would be able to "keep on foot amongst us a most efficient corps of spies, informers, suppliers, and aiders and abettors." He reflected that he ought to have arrested Robert E. Lee and people like him at the very beginning of the war. "I think the time not unlikely to come when I shall be blamed for having made too few arrests rather than too many," he said.[95]

Amid the Copperhead outcry against the war and emancipation, Lincoln kept alive his plan for colonization in the hope that it might contain the political danger. On April 14, a ship took 453 black volunteers to Île-à-Vache, the island off the coast of Haiti where some contractors had promised to resettle them. But Lincoln paid little attention to this effort, since he was far more interested in making provision for the free blacks and the liberated slaves who would decide to stay in America.

He took decisive actions to recruit black men for military service and to help the slaves whom his armies were beginning to liberate. As he tried to use colonization to tranquilize racists, he worked to shape public opinion in the hope that black military heroism in 1863 might pave the way for some measure of racial equality.

In March, Edwin Stanton dispatched the army's adjutant general, Lorenzo Thomas, to the Mississippi Valley to perform two tasks: to create a "refugee" policy for the freedmen and to start recruiting new black regiments. In support of this effort, Lincoln wrote to Andrew Johnson, who was serving as the occupation governor of Tennessee. "I am told you have at least *thought of* raising a negro military force," Lincoln began. In his own opinion, he continued, "the country now needs no specific thing so much as some man of your ability, and position, to go to this work. When I speak of your position, I mean that of an eminent citizen of a slave-state, and himself a slave-holder."

Lincoln said that "the colored population is the great *available* and yet *unavailed* of, force for restoring the Union. The bare sight of fifty thousand armed, and drilled black soldiers on the banks of the Mississippi, would end the rebellion at once. And who doubts that we can present that sight, if we but take hold in earnest?"[96]

Lincoln's initial idea had been to phase in military service for blacks—to get the public used to the idea by giving them auxiliary roles at the very beginning. He would start by using black troops to garrison some forts on the Mississippi River, and he would use them for similar duties elsewhere. In April, he sent a message to General Hunter congratulating him for the use of black troops in the occupation of Jacksonville, Florida. "It is important to the enemy that such a force shall *not* take shape, and grow," Lincoln wrote, "and in precisely the same proportion, it is important to us that it *shall*."[97]

As the news of Lincoln's Emancipation Proclamation spread, thousands of slaves made their way to the armies of Rosecrans and Grant, seeking freedom and military service. Able-bodied men were enrolled right away in black units. Throughout the occupied South and in parts of the North, black regiments were forming in the spring of 1863. Recruiting agents worked their way through one black community after another, seeking volunteers. In Boston, the Fifty-fourth Massachusetts Infantry, commanded by Robert Gould Shaw, a white officer, marched proudly through the streets on parade.

Here at last were Lincoln's black warriors, awaiting orders—seeking glory.

Their first combat action took place when Banks sent the Army of the Gulf to attack Port Hudson, Louisiana, and other rebel strongholds on the Mississippi River below Vicksburg. On May 27, black troops distinguished themselves in a brave attack against Port Hudson. Banks reported that "the severe test to which they were subjected, and the determined way in which they encountered the enemy, leaves upon my mind no doubt of their ultimate success."[98]

In early June, black troops showed bravery again in the battle of Milliken's Bend, Louisiana. These engagements were duly reported to Lincoln, who was duly impressed—and very pleased.

On April 27, in a mood of supreme confidence, Joseph Hooker led his army across the Rappahannock River. He had left a small detachment under the command of General John Sedgwick facing Fredericksburg in the hope that it would keep Lee distracted while the rest of the Union army crossed the river upstream. Hooker also sent a cavalry force under General George Stoneman to cut Lee's supply lines.

Lee's response was so masterful that it is generally regarded as his finest performance in the war. He split his own army, leaving a skeleton force to cover Fredericksburg while he took all the rest of his troops to attack Hooker's army near a small village called Chancellorsville—a village in a clearing surrounded by some very dense woods. Lee was outnumbered roughly two-to-one, but he was counting on his own audacity to even the odds.

He was fortunate, because as soon as Hooker realized that Lee had not been taken by surprise, his own confidence wavered. On May 1, he adopted a defensive posture against the wishes of many of his corps commanders. Lee could tell that his gamble had succeeded, so he split his own army again, sending Stonewall Jackson on a sweeping flank attack that erupted from the woods on May 2 with devastating results. To his credit, Hooker was aware of the danger of a surprise attack and he gave some orders to be watchful. But those orders went unheeded.

Meanwhile, Sedgwick's Union force crossed the Rappahannock and forced its way through Fredericksburg. So Lee sent a separate detachment to contain this pincer movement. Heavy fighting continued to rage around Chancellorsville on May 3. And then, in the midst of the battle, Hooker suffered an injury when a falling timber hit him on the head, most likely causing a concussion.

The casualties at Chancellorsville were very heavy: over seventeen thousand on the Union side and over thirteen thousand for the Confederates. The most grievous loss for the rebels was Stonewall Jackson, who was wounded by "friendly fire." His own troops had failed to recognize him in the darkness as he conducted a scouting maneuver at twilight. He died on May 10.

Nonetheless, this battle was a stunning Confederate victory. Hooker started to withdraw across the Rappahannock on May 5.

When Lincoln heard the news of this defeat, he was as shocked as he had been in the aftermath of Fredericksburg. "Had a thunderbolt fallen upon the President he could not have been more overwhelmed," Noah Brooks recorded, and Lincoln paced about the room crying out "My God! What will the country say!"[99]

But his spirits recovered, and then he got angry, reportedly declaring that if Hooker "had been killed by the shot which knocked over the pillar that stunned him, we should have been more successful."[100] A year later, however, he took a more charitable view of Hooker's performance, confessing that he might very well have faltered himself in the confusion (and terror) of battle. "When minie-balls were whistling, and those great oblong shells shrieking in my ear," he admitted, he might very well have "run away."[101]

By June, Lincoln felt more than ever that the time at his disposal was running out quickly. In roughly a year, the political conventions would choose the presidential candidates for the election of 1864. If military victory should still prove elusive by then—and if the white supremacist backlash continued and worsened—it was possible that a white supremacist Democrat would capture the presidency.

If that happened, who could say what sort of catastrophic results might follow? Re-Union on pro-slavery terms? Or an outright Confederate victory? Would the slaves who had been freed by Lincoln get sent right back to bondage?

By 1863, the anti-slavery mission of Lincoln had become the true centerpiece of his life, and the crusade to eradicate slavery was more important to him than any other political goal. In late summer he penned a reflection that is one of the most important and revealing things that he would say in the course of the entire war. It deserves to be far better known.

"Suppose," he wrote to himself, that "those now in rebellion should say: "We cease fighting: re-establish the national authority amongst us—customs, courts, mails, land-offices,—all as before the rebellion—we claiming to send members to both branches of Congress, as of yore, and to hold our slaves according to our State laws, notwithstanding anything or all things which have occurred during the rebellion." In other words, suppose the rebels *gave up as a way to save slavery?*

Lincoln answered this question as follows: "I shall dread, and I think we all should dread, to see 'the disturbing element' so brought back into the government. . . . During my continuance here, the government will return no person to slavery who is free according to the proclamation, or to any of the acts of Congress, unless such return shall be held to be a legal duty, by the proper court of final resort."[102]

In other words, Lincoln was saying to himself that *he did not want to win the Civil War* at the expense of emancipation. Important and crucial as victory was, that victory would turn out to be empty—in fact it would be downright sinister—if it led to pro-slavery Re-Union. And in 1863, Lincoln viewed that scenario as absolutely plausible. He had very good reasons for that belief, as we shall see momentarily.

His suggestion to Congress of constitutional amendments to protect emancipation had not led to any results. And now the Democrats possessed greater strength in the House, so it was very unlikely—if not impossible—for the supreme law of the land to be altered in a way that would make the Republicans' commitment to emancipation permanent.

And so a different strategic approach began to suggest itself to Lincoln: what if the occupation of slave states—or substantial parts of certain slave states—could be used to transform those states *into free states* by rewriting their state constitutions? West Virginia was formally admitted to the Union on June 23, 1863. A new free state had thus been added to the Union, so the free state majority in the United States was growing. Perhaps that majority could grow even faster if a series of occupied slave states could be changed into free states, one by one. But it would have to be done very quickly.

He decided to begin this experiment in occupied Louisiana with General Nathaniel Banks serving as his agent.

On May 1, a group of pro-slavery Louisiana Unionists gathered in New Orleans. They sent a delegation to call upon Lincoln requesting the "full recognition of all the rights of the State, as they existed previous to the passage of the act of secession, upon the principle of the existence of the State Constitution unimpaired." Lincoln would not be out-maneuvered by these people. He had learned that another group of Louisiana Unionists—whose leaders were Thomas J. Durant, Michael Hahn, and Benjamin Flanders—wished to call a constitutional convention to reorganize Louisiana as a free state.

Lincoln pounced upon this new opportunity. He told the pro-slavery Unionists on June 19 that since "reliable information has reached me that a respectable portion of the Louisiana people, desire to amend their State constitution, and contemplate holding a convention for that object," he would not comply with their request to recognize the existing state constitution.[103]

Lincoln quickly got Banks into an active partnership with the "free state" Louisiana leaders. Early in August he sent Banks a letter with between-the-lines instructions that were clear and that make for funny reading: he told Banks to give active assistance to the free state element while keeping his own presidential participation a secret to maintain deniability. "While I very well know what I would be glad for Louisiana to do," he began, "it is quite a different thing for me to assume direction of the matter." He continued:

> I would be glad for her to make a new Constitution recognizing the emancipation proclamation, and adopting emancipation in those parts of the state to which the proclamation does not apply. . . . If these views can be of any advantage in giving shape, impetus, and action there, I shall be glad for you to use them prudently for that

object. Of course you will confer with intelligent and trusty citizens of the State, among whom I would suggest Messrs. Flanders, Hahn, and Durant.[104]

Later on, having heard that Andrew Johnson had endorsed emancipation in Tennessee, Lincoln wrote to him as follows: "Not a moment should be lost. . . . I see that you have declared in favor of emancipation in Tennessee, for which, may God bless you. Get emancipation into your new State government—Constitution—and there will be no such word as fail for your case." Do it quickly, Lincoln said, for "it can not be known who is next to occupy the position I now hold, nor what he will do."[105]

On June 3, Lee moved his Army of Northern Virginia away from Fredericksburg and headed north. He was trying another invasion in the hope that he could undermine northern morale and—perhaps—reduce the pressure on Vicksburg.

Two days later, Hooker proposed an attack upon the rearguard of Lee's army, which was still below the Rappahannock. Lincoln said no, telling Hooker that he ought to be pursuing the main Confederate force, which was obviously heading north, and to avoid becoming "entangled upon the river, like an ox jumped half over a fence, and liable to be torn by dogs, front and rear, without a fair chance to gore one way or kick the other."[106]

When Hooker suggested ignoring Lee's invasion altogether and moving on Richmond, Lincoln snapped back that "*Lee's Army*, and not *Richmond*, is your true objective point." Follow Lee, Lincoln ordered Joseph Hooker—"follow on his flank, and on the inside track, shortening your lines, whilst he lengthens his. Fight him when the opportunity offers."[107]

Lee was moving toward the Shenandoah, with the obvious intention of using it as an invasion corridor. Union cavalry units that were tracking Lee's army collided with its cavalry at Brandy Station on June 9, and the result was the largest single cavalry battle of the war.

As Lee kept on, Lincoln started to worry that the Union garrison at Winchester, Virginia, might be captured. So he sent off orders on June 14 to have the Winchester garrison withdrawn to Harper's Ferry. He told Hooker to attack Lee's army on the march. "If the head of Lee's army is at Martinsburg," he wrote, "and the tail of it on the Plank road between Fredericksburg and Chancellorsville, the animal must be very slim somewhere. Could you not break him?"[108] But the Winchester troops were defeated on the very next day—and many of them got captured, just as Lincoln had feared.

Hooker began to complain in a manner that was all too reminiscent of George McClellan's behavior. He said that Halleck was failing to back him up and that he needed heavy reinforcements. When he asked to be given the ten thousand troops that were stationed at Harper's Ferry, the idea was vetoed by Halleck.

So Hooker resigned his command on June 27. His army had already crossed the Potomac.

The emergency that followed was comparable to what Lincoln had experienced at the beginning of Lee's prior invasion. The president sounded out the various corps commanders of the Army of the Potomac, but most of these generals said no when he asked if they would take Hooker's place. At last one of them, George Gordon Meade, agreed to assume the command. Meanwhile, Lee's men were roaming through lower Pennsylvania seeking supplies—and seizing free blacks, who would be shipped down South into slavery.

This was one of the various crimes against blacks that Confederate armies were inflicting as reprisals for emancipation. The Confederate Congress had warned that black troops would be captured and enslaved and that their white commanding officers would be shot. By 1864, the racist belligerence of the Confederates would lead them to commit gross atrocities.

The armies collided on July 1 near the little town of Gettysburg, Pennsylvania, and the result was a momentous battle that would soon become the most famous battle of the war. Union troops successfully occupied some high terrain below the town, and the place names along this particular stretch of ground—Culp's Hill, Cemetery Hill, Cemetery Ridge, Big Round Top, and Little Round Top—would be enshrined in American legend. Lee's attacks against the ends of this Union line were beaten back, though the fighting on Little Round Top became quite desperate. His flank attacks having failed, Lee committed a momentous blunder. On July 3, he unleashed a great frontal assault, Pickett's charge, against the center of the Union line. This position was all but impregnable.

The result was as catastrophic for Lee as the decision of Burnside at Fredericksburg. Lee's army began a slow retreat back to Virginia.

Gettysburg was without a doubt a great Union victory, and on the next day—the Fourth of July—Grant succeeded in capturing Vicksburg.

Then five days later the Confederate garrison at Port Hudson surrendered. The entire Mississippi River was now in Union hands and the rebel states of Arkansas and Texas were completely cut off from the rest of the Confederacy. Soon a great Union zone of occupation would extend all the way from Illinois to the Gulf of Mexico.

Serenaders called upon Lincoln, who seized the opportunity to link these victories to the nation's founding principles. Lincoln said, "I do most sincerely thank Almighty God for the occasion on which you have called. How long ago is it?—eighty odd years—since on the Fourth of July for the first time in the history of the world a nation by its representatives, assembled and declared as a self-evident truth that 'all men are created equal.'"

And now, he continued, "when we have a gigantic Rebellion, at the bottom of which is an effort to overthrow the principle that all men were created equal, we have the surrender of a most powerful position and army on that very day (cheers)." Lincoln was referring to Vicksburg. He went on to cite the victory at Gettysburg, when "those who opposed the declaration that all men are created equal, 'turned tail' and run."[109]

These events are often called the great "turning point" of the Civil War, and the battle of Gettysburg is called the "high water mark of the Confederacy." But without denying the great and obvious significance of these battles, the Confederates were closer to victory in the year before Gettysburg—1862—and they would be much closer to victory again in the year after Gettysburg—in 1864. From the outset, Confederate strategists had counted on infusions of force from elsewhere to help them overcome the power of the North. They had hoped for foreign intervention, and they sought all kinds of political assistance from the North's white supremacist Democrats. By 1863, the chances of intervention by a European power were increasingly remote.

Despite the triumphal tone that he adopted in public, Lincoln was enraged about the aftermath of Gettysburg. This was merely Antietam all over again: like McClellan, Meade allowed the Confederate army to escape.

Meade told his army that the task after Gettysburg was to "drive from our soil every vestige of the presence of the invader." When Lincoln found out about this message, he exclaimed, "*My God! Is that all?*" He called the message "a dreadful reminiscence of McClellan" and said "the whole country is *our* soil."[110]

On July 6, in a letter to Halleck, he expressed his extreme displeasure with Meade and said that he suspected Meade's purpose was merely "to get the enemy across the river again without a further collision." Lincoln wanted to "destroy him." "Please look to it," Lincoln told the general in chief and for the first time Halleck complied.[111]

Halleck—who was at last (belatedly) beginning to see the war in terms of Lincoln's total war vision—told Meade that the importance of attacking Lee's army before it could cross back into Virginia "is incalculable. Such an opportunity may not occur again."[112] Meade said he was afraid of committing the blunder that Lee had just committed when he ordered Pickett's Charge. Meade wanted to be certain he was not attacking an impregnable position.

According to Robert Todd Lincoln, the president sent Meade an unambiguous order, bypassing Halleck—an order "directing him to attack Lee's army with all his force immediately, and that if he was successful in the attack he might destroy the order, but if he was unsuccessful he might preserve it as his vindication."[113]

By July 12, Meade's army was catching up to Lee, who had finally reached the Potomac. Heavy rains had been swelling the river, and Lee, with his back to the wall, was trying desperately to build bridges strong enough for his army to use. Meade decided to wait and call a council of war. "Call no council of war," Halleck said; "it is proverbial that councils of war never fight."[114] But Lee's army escaped across the river on July 13 and 14. Meade's delay had permitted the escape.

Lincoln was livid. "We had only to stretch forth our hands & they were ours," he raged, adding bitterly that "if I had gone up there I could have whipped them myself."[115] It is an interesting prospect to wonder whether Lincoln should indeed have taken field command of the army. A few newspapers had been recommending that course of action. The Civil War might have ended much sooner with Lincoln giving orders directly to the troops, with no timid subordinates to undermine and interfere with his audacity.

On July 14 he wrote a long letter to Meade—a letter that he never chose to send. "I do not believe," he wrote, that "you appreciate the magnitude of the misfortune involved in Lee's escape. He was within your easy grasp, and to have closed upon him would, in connection with our other late successes, have ended the war. As it is, the war will be prolonged indefinitely. . . . Your golden opportunity is gone, and I am distressed immeasurably because of it."[116]

To fire Meade was out of the question, since many regarded him as the hero of Gettysburg. Northern confidence was surging again in the aftermath of the recent Union victories.

When Lincoln learned that Meade's corps commanders had opposed attacking Lee when his army was facing the flood-swollen river, his thoughts about treachery in the army's officer corps were rekindled. There was "bad faith somewhere," he brooded in a conversation with his secretary of the navy. "What does it mean, Mr. Welles," Lincoln asked: "Great God! What does it mean?"[117]

But Lincoln was thoroughly pleased with the work of Ulysses S. Grant and he told him so directly. On July 13, he sent a congratulatory telegram. "I do not remember that you and I ever met personally," he began, but he wished to acknowledge Grant's "inestimable service." Then he gave Grant the kind of compliment that only one strategic thinker can give to another:

> When you first reached the vicinity of Vicksburg, I thought you should do, what you finally did—march the troops across the neck, run the batteries with the transports, and thus go below. . . . When you got below, and took Port-Gibson, Grand Gulf, and vicinity, I thought you should go down the river and join Gen. Banks; and when you turned Northward East of the Big Black, I feared it was a mistake. I now wish to make the personal acknowledgement that you were right, and I was wrong.[118]

In July, two juxtaposed events offered stark and ironic commentary on the politics of emancipation. Riots convulsed New York City as draft resisters went on a rampage that turned into an ugly race riot that lasted from July 13–16. Vowing they would never fight to free "niggers," the rioters destroyed public buildings, attacked black homes, and then burned down the Colored Orphan Asylum at 44th Street and Fifth Avenue. Lincoln sent troops to quell the riots, in which over a hundred people were killed and more than three hundred were wounded. He supposedly said that before he would "abandon the draft at the dictation of the mob," he would "transfer Meade's entire army to the city of New York."[119] The Copperhead governor of New York, Horatio Seymour, expressed open sympathy for the mob.

Two days afterward, black troops of the Fifty-Fourth Massachusetts Infantry took heavy casualties in an attack against Fort Wagner, South

Carolina, a bastion the Confederates had built to guard the southern approaches to Charleston. Even though this Union attack was repulsed, the black troops performed valiantly.

Lincoln was determined to pay homage to these soldiers and he was revolted by the Confederate threats to murder or enslave them. On July 30, he drafted an order of retaliation proclaiming it "the duty of every government to give protection to its citizens, of whatever class, color, or condition. . . . To sell or enslave any captured person, on account of his color, and for no offense against the laws of war, is a relapse into barbarism and a crime against the civilization of the age." Consequently, he ordered,

> if the enemy shall sell or enslave anyone because of his color, the offense shall be punished by retaliation upon the enemy's prisoners in our possession. It is therefore ordered that for every soldier of the United States killed in violation of the laws of war, a rebel soldier shall be executed; and for every one enslaved by the enemy or sold into slavery, a rebel soldier shall be placed at hard labor.[120]

The treatment of black soldiers was an issue that prompted Frederick Douglass to visit Lincoln in August. Douglass set down a vivid account of their meeting in his memoirs. "I was induced to go to Washington," he remembered, "and lay the complaints of my people before President Lincoln and the secretary of war; and to urge upon them such action as should secure to the colored troops then fighting for the country a measure of fair play."

He recalled the trepidation that he felt when he requested this meeting: "The distance then between the black man and the white American citizen, was immeasurable. . . . I was an ex-slave, identified with a despised race; and yet I was to meet the most exalted person in this great republic. . . . I could not know what kind of a reception would be accorded to me. I might be told to go home and mind my business . . . or I might be refused an interview altogether."

But he was given an appointment with Lincoln on August 10, and as he walked into Lincoln's office, he found him "in a low arm chair, with his feet extended on the floor, surrounded by a large number of documents, and several busy secretaries. The room bore the marks of business, and the persons in it, the president included, appeared to be much over-worked and tired. Long lines of care were already deeply written in Mr. Lincoln's brow," but "his strong face lighted up as soon as my name was mentioned. As I approached and was introduced to him, he rose and extended his hand, and bade me welcome."

When Douglass explained the nature of his business, Lincoln asked him to "state particulars," so Douglass laid them out:

> First, that colored soldiers ought to receive the same wages as those paid to white soldiers. Second, that colored soldiers ought to receive the same protection when taken prisoners, and be exchanged as readily, and on the same terms, and if Jefferson Davis should shoot or hang colored soldiers in cold blood, the United States government should retaliate in kind and degree. . . . Third, when colored soldiers, seeking the "bauble-reputation at the cannon's mouth," performed great and uncommon service on the battle-field, they would be rewarded by distinction and promotion.

Lincoln "listened with patience and silence to all I had to say," Douglass recalled. "He was serious and even troubled by what I had said, and by what he had evidently thought himself before on the same points." Then Lincoln replied in a manner that reflected his usual method of phasing in volatile reforms by careful degrees:

> He began by saying that the employment of colored troops at all was a great gain to the colored people; that the measure could not have been successfully adopted at the beginning of the war; that the wisdom of making colored men into soldiers was still doubted; that their enlistment was a serious offense to popular prejudice; that they had larger motives for being soldiers than white men . . . that the fact that they were not to receive the same pay as white soldiers, seemed a necessary concession to smooth the way to their employment at all as soldiers; but that ultimately they would receive the same.[121]

Lincoln made his incremental strategy explicit to Douglass. Referring to the use of black troops, he said that the country "needed talking up to that point," and so he hesitated as long as his instincts told him that "the country was not ready." But once the "preparatory work had been done," Lincoln said, he went ahead and did the work with gusto.[122]

Lincoln never mentioned to Douglass the retaliation order he had drafted in response to Confederate atrocities. His conscience appeared to be troubling him as he pondered the cold impersonality of shooting prisoners at random in retaliation for the actions of others. He told Douglass that he feared such retaliation was a "terrible remedy," one which, "if once begun, there was no telling where it would end."[123]

A few weeks after his meeting with Douglass, Lincoln got a welcome letter from Grant extolling the value of African American troops. Lincoln had written to Grant to inform him that the adjutant general, Lorenzo Thomas, would be making another visit to the Mississippi Valley for the purpose of creating more black military units. Grant promised to cooperate, and he called the use of black soldiers "the heaviest blow yet given the Confederacy." He said that "they will make good soldiers and taking them from the enemy weakens him in the same proportion as they strengthen us."[124]

Three days after he received this letter, Lincoln sent off a letter of his own to his friend James Conkling in Springfield. Conkling had sent him an invitation to attend a meeting of Illinois Unionists, and while Lincoln declined, he decided to use this occasion for his own purposes: as an opportunity to issue a lengthy statement that would help the Republican cause. So he framed his reply to Conkling as a letter that was meant for public release. His letter to Conkling was a long manifesto on the war, emancipation, and race that he hoped the Republicans could use to undercut the Copperheads. This letter deserves to be much better known by Americans.

Though the letter was nominally sent to Conkling, Lincoln argued directly with the racist northern Democrats. "There are those who are dissatisfied with me," he began, and "to such I would say: You desire peace; and you blame me that we do not have it. But how can we attain it? There are but three conceivable ways. First, to suppress the rebellion by force of arms. This, I am trying to do. Are you for it? If you are, so far we are agreed." The second way was "to give up the Union. I am against this. Are you for it? If you are, you should say so plainly."

The third way, he said, was through compromise. Lincoln said that no compromise in his own opinion was possible, and his reason was power calculation. "The strength of the rebellion," he pointed out, "is its military—its army. That army now dominates all the country, and all the people, within its range." Any offer of compromise made by southerners within the range of that army was "nothing for the present" since the people in the South who disagreed with the rebellion had "no power to enforce their side of a compromise." And "no paper compromise, to which the controllers of Lee's army are not agreed" could have any force. There was no point in talking of a compromise when the Confederate armies were still on the loose, overpowering Unionists and intimidating southerner dissenters.

Then he turned to the issue of race. "To be plain," he wrote, "you are dissatisfied with me about the negro. Quite likely there is a difference between you and myself upon that subject." He continued:

> I certainly wish all men could be free, while I suppose you do not. Yet I have neither adopted, nor proposed any measure, which is not consistent with even your view, providing you are for the Union. I suggested compensated emancipation; to which you replied you wished not to be taxed to buy negroes. But I had not asked you to be taxed to buy negroes, except in such way, as to save you from greater taxation to save the Union exclusively by other means.

As to his Emancipation Proclamation, racists wanted it retracted and they called it unconstitutional. "I think differently," said Lincoln, since the "constitution invests its commander-in-chief, with the law of war, in time of war." The efficacy of the proclamation as a wartime measure was obvious. "Some of our commanders in the field who have given us our greatest successes," he pointed out, "believe the emancipation policy, and the used of colored troops, constitute the heaviest blow yet dealt to the rebellion." He was of course alluding to the letter he received from Grant.

As the tempo of his manifesto increased, Lincoln's anger at the racists grew stronger and became more obvious. "You say you will not fight to free negroes. Some of them seem willing to fight for you; but, no matter. Fight you, then, exclusively to save the Union. I issued the proclamation on purpose to aid you in saving the Union. Whenever you shall have conquered all resistance to the Union, if I shall urge you to continue fighting, it will be an apt time, then, for you to declare you will not fight to free negroes."

Peace, he concluded, "does not appear so distant as it did," and he added that he hoped that it would arrive in a form that would "be worth the keeping in all future time. . . . And then, there will be some black men who can remember that, with silent tongue, and clenched teeth, and steady eye, and well-poised bayonet, they have helped mankind on to this great consummation; while, I fear, there will be some white ones, unable to forget that, with malignant heart, and deceitful speech, they have strove to hinder it."[125]

This letter would be published in newspapers and reprinted many times in pamphlet form. Republicans would use these pamphlets during 1863 as an answer to the racist attacks of the Democrats.

Lincoln explored different ways to support and to empower all the slaves whom his armies were freeing. In August, he sent his friend Stephen Hurlbut to occupied Mississippi with instructions to initiate humanitarian efforts on behalf of the freedmen. While many "able bodied male contrabands are already employed by the Army," Lincoln said, many others were "in confusion and destitution."

Consequently, "if there are plantations near you which are abandoned by their owners, first put as many contrabands on such, as they will hold—that is, as can draw subsistence from them. If some still remain, get loyal men, of character in the vicinity, to take them temporarily on wages, to be paid to the contrabands themselves—such men obliging themselves to not let the contrabands be kidnapped, or forcibly taken away. Of course, if any voluntarily make arrangements to work for their living, you will not hinder them."[126]

Grant became a keen supporter of these efforts, and he set aside land in Davis Bend—including the plantation of Jefferson Davis—as a settlement for freedmen. This community of freed blacks had its own internal system of government, complete with elected judges and sheriffs. In October, Lincoln directed General James S. Wadsworth to investigate the living conditions of freedmen throughout the entire Mississippi Valley.

In occupied Louisiana, Banks issued labor regulations for freedmen that were more restrictive. Lincoln made it clear that these arrangements needed to be "probationary" (i.e., temporary). The goal, he explained to Banks, should be to "adopt some practical system by which the two races could gradually live themselves out of their old relation to each other, and both come out better prepared for the new." He added that "education for young blacks should be included in this plan."[127]

Congress had set aside portions of lands in the South that were seized for non-payment of taxes as a special "reserve" to be held for the use of former slaves. In September, Lincoln sent explicit orders to the federal tax commissioners in the Sea Islands off the coast of South Carolina and

Georgia. He told them to set aside lots of twenty acres for "the heads of families of the African race, one only to each, preferring such as by their conduct, meritorious services or exemplary character, will be examples of moral propriety and industry."[128] This order put Lincoln in direct support of the movement for land redistribution in the South. Here again was an action by Lincoln that was potent with significance for post-war Reconstruction.

Reconstruction was very much on Lincoln's mind in the autumn months of 1863. As he pondered the best-case and worst-case scenarios, he worked up conceptual terms for a splendid new beginning for America— one that would be worthy of the nation's ideals. "The Tycoon is in fine whack," wrote his secretary John Hay in early August. "He is managing this war, the draft, foreign relations, and planning a reconstruction of the Union, all at once. I never knew with what tyrannous authority he rules the Cabinet till now. The most important things he decides, and there is no cavil. . . . There is no man in the country, so wise, so gentle and so firm."[129]

Despite Lincoln's great frustration with the lack of military progress in Virginia and Tennessee, his popularity kept on increasing in the aftermath of the latest military victories. And this helped the Republicans to carry some off-year elections in 1863. A few of these elections helped to further the cause of emancipation in slave states where the Emancipation Proclamation did not apply.

The gubernatorial elections in Pennsylvania and Ohio were of special importance, though some of it was symbolic. Vallandigham was still the Democrats' candidate for the Ohio governorship. To help the Republicans in these and other states, the administration granted furloughs to Union soldiers so that they could go home and vote. New "Union Leagues" were organized outside of the Republican Party and they hammered away at Copperhead treachery.

The "Knights of the Golden Circle," the pro-slavery secret society that was organized in 1854, remained active in association with the Copperheads. The Knights pushed the idea of a secessionist Northwest Confederacy that would join with the slave-holding South to resist emancipation. The Union Leagues worked steadily to ferret out the activities of the "Knights."

The refusal of the Democratic legislatures of Indiana and Illinois to appropriate funds for the war was another easy target for the Union Leagues. Democratic war resistance looked increasingly bad in the aftermath of Gettysburg, Vicksburg, and Port Hudson, so Republicans went after the Democratic legislators of Illinois and Indiana, accusing them of being unpatriotic at best and traitors at worst.

Pennsylvania, however, was a rather close call, with Republican Governor Andrew Curtin facing a challenger, George W. Woodward, who had once called slavery an "incalculable blessing." Woodward was endorsed by none other than General George B. McClellan, who was seriously interested in the 1864 Democratic presidential nomination.

The Pennsylvania outcome was close because the supreme court of the state had ruled that the Union draft was unconstitutional. Pennsylvania judges issued writs of habeas corpus designed to help draft-age men resist. On September 17, Lincoln signed an executive order permitting army provost marshals to suspend these writs of habeas corpus in draft resistance cases.

The embattled Republican governor of Pennsylvania called this order "a heavy blow" that put his re-election at risk, but insofar as "it is right," Curtin said, "we can stand it."[130] He was narrowly re-elected by fifteen thousand votes.

But the Republican victory in Ohio was overwhelming. Vallandigham's supporters had mounted a grossly racist campaign that featured girls standing underneath banners that read "Father, save us from Negro Equality." On October 13, the Republican candidate for the Ohio governorship, John Brough, beat Clement Vallandigham by almost a hundred thousand votes.

In the slave state of Maryland, Republicans were actually pushing for immediate emancipation under the aegis of an "Unconditional Unionist" movement and they were winning. Slavery in Maryland was weakened when army recruiters were allowed to enroll male slaves. When the owners of the slaves protested, Lincoln made arrangements to pay them. The slaves became free as they entered military service.

General Robert C. Schenck, who was in charge of the Maryland recruiting, ordered his provost marshals to administer loyalty oaths to the voters and to guard the polling places, so that voters would not be intimidated. But the presence of these troops was somewhat intimidating in and of itself—to the Democrats. Democratic voter turnout in Maryland suffered accordingly.

The politics in Maryland thickened when Postmaster General Montgomery Blair delivered an incendiary speech in the city of Rockville denouncing the Radical Republicans. He called them extremists and he accused them of trying to force racial "amalgamation" on the nation's whites.

Lincoln accordingly distanced himself from this member of his cabinet as Radical Republicans called for his immediate ouster.

But the political situation in the slave state of Maryland was mild when compared to the situation in Missouri. Atrocities committed by pro-Confederate guerrillas had prompted scorched-earth reprisals from Union military commanders. And Missouri Republicans had divided into very bitter factions: Conservatives (known as "Claybanks") and Radicals (known as "Charcoals"). Both of these factions were in favor of emancipation, but the Claybanks favored gradualism while the Charcoals insisted on immediate and unconditional emancipation in the state.

In September, a Radical Union Emancipation Convention in Jefferson City, Missouri, chose a delegation to call upon Lincoln and demand that he endorse their policies. When Lincoln met with this delegation on September 30, he found the members' attitude so confrontational that he stood his own ground and refused to endorse their demands. He said that his preference for Missouri was gradual emancipation, and he said that he feared that the Radicals' activities might lead to a political backlash.

But even as he resisted these Radicals, Lincoln privately told John Hay that they were "nearer to me than the other side, in thought and sentiment, though bitterly hostile personally." He called them "the unhandiest devils in the world to deal with," but said that they possessed "the stuff which must save the state and on which we must mainly rely. If one side must be crushed out & the other cherished there could be no doubt which side we would choose as fuller of hope for the future. We would have to side with the Radicals."[131]

Lincoln's plans for the conversion of slave states to free states were very important to him, but his tactics would vary with the different situations in the different states. In Missouri, he believed that the Radicals needed to slow down. But in Louisiana, he wanted General Nathaniel Banks to hurry up.

Lincoln knew that the wave of political confidence resulting from the victories at Gettysburg and elsewhere would diminish. The most important objective in military terms was to put Lee's army out of action. The mere continued existence of Lee's army was a great potential threat to Lincoln's re-election chances. Even at the risk of more short-term defeats on the battlefield—defeats like Chancellorsville—Lee's army had to be engaged and then beaten.

But Meade continued to act like McClellan, though without the latter's ego and arrogance. Nothing was happening in Virginia in the autumn of 1863.

On October 16, Lincoln tried to spur Meade into action. Via Halleck, he wrote that if Meade would attack Lee "on a field no worse than equal for us, and will do so with all the skill and courage, which he, his officers and men possess, the honor will be his if he succeeds, and the blame may be mine if he fails."[132] But Meade wrote back that Lee's position—near the Rapidan and Rappahannock Rivers—was unassailable. Apparently the thought of even trying to flush Lee's army into a different position was inconceivable to Meade.

Lincoln was disgusted beyond endurance and he poured out his contempt for Meade in some off-the-record remarks. In a conversation with Gideon Welles, Lincoln said that it was "the same old story with the Army of the Potomac. Imbecility, inefficiency—don't want to *do*."[133]

And out in Tennessee, Rosecrans was also proving to be a disappointment to Lincoln. After the battle of Murfreesboro, he delayed, malingered, and complained for months on end. Urged to march against East Tennessee while Grant was conducting his campaign to capture Vicksburg, Rosecrans said that it was a very big mistake to fight two major battles at once. Such nonsense was too much even for Halleck, who ordered Rosecrans to start his campaign to attack Chattanooga in June.

Rosecrans finally acted on June 24, but all through July and August he continued to complain non-stop. He complained about the inadequate size of his cavalry forces, and the lack of support from Washington. Every dispatch that he sent was more quarrelsome than the last one.

Halleck's wishy-washiness was yielding to peremptory impatience as he read these foolish dispatches. He ordered Rosecrans to stop complaining and make use of the forces that he had. At last, by early September, Rosecrans got his army south of Chattanooga. The Confederate commander, Braxton Bragg, was afraid of being surrounded in the city and cut off. So he evacuated Chattanooga in order to regroup in a more defensible position. Rosecrans occupied the city and pursued Bragg's army across the state line into Georgia.

For a while, Lincoln exulted not only in the capture of Chattanooga but the liberation of East Tennessee in general. For the pincer movement of Burnside was beginning to penetrate the area, augmenting the operation of Rosecrans.

Then disaster struck. On September 19 and 20, Bragg attacked the army of Rosecrans at a place called Chickamauga Creek in northwest Georgia. Rosecrans bungled the command and a huge gap was opened in the Union lines. The Confederate attack was overwhelming. Rosecrans fled back to Chattanooga, while a Union commander with far more presence of mind, George Thomas, held off the Confederates. This prevented the Union defeat from becoming a rout. Thomas earned himself the nickname "Rock of Chickamauga" for this action.

Rosecrans was bottled up in Chattanooga as the Confederates proceeded to put the city under siege. Burnside bungled the opportunity to help, for he deployed his army in a different direction to attack the city of Jonesboro. "Damn Jonesboro," Lincoln exploded when he got this news, and he dashed off a furious dispatch to Burnside. "Yours of the 23rd. is just received, and it makes me doubt whether I am awake or dreaming," he wrote. "I have been struggling for ten days . . . to get you to go to assist Gen. Rosecrans in an extremity, and you have repeatedly declared you would do it, and yet you steadily move the contrary way."[134] But Lincoln chose not to send this message.

On the night of September 23, Stanton sent John Hay to summon Lincoln from the Soldiers' Home. Stanton was worried that Rosecrans could not hold his position much longer, so he and Lincoln decided to send reinforcements to Rosecrans and draw them from the Army of the Potomac. Since Meade seemed determined to do nothing, there was no good reason to keep his men pinned down while battles raged elsewhere.

Twenty thousand troops were sent to Chattanooga by train under the command of Joseph Hooker—who would thus be given a chance to redeem himself. Stanton urged Lincoln to replace William Rosecrans with George Thomas. Lincoln was inclined to take this advice, since the latest dispatches of Rosecrans made him seem as if, in Lincoln's words, he were "confused and stunned like a duck hit on the head."[135]

In mid-October Lincoln put Grant in command of all the Union armies in the West. He ordered Grant to go to Chattanooga, assess the situation, and then take charge of Union forces in person. Grant was authorized either to replace or retain Rosecrans at his own discretion.

Grant relieved Rosecrans immediately. Before he had even reached Chattanooga, Grant replaced him with George Thomas.

Lincoln felt the pressures of time closing in upon him more and more in the late weeks of autumn. In just a few months the politics of election year 1864 would start churning. Horace Greeley was encouraging others to run against Lincoln for the Republican nomination. It was an open secret that Salmon Chase might decide to challenge Lincoln's place at the head of the Republican ticket.

No one had ever been re-elected after serving a presidential term since Andrew Jackson back in 1832. And Lincoln remembered the eerie premonition that he had back in 1860 as he gazed at the double image in the mirror. Who could predict what awaited the nation or Lincoln in 1864 or in 1865? The theme of mortality continued to haunt him.

Back in June he had written to Mary—who was on a trip with Tad in Philadelphia—that she needed to be more careful with a miniature cannon that Captain John A. Dahlgren had constructed for Tad to play with. "Think you better put 'Tad's' pistol away," Lincoln wrote to Mary; "I had an ugly dream about him."[136] On July 2, Mary herself had had a nasty fall from a carriage.[137]

She continued her travels with Tad, and before very long Lincoln felt very lonely for the two of them. On September 21, he wrote to Mary and said he would be grateful if she would cut the trip short. "The air is so clear and cool, and apparently healthy," he wrote, "that I would be glad for you to come. Nothing very particular, but I would be glad to see you and Tad."[138] The next day his tone was more urgent; "I really wish to see you," he wrote. Then he added, "answer this on receipt."[139]

On the 24th, he had the duty of informing Mary that her brother-in-law, Ben Hardin Helm, had been killed at Chickamauga. Helm, who was married to Mary's half-sister Emilie, had fought for the Confederacy.

Mary returned, and the two of them went to a play together on October 30. Maggie Mitchell was the star in a performance of a play called *Fanchon, the Cricket*. The play was performed at Ford's Theatre. On November 9, Lincoln attended another play at the very same theater. The play was *The Marble Heart*.

The lead was played by John Wilkes Booth.

Lincoln went now and then to have his picture taken by Alexander Gardner, who established his own photographic studio after working for Mathew Brady. At a session on August 9, Lincoln was photographed standing with his hand upon a table, and this is one of the very best depictions that we have of his towering height. On November 8, he had his picture taken with his secretaries, Nicolay and Hay.

In the months that followed, some famous Lincoln images were produced at Brady's studio: a picture of Lincoln wearing spectacles and reading a book to his little boy Tad along with images of Lincoln that would later be used in the design of both U.S. currency and coin: the profile of Lincoln on the one-cent coin and the three-quarters portrait on the five-dollar bill.

That fall, he received two very interesting invitations. On November 2, he was invited to make brief remarks at the dedication of a new military cemetery in Gettysburg. The main speaker was to be the famed orator Edward Everett, who had been invited to speak at the ceremony almost two months earlier.

And on September 28, Lincoln was invited by Sarah Josepha Hale, the editor of the magazine *Godey's Lady's Book*, to issue a proclamation setting forth a day that would serve as a national celebration of thanksgiving. Hale had been advocating this idea for almost fifteen years.

Lincoln responded with alacrity to the invitation to compose and issue a proclamation of Thanksgiving Day. On October 3, he invited "the whole of the American people" to proclaim "with one heart and one voice" on "the last Thursday of November next" their thanks for God's blessings. "In the midst of a civil war of unparalleled magnitude and severity," he wrote, the nation's strength had providentially increased, as God continued to bless the American people. "The year that is drawing to a close has been filled with the blessings of fruitful fields and healthful skies," he wrote. Even war had "not arrested the plough, the shuttle or the ship."

"No human counsel hath devised nor hath any mortal hand worked out these great things," Lincoln said. No, they were "gifts of the most High God, who, while dealing with us in anger for our sins, hath nevertheless remembered mercy."

While submitting to the anger of the Lord, he continued—while acknowledging the "national perverseness and disobedience" that were certainly the cause of the carnage that was wiping out hundreds of thousands of northerners and southerners—we must commend to God's "tender care all those who have become widows, orphans, mourners or sufferers." We must "fervently implore the interposition of the Almighty Hand to heal the wounds of the nation."[140]

Here were the first meditations of the themes that would resound once again in Lincoln's Second Inaugural Address.

October 3, the day when Lincoln issued his thanksgiving proclamation, was the day when George Washington had issued the first presidential proclamation of thanksgiving in 1789. Lincoln was aware of this fact when he chose the day for issuing a proclamation of his own.

The creation of a national military cemetery at Gettysburg was the idea of a local attorney named David Wills. As the plans took shape, a number of people were suggesting to Lincoln that he make a speech on some convenient occasion that would present the war as a test of democracy itself. Consequently, he was probably thinking of the overall theme that he would use in his Gettysburg Address well before he received the invitation. It was a theme that he had used many times, not least of all in 1861 when he said that secession was a threat to the democratic principle.

Certain lines that he would use in the Gettysburg Address were drawn from older statements of his own. On August 17, 1858, he declared in the midst of his campaign against Douglas that the Founding Fathers had foreseen the need to "renew the battle" they started. The battle would have to be fought many times if the fundamental values of decency and mercy, the values that underlay the principle that all men are created equal, "might not be extinguished from the land."[141]

The classic formulation "of the people, by the people, for the people" was inspired perhaps by a statement that Daniel Webster had made in the course of the 1830 Webster-Hayne Debate. Webster spoke of the "people's government, made for the people, made by the people, and answerable to the people."

The beginning of the Gettysburg Address was clearly drawn from a passage in *Psalms* 90: 10: "The days of our years are threescore and ten; and if by reason of strength they be fourscore years, yet is their strength labour and sorrow; for it is soon cut off, and we fly away."

That would be the theme of this oration by Lincoln for the dedication of a graveyard: human life, so fragile and transient, compared to the time that was needed for the birth and growth of a nation. *Life* would be the theme of this tribute by Lincoln to the brave men who gave it up. They had given up their lives to extend the life of their nation—a nation that provided such hope to the world that the sacrifices made for its existence should be honored in relation to its purpose. That had been the purpose of Pericles of Athens in the fifth century B.C., when in his funeral oration for the men who were dying in the Peloponnesian War he declared that the democracy for which they were fighting, the democracy of Athens, was a power so worthy of its times that the sacrifices of its honored dead should be an inspiration to all.

Lincoln's little boy Tad had fallen seriously ill, so in order to make the trip to Gettysburg for the dedication ceremony on November 19, he would have to leave the bedside of his youngest surviving child.

He decided to go.

Despite the legend that Lincoln composed his address on the train as he traveled to the ceremony, he had probably started to write it earlier. He was accompanied to Gettysburg by Seward, Montgomery Blair, and other public officials, along with his secretaries Nicolay and Hay. They left Washington on November 18. Lincoln spent the night at the home of David Wills, the originator of the national cemetery project.

November 19 was "one of the most beautiful Indian Summer days ever enjoyed," according to Hay.[142] A vast crowd had jammed the roads into Gettysburg. Lincoln took an early morning tour of the battlefield along with Seward. Then he put a few finishing touches on his speech. At 10 a.m., Lincoln joined the great procession that was headed toward the cemetery.

Ward Hill Lamon led this procession and Lincoln rode along on horseback. The cheers from the crowd were almost deafening. One reporter wrote that Lincoln "sat up the tallest and grandest rider in the procession."[143] Benjamin Brown French was overwhelmed by the adulation of the crowd. However fragile his political support had become as the war casualties mounted—however much hatred and vilification the Democrats and Copperheads kept spewing in his direction—however much his Republican critics and rivals continued their interminable carping—the multitude in Gettysburg on November 19, 1863, appeared to be of one heart and mind in their feelings toward Abraham Lincoln.

They loved him.

French wrote that "anyone who saw & heard as I did, the hurricane of applause that met his every movement at Gettysburg would know that he lived in every heart." It was "a tumultuous outpouring of emotion."[144] One woman who was visiting from Virginia wrote that "such homage I never saw or imagined could be shown to any one person as the people bestow on Lincoln."[145]

As Lincoln and the other dignitaries reached the speakers' platform, the crowd had swelled to fifteen thousand. After Edward Everett spoke for two hours, Lamon rose to introduce Lincoln, who received another tremendous ovation. The president put on his reading glasses, drew forth the paper, and spoke in a voice so loud and so clear that it could be heard all the way to the outer edges of the crowd.

His opening sentence was majestic, but for all of its grandeur its rhythm was free-flowing, light, and without any trace of ostentation: "Four score and seven years ago our fathers brought forth upon this continent a new nation, conceived in liberty, and dedicated to the proposition that all men are created equal." Notes that were taken by journalists reveal that the crowd applauded immediately after Lincoln read the sentence.

No doubt the allusion to the biblical formulation of "three score and ten" found a ready reception. Lincoln had established his theme of human mortality—of the transience of human life—in the very first phrase of his speech.

Accounts make it clear that many people in the crowd were in tears as Lincoln set forth the purpose that brought them together: to dedicate a portion of the battlefield "as a final resting place for those who here gave their lives that the nation might live." The sublimity of his message increased as he contended that "the brave men, living and dead, who struggled here" had already consecrated this ground "far above our poor power to add or detract." And yet despite his disclaimer that, compared to such sacrifice, "we cannot dedicate, we cannot consecrate, we cannot hallow this ground," he went on to do precisely that in the passage that followed.

He called upon Americans to dedicate themselves to "the unfinished work," the "great task remaining before us"—to the cause for which the honored dead gave "the last full measure of devotion." They must not have died in vain, he declared, for their deaths must generate a "new birth of freedom," and Americans who understood the great meaning of the deaths must swear to themselves a sacred oath. They must "highly resolve" that America's task would be completed. And they must swear that "government of the people, by the people, for the people, shall not perish from the earth."[146]

According to one reporter, Lincoln's "calm but earnest utterance of this deep and beautiful address" stirred the "vast throngs before him" so much that amid the sustained applause "sobs of smothered emotion were heard on every hand."[147]

At 6 p.m. he boarded the next train for Washington. He was anxious to see how Tad was doing and he needed to attend to pressing business. His annual message to Congress required attention. Things were happening in Tennessee.

His health began to break, and the doctors diagnosed a mild case of smallpox. He was quarantined, but not for long. After just a few days he was up and about and back at work.

There was so much to do.

V

TRIUMPH

14

DEATH STRUGGLE

L incoln was delighted again with the performance of Ulysses S. Grant in November 1863. The forces under Grant's supervision turned the situation in Chattanooga around and delivered yet another great victory to Lincoln.

On November 24 and 25, Union troops attacked Confederate positions on the seemingly impregnable heights above Chattanooga. They stormed up Missionary Ridge and Lookout Mountain and drove the Confederates away. The Confederate siege of Chattanooga was lifted and the rebels retreated into Georgia.

Meanwhile, the new Congress elected back in November 1862 was about to convene. A long adjournment after congressional elections was standard in those days—unless the newly elected Congress were called into special session by the president. If not, the old Congress would wrap up its business and adjourn. The newly elected Congress would not convene until December 1 of the year that followed the elections.

On December 8, Lincoln sent his long annual message to Congress. He sought to merge the cause of emancipation with the imperative of saving the Union, to blend the objectives, to instill in the American public the conviction that saving the Union *required* the destruction of slavery. But he was careful to emphasize the point that preservation of the Union was the goal that justified his policies.

Looking back on the adoption of the emancipation policy and the use of black troops, he acknowledged that these kinds of revolutionary measures had incited tremendous controversy. "The policy of emancipation," he wrote, "and of employing black soldiers, gave to the future a new aspect, about which hope, and fear, and doubt contended in uncertain conflict." The announcement of emancipation "was followed by dark and doubtful days."[1]

But it was time to review what had happened. So he laid out the progress resulting from the merger of Unionism and the liberation of slaves:

> The rebel borders are pressed still further back, and by the complete opening of the Mississippi the country dominated by the rebellion is divided into distinct parts, with no practical communication between them. Tennessee and Arkansas have been substantially cleared of insurgent control, and influential citizens in each, owners of slaves and advocates of slavery at the beginning of the rebellion, now declare openly for emancipation in their respective states.[2]

In the case of Arkansas, he was alluding to the fact that after Union troops commanded by General Frederick Steele entered Little Rock in October, Arkansas Unionists called a convention to rewrite the state's constitution. Here was yet another slave state that was being converted to a free state.

Lincoln went on to pay tribute to the ongoing free state movements in Missouri and Maryland, "neither of which three years ago would tolerate any restraint upon the extension of slavery into new territories." But now in both of those states, he observed, the "only dispute" pertained to "the best mode of removing it within their own limits."[3]

As to his own emancipation efforts, he continued, the results were contributing to victory. "Of those who were slaves at the beginning of the rebellion," he said, "fully one hundred thousand are now in the United States military service . . . and supplying the places which otherwise must be filled with so many white men." They were doing very well as soldiers, and all of the fears about a bloody slave rebellion had proven to be groundless: "No servile insurrection, or tendency to violence or cruelty, has marked the measures of emancipation and arming the blacks."[4]

So the new birth of freedom was merging with defense of the Union, and people could see the connection. Even previous opponents were coming around to see the usefulness and the justice of what was being done. His policies were "fully discussed, supported, criticized, and denounced, and the annual elections following are highly encouraging to those whose official duty it is to bear the country through this great trial. Thus we have the new reckoning."[5]

One of the most important parts of this message was Lincoln's announcement of a preliminary policy for Reconstruction. This is one of the actions by Lincoln that is commonly cited by those who subscribe to the legend that Lincoln was nothing but a cautious "moderate," and that his policies for Reconstruction would have been undemanding if he had lived.

But Lincoln made it clear that he might turn to other measures in the future. The fact that he was announcing this particular plan did not necessarily commit him to use it indefinitely. "Saying that reconstruction will be accepted if presented in a specified way," he declared, was not equivalent to saying that "it will never be accepted in any other way."[6]

It is true that his policies of December 1863 could be said to have a lenient dimension. But there was also a hidden dimension—a secret dimension—and when closely examined, the provisions that Lincoln set forth in his plan show the outlines of a daring and audacious ploy. It was one of the very best schemes he had ever figured out in his long career as a tricky practitioner of law. It was a masterpiece of cunning.

What Lincoln announced would be known as his "Ten Percent Plan." It was attached to his 1863 message to Congress as a separate "Proclamation of Amnesty and Reconstruction." The Proclamation held out the following offers.

First, it proclaimed that every rebel who agreed to lay down his arms and swear a loyalty oath would receive a presidential pardon. Moreover, all of his seized property—except for slaves—would be returned. Exceptions were made in the case of those who in previous years had taken oaths to serve as officers of the United States or who had mistreated black troops when they were held as prisoners of war.

Second, Lincoln proclaimed that whenever at least one tenth of the people who voted in the 1860 election gave up the rebellion and took these loyalty oaths, they would be granted the power to "re-establish a State government" that Lincoln would recognize "as the true government of the State." Third, it provided that whenever these new state governments enacted laws to recognize the permanence of emancipation as well as to provide education for freedmen, those states would be allowed to create regulations or "provisions" in regard to the legal rights of former slaves. But Lincoln hastened to add that such provisions would be nothing more than a "temporary arrangement, with their present condition as a laboring, landless, and homeless class."[7]

The loyalty oath that the rebels had to swear consisted of more than a promise to "faithfully support, protect and defend the Constitution of the United States, and the Union of the states thereunder." It also forced them to swear that they would "abide by and faithfully support all acts of Congress passed during the existing rebellion with reference to slaves" along with "all proclamations of the President . . . having reference to slaves"—unless the Supreme Court overturned them.

These penitent rebels would conclude their oaths by intoning the words "So help me God."[8]

This insistence by Lincoln that the oaths to be sworn by the penitent rebels "in the presence of Almighty God" would commit them to support emancipation was overwhelmingly important. It was so important that he took some time to defend it in his message to Congress. His Emancipation Proclamation and the anti-slavery measures enacted by Congress were intended to subdue the rebellion, he said, and to give these measures "their fullest effect," some "pledge for their maintenance" had to be included in the loyalty oaths. He continued:

> To now abandon them would be not only to relinquish a lever of power, but would also be a cruel and astounding breach of faith. . . . While I remain in my present position I shall not attempt to retract or modify the emancipation proclamation; nor shall I return to slavery any person who is free by the terms of the proclamation, or by any of the acts of Congress. For these and other reasons it is thought best that support of these measures shall be included in the oath; and it is believed the Executive may lawfully claim it in return for pardon and restoration of forfeited rights, which he has clear constitutional power to withhold altogether, or grant upon the terms which he shall deem wisest for the public interest.[9]

There was certainly a lenient dimension to this first comprehensive Reconstruction policy of Lincoln's. He was trying an experiment to see whether easy terms would create an incentive for significant numbers of rebels to return to their allegiance. This would shrink the size of Confederate armies, undermine the authority of the Richmond regime, and shorten the war.

So much for the genuinely lenient or easy-going nature of Lincoln's famous Ten Percent Plan. But the hidden dimension of the plan was not lenient or permissive at all. It was high-handed action designed to facilitate the swift conversion of slave states into free states. It was nothing less than a strategic ploy that would hurry along the conversion process in Louisiana and elsewhere.

The loyalty oath that the penitent rebels had to swear would commit them—so help them God—to support emancipation. Any rebel who could not take this oath in the presence of God would be left out of Reconstruction. One had to take the oath if he wished to be a part of the electorate.

In other words, southerners who refused to recognize emancipation *would not be able to vote.* The electorate in the former Confederate states would consist entirely of anti-slavery whites. *Only the opponents of slavery would be allowed to vote in these states.* And *it would not take very many of them*—only 10 percent—to overpower the wishes of a 90 percent pro-slavery majority. Does the tricky dimension in Lincoln's Reconstruction policy now become clear?

It was a way to force fast abolition in approximately half a dozen slave states before the 1864 election put everything at risk.

Of all the occasions in his life when Lincoln used cunning to outmaneuver opponents, this was a virtuoso performance. In some respects, his Ten Percent Plan was precisely the reverse of what it seemed. It looked like a measure of forgiveness. But it was also a high-handed scheme to force emancipation down the throats of white supremacist southerners.

Early in November, Lincoln asked Banks to report on the plans to enroll a new Louisiana electorate to summon a state constitutional convention. Banks reported that the plans had bogged down. "This disappoints me bitterly," Lincoln replied. "There is a danger, even now," he said, "that the adverse element seeks insidiously to pre-occupy the ground"— that "a few professedly loyal men shall draw the disloyal around them, and colorably set up a State government, repudiating the emancipation proclamation, and re-establishing slavery."

So hurry, Lincoln told his agent Banks—work quickly and "lose no more time."[10] Banks would only have to enroll a mere tenth of Louisiana's

1860 voters to outmaneuver the advocates of slavery under the terms of Lincoln's Ten Percent Plan.

After Chattanooga, there was much talk in Washington about General Grant and how to use his talents. Grant realized that he had done very well for the country and himself, so he thought expansively about securing a larger role for himself in the overall war effort. He sent proposals up the chain of command—proposals relating to the issues of strategy that Lincoln was facing.

Halleck was cooperative. There appears to have been a transformation in General Halleck. He had started out as a sterile and treacherous bureaucrat, too feckless to do any good. But he slowly became a useful go-between for Lincoln to employ in his communications with field commanders. And it appears that Halleck was gradually becoming impressed by the total-war conceptions of Lincoln. The process was slow but unmistakable. So by the winter of 1864 he was ready to contribute to the execution of Lincoln's ideas. His previous jealousy of Grant was put aside.

In December, Grant proposed to take most of the army from east Tennessee and send it to New Orleans. From there, he would conduct an amphibious campaign against Mobile, Alabama. Grant also suggested that one of his own corps commanders should be given command in Virginia.

Grant entrusted these strategic proposals to a journalist named Charles A. Dana. Lincoln had used this reporter as an agent in the aftermath of Shiloh—as a source of undercover information. He told Dana to provide him with steady and reliable reports about the habits of Grant, whose critics claimed he was a drunkard. It was typical of Lincoln to use such methods to ascertain the truth when he could. He insisted on accuracy when he could get it.

Dana sent back glowing reports, and this enabled Grant to stage his come-back. Dana stayed with his army, and Grant came to trust this reporter's judgment almost as much as Lincoln did. So Grant sent his new proposals to Washington in the care of Dana.

Lincoln, Stanton, and Halleck discussed the proposals. Halleck reported to Grant that while the overall reaction was positive, the president was leery of stripping east Tennessee of so many troops.[11] Lincoln always did best-case and worst-case strategic planning simultaneously. He wanted to deploy his armies in a way that would permit them to switch from attack to defense, as the shifting contingencies and the behavior of the enemy might dictate. In the case of east Tennessee, he wanted to have enough force in the area to pursue the Confederates into Georgia while simultaneously guarding against a Confederate attempt to reassert control in Tennessee.

In January 1864, Grant modified some of his proposals in response to the feedback from Lincoln. Meanwhile, there was great talk in Washington about promoting Grant to general-in-chief. Much the wiser from experience, Halleck had no objections and behaved himself gracefully. He and Grant continued to correspond in January, when the scope of Grant's command of western armies was expanded to include the campaigns that were being conducted to the west of the Mississippi River.

On January 19, Grant made a big proposal for the eastern theater of the war. He proposed to send a force of sixty thousand by sea to conduct an invasion of North Carolina with the goal of cutting off supplies to Richmond.[12]

Halleck told Grant that in all probability Lincoln would reject the proposal. The troops for this campaign would have to be gathered at the expense of the Army of the Potomac, which would thus be diminished. And to weaken the Army of the Potomac might tempt Lee to strike at Washington. Besides, it was Lee's army, much more than Richmond, that constituted the proper target.[13]

One by one, Lincoln and the Radicals were lining up slave states to be converted into free states: the process was moving ahead in Louisiana, Tennessee, Missouri, Maryland, and Arkansas. Every state that could be subjected to this conversion—to be completed if possible before the next election—would subtract from the overall political strength of the institution of slavery. In December, Lincoln told Nathaniel Banks to "give us a free-state reorganization of Louisiana, in the shortest possible time."[14]

Since a Union attack was being planned in northern Florida, Lincoln sent John Hay to Florida with special instructions. Hay would follow up on the military operations by reorganizing the state per the terms of the Ten Percent Plan. To give Hay authority, Lincoln had him commissioned a major. Unfortunately, the military efforts in Florida would not be successful.

As this state-by-state assault upon slavery unfolded, Republicans took up the idea of amending the Constitution, as Lincoln had already suggested in his annual message to Congress in December 1862. A year later, Congressman James Ashley introduced an amendment that would outlaw slavery throughout the nation forever. Ashley introduced this Thirteenth Amendment in the House on December 14, 1863.

On January 11, 1864, Senator John B. Henderson of Missouri introduced a bill that called for a joint resolution on the amendment. The Senate Judiciary Committee, chaired by Lyman Trumbull, went to work. Charles Sumner and other Radicals pushed for expansive and open-ended wording in the draft of the amendment. They wanted to make this document as powerful as possible.

In Louisiana, Banks hit upon a plan for speeding up the free-state conversion. Since the effort to call a convention to amend the state's constitution was moving too slowly, Banks skipped the constitutional convention temporarily and ordered an election of state officers under the terms of the Ten Percent Plan. The elections were held on February 22, and the free state leader Michael Hahn was elected governor.

Free blacks in Louisiana had not been allowed to vote in these elections. On March 12, two of them—Arnold Bertonneau and Jean-Baptiste Roudanez—came to Washington and asked for a meeting with Lincoln. Their request was granted. They protested this denial of voting rights to African Americans in occupied Louisiana. Two days later, Lincoln wrote to Hahn and suggested that he think about phasing in voting rights for blacks. But he was to keep these efforts a secret for the time being.

"I congratulate you," Lincoln wrote, "on having fixed your name in history as the first free-state Governor of Louisiana. Now you are about to have a Convention which, among other things, will probably define the elective franchise." He continued in very careful language: "I barely suggest for your private consideration, whether some of the colored people may not be let in—as, for instance, the very intelligent and especially those who have fought gallantly in our ranks. They would probably help, in some trying time to come, to keep the jewel of liberty within the family of freedom. But this is only a suggestion, not to the public, but to you alone."[15]

The importance of this letter is overwhelming and it ought to be much better known. Here was a best-case possibility for post-war Reconstruction if Lincoln's work as a power orchestrator succeeded.

He was probing, as usual, the outer limits of the possible in advancing the revolution that he and the Radicals were leading, though in very different ways. Back in 1858, in the Lincoln-Douglas debates, he had said that "I have no purpose to introduce political or social equality between the white and black races." That was very tricky language, for the fact that he "had no purpose" *at the moment* was no guarantee that he might not embrace such a "purpose" sometime in the future.

And the time had arrived for beginning to explore that "purpose" when he wrote to Michael Hahn—to test the possibility of phasing in *political* equality for blacks. Of course he did this in secret. A year later, however, he would publicly endorse the idea and recommend the use of Louisiana as a model.

That recommendation would be duly noted by John Wilkes Booth and many others.

As he wrote to Hahn, Lincoln brought his experiment with "colonization" to an end. He sent a vessel to the colony at Île-à-Vache and brought the African American colonists back to America. He did it quietly.

In public, he continued to work to shape public opinion on the race issue. He gave a speech in Baltimore on April 18 in an effort to provide food for thought. He spoke about slavery, and likened himself to a shepherd protecting the sheep from the menace of wolves. "The world has never had a good definition of liberty," he began, "and the American people, just now, are much in want of one." He continued:

> With some the word liberty may mean for each man to do as he pleases with himself, and the product of his labor; while with others the same word may mean for some men to do as they please with other men, and the product of other men's labor. . . . The shepherd drives the wolf from the sheep's throat, for which the sheep thanks the shepherd as a liberator, while the wolf denounces him for the same act as a destroyer of liberty, especially as the sheep was a black one.[16]

Lincoln sent another agent to the South with a confidential mission in February. He directed a political general, Daniel Sickles, to "make a tour for me . . . by way of Cairo [Illinois] and New-Orleans, and returning by the Gulf and Ocean" to determine "what is being done, if anything, for reconstruction" and to "learn what you can as to the colored people—how they get along as soldiers, as laborers with their old masters, if there be such cases. Also learn what you can about the colored people within the rebel lines."[17]

For good reason many blacks were beginning to regard this white leader as "Moses." There was also good reason why some of them called him "Father Abraham."

A few days before Lincoln gave his speech in Baltimore, one of the worst atrocities of the war was perpetrated by Confederate troops under the command of General Nathan Bedford Forrest. Black troops were being used to garrison an installation on the banks of the Mississippi River in Tennessee, Fort Pillow. On April 12, Forrest's troops assaulted the fort and made its garrison surrender. After the African American troops had surrendered, the Confederates murdered them. Here was a war crime that would be worthy of the Nazi S.S., which would do the same thing to American servicemen after they surrendered in the Battle of the Bulge.

Forrest should have been hanged for this atrocity—before he went on to become one of the founders of the Ku Klux Klan. Here was graphic evidence of what was at stake in the election of 1864. What would happen to all the black soldiers if Lincoln were succeeded by a white-supremacist Democrat?

Lincoln's political position in the early months of 1864 was fairly strong. Many regarded his Proclamation of Amnesty and Reconstruction as a wise and judicious piece of work. The New York banker George Templeton Strong, whose observations were often astringent, wrote that "Uncle Abe is the most popular man in America today. . . . The weight of his personal character may do a great deal toward restoration of our national unity."[18]

Charles Eliot Norton concurred. "Once more," he wrote, "we rejoice that Abraham Lincoln is President." He and others made a point of praising the tone that Lincoln used in his message to Congress and Reconstruction Proclamation. "Lincoln will introduce a new style into state papers," Norton wrote; "he will make them sincere, and his honesty will compel even politicians to like virtue."[19] In a similar vein, Harriet Beecher Stowe wrote that Lincoln's messages "more resembled a father's talks to his children than a state paper. And they have had that relish and smack of the soil, which is a greater power in writing than the most artful devices of rhetoric."[20]

What Stowe and Norton failed to realize was that Lincoln's conversational tone was *precisely* one of his most "artful devices of rhetoric." When he wished to conceal a maneuver and give himself cover, his pose of innocence and candor was admirably suited to the purpose. This was one more feature of the overall genius that Lincoln displayed in so many of the things he said and did.

One of the people who was forcefully taken with Lincoln's achievements was the artist Francis Bicknell Carpenter. A painter who specialized in presidential portraits, he proposed an ambitious new painting: a depiction of the cabinet meeting when Lincoln first revealed his Emancipation Proclamation.

He arranged a meeting with Lincoln on February 6, and when Lincoln agreed to the project, Carpenter moved into the White House to work on it. As he labored on sketches of Lincoln and his cabinet members, he chatted with them. Later he produced an important book of reminiscences about these conversations.

Carpenter's painting, entitled "First Reading of the Emancipation Proclamation of President Lincoln," was finished by summer, and a private viewing was held in the State Dining Room on July 12. Carpenter had used this room as his studio. Afterward, the painting was exhibited to the public in the East Room.

Before Carpenter came to stay at the White House, Lincoln entertained another visitor, his sister-in-law Emilie Hardin Helm, whose husband—a Confederate officer—was killed at Chickamauga. After burying her husband, she made her way to Fortress Monroe and she telegraphed Lincoln in the hope that he could help her get back to Kentucky. Lincoln summoned her to Washington.

She stubbornly refused to abandon her Confederate loyalties, and as news of her visit leaked out, there was trouble for Lincoln. But he allowed the visit to continue, and for good reason. It gave Mary and Emilie a chance to commune about the loss of their loved ones. Mary continued to suffer from bouts of depression as she thought about her lost boy Willie. She saw Willie's ghost in her dreams, she reported, and she worried about Lincoln's health. She was also concerned about her eldest son Robert, who wished to take a break from his studies at Harvard and enlist in the army.[21]

Lincoln was keenly aware that his eldest son was conspicuously absent from military service. Mary kept saying she would never agree to let Robert enlist, for to lose another son would be more than she could bear. Lincoln did his best to convince her that they had to face up to this reality as thousands of other Americans were doing, but his wife refused to back down. So he dropped the matter.

In February, another kind of personal tragedy struck the Lincolns: the horses that belonged to their children were killed when the stable in which they were living caught fire. Flames appeared in the darkness outside of the White House on the evening of February 10. When told that the stable was burning, Lincoln bolted into action. A White House guard named Thomas W. McBride recalled that

> those of us who were on the ground saw a tall and hatless man come running from the direction of the White House. When he reached the boxwood hedge that served as an enclosure to the stables he sprang over it like a deer. As he approached the stable he inquired if the horses had been taken out. On learning that they had not, he asked impatiently why they had not, and with his own hands burst open the stable door. A glance within showed that the whole interior of the stable was in flames, and that the rescue of the horses was impossible. Notwithstanding this, he would apparently have rushed in had not those standing around caught and restrained him. It suddenly occurred to some one that possibly the stables had been fired for the purpose of bringing him out of the White House and giving an opportunity to assassinate him. Captain Bennett, of the Union Light Guard, and some others immediately hurried him into the White House.

Lincoln was overcome with sorrow. McBride later saw him in the East Room, "looking at the still burning stable and weeping. . . . His son Willie had died a short time before. He was his father's favorite, and the stable contained a pony that had belonged to the dead boy. The thought of his dead child had come to his mind as soon as he learned the stables were on fire, and he had rushed out to try to save the pony from the flames."[22]

Lincoln indulged little Tad and the two of them grew steadily closer. On the day before the stables burned, the famous photograph of Lincoln reading to Tad from a story book was produced at the Brady studio.

Even though Lincoln's popularity was high in the aftermath of the recent military victories, his chances of being elected to a second presidential term were far from certain. The anger of the Radical Republicans was being rekindled by the presidential aspirations of Salmon P. Chase.

Seward's jealousy toward Lincoln peaked and then crested in 1861. But Chase's jealousy was growing. By October 1863, according to the diary of Bates, Chase was using patronage to build up a formidable cadre of supporters in the treasury department.

Moreover, he cultivated Radical Republicans and inflamed their impatience with Lincoln. Chase endorsed the principle of black voting rights, and some Radicals had come to believe that their agenda might be advanced more quickly under Chase's leadership than under Lincoln's. Moderate and conservative Republicans were encouraged to believe that the end of the war would come sooner with a more energetic and determined man at the helm.

Charles Sumner—so imbued with confidence when he wrote back in 1862 about the "promise for the future" that Lincoln's leadership was providing—opposed another Lincoln term. Sumner was pushing the "state suicide" theory that he, along with Thaddeus Stevens and others, had propounded in 1862. Under this theory, Congress had the power to treat the conquered rebel states as territories and to reconstruct them from the top down and from the bottom up.

Though Lincoln signed bills in the spring of 1864 granting equal pay to black soldiers, allowing black witnesses to testify in federal courts, and outlawing segregation in the streetcar system of Washington, D.C., the Radicals wanted more and they wanted it quickly. Their initial approval of the Ten Percent Plan was being subjected to severe second thoughts in the early months of 1864.

Ashley was pushing his Thirteenth Amendment, which was quickly becoming his priority. He also introduced a bill on reconstruction in basic accord with Lincoln's Ten Percent Plan, while adding some provisions that would guarantee black voting rights and disfranchise former Confederates. This legislation was referred to a new House Committee on Reconstruction. By summer, this committee would be flatly opposed to Lincoln's Ten Percent Plan.

Chase's cultivation of the Radicals had been going on for a long time. He did it before the cabinet crisis of December 1862, and in the final months of 1863 he claimed again that the cabinet was riven by disunity and that Lincoln was a second-rate leader. On November 26, he lamented that Lincoln was "purposeless," and that there "must be a change in the White House."[23] In December, he wrote that he did not object to the fact that certain people were beginning to mention his name as a possible successor to Lincoln.

Lincoln knew about these machinations. He privately compared his treasury secretary to "a bluebottle fly" who lays "his eggs in every rotten spot he can find."[24]

In January, Chase announced publicly that he was available for the Republican nomination. A Chase-for-president organization was set up under the leadership of Senator Samuel Pomeroy of Kansas. Republican supporters of Chase ran the gamut from Radicals like Ashley to Conservatives like John Sherman. One of the subtler assets in Chase's possession was his daughter, Kate Chase Sprague. A strikingly beautiful woman, Kate would serve as the new first lady in a Chase administration since her father was a widower. She cut a winsome figure compared to Mary Todd Lincoln.

Lincoln's supporters urged him to take effective action to thwart the activities of Chase. Joseph Medill told him that "without your own assistance the efforts of your friends won't avail much. You have it in your power by a few simple moves on the chess board to defeat the game of your rivals."[25] Shelby Collum observed to Lincoln that everyone in Washington seemed to have turned against him. Lincoln replied that "it was not quite so bad as that," and then he flourished a list of the members of Congress that he was using to keep track of the "Chase Boom."[26]

Things came to a head in February, when a document known as the "Pomeroy Circular" appeared. The circular stated that Chase had "more of the qualities needed in a President during the next four years than are combined in any other available candidate," and it proclaimed that Lincoln could not be re-elected.[27] Sherman sent out copies of this document to his Ohio constituents and newspapers published it on February 20.

But the Pomeroy Circular backfired. Sherman was deluged with complaints when his constituents noticed that he mailed it out using his senatorial frank. Republican fence-sitters were impelled to play it safe when accused of complicity with an act that was treacherous or at the very least tasteless.

And Lincoln used his own political operatives—especially the members of the Blair family—to coordinate campaigns for his renomination in the state Republican conventions. He even got Simon Cameron, back from Russia after a very brief interlude as ambassador, to orchestrate Republican support in Pennsylvania.

After newspapers published the Pomeroy Circular, Chase offered to resign. Lincoln refused to accept this resignation, telling Chase that he had not read the circular and had no intention of doing so. Meanwhile, endorsements from the state party conventions rolled in. At last, after Ohio Republicans vowed to support Lincoln's renomination, Chase withdrew and the "Chase Boom" was over.

Though Lincoln had won, there was still a considerable amount of restlessness among Republicans who wanted a different candidate. One of the people who was being mentioned in this connection was Ulysses S. Grant. Indeed, some Democrats were trying to recruit this latest military hero as their own nominee.

In December, Congressman Elihu Washburne introduced a bill to revive the rank of lieutenant general—a rank that had only been held in the U.S. Army by George Washington and Winfield Scott—and bestow it on Grant.

Lincoln knew about the conversations regarding Grant in connection with the presidency, and he adopted a pose that was as nonchalant as the one he had used in the Chase Boom. If Grant "could be more useful than I in putting down the rebellion," Lincoln declared, "I would be quite content. He is fully committed to the policy of emancipation and employing negro soldiers; and with this policy faithfully carried out, it will not make much difference who is President."[28]

Privately, though, he was concerned, so he persuaded Washburne to ascertain whether Grant had political ambitions. "No man knows," Lincoln said, "when that presidential grub gets to gnawing at him, just how deep it will get until he has tried it; and I didn't know but what there was one gnawing at Grant."[29]

To Lincoln's relief, Grant disavowed presidential aspirations.

It was just as well, because Grant did not possess the kind of gifts that made Abraham Lincoln a statesman. In a curious episode in 1862, Grant issued an order barring Jews from doing business with the army. Such intolerance was not at all unusual at the time, especially among people who were influenced by the Know-Nothing movement in the 1850s. Jews, Catholics, and people of Irish and German descent were all targets for American nativists in the mid-nineteenth century. Grant's prejudice was mild compared to that of others, but it was revealing.

Grant's order brought a protest from Jews who sent a delegation to meet with Lincoln. They said they had "come unto Father Abraham for protection." And "this protection they shall have," Lincoln said as he rescinded Grant's order.[30] The president told Rabbi Isaac M. Wise that he "knows of no distinction between Jew and Gentile," and "that he feels no prejudice against any nationality." That was perfectly consistent with the stance that he had taken in opposing the Know-Nothings before the war.

But Wise also got the sense that Lincoln somehow "manifested a peculiar attachment" to those of Jewish birth.[31] It would have been consistent with the distinctly Old Testament emphasis of his late-blooming spirituality.

After receiving the news about Grant's lack of interest in presidential politics, Lincoln summoned him. Grant would be promoted, Lincoln said, not only to lieutenant general but also to general-in-chief, replacing Halleck, who would thereafter serve as Grant's chief of staff. Grant arrived in Washington on March 8, and he checked into Willard's Hotel. Then he went to the White House for a public reception that Lincoln had arranged in his honor.

Lincoln waited with the crowd in the East Room. He greeted Grant upon his arrival and shook him by the hand. Though shy on public occasions, Grant tried to gratify the interest of the White House guests, who crowded up to him en masse. Lincoln asked Seward to introduce Grant to Mary Lincoln.

After the reception, Lincoln talked to Grant about the ceremony to be held the following day: the ceremony when Grant would receive his promotion to lieutenant general. The ceremony would be memorable. After Lincoln conferred the promotion, the general replied that it would be his "earnest endeavor not to disappoint your expectations."[32]

Lincoln conferred with Grant during March and April as they worked out plans for a spring offensive. After Lincoln (via Halleck) over-ruled Grant's initial proposals for campaigns against Mobile and North Carolina, the president tried to appear deferential. He told Grant that "he did not pretend to know anything about the art of war, and it was with the greatest reluctance that he ever interfered with the movements of army commanders."[33] But Lincoln was not at all reluctant to exercise his natural talent for strategy. On this occasion he was simply trying to bolster Grant's morale.

In reality, he was pressing for a well-grounded meeting of minds with Grant. In the course of the discussions, Lincoln deftly made his wishes clear. Grant had promised not to disappoint Lincoln's expectations, since he knew very well that the president had a very definite set of expectations.

One of them was speed of movement. "Celerity," he observed to Grant, was "absolutely necessary." Another expectation was coordination of the armies' movements to orchestrate the use of force. All of the Union armies would have to move simultaneously under Grant's direction.

Lincoln had no trouble in securing Grant's agreement to these principles. The third and final expectation was to move against the armies of the enemy decisively and take them out of action.

After the war, Grant would reminisce that Lincoln had given him complete discretion in the 1864 campaign. That was not really true. Lincoln had enough confidence in Grant to let him handle *the specifics*, but he stayed ever watchful and Grant himself made sure to keep the president informed.

The two men agreed upon the following overall campaign.

The Army of the Potomac would strike at Lee's army and force it to surrender—or wipe it out. Grant developed a very neat solution to the problem of George Gordon Meade: he would ride along with Meade's army. He would establish his headquarters in the field. Grant thus became the new commander of the Army of the Potomac, though Meade remained in titular command. The army had been reinforced, and its troop strength was approximately 120,000.

In March, Grant established his headquarters in Culpeper Court House, Virginia. He rode back to Washington once a week to confer with Lincoln.

Other forces would be used in Virginia. These campaigns would be led by political generals whose followers needed to be courted for the coming presidential campaign. General Franz Sigel would occupy the Shenandoah Valley, then move toward Richmond. Benjamin Butler would advance toward Richmond from Fortress Monroe and cut the railroad links below Richmond that supplied Lee's army.

Meanwhile, the Union forces in the West, under Sherman, would move into Georgia. In addition to defeating the Confederate army—the army that retreated from Chattanooga—Sherman would strike toward Atlanta, with its vital rail connections, and do whatever was needed to take this important rebel stronghold out of the war. Sherman's army had been reinforced to approximately 112,000.

Finally, the Army of the Gulf under Banks would complete its ongoing military tasks and begin another operation. In January, Banks had begun to advance up the Red River toward Shreveport with the further objective of striking into Texas. One of the ancillary goals was to make a demonstration of force that would be felt in Mexico. Emperor Napoleon III of France had landed troops in Mexico—to collect some debts owed to France—and had set up a puppet regime under the nominal rule of an Austrian Archduke, Maximilian Ferdinand. The Confederates pledged to cooperate with France in return for the recognition of the Confederacy.

But Banks's Red River campaign would turn out to be a failure. In any case, Grant wanted Banks to finish the operation so the Army of the Gulf could be given a very different task: a campaign to take Mobile, Alabama, which Grant continued to regard as a worthy objective.

Here was the grand design that Lincoln and Grant worked out in the month of April. Lincoln told Hay that at last all the Union forces would be working together in the way he had always envisioned. He was "powerfully reminded," Hay wrote, of "his old suggestion so constantly made and so constantly neglected, to Buell & Halleck et al to move at once upon the enemy's whole line so as to bring into action to our advantage our great superiority in numbers." Grant's stated intention was "to make all the line useful—those not fighting could help the fighting." Lincoln said at one point as he was listening to Grant, "those not skinning can hold a leg."[34]

Significantly, Grant decided to reduce the number of troops defending Washington—in order to augment the size of the Army of the Potomac—and Stanton objected. The men took the issue to Lincoln, who decided to defer to Grant. Maybe Lincoln believed that the nation's capital would still be sufficiently protected since the army of Grant would remain between Washington and Richmond—positioned to attack or defend as needed, to serve as both a shield and a spearhead.

Robert E. Lee would take advantage of this situation later.

Lincoln's chances of prevailing at the Republican National Convention—scheduled in Baltimore during the first week in June—were improved when both Chase and Grant had been ruled out as rivals. But his troubles in the quest for the Republican nomination were far from over. Radical Republicans were flirting with some other candidates and wily Democrats were poised to take advantage of this situation.

Some of the Radicals had worked themselves into a state of such exasperation with Lincoln that nothing he could do was enough for them. What they failed to understand was how useful—and how necessary—his brand of leadership could be for themselves and the cause they espoused in a political situation that was fraught with danger.

Radical impatience for dramatic results was understandable, and Lincoln often observed that the Radicals were visionaries whose agitation was moving the country ahead. He tried to work in synergistic partnership with them. But as Lincoln gave credit to the Radicals, few of them returned the compliment.

The chief difference between Lincoln and the Radicals was their sense of political *timing* in relation to the worst-case contingencies that might threaten to undo their achievements. Lincoln had foreseen all the dangers of the 1864 election. He saw that military setbacks and war weariness could put a white supremacist Democrat in power. Consequently, he played his cards carefully. He sought to advance the social revolution that he and the Radicals were leading by practicing discretion as long as the volatile events of election year 1864 were still in play. He wanted to protect the Republicans' achievements.

But that was not the way that many of the Radicals saw things.

They began to play up to the ambitions of General Benjamin Butler and former General John C. Frémont. Butler was admired by the Radicals as the man who had refused to return the runaway slaves back in 1861 and who had put the defiant rebel city of New Orleans under stern and punitive rule. Frémont was lionized as the first Republican presidential candidate and the man who had boldly proclaimed emancipation in Missouri in August 1861.

Butler and Frémont enjoyed the admiration of the Radicals. But it was Frémont who posed the more serious threat to the renomination prospects of Lincoln. At a meeting in New York City on March 18, some dissident Republicans had launched a Frémont Campaign Club. Horace Greeley made a speech at this meeting—a speech recommending that the Republican national convention should be postponed.

The angriest Radicals rejected the idea of postponing their showdown with Lincoln. Reformers of all persuasions joined with these Radicals and vented their frustration with Lincoln in the springtime of 1864. "Let Abe finish up his jokes in Springfield," declared the angry feminist Elizabeth Cady Stanton, and let the Republicans put "Butler or Frémont . . . on their platform for the next President." She said, "We have had enough of 'Nero fiddling in Rome' in times like these, when the nation groans in sorrow, & mothers mourn their first born."[35]

Wendell Phillips wrote that "Old Abe is more cunning & slow than ever," that he "wishes to save slaveholders as much loss & trouble as he can."[36] It was time for a change, Phillips said, time to nominate a candidate who would carry out a bold campaign for reform. Even former Lincoln allies like Pennsylvania Governor Andrew Curtin and Massachusetts Governor John A. Andrew were becoming enthusiastic about the prospect of a Frémont candidacy.

On May 4, a "people's provisional committee" called for a convention in Cleveland to launch a new political party. Frederick Douglass supported this movement.

Meanwhile, pressure from the opposite side of the spectrum kept bearing in upon Lincoln. In March, a delegation of Kentucky conservatives came to the White House with the usual set of complaints: that Lincoln was needlessly radicalizing a war that should be fought for Union only. It bears noting that black soldiers were being recruited in Kentucky for the first time.

Lincoln's reply made a very strong impression on one of the delegates, an editor named Albert G. Hodges. So Hodges asked Lincoln to record what he told them, and to send him a copy in the mail. Some of Lincoln's most memorable—and subtle—observations on the war were contained in this letter.

Lincoln admitted he had always abominated slavery: "If slavery is not wrong," he wrote, "nothing is wrong," and he could "not remember when I did not so think, and feel." And yet he had "never understood that the Presidency conferred upon me an unrestricted right to act officially upon this judgment and feeling." Note the qualifying term: "*unrestricted.*"

He said all of his actions on slavery were meant to defend the Constitution. Since striking out at slavery would weaken the rebellion, he did so when no other course of action would suffice.

He claimed that it was only his duty to the nation that prompted him to lay "a strong hand upon the colored element." By freeing and arming the slaves, Lincoln said, the loyal people of the nation gained "a hundred and thirty thousand soldiers, seamen, and laborers."

Let any man who challenges the wisdom of these policies "test himself by writing down in one line that he is for subduing the rebellion by force of arms; and in the next, that he is for taking these hundred and thirty thousand men from the Union side, and placing them where they would be but for the measure he condemns."

After setting forth these justifications, Lincoln turned to the complaints that he had acted unconstitutionally. Here is where his letter to Hodges makes extremely interesting reading.

He had sworn to "preserve, protect, and defend the Constitution of the United States." But defending the Constitution in a time of civil war was much trickier business than it seemed. He said that his oath to defend the Constitution "imposed upon me the duty of preserving, by every indispensable means, that government—that nation—of which the constitution was the organic law."

Then he continued: "Was it possible to lose the nation, and yet preserve the constitution? By general law life *and* limb must be protected; yet often a limb must be amputated to save a life; but a life is never wisely given to save a limb. I felt that measures, otherwise unconstitutional, might become lawful, by becoming indispensable to the preservation of the constitution, through the preservation of the nation. Right or wrong, I assumed this ground, and now avow it."

Here was a breathtaking commentary on Lincoln's audacity on constitutional issues. This was more than just an exercise in architectonic thinking—in relating the parts to the whole. It was nothing less than intellectual alchemy.

In truth, it was the *Declaration of Independence* that Lincoln revered as the nation's founding document. The nation, *as imbued with the purposes and principles of Jefferson*, was for Lincoln the real supreme law. The Constitution, though important, was a package of derivative and mutable procedures of law that were easily manipulated one way or another—twisted through interpretation, construed according to the whims and inclinations of the nation's packed Supreme Court.

Lincoln's constitutional thinking was influenced during the war by a book that was written by a Boston abolitionist named William Whiting. This book, *The War Powers of the President*, appeared in 1862, and Lincoln obtained a copy and pondered its arguments with care. Whiting presented an argument for the expansive use of presidential power. It was of course no accident that Lincoln sent Whiting to the war department as solicitor.

More and more, the president decided he would judge for himself what was "constitutional" in this time of unprecedented crisis—subject, of course, to the constraints of the judicial process. Hence the striking proposition in his letter to Hodges that "measures, otherwise unconstitutional, might become lawful" to save the Constitution by saving the nation that gave the Constitution its meaning.

If the nation went down, who would care very much whether every constitutional procedure had been strictly upheld?

Lincoln closed this letter with a soon-to-be famous observation that requires careful reading since it raises some delicate issues. "I claim not to have controlled events," Lincoln wrote, "but confess plainly that events have controlled me." This observation was a prelude to one of his openly religious meditations.

"Now," Lincoln wrote, "at the end of three years struggle the nation's condition is not what either party, or any man devised, or expected. God alone can claim it. Whither it is tending seems plain. If God now wills the removal of a great wrong, and wills also that we of the North as well as you of the South, shall pay fairly for our complicity in that wrong, impartial history will find therein new cause to attest and revere the justice and goodness of God."[37]

Lincoln fervently believed what he was saying as a matter of spiritual *feeling*. He searched his own soul in regard to the providential meaning of the war. And in *practical* terms, he could attest to the fact that it was "all in God's hands" when he had reached the outer limits of his power. Lincoln's plans would come to nothing if events spun out of his control. Even Machiavellian strategists must sometimes simply cross their fingers and *hope*.

Lincoln knew this. But he also knew that he would go on using all the wits that God gave him to shape events as best he could. And to invoke the will of God—to claim that it was God as opposed to himself or any other human agent—who controlled the events of the war was a clever thing to say to Kentucky conservatives who hated the work that both Lincoln and the Radicals were doing.

Lincoln's statement regarding the providence of God was remarkable for this reason: he was being both "sincere" and "insincere" on this occasion *at the same time*. He believed what he was saying in a great many ways, but he also said it to be crafty. He believed that God's providence was guiding events and yet his work as a strategist continued.

He was playing a game with the Kentucky delegation, but he also meant some of what he told them.

He could only hope and pray that the results that he intended were indeed what the Lord was demanding. Like many who have struggled with the issues of theology, he thought about "destiny" versus "contingency," the omnipotence of God in relation to the feeling of human "free will." As he struggled so shrewdly with politics, his mind was absorbed in metaphysics—up in the clouds. Through it all, he reflected on mortality, the transience of life, both his own and the lives of many others. There was so much death to be accounted for.

On April 26, he was photographed in his office by Anthony Berger, one of Mathew Brady's assistants. The pictures have a ghostly quality about them because of the limited light in the room. He looks faded, like a being who may quickly melt away.

He had less than a year to live. Is it possible to gaze upon these pictures with tranquility in light of that?

On April 30, Grant was ready to lead the Army of the Potomac into battle with the Army of Northern Virginia and continue the attack until Lee's army was destroyed. Of significance to Lincoln was the fact that some African American troops would be participating in the battle. As they marched in review past the White House, Lincoln looked at them from a balcony. They cheered, and he bowed in response.

Lincoln wrote to Grant, expressing his "entire satisfaction with what you have done up to this time, so far as I understand it. The particulars of your plans I neither know, or seek to know. You are vigilant and self-reliant; and, pleased with this, I wish not to obtrude any constraints or restraints upon you."[38] Grant replied that he was honored by the confidence of Lincoln and grateful for all of the support he had received from the administration. He pointedly assured the president that if his plans did not succeed, "the fault is not with you."[39]

Everyone knew the importance of the coming campaign. It was crucial for Lincoln and his cause. Grant knew that time was of the essence. He had to force a wide-open battle with Lee—a battle where the powerful resources of the Army of the Potomac would be used for maximum effect. If Lee's army could be beaten before the Republican convention—or at least by the Fourth of July—all would surely be well.

Lincoln of course was in a state of great tension, and he sought to relieve it with his time-tested forms of relaxation. One night he was reading some selections by the English humorist Thomas Hood—a poet who had written and published a generation earlier—and he found them so good that he wandered down the corridor in nightshirt and slippers to seek out Nicolay and Hay. Then he read them the selection that tickled him the most: a piece entitled "An Unfortunate Bee-ing."

Lincoln augmented the stock of his humorous stories by reading aloud from the compositions of others. Sometimes he did it on the eve of important events to dissipate anxiety. When he revealed to his cabinet that he would issue the Emancipation Proclamation, he opened the cabinet meeting by reading them a selection from Artemus Ward's "A High-Handed Outrage at Utica." He also enjoyed the work of the humorist David Ross Lock, who adopted the pen name Petroleum Vesuvius Nasby.

Lincoln's detractors loved to pillory him as a man who injected low humor into bad situations. It would be interesting to know whether critics such as these ever lightened their own mental loads with a dose of good-natured humor.

On May 5, Grant plunged into battle with Lee in a spot that was adjacent to Chancellorsville. The armies collided in the densely forested tract that was known as "The Wilderness." As the battle raged, there was no news at all from the front, so Lincoln sought to distract himself—to relax in any way he could. One night he went to the theater to take his mind off the battle.

The battle of the Wilderness was a slaughter that was made more horrific by the fact that the woods caught fire from the intensity of shooting. Many perished in the flames. The casualties from this fight were so dreadful that some of the men in Grant's army presumed they would soon be retreating since the battle was more of a defeat for the Union than a stand-off.

But Grant had no intention of retreating. He decided to move around Lee's army to force him out into open ground. And that was exactly the kind of performance that Lincoln had always demanded from generals like McClellan, Hooker, and Meade. Now he had a commander who would keep on fighting and employ resourceful tactics as he did so.

On May 9, Grant sent the president a wire to explain what had happened. "I intend to fight it out on this line if it takes all summer," Grant wrote. Lincoln approved of Grant's attitude. "It is the dogged pertinacity of Grant that wins," he observed to John Hay.[40]

But Lincoln (like Grant) was appalled by the casualties, stricken by the magnitude of carnage. "Why do we suffer reverses," he asked Schuyler Colfax. "Could we have avoided this terrible, bloody war? Was it not forced upon us? Is it never to end?"[41]

That was the kind of reaction that Robert E. Lee wished to get from Lincoln and the public. For Confederate strategy would soon become obvious: they would fight a ghastly war of attrition, obstruct Union armies, force sickening casualties, and drag things out in the hope that the stalemate would ruin the morale of northern voters and destroy the Republicans' chances in the 1864 elections. They would stall until the clock ran out on Lincoln's presidency. They would put a white supremacist in power.

Was this to become the quintessence of Robert E. Lee's contribution to American history? Lee was hardly alone: the same strategy would be used by the new Confederate commander in Georgia, Joseph Johnston. The tactic of both of these commanders was to "dig in," retreat behind trenches, refuse to engage in open battle. The result was the same kind of warfare that would cause so many millions of casualties on the western front in World War I.

As soon as Lee realized that Grant was on the move, he acted quickly to dig in and block him. He knew that his army, not Richmond, was the target, and he knew this was a fight to the death.

So he would mete out all the death he could.

Grant attacked Lee's entrenchments at a place called Spotsylvania Courthouse. The fighting raged from May 8 until May 20, and the result was what Lee intended: more stalemate, with huge loss of life. Undaunted, Grant tried to move around Lee's army again, and the fighting resumed at the North Anna River from May 23 to 26. The result was just another deadlock.

The peripheral attacks in Virginia that were designed to put additional pressure on Lee—enough pressure to throw him off his balance and bring him out into the open—had also been failing. Franz Sigel in the Shenandoah Valley was defeated by Confederate forces in the battle of New Market on May 15, and Lincoln soon replaced him with David Hunter, who would also find himself stymied. Meanwhile, the forces under Benjamin Butler that were marching toward Richmond got trapped by the rebels near Bermuda Hundred, where the James and the Appomattox Rivers joined.

Butler's thirty-three-thousand-man "Army of the James" had been ordered to cut the Richmond and Petersburg railroad, a key supply line for Lee's army. The campaign began on May 5. The Confederate defenders of Richmond—eighteen thousand strong and under the command of General Beauregard—outmaneuvered Butler and constructed a line of entrenchments that bottled up his army at Drewry's Bluff, at the outermost defenses of Richmond.

The Virginia campaign was going wrong.

So Lincoln's re-election was at greater risk than ever and Republican divisions got worse. Democrats pounced upon the chance to exploit these divisions to the full. And so Confederate strategy was working. Rebel leaders had known from the beginning they would have to depend upon external help to prevail. The Democrats could give them that help in the summer of 1864.

Rebel armies didn't need to prevail any longer; all they had to do was hang on. Northern Democrats could do the rest. The Confederacy would never be closer to achieving its goal of independence than it was in the summer of 1864.

On May 29, a new political party was founded in Cleveland: the "Radical Democracy" Party. Delegates included disaffected Radical Republicans, abolitionists like Frederick Douglass, reformers like Elizabeth Cady Stanton, and a mixed assortment of Democrats, some of whom were out to make mischief by widening Republican divisions. The Radical Democrats nominated Frémont. The party's platform was a strange amalgam of Radical Republican and Democratic principles. It endorsed the Thirteenth Amendment—passed by the Senate in April but stalled in the House of Representatives. Yet the platform echoed the standard Democratic complaints about Lincoln's "dictatorial" actions like suspension of habeas corpus.

Wendell Phillips, though not in attendance, wrote a letter that was read to the delegates. He urged them to endorse the candidacy of Frémont. But support for Frémont among the Radical Republicans and abolitionists was not universal. Lydia Maria Child called Frémont a "selfish unprincipled adventurer."[42] And William Lloyd Garrison broke with Wendell Philipps and urged abolitionists to unite behind the leadership of Lincoln. Garrison's opinion of Lincoln had been slowly but decisively improving.

As early as March, he endorsed Lincoln's re-election in his famous anti-slavery publication *The Liberator*. Lincoln, like every politician, said Garrison, was "open to criticism and censure," but there was "much to rejoice over and be thankful for" in the achievements of a man who "at one blow, severed the chains of three millions."[43] In another editorial written for the *Philadelphia Press*, Garrison admitted that Lincoln "might have done more," but only at the risk of "inciting civil war at the North, and overturning the government." Look at what Lincoln accomplished, he said, for it was undeniable that

> his Emancipation proclamation of January 1, 1863, liberated more than three-fourths of the entire slave population; that since that period, emancipation has followed in Maryland, Western Virginia, Missouri, and the District of Columbia, and is being rapidly consummated in Kentucky and Tennessee, thus terminating the holding of property in man everywhere under the American flag . . . that no rebel State can be admitted to the Union, except on the basis of complete emancipation . . . that free negro schools are following wherever the army penetrates.[44]

This was a stunning turn-about for Garrison, who in previous years had viewed Lincoln with as much contempt as Wendell Phillips.

But a significant number of Radicals were flocking to the banner of Frémont, and that was bad news for Lincoln's re-election chances. Not the least of its effects was to push the Republican Party in a more conservative direction. With so many Radical defections, party leaders reached out to the Unionist Democrats, hoping to gain enough cross-over votes to make up for the Republicans' schism.

Meanwhile, Democratic saboteurs could not resist the chance to use every tactic they could think of, including deceit, in their campaign to undermine Lincoln. On May 18, some Democratic newspapers published a fraudulent document purporting to be a presidential proclamation. It called for four hundred thousand more Union volunteers and it designated May 26 as a day of national fasting and humiliation in light of the slaughter occurring on the battlefields.

Lincoln drafted an order directing the war department to suppress these newspapers and arrest their editors. But he later rescinded the order.

Grant was running out of time if he wished to give Lincoln the fast and decisive victory that he needed. On June 3, he confronted the army of Lee at a place called Cold Harbor. He decided to attack before Lee slipped away into the vast defenses of Richmond. By 1864, there were almost 120 miles of fortifications surrounding the Confederate capital. This defensive line contained numerous forts and batteries, built largely by slave labor. Lee himself had supervised the construction of this line back in 1861. He was sometimes called the "King of Spades" for this work.

Cold Harbor was alarmingly close to the Richmond defenses. Grant did not intend to permit Lee to go any further. So he ordered a frontal assault on June 3 and the Confederates were ready. Lee's men were, as usual, entrenched. This decision by Grant was catastrophic. The Union suffered thousands of casualties in half an hour. Here was a repetition of the very same mistake that was committed by Burnside at Fredericksburg and by Lee when he ordered Pickett's Charge.

And the timing could not have been worse. The Republican national convention met in Baltimore only four days after Cold Harbor. In just one month, Grant had lost almost half of his army. "The immense slaughter of our brave men," wrote Gideon Welles, "chills and sickens us all."[45] Welles wrote that line in his diary the day *before* Cold Harbor.

A few weeks later, Lincoln said in a speech that the war had "carried mourning into every home" and that (paraphrasing Shakespeare) it could "almost be said that the 'heavens are hung with black.'"[46]

Lincoln was renominated, but the delegates in Baltimore were running very scared. Perhaps in light of the overall weakness of his situation, Lincoln chose to adopt a hands-off policy regarding the work of this convention, with one important exception: he told the party's chairman, Edwin D. Morgan, that he wanted the anti-slavery Thirteenth Amendment to be the keynote of the platform.

In light of the Radical defections to the candidacy of Frémont, the delegates moved in the opposite direction and adopted an ultra-cautious strategy designed to woo all patriotic Unionists, even Democrats. They made the decision to change the name of the Republican Party—at least for the duration of the 1864 campaign—to the National Union Party. And they dumped Vice President Hannibal Hamlin in order to substitute a Unionist Democrat as Lincoln's running mate.

Lincoln sent John Nicolay to attend the convention. He said that he would prefer to keep the 1860 Republican ticket intact, but he would not interfere in the matter. He told Nicolay that

> all of the various candidates and their several supporters being his friends, he deemed it unbecoming in him to advocate the nomination of any one of them; but that privately and personally he would be best pleased if the convention would renominate the old ticket that had been so triumphantly elected in 1860.[47]

That was not what the delegates did. They replaced the Republican Hamlin with Andrew Johnson, the Unionist War Democrat from Tennessee. Few political decisions in our history have had such momentous and terrible consequences as this one.

After Cold Harbor, Grant had to change his strategy. His attempts to move around Lee's army, to hit him from the rear, to get between his army and Richmond—to "turn Lee's flank," to use a military term—had come to grief, since the Confederate commander had parried every thrust. So Grant decided to take his army across the James River and conduct a quick strike against Petersburg, a key railroad junction that was vital to supplying both the army of Lee and the city of Richmond.

On June 14, Grant's army crossed over the James using transports as well as a 2,200-foot-long pontoon bridge. Lincoln approved of this maneuver, despite the fact that it contained a significant drawback: the Army of the Potomac would no longer stand between Washington and Richmond.

But Grant's overland campaign against Lee had been thwarted, so Lincoln was ready to approve of this drastic change of plans. When Grant successfully crossed over the James before Lee figured out what was happening, Lincoln sent Grant the following message: "I begin to see it. You will succeed. God bless you all."[48]

But the attack on Petersburg was botched by subordinates of Grant. They commenced the attack on June 15 and it continued for three days. The Confederate line was initially thin, and a bolder attack might have seized the city and forced Lee to fight without entrenching. But the Union commanders on the scene were too slow, and Lee bolstered the defenses of Petersburg before Grant's army could break through. By June 18, it was obvious to Grant that he would have to conduct a long siege—a siege that might last for many months, since there were fewer troops at his disposal. His troop strength was massively depleted.

Down in Georgia, Sherman was confronted by the same Confederate strategy: obstruction. Sherman's flanking maneuvers were deftly overcome by the rebels' commander, Joseph Johnston. Every time Sherman attempted to force the Confederate army out into the open, the rebels found a way to fall back to a new line of defenses.

Sherman tried one frontal attack at Kenesaw Mountain, to the north of Atlanta, but he suffered heavy losses, so he never launched another attack like that one in his Georgia campaign. He conserved his advantage in troop strength, but it did him little good in the short run.

On June 21, Lincoln visited the Army of the Potomac, telling Grant that "I just thought I would jump aboard a boat and come down and see you."[49] He had no intention of pressuring Grant to change tactics. He probably just wanted to get some relief from the emotional pressure through a temporary change of scene. The opportunity to chat informally with his like-minded top commander might do him some good.

Gustavus Vasa Fox was nervous in regard to Lincoln's safety as he made this trip. Confederate gunners could have trained their sights upon Lincoln's vessel from a number of different positions.

Grant encouraged Lincoln to inspect the black troops in his army in the course of this visit. Hundreds of African American soldiers crowded up to see him when he came to their camp. A reporter observed that when they cheered him, it "was a genuine spontaneous outburst of love and affection for the man they looked upon as their deliverer from bondage."[50] When Lincoln spoke to these troops, his voice was "so broken by emotion that he could scarcely articulate the words. . . . The scene was affecting in the extreme, and no one could have witnessed it unmoved."[51]

Lincoln's troubles with dissidence among his fellow Republicans continued. Chase had become almost terminally quarrelsome. No doubt chagrined by the fact that Frémont had usurped his place as the foremost challenger to Lincoln, Chase fumed and caused no end of trouble.

All through June he feuded with Lincoln over patronage appointments, and he kept on using the ploy of threatening to leave the cabinet to gain leverage. Lincoln decided that enough was enough, and he decided on June 29 to accept the resignation of Chase.

He sent him a short and dignified letter on June 30. "Of all I have said in commendation of your ability and fidelity, I have nothing to unsay," he wrote, "and yet you and I have reached a point of mutual embarrassment in our official relation which it seems can not be overcome, or longer sustained."[52]

To succeed Chase, he nominated a former governor of Ohio (Chase's home state), David Tod, but congressional Republicans, shocked by Chase's departure, expressed their disapproval, so Tod withdrew. Lincoln finally nominated Senator William Pitt Fessenden as Chase's successor.

On July 2, the congressional Republicans pushed through a bill on Reconstruction that was written by Senator Benjamin Wade and Representative Henry Winter Davis. The Wade-Davis measure was a challenge to Lincoln's Ten Percent Plan. More demanding in certain respects, it required a majority of the registered voters in an occupied state to take an oath of allegiance before elections could be held. And only the voters who were able to swear an "ironclad oath"—an oath to the effect that they had *never* supported the rebellion—could be delegates at a state constitutional convention or vote upon a new constitution for the state.

As to those constitutions, they had to disfranchise former Confederates, repudiate Confederate war debts, and abolish slavery. Such requirements were grounded in the Radicals' state suicide theory—the theory giving Congress complete and unrestricted power to reform rebel states. Only after these new constitutions had been ratified could the rebel state in question participate in federal elections.

Lincoln chose not to sign this bill, which meant that he had exercised a "pocket-veto." He issued a proclamation on July 8 to explain his reasons for doing so. He said again—as he had said in his previous message to Congress back in December—that he would keep an open mind regarding other plans for Reconstruction. In general terms, he was "unprepared to be committed to any single plan of restoration." For the time being, however, he would stick to his Ten Percent Plan, for it was very important to him to keep the free state experiments in Louisiana and elsewhere moving along.

The Wade-Davis bill would abort the conversion process that was turning those states into free states. Reconstruction in those states would have to start all over again, and Lincoln was opposed to that scenario. He wrote that he was "unprepared to declare, that the free-state constitutions and governments, already adopted and installed in Arkansas and Louisiana, shall be set aside and held for nought."

But he made a concession to the authors of the bill when he said that the plan it contained was "a very proper plan for the loyal people of any State choosing to adopt it."[53]

The response of the Radicals was shrill—to put it mildly. Thaddeus Stevens declared that Lincoln's message was an "infamous proclamation."[54] Wade and Davis co-authored a scathing manifesto proclaiming that Lincoln's action was a usurpation of congressional prerogative. The "authority of Congress is paramount," they wrote, and the president should therefore "obey and execute, not make the laws." They hinted at impeachment: the supporters of constitutional procedure should "consider the remedy for these usurpations, and, having found it, fearlessly execute it."[55]

From that point on, the opposition of Radicals to Lincoln's re-election became almost frantic. Henry Winter Davis urged Radicals and abolitionists to find some way to get both Lincoln and Frémont out of the race so that someone better could be found. Sumner wanted Lincoln to resign. Chase naturally participated in this dump-Lincoln movement.

Lincoln saw plainly that his re-election prospects were in serious jeopardy. "To be wounded in the house of one's friends is perhaps the most grievous affliction that can befall a man," he told Noah Brooks.[56]

Lee made Lincoln's problems even worse when he launched yet another invasion of the North. Fifteen thousand raiders under the command of General Jubal Early marched through the Shenandoah Valley to do what Lincoln had dreaded since the earliest days of the war: put the city of Washington in peril. A successful attack against Washington, D.C., might seal Lincoln's fate with the voters.

The Army of the Potomac was no longer positioned to defend the city since Grant had taken the army south of Richmond. And the garrison manning the defensive perimeter of Washington was perilously weak. A state of hysteria gripped Washingtonians as Early and his Confederate raiders drew closer.

Stanton told Lincoln and his family to leave the Soldiers' Home immediately and return to the White House. Gustavus Fox prepared a steamer on the Potomac to evacuate the Lincolns if it should prove necessary.

Lincoln's response to this crisis was brave but in some respects eerie. He showed no sign of alarm about the possibility that Early might break through the city's defenses and sack the nation's capital even though the forts in the Washington defense perimeter were manned by only a few thousand militiamen, regular troops, and volunteers.

As usual, he regarded the Confederate army as a *target* that he wanted his own troops to destroy.

Union forces were heading toward Washington already from Cumberland, Maryland, as well as from some other points to the west. Grant detached a whole corps from the Army of the Potomac and he sent it up the Chesapeake Bay to rescue Washington. On July 9—two days before the fighting near Washington began—Grant offered to come in person.

Lincoln sent a reply that appears to have been dashed off in haste: "Now what I think is that you should provide to retain your hold where you are certainly, and bring the rest with you personally, and make a vigorous effort to destroy the enemy's force in this vicinity. I think there is really a fair chance to do this if the movement is prompt."[57]

The Sixth Corps of the Army of the Potomac came to the defense of Washington in the nick of time. On July 11, the Confederates attacked Fort Stevens, one of the sixty-eight forts that McClellan had constructed to defend the city back in 1862. Lincoln rode out to Fort Stevens to observe the fighting in person.

All of a sudden, in the midst of the fighting, he climbed upon the earthen parapet of Fort Stevens and looked at the enemy as bullets whistled all around him. Many people have tried to make sense of this extraordinary act.

We can never be certain in regard to the reasons that prompted him to do such a dangerous thing. We know that everything he wanted to achieve—saving the Union, freeing the slaves, seeing to it that the hundreds of thousands of military heroes had not died in vain—was in danger and the emotional pressure of this situation was excruciating.

He had come to believe that God's Providence was guiding events, and he prayed that his work would succeed. He had given orders that resulted in the termination of lives—hundreds of thousands of lives—and he wondered sometimes if he could face the same prospect of death without weakening or flinching. And here was a chance to find out—to test golden rule ethics in a do-or-die situation.

Noah Brooks was convinced that this accounted for his recklessness at Fort Stevens. What he did was "ample proof that he would not have dropped his musket and run, as he believed he certainly would, at the first sign of physical danger."[58] Lincoln was hardly the only public figure in American history to have put himself in harm's way. Theodore Roosevelt would do the same thing in the Spanish-American War, but that was three years before he was president. Lincoln is the only sitting president to have knowingly put himself in danger in a war zone.

Early's troops withdrew from Fort Stevens and crossed back into Virginia. Lincoln was completely disgusted that they got away.

Lincoln's determination to face the accumulating crises resolutely was demonstrated all through July. On July 18, he called for another five hundred thousand troops even though he knew that this would give additional ammunition to his critics. Weeks later, he said that "we must either have men, or the war must stop; I shall issue the call, and if the old ship goes down, it will be with the colors flying."[59]

Union forces under General Horatio G. Wright pursued Early's raiders into Virginia. Early defeated them, then turned and crossed over the Potomac again into Maryland. He intended to create more havoc. On July 30, his troops burned Chambersburg, Pennsylvania, in retaliation— or so he said—for attacks upon private property by Union forces in the Shenandoah Valley.

Early's raiders achieved their objective of spreading despair in the North. In New York, George William Curtis wrote that "the sense of absurdity and humiliation is very universal. These things weaken the hold of the administration upon the people." He foresaw "a reaction which may culminate in November and defeat Lincoln."[60]

Early in July, Horace Greeley urged Lincoln to open peace negotiations with the rebels. "Our bleeding, bankrupt, almost dying country," he told the president, "longs for peace" and "shudders at the prospect of fresh conscriptions, of further wholesale devastations, and of new rivers of human blood. And a widespread conviction that the Government [is] not anxious for peace ... is doing great harm now, and is morally certain, if not removed, to do far greater in the approaching elections. ... I entreat you, in your own time and manner, to submit overtures for pacification to the Southern insurgents."[61]

Lincoln had no intention of doing what Greeley recommended. He remained as defiant as ever when he told a Philadelphia audience that "this war has taken three years [and] as far as my knowledge enables me to speak, I say we are going through on this line if it takes three years more."[62]

Greeley suggested to Lincoln that he send representatives to talk with some Confederate agents who had just arrived on the Canadian side of Niagara Falls. Lincoln knew what these agents were up to: they were sent to cause trouble in collusion with the northern Democrats. So he instructed Greeley to go on up and determine for himself if these people were really peace emissaries or *agents provocateurs*. When Greeley demurred, Lincoln sent John Hay to convince him.

Greeley made the trip, and he discovered that Lincoln was right. So he asked for further instructions. Seizing the opportunity to put himself on record as a proponent of peace—on the non-negotiable terms of Union *and* emancipation—Lincoln sent Greeley the following statement:

> Any proposition which embraces the restoration of peace, the integrity of the whole Union, and the abandonment of slavery, and which comes by and with an authority that can control the armies now at war against the United States, will be received and considered by the Executive Government ... and will be met by liberal terms on other substantial and collateral points; and the bearer or bearers thereof shall have safe conduct both ways.[63]

Lincoln hastened to broadcast the news that the Confederate agents in Niagara Falls had *not* been sent to negotiate. On July 25, he told the journalist Abram Wakeman that "the men of the South, recently (and perhaps still) at Niagara Falls, tell us distinctly that they are *not* empowered to offer terms of peace. Does any one doubt what they *are* empowered to do, is to assist in selecting and arranging a candidate and a platform for the Chicago [Democratic] convention?"[64]

Lincoln even found a way to get his hands on some of the inflammatory language these rebels had drafted for use by the Democratic Copperheads.

Here is a representative sentence: "The stupid tyrant who now disgraces the Chair of Washington and Jackson," they wrote, "could, any day, have peace ... only that he persists in the war merely to free the slaves."[65]

Democrats pounced upon Lincoln's "Niagara Manifesto" as proof that the Republicans had hijacked the war and turned it into an abolition crusade that was wrecking the country. Lincoln's determination to bind the cause of saving the Union with emancipation was ridiculed by white supremacists. They condemned him for it over and over in the summer of 1864. "Tens of thousands of white men must bite the dust to allay the Negro mania of the President," they ranted.[66]

Meanwhile, soldiers at Petersburg developed a plan to break through the rebels' defenses. They dug a tunnel, placed an enormous amount of gunpowder there, and exploded it under the Confederates' lines. But this surprise attack on July 30 was botched because the Union attackers were sent down into the crater that resulted from the blast instead of around it. The troops just milled around in the hole as Confederate sharpshooters killed them. The "Battle of the Crater" was nothing more than another disappointment—another embarrassment—for Lincoln.

On August 1, he met with Grant down at Fortress Monroe and they devised a plan to destroy the rebel raiders of Early. Grant decided that the troops pursuing Early should be led by his cavalry commander Philip Sheridan. Lincoln approved of this decision, and he instructed Grant to make sure that this campaign would be remorseless.

"I have seen your dispatch," Lincoln wrote, "in which you say 'I want Sheridan put in command of all troops in the field, with instructions to put himself South of the enemy, and follow him to the death.' This, I think, is exactly right [but] ... I repeat to you it will neither be done nor attempted unless you watch it every day, and hour, and force it."[67] Lincoln trusted Grant's judgment, but he wanted his commander to be tough on subordinates who bungled and let him down.

Grant would keep most of his forces at Petersburg and maintain the siege. "I have seen your dispatch expressing your unwillingness to break your hold where you are," the president said. "Neither am I willing. Hold on with a bull-dog grip, and chew & choke, as much as possible."[68]

By August, the evidence was rolling in from all over the North that the Confederate strategy was working. The defeatist reaction resulting from war-weariness, frustration, and shock at all the carnage was eroding Lincoln's re-election prospects so greatly that Republican despair was becoming near-universal.

Thurlow Weed declared that Lincoln's re-election was "an impossibility," and he expressed the hope that Lincoln would drop out of the race.[69] Leonard Swett believed that "unless material changes can be wrought, Lincoln's election is beyond all possible hope. It is probably clean gone now."[70] On August 19, a Republican meeting in New York proposed that a second Republican convention should be held in Cincinnati on September 28. The purpose would be to choose a different presidential candidate. On August 25, Frémont offered to withdraw from the race if Lincoln would do the same thing.

The Democratic convention was scheduled to meet in Chicago on August 29–31. Democrats stoked the flames of racial hatred for weeks in advance. Leading the mob was the *New York World*, a Democratic newspaper that received financial assistance from August Belmont, a rich New York banker who was chairman of the Democratic National Committee.

The editors of the *World* laid the groundwork for their 1864 campaign months earlier—in December of the previous year, when they produced a pamphlet advocating racial intermarriage. This pamphlet was written to look like the work of an unnamed abolitionist. But it was actually written by Democratic journalists who sent out copies of the pamphlet— anonymously—to Republicans, asking them to endorse it, suggest their own ideas about accelerating and encouraging inter-racial sex, and then send their reactions to a post-office box in New York. They were trying to set these Republicans up for a political slaughter. The title of the pamphlet was *Miscegenation: The Theory of the Blending of the Races, Applied to the American White Man and Negro.*

Democrats in Congress denounced "miscegenation" in the months that followed. They reviled the "negro-loving, negro-hugging worshippers of Old Abe."[71] One Democratic editorial writer had this observation to share: "Abe Lincoln—passing the question as to his taint of Negro blood . . . is altogether an imbecile. . . . He is brutal in all his habits. . . . He is filthy. He is obscene. . . . He is an animal."[72]

Democratic cartoonists turned out scurrilous productions for weeks before the convention. One cartoon attacked "Abraham Africanus the First" while another depicted a "Miscegenation Ball" that was supposedly held at the "Headquarters of the Lincoln Central Campaign Club."

One night in August, as Lincoln was riding toward the Soldiers' Home, a shot rang out. His horse galloped, and when Lincoln arrived at his destination, a sentinel asked him what had happened. Lincoln told him of the shot. The sentry and one of his companions walked down the hill.[73] There was Lincoln's hat—lying on the road, with a bullet hole gaping in its side.

After that, Lincoln's friend and self-appointed bodyguard Ward Hill Lamon started sleeping on the floor outside of the president's bedroom in the White House. Around him, John Hay recalled, Lamon always made certain to arrange "a small arsenal of pistols & bowie knives."[74]

Amid all the racist abuse, Lincoln requested the black abolitionist Frederick Douglass to meet him at the White House. Douglass arrived for his meeting with Lincoln on August 19, and the president asked him to figure out a way to spread the word about emancipation behind rebel lines, so that slaves would intensify their efforts to flock to his armies while he still had the power to free them.

Douglass "agreed to undertake the organizing of a band of scouts, composed of colored men, whose business would be . . . to go into the rebel States, beyond the lines of our armies, and carry the news of emancipation, and urge the slaves to come within our boundaries."[75]

Three days later, Henry Raymond—the editor of the *New York Times* who was also serving as chairman of the Republican National Committee— wrote to Lincoln with a desperate suggestion. "I feel compelled to drop you a line concerning the political condition of the country," Raymond began. "I am in active correspondence with your staunchest friends in every state and from them all I hear but one report. The tide is setting against us."

Two causes accounted for this dreadful situation, Raymond continued: "the want of military successes, and the impression in some minds, the fear and suspicion in others, that we are not to have peace in any event under this administration until Slavery is abandoned. In some way or other the suspicion is widely diffused that we *can* have peace with Union if we would. It is idle to reason with this belief—still more idle to denounce it. It can only be dispelled by some authoritative act."

Therefore, Raymond suggested, Lincoln should reach out to Jefferson Davis with an offer. "Would it not be wise," he began, "to appoint a Commissioner, in due form, to make distinct proffers of peace to Davis, as the head of the rebel armies, on the sole condition of acknowledging the supremacy of the constitution,—all other questions to be settled in convention of the people of all the states?"

To be sure, Raymond said, this presidential offer would amount to something of a trick. "If the proffer were *accepted* (which I presume it would not be), the country would never consent to place the practical execution of it in any but loyal hands, and in those we should be safe. If it should be *rejected*, (as it would be), it would . . . dispel all the delusions about peace that prevail in the North."[76] The implication was reasonably clear: if Davis accepted the offer, the implementation could be dragged out for months until after the election was over and then an excuse could be found to abandon it.

Lincoln toyed with the idea. In fact, he had worked up a similar proposal of his own. "If Jefferson Davis wishes, for himself, to know what I would do if he were to offer peace and reunion, saying nothing about slavery," he had written in a letter to a Democratic editor, "let him try me."[77]

But Lincoln never sent the letter.

Had he reached the point of such total desperation that reunion without emancipation might really be acceptable to him? It seems unlikely.

He was probably thinking up a way to lure Jefferson Davis into a trap—to double-cross him. If so, he gave it up as implausible. When Raymond and some other members of the Republican National Committee paid a call upon Lincoln, he opposed negotiations with Davis. And he ruled out any kind of a deal that would undercut emancipation. It would be "worse than losing the Presidential contest," he declared; "it would be ignominiously surrendering it in advance."[78]

Instead, he wrote an odd memorandum that he sealed away in an envelope. Then he asked all the members of his cabinet to sign it without having read what it contained. Here is what Lincoln wrote: "This morning, as for some days past, it seems exceedingly probable that this Administration will not be re-elected. Then it will be my duty to so co-operate with the President elect, as to save the Union between the election and the inauguration, as he will have secured his election on such ground that he can not possibly save it afterwards."[79]

Many have wondered what Lincoln was doing when he wrote that strange memorandum. Later he would claim that he had written it to bolster his position in case he needed to convince his presidential successor to carry on the war.

But perhaps he had a more dynamic purpose. If a Democrat won the election, he might call for immediate negotiations and even an immediate cease-fire. *But Lincoln would refuse.* He would keep on urging his generals to devastate Confederate armies in the hope that he could force them to surrender before March 4, 1865.

He would try to win the war between the November election and the March inauguration—before he left office. He was probably hoping that victory, however belated, might serve to protect the legal status of the slaves whom his armies had freed.

If the Democrats complained that he had no mandate for doing such a thing—since his leadership had been repudiated—he could show them this memo, its date duly verified by the signatures upon the envelope, as proof that he always intended to work *in true partnership with his successor*, provided he could *do it in a manner that was loyal and patriotic.* Therefore, if his successor needed convincing that the war could still be won, it was his patriotic duty to provide him with the proof via battlefield results.

A far-fetched argument, perhaps, but at least it was a plan that might succeed.

In any case, he would not back down from his emancipation commitment. To some Republican visitors, he said that certain people had "proposed to me to return to slavery the black warriors of Port Hudson . . . to conciliate the South," but he would "be damned in time & in eternity for so doing."[80]

To defend himself against conservative opponents, he kept using the claim that he was nothing but a Unionist who did what he did about slavery to save the Union. "Any different policy in regard to the colored man, deprives us of his help," Lincoln wrote to some critics. "This is not a question of sentiment or taste, but one of physical force which may be measured and estimated as horse-power and steam-power are measured and estimated. Keep it and you can save the Union. Throw it away, and the Union goes with it."[81]

But there was little he could do in the final days of August to avert the disaster that was coming. One of two horrendous futures seemed to loom for his war-ravaged people: Confederate nationhood or reunion on terms as vindictive and harsh as the leaders of the slave states could make them. Either one of these futures would mean that the anti-slavery movement in America would fail.

It seemed that all of Lincoln's skill and all the bloodshed of hundreds of thousands would be for nothing—nothing except to make the long-term prospect of eradicating slavery more hopeless than ever.

When the Democrats convened in Chicago, they nominated George B. McClellan. The horrors that would follow his election are easy to imagine. He might have tried to re-enslave the black soldiers. That would probably have led to bloody rioting, draconian repression, and a race war. He might even have allowed the Confederates to have their independence. A new nation that was based upon master-race theory would be added to the sovereignties—to the empires—of the world.

Confederates saw McClellan as their last best hope for total victory. His election, proclaimed the *Charleston Mercury*, "must lead to peace and our independence [if] for the next two months *we hold our own*."[82]

But it was not to be, and the reason was perfectly simple: on September 2, Sherman captured Atlanta and the northern mood began to change.

At first, the rebels' Georgia campaign had gone well for them since their commander—Joseph Johnston—used the very same tactics of delay that were working in Virginia. In July, however, he prepared to attack Sherman's forces at Peachtree Creek, and on the very eve of this battle, an important decision was made by Jefferson Davis: to change his commanders. He put John Bell Hood, a more impetuous fighter, in command. The battle of Peachtree Creek on July 20 was a rebel defeat.

More desperate fighting occurred on July 21 and 22 when Sherman's forces succeeded in capturing a vital position between Atlanta and Decatur. Hood retreated into the defenses of Atlanta, and Sherman settled in for a siege.

The key was to shut off the railroad links that were keeping the city supplied. After weeks of maneuvers and counter-maneuvers, Sherman's men cut off a vital railroad link at Jonesboro, south of Atlanta. The two-day battle of Jonesboro began on August 31. Once again, the rebels were defeated. Hood abandoned Atlanta and Sherman's troops marched into the city on September 2.

When the news of this victory reached the North, things changed with astonishing speed. "Glorious news this morning," wrote the influential banker George Templeton Strong—"*Atlanta taken at last!!!* Coming at this political crisis," he continued, it was "the greatest event of the war."[83] He was absolutely right. Nicolay predicted that the "Atlanta victory alone ought to win the Presidential contest for us."[84] He told his fiancée that there had been "a perfect revolution in feeling. Three weeks ago, our friends everywhere were despondent, almost to the point of giving up the contest in despair. Now they are hopeful, jubilant, hard at work and confident of success."[85]

This was one of the great turning points of history.

On September 3, Lincoln sent an "Order of Thanks" to Sherman and his army, proclaiming that their victory would be "famous in the annals of war."[86] And he sent a meditation to a Quaker. "We had hoped for a happy termination of this terrible war," Lincoln wrote, and yet "God knows best, and has ruled otherwise." Still, he believed that God "intends some great good to follow this mighty convulsion."[87]

Dissident Republicans scrambled to get back into Lincoln's good graces and both Zachariah Chandler and Benjamin Wade strove to end the schism in the party. Chandler told his colleague that they ought to line up behind Lincoln and Wade was quick to agree—provided that the president agreed to dismiss Montgomery Blair from the cabinet.

Lincoln was indignant at first when he heard of this proposal. But the elder Francis Preston Blair—the old Jackson supporter who had come to embrace Free Soil and the Republican Party—stepped in and persuaded his son to resign. He told Lincoln that Montgomery Blair "would be very willing to be a martyr . . . if that would help."[88]

Lincoln began to come around. When Chandler offered to "get Frémont out of the way" if Lincoln would take Blair up on his offer to resign, Lincoln said, "Well, I think it may be done."[89]

Chandler was as good as his word. Relentlessly, he pushed Frémont to get "out of the way." On September 17, Frémont wrote out a peevish letter of withdrawal that was published a few days later. Lincoln followed up by thanking Montgomery Blair for his offer. For political reasons, Lincoln said, "the time has come," but "this proceeds from no dissatisfaction of mine with you personally or officially. Your uniform kindness has been unsurpassed by that of any friend."[90]

Meanwhile, Chase made it clear that he desired to be reconciled with Lincoln. He wanted to become the chief justice, for the old white supremacist Taney was terminally ill. So Hugh McCulloch—comptroller of the currency—worked hard in September to reconcile Lincoln and Chase, and the president said he was receptive.

The Republicans united, and the call for a second nominating convention in Cleveland was forgotten. Radical Republicans like Sumner and Stevens gave speeches for Lincoln, and Douglass helped to unify the abolitionists.

The mood of Republican triumphalism grew stronger, while the Democrats began to quarrel.

Lincoln claimed that he had foreseen that very possibility. He said the Democrats "must nominate a Peace Democrat on a war platform, or a War Democrat on a peace platform; and I personally can't say I care much which they do."[91] The party platform did include a "peace plank" that was written by Clement Vallandigham. It demanded a cease-fire followed by a great convention of the states. Consequently, McClellan—a War Democrat—was forced to campaign for a cease-fire with the rebels.

And the situation got worse for the Democrats as more and more Union victories occurred. So they lashed out at Lincoln in the only way they could: through coarse and vicious abuse. They suggested he was partly African and they offered him up as an example of where race-mixing would lead.

They sought to prey upon people who were grieving for the loss of their loved ones. The *New York World* published lies to the effect that when Lincoln toured the battlefield at Antietam he asked Ward Hill Lamon to sing him amusing songs. And they went after Lincoln's wife, reviving all the gossip about her wild spending.

These particular Democratic charges were largely correct.

Mary confessed to her friend and confidante Elizabeth Keckley that if Lincoln were defeated, the debts she had incurred would be impossible to repay. So she extorted contributions from lobbyists, money to be used for the ostensible purpose of supporting Lincoln's re-election. But she was building up a contingency fund that could be used to bail her out if it were time to make restitution.

She told Keckley she was not above subterfuge. "I have an object in view, Lizabeth," she said, and elaborated as follows:

> In a political canvass it is policy to cultivate every element of strength. These men have influence, and we require the influence to re-elect Mr. Lincoln. I will be clever to them until after the election, and then, if we remain at the White House, I will drop every one of them, and let them know very plainly that I only made tools of them. They are an unprincipled set, and I don't mind a little double-dealing with them.[92]

In September and October, the cavalry commander Philip Sheridan won electrifying victories in the Shenandoah.

Sent to pursue Early's raiders, he defeated them twice in September—at Winchester on September 19 and at Fisher's Hill on September 22. In consultation with Grant, he unleashed a demonstration of total-war tactics: a campaign of destruction in the Shenandoah Valley, burning farms to render them incapable of supporting Confederate armies. He sought to destroy the Shenandoah as a corridor for rebel invasions and to take it out of action as a source of food for the rebellion. No doubt the burning of Chambersburg by Early weighed heavily in the minds of Sheridan and Grant.

In October, Sheridan was ready to return a large portion of his army to Grant, who could use the men at Petersburg. He took a break from the fighting in order to confer with war department officials in Washington. Lincoln wondered whether this move might be risky. "I hope it will lay no constraint upon you," he wrote to Grant, "for me to say I am a little afraid lest Lee sends re-enforcements to Early, and thus enables him to turn upon Sheridan."[93]

Lincoln's fears were well-grounded. As Sheridan rode back to the Shenandoah on October 19, he heard the sounds of battle. Early had conducted a surprise attack upon his forces at Cedar Creek. As Sheridan approached, he encountered his own retreating troops. But through the force of sheer charisma, he rallied his troops, got them turned around, and led a charge against the rebels that was devastating. Early's army would almost cease to exist as a fighting force before long.

Lincoln issued another proclamation reaffirming that the "last Thursday in November" would be a time to thank God for his help and for inspiring the American people with "fortitude, courage and resolution sufficient for the great trial of civil war into which we have been brought by our adherence as a nation to the cause of Freedom and Humanity."[94]

In light of these victories, the candidacy of McClellan became nothing less than pitiful. He might have gone on to become one of the most sinister figures in American history—and world history. He might have led the United States into a race war or given the Confederates everything they wished.

As it was, he was destined to become a historical after-thought, a candle that flickered in its socket and died.

On October 12, Roger Taney of *Dred Scott* infamy was dead. On December 6, Lincoln sent to Congress the nomination of Salmon P. Chase as the nation's new chief justice. Taney had used the twisted logic of Calhoun to give the U.S. Constitution a pro-slavery reading. Chase had opposed these very doctrines of Calhoun in the 1840s and 1850s. Now he took the place of Roger Taney.

On October 29, Lincoln received a special caller at the White House: Sojourner Truth, the black abolitionist. He showed her a Bible that he had been given by a delegation of free blacks. She said that she had never been treated more kindly and cordially by a white person in her life.

The new free state constitution of Maryland was approved by the voters in October. Louisiana voters had approved their own constitution in September, and the new constitution for Arkansas had been instituted as early as March. Lincoln's state-by-state transformation had come a long way, and when the Maryland results were announced, serenaders came to the White House. Lincoln was in high and even mischievous spirits. "Most heartily to I congratulate you, and Maryland, and the nation, and the world, upon the event," he told the serenaders. "I sincerely hope its friends may fully realize all their anticipations of good from it; and that its opponents may, by its effects, be agreeably, and profitably disappointed."[95]

He was headed toward triumphal re-election, a landslide victory. Soldiers had been furloughed to vote, and they supported the president by huge, overwhelming margins. Despite the risk to themselves, these soldiers wanted to see the Civil War finished. And they voted to make certain that it would be.

On election night Lincoln and Hay walked over to the War Department through the rain. Lincoln calmly read the election returns in the telegraph office.

McClellan carried only three states: Kentucky, New Jersey, and Delaware. The vote in the Electoral College was 212 for Lincoln and only 21 for McClellan. The Republicans would dominate the new Congress by enormous margins: in the Senate by a margin of 42 to 10 and in the House by a margin of 145 to 40. Here was the Second American Revolution at the crest of its power.

On election night, Lincoln addressed another group of serenaders. He said he was "thankful to God for this approval of the people," adding that his gratitude was "free from any taint of personal triumph ... if I know my heart."[96] He urged Americans to use the Civil War as "philosophy to learn wisdom from," adding that "in any future great national trial, compared with the men of this, we shall have as weak and as strong; as silly and as wise; as bad and as good."[97]

He was supremely happy. And his activities in the following months would be suffused with energy—notwithstanding the obvious signs of fatigue that one could see in his face, his manner, his demeanor. But this fatigue would pass in due time. Another four-year presidential term would give him plenty of time to recuperate—or so he thought. There was just no telling how much he might accomplish with the Radicals, some of whom appeared to possess no clue that a master strategist would be helping them. But it made little difference if they knew it.

The danger that had come with this titanic struggle for the soul of America seemed to be over.

On December 20, 1864, the future Princeton University—which was still called the College of New Jersey at the time—awarded Lincoln, who had never been to college, a doctorate of laws. He simply took this compliment in stride. "Thoughtful men," he told the president of Princeton, know "that the fate of civilization upon this continent is involved in the issue of our contest." So he was thankful if his labor had saved the institutions "under which alone we can expect good government and in its train sound learning and the progress of the liberal arts."[98]

15

STOLEN FUTURE

few weeks before the election, a proposal from William Tecumseh Sherman crossed Lincoln's desk. Sherman was proposing to change his strategy and tactics. Both Lincoln and Grant were quite skeptical. But in light of the fact that Sherman's skill as a commander had rescued the nation from McClellan, Lincoln kept an open mind.

Sherman had been holding Atlanta since its capture, but John Bell Hood's Confederate army was still intact. Hood had been raiding Sherman's supply lines, hoping to draw him out of Atlanta. Sherman was sick of that game, so he suggested what appeared to be a risky experiment.

He would divide his huge army, sending thirty thousand men to Tennessee under George Thomas. If Hood entered Tennessee, he would find this army ready and waiting to confront him. Meanwhile, Sherman would march away from Atlanta and head for Savannah with sixty thousand men. If Hood decided to pursue him instead of striking Tennessee, Sherman would face him out in the open with vastly superior numbers.

Meanwhile, his army would live off the land and carry out a scorched-earth policy so devastating—so remorseless—as to break the back of the Confederacy. He would break the rebels' will to resist.

After hesitating, both Lincoln and Grant approved the "March to the Sea," and on November 15 Sherman left Atlanta after ordering its residents to leave. He set fire to everything in the city that might help the rebellion in the future.

As the campaign began, Lincoln wrote his long annual message to Congress. Everything had changed in political terms, so he sought a reconciliation with the Radicals. He wanted to push forward with gusto.

It was only a matter of time—and in all probability a short time—before the Confederacy would be extinguished. Five hundred thousand more troops were on the way, while the Confederates could not replace their losses. The territorial scope of their dominion had steadily shrunk. They were going down, and their rebellion would never rise again.

"The purpose of the people, within the loyal states, to maintain the integrity of the Union, was never more firm, nor more nearly unanimous, than now," Lincoln wrote. And "we have *more* men *now* than we had when the war *began*," so the people of the loyal states "may, if need be, maintain the contest indefinitely."[1]

He turned to Reconstruction and took the first steps toward adopting a more flexible policy. Per the terms of the Ten Percent Plan, Lincoln said, "the door has been, for a full year, open to all, except such as were not in condition to make free choice—that is, such as were in custody or under constraint." But "the time may come—probably will come—when public duty shall demand that it be closed, and that, in lieu, more rigorous measures than heretofore shall be adopted."[2]

Here was the first sign that Reconstruction under Lincoln would become more demanding. Those who subscribe to the legend that the Ten Percent Plan was Lincoln's one and only blueprint for Reconstruction should take note of this fact—and change their minds.

Then Lincoln got down to what was really on his mind: the opportunity to send the Thirteenth Amendment to the states before the lame-duck Congress adjourned. There was no doubt at all that the new Republican super-majorities would pass the amendment in time. But why wait? Here is what Lincoln had to say:

> At the last session of Congress a proposed amendment to the Constitution abolishing slavery throughout the United States, passed the Senate, but failed for lack of the requisite two-thirds vote in the House of Representatives. Although the present is the same Congress, and nearly the same members . . . I venture to recommend

the reconsideration and passage of the amendment at the present session. . . . The intervening election shows, almost certainly, that the next Congress will pass the measure if this does not. Hence, there is only a question of time as to when the proposed amendment will go to the States for their action. And as it is to so go, at all events, may we not agree that the sooner the better?[3]

He noted that additional free states were entering the Union: Nevada had just been admitted and Montana and Idaho would follow. The free state super-majority that Calhoun had dreaded was shaping up quickly.

And the tempo of Union victories began to quicken.

Hood invaded Tennessee in the hope that Sherman would pursue him. But Sherman refused. Besides, he had Tennessee covered—Hood was totally pre-empted since Thomas's army beat him to it. Even so, Hood decided to attack.

His campaign was a disaster. On November 30, he struck some Union forces in Franklin, Tennessee, and his men were slaughtered as he ordered them to keep on charging into murderous fire. He persevered and marched his men all the way to Nashville, where Thomas and his army were waiting. The two armies sat immobile, and Grant began to wonder whether Thomas was malingering. He wrote out an order relieving Thomas, but before he sent it, Thomas acted.

On December 15, Thomas struck the rebels front and rear with such pulverizing blows that the Confederate army shattered. Hood's troops began a headlong retreat in the direction of Mississippi.

Lincoln ordered Thomas to pursue the fleeing fragments of the army. "Please accept for yourself, officers, and men, the nation's thanks for your good work of yesterday," the president wrote. "You made a magnificent beginning. A grand consummation is within your easy grasp. Do not let it slip."[4]

Thomas did not let it slip; he pursued the rebels and he hunted them down so relentlessly that Hood's army would never fight again. The time when Lincoln's generals would let their fleeing enemies escape was over.

And Sherman's March to the Sea was going forward—meting out destruction. It was also liberating slaves. The effect of this scorched-earth plunge through Georgia would never be forgotten, and within a few months a new war song, "Marching through Georgia," was released to the public. The lyrics emphasized the liberating side of the march, about the soldiers who "bring the jubilee" and who hold aloft "the flag that makes you free."

Hordes of slaves had been flocking to Sherman's army and following it. The armies of Lincoln were sweeping all before them—bringing freedom to African Americans. The conquering armies of Lincoln would in time be positioned to enforce whatever policies the congressional Republicans and Lincoln chose to hand down.

Sherman reached Savannah on December 21, and he sent to the president a short and proud telegram presenting the city as a gift: a Christmas present. Other kinds of gifts were on the way. The industrialist George Pullman designed and built a luxury sleeping car that could double as an interim office for the president to use on his trips around the country—trips that he could take across the length and breadth of his newly reunified nation.

The war would soon be over—everybody knew it—and a new dispensation was coming.

The day after Christmas, Lincoln sent congratulations to Sherman. He admitted that "when you were about leaving Atlanta for the Atlantic coast, I was *anxious*, if not fearful; but feeling that you were the better judge, and remembering that 'nothing risked, nothing gained,' I did not interfere. Now, the undertaking being a success, the honor is all yours." This success "brings those who sat in darkness, to see a great light. But what next? I suppose it will be safer if I leave General Grant and yourself to decide."[5]

Sherman would soon propose to march north through the Carolinas, merge his army with Grant's, and then eradicate the army of Lee, which of course would bring the war to an end.

Grant—Sherman—Sheridan—Thomas—at last Lincoln had the commanders he had needed since the start of the war. And nothing could stop them.

Lincoln went to work in December to force the Thirteenth Amendment out of Congress. The Senate had passed it, and the challenge now was to incentivize enough House Democrats to back away from opposition. All they really had to do was stay home—simply fail to show up for the vote. All that Lincoln and the Radicals needed to have was a two-thirds majority of those who were *present* in order to win.

Lincoln worked with Congressman Ashley to woo enough House Democrats to prevail. He also used Seward as an agent to convert Democratic congressmen from New York. Seward was the last remaining member of Lincoln's original cabinet except for Gideon Welles. Bates decided to retire, and so Lincoln tapped James Speed, the brother of his old friend Joshua Speed, to be the new attorney general.

Rumors circulated that Seward and his cronies were turning to outright bribery to get Democrats in the House to do their bidding. There were also rumors that Ashley was engaging in influence-peddling in close coordination with Lincoln, offering patronage jobs to any Democrats who were willing to come around and support the Thirteenth Amendment.

We will never know the extent of these machinations. Lincoln had a vast range of jobs to give out, and he was once again besieged by a swarm of office-seekers. Unlike the situation in 1861, however, he could now turn this situation to advantage by using it for targeted strategic purposes.

And one of the arguments he used with the Democrats was to claim that the passage of the Thirteenth Amendment would shorten the war— shorten it by striking down its underlying cause. He told Missouri Congressman James S. Rollins that passage of the Thirteenth Amendment would "bring the war to a speedy close." The vote would be close, Lincoln said, and only "a few votes one way or the other will decide it." Rollins agreed to be supportive. He said he had "never seen any one evince deeper interest and anxiety upon any subject than did Mr. Lincoln upon the passage of this amendment."[6]

As this drama played out in the House of Representatives, another story was playing out in Washington and Richmond. Lincoln claimed that passing the Thirteenth Amendment would shorten the war. Many people were developing other ideas about shortening the war, and one of them was Francis Preston Blair Sr. He revived the old notion that perhaps the Confederacy and the Union could form an alliance against a foreign enemy. France was a convenient target, since its intervention in Mexican politics was a violation of America's Monroe Doctrine.

On December 28, Blair met with Lincoln and requested a pass so he could travel to Richmond. Lincoln agreed, and his reason was probably simple: here was a chance to gauge rebel opinion in Richmond and perhaps even smoke out divisions among the Confederate leaders. Blair arrived at Richmond on January 12.

Davis rejected the idea of a joint campaign in Mexico, but he expressed his willingness to entertain an agreement bringing "peace to the two countries." When Blair reported this to Lincoln on January 18, the president, no doubt smiling to himself, dashed off a reply to the effect that he too would like to bring peace to "our one common country."[7]

Other Confederate leaders had different ideas, and Alexander Stephens recommended the appointment of a peace commission to meet with Lincoln himself. So Davis appointed three commissioners: Stephens, Senator Robert M. T. Hunter, and Assistant Secretary of War John A. Campbell. He told them to seek safe conduct to Washington, D.C.

When the news of these developments leaked, Republicans were angry and alarmed. Gideon Welles observed in his diary that "the President, with much shrewdness and good sense, has often strange and incomprehensible whims."[8] Yet there is reason to believe that Lincoln's reasoning was not incomprehensible.

He had floated the idea that the war could be shortened by the Thirteenth Amendment. One Democrat, Congressman Samuel S. Cox of Ohio, replied that the key to obtaining support for the amendment was a good-faith effort at negotiating with the rebels. Cox promised to work hard for the Thirteenth Amendment if such an effort were made.

This was a double-sided proposition for Lincoln: peace negotiations with the rebels might undermine as well as support his efforts to gain passage of the Thirteenth Amendment. And the issue came to a head in the last week of January.

The vote on the Thirteenth Amendment was impending, and Ashley, in a state of great alarm, wrote to Lincoln as follows: "The report is in circulation in the House that peace Commissioners are on their way or are in the city, and is being used against us. If it is true, I fear we shall lose the bill. Please authorize me to contradict it, if not true."[9] Lincoln sent back the following laconic message: "So far as I know, there are no peace commissioners in the city, or likely to be in it."[10]

This exchange of messages took place on January 31. Ashley later told Herndon he was worried that the Democrats might bolt and turn against the Thirteenth Amendment "on the ground that the passage of such a proposition . . . would have been offensive to the Commissioners."[11]

The amendment squeaked through the House by a very narrow margin on January 31. Immediately cheers erupted from the crowd that was packing the galleries. Whites and blacks embraced one another, shouted, threw their hats in the air, and waved down to the House floor. When a delegation of congressmen led by Isaac S. Arnold informed Lincoln, he beamed with pleasure. He signed his name to the amendment, though the law requires no such action.

When some serenaders called, he said that the amendment would soon provide "the King's cure for all the evils." The occasion was "one of congratulation to the country and to the whole world." The amendment would settle any lingering disputes about the scope and validity of his Emancipation Proclamation. After all, the president admitted to the crowd, that document

> falls far short of what the amendment will be when fully consummated. A question might be raised whether the proclamation was legally valid. It might be added that it only aided those who came into our lines and that it was inoperative as to those who did not give themselves up, or that it would have no effect upon the children of the slaves.

But those arguments would soon be moot forever—at least when three quarters of the states had approved the amendment. It bears noting that this was exactly how John C. Calhoun feared that slavery would end.

William Lloyd Garrison could not restrain his joy when he wrote to the president as follows: "God save you, and bless you abundantly! As an instrument in his hands, you have done a mighty work for the freedom of the millions who have so long pined in bondage in our land—nay, for the freedom of all mankind. I have the utmost faith in the benevolence of your heart, the purity of your motives, and the integrity of your spirit."[12]

Garrison spoke the following words to a Boston crowd on February 4: "And to whom is the country more immediately indebted for this vital and saving amendment of the Constitution than, perhaps to any other man? I believe I may confidently answer—to the humble railsplitter of Illinois—to Presidential chain-breaker for millions of the oppressed—to Abraham Lincoln!"[13]

In April, Lincoln returned the compliment, observing that abolitionists like Garrison deserved most of the credit. "I have only been an instrument," he said. "The logic and moral power of Garrison, and the anti-slavery people of the country and the army have done it all."[14]

In February, Lincoln returned to the photographic studio of Alexander Gardner to have his picture taken with Tad. These photographs tell us all we need to know about his mood at this particular time. He looks radiant. He is smiling with the deep inner pleasure of a man who is basking in triumph, a man who knows that he has won.

As Sherman prepared to march north into South Carolina, he had to make provision for the slaves who were following his army—and slowing it down. He wanted to get them settled so his army could move north quickly.

On January 12, he held a meeting with some black Methodist and Baptist ministers from Savannah. Secretary of War Stanton sailed down to attend this meeting. What emerged was a potentially transformative order that was handed down by Sherman: "Special Field Order Number 15." It established a huge "reservation" of seized rebel lands—four hundred thousand acres in size—that would extend all the way from Charleston, South Carolina, to Jacksonville, Florida. Forty acres would be given to each black family. The titles to the land would be "possessory" until such time as Congress made them permanent.

It is hard to believe that Lincoln had no knowledge of this order since Stanton helped to frame it. In any case, Lincoln never countermanded the order.

But what of his previous claim to the effect that the permanent seizure of land as a punishment for treason (as opposed to non-payment of taxes) was unconstitutional, a "bill of attainder"? According to Congressman George Julian, who met with Lincoln in the previous summer to discuss the issue of land redistribution, Lincoln said that he had changed his mind. He said that the arguments of William Whiting in his book about presidential war powers had broadened his views on all sorts of constitutional issues.

Here was a preview of the kind of Reconstruction that Lincoln was beginning to support: a Radical Reconstruction. A massive program of land redistribution in the South would alter race relations permanently. Freed slaves would be given a substantial and powerful new basis for supporting themselves. Other rights could be conferred—just as quickly as the ever-shifting contingencies of politics permitted. And Lincoln was just the right man to determine how quickly the process could move.

On January 30, the Confederate peace commissioners arrived at Grant's lines below Petersburg. Lincoln sent an agent, Major Thomas Eckert, to confer with these commissioners and see if they were ready to abandon the Confederates' claim to nationhood. The commissioners requested Grant to give them safe passage so they could set up a meeting with Lincoln "in pursuance of the course indicated by him in his letter to Mr. F.P. Blair of January 18, 1865."[15] Grant permitted the commissioners to enter his lines.

Lincoln sent Seward to confer with the commissioners at Hampton Roads. He told him to see if the rebels were prepared to abandon Confederate nationhood—and also slavery. He told Seward to test them without committing himself (or Lincoln) to any agreement. In the meantime, Eckert, Lincoln's agent, returned on February 1 and said that he had not received satisfactory assurances from the rebels. But Grant wrote to Stanton and said that the commissioners' "intentions are good and their desire sincere to restore peace and union."[16]

So Lincoln decided to go down to Hampton Roads and cross-examine these rebels himself. He took a train to Annapolis, Maryland, and boarded the steamer *River Queen*, which took him down the bay to Hampton Roads. The conference with the rebels took place aboard the ship on February 3.

Radicals were in a state of indignation back in Washington. Zachariah Chandler fumed that "nothing but evil *can* come of this nonsense."[17] The Radicals worried that Lincoln might somehow sell them out or give away too much. The president observed in response that "some of my friends in Congress act as if they were afraid to trust me with a dinner, yet I shall never compromise the principles upon which I was elected."[18]

There were no notes taken in the course of the "Hampton Roads Conference," and accounts of the meeting by participants have been questioned by historians. Nonetheless, there is general agreement on some of the details.

Lincoln projected a friendly attitude and he exchanged some harmless banter with Stephens, whom he remembered from their years together in Congress. When Stephens came aboard the *River Queen*, he was bundled up in an enormous overcoat. "Now, gentlemen," Lincoln quipped, you see what a large amount of 'shuck' Stephens has—just wait a minute and you will be surprised to find what a small 'nubbin' he is."[19]

When the men got down to business, the gist of the meeting was as follows: Lincoln shot down the idea of a joint operation against the French in Mexico and he refused to budge on the principle of permanent Union. "The restoration of the Union is a *sine qua non* with me," he said.[20] He said that as soon as the rebels stopped fighting, he would expedite "practical relations" between their states and the rest of the Union and show them the "utmost liberality," with one proviso: he would "never change or modify the terms" of the Emancipation Proclamation.[21]

At this point Seward mentioned the Thirteenth Amendment. According to some accounts, he told the commissioners that if the rebels ceased fighting they might be able to prevent its ratification. According to Stephens, Lincoln said something different: that the ex-rebel states might ratify the Thirteenth Amendment in such a way as to delay its effects. "Get the Governor of the State to call the Legislature together," he supposedly said, "and get them to recall all the State troops from the war; elect Senators and Representatives to Congress, and ratify the Constitutional Amendment prospectively, so as to take effect—say in five years."[22]

Many Civil War scholars have doubted the likelihood that Lincoln would have said such a thing.

According to another account, Stephens said that "negroes will not work, unless forced to it, and . . . we shall all starve together." Lincoln answered that southern whites should indeed "go to work like honest people or starve."[23]

There is little doubt about one thing that Lincoln reportedly said: he said that both the North and the South were complicit in slavery and he continued to support the idea that southern whites should be compensated for their slaves. He added that he "knew some who were in favor of an appropriation as high as Four Hundred Millions of Dollars for that purpose."[24]

The meeting broke up with no agreement.

For his own part, Jefferson Davis poured contempt upon the offers of Lincoln. And the Radical Republicans were angry for reasons of their own. Zachariah Chandler wrote that "the peace fizzle has ended as I supposed it would in national disgrace." He said it was "ridiculous for the President to go 200 miles to meet the representatives of these accursed Rebels." Congressional leaders demanded a report, and so Lincoln composed and submitted a report that was read aloud to the House of Representatives on February 10. This report was extremely amusing.

The rebels, Lincoln wrote, never said that "they *ever* would consent to re-union, and yet they equally omitted to declare that they *never* would so consent." Instead, "they seemed to desire a postponement of that question, and the adoption of some other course first, which, as some of them seemed to argue, might, or might not, lead to re-union, but which course, we thought, would amount to an indefinite postponement. The conference ended without result."[25]

Noah Brooks was in the gallery when the clerk read the president's report. The expressions of the congressmen changed as they listened, and some of them began to chuckle. They "smilingly exchanged glances as they began to appreciate Lincoln's sagacious plan for unmasking the craftiness . . . of the rebel leaders." When the presentation was completed, "an instant and irrepressible storm of applause" began.[26]

The Radicals calmed down. Thaddeus Stevens wrote that "the President thought it was best to make the effort, and he had done it in such masterly style" that people would "applaud his action."[27] The *New York Times* concluded that no harm had been done, "due to the practical good sense of President Lincoln."[28] The *New York Herald* called him "one of the shrewdest diplomats of the day."[29]

Behind the scenes, Lincoln pursued the idea of paying $400 million in compensation for the slaves and he expanded it into a far more creative and extraordinary proposal: he would *pay* the slave states to ratify the Thirteenth Amendment. He wrote it all out and presented it to his cabinet on February 6. He drafted the proposal in the form of a congressional resolution. Here is what it said:

> The President of the United States is hereby empowered, at his discretion, to pay four hundred millions of dollars to the States of Alabama, Arkansas, Delaware, Florida, Georgia, Kentucky, Louisiana, Maryland, Mississippi, Missouri, North Carolina, South Carolina, Tennessee, Texas, Virginia, and West-Virginia . . . on the conditions following, to wit: . . . All resistance to the national authority shall be abandoned and cease, on or before the first day of April next; and upon such abandonment and ceasing of resistance, one half of said sum to be paid . . . and the remaining half to be paid only upon the amendment of the national constitution recently proposed by congress, becoming valid law, on or before the first day of July next, by the action thereon of the requisite number of states.[30]

As one more demonstration of Lincoln's audacity, this document is breathtaking. Would any other president dream of attempting to *pay off* the states for the ratification of a constitutional amendment? Would such an action itself be constitutional? There is nothing in the Constitution permitting it.

But there is nothing in the Constitution forbidding it either. So why not go ahead and do it?

Lincoln's cabinet disapproved of the proposal, so Lincoln filed it away. But the proposal provides more evidence of how sweeping and revolutionary Reconstruction might have become under Lincoln's leadership. He might have found a way to revive the idea later on as a way to inject massive economic investment into the erstwhile slave states, creating purchasing power that would "lift all boats" toward prosperity.

Gideon Welles reminisced that Lincoln "frequently expressed his opinion that the condition of affairs in the rebel States was deplorable, and did not conceal his apprehension that, unless immediately attended to, they would, in consequence of their disturbed civil, social, and industrial relations, be worse after the rebellion was suppressed."[31]

Lincoln apparently wanted to give the South economic assistance to rebuild—or, to put the matter differently, to build anew.

Another $400 million would be pumped into the southern economy. Price was really no object for Lincoln. His economic thinking was expansive and bold enough to recognize the fact that the nation's aggregate buying power would increase with the growth of its population and productivity. Back in 1862, he had justified the cost of a gradual phase-out of slavery by recommending deficit spending as the finance method that could pay for it. He said that the American economy could handle the challenge with ease. By 1900, he argued, "we shall probably have a hundred million people to share the burden, instead of thirty one millions, as now."[32]

One more thing: knowing money and banking as well as he did, Lincoln knew how money was created—via methods that went far beyond the process of precious-metal coinage. And he knew that the money supply of the nation could grow in all sorts of ways. He knew, for example, that upwards of $430 million had been created by Congress, then spent right into circulation through the legal tender acts. True, these "Greenbacks" were supposed to be exchanged for gold coin sometime in the future. But by 1865, there were serious proposals to keep them in circulation indefinitely. There were all sorts of ways to expand the sheer money supply of the nation.

By 1865, it seemed that almost anything might become possible.

All through February, Sherman turned his wrath against South Carolina, for years the most militant slave state. His army's punishment of

South Carolina made his treatment of Georgia look mild. When his men reached Columbia, South Carolina, they destroyed things of military value as they had in Atlanta. Then the city burned, though it has never been proven whether Sherman's men set the fire. Meanwhile, Charleston had been heavily damaged by months of bombardment.

Political battles were raging in Congress as the lame-duck session played out. The Radicals refused to accept the new free state constitutions of Louisiana and Arkansas—in part because those constitutions failed to provide for black voting rights and in part because they wanted to establish the principle that Congress, and not the president, should determine the law when it came to Reconstruction.

In January, new senators and congressmen from Louisiana asked to be seated. Lincoln argued that Congress should admit them. In a letter to Lyman Trumbull, who chaired the Senate Judiciary Committee, he framed the issue by means of the following question: "Can Louisiana be brought into proper practical relations with the Union sooner by *admitting* or by *rejecting* the proposed Senators?"[33]

The committee sent a favorable report to the Senate. But then a filibuster led by Charles Sumner prevented the Louisiana senators from taking their seats. Conservative and moderate Republicans were outraged by Sumner's behavior, and Lincoln himself was becoming rather angry with Sumner. Just the same, he knew that he would have to work with Sumner and the Radicals when the new Congress convened in December, 1865. And he was perfectly inclined to do so. In the meantime, though, he preferred to protect the existing Ten Percent regimes. Lincoln viewed them—especially the Hahn government in Louisiana—as valuable laboratory experiments for trying out cutting-edge ideas.

In December, James Ashley had introduced a bill that would require Louisiana to enfranchise blacks before Congress would recognize its new free-state constitution. That constitution already empowered the Louisiana legislature to extend voting rights to blacks. Lincoln believed that black voting rights ought to be phased in—so as not to trigger a violent reaction among whites. He had recommended such a phase-in to Hahn in his secret letter of March 13, 1864.

Ashley agreed to revise his legislation to mollify Lincoln. He was willing to stipulate that voting rights would be extended at first to blacks who had served the nation in uniform. No action could be taken on this bill before Congress adjourned. But Lincoln began to reveal his Hahn letter to selected Radical Republicans to show them he was working already on a plan that would initiate the great reform.

Ashley agreed to work with Lincoln on some new Reconstruction legislation for the new Congress to consider. He and Lincoln supposedly struck the following deal: if Congress would agree to preserve the existing Ten Percent regimes, then Lincoln in return would support a Wade-Davis approach in the rest of the ex-rebel states.

Lincoln wholeheartedly agreed to one Radical measure that Congress passed just before adjournment: the Freedmen's Bureau Act that Congress passed on March 3. This act created a new federal agency— the Bureau of Refugees, Freedmen, and Abandoned Lands—in the war department. The agency would extend direct help of all kinds to former slaves: legal, medical, and educational assistance.

And the bureau was also charged with the task of surveying "abandoned" or confiscated lands to which the federal government was acquiring title. These lands would be surveyed into forty-acre tracts that would be set aside for the use of former slaves as well as white refugees. Lincoln signed this bill—further evidence that he intended to support a program of land redistribution in the South.

Inauguration Day, March 4, was dark and rainy in Washington. The president went to the Capitol early to sign legislation, so the grand procession departed from the White House without him. In the presidential carriage were his wife, his eldest son Robert, and Senator James Harlan of Iowa, whose daughter and Robert would marry a few years later.

Robert was finally enrolled in the army. His entreaties from Harvard took their toll on Mary, and so did some inquiries from prominent Washingtonians as to why her eldest son was not doing his duty.

She relented in January, so Lincoln wrote to Grant and requested a place for Robert at Petersburg. "Please read and answer this letter as though I was not President, but only a friend," Lincoln wrote. Robert, said Lincoln, "wishes to see something of the war before it ends." But he was not seeking a commission—only "some nominal rank."[34] Grant of course agreed. He made Robert a captain and a member of his personal staff. A major source of embarrassment for Lincoln was thus removed.

The crowds along Pennsylvania Avenue and at the Capitol were estimated to be twice as large as the ones at Lincoln's first Inauguration. Many blacks were in the audience. Once again, the security issue was paramount, and Stanton had taken extraordinary precautions to keep the city—and the president—safe.

After Lincoln and the delegation came into the Senate chamber, the swearing in of the new vice president, Andrew Johnson, was the order of business. At noon, Vice President Hannibal Hamlin prepared to relinquish his office. But before Johnson took the oath, he subjected the crowd to a shocking and disgraceful performance. He was obviously intoxicated as he bragged, lectured, and harangued those present, telling government officials that they owed their power to the people. He singled them out by name and pointed to them. He went on and on, as Lincoln just closed his eyes and listened.

Attorney General Speed said that Johnson's performance was "in wretched bad taste," and Welles said to Stanton that "Johnson is either drunk or crazy."[35] Zachariah Chandler sent this recollection to his wife: "I was never so mortified in my life. Had I been able to find a small hole I should have dropped through it out of sight."[36] At last it was over. When Lincoln prepared to walk out to the ceremonial platform on the Capitol building's East Front, he whispered to one of the marshals, "Do not permit Johnson to speak a word during the exercises that are to follow."[37]

As Lincoln and the dignitaries filed onto the platform, cheering broke out and the surging crowd swarmed close. Just as the president rose to give his speech, the sun broke through the clouds. According to Noah Brooks, Lincoln recalled that he was "just superstitious enough to consider it a happy omen."[38]

Lincoln's second Inaugural Address was his greatest oratorical masterpiece. Biblical in tone, it distilled the theological and spiritual emotions that he had been expressing since 1862. Lincoln crafted his thoughts into beautiful lines that made the cause of the war divine wrath. All were being punished. Slavery was such a gross violation of justice that carnage was the price that God demanded.

He began with some quiet disclaimers, saying that no detailed account of any recent event would be needed. "The progress of our arms," he said, "upon which all else chiefly depends, is as well known to the public as to myself; and it is, I trust, reasonably satisfactory and encouraging to all. With high hope for the future, no prediction in regard to it is ventured."

Then he talked about the war and reminisced about the state of affairs when he was first sworn into office. "All thoughts were anxiously directed to an impending civil war," Lincoln said. "All dreaded it—all sought to avert it." But while he was trying to save the Union without war, rebel agents were "seeking to *destroy* it without war—seeking to dissolve the Union."

"Both parties deprecated war," he continued, "but one of them would *make* war rather than let the nation survive; and the other would *accept* war rather than let it perish. And the war came."

He talked about its cause: "One eighth of the whole population were colored slaves, not distributed generally over the Union, but localized in the Southern part of it. These slaves constituted a peculiar and powerful interest. All knew that this interest was, somehow, the cause of the war." The rebels insisted on protecting and extending this "interest," while "the government claimed no right to do more than to restrict the territorial enlargement of it."

The war grew beyond what anyone had foreseen and it began to transform the American people. "Neither party expected for the war, the magnitude, or the duration, which it has already attained. Neither anticipated that the *cause* of the conflict might cease with, or even before, the conflict itself should cease." Lincoln was probably alluding to the passage of the Thirteenth Amendment.

Then he shared his religious reflections and the sentences that followed were written in such powerful prose that they demand to be presented complete:

> Each looked for an easier triumph, and a result less fundamental and astounding. Both read the same Bible, and pray to the same God; and each invokes His aid against the other. It may seem strange that any men should dare to ask a just God's assistance in wringing their bread from the sweat of other men's faces; but let us judge not that we be not judged. The prayers of both could not be answered; that of neither has been answered fully. The Almighty has His own purposes. "Woe unto the world because of offences! for it must needs be that offences come; but woe to that man by whom the offence cometh!" If we shall suppose that American Slavery is one of those offences which, in the providence of God, must needs come, but which, having continued through His appointed time, He now wills to remove, and that He gives to both North and South, this terrible war, as the woe due to those by whom the offense came, shall we discern therein any

departure from those divine attributes which the believers in a Living God always ascribe to him?

The next passage possesses such terrible beauty that the crowd must have stood transfixed:

> Fondly do we hope—fervently do we pray—that this mighty scourge of war may speedily pass away. Yet, if God wills it to continue, until all the wealth piled by the bond-man's two hundred and fifty years of unrequited toil shall be sunk, and until every drop of blood drawn with the lash, shall be paid by another drawn with the sword, as was said three thousand years ago, so still it must be said, "the judgments of the Lord, are true and righteous altogether."

A "scourge" is a whip.

So Lincoln was saying that the *war* was a whip and that America would have to be lashed until the land was running red with the blood of atonement—until the land became as bloody as the backs of all the millions of slaves who had been whipped in the land of the free.

And then the incomparable lines that would make this speech so very famous:

> With malice toward none; with charity for all; with firmness in the right, as God gives us to see the right, let us strive on to finish the work we are in; to bind up the nation's wounds; to care for him who shall have borne the battle, and for his widow, and his orphan—to do all that may achieve and cherish a just, and a lasting peace, among ourselves, and with all nations.[39]

After Lincoln finished, he took the oath of office from Chief Justice Chase, kissed the Bible, and bowed to the audience. Deafening applause that was punctuated by artillery salutes filled the air.

At the reception that followed, Frederick Douglass called upon Lincoln. Presumably because of his color, two guards at the White House blocked his entrance—even though some other blacks had been admitted to the New Year's reception at the White House a few months earlier. Douglass asked a companion to see that Lincoln was informed about the situation. Within a few minutes, Douglass was ushered in.

"I could not have been more than ten feet from him," Douglass recalled, "when Mr. Lincoln saw me; his countenance lighted up, and he said in a voice which was heard all around: 'Here comes my friend Douglass.' As I approached him he reached out his hand, gave me a cordial shake, and said: 'Douglass, I saw you in the crowd to-day listening to my inaugural address. There is no man's opinion that I value more than yours: what do you think of it?'" Douglass called the speech "a sacred effort."[40]

Many people were stunned by the elegance and power of Lincoln's Second Inaugural Address. William Gladstone proclaimed that he was "taken captive by so striking an utterance as this." He said that "the address gives evidence of a moral elevation most rare in a statesman, or indeed in any man."[41]

After Thurlow Weed congratulated Lincoln on the Second Inaugural Address, he sent this answer: "Every one likes a compliment. Thank you for yours on . . . the recent Inaugural Address." Lincoln said that he expected it "to wear as well as—perhaps better than—any thing I have produced; but I believe it is not immediately popular. Men are not flattered by being shown that there has been a difference of purpose between the Almighty and them. To deny it, however, in this case, is to deny that there is a God governing the world. It is a truth which I thought needed to be told; and as whatever of humiliation there is in it, falls most directly on myself, I thought others might afford for me to tell it."[42]

There were many signs that fatigue with a touch of depression was wearing Lincoln down. The sheer exhaustion resulting from his duties would have staggered any man. And perhaps there was something of a letdown after all the euphoria that he experienced in the aftermath of his re-election and the passage of the Thirteenth Amendment. But there were probably other reasons for the onset of gloom and ill-health.

A reporter for the *Chicago Tribune* recorded that many people were struck by Lincoln's "gaunt, skeleton-like appearance."[43] Lincoln's old friend Joshua Speed came to call and Lincoln told him that "my feet and hands are always cold—I suppose I ought to be in bed."[44]

One source of aggravation and demoralization was Mary's bad behavior, a source of steady stress. Her behavior in fact was growing steadily worse; her jealousy of any other woman who came within Lincoln's proximity was becoming almost maniacal. Burdened, no doubt, by the knowledge that her debts had climbed above $27,000, she perhaps—like a great many other guilty people—turned her thoughts away from her own guilty conscience by accusing others of treachery.

Elizabeth Keckley reminisced about the conversations between the Lincolns that she often overheard. Once, for example, they were dressing for dinner and exchanged the following rapid-fire questions and answers:

> Well, mother, who must I talk with to-night—shall it be Mrs. D?
>
> That deceitful woman! No, you shall not listen to her flattery.
>
> Well, then, what do you say to Miss C.? She is too young and handsome to practice deceit.
>
> Young and handsome, do you call her! You should not judge beauty for me. No, she is in league with Mrs. D., and you shall not talk with her.
>
> Well, mother, I must talk with some one. Is there any one that you do not object to?
>
> I don't know as it is necessary that you should talk to anybody in particular. You know well enough, Mr. Lincoln, that I do not approve of your flirtations with silly women.[45]

Beyond the pressure of such marital friction, Lincoln was increasingly haunted by thoughts about his own mortality. He told Harriet Beecher Stowe that no matter how the war ended, "I have the impression that *I* shan't last long after it's over."[46] He told Owen Lovejoy much the same thing: "I have a strong impression that I shall not live to see the end."[47]

No doubt the attempt upon his life as he rode alone to the Soldier's Home the previous August was ever on his mind. He had lived with the threat of assassination since 1860 and the death threats started just as soon as he had won the election.

He began reminiscing about such things in the autumn of 1864. He told Noah Brooks about the moment when he looked in the mirror and beheld the two reflections of himself, one healthy and the other pale as death. In December he told two visitors—Benson J. Lossing and Isaac N. Arnold—the details about how he changed trains in Baltimore and wore a disguise to avoid being killed.[48]

All through his presidency he had struggled to reduce his anxiety about this threat by adopting a carefree attitude. "Oh, there is nothing like getting *used* to things," he had told Francis Carpenter after describing the hate mail that he received on a regular basis. At first these letters made him "a little uncomfortable," he admitted, "but they have ceased to give me apprehension."[49] He said that he kept a large file marked "assassination letters."

He told Brooks that he had made up his mind that "if anybody wants to kill me, he will do it. . . . There are a thousand ways of getting at a man if it is desirable that he should be killed."[50] He said he would refuse to "lock myself up in a box" or "be shut up in an iron cage and guarded."[51]

After his re-election, the assassination threats increased. And even before the election Democratic newspapers were calling for his murder. In August, the La Crosse, Wisconsin *Democrat* editorialized that if Lincoln "is elected to misgovern for another four years, we trust some bold hand will pierce his heart with dagger point for the public good."[52] The Greensburg, Pennsylvania *Argus* said that his "defeat or his death is an indispensable condition to an honorable peace."[53]

Newspapers in the Confederate states were saying much the same thing.

Stanton was preoccupied with ensuring the president's safety. He arranged to have troops on the White House grounds and at the Soldiers' Home. He also arranged for the Washington police department to assign some plain clothes officers and detectives to help guard the president. Ward Hill Lamon, Lincoln's self-appointed bodyguard as well as the marshal of the District of Columbia, worried constantly about the president's safety and kept himself as close to Lincoln as he could.

"*You are in danger,*" he warned. "You know, or ought to know, that your life is sought after, and will be taken unless you and your friends are cautious; for you have many enemies within our lines."[54] Lincoln confided to Seward that he knew he was in danger. But he refused to let himself worry. Seward agreed with this attitude, observing that no American president had ever been murdered.

Lincoln's wanderings—he liked to make impromptu visits and even walk the streets of Washington, a practice that presidents would continue right up to the time of Harry Truman—were enjoyable, and they probably derived from his behavior long ago when he would seize upon any excuse to get out and about.

But in the atmosphere of 1864 and 1865, such behavior was a form of psychological denial—a dangerous emotional strategy for staving off anxiety. "Oh, they wouldn't hurt *me*," he told a general who had warned him against the practice of walking alone from the White House to the red-brick War Department building next door down a dark and shaded path.[55]

Denial may be helpful and comforting at times—even useful—but the unconscious mind will continue to engage itself with real and justified fears. In early April Lincoln spoke about a morbid dream—according to Ward Hill Lamon, who wrote down all the details. Lincoln told Lamon and others that this dream had been haunting him, that it had "got possession of me."

He told them the details. In his dream there "was a death-like stillness about me. Then I heard subdued sobs, as if a number of people were weeping. I thought I left my bed and wandered downstairs. There the silence was broken by the same pitiful sobbing, but the mourners were invisible." He was determined to find out what was wrong.

> I went from room to room; no living person was in sight, but the same mournful sounds of distress met me as I passed along. It was light in all the rooms; every object was familiar to me; but where were all the people who were grieving as if their hearts would break? I was puzzled and alarmed. What could be the meaning of all this? Determined to find the cause of a state of things so mysterious and so shocking, I kept on until I arrived at the East Room, which I entered. There I met with a sickening surprise. Before me was a catafalque, on which rested a corpse wrapped in funeral vestments. Around it were stationed soldiers who were acting as guards; and there was a throng of people, some gazing mournfully upon the corpse, whose face was covered, others weeping pitifully. "Who is dead in the White House," I demanded of one of the soldiers. "The President," was his answer; "he was killed by an assassin."[56]

Sherman's troops were storming into North Carolina and the end of the war was drawing near. The Confederates had gathered a force of approximately twenty thousand under the command of Joseph Johnston to try and slow Sherman down. But it was hopeless. The rebel troops were outnumbered almost ten-to-one.

In Petersburg, Lee knew that time was closing in. In early March he sent overtures to Grant to explore some tentative peace terms. Stanton sent back Lincoln's order forbidding it. Only the unconditional surrender of Lee's army would be acceptable. The president "instructs me," wrote Stanton, "to say that you are not to decide, discuss, or confer upon any political questions; such questions the President holds in his own hands."[57]

On March 20, Grant invited Lincoln to visit the front for a few days. Lincoln jumped at the invitation. Gustavus Fox made arrangements for him to travel aboard a powerfully armed naval vessel, the USS *Bat*.

But then Mary decided that she had to come along, and so a different vessel with accommodations that would meet her exacting standards would have to be found. The steamer *River Queen* was chartered. But the *Bat* came along for protection. On March 23, Lincoln, Mary, and Tad set off for City Point, Grant's huge supply depot and headquarters on the James River. They arrived at City Point the next day.

Mary immediately started quarreling with almost everyone in sight. Though some historians believe that accounts of her misbehavior in the course of this visit were exaggerated, she clearly behaved very badly. When General Grant's wife Julia sat down next to Mary, the indignant first lady reportedly said, "How dare you be seated until I invite you!" That set the tone for the rest of the visit.

Lincoln's spirits began to improve as he got a chance to meet some new people. But Mary would always find ways to cut his conversations short and keep him attentive—and submissive. A journalist named Sylvanus Cadwallader observed an occasion when Lincoln was right in the middle of an interesting conversation when Tad, sent by his mother, tugged at him and said, "come, come, come now, mama says you must come instantly." As Lincoln left, he muttered, "My God, will that woman never understand me?"[58]

The great showdown between Grant and Lee was shaping up in the course of Lincoln's visit.

On March 25, Lee attempted a breakout from Petersburg. Lincoln wanted to observe the fighting, but Grant said no. Afterward, though, he took Lincoln to the scene of the fighting. The president rode on horseback over devastated terrain watching burial squads dispose of corpses. He said that he had "seen enough of the horrors of war" and "he hoped this was the beginning of the end."[59] When they returned to City Point, Lincoln sat around a campfire with Grant and his officers.

The next day, he received an invitation to review some troops from different units—some of Sheridan's men who had returned from the Shenandoah Valley as well as the Army of the James, no longer commanded by

Benjamin Butler, who had since been replaced by General Edward O. C. Ord.

While Mary's carriage was on its way to the campsite, the wife of General Ord rode up to greet Lincoln, who was also on horseback. Upon arriving, Mary unleashed a torrent of rage. To Adam Badeau, an aide to Grant, she reportedly said, "What does the woman mean by riding by the side of the President? And ahead of me?" When she arrived at Ord's headquarters, she subjected Ord's wife to a tirade. Badeau claimed that Mary Lincoln

> positively insulted her, called her vile names in the presence of a crowd of officers, and asked what she meant by following up the President. The poor woman burst into tears and inquired what she had done, but Mrs. Lincoln refused to be appeased, and stormed till she was tired.... Everybody was shocked and horrified.[60]

At dinner that night, she said that Ord should be relieved of command. If Badeau's account can be believed, "she repeatedly attacked her husband" that evening. "I have never suffered greater humiliation and pain," Badeau wrote, "than when I saw the Head of State, the man who carried all the cares of the nation in such a crisis—subjected to this inexpressible public mortification." Lincoln bore it with an expression of pain and sadness that "cut one to the heart."[61]

General Sherman arrived for a visit with Lincoln and Grant on March 27. They met aboard the *River Queen*. Sherman observed that while the president at first looked discouraged, he brightened up as they began to talk strategy.

Grant said that Sheridan was about to launch a flanking maneuver that would make Lee's position untenable. The Union army had been greatly reinforced and Grant was steadily extending his lines. Lee would probably decide to abandon Petersburg and move south in an effort to link up with Johnston's forces. Grant said that he was confident that he could block such a break-out by Lee.

Lincoln wondered whether Sherman's absence might permit the Confederates in North Carolina to escape. Sherman said that Johnston's army was contained so effectively that in order to move he would have to break the army into units so small that it could never be reassembled.[62]

The final assault upon Petersburg began and Lincoln was on hand to observe from a distance. He listened to a "furious cannonade" and saw "flashes of guns upon the clouds."[63]

Mary returned to Washington on April 1. On the same day, Sheridan achieved a victory in the battle of Five Forks—a victory so decisive that it forced Lee to order the evacuation of Petersburg. The last railroad that had been supplying the city was cut.

When Lincoln got the news and was presented with some captured Confederate battle flags, he said, "Here is something material—something I can see, feel, and understand. This means victory. This *is* victory."

He toured Petersburg and walked its streets with little Tad. He told Grant that "I had a sort of sneaking idea all along that you would so maneuver as to have Sherman come up and be near enough to cooperate with you." Grant replied that he had intended to issue such an order at first but then decided that he ought to give the star-crossed Army of the Potomac a chance to finish off the army of Lee on its own, for the sake of its honor.[64]

Lincoln told Grant that he wanted the Confederate troops to be given lenient treatment after they had surrendered.

At one point during Lincoln's City Point visit, Andrew Johnson and a friend came to visit. Lincoln said, "Don't let those men come into my presence. I won't see either of them; send them away. . . . I won't see them now, and never want to lay eyes on them. I don't care what you do with them . . . but don't let them come near me!"[65]

The Confederates evacuated Richmond on April 2. Davis and most of the other Confederate officials fled south in the direction of Danville. They ordered their troops to set fire to the bridges, the armory, and warehouses. This fire spread out of control, and large parts of the city were destroyed. Union troops entered Richmond under the command of General Godfrey Weitzel and General Ord.

When Lincoln heard that Richmond had fallen, he said, "Thank God that I have lived to see this! It seems to me that I have been dreaming a horrid dream for four years, and now the nightmare is gone. I want to see Richmond."[66]

On April 4, he visited the city. He and Tad set off aboard the *River Queen*, but due to the mines and defensive obstructions that Confederates had placed in the river, the final approach was made by barge.

The scene that day in the city of Richmond was extraordinarily moving. As Lincoln and his party walked the streets, they were greeted by throngs of joyous slaves, who cried, "Bless the Lord" and "Hallelujah!" When some of them knelt in his presence, Lincoln said, "Don't kneel to me. That is not right."[67]

Even whites rushed up to bid him welcome. A white girl handed him a bouquet of roses with a card that read "From Eva to the Liberator of the Slaves."[68] A white man shouted, "Abraham Lincoln, God bless you! You are the poor man's friend!"[69] Journalist Charles C. Coffin described the scene:

> No written page or illuminated canvas can give the reality of the event—the enthusiastic bearing of the people—the blacks and poor whites who have suffered untold horrors during the war, their demonstrations of pleasure, the shouting, dancing, the thanksgiving to God, the mention of the name of Jesus—as if President Lincoln were next to the son of God in their affections—the jubilant cries, the countenances beaming with unspeakable joy, the tossing up of caps, the swinging of arms of a motley crowd—some in rags, some bare-foot, some wearing pants of Union blue, and coats of Confederate gray.[70]

Weitzel moved into the "Confederate White House" and used it as his headquarters. Lincoln joined him there and he sat for a moment in the chair of Jefferson Davis. Then he went to a balcony and looked down upon the cheering crowd. Afterward, Lincoln, Weitzel, and others took a tour of Richmond in a horse-drawn carriage.

Lincoln made an impromptu speech to a huge crowd of blacks who had gathered at Capitol Square. "My poor friends," he told them, "you are free—free as air. You can cast off the name of slave and trample upon it; it will come to you no more. Liberty is your birthright. God gave it to you as he gave to others, and it is a sin that you have been deprived of it for so many years."[71]

Lincoln readily admitted what a dangerous thing he had done when he walked the streets of Richmond. "Anyone could have shot me from a second-story window," he said.[72]

Mary returned on April 6. She was sorry she had missed the excitement, so she made a tour of Richmond on her own—with an entourage that included Senator Sumner—and then she had Lincoln escort her around Petersburg.

Meanwhile, Grant's army was blocking the path that Lee had been hoping to use to head south. The Army of the Potomac drove him steadily westward, all the while outracing his advance units and surrounding them. Lincoln was kept steadily informed. On April 7, he sent Grant the following message: "Gen. Sheridan says 'If the thing is pressed I think that Lee will surrender.' Let the *thing* be pressed."[73]

They returned to Washington on April 8, and just before he left, Lincoln toured some military hospitals. He was interested in talking to wounded Confederate prisoners of war. Before the *River Queen* departed, Lincoln asked a military band to play "Dixie." "That tune is now Federal property," he said, and "it is good to show the rebels that with us they will be free to hear it again."[74]

Mary continued to create ugly scenes. Thomas Stackpole, a White House servant, reported that she slapped Lincoln's face on the trip back to Washington and she cursed him. Lincoln sought refuge in the company of others; to some of his shipboard companions he read aloud from Shakespeare's *Macbeth* and he talked of how he wanted to return to Springfield after his presidency. "Mary does not expect ever to go back there," he said, "but I do—I expect to go back and make my home in Springfield for the rest of my life."[75]

Lee surrendered to Grant at Appomattox on April 9. Euphoria spread through the nation's capital.

But Lincoln was eager to get on with the work of creating the post-war future. He had no interest whatsoever in treason prosecutions. Let people like Mary be punitive. Lincoln preferred to be positive—ever positive.

On April 10, an immense crowd of well-wishers congregated at the White House and called for Lincoln. He asked them to return the next evening; he would give them a speech on Reconstruction—a speech in which he would lay out the basis for cooperating with the Radicals.

It was obvious to many that his Ten Percent Plan might have to be discarded. But before he joined forces with the Radicals, he intended to keep on using Louisiana as a laboratory for social reform.

His speech on April 11 was nothing less than remarkable. It contained a unique blend of humor, moral grandeur, and . . . cunning.

Lincoln gave his speech from a window on the north side of the White House, which was all lit up. The crowd below was so vast that it spilled over from 15th Street on the east to 17th Street on the west. Lincoln's speech would be reprinted in full the next day in the newspapers—as front-page copy.

"We meet this evening," he began, "not in sorrow, but in gladness of heart. The evacuation of Petersburg and Richmond, and the surrender of the principal insurgent army, give hope of a righteous and speedy peace whose joyous expression cannot be restrained."[76]

"By these recent successes," he continued, "the re-inauguration of the national authority—reconstruction—is pressed much more closely upon our attention." It was a matter "fraught with great difficulty."[77]

Right away he discussed Louisiana. And the impish deception that he used merits comment. He must have found it a challenge to keep a straight face as he intoned the following words: it had come to his attention, he said, that he was "much censured for some supposed agency in setting up, and seeking to sustain, the new State Government of Louisiana. In this I have done just so much as, and no more than, the public knows."[78]

Of course he had worked behind the scenes in that state to an extent that few people could imagine. But he probably figured that his letters to Banks and Hahn would stay hidden for a great many years—as of course they did.

"In the Annual Message of Dec. 1863," he explained, "I presented *a* plan of re-construction (as the phrase goes) which, I promised, if adopted by any State, should be acceptable to, and sustained by, the Executive government of the nation. I distinctly stated that this was not the only plan which might possibly be acceptable; and I also distinctly protested that the Executive claimed no right to say when, or whether members should be admitted to seats in Congress from such States."

His Ten Percent offer, he continued, was received with some interest in Louisiana, so he let the events play out: "When the Message of 1863, with the plan before mentioned, reached New Orleans, Gen. Banks wrote me that he was confident the people, with his military co-operation, would reconstruct, substantially on that plan. I wrote him, and some of them to try it; they tried it, and the result is known. Such only has been my agency in getting up the Louisiana government. As to sustaining it, my promise is out."[79]

Then he made a statement that perhaps no one else in public life would ever risk. Listen: "But, as bad promises are better broken than kept, I shall treat this as a bad promise, and break it, whenever I shall be convinced that keeping it is adverse to the public interest. But I have not yet been so convinced."[80]

Could anyone but Lincoln interweave such breathtaking audacity with common sense? He was getting people used to the idea that he was willing to turn about-face, embrace a policy change with nonchalance. He might very well be ready to abandon his Ten Percent Plan—abandon it without a qualm—but before he did so he would use it for all that it was worth in Louisiana as a laboratory experiment.

Before returning to the subject of Louisiana, he made some statements that were even more startling. He began with self-effacing humor. "I have been shown a letter," he said, "supposedly an able one, in which the writer expresses regret that my mind has not seemed to be definitely fixed on the question whether the seceded States, so called, are in the Union or out of it. It would, perhaps, add astonishment to his regret, were he to learn that . . . I have *purposely* forborne any public expression upon it."[81]

Astonishment? Anyone taking a moment to reflect upon the statement would feel a great deal more than astonishment. Over and over Lincoln put himself on record since 1860 in regard to that particular question. In his First Inaugural Address he had stated in no uncertain terms that the "seceded states," so-called, were definitely *in* the Union, not out of it. Secession, he had said, was impossible. He said the same thing even more forcefully in his message to Congress of July 4, 1861.

But now he was claiming—or pretending—that he had never ever taken a position on the issue. He said that he had never even addressed that particular question.

Why?

We can never know for sure, but perhaps he was sending a signal to the Radicals, a hint that he was ready and willing to do business with them when the new Congress convened. If Sumner and others wished to push their state-suicide theory, he would yield and cooperate. As to the constitutional metaphysics, he was ready to turn on a dime, since the issues didn't matter to him.

At least that was what he said.

"We all agree," he observed, "that the seceded States, so called, are out of their proper practical relation to the Union; and that the sole object of the government, both civil and military, in regard to those States, is to again get them into that proper practical relation. I believe it is not only possible, but in fact, easier, to do this, without deciding, or even considering, whether these states have even been out of the Union. . . . Let us all join in doing the acts necessary to restoring the proper practical relations between these States and the Union; and each forever after, innocently indulge his own opinion whether, in doing the acts, he brought the States from without, into the Union, or only gave them proper assistance, they never having been out of it."[82]

Then he returned to the issues of Louisiana and he laid out a case for allowing his experiment there to continue. "Some twelve thousand persons in the heretofore slave-state of Louisiana," he pointed out, had "adopted a free-state constitution, giving the benefit of public schools equally to black and white, and empowered the Legislature to confer the elective franchise upon the colored man. Their Legislature has already voted to ratify the constitutional amendment recently passed by Congress, abolishing slavery throughout the nation."[83]

Then he came right out into the open and endorsed black voting rights himself. He admitted it was "unsatisfactory to some that the elective franchise is not given to the colored man. I would myself prefer that it were now conferred on the very intelligent, and on those who serve our cause as soldiers."[84]

There it was—the irrevocable step.

As always, he intended to phase in reform using incremental methods, beginning with soldiers to establish a precedent that could later be extended to others. In any case, he said, "the question is not whether the Louisiana government, as it stands, is quite all that is desirable. The question is, 'Would it be wiser to take it as it is, and help to improve it; or to reject, and disperse it?'"[85]

Then he began to get passionate. He said that if the nation should accept the Louisiana achievement, "we encourage the hearts, and nerve the arms of the twelve thousand to adhere to their work, and argue for it, and proselyte for it, and fight for it, and feed it, and grow it, and ripen it to complete success. The colored man, too, in seeing all united for him, is inspired with vigilance, and energy, and daring to the same end."[86]

The implication was very clear: Lincoln wanted to see black voting rights tested in Louisiana. He was hoping that the state would become a new model for other states to copy: "What is said of Louisiana," he observed, "will apply generally to other States."

Then he took another turn and made it clear that Reconstruction might become more radical—more demanding. After saying that

Louisiana's situation could apply to other states, he said that "so great peculiarities pertain to each state; and such important and sudden changes can occur in the same state; and, withal, so new and unprecedented is the whole case, that no exclusive, and inflexible plan can safely be prescribed as to details and collaterals."[87]

The next statement was as strong as he could make it. "In the present 'situation' as the phase goes, it may be my duty to make some new announcement to the people of the South. I am considering, and shall not fail to act, when satisfied that action will be proper."[88]

So: he had endorsed black voting rights and summoned its advocates to show "vigilance, and energy, and daring." He said that he might have to make a new announcement to the people of the South. Was there any doubt at all about the way in which his policies were changing?

In the audience was John Wilkes Booth. "That means nigger citizenship," he said to his companions, Lewis Paine and David Herold. "Now, by God, I'll put him through. That is the last speech that he will ever make."[89]

How do we know that Booth said this? When his accomplices were tried, they had attorneys. And in the memoirs of these attorneys are cross-corroborations of the words that Booth spoke when the president had finished his speech.

Lincoln's speech created a sensation. Journalist Whitelaw Reid was in the audience and he wrote that, notwithstanding its elements of humor, the speech was delivered "with all the deliberation of a grave political manifesto."[90] The fact that Lincoln had endorsed black voting rights elicited international commentary. The abolitionist Moncure Daniel Conway was accosted on the subject in the course of a visit to London.

Salmon Chase sent Lincoln a letter of support and urged him to go all the way and support universal voting rights "without regard to complexion." Once, he said, "I should have been . . . contented with suffrage for the intelligent and for those who have been soldiers; now I am convinced that universal suffrage is demanded by sound policy and impartial justice."[91] Reid reported that Lincoln, after reading this letter, "showed it to a leading member of his cabinet; and it was so well known as to have been . . . talked of among Administration leaders at Washington at the cabinet meeting that day. . . . Mr. Lincoln's expressions of liberality toward negro citizens . . . were fuller and more emphatic" than ever.[92]

The day of the cabinet meeting was April 14—Good Friday. People who encountered the president were stunned by his good appearance: he looked healthy, rested, and serene. Hugh McCulloch, who had succeeded William Pitt Fessenden as treasury secretary, said he "never saw Mr. Lincoln so cheerful and happy."[93] James Harlan, the new secretary of the interior-designate, said Lincoln was "transfigured." His face bore an "indescribable expression of serene joy, as if conscious that the great purpose of his life had been achieved."[94]

At the cabinet meeting black voting was discussed along with a proposal from Stanton for extended military occupation in ex-rebel states. Lincoln generally approved of this approach; he wanted the rights of the freedmen protected and he was concerned about the possibility of guerrilla warfare.

Lincoln and Mary took a carriage ride in the afternoon, and she told him "you startle me by your great cheerfulness." "And well I may feel so, Mary," he replied, for "I consider *this* day the war has come to a close. We must both, be more cheerful in the future—between the war and the loss of our darling Willie—we have both, been very miserable."[95]

He was affectionate toward her, and worked to soothe her, calm her down, as he had done in the past. Later that afternoon they visited the Navy Yard, and still later, when Illinois visitors came to call, Lincoln read aloud some humorous selections from the latest book by Petroleum Vesuvius Nasby.

They planned a trip to the theater that evening. Lincoln invited the Grants, but when they said they had other plans, Mary invited Major Henry R. Rathbone and his step-sister, Clara Harris.

After dinner, Lincoln met with Schuyler Colfax, who said he would be traveling to California. Lincoln said that he would love to visit California. He was interested in developing the nation's mineral wealth. The mining and coining of gold would make it easier to service the national debt when it was time to redeem all the war bonds.

At 8:30, the Lincolns left for Ford's Theatre to see a new comedy by Tom Taylor, *Our American Cousin*. It starred the famous British actress Laura Keene. Ward Hill Lamon, who insisted on protecting the president, was out of town—on an errand. Lincoln would be guarded by a Metropolitan policeman, John F. Parker, and by a messenger named Charles Forbes. But Parker drifted off before the actor John Wilkes Booth made his way to the presidential box. And Forbes admitted Booth to the anteroom behind the box when Booth displayed an identification card from the theater.

Booth approached the wooden door that opened to the rear of where Lincoln was seated. He looked through a very small peephole he had drilled a few hours before. Then he opened the door, sneaked up behind the rocking chair in which the president was sitting, and shot him point-blank in the head.

He extinguished forever the mind that might have given us a real civil rights revolution. He cost the American people nothing less than a century of progress when he did.

Radical Republicans would do their very best to make the former slaves American citizens—citizens in full—but a hundred years would elapse before decisive results could be achieved. Could Lincoln have produced such results?

We can easily imagine what Lincoln could have done in four years. And so could millions of blacks when they heard the news of Lincoln's death.

Booth was a vicious white supremacist and Confederate sympathizer. Since he never enlisted to fight for the Confederacy, he was often ridiculed as a coward. The shame of this ate at his psyche. His renowned brother Edwin Booth—also an actor, and a famous one—said that Lincoln's assassin was deranged since his earliest years. As an adult, he became an alcoholic as well.

In the autumn of 1864, he hatched a plot to kidnap Lincoln. Some historians believe that he did this in collusion with Confederate agents. He gathered around him an assortment of malcontents to help. John Surratt, a Confederate spy, helped to organize this ring. But the kidnapping scheme came to nothing. In March, when they planned to seize Lincoln on his way to the Soldiers' Home, he did not show up.

After Lee's surrender, Booth determined that the president would have to be killed. He summoned what remained of his fellow conspirators: David Herold, George Atzerodt, and Lewis Powell—alias Paine. Booth decided to kill not only Lincoln, but Johnson and Seward as well. When he heard on April 14 that the president would be attending Ford's Theatre that very evening, he made up his mind to go ahead.

After Booth shot Lincoln, Major Rathbone attempted to grab him. Booth stabbed and wounded the major, then jumped from the box to the stage, shouting "Sic semper tyrannus"—"thus ever to tyrants," the Virginia motto. Racing out the back door, he jumped upon a horse and then fled to southern Maryland.

Meanwhile, Lewis Paine broke into the Seward residence and tried to kill the secretary of state.

Lincoln was carried across the street to the Peterson house on Tenth Street. Mary followed and she tried to get Lincoln to speak to her. But he would never speak to anyone again. Tad, who had been taken to a different theater, was returned to the White House by his tutor. "They've killed papa dead," the boy sobbed. Robert and John Hay were both called to the Peterson house, and then Senator Sumner arrived. Slowly, the room in which Lincoln was dying filled up with his cabinet members. At 7:22 the next morning, Lincoln stopped breathing. "Now he belongs to the ages," said Stanton, who began to weep.

Booth and the other conspirators were all pursued. Booth was killed before he could be taken, but the others were apprehended, tried, and hanged.

The news of Lincoln's murder spread faster than the telegraphs could send it. Millions were plunged into shock, and then the shock gave way to rage and sorrow. No president had ever been murdered before, and to lose this particular president—especially at this moment in his life, and in the life of the nation—was a blow that words could hardly express.

But words came: in newspaper headlines, public banners, letters and diaries, speeches, conversations, eulogies. Surely there were people who had hated and detested him, but millions of Americans loved him. Even those who grasped the tricky side of his nature saw an honesty of purpose that was real: real enough to make people all over the world pay attention. Lincoln was *dedicated* and *true* to the highest ideals. He had a brilliant mind, but he was free of vainglory or pomp. He spoke to everyone in words that could inspire them—or comfort them—or enlighten them. He was a teacher in the very best sense, and he was also a guardian—a protector. He was a moral leader who could touch the hearts of millions as he helped and empowered millions more.

He was a gift to the world—and he was gone.

On April 19, Lincoln's body lay in the East Room of the White House. The premonition he had dreamt had come true. His open coffin was placed upon a catafalque covered with flowers. Mary wept in her room as Elizabeth Keckley and Tad did their best to console her. She was far too distraught to come down and attend her husband's funeral.

But almost everybody else was there: Andrew Johnson, Ulysses S. Grant, Salmon Chase, the cabinet, congressmen, diplomats, military leaders, Lincoln's cavalry escort, and his personal assistants and friends: Nicolay, Hay, and Noah Brooks. After four ministers prayed, Lincoln's coffin was carried to the funeral car for the procession that would take his body to the Capitol.

Church bells tolled throughout the city and artillery salutes filled the air. Bands played dirges. To the beat of muffled drums, Lincoln's funeral car moved along, with a riderless horse beside it. Four thousand black citizens marched among the mourners and African American troops led the funeral procession. Wounded soldiers left hospital beds so they could march in tribute to their leader.

The next day he lay in state in the Capitol rotunda as a vast stream of mourners passed by. On April 21, he was taken on a nine-car funeral train through one city after another on his way back to Springfield. Willie's coffin was unearthed from the Georgetown cemetery and placed beside his father's coffin in the funeral car.

Eighty-five thousand people turned out in New York City, and a very young Theodore Roosevelt watched as the funeral procession worked its way through the street below. Lincoln's coffin lay in state in Albany. Then the funeral train moved west. One hundred fifty thousand mourners turned out in Cleveland, bonfires lit up the night as the train moved to Indianapolis and Chicago, and finally the bodies of Abraham and Willie were laid to rest together in a vault within the Oak Ridge cemetery in Springfield on May 4, 1865.

Walt Whitman composed some new verse to be added to his steadily expanding opus, *Leaves of Grass*—a new section entitled "Memories of President Lincoln," and within this section was a poem about a ship whose captain fell "cold and dead" at the instant when his ship returned safely.

"Memories of President Lincoln" drew upon so many of Whitman's emotions.

He wrote of "the sweetest, wisest soul of all my days and lands," of how "ever-returning spring" would lead him for the rest of his life to remember the "powerful western fallen star" and the "moody, tearful night"—that night when it vanished from the sky.

But he tried to console himself in any way he could, and so he put these lines into his poem:

Come lovely and soothing death,
Undulate round the world, serenely arriving, arriving,
In the day, in the night, to all, to each,
Sooner or later delicate death.

It did not take long for Americans to elevate Lincoln to the stature of legend. Many see in him our very greatest president—which he was.

But to see his life accurately requires effort since the memories of people who knew him would fade and those people would themselves die away. It was vital to record what they remembered. Herndon began right away to gather up facts and to interview people who had known and worked with Lincoln. Biographies began to appear: Herndon and Ward Hill Lamon wrote one-volume works and then Hay and Nicolay produced a ten-volume series that was published in 1890. The six-volume life of Lincoln that was written by Carl Sandburg became a classic by the 1930s. But Sandburg had never known Lincoln, whereas Hay and Nicolay had known him.

Lincoln's life would inspire many presidents. Perhaps the most important was Theodore Roosevelt, who was able to confer with some people who had really known Lincoln while he lived. When Roosevelt became president in 1901—after the assassination of William McKinley—he inherited as secretary of state none other than John Hay. Roosevelt strove to bring Lincolnesque leadership back to the Republican Party, and Hay watched with interest and approval. "Lincoln is my hero," Roosevelt told a friend in 1905, and in the very same year Hay told him he was "one of the men who most thoroughly understand and appreciate Lincoln."[96] Hay presented the president with a ring containing strands of Lincoln's hair—hair that was shorn on the night he passed away and then treasured as a personal keepsake.

Roosevelt kept that ring until he died.

EPILOGUE

When Americans think about Abraham Lincoln, they think that they know him very well. A picture may enter their minds: a picture of the Lincoln Memorial in Washington, the shrine to his memory.

They ponder the theme that this masterpiece of architecture expresses—a theme in our cultural memory, a theme that they associate with Lincoln for reasons that are perfectly understandable.

They know him as the savior of the Union. They see him sculpted in marble by Daniel Chester French, and right behind the statue are these famous and elegant lines:

In this temple
As in the hearts of the people
For whom he saved the Union
The memory of Abraham Lincoln
Is enshrined forever.

People who revere the memory of Lincoln read over those lines with satisfaction. They were written by an art historian named Royal Cortissoz, and they seem to be absolutely perfect. Except they aren't—because they leave out the issue of slavery.

Lincoln saved the Union—that part of the verse composition is correct—but he only had to save it when secessionists attempted to leave, and they did so because of his non-negotiable position on slavery. The inscription says nothing at all about that.

The most popular impression to this day is that Lincoln was a moderate Unionist. Buffeted by horrible events, he reacted with fortitude: he endured what he had to endure to keep the Union together. He "freed the slaves" for the ostensible reason he gave in his famous open letter to Horace Greeley in 1862: to save the Union. Those were his words, and surely "Honest Abe" meant it.

The truth is of course more complex. Lincoln's Unionism must be seen in the context of what that Union would *stand for*. And that issue had become the all-important one for Lincoln by the time that he changed world history.

He rose to greatness when he joined the Free Soilers and condemned the Kansas-Nebraska Act as an atrocity. He stood with his fellow Free Soilers through the nightmare of *Dred Scott*. And in the course of his long campaign against Douglas, he rose to the leadership position in the national Free Soil movement and the brand new party it created.

That took him to his presidential destiny. And his election as president triggered the outbreak of secession, the outbreak of war.

Lincoln occupies a titanic position in the long and grueling crusade to terminate slavery. The events were set in motion by the abolitionists, who kept up the pressure to the end. They were heroes, and Lincoln acknowledged that fact many times in the course of the war. But final victory depended on the presence of a mind that was capable of orchestrating power—a mind that could *visualize* power and direct it. Lincoln possessed that sort of a mind—a *strategic* mind—and he used it.

He beheld the evil of slavery rising to national dimensions: he foresaw that it could spread to every state. It takes a vigorous effort these days to imagine that "unthinkable" future, but Lincoln perceived it, and he sounded the alarm as early as 1854 in his Peoria speech. He warned his fellow citizens that slavery could spread beyond the South, and that slaves could be used for any purpose. He told the Illinois voters to look across the Mississippi River for proof—in Missouri, where slavery was thriving—if they needed any proof. Slavery had *already* spread beyond the South.

The use of slave labor for industrial production was a fact by the 1840s. Slaves had been used as rented strike-breakers at the Tredegar Iron Works in Richmond. Here was a formula that could have been replicated anywhere—in New York, in Chicago, or in Boston.

Anywhere.

The state constitutions of the northern free states would not keep it out for very long. Not after the *Dred Scott* decision laid the groundwork for overturning those constitutions. *Dred Scott* gave a twist to the language of the Fifth Amendment that would soon force a pro-slavery reading of the entire Constitution. The Constitution—the supreme law of the land. No state constitution could conflict with it.

Only one more decision would be needed to construe the Constitution in a way that would strike down the prohibition on slavery in the free states. Lincoln said so clearly in his House Divided speech. The events of the 1850s were part of a stupendous struggle for control of the federal government—and for control of the American way of life. The leaders of the slave states would not give up, and so they had to be stopped.

They were stopped—by Lincoln's leadership. And it was Lincoln's leadership that triggered secession.

He possessed the unique combination of qualities that were needed during this emergency. His nearest competitor for the Republican nomination proved weak when the crisis arrived. In fact, all of his political rivals were comparatively weak by the standards of Lincoln. Both William Seward and Salmon Chase would reveal the kind of character flaws that were disastrous. Who can say what kind of calamities would follow if they, instead of Lincoln, were in power?

But Lincoln was in power. And his formidable skill as a power orchestrator was shown right away. He had the judgment to know when to use overwhelming force and when to pause, play for time, and let the enemy walk into a trap. He could juxtapose honesty and brilliant deception to outmaneuver enemies and deliver the results that would thwart Confederate nationhood and liberate millions.

Confederate nationhood would have been a world-historical catastrophe. There can be little doubt about what would have happened if they won. Their plans for aggression and conquest were already in place as they proclaimed independence. They could have spread their master-race ideology far and wide—into the Caribbean, through Central America, and into the upper tier of South America. Within decades, they might have put their slaves to work extracting products like rubber and oil that could be used for industrial production, products for export, products for use by the war machines of the totalitarian states that would emerge in the twentieth century.

Alexander Stephens proclaimed that the Confederacy was the first nation in the history of the world to be based upon the principle of race. One shudders to think about the twentieth-century global situation as warped by the presence of a powerful slave-holding nation in the middle of the western hemisphere broadcasting its principles of white supremacy and racial domination. Their evil experiment in race-based nationhood might have grossly disfigured our world.

Lincoln's skill as a leader prevented this. It took him time to find commanders who could carry out his plans—and he almost ran out of time in the dangerous election of 1864. But he prevailed, and the Confederacy died.

Lincoln orchestrated power and ideals at one of the single greatest turning points in history. He prevented the emergence of a future so dark that we are forced to regard the great achievement of his life in terms that measure up to the issues.

In the hour of his victory, he turned with anticipation to the prospect of working with the Radicals to advance their social revolution—to push it, perhaps, to the threshold of full black equality. The new birth of freedom was emerging unmistakably and powerfully in 1865. A brilliant future seemed to beckon after all of the suffering and death.

With another four years at his disposal, with Republicans controlling both houses of Congress by super-majorities, the prospects were breathtaking when Lincoln was sworn into office again. His mind was turning already to the demonstration of black voting rights that he intended to guide in the summertime of 1865, using his laboratory state of Louisiana as the model. It is not at all fanciful to say that America's civil rights revolution could have happened a hundred years sooner if Lincoln had lived.

Neither financial constraints nor constitutional haggling would have slowed Lincoln down in the dynamic partnership that he was building with Radical Republicans. James Ashley was emerging as a deal-making player for Lincoln in Radical circles, and the president's consummate skill would almost certainly have led to a party-wide Republican consensus on policy issues when the new Congress convened. Lincoln would have set the tone quickly enough in his annual message to Congress.

And the benefits of a Lincoln-guided Reconstruction might have helped many millions of whites as well as blacks. The South's economy could have been transformed by a huge public works campaign that might very well have been launched in accordance with the Civil War Republicans' "internal improvements" program—a program that some historians have seen as nothing less than the "blueprint for modern America," the program that began with the building of the transcontinental railroad right in the middle of the Civil War. Heroic building with opportunities for all might have made the American Gilded Age different. It would not have been a "gilded" age at all—it could have been golden.

Without the fight between Congress and Lincoln's successor Andrew Johnson—an angry white supremacist Democrat—who can say how far this transformation might have gone? An extraordinary future was stolen from America when John Wilkes Booth put an end to Lincoln's life in Ford's Theatre. The times were nothing less than revolutionary after Robert E. Lee had surrendered, and Lincoln was determined to make the most of this tremendous opportunity.

It was never to be.

But we can easily recapture the expectations that millions were beginning to feel in the springtime of 1865. A writer from a little town in Massachusetts sent Lincoln this letter on the day when he took the presidential oath for the second time:

Dear Sir:

I only wish to thank you for being so good—and to say how sorry we all are that you must have four years more of this terrible toil. But remember what a triumph it is for the right, what a blessing to the country—and then your rest shall be glorious when it does come!

You can't tell anything about it in Washington where they make a noise on the slightest provocation—but if you had been in this little speck of a village this morning and heard the soft, sweet music of unseen bells rippling through the morning silence from every quarter of the far off horizon, you would have better known what your name is in this nation.

May God help you in the future as he has helped you in the past; and a people's love and gratitude will be but a small portion of your exceeding great reward.

Most respectfully,
Mary A. Dodge[1]

What Lincoln accomplished was enough to make his name immortal: he brought his nation through the firestorm to safety. This achievement would come at a terrible cost, yet he gave the United States a chance to push on with its noble experiment: to continue the struggle of advancing the cause of human rights. As we mourn for him, we must celebrate the many priceless gifts that he gave to his fellow Americans as well as to ourselves and our children.

He redeemed the American promise, made it real as no other man has. Our praise should not become extravagant. And yet we come away better and stronger if we take the time to ponder his life—and everything it meant.

We take heart from the example that he set as he strengthened himself and went on to the rescue of others. His achievement in surmounting depression, a difficult marriage, the loss of a sweetheart, the loss of two children, built him into such formidable man that he could brave the greatest crisis in our history. Through the use of his gifts and by attaining self-mastery, he showed us what a blessing life can be. He grew stronger as he faced every challenge.

He will stand for all time as an exemplar of human life fulfilled.

NOTES

Preface

1. See Michael Burlingame, *The Inner World of Abraham Lincoln* (Urbana and Chicago: University of Illinois Press, 1994), Douglas L. Wilson, *Honor's Voice: The Transformation of Abraham Lincoln* (New York: Alfred A. Knopf, 1998), and Joshua Wolf Shenk, *Lincoln's Melancholy: How Depression Changed a President and Fueled his Greatness* (Boston: Houghton Mifflin, 2005).

2. Michael Burlingame, *Abraham Lincoln: A Life* (Baltimore, MD: Johns Hopkins University Press, 2008), two volumes.

3. Benjamin Thomas, *Abraham Lincoln* (New York: Alfred A. Knopf, 1952), Borzoi edition, 22.

4. David Herbert Donald, *Lincoln* (New York: Simon & Schuster, 1995), 14–15.

Chapter 1

1. John L. Scripps to William Herndon, June 24, 1865, in *Herndon's Informants: Letters, Interviews, and Statements about Abraham Lincoln*, eds. Douglas L. Wilson and Rodney O. Davis (Urbana: University of Illinois Press, 1998), 57.

2. J. J. Wright to Ida Tarbell, April 18, 1896, Ida M. Tarbell Papers, Allegheny College.

3. Abraham Lincoln to Jesse W. Fell, Enclosing Autobiography (autobiography written for Jesse W. Fell), December 20, 1859, *Collected Works of*

Abraham Lincoln, ed. Roy P. Basler (New Brunswick, NJ: Rutgers University Press, 1953), III, 511.

4. William H. Herndon to Ward Hill Lamon, February 25, 1870, Lamon Papers, Huntington Library, San Marino, California.

5. William H. Herndon, "Nancy Hanks," notes written circa August 1887, Herndon-Weik Papers, Library of Congress.

6. Abraham Lincoln, Autobiography Written for John L. Scripps, circa June 1860, *Collected Works*, IV, 61.

7. Dennis Hanks to William H. Herndon, interview in Chicago, June 13, 1865, *Herndon's Informants: Letters, Interviews, and Statements about Abraham Lincoln*, eds. Douglas L. Wilson and Rodney O. Davis (Urbana: University of Illinois Press, 1998), 39.

8. Interview with Sarah Bush Lincoln, Bloomington *Pantagraph*, December 17, 1867.

9. Augustus H. Chapman, statement for William H. Herndon, *Herndon's Informants*, 99.

10. Sarah Bush Lincoln, interview with Herndon, September 8, 1865, ibid., 106–7.

11. William H. Herndon and Jesse W. Weik, *Herndon's Lincoln*, ed. Douglas L. Wilson and Rodney O. Davis (1889; Urbana: University of Illinois Press, 2006), 35n. Some words are in order regarding the provenance and context of the original work just cited. The 1889 volume *Herndon's Lincoln*, recently edited and re-issued by Wilson and Davis, was one of a number of early biographies or reminiscences of Lincoln, which varied greatly in quality and reliability. One of the earliest biographies of Lincoln was Josiah B. Holland's *The Life of Abraham Lincoln* (1866). Far more important was Ward Hill Lamon's *Life of Abraham Lincoln* (1872), which was heavily based upon material supplied by Lincoln's old Springfield law partner William H. Herndon. Lamon, who was Lincoln's friend and self-appointed bodyguard, left his own reminiscences of Lincoln to his daughter, Dorothy Lamon Teillard, who published these records in 1896 under the title of *Recollections of Abraham Lincoln, 1847–1865*. Another biography that was based upon Herndon's recollections appeared in 1889: the afore-mentioned *Herndon's Lincoln: The True Story of a Great Life*, by Jesse W. Weik. Various selected items from Herndon's papers were published later on in a book entitled *The Hidden Lincoln, From the Letters and Papers of William H. Herndon* (1938) by Emanuel Hertz.

12. Augustus H. Chapman, statement for Herndon, *Herndon's Informants*, 99.

13. Sarah Bush Lincoln, interview with Herndon, September 8, 1865, ibid., 107.

14. John P. Gulliver, "A Talk with Abraham Lincoln," New York *Independent*, September 1, 1864.

15. Sarah Bush Lincoln, interview with Herndon, September 8, 1865, *Herndon's Informants*, 107.

16. Pages from some of Lincoln's childhood workbooks are in the collections of the Library of Congress, Chicago Historical Society, the Brown University Library, and the Columbia University Library, and a number of these pages are reproduced in Volume I of the *Collected Works* of Lincoln.

17. *Collected Works*, III, 362–63.

18. Joshua Speed, *Reminiscences of Abraham Lincoln and Notes of a Visit to California: Two Lectures* (Louisville, KY: John P. Morton, 1884), 25–26.

19. Reminiscences of John Roll, Chicago *Sunday Times-Herald*, August 25, 1895.

20. This anecdote is based upon interviews with Gentry family descendants. These interviews, conducted in 1936 by Francis Marion Van Natter, are in the Van Natter Papers at Vincennes University.

21. Dennis Hanks to William H. Herndon, December 27, 1865, *Herndon's Informants*, 147.

22. Sarah Bush Lincoln, interview with Herndon, September 8, 1865, ibid., 107.

23. Henry C. Whitney, "Lincoln a Fatalist," Rockport, Indiana *Journal*, February 11, 1898.

24. Accounts of this affair are contained in a series of interviews conducted by Herndon with surviving participants in 1865. See ibid., 114, 120, 127.

25. Francis Marion Van Natter, *Lincoln's Boyhood: A Chronicle of his Indiana Years* (Washington, DC: Public Affairs Press, 1963), 36, and Elizabeth Crawford, interview with Herndon, September 16, 1865, *Herndon's Informants*, 127.

26. William Butler, interview with John G. Nicolay, June 13, 1875, in Michael Burlingame, ed., *An Oral History of Abraham Lincoln: John G. Nicolay's Interviews and Essays* (Carbondale: Southern Illinois University Press, 1996), 20.

27. John Hanks, interview with Herndon, *Herndon's Informants*, 456.

28. Clark E. Carr, *My Day and Generation* (Chicago: McClurg, 1908), 107.

29. Abner Y. Ellis to Herndon, January 23, 1866, *Herndon's Informants*, 174.

30. For an extensive critical comparison of the different accounts of this wrestling match, see Douglas L. Wilson, *Honor's Voice: The Transformation of Abraham Lincoln* (New York: Alfred A. Knopf, 1998), Vintage Edition, 19–51.

31. Quoted in Belleville, Illinois *Advocate*, January 5, 1866.

32. Abraham Lincoln to James H. Hackett, August 17, 1863, *Collected Works*, VI, 392.

33. Robert B. Rutledge, son of James Rutledge, to Herndon, 1866, *Herndon's Informants*, 384–85.

Chapter 2

1. Jason Duncan to Herndon, 1866–1867, *Herndon's Informants: Letters, Interviews, and Statements about Abraham Lincoln*, eds. Douglas L. Wilson and Rodney O. Davis (Urbana: University of Illinois Press, 1998), 539.

2. Ben Perley Poore in Allen Thorndike Rice, ed., *Reminiscences of Abraham Lincoln by Distinguished Men of His Time* (New York: North American Review, 1888), 218–19.

3. William Greene to William Herndon (interview), 1865, *Herndon's Informants*, 18–19.

4. Reminiscence of conversation in Lincoln's home, Risdon M. Moore, "Mr. Lincoln as a Wrestler," *Transactions of the Illinois State Historical Society* 9 (1904), 434.

5. John Todd Stuart, interview with Herndon, circa 1865–1866, *Herndon's Informants*, 481.

6. Abraham Lincoln, Speech in the House of Representatives, July 27, 1848, *Collected Works*, I, 509–10.

7. Stephen T. Logan, interviewed by John G. Nicolay, July 6, 1875, in Michael Burlingame, ed., *An Oral History of Abraham Lincoln: John G. Nicolay's Interviews and Essays* (Carbondale: Southern Illinois University Press, 1996), 35.

8. Abraham Lincoln, Autobiography written for John Locke Scripps, June 1860, *Collected Works*, IV, 65.

9. Leonard Swett in Rice, ed., *Reminiscences of Abraham Lincoln*, 465–66.

10. John Moore Fisk, interview with Herndon, 1887, *Herndon's Informants*, 715.

11. Abraham Lincoln, Autobiography written for John Locke Scripps, *Collected Works*, IV, 62.

12. Abraham Lincoln to George B. McClellan, October 13, 1862, *Collected Works*, V, 460–61.

13. Russell Godbey, interview with Herndon, 1865-1866, *Herndon's Informants*, 450.

14. Abner Y. Ellis to Herndon, 1866, *Herndon's Informants*, 501.

15. Edward D. Baker, speech in the United States Senate, January 3, 1861, *Congressional Globe*, 36th Congress, 2nd Session, 238.

16. Benjamin Thomas, *Abraham Lincoln* (New York: Alfred A. Knopf, 1952), Borzoi edition, 51.

17. Stephen B. Oates, *With Malice Toward None: A Life of Abraham Lincoln* (New York: Harper & Row, 1977), HarperPerennial edition, 19.

18. John Evangelist Walsh, *The Shadows Rise: Abraham Lincoln and the Ann Rutledge Legend* (Urbana and Chicago: University of Illinois Press, 1993).

19. Douglas L. Wilson, *Honor's Voice: The Transformation of Abraham Lincoln* (New York: Alfred A. Knopf, 1998), Vintage Books edition, 114.

20. Interview with Nancy Rutledge Prewitt, conducted by Margaret Flindt, Chicago *Inter-Ocean*, Febuary 12, 1899.

21. Eliza Armstrong Smith, Lerna, Illinois *Eagle*, September 19, 1930.

22. Elizabeth Abell to Herndon, February 15, 1867, *Herndon's Informants*, 556–57.

23. William G. Greene, interview with Herndon, 1865, ibid., 21.

24. George U. Miles to Herndon, March 23, 1866, ibid., 236.

25. John Hill to Ida M. Tarbell, February 6 and 17, 1896, Tarbell Papers, Allegheny College.

26. Henry McHenry to Herndon, January 8, 1866, ibid., 155–56.

27. Wilson, *Honor's Voice*, 119.

28. Isaac Cogdall, interview with Herndon, 1865–1866, *Herndon's Informants*, 440.

29. Joshua Wolf Shenk, *Lincoln's Melancholy: How Depression Challenged a President and Fueled His Greatness* (Boston and New York: Houghton Mifflin, 2005), Mariner edition, 18–21, passim.

Chapter 3

1. Sarah Bush Lincoln, interview with William Herndon, 1865, *Herndon's Informants: Letters, Interviews, and Statements about Abraham Lincoln*, eds. Douglas L. Wilson and Rodney O. Davis (Urbana: University of Illinois Press, 1998), 108.

2. William Herndon to Jesse W. Weik, January 23, 1890, in Emanuel Hertz, *The Hidden Lincoln: From the Letters and Papers of William H. Herndon* (New York: Viking, 1938), 247.

3. Abner Y. Ellis, interview with Herndon, 1866, Herndon's Informants, 170.

4. Polly Richardson Egnew, in J. Edward Murr, "Lincoln in Indiana," *Indiana Magazine of History* 14 (1918), 57.

5. See, for example, Clarence A. Tripp, *The Intimate World of Abraham Lincoln* (New York: Free Press, 2005).

6. Charles B. Strozier, *Your Friend Forever, A. Lincoln: The Enduring Friendship of Abraham Lincoln and Joshua Speed* (New York: Columbia University Press, 2016), 33, 34.

7. Strozier has castigated Michael Burlingame for concluding that Lincoln was indeed a member of the group who visited the prostitutes in Galena. See ibid., 267, n. 7.

8. Douglas L. Wilson has taken the position that Herndon's story of the Beardstown episode may well be true. See Douglas L. Wilson, *Honor's Voice: The Transformation of Abraham Lincoln* (New York: Alfred A. Knopf, 1998), Vintage Books edition, 127–29.

9. James Taylor, interview with Herndon, 1865–1866, *Herndon's Informants*, 482.

10. Hannah Armstrong, interview with Herndon, 1865–1866, ibid., 527.

11. N. W. Branson to Herndon, 1865, ibid., 90.

12. Douglas L. Wilson, *Honor's Voice*, 127.

13. Abraham Lincoln to Mrs. Orville Browning, April 1, 1838, *Collected Works of Abraham Lincoln*, ed. Roy B. Basler (New Brunswick, NJ: Rutgers University Press, 1953), I, 117.

14. Ibid.

15. *Collected Works*, I, 118.

16. Ibid.

17. Abraham Lincoln to Mary S. Owens, August 16, 1857, *Collected Works*, I, 94.

18. Lincoln to Mrs. Orville Browning, April 1, 1838, *Collected Works*, I, 119.

19. Abraham Lincoln, "To the Editor of the *Sangamo Journal*," June 13, 1836, ibid., 48.

20. Undated handbill [ca. July 1836], *Collected Works*, VIII, 429.

21. See Michael Burlingame, *Abraham Lincoln: A Life* (Baltimore: Johns Hopkins University Press, 2008), I, 107.

22. See ibid., 108–9.

23. William Herndon to C. O. Poole, January 5, 1886, Herndon-Weik Papers, Library of Congress.

24. Abraham Lincoln, "Speech in the Illinois Legislature Concerning the State Bank," January 11, 1837, *Collected Works*, I, 65–66.

25. Ibid., 63–64.

26. Abraham Lincoln and Dan Stone, "Protest in Illinois Legislature on Slavery," March 3, 1837, ibid., I, 74–75.

27. Don E. Fehrenbacher, "Only His Stepchildren: Lincoln and the Negro," *Civil War History* 20 (December 1974), 300–301.

28. William Butler, interview with John Nicolay, in Michael Burlingame, ed., *An Oral History of Abraham Lincoln: John G. Nicolay's Interviews and Essays* (Carbondale: Southern Illinois University Press, 1996), 22–23.

29. Joshua Speed to Herndon, 1882, *Herndon's Informants*, 589–90, Speed, *Reminiscences of Abraham Lincoln and Notes of a Visit to California: Two Lectures* (Louisville, KY: John P. Morton, 1884), 21–22.

30. Speed, *Reminiscences*, 34.

31. Abraham Lincoln to Mary S. Owens, May 7, 1837, *Collected Works*, I, 78–79.

32. Speed, *Reminiscences*, 25.

33. Ibid., 23.

34. Edmund Wilson, "Abraham Lincoln: The Union as Religious Mysticism," in *Eight Essays* (New York: Doubleday and Anchor Books, 1954), 190–91, 202.

35. Abraham Lincoln, "Address to the Young Men's Lyceum of Springfield, Illinois," January 27, 1838, *Collected Works*, I, 108–15.

36. Abraham Lincoln, "Speech on the Sub-Treasury," December 26, 1839, ibid., 159–79.

37. Orville Browning, interview with John G. Nicolay, 1875, in *An Oral History of Abraham Lincoln*, 2.

38. Ninian Edwards, interview with Herndon, 1865, *Herndon's Informants*, 133.

39. Martin McKee to John J. Hardin, January 22, 1841, quoted in *Collected Works*, I, 228–29, n. 3.

40. Jane D. Bell to Anne Bell, January 27, 1841, Lincoln files, "Wife" folder, Lincoln Memorial University, Harrogate, Tennessee.

41. Abraham Lincoln to John Todd Stuart, January 20, 1841, *Collected Works*, I, 228.

42. Abraham Lincoln to John Todd Stuart, January 23, 1841, ibid., 229.

43. Orville Browning, interview with Nicolay, 1875, *Oral History*, 1–2.

44. Joshua Speed, interview with Herndon, 1865–1866, *Herndon's Informants*, 474–75.

45. Abraham Lincoln, "Temperance Address, Delivered before the Springfield Washington Temperance Society, on the 22nd February, 1842," *Collected Works*, I, 271–79.

46. Abraham Lincoln to Mary Speed, September 27, 1841, ibid., I, 259–61.

47. Abraham Lincoln to Joshua F. Speed, February 3, 1842, *Collected Works*, I, 267–68.

48. Abraham Lincoln to Joshua F. Speed, February 13, 1842, ibid., I, 269–70.

49. Abraham Lincoln to Joshua F. Speed, March 27, 1862, ibid., I, 282–83.

50. Abraham Lincoln to Joshua F. Speed, July 4, 1842, ibid., I, 288–90.

51. "The 'Rebecca' Letter," August 27, 1842, ibid., I, 291–97.

52. Abraham Lincoln, Memorandum of Duel Instructions to Elias H. Merryman, September 19, 1842, *Collected Works*, I, 300–301.

Chapter 4

1. James Matheny, interview with William Herndon, May 3, 1866, in *Herndon's Informants: Letters, Interviews, and Statements about Abraham Lincoln*, eds. Douglas L. Wilson and Rodney O. Davis (Urbana: University of Illinois Press, 1998), 215.

2. Wayne C. Temple, *Abraham Lincoln: From Skeptic to Prophet* (Mahomet, IL: Mayhaven Publishing, 1995), 27–28.

3. Mary Lincoln to Abram Wakeman, January 30, 1865, in Justin C. Turner and Linda Levitt Turner, eds., *Mary Todd Lincoln: Her Life and Letters* (New York: Alfred A. Knopf, 1972), 200.

4. William H. Herndon and Jesse W. Weik, *Herndon's Lincoln*, Douglas L. Wilson and Rodney O. Davis, eds. (1889; Urbana: University of Illinois Press, 2006), 134.

5. Herndon to Jesse W. Weik, January 16, 1886, Herndon-Weik Papers, Library of Congress.

6. Abraham Lincoln to Joshua F. Speed, February 25, 1842, *Collected Works of Abraham Lincoln*, ed. Roy B. Basler (New Brunswick, NJ: Rutgers University Press, 1953), I, 280.

7. Henry B. Stanton, *Random Recollections* (New York: Harper and Brothers, 1887), 221.

8. William H. Herndon and Jesse W. Weik, *Herndon's Lincoln*, ed. Douglas L. Wilson and Rodney O. Davis (1889; Urbana: University of Illinois Press, 2006), 194.

9. Herndon to Isaac S. Arnold, October 24, 1883, Lincoln Collection, Chicago History Museum.

10. Herndon to Jesse W. Weik, December 1, 1885, Herndon-Weik Papers, Library of Congress.

11. Abraham Lincoln to John T. Stuart, January 21, 1840, *Collected Works*, I, 195, n. 2.

12. Resolutions at a Whig Meeting, March 1, 1843, *Collected Works*, I, 307–08.

13. Abraham Lincoln to Martin S. Morris, April 14, 1843, ibid., 320.

14. Ibid.

15. James Madison to Robert J. Evans, June 15, 1819, in Gaillard Hunt, ed., *The Writings of James Madison* (New York: G.P. Putnam's Sons, 1900–1910), VIII, 437-439.

16. Abraham Lincoln to Williamson Durley, October 3, 1845, *Collected Works*, I, 347.

17. Ibid., 348.

18. William Herndon to Theodore Parker, November 24, 1858, Herndon-Parker Papers, University of Iowa.

19. Isaac N. Arnold, "Reminiscences of the Illinois Bar Forty Years Ago: Lincoln and Douglas as Orators and Lawyers," speech before the Bar Association of the State of Illinois, Springfield, January 7, 1881 (Chicago: Fergus, 1881), 20.

20. William Herndon to Mrs. Leonard Swett, February 20, 1890, Swett Papers, Abraham Lincoln Presidential Library and Museum, Springfield, Illinois.

21. "May Term of the Urbana Court," Danville *Illinois Citizen*, May 29, 1850.

22. *DeKalb County Sentinel*, no date, in J.G. Randall Papers, Library of Congress.

23. Unattributed manuscript, Ida Tarbell Papers, Allegheny College. Lincoln scholar Michael Burlingame has suggested that this account was probably written by attorney James C. Robinson.

24. Lecture by Leonard Swett, Chicago, February 20, 1876, *Chicago Times*, February 21, 1876.

25. Leonard Swett, quoted in Henry Clay Whitney, *Life on the Circuit with Lincoln* (Boston: Estes and Lauriat, 1892), 251.

26. John M. Scott, "Lincoln on the Stump and at the Bar," undated manuscript enclosed in Scott to Ida Tarbell, August 14, 1895, Tarbell Papers.

27. Samuel C. Parks to William Herndon, March 25, 1866, in *Herndon's Informants*, 239.

28. Reminiscences of Adlai E. Stevenson, in Frederick T. Hill, *Lincoln the Lawyer* (New York: Century 1906), 219.

29. For accounts of this case, see Jesse W. Weik, "Lincoln and the Matson Negroes: A Vista into the Fugitive-Slave Days," *Arena*, April 1897, 753, Duncan T. McIntyre, "Lincoln and the Matson Slave Case," *Illinois Law Review*, 1, 1906–1907, 390–91, Paul M. Angle, "Aftermath of the Matson Slave Case," *Abraham Lincoln Quarterly*, 3, 1944, 148, and Mark E. Steiner, *An Honest Calling: The Law Practice of Abraham Lincoln* (DeKalb: Northern Illinois University Press, 2006), 121.

30. David Dudley Field, "The Study and Practice of the Law," *United States Magazine and Democratic Review*, 14, 1844, 347.

31. Abraham Lincoln, "Speech in the United States House of Representatives: The War with Mexico," January 12, 1848, *Collected Works*, I, 432.

32. *Congressional Globe*, 29th Congress, 2nd Sess. Appendix 317 (1847).

33. John Todd Stuart, interview with Herndon, *Herndon's Informants*, 576.

34. William Herndon to Ward Hill Lamon, February 25, 1870, Lamon Papers, Huntington Library, San Marino, California.

35. Abraham Lincoln, "Handbill Replying to Charges of Infidelity," July 31, 1845, *Collected Works*, I, 382.

36. Judge Samuel Treat, statement to William Herndon, *Herndon's Informants*, 483.

37. Thomas J. McCormack, ed., *Memoirs of Gustave Koerner, 1809–1896* (Cedar Rapids, IA: Torch Press, 1909), I, 443–44.

38. Abraham Lincoln to Andrew Johnston, April 18, 1846, *Collected Works*, I, 377–79.

39. Abraham Lincoln to Andrew Johnston, February 25, 1847, ibid., I, 392.

Chapter 5

1. Charles H. Brainard, "Reminiscences of Abraham Lincoln," *Youth's Companion*, December 9, 1880, 435–36.

2. "Washington Correspondence by X," *New York Tribune*, December 15, 1848.

3. David Rankin Barbee to Stephen I. Gilchrist, no date, William H. Townsend Papers, University of Kentucky.

4. Abraham Lincoln to Mary Todd Lincoln, April 16, 1848, Collected Works of Abraham Lincoln, ed. Roy B. Basler (New Brunswick, NJ: Rutgers University Press, 1953), I, 465–66.

5. Ibid.

6. Ibid.

7. Ibid.

8. Mary Todd Lincoln to Abraham Lincoln, May 1848, Justin G. Turner and Linda Levitt Turner, *Mary Todd Lincoln: Her Life and Letters* (New York: Alfred A. Knopf, 1972), 38.

9. Abraham Lincoln to Mary Todd Lincoln, June 12, 1848, *Collected Works*, I, 477–78.

10. Abraham Lincoln, "'Spot' Resolutions in the United States House of Representatives," December 22, 1847, *Collected Works*, I, 420–22.

11. Abraham Lincoln, Speech in the United States House of Representatives: The War with Mexico," January 12, 1848, ibid., I, 431–42.

12. Abraham Lincoln to William H. Herndon, February 1, 1848, ibid., I, 446–48.

13. Abraham Lincoln to Thomas S. Flournoy, February 17, 1848, ibid., 452.

14. Abraham Lincoln to Jesse Lynch, April 10, 1848, ibid., 463–64.

15. Abraham Lincoln, "Fragment: What General Taylor Ought to Say," March [?] 1848, ibid., I, 454.

16. Abraham Lincoln to William H. Herndon, June 12, 1848, ibid., I, 476–77.

17. Abraham Lincoln to William H. Herndon, June 22, 1848, ibid., I, 490–92.

18. Abraham Lincoln, Speech in the U.S. House of Representatives on Internal Improvements, June 20, 1848, ibid., I, 480–89.

19. Abraham Lincoln, Speech in the U.S. House of Representatives on the Presidential Question, July 27, 1848, ibid., I, 501–16.

20. Abraham Lincoln, Speech at Worcester, Massachusetts, September 12, 1848, *Collected Works*, II, 1–5.

21. Abraham Lincoln, Speech at Boston Massachusetts, September 15, 1848, ibid., II, 5.

22. Abraham Lincoln, Speech at Lowell, Massachusetts, September 16, 1848, ibid., II, 6.

23. Abraham Lincoln, Speech at Taunton, Massachusetts, September [21?] 1848, ibid., II, 6–9.

24. Samuel P. Hadley, "Recollections of Lincoln at Lowell in 1848," in Frederick W. Coburn, *History of Lowell and Its People* (New York: Lewis Historical Co., 1920), I, 235–36.

25. Frederick W. Seward, *Seward at Washington as Senator and Secretary of State: A Memoir of His Life, with Selections from His Letters* (New York: Derby and Miller, 1891), I, 180.

26. Abraham Lincoln, Fragment: Niagara Falls [c. September 25–30, 1848], *Collected Works*, II, 10–11.

27. John Wentworth to Edmund S. Kimberly, June 26, 1848, in Don E. Fehrenbacher, *Chicago Giant: A Biography of "Long John" Wentworth* (Madison, WI: American History Research Center, 1957), 79.

28. Abraham Lincoln, Speech at Peoria, Illinois, October 16, 1854, *Collected Works*, II, 253.

29. John C. Calhoun, "Address of Southern Delegates in Congress to their Constituents," January 22, 1849, accessible on-line via http://facweb.furman.edu/~benson/docs/calhoun.htm.

30. John C. Calhoun to Virgil Maxcy, September 11, 1830, Galloway-Maxcy-Markoe Papers, Library of Congress, cited in William W. Freehling, *Prelude to Civil War: The Nullification Controversy in South Carolina, 1816–1836* (New York: Harper & Row, 1965), 257.

31. James Quay Howard, notes of an interview with Lincoln, May 1860, Abraham Lincoln Papers, Library of Congress.

Chapter 6

1. Mary Todd Lincoln to James Smith, June 8, 1870, Justin G. Turner and Linda Levitt Turner, *Mary Todd Lincoln: Her Life and Letters* (New York: Alfred A. Knopf, 1972), 567–68.

2. Abraham Lincoln to John D. Johnston, January 12, 1851, *Collected Works of Abraham Lincoln*, ed. Roy B. Basler (New Brunswick, NJ: Rutgers University Press, 1953), II, 96–97.

3. Abraham Lincoln to John D. Johnston, November 4, 1851, ibid., II, 111–12.

4. Abraham Lincoln to Jesse W. Fell, Enclosing Autobiography (autobiography written for Jesse W. Fell), December 20, 1859, *Collected Works of Abraham Lincoln*, ed. Roy P. Basler (New Brunswick, NJ: Rutgers University Press, 1953), III, 512.

5. William Herndon, quoted in Emanuel Hertz, *The Hidden Lincoln, from the Papers of William H. Herndon* (New York: Viking Press, 1938), 261.

6. Zachary Taylor, Annual Message to Congress, December 4, 1849, http://www.presidency.ucsb.edu/ws/index.php?pid=29490.

7. John C. Calhoun, Speech in the U.S. Senate, March 4, 1850, *Congressional Globe*, 31st Congress, 1st Session, 451, https://memory.loc.gov/cgi-bin/ampage?collId=llcg&fileName=022/llcg022.db&recNum=538.

8. Thurlow Weed, Thurlow Weed Barnes, ed., *Memoir of Thurlow Weed* (Boston: Houghton Mifflin, 1884), 177.

9. Abraham Lincoln, "Eulogy on Henry Clay," July 6, 1852, *Collected Works*, II, 130, 132.

10. Ibid., 123.

11. See Eugene D. Genovese, *The Political Economy of Slavery: Studies in the Economy and Society of the Slave South* (New York: Random House, 1965), 255–64.

12. M. W. McCluskey, ed., *Speeches, Messages, and Other Writings of the Hon. Albert Gallatin Brown, a Senator in Congress from the State of Mississippi* (Philadelphia: J.B. Smith & Co., 1859), 588–99.

13. *Selections from the Writings and Speeches of Hon. Thomas L. Clingman, of North Carolina* (Raleigh, NC: J. Nichols, printer, 1877), 239.

14. Thomas Jefferson to Roger Weightman, June 24, 1826, Library of Congress, accessible via https://www.loc.gov/exhibits/jefferson/214.html.

15. George Fitzhugh, *Sociology for the South—Or, the Failure of Free Society* (Richmond, VA: A. Morris, Publisher, 1854), Burt Franklin Research and Source Book Series, No. 102, 179.

16. Lewis Lehrman, *Lincoln at Peoria: The Turning Point* (Mechanicsburg, PA: Stackpole Books, 2008), xvi.

17. Abraham Lincoln, Speech at Peoria, Illinois, October 16, 1854, *Collected Works*, II, 247–48.

18. Ibid., 274.

19. Ibid., 265–66.

20. Ibid., 271.

21. Ibid., 282.

22. Joseph Gillespie, quoted in Josephine G. Pricket, "Joseph Gillespie," *Transactions of the Illinois State Historical Society for the Year 1912* (publication no. 17 of the Illinois State Historical Library), 108.

23. Reminiscences of James A. Connolly, Peoria, Illinois *Journal*, February 11, 1910.

24. Reminiscences of Peter van Duchene, Milwaukee *Free Press*, February 3, 1909.

Chapter 7

1. Speech at Peoria, Illinois, October 16, 1854, *Collected Works of Abraham Lincoln*, ed. Roy B. Basler (New Brunswick, NJ: Rutgers University Press, 1953), II, 271.

2. Abraham Lincoln to Joshua F. Speed, August 24, 1855, ibid., II, 320–23.

3. Abraham Lincoln to George Robertson, August 15, 1855, ibid., II, 317–38.

4. Ibid.

5. George Harding, quoted in Robert Henry Parkinson, "The Patent Case that Lifted Lincoln into a Presidential Candidate," *Abraham Lincoln Quarterly*, 4 (1946), 113–15.

6. Donn Piat in Benjamin P. Thomas and Harold M. Hyman, *Stanton: The Life and Times of Lincoln's Secretary of War* (New York: Alfred A. Knopf, 1962), 66, and Benjamin Rush Cowen, *Abraham Lincoln: An Appreciation by One Who Knew Him* (Cincinnati: Robert Clarke, 1909), 10–12.

7. Lincoln to Speed, August 24, 1855, *Collected Works*, II, 320–23.

8. John Locke Scripps, *Life of Abraham Lincoln*, Roy P. Basler and Lloyd Dunlap, editors (1860; Bloomington: University of Indiana Press, 1961), 121.

9. Henry Clay Whitney, *Life on the Circuit with Lincoln*, Paul M. Angle, ed. (1892; Caldwell, ID: Caxton Printers, 1940), 92, and Whitney, Lincoln the Citizen, *A Life of Lincoln*, Marion Mills Miller, editor (New York: Baker and Taylor, 1908), I, 259.

10. Thomas J. Henderson to Ida Tarbell, September 12, 1895, Tarbell Papers, Allegheny College.

11. John M. Scott, "Lincoln on the Stump and at the Bar."

12. John Locke Scripps, *Chicago Democratic Press*, May 31, 1856, in Ezra M. Prince, ed., *Meeting of May 29, 1900 Commemorative of the Convention of May 29, 1856 that Organized the Republican Party in the State of Illinois,*, Transactions of the McLean County Historical Society, III, 174.

13. Henderson to Tarbell.

14. Scott, "Lincoln on the Stump and at the Bar."

15. Abraham Lincoln, "Speech at Galena, Illinois," July 23, 1856, *Collected Works*, II, 353–55.

16. Abraham Lincoln, "Fragment on Sectionalism," ca. July 23, 1856, ibid., II, 352.

17. Roger B. Taney, Opinion of the Court, *Scott v. Sandford*, 60 U.S. 393, March 6, 1857, Legal Information Institute, Cornell Law School, accessible via https://www.law.cornell.edu/supremecourt/text/60/393#writing-USSC_CR_0060_0393_ZO.

18. Ibid.

19. Ibid.

20. For a full explication of my views on this subject, see Richard Striner, *Lincoln and Race* (Carbondale: Southern Illinois University Press, 2012).

21. Arthur C. Cole, ed., *The Constitutional Debates of 1847* (Springfield: Illinois State Historical Library, Illinois Historical Collections, 1919), XIV, 216–17.

22. *Chicago Herald*, April 18, June 7, 1860.

23. Abraham Lincoln, "Speech at Springfield," June 26, 1857, *Collected Works*, II, 405.

24. Ibid.

25. Ibid., 407.

26. Ibid., 408.

27. David R. Locke, quoted in Rice, Allen Thorndike, ed., *Reminiscences of Abraham Lincoln by Distinguished Men of His Time* (New York: North American Review, 1886), 446–47.

28. Abraham Lincoln, "Fragment on Slavery," ca. July 1, 1854, *Collected Works*, II, 222–23.

29. Abraham Lincoln, "Speech at Peoria, Illinois," October 16, 1854, ibid., 255–56.

30. Lincoln, Speech at Springfield, June 26, 1857, ibid., II, 405–6.

31. Ibid., 404.

32. Mary Lincoln to Emilie Todd Helm, September 20, 1857, Justin G. Turner and Linda Levitt Turner, eds., *Mary Todd Lincoln: Her Life and Letters* (New York: Alfred A. Knopf, 1972), 50.

33. Colonel Peter A. Dey, quoted in Frederick T. Hill, *Lincoln the Lawyer* (New York: Century, 1906), 260–61.

34. Abraham Lincoln, "Fragment of a Speech," ca. May 18, 1858, *Collected Works*, II, 453.

35. Abraham Lincoln, "Fragment of a Speech," ca. May 18, 1858.

36. Abraham Lincoln, "A House Divided," Speech at Springfield, Illinois, June 16, 1858, ibid., II, 461.

37. Ibid., 464–65.

38. Ibid., 467.
39. Ibid., 465–66.
40. Ibid., 468.

Chapter 8

1. Abraham Lincoln, "Speech at Chicago, Illinois," July 10, 1858, in *Collected Works of Abraham Lincoln*, ed. Roy B. Basler (New Brunswick, NJ: Rutgers University Press, 1953), II, 500.
2. Ibid.
3. Ibid.
4. Ibid., 500–1.
5. Ibid., 501.
6. Abraham Lincoln to Lyman Trumbull, June 23, 1858, ibid., 472.
7. Ezra Prince, "A Day and a Night with Abraham Lincoln," 10, Herndon-Weik Papers, Library of Congress.
8. John W. Forney, *Anecdotes of Public Men* (New York: Harper & Brothers, 1881), II, 179.
9. Abraham Lincoln, "Fragment on the Struggle Against Slavery," ca. July 1858, *Collected Works*, II, 482.
10. Stephen Douglas, speech at Springfield, July 17, 1858, in Paul M. Angle, ed., *Created Equal? The Complete Lincoln-Douglas Debates of 1858* (Chicago: University of Chicago Press, 1958), 62–65.
11. Abraham Lincoln, "Speech at Springfield, Illinois," July 17, 1858, *Collected Works*, II, 519–20.
12. William Walker to William Herndon, June 1865, in *Herndon's Informants: Letters, Interviews, and Statements about Abraham Lincoln*, eds. Douglas L. Wilson and Rodney O. Davis (Urbana: University of Illinois Press, 1998), 22–23.
13. Abraham Lincoln, "Speech at Lewistown," August 17, 1858, *Collected Works*, II, 546–47.
14. *Chicago Press and Tribune*, August 21, 1858, "Douglas at Centralia," *Chicago Press and Tribune*, September 21, 1858.
15. Stephen Douglas, undated interview with Henry T. Glover, Ida M. Tarbell Papers, Allegheny College.
16. *Chicago Press and Tribune*, July 28, 1858.
17. Recollections of George Beatty, Ida M. Tarbell Papers, Allegheny College.
18. Stephen A. Douglas, "Mr. Douglas's Speech," in "First Debate with Stephen A. Douglas at Ottawa, Illinois," August 21, 1858, *Collected Works*, III, 9–10.

19. Ibid., 5.

20. Abraham Lincoln, "Mr. Lincoln's Reply," ibid., 16.

21. Stephen A. Douglas, "Mr. Douglas's Reply," ibid., 35.

22. Abraham Lincoln, "Mr. Lincoln's Speech," in "Second Debate with Stephen A. Douglas at Freeport, Illinois," August 27, 1858, ibid., 39.

23. Ibid., 40–41.

24. Ibid., 40.

25. Ibid., 43.

26. Stephen A. Douglas, "Mr. Douglas's Speech," August 27, 1858, ibid., 51–52.

27. Ibid., 53–54.

28. Ibid., 55–56.

29. Stephen A. Douglas, "Mr. Douglas's Speech," in "Third Debate with Stephen A. Douglas at Jonesboro, Illinois," September 15, 1858, ibid., 105.

30. Abraham Lincoln, "Mr. Lincoln's Speech," September 15, 1858, ibid., 134–35.

31. Stephen A. Douglas, "Senator Douglas's Speech," in "Fourth Debate with Stephen A. Douglas at Charleston, Illinois" on September 18, 1858, ibid., 176.

32. Abraham Lincoln, "Mr. Lincoln's Speech," September 18, 1858, ibid., 146.

33. Abraham Lincoln, "Mr. Lincoln's Reply," in "Fifth Debate with Stephen A. Douglas at Galesburg, Illinois" on October 7, 1858, ibid., 225.

34. Ibid., 230–31.

35. Ibid., 233.

36. Stephen A. Douglas, "Senator Douglas's Reply," in "Sixth Debate with Stephen A. Douglas at Quincy, Illinois," October 13, 1858, ibid., 265.

37. Ibid., 274.

38. Ibid., 267.

39. Abraham Lincoln, "Mr. Lincoln's Rejoinder," October 13, 1858, ibid., 278.

40. Abraham Lincoln, "Mr. Lincoln's Reply," in "Seventh and Last Debate with Stephen A. Douglas at Alton, Illinois," October 15, 1858, ibid., 304.

41. Abraham Lincoln to Norman B. Judd, October 20, 1858, ibid., 329–30.

42. Abraham Lincoln to Anson G. Henry, November 19, 1858, ibid., 339.

43. Abraham Lincoln to Charles H. Ray, November 20, 1858, ibid., 342.

44. Abraham Lincoln to Anson S. Miller, November 19, 1858, ibid., 340.

45. Jesse W. Fell in Osborn H. Oldroyd, ed., *The Lincoln Memorial: Album-Immortelles* (New York: G. W. Carleton, 1882), 476.

46. Abraham Lincoln to Lyman Trumbull, December 11, 1858, ibid., 345.

47. Abraham Lincoln, "Speech at Chicago, Illinois," March 1, 1859, ibid., 367.

48. Abraham Lincoln to Samuel Galloway, July 28, 1859, ibid., 394–95.

49. Abraham Lincoln, to Henry L. Pierce and Others, April 6, 1859, ibid., 375–76.

50. Abraham Lincoln, "Notes for Speeches at Columbus and Cincinnati, Ohio," September 16, 17, 1859, ibid., 435.

51. Stephen Douglas, speech in Memphis, Tennessee, November 30, 1858, *Chicago Times*, December 8, 1858.

52. Abraham Lincoln, "Notes for Speeches at Columbus and Cincinnati, Ohio," September 16, 17, 1859, *Collected Works*, III, 431–32.

53. Ibid., 434.

54. Abraham Lincoln, Speech at Columbus, Ohio, September 18, 1859, ibid., 423.

55. Ibid., 423–24.

56. Ibid., 424.

57. William Herndon to Jesse Weik, February 18, 1887, Herndon-Weik manuscripts, Library of Congress.

58. Mary Todd Lincoln, interview with Herndon, September 1866, in *Herndon's Informants: Letters, Interviews, and Statements about Abraham Lincoln*, eds. Douglas L. Wilson and Rodney O. Davis (Urbana: University of Illinois Press, 1998), 359.

Chapter 9

1. Abraham Lincoln, "Speech at Cincinnati, Ohio," September 17, 1859, *Collected Works of Abraham Lincoln*, ed. Roy P. Basler (New Brunswick, NJ: Rutgers University Press, 1953), III, 440.

2. Ibid., 453.

3. Ibid.

4. Ibid.

5. Ibid., 453–54.

6. Abraham Lincoln, "Speech at Leavenworth, Kansas," December 3, 1859, ibid., III, 502.

7. William Pitt Fessenden, to Elizabeth Warriner, March 16 and April 1, 1860, and to William Fessenden (his son), March 19, 1860, Fessenden Family Papers, Bowdoin College.

8. Abraham Lincoln to William E. Frazer, November 1, 1859, *Collected Works*, III, 491.

9. Norman Judd, interview with John G. Nicolay, February 28, 1876, Michael Burlingame, ed., *An Oral History of Abraham Lincoln: John G. Nicolay's Interviews and Essays* (Carbondale: Southern Illinois University Press, 1996), 46.

10. Leonard Swett, Reminiscences, Correspondence of "Jerome," *Indiana Journal*, February 6–February 10, 1879.

11. William Herndon to Horace White, April 25, 1890, White Papers, Abraham Lincoln Presidential Library and Museum, Springfield, Illinois.

12. Harold Holzer, *Lincoln at Cooper Union: The Speech that Made Abraham Lincoln President* (New York: Simon & Schuster, 2004).

13. Undated reminiscences of Mrs. Theodore Gowdy, Ida M. Tarbell Papers, Allegheny College.

14. Richard C. McCormick, reminiscences, *New York Evening Post*, May 3, 1865.

15. Cornelius A. Runkle, quoted by Noah Brooks, *Abraham Lincoln and the Downfall of American Slavery* (New York: Putnam's, 1894), 186.

16. Abraham Lincoln, "Address at Cooper Institute, New York City," February 27, 1860, *Collected Works*, III, 538.

17. Ibid., 546–47.

18. Ibid., 547–48.

19. Ibid., 549–50.

20. William Cullen Bryant, quoted in Charles H. Brown, *William Cullen Bryant* (New York: Scribner, 1971), 419.

21. Horace Greeley, "Greeley's Estimate of Lincoln: An Unpublished Address by Horace Greeley," *Century Magazine*, 42 (July 1891), 373.

22. Abraham Lincoln to Schuyler Colfax, July 6, 1859, *Collected Works*, III, 390–91.

23. Abraham Lincoln, "Speech at New Haven, Connecticut," March 6, 1860, ibid., IV, 18.

24. Abraham Lincoln, "Speech at Hartford, Connecticut," March 5, 1860, ibid., IV, 7.

25. Concord, New Hampshire *Independent Democrat*, March 8, 1860.

26. Abraham Lincoln to Samuel Galloway, March 24, 1860, *Collected Works*, IV, 34.

27. Abraham Lincoln to Lyman Trumbull, April 29, 1860, ibid., 45.

28. Mark A. Plummer, *Lincoln's Rail-Splitter: Governor Richard J. Oglesby* (Urbana: University of Illinois Press, 2001) 41–42.

29. Leonard Swett, reminiscences, *St. Louis Globe-Democrat*, June 27, 1888.

30. Leonard Swett to the editor, *Chicago Tribune*, July 14, 1878.

31. Nathan M Knapp to Lincoln, May 14, 1860, Abraham Lincoln Manuscripts, Library of Congress.

32. "Lincoln Endorsement," May 17, 1860, *Collected Works*, IV, 50.

33. Marion Mills Miller and Henry Clay Whitney, *Life of Lincoln the Citizen* (New York: Baker and Taylor, 1908), I, 289.

34. Leonard Swett to Abraham Lincoln, May 25 and November 30, 1860, Abraham Lincoln Manuscripts, Library of Congress.

35. Isaac H. Bromley, "Historic Moments: The Nomination of Lincoln," *Scribner's Magazine* 14 (November 1893), 647.

36. Murat Halstead, report in the *Cincinnati Commercial*, May 21, 1860.

37. Ibid.

38. John A. Andrew, speech of May 25, 1860 in Faneuil Hall, *Chicago Press and Tribune*, May 30, 1860.

39. Paul M. Angle, *"Here I Have Lived:" A History of Lincoln's Springfield* (Springfield, IL: Abraham Lincoln Association, 1935), 237.

40. Joshua Giddings to Abraham Lincoln, May 19, 1860, Abraham Lincoln Manuscripts, Library of Congress.

41. Theodore Calvin Pease and James G. Randall, eds., *The Diary of Orville Hickman Browning* (Springfield: Illinois State Historical Library, 1925–1933), I, 415.

42. Jeriah Bonham, *Fifty Years' Recollections* (Peoria, IL: J.W. Franks & Sons, 1883), 182.

43. John A. Kasson to Horace Greeley, July 1, 1860, Greeley Papers, New York Public Library.

44. Letter from "An Intelligent and Substantial Farmer in Union County, Ohio," *New York Tribune*, June 6, 1860.

45. *Charleston Mercury*, October 11, 1860.

46. Abraham Lincoln to John B. Frye, August 15, 1860, *Collected Works*, IV, 95.

47. Abraham Lincoln to William S. Speer, October 23, 1860, ibid., IV, 130.

48. *Atlanta Southern Confederacy*, no date, copied in the *Illinois State Democrat*, September 19, 1860.

49. Lydia Maria Child to Charles Sumner, May 27, 1860, in Milton Meltzer and Patricia G. Holland, eds., *Lydia Maria Child: Selected Letters, 1817–1880* (Amherst: University of Massachusetts Press, 1982), 352.

50. Gerrit Smith to Joshua Giddings, June 2, 1860, Giddings Papers, Ohio Historical Society.

51. *Douglass's Monthly*, June 1860, 276.

52. Frederick Douglass, speech at Geneva, New York, August 1, 1860, in John W. Blassingame, ed., *The Frederick Douglass Papers, Series One: Speeches, Debates, and Interviews* (New Haven: Yale University Press, 1979–1992, III, 381–82.

53. *Chicago Herald*, July 17, 1860.

54. *Illinois State Register*, August 14, 1860.

55. *Indianapolis Daily Journal*, quoted in Emma Lou Thornbrough, *Indiana in the Civil War Era, 1850-1880* (Indianapolis: Indiana Historical Bureau, 1965), 92–93.

56. William Cullen Bryant II, *Power for Sanity: Selected Editorials of William Cullen Bryant* (New York: Fordham University Press, 1994), 380.

57. Declaration of the Immediate Causes Which Induce and Justify the Secession of South Carolina from the Federal Union. Accessible via http://avalon.law.yale.edu/19th_century/csa_scarsec.asp.

Chapter 10

1. Hawkins Taylor to Benjamin F. Wade, December 25, 1860, Wade Papers, Library of Congress.

2. Noah Brooks, "Personal Recollections of Abraham Lincoln," *Harper's New Monthly Magazine*, 30, No. 182 (July, 1865), 225.

3. Ward Hill Lamon, *Recollections of Abraham Lincoln, 1847–1865*, Dorothy Lamon Teillard, ed. (Washington, DC: The Editor, 1911), 112–13.

4. John W. Bunn to Isaac N. Phillips, November 8, 1910, in Isaac N. Phillips, ed., *Abraham Lincoln by Some Men Who Knew Him* (Bloomington, IL: Pantagraph, 1910), 163–64.

5. *Albany Evening Journal*, December 24, 1860.

6. Abraham Lincoln to Alexander Stephens, December 22, 1860, *Collected Works of Abraham Lincoln*, ed. Roy P. Basler (New Brunswick, NJ: Rutgers University Press, 1953), IV, 160.

7. Abraham Lincoln, "Remarks Concerning Concessions to Secession," circa January 19–21, 1861, ibid., IV, 175–76.

8. "J H v A" [James H. Van Allen] to Horace Greeley, December 21, 1860, Greeley Papers, New York Public Library.

9. Abraham Lincoln to William Kellogg, December 11, 1860, *Collected Works*, IV, 150.

10. Abraham Lincoln to Elihu B. Washburne, December 13, 1860, ibid., 151.

11. Abraham Lincoln to Lyman Trumbull, December 17, 1860, ibid., 153.

12. Abraham Lincoln to John A. Gilmer, December 15, 1860, ibid., 151–52.

13. Abraham Lincoln to Elihu B. Washburne, December 21, 1860, ibid., 159.

14. Abraham Lincoln to Duff Green, December 28, 1860, ibid., 162–63.

15. Alexander H. Stephens, speech delivered in Savannah, Georgia, March 21, 1861, in Henry Cleveland, *Alexander H. Stephens, in Public and Private with Letters and Speeches, Before, During, and Since the War* (Philadelphia: National Publishing, 1866), 722.

16. Silas Noble to E. B. Washburne, December 17, 1860, Washburne Papers, Library of Congress, John G. Nicolay, memorandum, December 15, 1860, in Michael Burlingame, ed., *With Lincoln in the White House: Letters, Memoranda, and Other Writings of John G. Nicolay, 1860–1865* (Carbondale: Southern Illinois University Press, 2000), 17–19.

17. Abraham Lincoln to Simon Cameron, January 3, 1861, *Collected Works*, IV, 170.

18. Abraham Lincoln to Salmon P. Chase, December 31, 1860, ibid., IV, 168.

19. Salmon P. Chase to James Shepherd Pike, January 10, 1861, Pike Papers, University of Maine.

20. Abraham Lincoln, Remarks to a Pennsylvania Delegation, January 24, 1861, *Collected Works*, IV, 180–81.

21. Abraham Lincoln to William Seward, January 19, 1861, ibid., IV, 176.

22. Joseph Gillespie, "Lincoln's Time of Agony," *New York Tribune*, February 5, 1888.

23. Abraham Lincoln to William Seward, February 1, 1861, *Collected Works*, IV, 183.

24. Jesse W. Weik, "How Lincoln Was Convinced of General Scott's Loyalty," *Century Magazine*, February 1911, 594.

25. William H. Herndon and Jesse W. Weik, *Herndon's Lincoln: The True Story of a Great Life* (1921), Douglas L. Wilson and Rodney O. Davis, eds. (Urbana: University of Illinois Press, 2007), 289–90.

26. W. H. L. Wallace to Ann Wallace, January 11, 1861, Wallace-Dickey Papers, Abraham Lincoln Presidential Library and Museum.

27. Abraham Lincoln, Farewell Address, February 11, 1861, *Collected Works*, IV, 190.

28. Abraham Lincoln, "Speech from the Balcony of the Bates House at Indianapolis, Indiana," February 11, 1861, ibid., IV, 195–96.

29. Abraham Lincoln, "Speech at Cincinnati, Ohio," February 12, 1861, ibid., IV, 199.

30. Abraham Lincoln, "Speech at Pittsburgh, Pennsylvania," February 15, 1861, ibid., IV, 212.

31. John G. Nicolay, "Some Incidents in Lincoln's Journey," Burlingame, ed., *An Oral History of Abraham Lincoln: John G. Nicolay's Interviews and Essays* (Carbondale: Southern Illinois University Press, 1996), 109–10.

32. Ward Hill Lamon, *Recollections of Abraham Lincoln*, 36.

33. "Lincoln's Beard," *Washington Post*, October 14, 1910.

34. Harry E. Pratt, ed., *Concerning Mr. Lincoln, in Which Abraham Lincoln Is Pictured As He Appeared to Letter Writers of His Time* (Springfield, IL: Abraham Lincoln Association, 1944), 54.

35. Abraham Lincoln, "Reply to Mayor Fernando Wood, at New York City," February 20, 1861, ibid., IV, 233.

36. Abraham Lincoln, "Address to the New Jersey General Assembly at Trenton," February 21, 1861, ibid., IV, 237.

37. Abraham Lincoln, "Reply to Mayor Alexander Henry at Philadelphia, Pennsylvania," February 21, 1861, IV, 239.

38. Abraham Lincoln, "Speech in Independence Hall, Philadelphia, Pennsylvania," February 22, 1861, ibid., IV, 240.

39. Isaac N. Arnold, *The History of Abraham Lincoln and the Overthrow of Slavery* (Chicago: Clarke, 1866), 171.

40. William H. L. Wallace to Ann Wallace, February 27, 1861, Wallace-Dickey Papers, Abraham Lincoln Presidential Library and Museum.

41. *Richmond Enquirer*, March 16, 1861.

42. Orville H. Browning to Abraham Lincoln, February 17, 1861, Abraham Lincoln Papers, Library of Congress.

43. Washington Correspondence, *Philadelphia Inquirer*, March 4, 1861.

44. John Hay, "The Heroic Age in Washington," in Michael Burlingame, ed., *At Lincoln's Side: John Hay's Civil War Correspondence and Selected Writings* (Carbondale: Southern Illinois University Press, 2000), 119.

45. Abraham Lincoln, "First Inaugural Address—Final Text," March 4, 1861, *Collected Works*, IV, 262–63.

46. Ibid., 264–65.

47. Ibid., 265–66.

48. Ibid., 266.

49. Ibid., 268.

50. Ibid., 267.

51. Ibid., 268.

52. Ibid., 271.

53. Ibid.

54. Ibid., 269–70.

55. John A. Bingham, "Abraham Lincoln," speech in Cadiz, Ohio, April 15, 1886, *The Current* (Chicago), April 24, 1886, 282.

56. Edwin Stanton to John A. Dix, March 19, 1861, Dix Papers, Columbia University.

57. William B. Plato to Lyman Trumbull, March 29, 1861, Trumbull Papers, Library of Congress.

58. Henry J. Raymond, *The Life and Public Services of Abraham Lincoln* (New York: Derby and Miller, 1865), 720.

59. William Pitt Fessenden to Elizabeth Warriner, March 17, 1861, Fessenden Papers, Bowdoin College.

60. Henry Villard, *Memoirs of Henry Villard, Journalist and Financier, 1838–1900* (Boston: Houghton Mifflin, 1904), I, 156.

61. John W. Starr, "Lincoln and the Office Seekers," unpublished manuscript, 1936, Lincoln Files, "Patronage" folder, Lincoln Memorial University, Harrogate, Tennessee.

62. James C. Conkling to Lyman Trumbull, June 20, 1862, Trumbull Papers, Library of Congress.

63. Charles A. Dana, *Recollections of the Civil War: With the Leaders at Washington and in the Field in the Sixties* (New York: D. Appleton, 1898), 3.

64. Charles Francis Adams Jr. to Frederic Bancroft, October 11, 1911, Allan Nevins Papers, Columbia University.

65. Ibid.

66. Stephen A. Hurlbut to Abraham Lincoln, March 27, 1861, Abraham Lincoln Papers, Library of Congress, and Stephen A. Hurlbut, interview with John G. Nicolay, May 4, 1876, in Michael Burlingame, ed., *An Oral History of Abraham Lincoln: John G. Nicolay's Interviews and Essays* (Carbondale: Southern Illinois University Press, 1996), 64.

67. James M. McPherson, *Battle Cry of Freedom: The Civil War Era* (New York and Oxford: Oxford University Press, 1988), 271–72.

68. Abraham Lincoln to William H. Seward, April 1, 1861, *Collected Works*, IV, 316–17.

Chapter 11

1. Abraham Lincoln to Andrew G. Curtin, April 8, 1861, *Collected Works of Abraham Lincoln*, ed. Roy P. Basler (New Brunswick, NJ: Rutgers University Press, 1953), IV, 324.

2. Abraham Lincoln to Reverdy Johnson, April 24, 1861, ibid., IV, 342–43.

3. Diary of Clifford Arrick, April 20, 1861, Frontier Guard Records, Library of Congress.

4. Henry Villard, *Memoirs of Henry Villard, Journalist and Financier, 1838–1900* (Boston: Houghton Mifflin, 1904), I, 169–70.

5. Philip B. Fouke, quoted in *New York Herald*, April 24, 1861.

6. John G. Nicolay and John Hay, *Abraham Lincoln: A History* (New York: The Century Company, 1890), IV, 152.

7. Abraham Lincoln, Reply to Baltimore Committee, *Collected Works*, IV, 341–42.

8. Michael Burlingame and John R. Turner Ettlinger, eds., *Inside Lincoln's White House: The Complete Civil War Diary of John Hay* (Carbondale: Southern Illinois University Press, 1997), 11, entry for April 24, 1861.

9. Abraham Lincoln to Gideon Welles, April 29, 1861, ibid., IV, 348.

10. Abraham Lincoln to Winfield Scott, April 25, 1861, ibid., IV, 344.

11. Abraham Lincoln to the Senate and House of Representatives, May 26, 1862, ibid., V, 241.

12. William O. Stoddard, *Inside the White House in War Times: Memories and Reports of Lincoln's Secretary,* Michael Burlingame, ed. (1890; Lincoln: University of Nebraska Press, 2000), 149.

13. William H. Russell, *My Diary North and South* (New York: Harper and Brothers, 1863), 22.

14. Frederick Law Olmsted to Mary Perkins Olmsted, July 2, 1861, in Charles Capen McLaughlin, et al., eds., *The Papers of Frederick Law Olmsted* (Baltimore: Johns Hopkins University Press, 1977–1992), IV, 126.

15. Howard K. Beale, ed., *The Diary of Edward Bates, 1859–1866* (Annual Report of the American Historical Association for the Year 1930, IV; Washington, DC: U.S. Government Printing Office, 1933), 177.

16. Herman Melville to Elizabeth Shaw Melville, March 24, 1861, Merrell R. Davis and William H. Gilman, eds., *The Letters of Herman Melville* (New Haven, CT: Yale University Press, 1960), 210.

17. John Hay, "Life in the White House," Michael Burlingame, ed., *At Lincoln's Side: John Hay's Civil War Correspondence and Selected Writings* (Carbondale: Southern Illinois University Press, 2000), 135.

18. Russell, *My Diary North and South*, 22.

19. Gustavus Vasa Fox to his wife, March 27, 1861, Robert Means Thompson and Richard Wainwright, eds., *Confidential Correspondence of Gustavus Vasa Fox, Assistant Secretary of the Navy, 1861–1865* (New York: De Vinne Press, 1918–1919), I, 11.

20. "Union" to Lincoln, June 26, 1861, typed copy, Abraham Lincoln Presidential Library and Museum.

21. Orville Browning, interview with Nicolay, June 17, 1875, in Burlingame, ed., *An Oral History of Abraham Lincoln: John G. Nicolay's Interviews and Essays* (Carbondale: Southern Illinois University Press, 1996), 3.

22. John Hay, "Life in the White House," in Burlingame, ed., *At Lincoln's Side*, 135–36.

23. Ibid.

24. John Hay, "Tad Lincoln," *New York Tribune*, July 19, 1871, Ibid., 112.

25. John Hay, "Ellsworth," *Atlantic Monthly*, July 1861, 124.

26. Washington Correspondence, *New York Tribune*, May 24, 1861, and *New York Herald*, May 25, 1861.

27. Abraham Lincoln to Ephraim and Phoebe Ellsworth, May 25, 1861, *Collected Works*, IV, 385–86.

28. Abraham Lincoln, Message to Congress in Special Session, July 4, 1861, ibid., IV, 434–35.

29. Ibid., 432–33.

30. Ibid., 437.

31. Ibid., 438.

32. Ibid., 439.

33. Ibid., 429–31.

34. Ibid., 441.

35. Abraham Lincoln, "Speech at Cincinnati, Ohio," September 17, 1859, *Collected Works*, III, 453–54.

36. George B. McClellan to his wife, July 27, 1861, in Stephen W. Sears, ed., *The Civil War Papers of George B. McClellan Selected Correspondence, 1860–1865* (New York: Ticknor & Fields, 1989), 70.

37. George B. McClellan to Abraham Lincoln, August 2, 1861, ibid., 74–75.

38. John G. Nicolay, memorandum of November 20, 1861, in Michael Burlingame, ed., *With Lincoln in the White House: Letters, Memoranda, and Other Writings of John G. Nicolay, 1860–1865* (Carbondale: Southern Illinois University Press, 2000), 62.

39. McClellan to his wife, August 8, 1861, *The Civil War Papers of George B. McClellan*, 81.

40. Benjamin Butler, *Autobiography and Personal Reminiscences of Major-General Benjamin F. Butler: Butler's Book* (Boston: A.M. Thayer, 1892), 287–88.

41. Joshua Speed to Abraham Lincoln, September 9, 1861, Abraham Lincoln Papers, Library of Congress.

42. Robert Anderson to Abraham Lincoln, September 13, 1863, ibid.

43. Abraham Lincoln to John C. Frémont, September 2, 1861, *Collected Works*, IV, 506.

44. Abraham Lincoln to John C. Frémont, September 11, 1861, ibid., 518.

45. Joseph Medill to Salmon P. Chase, September 15, 1861, in John Niven, ed., *The Salmon P. Chase Papers* (Kent, OH: Kent State University Press, 1993–1998), III, 97–98.

46. Abraham Lincoln to Orville H. Browning, September 22, 1861, *Collected Works*, IV, 531–32.

47. John C. Frémont to Edward D. Townsend, September 16, 1861, Abraham Lincoln Papers, Library of Congress.

48. Abraham Lincoln to David Hunter, September 9, 1861, *Collected Works*, IV, 513.

49. Richard Smith to Salmon Chase, November 7, 1861, Chase Papers, Library of Congress.

50. Burlingame and Ettlinger, eds., *Hay Diary*, 30, entry for November 1, 1861.

51. McClellan to his wife, November 17, 1861, *The Civil War Papers of George B. McClellan*, 135–36.

52. *Hay Diary*, 32 (entry for November 13, 1861).

53. Washington Correspondence, Springfield, Massachusetts, *Republican*, November 8, 1861.

54. Ibid., November 1, 1861.

55. Jacob W. Schuckers to Whitelaw Reid, October 3, 1872, Reid Family Papers, Library of Congress.

56. Howard K. Beale and Alan W. Brownsword, eds., *Diary of Gideon Welles, Secretary of the Navy under Lincoln and Johnson* (New York: W.W. Norton, 1960), I, 127, entry for September 12, 1862.

57. Gideon Welles, *Lincoln and Seward* (New York: Sheldon, 1874),185–87.

58. Abraham Lincoln, "Draft of a Dispatch in Reply to Lord John Russell, Concerning the Trent Affair [December 10?] 1861, *Collected Works*, V, 62–64.

59. *The Diary of Edward Bates: 1859–1866*, Howard K. Beale, ed. (Washington: Government Printing Office, 1933), 216, entry for December 25, 1861.

60. *Chase Papers*, I, 319–20, entry for December 25, 1861.

61. Orville H. Browning, manuscript diary, March 3, 1862, Abraham Lincoln Presidential Library and Museum.

62. James H. Upperman to Caleb Smith, October 21, 1861, Records of the U.S. Senate, Committee on Public Buildings and Grounds, 37th Congress, Record Group 46, National Archives and Records Administration.

63. David Davis to his wife, February 19, 1862, David Davis Papers, Abraham Lincoln Presidential Library and Museum.

64. Benjamin Brown French to Pamela French, December 24, 1861, Benjamin French Papers, Library of Congress, and Benjamin Brown French, *Witness to the Young Republic: A Yankee's Journal, 1828–1870*, ed. Cole and McDonough (Hanover, NH: University Press of New England, 1989), 382.

65. William Lloyd Garrison to Oliver Johnson, October 7, 1861, Walter M. Merrill, ed., *The Letters of William Lloyd Garrison* (Cambridge, MA: Harvard University Press, 1971–1981), V, 37.

66. William Herndon to Joseph Gillespie, February 20, 1866, Chicago Historical Society.

67. Charles Edwards Lester, *Life and Public Services of Charles Sumner* (New York: United States Publishing Company, 1874), 359–60.

68. W. A. Croffut, *An American Procession, 1855–1914: A Personal Chronicle of Famous Men* (Boston: Little, Brown, 1931), 73.

69. Moncure Daniel Conway, *Autobiography: Memories and Experiences of Moncure Daniel Conway* (London: Cassell, 1904), I, 380.

70. Abraham Lincoln, "Drafts of a Bill for Compensated Emancipation in Delaware," ca. November 26, 1861, *Collected Works*, V, 29–30.

71. David Davis to Leonard Swett, November 26, 1862, David Davis Papers, Lincoln Presidential Library and Historical Museum.

72. Abraham Lincoln, "Annual Message to Congress," December 3, 1861, *Collected Works*, V, 52.

73. Ibid., 51.

74. Ibid., 48–49.

75. Ibid., 49.

76. Ibid., 48.

77. Ibid., 53.

78. Charles Sumner, "Letter to Governor Andrew, of Massachusetts," December 27, 1861, *The Works of Charles Sumner* (Boston: Lee and Shepard, 1870–1873), VI, 152.

Chapter 12

1. Abraham Lincoln to Simon Cameron, January 10, 1862, *Collected Works of Abraham Lincoln*, ed. Roy P. Basler (New Brunswick, NJ: Rutgers University Press, 1953), V, 95.

2. "General M.C. Meigs on the Conduct of the War," *American Historical Review*, XXVI, January, 1921, 292–93.

3. Abraham Lincoln to Don C. Buell, January 13, 1862, *Collected Works*, V, 98.

4. *The Diary of Edward Bates: 1859–1866*, Howard K. Beale, ed. (Washington: Government Printing Office, 1933), 218, entry for December 31, 1861.

5. Francis B. Carpenter, *The Inner Life of Abraham Lincoln: Six Months at the White House* (New York: Hurd and Houghton, 1867), 258–59.

6. Moncure Daniel Conway, *Autobiography, Memories and Experiences* (New York: Houghton Mifflin Company, 1904), I, 345–46.

7. Wendell Phillips to his wife Ann, March 31, 1862, Phillips Papers, Harvard University.

8. Abraham Lincoln, "President's General War Order No. 1," January 27, 1862, *Collected Works*, V, 111–12.

9. Abraham Lincoln to George B. McClellan, February 3, 1862, *Collected Works*, V, 118–19.

10. For a long analysis of the documentary record of this entire episode by the editors of Lincoln's papers, see ibid., V, 119–25, n. 1.

11. Henry Wilson, interview with Nicolay, November 16, 1875, in Michael Burlingame, ed., *An Oral History of Abraham Lincoln: John G. Nicolay's Interviews and Essays* (Carbondale: Southern Illinois University Press, 1996), 84.

12. Henry A. Wise to A. H. Foote, January 31, 1862, *Collected Works of Lincoln*, V, 108, n. 1.

13. John G. Nicolay, February 20, 1862, in Michael Burlingame, ed., *With Lincoln in the White House: Letters, Memoranda, and Other Writings of John G. Nicolay, 1860–1865* (Carbondale: Southern Illinois University Press, 2000), 71.

14. Elihu Washburne to his wife, February 21, 1862, Washburne Family Papers, Washburne Memorial Library, Norlands, Maine.

15. Anna L. Boyden, *Echoes from Hospital and White House: A Record of Mrs. Rebecca R. Pomroy's Experience in War* (Boston: D. Lothrop, 1884), 56.

16. Michael Burlingame, ed., *Dispatches from Lincoln's White House: The Anonymous Civil War Journalism of Presidential Secretary William O. Stoddard* (Lincoln: University of Nebraska Press, 2002), 66.

17. David B. Chesebrough, *No Sorrow Like Our Sorrow: Northern Protestant Ministers and the Assassination of Lincoln* (Kent, OH: Kent State University Press, 1994), 135.

18. William Fleurville to Lincoln, December 27, 1863, Abraham Lincoln Papers, Library of Congress.

19. Elizabeth Todd Edwards, interview with Herndon, *Herndon's Informants*, 444–45.

20. Elizabeth Keckley, *Behind the Scenes: or, Thirty Years a Slave and Four Years in the White House* (New York: G. W. Carleton, 1868), 104–5.

21. Abraham Lincoln, "Message to Congress," March 6, 1862, *Collected Works*, V, 144–46.

22. Ibid.

23. Ibid.

24. Abraham Lincoln to Henry J. Raymond, March 9, 1862, ibid., V, 152–53.

25. Wendell Phillips, lecture at Smithsonian Institution, March 14, 1862, in *New York Tribune*, March 18, 1862, and *Washington Evening Star*, March 15, 1862.

26. Moncure D. Conway to his wife Ellen, March 8, 1862, Conway Papers, Columbia University.

27. *New York Tribune*, March 7, March 8, 1862.

28. Elihu Burritt to Abraham Lincoln, June 2, 1862, Abraham Lincoln Papers, Library of Congress.

29. Abraham Lincoln, "President's General War Order Number Three," March 8, 1862, ibid., V, 151.

30. Abraham Lincoln to George B. McClellan, April 6, 1862, ibid., V, 182.

31. Abraham Lincoln to George B. McClellan, April 9, 1862, ibid., 184–85.

32. William F. Moore and Jane Ann Moore, eds., *His Brother's Blood: Speeches and Writings of Owen Lovejoy, 1838–1864* (Urbana: University of Illinois Press, 2004), 345.

33. Memorandum by John W. Crisfield, March 10, 1862, published in *Louisville Democrat*, October 26, 1862.

34. George W. Smalley to Sydney Howard Gay, June 21, 1862, Gay Papers, Columbia University.

35. Abraham Lincoln, "Proclamation Revoking General Hunter's Order of Military Emancipation of May 9, 1862," May 19, 1862, ibid., 222–23.

36. Ibid.

37. Abraham Lincoln, "Remarks to a Delegation of Progressive Friends," June 20, 1862, ibid., 278–79.

38. Matilda Johnston Moore, interview with Herndon, 1865, *Herndon's Informants*, 109.

39. *New York Tribune*, May 13, 1862, *New York Herald*, May 13, 1862.

40. Joseph B. Carr, "Operations of 1862 around Fort Monroe," Robert Underwood Johnson and Clarence Clough, eds., *Battles and Leaders of the Civil War* (New York: Century, 1887–1888), II, 152.

41. Captain Wilson Barstow to Elizabeth Barstow Stoddard, May 12, 1862, Barstow Papers, Library of Congress.

42. William F. Keeler to his wife, aboard the *Monitor*, May 9, 1862, in Robert W. Daly, ed., *Aboard the USS Monitor, 1862: The Letters of Acting Paymaster William Frederick Keeler, U.S. Navy, to his Wife, Anna* (Annapolis, MD: U.S. Naval Institute, 1964), 115.

43. Salmon P. Chase to his daughter Janet, aboard the steamer "Baltimore," May 11, 1862, John Niven, ed., *The Salmon P. Chase Papers* (Kent, OH: Kent State University Press, 1994), III, 197.

44. Abraham Lincoln to John C. Frémont, May 24, 1862, *Collected Works*, V, 231.

45. Abraham Lincoln to John C. Frémont, May 30, 1862, ibid., 250.

46. Abraham Lincoln to George B. McClellan, May 25, 1862, ibid., 235–36.

47. *Congressional Globe*, 37th Congress, 2nd Session, 26 (1861).

48. Charles Sumner, "'Stand by the Administration,' Letter to _____," June 5, 1862, *The Works of Charles Sumner* (Boston: Lee and Shepard, 1870–1873), VII, 116–18.

49. Washington Correspondence, Springfield, Massachusetts, *Republican*, June 27, 1862.

50. *Opinion of Attorney General Bates on Citizenship* (Washington, DC: 1862), 26.

51. McClellan to his wife, June 2, 1862, George B. McClellan, *McClellan's Own Story* (New York: Charles L. Webster and Company, 1887), 398.

52. Abraham Lincoln, "Order Constituting the Army of Virginia," June 26, 1862, *Collected Works*, V, 287.

53. *War of the Rebellion: A Compilation of Official Records of the Union and Confederate Armies* (Washington, DC: Government Printing Office, 1880–1901), Series 1, Volume 11, Part 1, 61. Also cited in *Collected Works*, V, 290, f. 1.

54. Abraham Lincoln to George B. McClellan, *Collected Works*, V, 289–90.

55. Abraham Lincoln to William H. Seward, June 28, 1862, ibid., 291–92.

56. Charles Sumner to John Bright, August 5, 1862, Bright Manuscripts, British Museum, London.

57. Abraham Lincoln, "Appeal to Border State Representatives to Favor Compensated Emancipation," July 12, 1862, *Collected Works*, V, 317–19.

58. Gideon Welles, *Diary of Gideon Welles, Secretary of the Navy under Lincoln and Johnson* (New York: Houghton Mifflin Company, 1911), I, 70–71, and idem., "History of Emancipation," *Galaxy* (December 1872), 842–43.

59. Abraham Lincoln, "Emancipation Proclamation—First Draft," July 22, 1862, ibid., 336–37.

60. Francis Carpenter, *Inner Life of Abraham Lincoln*, 21–22.

61. Mary Lincoln to Mrs. Charles Eames, July 26, 1862, Justin G. Turner and Linda Levitt Turner, eds., *Mary Todd Lincoln: Her Life and Letters* (New York: Alfred A. Knopf, 1972), 130.

62. Walt Whitman, "Abraham Lincoln," Number 45, August 12, 1863, *Specimen Days* in *Prose Works* (Philadelphia: David McKay, 1892), 37.

63. Ibid.

64. Abraham Lincoln to Cuthbert Bullitt, July 28, 1862, *Collected Works*, V, 345–46.

65. Abraham Lincoln to August Belmont, July 31, 1862, ibid., 350.

66. *Congressional Globe*, June 2, 1862, 37th Congress, Third Session, 2504.

67. Joseph Enoch Williams et al., to the Honorable Senate and House of Representatives, April 1862, in Select Committee on Emancipation, Petitions & Memorials, Series 467, 37th Congress.

68. Abraham Lincoln, "Address on Colonization to Deputation of Negroes," August 14, 1862, *Collected Works*, V, 371–72.

69. Ibid., 372.

70. Ibid., 374–75.

71. Ibid., 375.

72. Abraham Lincoln to Horace Greeley, August 22, 1862, ibid., V, 388–89.

73. John G. Nicolay, journal entry for March 9, 1862, in Michael Burlingame, ed., *With Lincoln in the White House: Letters, Memoranda, and Other Writings of John G. Nicolay, 1860–1865* (Carbondale: Southern Illinois University Press, 2000), 73.

74. McClellan to his wife, August 10, 1862, in Stephen W. Sears, ed., *The Civil War Papers of George B. McClellan Selected Correspondence, 1860–1865* (New York: Ticknor & Fields, 1989), 389–90.

75. McClellan to Lincoln, August 29, 1862, ibid., 416.

76. Edward Bates, memorandum, September 2, 1862, Abraham Lincoln Papers, Library of Congress.

77. Whitelaw Reid, writing under the pseudonym "Agate," September 10, 1862, *Cincinnati Gazette*, in James G. Smart, ed., *A Radical View: The "Agate" Dispatches of Whitelaw Reid, 1861–1865* (Memphis, TN: Memphis State University Press, 1976), I, 227.

78. George Templeton Strong, diary entry for September 7, 1862, in Allan Nevins and Milton Halsey, eds., *The Diary of George Templeton Strong* (New York: Macmillan, 1952), III, 253.

79. John Hay, in Michael Burlingame and John R. Turner Ettlinger, eds., *Inside Lincoln's White House: The Complete Civil War Diary of John Hay* (Carbondale: Southern Illinois University Press, 1997), 36–37, diary entry of September 1, 1862.

80. Ibid., 37–38.

81. William D. Kelley, *Lincoln and Stanton: A Study of the War Administration of 1861 and 1862* (New York: G.P. Putnam's Sons, 1885), 74–75.

82. Burlingame and Ettlinger, *Hay Diary*, 38–39, diary entry of September 5, 1862.

83. Abraham Lincoln, "Meditation on the Divine Will," ca. September 2, 1862, *Collected Works*, V, 403–4.

84. Robert E. Lee to Jefferson Davis, September 8, 1862, in Clifford Dowdey and Louis H. Manarin, eds., *The Wartime Papers of R.E. Lee* (New York: Bramhall House, 1961), 301.

85. *War of the Rebellion: A Compilation of Official Records of the Union and Confederate Armies*, Series I, Vol. 19, Part 2, 601–2.

86. Abraham Lincoln, "Reply to Emancipation Memorial Presented by Chicago Christians of All Denominations," September 13, 1862, *Collected Works*, V, 420, 421, 425.

87. Salmon Chase, diary entry for September 22, 1862, in Niven, ed., *Chase Papers*, I, 393–94.

88. Abraham Lincoln, "Preliminary Emancipation Proclamation," September 22, 1862, *Collected Works*, V, 433–36.

89. Burlingame and Ettlinger, *Hay Diary*, 41, diary entry for September 24, 1862.

Chapter 13

1. Abraham Lincoln, "Reply to Serenade in Honor of Emancipation Proclamation," September 24, 1862, *Collected Works of Abraham Lincoln*, ed. Roy P. Basler (New Brunswick, NJ: Rutgers University Press, 1953), V, 438–39.

2. *New York Tribune*, September 24, 1862.

3. Theodore Tilton to William Lloyd Garrison, September 24, 1862, Garrison Papers, Boston Public Library.

4. *The Works of Charles Sumner* (Boston: Lee and Shepard, 1870–1873), VII, 199.

5. Ralph Waldo Emerson, "The President's Proclamation," *The Atlantic Monthly*, November, 1862, 639–40.

6. *New York Times*, September 28, 1862.

7. *Pittsburgh Gazette*, September 24, 1862.

8. Lydia Maria Child to Sarah Shaw, October 30, 1862, in Milton Meltzer and Patricia G. Holland, eds., *Lydia Maria Child: Selected Letters, 1817–1880* (Amherst: University of Massachusetts Press, 1982), 419.

9. *Douglass's Monthly*, October 1862.

10. *Douglass's Monthly*, January 1863.

11. *Louisville Democrat*, September 24, 1862.

12. *Louisville Journal*, no date, reprinted in Springfield (Massachusetts) *Republican*, October 2, 1862.

13. Charles Mason, diary entry for September 23, 1862, in Hubert H. Wubben, *Civil War Iowa and the Copperhead Movement* (Ames: Iowa State University Press, 1980), 84.

14. George McClellan to Ellen Marcy McClellan, September 25, October 5, 1862, in Stephen W. Sears, ed., *The Civil War Papers of George B. McClellan: Selected Correspondence, 1860–1865* (New York: Ticknor & Fields, 1989), 481–82.

15. *War of the Rebellion: A Compilation of Official Records of the Union and Confederate Armies*, Series I, Vol. XIX, Part 2, 395–96.

16. Dunbar Rowland, ed., *Jefferson Davis, Constitutionalist: His Letters, Papers, and Speeches* (Jackson: Mississippi Department of Archives and History, 1923), V, 409.

17. *Richmond Enquirer*, October 1, 1862, reprinted in *New York Herald*, October 4, 1862.

18. *London Times*, October 7, 1862.

19. *London Morning Star*, October 6, 1862.

20. John Stuart Mill to John Lothrop Motley, October, 1862, in Henry Donaldson Jordan and Edwin J. Pratt, *Europe and the American Civil War* (Boston: Houghton Mifflin, 1931), 139.

21. Henry Adams to Charles Francis Adams Jr., January 23, 1863, in J. C. Levenson, ed., *The Letters of Henry Adams* (Cambridge: Harvard University Press, 1982), I, 327.

22. William E. Gladstone, speech at Newcastle-on-Tyne, October 7, 1862, *London Times*, October 9, 1862.

23. Lord Palmerston to Lord John Russell, October 2, October 22, 1862, in Ephraim Douglas Adams, *Great Britain and the American Civil War* (New York: Longmans, Green & Company, 1925), II, 43–44, 54–55.

24. Adams S. Hill to Sydney Howard Gay, October 13, 1862, in Louis Morris Starr, *Bohemian Brigade: Civil War Newsmen in Action* (New York: Alfred A. Knopf, 1954), 152.

25. Headquarters of the Army of the Potomac correspondence, *New York Herald*, October 7, 1862.

26. John L. Parker, *Henry Wilson's Regiment* (Boston: Rand Avery, 1887), 205.

27. Washington correspondence by "W," *Cincinnati Commercial*, October 8, 1862.

28. John Hay, in Michael Burlingame and John R. Turner Ettlinger, eds., *Inside Lincoln's White House: The Complete Civil War Diary of John Hay* (Carbondale: Southern Illinois University Press, 1997), 232, diary entry of September 25, 1864.

29. Anonymous letter to "B.F.M.," Washington correspondence of B.F.M., *Cincinnati Gazette*, October 30, 1862.

30. William M. Dickson, "A Leaf from the Unwritten History of the Rebellion," no date, Dickson Papers, William L. Clements Library, University of Michigan.

31. O. M. Hatch, interview by John Nicolay, June 1875, in Michael Burlingame, ed., *An Oral History of Abraham Lincoln: John G. Nicolay's Interviews and Essays* (Carbondale: Southern Illinois University Press, 1996), 16.

32. Allan Nevins, ed., *A Diary of Battle: The Personal Journals of Colonel Charles S. Wainwright, 1861–1865* (New York: Harcourt, Brace & World, 1962), 109, diary entry for October 2, 1862.

33. Abraham Lincoln to George B. McClellan, October 13, 1862, *Collected Works*, V, 460.

34. Ibid.

35. Ibid., 461.

36. Ibid., 460.

37. Abraham Lincoln to George B. McClellan, October 24 or 25, 1862, ibid., 474.

38. Abraham Lincoln to John Ross, September 25, 1862, ibid., 439–40.

39. Abraham Lincoln to Carl Schurz, November 10, 1862, ibid., 493–94.

40. Washington correspondence by "Van" (D. W. Bartlett), Massachusetts *Republican*, November 28, 1862.

41. Abraham Lincoln, "Remarks to Kentucky Unionists," November 21, 1862, ibid., 503.

42. Abraham Lincoln to Henry Halleck, November 27, 1862, ibid., 514–15.

43. Abraham Lincoln, "Annual Message to Congress," December 1, 1862, ibid., 530.

44. Ibid., 535.

45. Ibid., 537.

46. William Henry Wadsworth to S. L. M. Barlow, December 16, 1862, Barlow Papers, Huntington Library.

47. William O. Stoddard, "White House Sketches No. VII," New York Citizen, September 29, 1866, in Stoddard, *Inside the White House in War Times: Memoirs and Reports of Lincoln's Secretary*, Michael Burlingame, ed. (1890; Lincoln: University of Nebraska Press, 2000), 171.

48. Adam S. Hill to Sydney Howard Gay, September 8, 12, 1862, Gay Papers, Columbia University.

49. Zachariah Chandler to Lyman Trumbull, September 10, 1862, Trumbull Papers, Library of Congress.

50. Oliver P. Morton to Abraham Lincoln, October 27, 1862, in W. H. H. Terrell, *Indiana in the War of the Rebellion: Report of the Adjutant General* (Indianapolis: Douglass and Conner, 1869), 26.

51. Carl Schurz to Abraham Lincoln, November 8, 1862, Abraham Lincoln Papers, Library of Congress.

52. Abraham Lincoln to Carl Schurz, November 10, 1862, *Collected Works*, V, 493–95.

53. Carl Schurz to Lincoln, November 20, 1862, Lincoln Papers.

54. Lincoln to Schurz, November 24, 1862, *Collected Works*, 509–10.

55. Zachariah Chandler to his wife, December 18, 1862, Chandler Papers, Library of Congress.

56. Ibid.

57. Joseph Medill to Schuyler Colfax, no date, O.J. Hollister, *Life of Schuyler Colfax* (New York: Funk & Wagnalls, 1886), 200.

58. Theodore Calvin Pease and James G. Randall, eds., *The Diary of Orville Hickman Browning* (Springfield: The Trustees of the Illinois State Historical Library, 1925), I, 597, entry for December 16, 1862, and William Pitt Fessenden, manuscript account of 1862 cabinet crisis, Fessenden Papers, Bowdoin College.

59. Washington correspondence, *New York Times*, December 22, 1862.

60. *Browning Diary*, I, 602, entry for December 19, 1862.

61. Washington correspondence, "Henry J.R." (Henry J. Raymond), *New York Times*, December 22, 1862.

62. Fessenden, manuscript account of cabinet crisis.

63. Francis Fessenden, *Life and Public Services of William Pitt Fessenden* (Boston: Houghton Mifflin, 1907), II, 244.

64. Gideon Welles, *Diary of Gideon Welles, Secretary of the Navy under Lincoln and Johnson* (New York: Houghton Mifflin Company, 1911), I, 201–2, entry for December 20, 1862.

65. Fredrick Seward, interviewed by Nicolay, January 9, 1879, in Burlingame, ed., *Oral History of Lincoln*, 87.

66. Washington correspondence by "Agate" (Whitelaw Reid), *Cincinnati Gazette*, March 26, 1863.

67. Abraham Lincoln, "Opinion on the Admission of West Virginia into the Union," December 31, 1862, *Collected Works*, VI, 27.

68. Ibid.

69. Ibid.

70. Ibid.

71. Ibid., 28.

72. Ibid.

73. Abraham Lincoln, "Emancipation Proclamation," January 1, 1863, ibid., 28.

74. Ibid.

75. George Alfred Townsend, *Washington, Outside and Inside* (Cincinnati: Betts, 1874), 715.

76. W. North Brown and Randolph C. Downes, eds., "A Conference with Abraham Lincoln: From the Diary of Reverend Nathan Brown," *Northwest Ohio Quarterly*, 22 (1949–1950), 61–62.

77. Francis Carpenter, *The Inner Life of Abraham Lincoln: Six Months at the White House* (New York: Hurd and Houghton, 1867), 269–70, Frederick Seward, *Reminiscences of a War-Time Statesman and Diplomat, 1830–1915* (New York and London: G.P. Putnam's Sons, 1916), 226–27.

78. Frederick Seward, *Reminiscences*, 227.

79. Jefferson Davis, Message to the Confederate Congress, January 12, 1863, J. D. Richardson, ed., *Messages and Papers of Jefferson Davis and the Confederacy* (Nashville: United States Publishing Company, 1905), I, 290–93.

80. Frederick Douglass, *Life and Times of Frederick Douglass, written by himself* (Hartford, CT: Park Publishing Co., 1881, facsimile edition, Secaucus, NJ: Citadel Press, 1983), 359–60.

81. Abraham Lincoln to William S. Rosecrans, January 5, 1863, *Collected Works*, VI, 39.

82. *Browning Diary*, I, 613, entry for January 12, 1863.

83. Ibid., 152–53, n. 1.

84. Abraham Lincoln, "Speech to Indians," March 27, 1863, ibid., 151–53.

85. Abraham Lincoln to Isaac N. Arnold, May 26, 1863, ibid., 230.

86. A.D. Richardson to Sydney Howard Gay, March 20, 1863, Gay Papers, Columbia University.

87. Noah Brooks, Washington correspondence, *Sacramento Daily Union*, May 8, 1863, in in Michael Burlingame, ed., *Lincoln Observed: Civil War Dispatches of Noah Brooks* (Baltimore: Johns Hopkins University Press, 1998), 43.

88. Ibid., 42.

89. Abraham Lincoln, "Memorandum on Joseph Hooker's Plan of Campaign against Richmond," ca. April 6–10, 1863, *Collected Works*, VI, 164–65.

90. Abraham Lincoln, "Proclamation Suspending the Writ of Habeas Corpus," September 24, 1862, *Collected Works*, V, 436–37.

91. *Congressional Globe*, 37th Congress, 2nd Session, Appendix 52–60.

92. *War of the Rebellion: A Compilation of Official Records of the Union and Confederate Armies*, Series II, Vol. 5, 636, 641.

93. *American Annual Cyclopaedia and Register of Important Events of the Year 1863* (New York: C. Appleton, 1864), 689.

94. Ibid., 474.

95. Abraham Lincoln to Erastus Corning & Others, June 12, 1863, *Collected Works*, VI, 260–69.

96. Abraham Lincoln to Andrew Johnson, March 26, 1863, ibid., 149–50.

97. Abraham Lincoln to David Hunter, April 1, 1863, ibid., 158.

98. *War of the Rebellion: A Compilation of Official Records of the Union and Confederate Armies*, Series I, Vol. 26, Part 1, 45.

99. Noah Brooks, Washington Correspondence, *Sacramento Daily Union*, June 5, 1863, in Burlingame, ed., *Lincoln Observed*, 50.

100. *Welles Diary*, I, 336, entry for June 20, 1863.

101. Francis Carpenter, *Inner Life of Abraham Lincoln*, 220–21.

102. Abraham Lincoln, "Fragment," circa August 26, 1863, *Collected Works*, VI, 410–11.

103. Abraham Lincoln to E. E. Malhiot, Bradish Johnson, and Thomas Cottman, June 19, 1863, ibid., 288.

104. Abraham Lincoln to Nathaniel Banks, August 5, 1863, ibid., 364–65.

105. Abraham Lincoln to Andrew Johnson, September 11, 1863, ibid., 440.

106. Abraham Lincoln to Joseph Hooker, June 5, 1863, ibid., 249.

107. Abraham Lincoln to Joseph Hooker, June 10, 1863, ibid., 257.

108. Abraham Lincoln to Joseph Hooker, June 14, 1863, ibid., 273.

109. Abraham Lincoln, "Response to a Serenade," July 7, 1863, ibid., 319–20.

110. *Hay Diary*, 62, entry for July 14, 1863.

111. Abraham Lincoln to Henry W. Halleck, July 6, 1863, *Collected Works*, VI, 318.

112. John F. Marszalek, *Commander of All Lincoln's Armies: A Life of General Henry W. Halleck* (Cambridge: Harvard University Press, 2004), 179.

113. Robert Todd Lincoln, memo to John Nicolay, January 5, 1885, in Burlingame, ed., *Oral History of Lincoln*, 88–89.

114. *War of the Rebellion: A Compilation of Official Records of the Union and Confederate Armies*, Series I, Vol. 27, Part 1, 92.

115. *Hay Diary*, 62, 63, entries for July 14 and July 15, 1863.

116. Abraham Lincoln to George Gordon Meade, July 14, 1863, *Collected Works*, VI, 327–28.

117. *Welles Diary*, I, 370-371, entry for July 14, 1863.

118. Abraham Lincoln to Ulysses S. Grant, July 13, 1863, *Collected Works*, VI, 326.

119. Washington Correspondence, *New York Independent*, July 30, 1863.

120. Abraham Lincoln, "Order of Retaliation," July 30, 1863, *Collected Works*, VI, 357.

121. Frederick Douglass, *Life and Times of Frederick Douglass* (Hartford, CT: Park Publishing Company, 1881), 350–53.

122. Frederick Douglass to George Luther Stearns, August 12, 1863, Records of the Free Military School for Command of Colored Regiments, Historical Society of Pennsylvania, and Douglass, speech of December 4, 1863 in John W. Blassingame et al., eds., *The Frederick Douglass Papers, Series One: Speeches, Debates, and Interviews* (New Haven, CT: Yale University Press, 1979–1992), III, 606–8.

123. *Life and Times of Frederick Douglass*, 353.

124. Ulysses S. Grant to Lincoln, August 23, 1863, Abraham Lincoln Papers, Library of Congress.

125. Abraham Lincoln to James C. Conkling, August 26, 1863, *Collected Works*, VI, 406–10.

126. Abraham Lincoln to Stephen A. Hurlbut, ca. August 15, 1863, ibid., 387.

127. Abraham Lincoln to Nathaniel P. Banks, August 5, 1863, ibid., 365.

128. Abraham Lincoln, "Instructions to Tax Commissioners in South Carolina," September 16, 1863, ibid., 457.

129. John Hay to John Nicolay, August 7, 1863, in Michael Burlingame, ed., *At Lincoln's Side: John Hay's Civil War Correspondence and Selected Writings* (Carbondale: Southern Illinois University Press, 2000), 49.

130. Andrew G. Curtin to Lincoln, September 18, 1863, Abraham Lincoln Papers, Library of Congress.

131. *Hay Diary*, 101, entry for October 28, 1863.

132. Abraham Lincoln to Henry Halleck, October 16, 1863, *Collected Works*, VI, 518.

133. *Welles Diary*, I, 439, entry for September 21, 1863.

134. Abraham Lincoln to Ambrose Burnside, September 25, 1863, *Collected Works*, VI, 480–81.

135. *Hay Diary*, 99, entry for October 24, 1863.

136. Abraham Lincoln to Mary Todd Lincoln, June 10, 1863, ibid., 256.

137. Abraham Lincoln to Robert Todd Lincoln, July 3, 1863, ibid., 314.

138. Abraham Lincoln to Mary Todd Lincoln, September 21, 1863, ibid., 471.

139. Abraham Lincoln to Mary Todd Lincoln, September 22, 1863, ibid., 474.

140. Abraham Lincoln, "Proclamation of Thanksgiving," October 3, 1863, ibid., 496–97.

141. Abraham Lincoln, "Speech at Lewistown," August 17, 1858, *Collected Works*, II, 546–47.

142. *Washington Daily Morning Chronicle*, November 21, 1863.

143. *Philadelphia Press*, November 20, 1863.

144. Benjamin Brown French, *Witness to the Young Republic: A Yankee's Journal, 1828–1870*, Donald B. Cole and John J. McDonough, eds. (Hanover, NH: University Press of New England, 1989), 435–36.

145. Josephine Forney Roedel, diary entry, November 19, 1863, Library of Congress.

146. Abraham Lincoln, "Gettysburg Address," November 19, 1863, *Collected Works*, VII, 17–23.

147. *Ohio State Journal*, November 23, 1863.

Chapter 14

1. Abraham Lincoln, Annual Message to Congress, December 8, 1863, *Collected Works of Abraham Lincoln*, ed. Roy P. Basler (New Brunswick, NJ: Rutgers University Press, 1953), VII, 49.

2. Ibid.

3. Ibid.

4. Ibid., 49–50.

5. Ibid., 50.

6. Ibid., 52.

7. Abraham Lincoln, Proclamation of Amnesty and Reconstruction, December 8, 1863, ibid., 55.

8. Ibid., 54.

9. Annual Message to Congress, December 8, 1863, ibid., 51.

10. Abraham Lincoln to Nathaniel Banks, November 5, 1863, ibid., 1–2.

11. Henry Halleck to Ulysses S. Grant, December 21, 1863, *War of the Rebellion: A Compilation of Official Records of the Union and Confederate Armies* (Washington, DC: Government Printing Office, 1880–1901), Series 1, Volume XXXI, Part 3, 458.

12. Ulysses S. Grant to Henry Halleck, January 19, 1864, ibid., XXXIII, Part 2, 394–95.

13. Henry Halleck to Ulysses S. Grant, February 17, 1864, ibid., XXXII, Part 2, 411–13.

14. Abraham Lincoln to Nathaniel Banks, December 24, 1863, *Collected Works*, VII, 90.

15. Abraham Lincoln to Michael Hahn, March 13, 1864, ibid., VII, 243.

16. Abraham Lincoln, "Address at Sanitary Fair, Baltimore, Maryland," April 18, 1864, ibid., VII, 301–2.

17. Abraham Lincoln to Daniel E. Sickles, February 15, 1864, ibid., VII, 185.

18. Allan Nevins and Milton Halsey, eds., *Diary of George Templeton Strong, 1835–1875* (New York: Macmillan, 1952), III, 379, entry for December 11, 1863.

19. Charles Eliot Norton to G. W. Curtis, December 10, 1863, Sara Norton and M. A. De Wolf Howe, eds., *Letters of Charles Eliot Norton* (Boston: Houghton Mifflin, 1913), I, 266.

20. Harriet Beecher Stowe, "Watchman and Reflector," *Little's Living Age*, February 6, 1864, 283.

21. Katherine Helm, *The True Story of Mary, Wife of Lincoln: Containing the Recollections of Mary Lincoln's Sister Emilie (Mrs. Ben Hardin Helm), Extracts of her War-Time Diary, Numerous Letters and Other Documents* (New York: Harper and Brothers, 1928), 222–32.

22. Robert Wesley McBride, *Lincoln's Body Guard: The Union Light Guard of Ohio, with Some Personal Recollections of Abraham Lincoln* (Indianapolis, IN: Edward J. Hecker, 1911), 26–27.

23. Diary of William T. Coggeshall, November 26, 1863, in Freda Postle Koch, *Colonel Coggeshall: The Man Who Saved Lincoln* (Columbus, Ohio: Poko Press, 1985), 63.

24. John Hay, in Michael Burlingame and John R. Turner Ettlinger, eds., *Inside Lincoln's White House: The Complete Civil War Diary of John Hay* (Carbondale: Southern Illinois University Press, 1997), 93, 103, entries for October 18 and 29, 1863.

25. Joseph Medill to Abraham Lincoln, February 17, 1864, Abraham Lincoln Papers, Library of Congress.

26. Shelby M. Cullom, *Fifty Years of Public Service: Personal Recollections* (Chicago: A. C. McClurg, 1911), 98.

27. *The American Annual Cyclopedia of Important Events in the Year 1864* (New York: D. Appleton, 1869), 784.

28. Albert D. Richardson, *A Personal History of Ulysses S. Grant* (Hartford, CT: American Publishing Company, 1868), 413.

29. J. Russell Jones, quoted in Ida M. Tarbell, *The Life of Abraham Lincoln, drawn from original Sources and containing many Speeches, Letters, and Telegrams, hitherto unpublished* (New York: The Doubleday & McClure Company, 1900), II, 188.

30. Isaac Markens, *Abraham Lincoln and the Jews* (New York: published by the author, 1909), 12.

31. Washington Correspondence, Isaac M. Wise, The Cincinnati *Israelite*, January 16, 1863, ibid., January 23, 1863.

32. *The American Annual Cyclopedia and Register of Important Events for the Year 1864* (New York: D. Appleton, 1865), 67.

33. Horace Porter, "Lincoln and Grant," in Peter Cozzens, ed., *Battles and Leaders of the Civil War* (Urbana: University of Illinois Press, 2004), VI, 79.

34. *Hay Diary*, 193–94, entry for April 30, 1864.

35. Elizabeth Cady Stanton to Lydia Maria Child, ca. April 22, 1864 in Ann D. Gordon, ed., *The Selected Papers of Elizabeth Cady Stanton and Susan B. Anthony* (New Brunswick, NJ: Rutgers University Press, 1997–2006), I, 514.

36. Wendell Phillips to Moncure Daniel Conway, March 16, 1864, Conway Papers, Columbia University.

37. Abraham Lincoln to Albert G. Hodges, April 4, 1864, *Collected Works*, VII, 281–82.

38. Abraham Lincoln to Ulysses S. Grant, April 30, 1864, Ibid., 324.

39. Ulysses S. Grant to Abraham Lincoln, May 1, 1864, in John Y. Simon, ed., *The Papers of Ulysses S. Grant* (Carbondale: Southern Illinois University Press, 1967–2005), X, 380.

40. *Hay Diary*, 195, entry for May 9, 1864.

41. Schuyler Colfax, in Allen Thorndike Rice, ed., *Reminiscences of Abraham Lincoln by Distinguished Men of his Time* (New York: North American, 1886), 337.

42. Lydia Maria Child to Gerrit Smith, July 23, 1864, in Milton Meltzer and Patricia G. Holland, eds., *Lydia Maria Child: Selected Letters, 1817–1880* (Amherst: University of Massachusetts Press, 1982), 445.

43. William Lloyd Garrison, *The Liberator*, March 18, 1864.

44. William Lloyd Garrison, *Philadelphia Press*, March 17, 1864.

45. Gideon Welles, *Diary of Gideon Welles, Secretary of the Navy under Lincoln and Johnson* (New York: Houghton Mifflin Company, 1911), II, 44–45, entry for June 2, 1864.

46. Abraham Lincoln, "Speech at Great Central Sanitary Fair, Philadelphia, Pennsylvania," June 16, 1864, *Collected Works*, VII, 394.

47. John G. Nicolay to Charles Eugene Hamlin, February 24, 1896, in C. E. Hamlin, *The Life and Times of Hannibal Hamlin* (Cambridge: Riverside Press, 1899), 593–94.

48. Abraham Lincoln to Ulysses S. Grant, June 15, 1864, *Collected Works*, VII, 393.

49. Horace Porter to his wife, June 24, 1864, Porter Papers, Library of Congress.

50. Sylvanus Cadwallader, *Three Years with Grant*, ed. Benjamin Thomas (New York: Knopf, 1955), 233.

51. Horace Porter to his wife, June 24, 1864 Porter Papers.

52. Abraham Lincoln to Salmon Chase, June 30, 1864, *Collected Works*, VII, 419.

53. Abraham Lincoln, Proclamation Concerning Reconstruction," July 8, 1864, ibid., 433–34.

54. Thaddeus Stevens to Edward McPherson, July 10, 1864, in Beverly Wilson Palmer, ed., *The Selected Papers of Thaddeus Stevens* (Pittsburgh: University of Pittsburgh Press, 1997–1998), I, 500.

55. *The American Annual Cyclopedia and Register of Important Events of the Year 1864* (New York: D. Appleton, 1865), 308–310.

56. Noah Brooks, *Washington, D.C. in Lincoln's Time* (New York: The Century Company, 1896), 156.

57. Abraham Lincoln to Ulysses S. Grant, July 10, 1864, *Collected Works*, VII, 437.

58. Noah Brooks, *Washington, D.C. in Lincoln's Time*, 162.

59. Washington Correspondence by R.S.B., *Philadelphia Inquirer*, August 22, 1864.

60. George William Curtis to Charles Eliot Norton, July 12, 1864, Curtis Papers, Harvard University.

61. Horace Greeley to Abraham Lincoln, July 7, 1864, *Collected Works*, VII, 435, n. 1.

62. Abraham Lincoln, Speech at Great Central Sanitary Fair, Philadelphia, Pennsylvania, June 16, 1864, ibid., 395.

63. Abraham Lincoln, To Whom It May Concern, July 18, 1864, ibid., 451.

64. Abraham Lincoln to Abram Wakeman, July 25, 1864, ibid., 461.

65. Abraham Lincoln, "Memorandum on Clement C. Clay," ca. July 25, 1864, ibid., 459.

66. *Columbus Crisis*, August 3, 1864.

67. Abraham Lincoln to Ulysses S. Grant, August 3, 1864, ibid., 476.

68. Abraham Lincoln to Ulysses S. Grant, August 17, 1864, ibid., 499.

69. Thurlow Weed to William Seward, August 22, 1864, Abraham Lincoln Papers, Library of Congress.

70. Leonard Swett to his wife, no date, in Ida Tarbell, *Life of Abraham Lincoln*, II, 201–2.

71. *Columbus Crisis*, August 3, 1864.

72. *Freeman's Journal*, August 20, 1864.

73. Ward Hill Lamon, *Recollections of Abraham Lincoln, 1847–1865*, ed. Dorothy Lamon Teillard (Washington, DC.: Lamon Teillard, 1911), 267–69, *New York Times*, April 6, 1887.

74. *Hay Diary*, 246, entry for November 8, 1864.

75. Frederick Douglass, *Life and Times of Frederick Douglass* (Hartford, CT: Park Publishing Company, 1881), 363–64.

76. Henry J. Raymond to Abraham Lincoln, August 22, 1864, *Collected Works*, VII, 517–18, n. 1.

77. Abraham Lincoln to Charles D. Robinson, August 17, 1864, ibid., 501.

78. John G. Nicolay to John Hay, August 25, 1864, Michael Burlingame, ed., *With Lincoln in the White House: Letters, Memoranda, and Other Writings of John G. Nicolay, 1860–1865* (Carbondale: Southern Illinois University Press, 2000), 152–54.

79. Abraham Lincoln, Memorandum Concerning His Probable Failure of Re-election, August 23, 1864, *Collected Works*, VII, 514.

80. Abraham Lincoln, "Interview with Alexander W. Randall and Joseph T. Mills," August 19, 1864, ibid.

81. Abraham Lincoln to Isaac M. Schermerhorn, September 12, 1864 ibid., VIII, 1–2.

82. *Charleston Mercury*, September 5, 1864.

83. George Templeton Strong, diary entry for September 3, 1864, in Allan Nevins and Milton Halsey, eds., *The Diary of George Templeton Strong* (New York: Macmillan, 1952), III, 480–81.

84. John G. Nicolay to Theodore Tilton, September 6, 1864, Burlingame, ed., *With Lincoln in the White House*, 158.

85. Nicolay to Therena Bates, September 11, 1864, ibid.

86. Abraham Lincoln, "Order of Thanks to William T. Sherman and Others," September 3, 1864, *Collected Works*, VII, 533.

87. Abraham Lincoln to Eliza P. Gurney, September 4, 1864, ibid., 535.

88. Elizabeth Blair Lee to Samuel Phillips Lee, September 24, 1864, Virginia Jeans Laas, ed., *Wartime Washington: The Civil War Letters of Elizabeth Blair Lee* (Urbana: University of Illinois Press, 1991), 433.

89. Zachariah Chandler to his wife, September 8, 1864, Chandler Papers, Library of Congress.

90. Abraham Lincoln to Montgomery Blair, September 23, 1864, *Collected Works*, VIII, 18.

91. Noah Brooks, *Washington, D.C. in Lincoln's Time*, 164.

92. Elizabeth Keckly, *Behind the Scenes: or, Thirty Years a Slave and Four Years in the White House* (New York: G. W. Carleton, 1868), 145.

93. Abraham Lincoln to Ulysses S. Grant, September 29, 1864, *Collected Works*, VIII, 29.

94. Abraham Lincoln, "Proclamation of Thanksgiving," October 20, 1864, ibid., 55.

95. Abraham Lincoln, "Response to a Serenade," October 19, 1864, ibid., 52.

96. Abraham Lincoln, "Response to a Serenade, November 8, 1864, ibid., 96.

97. Abraham Lincoln, "Response to a Serenade," November 10, 1864, ibid., 100–101.

98. Abraham Lincoln to John Maclean, December 27, 1864, ibid., 183–84.

Chapter 15

1. Abraham Lincoln, "Annual Message to Congress," December 6, 1864, *Collected Works of Abraham Lincoln*, ed. Roy P. Basler (New Brunswick, NJ: Rutgers University Press, 1953), VIII, 151.

2. Ibid., 152.

3. Ibid., 149.

4. Abraham Lincoln to George H. Thomas, December 16, 1864, ibid., 169.

5. Abraham Lincoln to William T. Sherman, December 26, 1864, ibid., 181–82.

6. James S. Rollins in Osborn H. Oldroyd, ed., *The Lincoln Memorial: Album-Immortelles* (New York: G. W. Carleton, 1882), 492–93.

7. Abraham Lincoln to Francis P. Blair, Sr., January 18, 1865, *Collected Works*, VIII, 220–21.

8. Gideon Welles, *Diary of Gideon Welles, Secretary of the Navy under Lincoln and Johnson* (New York: Houghton Mifflin Company, 1911), II, 231.

9. James Ashley to Lincoln, January 31, 1865, *Collected Works*, VIII, 248.

10. Abraham Lincoln to James Ashley, January 31, 1865, ibid.

11. Ashley to William Herndon, November 23, 1866, Herndon-Weik Collection, Library of Congress.

12. William Lloyd Garrison to Abraham Lincoln, February 13, 1865, Abraham Lincoln Papers, Library of Congress.

13. *The Liberator*, February 10, 1865.

14. *New York Tribune*, November 4, 1883.

15. Alexander Stephens, John A. Campbell, and Robert M. T. Hunter to Ulysses S. Grant, January 30, 1865, in *The War of the Rebellion: A Compilation of the Official Records of the Union and Confederate Armies* (Washington, DC: Government Printing Office, 1880–1901), Series I, Vol. 46, Part 2, 297.

16. Ulysses S. Grant to Edwin Stanton, February 1, 1865, *Collected Works*, VIII, 282.

17. Zachariah Chandler to his wife, January 25, 1865, Chandler Papers, Library of Congress.

18. Washington Correspondence, *New York World*, February 11, 1865.

19. Reminiscence of Alexander Stephens to Evan P. Howell, 1882, in Howell to Henry Watterson, *Louisville Courier-Journal*, clipping in collection of Lincoln Museum, Fort Wayne, Indiana.

20. Alexander Stephens, *A Constitutional View of the Late War between the States: Its Causes, Character, Conduct, and Results, Presented in a Series of Colloquies at Liberty Hall* (Philadelphia: National Publishing Company, 1868–1870), II, 599–601.

21. Augusta, Georgia *Chronicle and Sentinel*, June 7, 1865.

22. Ibid.

23. Springfield, Massachusetts *Republican*, February 25, 1865.

24. Stephens, *Constitutional View*, II, 617.

25. Abraham Lincoln, "Message to the House of Representatives," February 10, 1865, *Collected Works*, VIII, 274–85.

26. Noah Brooks, *Washington in Lincoln's Time* (New York: Rinehart, 1958), 206–7.

27. *Congressional Globe*, 38th Congress, 2nd Session, February 10, 1865, 733.

28. *New York Times*, February 7, 1865.

29. *New York Herald*, February 8, 1865.

30. Abraham Lincoln, "To the Senate and House of Representatives," February 5, 1865, *Collected Works*, VIII, 260.

31. Gideon Welles, "Lincoln and Johnson: Their Plan of Reconstruction and the Resumption of National Authority," *Galaxy* 13 (April, 1872), 522.

32. Abraham Lincoln, "Annual Message to Congress," December 1, 1863, *Collected Works*, V, 532.

33. Abraham Lincoln to Lyman Trumbull, January 9, 1865, *Collected Works*, VIII, 207.

34. Abraham Lincoln to Ulysses S. Grant, January 19, 1865, ibid., 223.

35. Welles diary, II, 252, entry for March 4, 1865.

36. Zachariah Chandler to his wife, March 6, 1865, Chandler Papers.

37. Ervin Chapman, *Latest Light on Abraham Lincoln* (New York: Fleming H. Revell, 1917), 294.

38. Noah Brooks, *Washington, D.C. in Lincoln's Time* (New York: The Century Company, 1896), 74.

39. Abraham Lincoln, "Second Inaugural Address," March 4, 1865, *Collected Works*, VIII, 332–33.

40. Frederick Douglass, *Life and Times of Frederick Douglass* (Hartford, CT: Park, 1881), 444.

41. James Grant Wilson, "Recollections of Lincoln," *Putnam's Monthly*, 5 (February, 1909), 675.

42. Abraham Lincoln to Thurlow Weed, March 15, 1865, *Collected Works*, VIII, 356.

43. *Chicago Tribune*, March 22, 1865.

44. Joshua Speed to William Herndon, January 12, 1866, Herndon-Weik Collection.

45. Elizabeth Keckley, *Behind the Scenes: or, Thirty Years a Slave and Four Years in the White House* (New York: G. W. Carleton, 1868), 124–26.

46. Harriet Beecher Stowe, *Men of Our Times* (Hartford, CT: Hartford Publishing Company, 1868), 73.

47. Francis B. Carpenter, *The Inner Life of Abraham Lincoln: Six Months at the White House* (New York: Hurd and Houghton, 1867), 17.

48. Don E. Fehrenbacher and Virginia Fehrenbacher, eds., *Recollected Words of Abraham Lincoln* (Stanford, CA: Stanford University Press, 1996), 305–7.

49. Carpenter, *Inner Life of Lincoln*, 62–63.

50. Brooks, *Washington in Lincoln's Time*, 38.

51. Nicolay interview, *Chicago Herald*, December 4, 1887.

52. La Crosse *Daily Democrat*, August 25, 1864.

53. Greensburg, Pennsylvania *Argus*, August 10, 1864.

54. Ward Hill Lamon, *Recollections of Abraham Lincoln, 1847–1865*, Dorothy Lamon Teillard, ed. (Washington, DC: 1911), 263–81.

55. J. H. Van Alen to the editors of the New York *Evening Post*, May 11, 1865.

56. Lamon, *Recollections of Lincoln*, 115–18.

57. Edwin Stanton to Ulysses S. Grant, March 3, 1865, John Y. Simon, ed., *The Papers of Ulysses S. Grant* (Carbondale: Southern Illinois University Press, 1967–2012), XIV, 91.

58. Sylvanus Cadwallader, *Three Years with Grant*, Benjamin P. Thomas, ed. (New York: Alfred A. Knopf, 1955), 282.

59. John S. Barnes, "With Lincoln from Washington to Richmond in 1865," *Appleton's Magazine* 9 (May 1907), 522.

60. Adam Badeau, *Grant in Peace, from Appomattox to Mount McGregor: A Personal Memoir* (Hartford, CT: S.S. Scranton, 1887), 362.

61. Ibid.

62. William Tecumseh Sherman, *Memoirs of General W. T. Sherman* (New York: C.L. Webster, 1891–1892), II, 325–27.

63. Abraham Lincoln to Edwin Stanton, March 30, 1865, *Collected Works*, VIII, 377.

64. Horace Porter, *Campaigning with Grant* (New York: Century, 1897), 450–51.

65. David D. Porter, *Incidents and Anecdotes of the Civil War* (New York: D. Appleton, 1885), 287.

66. Ibid., 294.

67. Ibid., 295.

68. Porter, *Incidents and Anecdotes*, 300–301.

69. Ibid.

70. Charles Carleton Coffin in the Boston Journal, Herbert Mitgang, ed., *Abraham Lincoln: A Press Portrait* (Chicago: Quadrangle Press, 1971), 453–54.

71. Porter, *Incidents and Anecdotes*, 297–98.

72. Ervin Chapman, *Latest Light on Abraham Lincoln: And Wartime Memories* (New York: Fleming H. Revell, 1917), II, 500.

73. Abraham Lincoln to Ulysses S. Grant, April 7, 1865, *Collected Works*, VIII, 392.

74. Marquis de Chambrun, "Personal Recollections of Mr. Lincoln," *Scribner's Magazine*, January, 1893, 28.

75. John Todd Stuart, interviewed by Nicolay, June 24, 1875, in Michael Burlingame, ed., *An Oral History of Abraham Lincoln: John G. Nicolay's Interviews and Essays* (Carbondale: Southern Illinois University Press, 1996), 14.

76. Abraham Lincoln, "Last Public Address," April 11, 1865, *Collected Works*, VIII, 399.

77. Ibid., 400.

78. Ibid., 401.

79. Ibid., 401–2.

80. Ibid., 402.

81. Ibid., 402–3.

82. Ibid., 403.

83. Ibid.

84. Ibid.

85. Ibid.

86. Ibid., 404.

87. Ibid.

88. Ibid., 405.

89. Edward Steers, Jr., *Blood on the Moon: The Assassination of Abraham Lincoln* (Lexington: University Press of Kentucky, 2001), 91.

90. "Agate," in *Cincinnati Gazette*, July 23, 1865.

91. Salmon P. Chase to Lincoln, April 12, 1865, in Jacob W. Schuckers, *Life And Public Service of Salmon Portland Chase* (New York: Appleton, 1874), 516–18.

92. "Agate," quoted in Harold M. Hyman, "Lincoln and Equal Rights for Negroes," *Civil War History* 12 (September 1966), 255–56.

93. Hugh McCulloch, *Men and Measures of Half a Century: Sketches and Comments* (New York: Charles Scribner's Sons, 1888), 222.

94. Ida M. Tarbell, *The Life of Lincoln* (New York: McClure, Phillips, 1900), II, 232.

95. Mary Lincoln to Francis B. Carpenter, November 15, 1865, in Justin G. Turner and Linda Levitt Turner, *Mary Todd Lincoln: Her Life and Letters* (New York: Alfred A. Knopf, 1972), 284–85.

96. Theodore Roosevelt to George Otto Trevelyan, March 9, 1905, in Elting E. Morison, ed., *The Letters of Theodore Roosevelt* (Cambridge: Harvard University Press, 1951), IV, 1132, and idem, IV, 1131, n. 1.

Epilogue

1. Mary A. Dodge to Abraham Lincoln, March 4, 1865, Abraham Lincoln Papers, Library of Congress.

INDEX

Abell, Elizabeth, 29
Abolitionism and abolitionists, 36,
    40, 152, 182–83, 265–68, 276–77,
    285, 294, 323, 325, 346–347,
    408, 434, 464; Lincoln and, 36,
    39–40, 172, 181, 182–83, 265–68,
    276–77, 285, 294, 323, 327–28,
    346–47, 408, 434
Adams, Charles Francis, Sr., 209,
    233
Adams, Henry, 329
Adams, John Quincy, 88
African Americans, 9, 33, 35–36,
    39–40, 48–49, 61–62, 65, 99–100,
    104, 106–7, 121, 125–30, 144–45,
    148–49, 152–53, 154, 161–63,
    183, 250–52, 300–1, 311–13,
    334–35, 337–338, 345–46,
    355–56, 361, 364–67, 369–70,
    390–92, 395, 405, 411–12, 418,
    421, 426, 433–34, 452, 456–57,
    459, 460; diversity of opinions
    among, 63, 311–12; leadership
    of, 311–12; military service of,

345–46, 355–56, 361, 364–67,
    384, 405, 411–12, 421; persecu-
    tion of, 105–6, 121, 125–30, 163,
    183, 312, 361, 364, 365, 392, 418,
    452; voting rights for, 390–91,
    440, 456–57
Agassiz, Louis, 106
Alabama, 195, 388, 400
Allen, John, 12
"Almanac Trial," 71, 145–46
Alton, Illinois: Lincoln-Douglas
    debate in, 156; murder of Elijah
    Lovejoy and, 35
amendments to the Constitution.
    See constitutional amendments
American Party. See Know-Nothing
    Party
Anaconda Plan, 244, 252
Anderson, (Major) Robert, 221, 236,
    257, 275
Andrew, John A., 178, 401
Antietam: battle of, 324, 329;
    and Emancipation Proclama-
    tion, 324–25; international

significance of, 329; McClellan's incompetence in, 323–24; political significance of, 324, 329

antislavery movement, 36, 40, 61–65, 66, 73–74, 87–92, 111–30, 132–39, 140–63, 172, 181, 182–83, 250–52, 256–59, 265–71, 276–77, 282–85, 292–96, 305–9, 323–29, 337, 345–47, 358–60, 389–92, 421, 429–30 433–34, 464–66

Appomattox Court House surrender, 453

Arkansas, 234, 384, 389, 426

Armstrong, Hannah, 13, 23, 28, 224

Armstrong, Jack, 13, 28

Armstrong, William "Duff," 71, 145–46

Army of the Potomac: creation of, 249, 255; leadership of, 249, 261, 274, 278, 287–88, 303, 310, 321–22, 331–32, 336–39, 359–60, 373, 399, 405, 410–11, 413, 451

Articles of Confederation and Perpetual Union, 61, 123, 198

Ashley, James M., 271, 283, 292, 345, 389, 395, 431–33, 440–41, 466

Atlanta, Georgia, 399, 422–23, 428–29, battle of Atlanta as turning point in Civil War, 422–23, Sherman's leadership, 422–23

Atzerodt, George, 459

Badeau, Adam, 450

Baker, Edward D., 20, 42, 58, 59, 60, 72, 93, 177, 213, 260

Baldwin, John B., 227

Baltimore, Maryland, 174, 231, 232, 235; during secession crisis,

207–8, 231, 232, 235; Lincoln's speech on liberty in, 390

Bank of the United States, Second, 21–22, 44

banks and banking, 21–22, 43–45, 50–51, 273, 285

Banks, Nathaniel P., 197, 297–98, 302, 330, 356, 359–360, 369, 387–390, 399, 454

Barret v. Alton and Sangamon Railroad Company, 96

Bates, Edward M., 166, 176, 177, 195, 212, 222, 232, 239, 274, 302, 308, 318, 394

battles: Antietam, 324, 329; Atlanta, 422–23; Ball's Bluff, 260; Brandy Station, 360; Cedar Creek, 425; Chancellorsville, 356–57; Chattanooga, 383; Chickamauga, 374; Cold Harbor, 409; Corinth, 329; Fair Oaks, 302; Fisher's Hill, 425; Five Forks, 451; Franklin, 430; Fredericksburg, 338–39; Gettysburg, 320, 360–61, 362; Iuka, 329; Kernstown, 298; Logan's Crossroads, 276, 280; Malvern Hill, 304; Manassas, first battle of, 248–50; Manassas, second battle of, 317–18; Murfreesboro, 347; Nashville, 430; Pea Ridge, 286, 334; Perryville, 329; Seven Pines, 302; Shiloh, 288–89; Spotsylvania Court House, 407; Stone's River, 347; Wilderness, 406; Wilson's Creek, 252

Beauregard, P. G. T., 228, 244, 248–49, 288–89, 407

Bedell, Grace, 202, 204–5

Beecher, Henry Ward, 113, 167

Bell, John, 174, 183, 191
Belmont, August, 311, 418
Berry, William F., 18–19
Bertonneau, Arnold, 390
Bickley, George, 101
Biddle, George, 312
Bingham, John A., 220
Birney, James G., 66
Black Hawk War, 16–18, 87
Blacks. *See* African Americans
Blair, Francis Preston, Sr., 197, 231, 423, 432
Blair, Frank (Francis Preston Blair, Jr.), 197, 236–37, 250, 258–59, 271, 315
Blair, Montgomery, 197, 212, 221–222, 226, 250, 259, 262, 263, 308, 371–72, 378, 423
Bloomington, Illinois, Convention, 117–18
Booth, John Wilkes, 375, 457–60, 467
border slave states, 190, 234–37, 284–85, 292–96, 305–7
Brady, Mathew, 169, 331, 394
Bragg, Braxton, 316, 329, 347, 373–74
Breckinridge, John C., 183, 271
Britain, 143–144, 233, 263–64, 283, 308–9, 328–29
Brooks, Noah, 169, 352, 357, 413, 438, 447, 461
Brooks, Preston, 117
Brown, Albert Gallatin, 101
Brown, John, 116, 118, 163, 165–66, 171, 181, 332
Browning, Eliza, 29, 31
Browning, Orville H., 33, 47, 176, 177, 211–212, 225, 240, 257–58, 281, 294, 342, 345, 349

Bryant, William Cullen, 169, 172, 184
Buchanan, James, 83, 101, 117, 119, 121, 124, 132–133, 149–50, 158, 192, 208, 213
Buell, Don Carlos, 261, 273, 275–76, 280, 288–89, 316, 329, 349
Buffalo, New York, 204
Bullitt, Cuthbert, 311
Bull Run. *See* Manassas Junction, Virginia
Burlingame, Michael: Lincoln scholarship of, ix, x; opinion regarding Mary Lincoln, 56
Burns, Robert, 13
Burnside, Ambrose E., 280, 321, 336–37, 338–339, 348, 355, 374
Butler, Benjamin F., 235, 250–252, 256, 292, 330, 399, 401, 407, 450
Butler, William, 37, 48

cabinet: crisis of 1862, 341–43; formation of by Lincoln, 190–91, 195–97, 212, 341–43; meetings of, 221, 222, 225–26, 308, 318–19, 324, 342–43, 458
Cadwallader, Sylvanus, 449
Calhoun, John, 19
Calhoun, John C., 40, 64, 91–92, 97, 98, 99, 120, 135, 181, 426, 434
California, 91, 97, 98, 100, 118, 229
Cameron, Simon, 167, 175, 176, 177, 196, 197, 212, 222, 226, 237, 261–62, 271, 273, 275, 396
Carpenter, Francis B., 308, 392–93, 446–47
Cartwright, Peter, 11, 74–75
Cass, Lewis, 17–18, 83, 84, 86–87
Chandler, Zachariah, 251, 256, 339, 341, 423, 436–37, 442

Channing, William Henry, 276–77, 306, 314

Charleston Mercury, 132, 181, 219, 422

Charleston, South Carolina, 210, 212, 221–23, 225–28, 244, 352, 365, 440

Chase, Salmon P., 92, 158, 173–174, 175, 176, 190, 196–197, 212, 222, 226, 264, 273–274, 286, 296–97, 308, 318, 320, 321, 324–25, 341–43, 375, 394–96, 412, 423, 426, 444, 457, 460, 461, 465

Chattanooga, Tennessee, 316, 347, 373–74, 383, battle of, 383

Cherokee Indians, 334

Chicago Herald, 125, 183

Chicago, Illinois, 21, 140–43, 166, 175–78, 191

Chicago Press and Tribune, 147

Chicago Times, 125

Chicago Tribune, 150, 257, 445

Child, Lydia Maria, 182–83, 327, 408

Chiriqui province of Panama, 313, 335

civil liberties during Civil War, 234–35, 353–55

Civil War: attempts to avert, 192, 193–195, 199–201, 208–12, 224–27; casualties in, 191, 223, 242–243, 249, 289, 295, 302–303, 339, 377–379, 406–7, 409, 415, 442–44; Lincoln's leadership in, 229–37, 269–80, 287–99, 302–4, 305–15, 318–20, 321–26, 330–38, 348–49, 352–53, 360–62, 383–88, 398–400, 417–27, 465–66; meaning of, 191, 271, 294–96, 314, 325, 338, 357–58, 362, 376–80, 421–22, 425, 442–44, 465–66; military leadership in, 231, 236–37, 242,

243–44, 248–50, 252, 253–56, 269–73, 275, 278–80, 287–92, 296–99, 305, 310, 318–20, 321–24, 329–33, 338–41, 347–49, 352–53, 356–57, 360–62, 388–89, 398–400, 405–7, 409–11, 425; political dimensions of, 230, 237–38, 245–48, 249–50, 251–52, 253, 256–59, 269–71, 282–85, 292–96, 305–9, 311–16, 318, 320, 327–31, 335–36, 357–60, 401, 405–7, 409, 413–14, 415–27, 422–23; strategic contingencies of, 231, 233–38, 258, 289–90, 315–16, 320, 329, 357–60, 362, 401, 405–7, 409, 413–14, 415–17, 422–23

Clary's Grove Boys, 12, 13, 16

Clay, Cassius M., 231–232

Clay, Henry, 15–16, 21, 31, 39, 45, 60–61, 63, 64, 66, 79, 83, 97, 99, 100, 107, 178, 268, 299, 311

Clingman, Thomas L., 101

Coffin, Charles C., 452

Cogdal, Isaac, 24, 224

Colfax, Schuyler, 406, 458

Collum, Shelby, 396

colonization controversies and proposals, 63, 99–100, 292, 311–13, 334–35, 337–38, 355, 390

Compromise of 1850, 99, 100, 104

Confederate States of America, 195, 208–9, 225, 229–30, 233–34, 245–46, 267, 269, 284, 286, 308, 315–16, 320, 328–29, 362, 365, 406–7, 415–17, 421–22, 429, 451; and foreign relations, 233, 262, 316, 320, 328–29, 362, 415–17; and race, 195, 267, 308–9, 328, 361, 365, 466; and northern Democrats, 233, 309, 316, 320, 322, 362, 406–7, 432–33, 435–38,

459, 465–66; and slavery, 195, 267, 308–9, 328, 361, 365, 465–66; strategic strengths and weaknesses of, 233, 308–9, 362; war crimes and atrocities of, 361, 365, 392

Confederation Congress, United States, 61, 170

Confiscation Act, first, 251–52, 257, 270

Confiscation Act, second, 301, 307, 309

Congress, United States, 39–40, 59, 60, 62, 72–73, 74, 75, 122–23, 151, 158, 160, 170, 193, 198, 230, 235, 245–48, 268–71, 283–85, 299–302, 307, 337–38, 383–87, 413, 429–32, 440–41

Conkling, James C., 38, 224, 367–69

constitutional amendments, 64, 91, 98, 185, 193–94, 199, 209, 217, 337, 358, 389–90, 395, 410, 429–32, 433–34,

Constitutional Union Party, 174

Constitution, United States, 35, 61–62, 64, 91, 92, 106, 120–24, 134–35, 137, 151, 154–55, 170, 185–86, 193–94, 198, 235, 247, 307, 323, 337, 344, 354, 402–3, 410, 429–32, 433–34, 435, 438–39, 465, as interpreted by both sides in slavery contro- versy, 92, 120–24, 134–35, 137, 151, 154–55, 160–61, 170, 465, Lincoln's views of, 84, 235–36, 247, 323, 354, 402–3, 435

Conway, Moncure D., 267, 276–77, 285, 306, 314, 457

Copperheads, 350, 353–55, 364, 367, 370–71, 414–17

corruption, political, 175, 179, 196, 261–62

Corwin Amendment, 199, 209, 211, 217–20, 268

Corwin, Thomas, 209

Cox, Samuel S., 433

Crawford, Elizabeth, 10

Crisfield, John W., 293

Crittenden Compromise, 193–94, 209, 210, 314

Crittenden, John J., 193, 251

Crittenden-Johnson Resolutions, 251, 270–71

Cuba, annexation of, 100, 101, 158

Curtin, Andrew G., 229–30, 339, 371, 401

Curtis, George William, 415

Curtis, Samuel R., 286

Dahlgren, John A., 287, 375

Dana, Charles A., 388

Davis, David, 58, 116, 167, 176–77, 196, 264, 269, 300

Davis, Henry Winter, 197, 412–13

Davis, Jefferson, 161, 195, 213, 228, 275, 288–89, 322, 328, 336, 346, 369, 419–20, 422, 432–33, 437, 451–52

Decatur, Illinois, 115, 174–75

Declaration of Independence, United States, 113–14, 121, 126, 129–30, 140–43, 144, 162, 206, 403; Lincoln's emphasis on, 113–14, 126, 129–30, 140–43, 144, 162, 206, 403

Delaware, 234, 268–69, 276, 282

Democratic convention: in 1860, 174, in 1864, 416, 418, 422

Democratic Party, 15, 32–34, 39, 44, 59, 66, 73–74, 82, 84, 86, 88–89, 100, 103, 111–12, 117–18, 119,

167, 174, 183, 245, 251, 270–71,
285, 292, 309, 315–16, 320, 326,
328, 335–37, 350, 370–72, 400,
406–7, 409, 416–19, 422, 424,
431–32; anti–government creed
of, 15, 39, 84–85, 184, 190; free
soil schisms within, 88, 103,
111–12; racism of, 183, 285, 292,
309, 327–28, 350, 371, 417–18,
424; schism between War Democrats and Peace Democrats, 326,
350, 424
District of Columbia. See Washington, D.C.
Dixon, Archibald, 102
Dodge, Mary A., 467–68
Donald, David Herbert, Lincoln
biography of, xi, 469n4
Douglas, Stephen A., 22, 34, 42,
48, 59, 97–98, 99, 102–103, 111,
117, 124–25, 126–27, 129–31,
132–133, 135–36, 140–63, 167,
174, 183, 191, 200, 210, 213, 220,
230, 243, 300; as Democratic
leader in Illinois, 22, 34, 42, 48,
59; debates with Lincoln, 104–7,
146–56; Popular Sovereignty
doctrine of, 104, 124–25, 141,
148, 158, 161, 164, 167, 174, 200;
presidential aspirations of, 117,
158, 167, 174, 183; racism of,
104, 124–43, 144–45, 148–49,
151–55
Douglass, Frederick, 152, 183, 311,
327–28, 346–47, 365–67, 401,
408, 419, 424, 444–45; criticism
of Lincoln, 327–28, 401; meetings with Lincoln, 365–67, 419;
praise of Lincoln, 183, 346–47,
445
draft, Confederate, 289
draft, Union, 289, 353, 364, 371

Dred Scott v. Sandford, 120–25,
134–35, 137, 141, 155, 156, 168,
170, 185, 300, 302, 464–65;
Curtis, Benjamin, dissent from
decision, 123, 168
Dresser, Charles N., 55, 58
Duncan, Jason, 15, 39
Du Pont, Samuel Francis, 352
Durant, Thomas J., 359–60

Early, Jubal, 413–15, 417, 425
Eckert, Thomas, 435–36
Edwards, Elizabeth Todd, 46, 51,
282
Edwards, Ninian W., 34, 46, 47, 51
"Effie Afton" case, 131–132
Ellis, Abner Y., 12, 20, 26
Ellsworth, Elmer Ephraim, 180,
202, 203, 241–43
emancipation, compensated and
gradual, 61–63, 268–69, 276–77,
282–85, 292, 301–2, 305–6, 337,
372
emancipation, immediate, 253,
256–59, 271, 282, 292–94, 306,
372
emancipation in Washington, D.C.,
92–93, 282, 292–93
Emancipation Proclamation, 306,
308, 321, 323–329, 332, 335–37,
345–47, 368, 384–85, 434; limitations of, 306, 308; reactions to,
327–29, 332, 335, 346–47, 349,
434, 436; revolutionary nature
of, 306–8, 324–25, 336, 345–47,
scope of, 306–8, 324–26, 345–47,
434
Emerson, Ralph Waldo, 327
Everett, Edward, 376, 379

Falmouth, Virginia, 352–53
Farragut, David, 291–92, 315

Fell, Jesse W., 159, 167, 176
Fessenden, William Pitt, 166, 223,
    412, 458
filibusterers, 101, 194
Fillmore, Millard, 99, 100, 115
Fisher, George P., 269, 282
Fitzhugh, George, 103
Flanders, Benjamin, 359–60
Fleurville (or Florville), William,
    127, 281–82, 312
Florida, 195, 389
Foote, Andrew H., 280
Forbes, Charles, 458
Ford's Theatre, 458–59
Forrest, Nathan Bedford, 316, 347,
    392; and Fort Pillow massacre,
    392
Fort Donelson, 280
Fort Henry, 280
Fort Pillow massacre, 392
Fort Stevens, 414–15
Fort Sumter, 210, 212, 221–23,
    225–29
Fort Wagner, 364–365
Fortress Monroe, 230, 244, 250, 286,
    288, 296
Founding Fathers, 41, 61, 105, 146,
    165, 170, 204, 206, 338, 380; and
    American ideals, 146, 206, 338,
    380; and slavery, 61, 105–6, 121,
    146, 154, 165, 170
Fox, Gustavus Vasa, 222, 225, 239,
    256, 279, 411, 414
France, 233, 309, 329, 399
Francis, Simeon, 51
Franklin, William B., 273
Fredericksburg, Virginia, 336–37;
    battle of, 338–39
Freedmen's Bureau, 441
free labor system, 173, 246, 269
Free Soil movement, viii, 61, 65,
    73–74, 87–92, 101–8, 111–30,

132–39, 140–63, 170, 183–84,
    193–94, 300, 464
Free Soil Party, 88, 90, 115
Frémont, John C., 118, 252–53,
    256–59, 265, 267–68, 279, 293,
    299, 302, 401, 408–9, 418, 423
French, Benjamin Brown, 265,
    378–79
Fugitive Slave Act of 1850, 99, 165,
    199, 250–52

Gamble, Hamilton R., 237
Gardner, Alexander, 331, 375–76,
    434
Garnet, Henry Highland, 312
Garrison, William Lloyd, 40, 118,
    265, 266–67, 285, 408, 434;
    praise of Lincoln, 408, 434
General Land Office, commission-
    ership of, 93–94
Gentry, Allen, 9
Gentry, James, 9
Gentry, Matthew, 61, 77–78
Georgia, 191, 195, 406, 411, 428–31
German-Americans, 141, 177, 236
Gettysburg, battle of, 320, 360–61,
    362; Lincoln's reactions to,
    362–64; strategic significance of,
    362
Giddings, Joshua R., 79, 153, 161,
    179, 183
Gilmer, John A., 194
Gladstone, William E., 322, 329,
    445
Globe Tavern, 55, 58
Goldsborough, Louis M., 280, 296
Gosport Navy Yard, 286–87
Graham, Mentor, 12, 13, 19
Grant, Julia, 449, 458
Grant, Ulysses S., 252, 258, 275,
    279–80, 286, 288–89, 316,
    329–30, 347–48, 349, 351–52,

361, 364, 367, 369, 374–75, 383,
    388–89, 397–400, 404–7, 409–11,
    414, 417, 425, 428, 435–36, 441,
    448–51, 453, 458, 461
Gray, Thomas, 4
Great Britain. *See* Britain
Greeley, Horace, 135, 172, 175,
    313–15, 327, 375, 415–16
Green, Bowling, 12, 20, 23
Green, Duff, 194
Greenbacks, 285–86, 439
Grigsby family, 10

habeas corpus, writ of, 234–35,
    247–48, 353–55, 371
Hahn, Michael, 359–60, 390–91,
    440
Haiti, 302, 335, 355
Halleck, Henry W., 260–261, 271,
    273, 279–80, 286, 305, 310,
    317–18, 322, 336–37, 348, 361,
    363, 373, 388–89, 398
Hamilton, Alexander, 84, 299
Hamlin, Hannibal, 178, 191, 213,
    292, 410, 442
Hampton Roads Conference,
    432–33, 435–38
Hanks, Dennis, 5, 6, 9
Hanks, John, 10, 11, 174
Hanks, Nancy. *See* Lincoln, Hancy
    Hanks
Hardin, John J., 59, 60, 72
Harper's Ferry, 163, 164, 166, 171,
    243, 245, 297, 323, 360
Harrison, William Henry, 45, 83
Harvey, James E., 227
Hay, John, 180, 202, 213, 221,
    223–24, 241, 261, 276, 319–20,
    325, 330, 370, 372, 374, 376, 378,
    389, 400, 405, 406, 416, 419, 426,
    460, 461, 462

Helm, Benjamin Hardin, 375
Helm, Emilie, 375, 393
Henderson, Thomas J., 117
Henry, Anson, 47, 94
Herndon, William H., 5, 12, 22,
    26–28, 55, 56, 57, 58, 68–69, 82,
    84, 116, 132, 135, 163, 167, 182,
    201–2, 266, 462
Herold, David, 457, 459
Hitchcock, Ethan Allen, 288
Hodgenville, Kentucky, 3
Hodges, Albert G., 402
Holman, William Steele, 271
Homestead Act, 178, 299
Hood, John Bell, 422–23, 428, 430
Hood, Thomas, 405
Hooker, Joseph, 321, 336, 348–49,
    352–53, 356–57, 359–60
Hunter, David, 259, 261, 293–94,
    355–56
Hurd v. The Rock Island Bridge Com-
    pany. See "Effie Afton" case
Hurlbut, Stephen, 222, 225–26, 369

Île-à-Vache, 335, 355, 390
Illinois, 10, 15, 18, 20–22, 32–38,
    42–43, 46–51, 55, 57–60, 68–72,
    74–75, 93–94, 104–8, 111,
    115–17, 124, 125–26, 135–39,
    140–57, 167, 173, 174–75, 184,
    335, 370–71
Illinois and Michigan Canal, 21
Illinois Central Railroad Company
    v. McLean County, Illinois and
    Parke, 131
Illinois legislature, 15, 18, 20–22, 32,
    33–34, 35, 48, 111, 131, 143, 157,
    335, 370
Illinois state bank, 21, 34, 43, 46, 48
Illinois Supreme Court, 48, 105,
    131, 156

Inaugural Address, Lincoln's first.
See Lincoln, Abraham, addresses
made by Lincoln
Inaugural Address, Lincoln's second.
See Lincoln, Abraham, addresses
made by Lincoln
Indiana, 5–6, 9, 61, 76–78, 176–77,
196, 370–71
Indians, American. See Native
Americans, Lincoln and
Indian Territory, 334
internal improvements, 15, 39, 43,
84–85, 178, 299, 467
Island Number Ten, 286, 291

Jackson, Andrew, 15, 21, 31–32, 44,
86, 232
Jackson, Claiborne F., 236–37
Jackson, Mississippi, 352
Jackson, Thomas J. ("Stonewall"),
248, 290, 297–99, 317, 323, 357
Jefferson, Thomas, 61, 103, 160
Jews, 397
Johnson, Andrew, 237, 251, 355,
360, 442, 451, 459, 460, 461, 467;
and emancipation, 251, 355, 360,
410; as Lincoln's successor, 467; as
occupation governor of Tennessee,
355, 360; as vice presidential
candidate, 410; in Congress, 251
Johnson, Reverdy, 230
Johnston, Albert Sidney, 275,
288–289
Johnston, John D. (stepbrother), 9, 6,
9, 11, 95–96
Johnston, Joseph E., 243, 245, 275,
289, 296, 297, 302, 406, 411, 422,
448, 450
Johnston, Matilda, 6, 295
Johnston, Sarah Bush. See Lincoln,
Sarah Bush Johnston

Judd, Norman B., 132, 146–47, 150,
156–57, 166, 167, 176, 207
Julian, George, 435

Kansas, 102, 105, 112–14, 116, 118,
132–33, 135, 140, 158, 165–66,
206
Kansas-Nebraska Act, 102–8, 112,
117
Keckly, Elizabeth, 238, 312, 424,
446, 460
Kelley, William D., 319
Kellogg, William D., 193
Kelso, Jack, 12, 13
Kentucky, 3–4, 63, 105, 164, 234,
236, 256–57, 258, 275, 316, 329,
402
Keynes, John Maynard, 43
King, Preston, 178
Knapp, Nathan M., 176
Knights of the Golden Circle, 101,
370
Knob Creek (Kentucky), 4
Know-Nothing Party, 115, 177
Kock, Bernard, 335
Koerner, Gustave, 76, 177

Lamon, Ward Hill, 176, 190, 203,
208, 222, 378, 419, 424, 447–48,
458, 462
land redistribution to freedmen,
369–70, 435, 441
Lane, Henry, 177
Lane, James, 232
Lecompton Constitution for Kansas, 132–133
Lee, Robert E., 231, 243, 244,
253–54, 275, 289, 290, 302–4,
310, 316–17, 321–24, 336–37,
355, 356–57, 360–61, 372–73,
405–7, 409–11, 413, 448–49, 453

Legal Tender Act, 285–86
Liberia, 302, 313
Liberty Party, 66, 88
Lincoln, Abraham: and alcohol, 48; and Ann Rutledge, 22–25, 56 and George McClellan, 255, 260–261, 272–75, 278–80, 287–92, 296–99, 303–5, 310, 318–24, 330–33, 336; and Joshua Speed, 37–38, 48–50, 113–14, 256–57; and Mary Todd Lincoln, 46–47, 50, 51, 55–58, 80–81, 94, 95, 131, 239–40, 265, 280–82, 304, 309, 341, 346, 353, 375, 393, 424, 441, 445–46, 449–50, 458; and Salmon Chase, 196–97, 341–43, 394–96, 412, 423, 457; and slavery, viii, 9, 35–36, 40, 66–67, 72, 87, 90–91, 92–93, 99–100, 103–8, 113–14, 130, 134–39, 140–63, 191, 258, 265–71, 282–85, 292–96, 305–8, 311–15, 321–26, 358–60, 389–92, 402, 408, 410, 429–30, 433–34, 442–44, 452, 464–66; and Stephen Douglas, 42, 103–7, 125, 126–27, 131, 133, 140–63, 164; and Ulysses S Grant, 352, 364, 397–400, 404–6, 411, 414, 417; and William Herndon, 68–69, 82, 84, 163, 201–2; and William Seward, 89, 178, 191, 195, 199–200, 208–12, 224–27, 341–43; anger of, 10, 71, 204, 274–75, 340–41, 357, 362–64, 368, 373; appearance of, 8, 26–27, 75–76, 81, 145, 163, 202, 213, 239, 310, 331, 375–76, 434, 445, 458; assassination threats and murder of, 189–90, 201, 207–8, 419, 446–48, 457–60; audacity of, 20, 231, 243, 274–76, 291, 296–97, 298–99, 332–33, 363, 387, 438–39, 453–57; biographers' misunderstandings of, vii–xi; character of, vii–xi, 4, 7–8, 9–10, 12–13, 24, 30–31, 33, 38, 50, 56–57, 179, 210–11, 265–66, 333, 420, 460–68; childhood of, 3–7; congressional service of, 17, 79–94; deceptions of, 69–71, 74–75, 125–28, 144–45, 149, 150–51, 210–11, 218–20, 226–28, 276–77, 293, 313–14, 323, 359–60, 385–88, 390–92, 402–4, 453–57; depression and, ix–x, 22–25, 46–51, 280–82, 445–46; economic views of, 21, 39, 43–45, 50–51, 439; education of, 4, 6–8, 15, 20, 168–69, 179, 427, emotions of, ix, 8,10, 12, 22–25, 26–31, 37–38, 46–51, 55–57, 240, 242–43, 260, 265–66, 280–82, 289, 294–96, 340–41, 375, 394, 405–6, 411, 427, 434, 445–48, 451–52, 458; empathy of, 8, 9, 48–49, 60, 106–7, 113, 130, 161–63, 312, 452; ethics of, 7–8, 17, 30–31, 50, 82, 106–7, 113–14, 159–63, 442–44; friendships of, 4, 11–12, 37–39, 46, 48–50, 58, 59, 113–14; grieving and responses to death, 4, 10, 22–25, 27, 56, 242–243, 260, 280–82, 289, 294–96, 406, 409; humor of, 9, 10, 12, 13, 17–18, 28–29, 33, 34–35, 70–71, 80, 86–87, 105, 127, 153, 154, 156, 239, 277, 405, in Chicago, 140–43, 173; incremental methods of, 218–20, 258, 265–71, 276–77, 292–96, 366; in Illinois

legislature, 21,33–36; in Indiana, 5–10, 61, 76–78; in Kentucky, 3–4, 79; in New England, 88–89, 172–73; in New York City, 131, 168–72, 205–6; in Philadelphia, 206–7; intellectual gifts of, xi, 5, 6–8, 19–20, 38–39, 67, 69–71, 75, 262, 274–75, 392, 404; journey from Springfield to Washington, 201–8; law practice of, 31, 36, 38, 42, 48, 57–58, 68–72, 96, 115, 131–32, 202; leadership abilities of, 12, 16, 34, 41–42, 59–60, 83, 84, 115–17, 135–39, 158–61, 172, 190–94, 269–71, 311–15, 341–43, 348–49, 358–64, 367–70, 373–74, 383–93, 397–400, 415–17; literary gifts of, 13, 15, 41–42, 75–78, 138, 377–80, 392, 442–45; love and courtships of, 22–25, 29–31, 46–51; mental power of, vii, 19, 38–39, 67, 69–71, 75, 262, 266, 274–76, 460; military instincts of, 118, 191, 194, 231, 234–35, 244–45, 274–76, 278–80, 287–92, 298–99, 303–4, 332–33, 348–49, 352–53, 360–62, 362–64, 372–74, 388–89, 398–400, 417, 430; move to Illinois, 10–11; move to Springfield, 36–39; New Salem years, 11– 36; oratorical power of, 79, 86–87, 89, 117, 132, 137–39, 140–43, 145–46, 161–63, 169–70, 172; party politics and, 33, 34–35, 42–43, 59–60, 66, 72, 83–89, 158–61, 115–17, 135–39, 157–59, 161, 166–67, 172–80, 183–84, 190, 195–97, 245, 285, 301, 308, 316, 328, 335–37, 339–43, 369, 370–72, 375,

394–97, 400–1, 407–10, 412–13; personality of, viii–ix, 3–14, 23–25, 26–31, 37–39, 56–57, 67, 76–78, 80–81, 179, 190–91, 205, 223–24, 238–42, 243, 262, 265–66, 274–77, 280–82, 294–96; political campaigns of, 15–18, 20–21, 32–33, 42–43, 45–46, 59–60, 72, 74–75, 111–12, 135–39, 166–79, 183–84, 394–97, 400–1, 407–10, 417–27; political philosophy of, 15–16, 40–42, 84–85, 113–14, 128–30, 136–39, 140–43, 146, 159–63, 171–72, 215, 246–47, 338, 376–80, 425; presidential leadership of, vii, 190–228, 229–38, 245–48, 253, 260–80, 282–85, 287–99, 304, 310–15, 318–26, 330–38, 339–43, 348–49, 357–62, 367–69, 383–88, 398–400, 402–4, 414–17, 429–38, 465–68; reconstruction plans of, 344–45, 369–70, 385–88, 391–92, 412–13, 429, 435, 437–38, 440–41, 453–57, 466–67; relations with children, 58, 80–81, 240–42, 280–81, 375, 363, 376, 378, 393–94, 441; relations with father, 3–6 , 8–11, 57, 95; relations with women, 8, 22–25, 26–31, 46–51; religious views of, 9–10, 74–75, 95, 202, 284, 294–96, 320–21, 324, 346, 376–77, 397–98, 403–4, 423, 425, 443–44; Republican Party leadership of, 117–18, 136–39, 158–61, 193–97, 335, 339–43, 367, 371–72, 394–97, 400, 407–10, 412–13, 423; Republican presidential nomination in 1860,

166–78; sexual orientation of, 26–29, strategic sense of, viii–ix, 67, 69–72, 127–28, 174, 178, 191, 209–12, 218–20, 226–28, 250, 258, 266–71, 274–77, 293, 298–99, 303–4, 306, 311–15, 319, 330–31, 332–33, 341–43, 385–89, 392, 398–401, 420–21, 435–38, 453–57, 464; superstitions of, 9–10, 189–90, 375, 448; unionism of, 118, 205–6, 214–15, 245–46, 314–15, 358, 367–69, 383–84, 455–56, 464; views on race, 33, 36, 125–30, 140–43, 144–45, 302, 311–12, 338, 355–56, 365–69, 391, 411–12 wartime leadership of, ix, 229–37, 245–48, 250, 256–59, 260–71, 278–80, 282–85, 287–99, 303–4, 310–15, 318–26, 330–38, 348–49, 352–53, 355–56, 357–64, 367–69, 372–74, 383–88, 398–401, 402–4, 414–17, 428–30, 465–66

Lincoln, Abraham, addresses made by Lincoln: First Inaugural Address, 201, 204, 211, 214–20; Gettysburg Address, 205, 376–80; Second Inaugural Address, 442–45

Lincoln, Abraham, scholarship on Lincoln by: Burlingame, Michael, ix, x; Fehrenbacher, Don, 36; Holzer, Harold, 168; Lehrman, Lewis, 104; Shenk, Joshua Wolf, Lincoln scholarship of, ix, 24; Strozier, Charles B., 27; Temple, Wayne C., 55; Walsh, John E., 22; Wilson, Douglas, ix, 22–24, 28

Lincoln, Abraham, speeches: in Baltimore, Maryland, 390; in Cincinnati, Ohio, 164–65, 204, 250; in Columbus, Ohio, 161–63, 266; the Cooper Union speech, 167–72; the Farewell speech (Springfield), 202; in Harrisburg, Pennsylvania, 207; the House Divided speech, 136–39, 145, 154, 155, 180, 205, 218, 267; at Independence Hall, 206; in Indianapolis, Indiana, 203; the Lost Speech, 117; the Lyceum speech, 40–42; in New Haven, Connecticut, 173; in New York City, 167–172, 205–6; the Peoria speech, 104–7, 128–29; in Philadelphia, Pennsylvania, 206–207; in Pittsburgh, Pennsylvania, 204; in Trenton, New Jersey, 206

Lincoln-Douglas debates, 146–56; in Alton, Illinois, 156; in Charleston, Illinois, 153–54; in Freeport, Illinois, 150–52; in Galesburg, Illinois, 154–55; in Jonesboro, Illinois, 152–53; in Ottawa, Illinois, 147–50; in Quincy, Illinois, 155–56

Lincoln, Edward Baker ("Eddy"), 58, 80, 94, 95

Lincoln, Nancy Hanks (mother), 3–6

Lincoln, Mary Todd, 46–51, 55–58, 69, 80–81, 94, 95, 131, 190, 201, 221, 238, 239–40, 264–65, 280–82, 304, 309, 341, 346, 353, 375, 393, 424, 441, 445–46, 449–53, 458, 460; as mother, 80–81, 201, 253, 280–82, 375, 393, 441, as wife, 55–58, 80–81, 240, 353, 375, 445–46, 449–50, 453; controversies surrounding, 56, 239–40, 264–65, 424, 449–50, 453; emotional problems of, 56–57, 240, 353, 445–46, 449–50;